International Relations: A Political Dictionary

International Relations: A Political Dictionary

Fifth Edition
Lawrence Ziring
Jack C. Plano
Roy Olton
Western Michigan University

ABC-CLIO

Santa Barbara, California
Denver, Colorado
Oxford, England

Library of Congress Cataloging-in-Publication Data
Ziring, Lawrence, 1928–
    The international relations dictionary / Lawrence Ziring, Jack C. Plano, Roy Olton. — 5th ed.
        p. cm. — (Clio dictionaries in political science)
    Plano's name appeared first on previous edition.
    Includes bibliographical references and index.
        1. International relations—Dictionaries. I. Plano, Jack C. II. Olton, Roy, 1922– . III. Title. IV. Series.
JX1226.P55   1995   327'.03—dc20   95-37359

ISBN 0-87436-897-9 (hc)
ISBN 0-87436-791-3 (pbk)

01 00 99 98 97 96 95   10 9 8 7 6 5 4 3 2 1

ABC-CLIO, Inc.
130 Cremona Drive, P.O. Box 1911
Santa Barbara, California 93116-1911

This book is printed on acid-free paper ∞.
Manufactured in the United States of America

For
Jack C. Plano
and
Roy Olton
Creative Lexicographers
and
Dear Friends
and
Raye
My Inspiration and Support

Contents

Preface
to the Fifth Edition

This fifth edition of *International Relations: A Political Dictionary* (formerly *The International Relations Dictionary*) mirrors a different world from that of the previous four editions. The current volume draws from virtually all the rich material contained in the previous presentations, but it centers attention on a world of nations irreversibly changed by the dramatic disappearance of the Union of Soviet Socialist Republics and the passing of the global superpower rivalry otherwise known as the Cold War. Post–Cold War international relations continue to function much as they have in the past, but the framework that focused relationships and associations no longer exists. Terms once intelligible within the context of the Cold War are no longer so clearly defined. In many ways, the world of today is a more complex place, and therefore more unpredictable. The international certainties inherent in the ideological clash between the Soviet Union and the United States are far less clear in an era devoid of superpowers, an age when small nations—and indeed, even smaller nations within nations—set exclusive and particularistic courses with hardly a glance toward international limitations on their often self-proclaimed prerogatives.

This fifth edition tries to account for the many changes occurring in a world seemingly trapped between centrifugal and centripetal forces—those that would shatter an international arrangement founded on established states, and others that address the limitations of the nation-state system and press a design that is more politically integrative. This volume attempts to capture the sweep of both international relations theory and practice as the world proceeds inexorably toward the twenty-first century. Nineteenth-century issues of ethnicity and nationalism collide with twenty-first-century dilemmas of ecosystem override and abuse. Never has there been a greater need for enhancing the diplomatic method, but no instrument has suffered more in the calamitous developments of the twentieth century. Technological innovation dominates thought and action, but it also demands that attention be given the human condition, which is so much more at risk today than during the years of the Cold War.

As with the previous four editions, hopefully there is much for the student of international relations in this fifth edition. The volume follows the identical format created by Jack C. Plano and Roy Olton, and should be as user-friendly as those earlier renditions. But there is something more that needs saying concerning this edition. Jack C. Plano and Roy Olton, whose book this is, entrusted the fifth edition solely to my care. I have tried to be faithful to their renderings and can only hope that my work is true to the intent and purpose of their *International Relations Dictionary*. Finally, I am ever mindful of the reader, especially student readers of international relations. I hope this volume will serve them well in grasping a critical body of knowledge on a subject that touches all their lives.

The writing, revising, and updating of this fifth edition has been a solitary matter, but nevertheless, I am indebted to Amy Catala of ABC-Clio for her patience and expertise in preparing the book for publication. I also must note the research assistance received from my graduate students, Chien-Hong Lee and Robert Dibie, and the constant inspiration and, no less important, critical technical help of my wife Raye, who led me through the electronic maze of manuscript preparation. Considering the sheer volume of this assignment, the book would not have been possible without her help and forbearance. This fifth edition of *International Relations: A Political Dictionary* is dedicated to her—and of course to Jack and Roy, whose confidence I deeply treasure.

Lawrence Ziring
11 October 1995

International
Relations:
A Political
Dictionary

The Nature
and Role
of
Foreign Policy

Balance of Power | 1 |
A concept that describes how states deal with problems of national security in a context of shifting alliances and alignments. The balance system is produced by the clustering of related individual national interests in opposition to those of other states. The system originates when anti–status quo states threaten the security of the status quo powers. The balance-of-power concept in the relations of states can be expressed in terms of a power equation. The actors (states) on each side of the equation may be in a situation of approximate equilibrium, or one side may possess a temporary preponderance of power over the other. Because states are largely particularistic and exclusive and seek to maximize their individual national interests, the balance of power is normally in a condition of flux. States may pursue conscious balance-of-power policies, as Great Britain did during the nineteenth century. From a period following the Napoleonic wars until the outbreak of World War I, Great Britain utilized the existing balance-of-power system to maximize its imperial advan-

tages. The strategy it chose involved playing the role of the "balancer" to maintain a power equilibrium among rival imperial powers, notably in Europe but more generally worldwide. Britain's strategy focused on shifting its power from one side to another, depending on where its support was most needed to assist the perceived weaker side against a more formidable foe. By acting in this manner, Great Britain prevented major changes in the prevailing balance of power, which favored its interests. *See also* FOREIGN-POLICY APPROACH: REVISIONIST (9); FOREIGN-POLICY APPROACH: STATUS QUO (10); NEUTRALISM (74).

Significance
The balance-of-power phenomenon pervades international politics and is the central feature in the ongoing power struggle, but it is not mathematically predictable, and references to its exactitude are overstatement. The balance of power is a dominant concept in the relations of states, but if opposed states or groupings of states acknowledge the other's capability but avoid testing the other, it is an assumed condition or perception that

3

ensures the balance between them, not the quantitative character of their rivalry. In a workable balance, states on both sides of the equation largely overestimate the capability of their rival(s), and thus decide to refrain from upsetting the existing equilibrium. The United States and the Soviet Union operated on just such a principle throughout the Cold War period, and although they challenged one another repeatedly, they avoided bringing their forces into direct conflict. On the other hand, the balance of power is the net effect, or result, produced by a state system in which the independent sovereign members are free to join, or to refrain from joining, alliances and alignments as each endeavors to enhance its security and advance its national interests. The balance of power is not the profession of an abstraction, such as peace; peace may or may not serve individual national interests, depending on the time, place, and situation. The balance of power has no central organization to guide it, and the combinations of states that comprise the balance are usually characterized by a shifting membership—some brief, and some of longer duration—and limited objectives. A multiple balance of power prevailed from the seventeenth to the mid-twentieth centuries. It was dominated by shifting combinations of at least five great powers, which tended to ensure flexibility, limited objectives, and the preservation of the participants. A simple or bipolar balance emerged after World War II that was dominated by the Soviet Union and the United States. This configuration was considered inherently dangerous because it prevented the development of a "balancer" and the needed maneuverability to adjust rival power claims. The Cold War balance of power, however, proved to be less rigid than the pundits had feared. Despite ideological divisions, the creation of rival blocs, and frequent testing of the balance through "limited wars" in places such as Korea, Indochina, and Afghanistan, the superpower equilibrium was sustained, and because it was, a general, wider war between the major actors was avoided.

The collapse of the Soviet Union in 1991, without a clash of arms between the major contenders, is testimony to the successful operation of the global balance of power fashioned by the United States and, curiously, by the Soviet Union as well. Indeed, global equilibrium was sustained, despite the numerous peripheral wars that punctuated the Cold War period. Most significantly, Europe (especially Western Europe) enjoyed its longest period of peace in several centuries. The post–Cold War era, however, calls for still another balance-of-power configuration. The breakup of the Soviet Union into 15 independent and sovereign republics, like the disintegration of the Yugoslav Federation, is not without its problems. The ethnic and civil wars that followed in the wake of the Cold War, e.g, Chechnya, Georgia, Bosnia, and Croatia, illustrate the passing of the old balance of power, as well as the failure to find its replacement. The burden placed upon the United Nations as the world's principal peacekeeper reflects reluctance on the part of the major powers to assume responsibility for a new balance of power. UN peacekeeping operations mask rather than circumvent the obligations of the more powerful nations. In a world still driven by independent, sovereign nation-states, it can be argued that the creation of workable regional as well as global equilibrium is still the task of the major actors.

Balance of Power: Bipolarity   2

A rigid balance-of-power system in which power is polarized into two rival power centers. Bipolarity is the converse of polycentrism, which is the development of a number of power centers, allowing greater flexibility for keeping the balance system in equilibrium. The bipolar model tends to evolve when, for the sake of security needs or ideological or political dependence, states are forced to commit themselves to one side of a power configuration dominated by two great powers. *See also* BALANCE OF POWER (1); BALANCE OF POWER: POLYCENTRISM (3).

Significance
Rigid bipolarity characterized the balance-of-power system that emerged almost immediately after World War II. Two superpowers, the United States and the Soviet Union, dominated the rival military, political, economic, and social camps—the "Free World" and the Communist bloc. The early monopoly of nuclear weapons and the substantial conventional military forces held by each superpower compelled other nations to accept positions of dependence for their individual security, in effect polarizing them into separate camps, and leaving key decision-making processes on questions of peace and war to the two principals. Neutral states were pressured by the prevailing circumstances to submit to superpower hegemony through alliances and other arrangements, ostensibly created for protection against the allegedly aggressive designs of the rival bloc. In time, the rigidity of the bipolar model was moderated by the impact of growing polycentrism. The passing from a rigid to a more flexible multipolar balance of power contributed in many ways to the events terminating the Cold War. The revival of political and economic nationalism, the proliferation of nuclear weapons, the weakening of superpower hegemonic control by political change (and especially economic change elsewhere), the general success of nuclear-deterrence policies, and the splintering of alliances in each camp signaled the end of bipolarity and ultimately the self-destruction of one of its major poles, the Soviet Union.

Balance of Power: Polycentrism $\boxed{3}$

An international balance-of-power situation characterized by a number of power centers. Polycentrism, or a flexible balance, is reminiscent of the nineteenth century in that it is composed of a number of active participants. It replaced the post–World War II bipolar balance controlled by the Soviet Union and the United States, but the polycentrism of the post–Cold War era has yet to produce the nec-

essary confidence within the world of nations that polycentrism can manage the "peace." *See also* BALANCE OF POWER: BIPOLARITY (2); COMMUNIST DOCTRINE: TITOISM (89).

Significance
The return to polycentrism challenged and finally terminated U.S.-Soviet hegemony. Causal factors for superpower decline and the rise of polycentrism included: (1) the nuclear "balance of terror" between the United States and the Soviet Union, which reduced the credibility of their promises to defend their allies; (2) economic prosperity in Western Europe and the desire to replicate that experience in Eastern Europe reduced trade barriers between East and West, which lessened economic dependence on the superpowers; (3) the resurgence of nationalism throughout the world and the increasing demand for self-government; and (4) the emergence of a large number of new states, whose leaders saw their national interests in economic, social, and political modernization rather than in terms of Cold War rivalry. Polycentrism meant that an increasing number of states assumed the right to make independent decisions, and a new sense of independence impacted the ideological contest by lowering existing international tensions and opening the world to a larger range of cooperative and accommodative ventures. That cooperative spirit, however, is threatened by internecine and civil conflict in the post–Cold War era, and many observers fear that the polycentrism emerging from the Cold War will only usher in an age of increased anarchy.

Foreign Office $\boxed{4}$

An executive agency charged with the formulation and implementation of foreign policy. Other names for the foreign office include foreign ministry, ministry of foreign affairs, and department of state. Foreign offices are presided over by a foreign secretary, foreign minister, or secretary of state. In large states, foreign offices tend to be organized on both geographical and functional lines. *See also* FOREIGN-POLICY PROCESS: DECISIONMAKERS (16); SECRETARY OF STATE (673).

Significance

The foreign office of any state is the vehicle through which the bulk of relations with other countries is conducted. Reports from diplomats in the field are received, collated, and evaluated as the raw materials of foreign policy in the foreign office. Policy instructions are drafted in the foreign office and dispatched to the diplomat in the field. Once relatively small operations, foreign offices in the major states have become huge bureaucratic institutions employing thousands of persons at home and abroad. Formerly, foreign-office personnel were amateurs recruited haphazardly. However, the complexity, diversity, and volume of interstate relations in the modern world require increasingly higher degrees of education, selectivity, training, and professionalism.

Foreign Policy $\boxed{5}$

A strategy or planned course of action developed by the decisionmakers of a state vis-à-vis other states or international entities to achieve specific goals defined in terms of national interest. A specific foreign policy carried on by a state may be the result of an initiative by that state or may be a reaction to initiatives undertaken by other states. Foreign policy involves a dynamic process of applying relatively fixed interpretations of national interest to the highly fluctuating situational factors of the international environment in order to develop a course of action, followed by efforts to achieve diplomatic implementation of the policy guidelines. Major steps in the foreign-policy process include (1) translating national interest considerations into specific goals and objectives, (2) determining the international and domestic situational factors related to the policy goals, (3) analyzing the state's capabilities of achieving the

desired results, (4) developing a plan or strategy for using the state's capabilities to deal with the variables in pursuit of the goals, (5) undertaking the requisite actions, and (6) periodically reviewing and evaluating progress made toward the achievement of the desired results. The process seldom proceeds logically and chronologically; often, several steps in the process may be carried on simultaneously, and fundamental issues may be reopened when conditions change or setbacks occur. Because the international situation is in constant flux, the policy process is continuous.

Significance

Although it cannot be wholly separated from domestic policy, foreign policy has assumed a major role in the decision processes of most states. In general, the more powerful states devote far greater efforts and resources to the development and implementation of foreign policy than medium-sized or small powers. Although often used in a generic sense to encompass all foreign programs carried on by a state, the term *foreign policy* can be applied more precisely to describe a single situation and the actions of a state to accomplish a limited objective. Consequently, a state must pursue numerous policies, identify many goals, map out various strategies, evaluate different kinds of capabilities, and initiate and evaluate specific decisions and actions. A semblance of coordination must be maintained among policies so that all planning and actions fall within the broad framework of national-interest guidelines. Most such activities are carried on within a state's foreign ministry by a foreign secretary or secretary of state through a bureaucracy divided into regional and country units. Foreign-policy actions are difficult to evaluate because (1) short-range advantages or disadvantages must be weighed in relation to long-range consequences, (2) their impact on other nations is difficult to evaluate, and (3) most policies result in a mixture of successes and failures that are hard to disentangle.

Foreign-Policy Approach: Liberalism 6

A theory in international relations emphasizing the interdependence of nations in economic, financial, and technological endeavors. The liberal theorists cite the growth in transnational activities, the emergence of thousands of internationally oriented nongovernmental organizations that interact with the state system and the larger umbrella or coordinating organizations, e.g., the Environmental Liaison Center International (ELCI) that works with the United Nations Environment Program (UNEP), had 726 member organizations in 1993. Liberal theorists describe power in complex terms, and serious efforts are directed at minimizing the military component. Indeed, military power is neither a substitute for nor the dominant element in equations concerned with economic, financial, technological, and political power. Liberals note the tendency toward a borderless world and the developments that are beginning to further that condition. Security is no longer perceived in strictly zero-sum terms, and states are envisaged as forming more cooperative unions, which would appear helpful in dispelling self-aggrandizing policies. Although the realists acknowledge the sustained interest in national sovereignty, they are nonetheless convinced that mutual self-interest dictates greater displays of accommodation and therefore a willingness to sacrifice some aspects of national privilege for still greater gain. Liberal theorists conclude that more genuine, voluntaristic communities of states will produce more significant adherence to rules, principles, and processes, and thus enhance the flowering of international law and organization. *See also* FOREIGN-POLICY APPROACH: REALIST-IDEALIST DICHOTOMY (8).

Significance

The liberal theorists in international relations reject a return to older thinking and behavior. They believe that nations will forgo the temptation to develop nuclear weapons. What is needed, they argue, is more stress on confidence-building measures, and that this can be accomplished by creating international institutions that minimize threat and maximize security. Liberal theorists recognize the importance of leadership in this scenario, and especially how states' leaders manage domestic opinion in bridging the gulf between their vision of the future and their population's everyday reality. The liberal/idealistic optimism represented in this theoretical construct insists that antagonists can be won over when the benefits of cooperation and sharing begin to influence the larger public in positive directions. Security in such circumstances is not measured in nuclear arsenals or in the capability of procuring conventional weapons, but in improving the physical and psychological well-being of society. Economic development, not political rivalry, is the emphasis of this interpretation. Balance-of-power arrangements are no longer expressed in geopolitical terms, but rather in geoeconomic circumstances. Moreover, material satisfaction has its own rewards, and a reduced emphasis on national security gives greater opportunities to democratic political forces within societies heretofore constrained by overbearing military establishments.

Foreign-Policy Approach: Realism 7

Concern with human nature as it really is, and with historic processes as they emerge and run their course. Realism is one of the more enduring theories of international relations. Proponents of the realist school posit a state-centric international system characterized by structural anarchy and competition for power and influence in which military power is the most important factor. They argue that, with the end of the Cold War and its bipolar military system, the world of nation-states will inexorably return to their individual pursuits for power and status in the global community. The inevitable consequence of their actions is an insatiable appetite for state-of-the-art weaponry, and more significantly, the acquisition of nuclear-weapons capabilities. Realists view the structure of the global system as the essential factor; they contend that state behavior is predicated on exclusive representations of national sovereignty. and that states believe their security is dependent on finding a place in a systemic equilibrium, centered on a balance of power that is diplomatically and militarily driven, not legally arranged. *See also* NUCLEAR DIPLOMACY: NORTH KOREA–UNITED STATES (433); PATTERNS OF POWER: MUTUAL SECURITY (23).

Significance
In the more than four decades following World War II, the bipolar international power structure was framed by a worldwide Soviet-U.S. rivalry that also engendered a successful balance of power. Realists would argue that this balance provided relative global security in nuclear matters. Superpower deterrence policies realistically avoided direct confrontation between the major contenders, contained ideological extremism, and convinced an overwhelming majority of lesser states to avoid developing nuclear arsenals of their own. In the post–Cold War period, however, realists see a new, more concerted shift to multipolar actions and, indeed, enhanced individual state actions that present new obstacles to international equilibrium. The crosscutting and multiple rivalries that prevailed during the nineteenth and early twentieth centuries have reappeared, and regional and/or ethnic conflict has multiplied. States heretofore constrained from joining the nuclear club now see their admission to that circle as the only serious guarantee of their power status—and, in some cases, their very survival as independent states. International observers believe that nuclear weapons will be the security system of choice for numerous states. The efforts launched by India, Israel, North Korea, Iraq, Iran, and Pakistan to establish themselves as nuclear-weapons powers are only some of the more glaring examples in a world obsessed by security needs. The first casualty of this increasing emphasis on nuclear assertiveness is the failure to gain universal approval for the Nuclear Non-Proliferation Treaty (NPT). Even after the NPT's indefinite extension in May 1995, a number of prominent states refused to sign the pact, let alone accept limitations on their sovereign prerogative to construct nuclear weapons. Nor have the nuclear-club states—the United States, Russia, Great Britain, France, and China—agreed to liquidate their arsenals. The continuing role of these countries as nuclear-weapons powers fuels the ambitions of other states wishing to emulate their example. The proliferation of nuclear weapons in the post–Cold War world makes a future ban even more problematical. The spread of nuclear weapons also raises the likelihood of their eventual use by nations desperate enough to resort to them.

Foreign-Policy Approach: Realist-Idealist Dichotomy   8
Alternative approaches of decisionmakers in forming foreign policy. The realist approach is fundamentally empirical and pragmatic, whereas the idealist approach is based on abstract, traditional foreign-policy principles involving international norms, legal codes, and moral/ethical values. The realist school assumes that the key factor prevalent in all international relationships is power. The wise and efficient use of power by a state in pursuit of its national interest is, therefore, the main ingredient of a successful foreign policy. The idealist, on the other hand, believes that foreign policies based on moral principles are more effective because they promote unity and cooperation rather than competition and conflict among states. According to the idealist, moral power is more effective than physical power because it is more durable. In place of force and coercion, it involves winning over people's minds and allegiances to accept principles that ought to govern state conduct. *See also* DIPLOMACY, MACHIAVELLIAN (412).

Significance
The realist-idealist dichotomy relates particularly to the debates over the "best"

approach to foreign-policy making in the United States. Many realists regard the United States as the leading, if not the only, state in the world misled by popular attitudes and moral self-righteousness into adopting idealistic guidelines to govern the making of foreign-policy decisions. The result, according to the realists, is the inability of the United States to compete effectively with other states that base their policies on the hard realities of national self-interest. Idealists tend to reject the power-centered realist approach as a pseudoscientific Machiavellianism likely to produce only minor, short-lived gains for the nation. The idealists consider the most successful policies to be those based on principles and moral values, policies that they feel have won support from millions of people from other nations. Examples of idealist approaches include the Fourteen Points enunciated by Woodrow Wilson in World War I, the Atlantic Charter proclaimed by Franklin Roosevelt and Winston Churchill in World War II, and, between the two global conflicts, the Kellogg-Briand Pact, which was aimed at the renunciation of war as an instrument of national policy. In practice, most policies are a mixture of realism and idealism. The realist approach specifies the means for achieving goals, and the idealist approach justifies and wins support for the policies adopted.

Foreign-Policy Approach: Revisionism $\boxed{9}$

Any foreign policy by which a state seeks to alter the existing international territorial, ideological, or power distribution to its advantage. A revisionist policy is basically expansionist and acquisitive in nature; hence a state will be likely to pursue such a policy if its decisionmakers are dissatisfied with the status quo and believe that the state has the ability to achieve its objectives. *See also* BALANCE OF POWER (1); FOREIGN-POLICY APPROACH: STATUS QUO (10).

Significance

Typically, a revisionist policy is pursued by a "have not" or "unsatiated" state that attempts to improve its relative international position by undertaking strategic initiatives. Although it uses various non-belligerent offensive tactics in seeking its objectives, ultimately a revisionist state may commit acts of aggression or declare war in its effort to change the status quo. By its very nature, revisionism tends to produce defensive policies in status quo states. The power alignments that result from revisionist–status quo divisions among states encourage the formation of alliances and counteralliances. Revisionist states tend to view diplomacy, treaties, international law, and international organizations as means for gaining advantages in the power struggle rather than for ameliorating conflicts and resolving issues. For example, Nazi Germany rearmed in violation of the Treaty of Versailles; in numerous acts of duplicity, it threatened and then launched undeclared wars against considerably weaker governments. A significant example of Nazi revisionist policy was Hitler's aggressive diplomacy at Munich in 1938. Great Britain, led by Neville Chamberlain, capitulated to German demands and sold out Czechoslovakia, preparing the way for Germany's invasion of Poland and the beginning of World War II.

Foreign-Policy Approach: Status Quo $\boxed{10}$

Any foreign policy aimed at maintaining the existing international territorial, ideological, or power distribution. A status quo policy is basically conservative and defensive in nature. If a state enjoys an advantageous position in world politics, it will pursue such a policy and seek stability rather than change in order to maintain its existing advantages. *See also* FOREIGN-POLICY APPROACH: REVISIONIST (9).

Significance

A defensive status quo policy is typically pursued by a "satiated" or "have" state or bloc in direct opposition to an offensive or revisionist policy carried on by a "have not" or expansionist state or bloc. The power alignments that emerge out of status quo–revisionist divisions among states encourage the formation of alliances and counteralliances and the development of a balance-of-power system. Status quo states tend to react to the initiatives of revisionist states, avoid open conflict or escalation of military actions, emphasize orderly diplomatic procedures, and seek negotiated agreements that will leave them in possession of whatever advantages they enjoyed prior to the emergence of the rival bloc. International law as a conservative force in world affairs is frequently invoked by status quo states to defend existing rights. During the Cold War, more than 40 states were at one time or another allied militarily with the United States, ostensibly to defend the status quo by deterring aggression or other forms of violent, revolutionary change initiated by anti–status quo Communist states. The Soviet Union challenged the U.S.-generated status quo in ideological terms that pitted the forces of capitalism against those of revolutionary, Marxist-inspired communism. Each side regarded the other's policy as an expansionist imperialism, although the revisionist, anti–status quo Soviets insisted that their cause had the popular support of people everywhere. The failure of the Soviet Marxist appeal, however, was witnessed in the collapse of the Berlin Wall in 1989, the abandonment of Communist systems in Eastern Europe, and finally, in the self-destruction of the Soviet Union in 1991. It could be said, therefore, that the status quo prevailed over revisionism during the era of the Cold War.

Foreign-Policy Components: Elements of National Power | 11 |
The factors that collectively constitute the power-in-being and the power potentiality of a state. Some elements of national power are natural factors not ordinarily subject to human control or alteration, while others are variables that depend on human impulses, organization, and capacities. Major components in the power equation include (1) the size, location, climate, and topography of the national territory; (2) the natural resources, energy sources, and foodstuffs that can be pro-

duced; (3) the population size, density, and per capita relationship to national income; (4) the size and efficiency of the industrial plant; (5) the extent and effectiveness of the transportation system and communications media; (6) the educational system, research facilities, and the number and quality of the scientific and technical elite; (7) the size, training, equipment, and spirit of the military forces; (8) the nature and strength of the nation's political, economic, and social system; (9) the quality of its diplomats and diplomacy; (10) the policies and attitudes of the nation's leaders; and (11) the national character and morale of its people.

Significance
No single element of national power is likely to be decisive in determining a country's power potential or the outcome of a struggle with other nations. It is therefore absolutely essential to avoid the fallacy of single-factor analysis in evaluating international rivalries. Most power factors are relative in regard to time and the strength of rivals. An assessment of national capabilities that omits consideration of the comparative nature of the elements may be dangerous to a nation's security. In 1940, for example, France was militarily and psychologically prepared to fight a previously successful 1914–1918 type of war, but new developments in the technology and tactics of warfare made France's "Maginot line" thinking antiquated and led to its early defeat in World War II. The effectiveness with which national power is employed to achieve a state's objectives depends mainly on how capably the nation's leaders marshal, integrate, and direct the elements of national power in pursuit of its goals. Moreover, a nation's capabilities depend on how other states perceive and assess its elements of national power. In the nuclear age, weapons of mass destruction give the nuclear-weapons states unprecedented power-in-being, but because their catastrophic destructive power inhibits their use, other elements may outweigh nuclear weapons in computing national power in specific situations.

Foreign-Policy Components: National Interest | 12 |

The fundamental objective and ultimate determinant that guides the decision-makers of a state in forming foreign policy. The national interest of a state is typically a highly generalized conception of those elements that constitute the state's most vital needs, including self-preservation, independence, territorial integrity, military security, and economic well-being. Because no single interest dominates the policy-making functions of a government, the concept might be referred to more accurately in the plural as national interests. When a state bases its foreign policy solely on the bedrock of national interest with little or no concern for universal moral principles, it can be described as pursuing a realistic policy, in contradistinction to an idealistic one. *See also* FOREIGN POLICY (5).

Significance
Each of the approximately 180 nations in the contemporary state system interacts with other members as it develops policies and carries on diplomatic actions in pursuit of its subjectively defined national interest. When their interests are harmonious, states often act in concert to solve mutual problems. When their interests conflict, however, competition, rivalry, tension, fear, and ultimately war may result. Techniques developed in the state system to reconcile conflicts of national interest include diplomacy, peaceful settlement, international law, regional organizations, and global institutions such as the United Nations and its agencies. The key problem of foreign-policy making and diplomacy is that of translating the relatively vague and general interests of a nation into concrete, precise objectives and means. Although decisionmakers must deal with many variables in the international milieu, the concept of national interest usually remains the most constant factor and serves as a guidepost for decisionmakers in the policy process. The post–Cold War debate in the United States between those promoting international peacekeeping and those opposed to it centers on the question of national interest. For example, given the absence of a major adversary, in what way is U.S. national interest involved in the strife in Bosnia, Rwanda, or places like Kashmir and Cyprus? National interest in international relations is not easily defined, but it apparently says something about the domestic condition, i.e., public opinion and public perception, and how it influences foreign-policy decision making.

Foreign-Policy Components: Objectives | 13 |

The ends that foreign policy is designed to achieve. Foreign-policy objectives are concrete formulations derived from relating the national interest to the prevailing international situation and to the power available to the state. The objectives are selected by decisionmakers seeking to change (revisionist policy) or preserve (status quo policy) a particular state of affairs in the international environment. *See also* FOREIGN-POLICY PROCESS: CAPABILITY ANALYSIS (15).

Significance
Foreign-policy objectives are produced from an analysis of ends and means. Logically, the ends sought should determine the means selected for their achievement. Where several courses of action are feasible, the method that will most clearly advance the national interest should be adopted. The reverse situation sometimes prevails, however, and the means available may determine what objective a state ought to seek, just as events sometimes seem to outrun policy. Although concrete foreign-policy objectives vary from state to state, they tend to involve such abstract goals as self-preservation, security, national well-being, national prestige, the protection and advancement of ideology, and the pursuit of power.

Foreign-Policy Components: Situational Factors | 14 |

The international and national variables considered by decisionmakers when making foreign policy. Situational factors include (1) the general international setting or environment, including the attitudes, actions, and national-interest considerations of policy officials in other states; (2) the relative power or capability of the state as calculated by its decisionmakers; and (3) the specific actions and reactions undertaken by other states related to the policy decision and its execution. *See also* FOREIGN POLICY (5).

Significance
Analysis of situational factors that influence decisions is a crucial stage in the foreign-policy process. Although no policymaker is capable of recognizing or analyzing all factors that may impinge upon the decision process, identifying and understanding the more crucial ones and their relationship to the means and objectives of the state increase the chances for success. Still, because situational factors remain largely imponderables, incomplete and incapable of precise measurement, the judgments of decisionmakers must often be based on fragmentary knowledge and subjective evaluation of available data. Consequently, the foreign-policy process is more of an art than a science.

Foreign-Policy Process: Capability Analysis $\boxed{15}$
The systematic evaluation by a state of its military, political, diplomatic, and economic abilities to achieve its national-interest objectives. Before undertaking a planned initiative, decisionmakers analyze the capability or power potentiality of their state within the framework of the international system and relative to states directly affected. All the major elements of state power—both tangible and intangible—may be involved in determining the feasibility of a policy. An analysis of tangible factors may include geography (relative size, location, topography, and climate), population (size, age and sex composition, and human reserves), natural resources (availability of raw materials), economic strength (agricultural and industrial output), administrative organization (the nature and effectiveness of governmental machinery), and mili-

tary power (the relative size, organization, equipment, training, and reserves of the armed forces). Intangible factors, always more difficult to assess because they cannot be measured accurately, might include such considerations as national character and morale, the quality of diplomacy, relationships among the leaders of various states, and the reaction levels of states. *See also* FOREIGN-POLICY COMPONENTS: ELEMENTS OF NATIONAL POWER (11); POWER (26).

Significance
An effective capability analysis must involve a realistic appraisal of a state's ability to accomplish a specific objective vis-à-vis other states within the context of the international milieu. Capability never exists in a general or absolute sense; it is always relative to the interactions and capabilities of other states, and is subject to time changes that inexorably modify calculations. Therefore, capability should never be equated with national interest; for example, simply because a country has the capability to send its armed forces to remote regions of the world, it is not logical to conclude that it has a national interest in that region. The United States had the capability (that is, the extension) to involve itself in Vietnam in the 1960s, but it did not follow that it also had a vital national interest in doing so. In fact, because capability analysis determined U.S. policy, the United States was compelled to develop justifications for such involvement. Capability analysis can be of critical importance, but policymakers must be aware of its influence on their thinking and actions.

Foreign-Policy Process: Decisionmakers $\boxed{16}$
Those individuals in each state who exercise the powers of making and implementing foreign-policy decisions. Official decisionmakers may be influenced—sometimes decisively—by private individuals and groups serving as consultants or functioning as unofficial members of the nation's "establishment." Opinion elites and the general public may also

affect foreign-policy actions by setting limits on the decisionmakers through support for some policies and rejection of others. In most states, the chief of government—president, prime minister, premier, or chairperson—plays the key role in the decision process. In others, the highest decisionmaker may be the leader of the single party that controls power, as in Communist states, or the dictator or oligarchs who hold no official position but control the decision process, as in some Fascist states. Others who function as high-ranking decisionmakers in most states include the minister of foreign affairs, sometimes called secretary of state, and the bureaucracy that functions under his or her direction in the state's foreign office. Other ministries, particularly defense, and high military officers contribute to decision making. In many democratic states, key legislators of the majority party or coalition also play a role in making foreign-policy decisions, and in some—such as the United States—leaders of the opposition party or parties may also participate in the process. *See also* FOREIGN OFFICE (4); PUBLIC OPINION (138).

Significance
Although states are the actors in international politics, it is human beings in their role as decisionmakers who act and react to the stimuli of the international environment. It is individuals, not abstract entities called states, who define and interpret the concept of national interest, plan strategies, perceive issues, make decisions to act, and evaluate actions undertaken. Psychological factors are crucial in the decision process because individuals tend to act and react differently to the same stimuli. Consequently, changes in governmental personnel may result in new approaches to foreign-policy problems. In those states where officials holding the formal powers to make decisions are not the actual decisionmakers, however, changes in governments or officials may not influence policy decisions. In addition, all decisionmakers are conditioned and limited in their actions by the domestic and international environment

related to specific decisions or to the process of making them.

Foreign-Policy Process: Intelligence $\boxed{17}$
Information gathered by a government about other states' capabilities and intentions. Military or strategic intelligence is concerned with uncovering the strength and location of land, sea, and air forces; new weapons and weapons development; troop morale and combat qualities; strategic and tactical plans; secret alliances and agreements; and civilian attitudes and morale. At the same time, counterintelligence units actively ferret out espionage agents carrying on military intelligence activities for other nations. Most nations also conduct nonstrategic intelligence efforts to secure pertinent political, diplomatic, economic, and social data to aid their governments in pursuit of national-interest objectives. Most intelligence is secured openly through careful scrutiny of public documents and private news and data sources, but the more critical strategic information often requires the use of clandestine "cloak-and-dagger" methods. Today, spying can be accomplished at great distances by satellites and planes equipped with special radar and photo equipment operating in friendly or neutral airspace. *See also* CENTRAL INTELLIGENCE AGENCY (CIA) (624).

Significance
Most nations are engaged in widespread intelligence-gathering activities in pursuit of useful data about the activities and plans of friends and allies as well as potential enemies. The U.S. government, for example, assigns major intelligence responsibilities to at least nine military and civilian agencies and uses many others for supplementary work in the field. Much of the open intelligence work, as well as some covert activity, is carried on by diplomatic representatives and their staffs, particularly by military and other attachés. Revolutionary developments in warfare technology have greatly expanded the need to obtain vital information related to the security of nations.

When intelligence agents fail to uncover information concerning a potential enemy's intentions and strategic plans, a decisive defeat may result. In the 1967 Israeli attack on the United Arab Republic, for example, the element of surprise permitted the destruction of many Egyptian aircraft on the ground; the Israelis' resulting air superiority proved decisive. A surprise Arab attack on Israel in 1973 also produced some early military successes. An erroneous assessment of a foreign situation—as in the U.S. assumption that the Bay of Pigs assault on Cuba in 1961 would trigger a mass uprising— may also place a nation's vital security interests in danger. It is interesting to note that no one in the Western intelligence community foresaw the tearing down of the Berlin Wall, let alone the demise of the Soviet Union.

Foreign-Policy Process: National Style   18

The characteristic behavior patterns of a state as it attempts to deal with its foreign-policy problems. National style can be described as a function of ideological values, common historical experiences, traditions, and precedents. Thus, in established countries, a change in regime is not likely to result in a drastically altered approach to international problems. However, a conscious and explicit effort can be made to alter the national style. For example, under the constitution of the Fifth French Republic, the personalized executive leadership style of President Charles de Gaulle weakened legislative dominance in French national life.

Significance
Ascertaining the national style of another country may prove helpful as a guide in the conduct of relations with that country, but there is no guarantee that it will always act in a predictable fashion. Situational factors related to a specific problem may be similar over time, but they are never exactly the same. Nevertheless, in the diplomatic arena, where the variables

are not subject to scientific controls, no guide to action and reaction should be overlooked. The differences in national style between the United States and most other nations is observed in U.S. impatience in matters involving international commitment; by and large, the collective U.S. attitude anticipates quick solutions to a problem. This expectation often causes difficulties with the United States' partners, who argue the complexity of a given situation, the need to act incrementally, and their opposition to the U.S. penchant for immediate results.

Fourth World   19

A United Nations term that lumps the least developed countries (LDCs) into a category of those nations needing special treatment in aid and development projects. Many of the people of the Fourth World live under conditions described by World Bank economists as below the income level that provides the bare essentials of food, clothing, and shelter. Whereas many Third World states have demonstrated persistent growth and increasing economic viability, Fourth World countries are mired in poverty and unable to develop the resources and technical capabilities to reach the stage of self-sustaining economic growth. The help provided to Fourth World countries has been reduced by increasing bilateralism in aid and the need to support major debtor countries, and particularly by a greater reluctance on the part of "have" nations to provide assistance to the "have not" states. In 1995, with the Cold War over, a newly elected U.S. Congress made drastic reduction in its foreign-aid budget a major feature of its legislative program. *See also* THIRD WORLD (27).

Significance
The developing states are finding it increasingly difficult to maintain their longstanding unity on economic issues because of growing disparities between the Third and Fourth Worlds. The First and Third Worlds have concluded a num-

ber of arrangements and agreements, such as the Lomé Convention, the Caribbean Basin Initiative, and the Generalized System of Preferences, that provide preferential access to Western markets, often at the expense of Fourth World exporters. According to a United Nations classification, the "least developed" or Fourth World group includes Bangladesh, Benin, Bhutan, Botswana, Burundi, Cape Verde, Central African Republic, Chad, Comoros, Gambia, Guinea, Haiti, Lesotho, Malawi, Maldives, Mali, Nepal, Rwanda, Somalia, Sudan, Tanzania, Uganda, Upper Volta, Western Samoa, and the Yemen Arab Republic.

Patterns of Power $\boxed{20}$
The ways in which individual states organize and use their power to maximize their security and achieve their national interests in competition with other states. The patterns of power involve the characteristic responses available to the state in an international system in which the power of other states represents an actual or potential threat. The patterns include (1) unilateralism—dependence on one's own power; (2) alliances—the power configuration of group against group; (3) mutual security—the conscious effort by two rivals or groups of rivals to avoid displays of power that mortally threaten the other, while at the same time establishing those techniques and methods that aim at building confidences between them; (4) collective security—a universalized power system of "one for all, and all for one"; and (5) world government—a cooperative federal structure, or a world empire dominated by one government. *See also* PATTERNS OF POWER: ALLIANCES (21); PATTERNS OF POWER: MUTUAL SECURITY (23); POWER (26).

Significance
The patterns of power offer options to decisionmakers who must cope with a state system that acknowledges sovereignty as its central feature. Sovereignty involves the power of the state to make

final decisions, and a state system so organized implies that the use of power is spread among the states; consequently, each state may constitute a threat to every other state. Each, therefore, must use its power to meet potential threats by pursuing policies through one or more of the available patterns. The choice will hinge on the state's formulation of its national interest, its perception of the interests of other states, and its assessment of its own power compared to the power of other states in a specific time, place, and situation. The choice for the patterns of unilateralism or alliances implies a decision to operate within the state system as it exists. The choice of mutual security is judged risky for the individual state, but in an age of weapons of mass destruction, the transcending of ideological and psychological differences has become a higher imperative. In a condition of mutual security, the Soviet Union ultimately dissolved itself rather than sustain an ideological hostility it no longer deemed relevant. The choice for collective security or a form of world government implies a decision to seek security by changing the nature of the state system; these patterns require the diminution or elimination of individual state sovereignty.

Patterns of Power: Alliances $\boxed{21}$
A configuration of power wherein the state seeks security and the opportunity to advance its national interests by linking its power with that of one or more states with similar interests. The alliance pattern implies a decision by a state to alter or maintain a local, regional, or global power equilibrium. Such action usually leads to the seeking of alliance partners by the other side. Thus, the alliance pattern presents the typical appearance of bloc versus bloc. The pattern is most often established by formal treaties of alliance, but less formal understandings or ententes are also possible. Post–World War II alliances proved to be significantly different from those preceding World War I, when alliances were generally

arranged secretly and formed as a consequence of war. Such alliances largely dissolved once the war was terminated.
Post–World War II alliances, however,
were public, arranged in relative peacetime, and publicized as being defensive in
nature. The North Atlantic Treaty Organization (NATO) was formed as such
an alliance in 1949, and even after the
demise of the Soviet Union whose aggressive intentions it had been organized to
thwart, it was sustained and in fact expanded. The 1994 creation of the Partnership for Peace (PFP), linked with NATO,
represented still another pattern of
power, one which is more likely understood as "mutual security." *See also* ALLI-
ANCE (276); PATTERNS OF POWER: MUTUAL
SECURITY (23).

Significance
The pattern of alliances is the most widely
used technique by which states augment
their individual national powers in the
interest of national security. Some critics,
such as former U.S. president Woodrow
Wilson, argued that the balancing of power
by means of military alliances is counterproductive in that it actually encourages
war and is ultimately antithetical to security. This theory is often explained in
terms of a security-insecurity paradox:
When one state increases its security with
an alliance, the security of the other side
is weakened, thereby leading to efforts to
strengthen it. Russia's concern that
NATO will include members that are its
immediate neighbors represents a problem wherein the security of Russia's
neighbors must be weighed against that
of Russia itself. The post–Cold War world
can ill afford a heightening of tensions in
Central and Eastern Europe. Moreover,
the nuclear age demands a more neutral
approach to alliance strategies, and the
fact that neither Russia nor the United
States targets the other necessitates doing
all that can be done to build confidence
between former rivals. Seen in that light,
it either becomes necessary to expand
NATO to include Russia, or to avoid taking actions that may appear to promise
regional security to small states, but

which only elevate tensions and suspicions, and hence threaten the prevailing
equilibrium. Alliance patterns nevertheless persist in the Western world because
(1) unilateralism is perceived to have
limitations in an increasingly technological era and (2) the state system fails to
establish the conditions essential for the
operation of either a proof-positive mutual-
security system, a universal collective-
security system, or a cooperative system of
world government.

Patterns of Power: Collective Security   22

A power system in which each state of the
world would guarantee the security and
independence of every other state. The
key to the collective-security pattern is
universality of participation and obligation. Under these conditions, an aggressor
nation would face the united opposition of
the entire community. This fundamental
assumption was written into the Covenant of the League of Nations and the
United Nations Charter. The term *collective security* sometimes is used inaccurately to describe regional or bloc security
arrangements. Such groupings as NATO,
the now defunct Warsaw Pact, and the
Rio Pact often are referred to as regional
collective-security arrangements; not only
are they permitted by the United Nations
Charter, they are available for use at the
direction of the United Nations (for example, NATO was called to the service of
the United Nations in Bosnia). The concept of regional collective-security arrangements is a contradiction in terms,
however, since it does not fulfill the requirement of universality. Such organizations are examples of alliances, not the
pattern of collective security. *See also*
UNITED NATIONS: COLLECTIVE SECURITY
(576).

Significance
Collective security is only a theoretical
pattern of power. As an idea, it has ex-
cited the attention of statesmen and scholars since World War I, but in fact such a
security system has never operated effec-

tively. The League of Nations system never fulfilled the requirement of universality; even the great powers were not all under the same obligation at the same time. The United Nations system did not achieve unanimity among the permanent powers of the Security Council during the years of the Cold War until action was taken against Iraq for its aggression against Kuwait in 1990–1991. Even then, the Soviet Union did not join the alliance against Iraq, and China simply agreed not to veto the action. With the demise of the Soviet Union and the emergence of the Russian federation as the fifth permanent power on the Security Council, unanimity of action is still difficult to obtain; even the Western allies have differences over courses of action in Iraq, Bosnia, and other world trouble spots.

Patterns of Power: Mutual Security | 23 |

The belief that the security of one nation cannot be bought at the expense of others'. Mutual security emerged as a concept with the 1982 publication of the "Report of the Commission on Disarmament and Security Issues," generally cited as "The Palme Report" after the commission's chairman, Olaf Palme of Sweden. The report was published as a book with the title *Common Security*. Mutual security was the basic idea that undergirded U.S.-Soviet relations during the later years of the Cold War. Its purpose was the prevention of war while enhancing the two superpowers' mutual security. After Mikhail Gorbachev assumed the leadership of the Soviet Union in 1985, the idea of mutual security became an important element in the "new thinking" that Gorbachev and his supporters pledged to bring to Soviet foreign policy. By February 1986 mutual security was part of the declaratory policy of the USSR. By the late 1980s, Soviet and Western writers began employing the term *common security* to refer to the security of all nations, reserving the term *mutual security* to refer to East-West security. The confusion in terminology can be traced to

the much-used term in the West of *collective security,* a concept meaning security for all, as well as the roughly synonymous term *global security*. To understand how *mutual security* is different from these other Western-designed concepts, it is necessary to drop the term *common security* altogether. Thus, *mutual security* can be defined as a policy aimed at improving the security of both sides, under conditions of acknowledged mutual insecurity. The two sides may be two nations, or two loose or tight groupings of nations. In principle, mutual-security policy applies to any two actors who are able to threaten each other and are presently in a state of mutual insecurity, but who nonetheless truly seek to avoid direct conflict.

Significance

Mutual-security policy is more than a semantic expression. It is the foundation for the construction of international stability in the post–Cold War world. The policy focuses on the need for more successful communication among states. It stresses the point that international security cannot be achieved unilaterally. It notes that the security of one nation cannot be purchased at the expense of others. The mere existence and spread of nuclear weapons underlines the validity of the proposition. Nations confront common dangers; they must therefore promote mutual security. The matter of "interlinking" is important in understanding mutual-security policy. By linking their national security with practices of mutual security, rival actors more realistically acknowledge their mutual vulnerability, and hence develop postures that avoid or diminish the emphasis given to policies that perceive rivalry as irreconcilable, or that assume a nation can effect decisive, war-winning superiority, e.g., overwhelming first-strike capability. Unlike these latter policies, mutual security emphasizes the genuine willingness of the rivals to build accommodative measures that in time could diminish their rivalry. It is suggested that the success of the policy of mutual security pursued by Mikhail Gorbachev and acceded to by the United

States was primarily responsible for terminating the Cold War.

Patterns of Power: Unilateralism | 24 |

A policy whereby a state depends completely on its own resources for security and the advancement of its national interest. Unilateralism can take a variety of forms. Isolationism or neoisolationism implies a decision not to participate in or to severely limit participation in international relations. Neutrality involves giving up, by unilateral act or by treaty, the option of military participation in international affairs unless attacked. States that participate actively in international politics but rely on their own wits and strength are also engaged in unilateralism. Nonalignment describes the current disinclination, mainly among the developing countries, to commit themselves exclusively to the interests of one great power.

Significance

Unilateralism, once the most common pattern of power, has become increasingly difficult to pursue. Historically, it has been most successful for states well-placed geographically but hard to reach with existing methods of transportation, communication, and military technology. Great Britain, Japan, and the United States are classic examples of states that have long benefited from this techno-geographical situation. States in continental Europe do not enjoy the same advantage; formerly, they entered into alliances only on a temporary and emergency basis because the military technology then available allowed sufficient time to make arrangements after a threat arose or even after a war had begun. The industrial, scientific, and technological revolutions, however, make unilateralism less attractive for maximizing security and advancing the national interest. The motorization of land and sea travel and the development of the airplane and the rocket make states more readily accessible to one another; distance no longer

offers protection. Also, science has increased the economic cost and the destructiveness of arms and warfare so much that most states are increasingly hard-pressed to undertake their own defense unaided. Although reliance on unilateralism has declined, and states are increasingly dependent on regional security arrangements, in 1995 the U.S. House of Representatives approved a National Security Revitalization Act that would prevent the United States from engaging in UN peacekeeping missions and recommended unilateral U.S. actions unencumbered by UN command structures.

Patterns of Power: World Government | 25 |

The concentration in a single supranational authority of a monopoly of force and the power to make policies binding on individual states and their citizens. World government requires the surrender of sovereignty as it is now exercised by nation-states. It is theoretically possible to create such a superstate either through military conquest or by cooperative effort. Although World Federalists continue to promote a one-world concept, no serious effort has ever been made to establish a world government by peaceful international cooperation. President George Bush's call for "a new world order" following the successful war against Iraq in 1991 did not suggest the creation of a world government, although extreme political elements in the United States spread the word that the United States was being sold out to the "one-world advocates" and that the United Nations was a part of the conspiracy and needed to be resisted. The intensity of opposition in the United States to even the hint of world government was demonstrated in April 1995 when U.S. extremists bombed the Federal Building in Oklahoma City, killing 169 people and injuring hundreds. Although only one of the many complaints registered by the extremists as justification for the bombing, their opposition to world government was nonetheless a principal issue influencing their violent behavior. World government may be an ideal solution to the problem of war for some, but to others it is apparently a call to violent action. *See also* POLITICAL COMMUNITY: WORLD GOVERNMENT (544).

nation-state. Thus, despite a conflicted and threatened world, the general belief persists that only the nation-state can service the multidimensional needs of its citizens.

Significance
For those promoting the world government idea, such as the World Federalist Association, the plan would appear to solve the international power problem, but only by eliminating the international sovereign-state system. In the atomic age, any effort to create a world government by coercive power would likely trigger mutual annihilation. The only other alternative is a form of world federation. The belief that the United Nations could be converted into a world government indicates lack of understanding of the nature of that organization. The United Nations is a confederation in which certain limited powers have been conferred on the Security Council, powers that are themselves circumscribed by the veto power that is reserved to the permanent powers (the United States, Russia, Great Britain, China, and France). National sovereignty continues to dominate the thinking and action of each individual member state, and each jealously guards its independent actions. In a federation, sovereignty resides in the collectivity, and each individual unit is subordinate to the authority of the whole. Because states in the international community do not agree on fundamental values, objectives, or aspirations, they will not contemplate surrendering sovereignty. The writing of a world constitution is not the answer. Constitutions do not create mutual trust; they are only its product. Nor does it seem likely that world government can evolve out of wider regional agreements. Even the European Union, no longer motivated by the Cold War, confronts older problems of nationalism and exclusivity. Needless to say, even cooperative government at the world level is doubtful in a climate that emphasizes the emotional and sentimental importance of the

Power $\boxed{26}$
Influence and control exercised by one nation over others. Power is both the means used and the goal sought by states in political, military, economic, and social competition with one another. Although not every state action is motivated by power considerations, those directly related to enhancing or defending the national interest are always deeply involved in power politics. The exercise and pursuit of power are carried on by decision-makers who use the governmental machinery of the state to develop and implement foreign policy. Political power, therefore, involves a psychological relationship between the elites who exercise it and those who are influenced or controlled by it. The exercise of power takes many forms, including persuasion, ideological and psychological warfare, economic coercion, moral suasion, cultural imperialism, legally recognized measures short of war, and, ultimately, war. *See also* FOREIGN-POLICY COMPONENTS: ELEMENTS OF NATIONAL POWER (11); FOREIGN-POLICY PROCESS: CAPABILITY ANALYSIS (15).

Significance
The exercise of political power has been the central feature of the state system since the emergence of the concept of sovereignty. Major states have always exercised and sought power more frequently and effectively than smaller states, with the success for each policy dependent on the relative capabilities of the state. As one state seeks more power, however, those nations threatened or attacked by its policies react by building up their own power. The power of states that act most aggressively, therefore, tends to be brought under control by the development of

countervailing power on the part of those threatened, resulting in the evolution of a balance of power. In addition, there are institutional restraints on the exercise of power in the state system: international law, world opinion, disarmament and arms-control agreements, and collective-security arrangements such as the United Nations system.

Third World 27

The economically underdeveloped and developing countries. The Third World differs materially from the First World (the United States and its industrialized allies and partners), and, during the era of the Cold War, from the Second World (the Soviet Union and its East European adherents—stalwarts of Marxism-Leninism). The United Nations also identifies a Fourth World, composed of those countries with an exceptionally small annual per capita income. Third World countries are located mainly in Africa, Asia, Latin America, and the Pacific. *See also* DEVELOPMENT STRATEGY: GROUP OF SEVENTY-SEVEN (G-77) (211); FOURTH WORLD (19).

Significance
More than 100 countries, containing the majority of the world's population, have achieved independent status since the end of World War II. Most are poor, weak, and inexperienced. Typically, they produce primary and semifinished products, and their population growth impedes economic progress (measured by living standards in already developed countries). As a consequence, Third World countries are generally dependent on those representing the First World. Moreover, the end of the Cold War and the rejection of Communist systems in a majority of Second World states have eliminated many of the differences between the Third and Second World nations. Indeed, with the breakup of the Soviet Union many new nations have become included in the classification commonly described as Third World.

Third World: Nonaligned Movement (NAM) 28

A group of nations organized during the Cold War era and including more than 100 members that claimed to be neutral in the confrontation between the Western bloc led by the United States and the Eastern bloc dominated by the Soviet Union. The nonaligned movement had its roots in Bandung, Indonesia, where leaders of 25 Asian and African countries met in 1955 and proclaimed themselves to be a third force in the realm of world affairs. Marshal Josip Broz Tito of Yugoslavia and Prime Minister Pandit Jawaharlal Nehru of India emerged as the leaders of the new movement, along with Sukarno of Indonesia and Gamal Abdel Nasser of Egypt. At its first formal Conference of Nonaligned Countries, held in Belgrade in 1961, the participants adopted a definition of nonalignment, which states that a nonaligned country must (1) pursue an independent policy based on peaceful coexistence, (2) not participate in any multilateral military alliance, and (3) avoid even bilateral military alliances with any of the superpowers. *See also* THIRD WORLD (27).

Significance
The nonaligned movement received its impetus from the desire of many Third World nations to remain aloof from East-West conflicts. But the movement lost its raison d'être when the Cold War ended and the Soviet Union disintegrated. If the movement is to survive, it will have to find a different focus. Considering the fractures within the movement, even during its formative period, it is doubtful that the Third World states can muster the necessary enthusiasm to perpetuate the organization under a credo to which they can jointly respond. Moreover, the time has passed when the NAM states could successfully play off one superpower against another as a method for achieving material benefits. In point of fact, it is impossible to say that the NAM is a genuinely neutral body, dominated as it has been by states that appeared to favor the Soviet Union, though only one of these

was truly Marxist (Cuba). India became a major recipient of Soviet arms, but remained a major actor in the organization. Only those developing states formally allied with the West, such as Pakistan, were prevented from joining the NAM. North Korea was granted membership, while South Korea, like the Philippines, was rejected on the ground that it had aligned with the United States.

Third World: North-South Relations 　29

The continuing political, economic, and social relationship between the industrialized, developed countries (the "North") and largely poor, developing countries (the "South"). The term *North-South relations* is used to describe this relationship because most of the rich, developed countries are located geographically north of the Third and Fourth World countries. Countries of the South are mainly African, Asian, and Latin American, whereas countries of the North are European, North American, Japanese, and Oceanic. The North develops joint policies and approaches through organizations such as the 24-member Organization for Economic Cooperation and Development (OECD). The South coordinates policies and develops a common approach largely through the workings of the Group of Seventy-Seven (G-77), which functions as a caucus for the approximately 130 nations of the South. *See also* DEVELOPMENT AGENCY: UNITED NATIONS CONFERENCE ON TRADE AND DEVELOPMENT (UNCTAD) (204); DEVELOPMENT STRATEGY: NEW INTERNATIONAL ECONOMIC ORDER (NIEO) (212).

Significance
The North was mainly concerned with keeping countries of the South free from Soviet influence and open to trade and investment by its private companies, mostly multinationals. The South has been primarily concerned with achieving economic development and modernization, ending colonialism and neocolonialism, and protecting human rights,

especially by ending racial discrimination. In foreign aid to the South, the North prefers to offer technical assistance and infrastructure aid, leaving actual development in the hands of private capital, especially multinational corporations. The South, on the other hand, prefers grants and low-interest loans, increased trade, and higher prices for their raw materials as means for obtaining the capital to produce economic growth. To improve their position vis-à-vis the North, over the years countries of the South have campaigned for programs that would better meet their economic needs. These campaigns have included (1) the Special United Nations Fund for Economic Development (SUNFED) proposal in the United Nations to set up a huge capital fund from which the South could receive grants or obtain low-interest loans; (2) the establishment of the United Nations Conference on Trade and Development (UNCTAD) to increase the South's export trade with the North to earn more capital for development; (3) the creation of the International Development Association (IDA) as an affiliate of the World Bank, to grant soft loans (no interest charged and 50 years to repay); and (4) the creation of a New International Economic Order (NIEO), which would replace the existing world economic system with one in which the nations of the South would receive fairer treatment and higher prices for their commodities. These and other campaigns aimed at improving the South's opportunities to develop and modernize have generally failed because of the North's refusal to participate or, in some cases, offers of only half-hearted support. In the case of SUNFED, for example, after a campaign of many years the South finally had the votes to secure a two-thirds majority in the General Assembly. Using this power, the South created a SUNFED-type United Nations Capital Development Fund (UNCDF) to disburse grants and loans of capital, but the North declined to contribute to the new fund. This case demonstrates that, in North-South relations, the South has achieved the ability to garner the votes through sheer numbers, but lacks the ability to compel the North to honor the decisions of the voting majority and to give them full support.

Third World: Privatization   30

The trend away from Third World socialism toward the encouragement of foreign and domestic private investment as a means of achieving substantial economic growth. Third World privatization is a pragmatic policy aimed at changing political and economic conditions in a manner likely to attract capital from the developed world. The end of the Cold War and the attraction of privatization has led many Third World states to change their basic outlook. Instead of regarding foreign capital investment as "neocolonialism" and "neoimperialism," developing countries are removing many disincentives to foreign private-capital investment. In effect, these actions are a recognition that private capital is likely to flow to those areas and countries where earnings and the repatriation of profits are least controlled. In some Third World countries, unique programs, such as Nigeria's "Make or Buy" policy, promote privatization and joint ventures, and involve a working partnership between government, private companies, and some multinational corporations. *See also* CAPITALISM (81).

Significance
Third World privatization is a product of both external and internal forces. In the 1980s the industrialized countries of the West, with President Ronald Reagan providing the ideological and political leadership, pushed for a global free-market system for trade and investment. As a practical matter in their search for capital, Third World states eventually followed the lead of the West and changed their long-standing policies of state control over, and in many cases operation of, their national economies. The termination of the Cold War gave these economic programs even greater emphasis. Another influential factor encouraging privatization is the great economic success enjoyed by those Third World countries that have adopted policies to encourage the private sector. Examples of success based on privatization include South Korea, Taiwan, Singapore, Hong Kong, and Brazil. Today, most African countries accept a formula of economics that moves the developing states from their almost exclusive dependence on government-managed corporations and state-owned enterprises. Even Communist-led China pursues a program that encourages free enterprise and foreign corporate investment. China's success in this area of privatization is read in its huge balance-of-payments surplus with the United States.

Ethnicity, Nationalism, and Interdependencies

Apartheid

31

The Republic of South Africa's official policy of racial segregation established through openly discriminatory legislation following World War II. The apartheid (apartness) policy was designed to perpetuate control of the state by the European minority. South Africa's population of about 40 million is approximately 73 percent African (black), 12 percent European (white), 13 percent colored (mixed), and 2 percent Asian. Its white minority, much dependent on black labor, transformed the country into a relatively modern state, with an economy said to represent about one-third of Africa's total income. Otherwise judged a major economic success, considering that South Africa constituted only 4 percent of the continent and 6 percent of the population, the apartheid policy nevertheless demonstrated the political backwardness of the country. Apartheid's deliberate and official separation of the races denied the majority black African population representation and participation in their country's political life. Moreover, policies designed by the white-dominated government to create black "homelands" were no substitute for black self-government. The African National Congress (ANC), led by Nelson Mandela from his prison cell, articulated the demand for black rights. Supported by a majority of the world's nations, the ANC cause was pressed in the United Nations and by individual governments refusing to do business with South Africa if the white Afrikaner government did not abandon its apartheid policy. Although it required almost five decades to force the white minority to discard its racist policy, the goal was achieved when Mandela was released from his 28-year imprisonment and led the movement that won for the black population the right to elect the country's leaders. Apartheid was officially terminated in 1994 when black South African voters went to the polls and elected Nelson Mandela president of South Africa. *See also* NATIONALIST MOVEMENT: AFRICAN NATIONAL CONGRESS (ANC) (64); NATIONALIST MOVEMENT: NAMIBIA (69).

Significance
The harshness of white rule provoked an extended period of violence and counterviolence, but in the end the transfer of

power to the black majority was largely peaceful. Few observers could have anticipated the relative tranquility with which the Afrikaners yielded power. Moreover, the pacific manner of the change process encouraged the formation of a government comprised of all the races, with the white minority holding prominent positions and, no less significant, able to successfully manage their business ventures. Although apartheid had been demonstrably abolished, complex problems, notably of a socioeconomic character, continued to haunt the country. Moreover, Mandela's looming presence provided the bridge for the commingling of the races, but his advanced age raised the question of a successor. It was all too apparent that no one could be expected to play the charismatic role he had fashioned over a lifetime of demonstrated selflessness and personal sacrifice. Mandela's achievement in moving South Africa from apartheid to political integration is only the initial stage in a continuing campaign aimed at transforming South Africa into a successful multicultural and multiracial society.

Charismatic Leadership   32

Leadership characterized by a mystical or spiritual messianic quality that elicits widespread emotional popular support often bordering on reverence. Charismatic leadership tends to merge with the spirit of nationalism and to become identified with or symbolic of the state itself. The charismatic leader, particularly in newly emergent nations, appears to followers as the personification of truth, one who is beyond the fears and ambitions of ordinary mortals, the chosen instrument for the realization of the nation's destiny. Charismatic leaders can be separated into two major categories: those who are genuinely concerned with leading a people to a noble sense of responsibility and community, and those who use their magnetic charm to capture the loyalty of a desperate people searching for a human savior. In the first category are Mahatma Mohandas Gandhi, Martin Luther King, Jr., and Nelson Mandela. In the second are the demagogues, amply represented by Josef Stalin, Adolf Hitler, and Benito Mussolini. *See also* NATIONALISM (57).

Significance
Charismatic leadership is linked inextricably with human society's fascination with leaders, heroes, and celebrities. Political organizations have always formed around personalities, and the institutionalization of leadership in contemporary history has not necessarily supplanted the popular need for the all-knowing, all-seeing leader who demonstrates a facility for articulating a people's deepest sentiments. In the midst of significant upheaval, societies too often bestow godlike qualities on charismatic leaders. The post–World War I period proved to be one of considerable stress, exacerbated by a worldwide economic depression that tore national societies apart and ultimately destroyed plans for political reorganization. Adolf Hitler and Franklin D. Roosevelt achieved political power at roughly the same time, and under essentially the same conditions of economic dislocation and social demoralization. Both men assumed charismatic qualities in that both enjoyed the considerable support of their desperate populations. Hitler's response to a strife-torn and destabilized nation was a narrowly conceived nationalism rooted in revenge, scapegoating, and violence. Roosevelt's efforts, by contrast, centered on the pooling of human talents and labor, and the bridging of human differences to enhance the voluntary growth of an expanding community. Hitler exploited fear; Roosevelt sought to dispel it. The importance of charismatic leaders is seen in their capacity to mobilize societies for either negative or positive purposes. In the modern world, charismatic leaders may either lead their people to accept new forms of human bondage, e.g., totalitarianism, or find ways to advance the cause of democratic development despite the enormous obstacles in their path.

Charismatic Leadership: Iran-Iraq War | 33 |

A war conducted by leaders whose followers display blind faith and almost total obedience. The war between Iran and Iraq in 1980 can be attributed to the charismatic leadership of both Saddam Hussein of Iraq and Ayatollah Khomeini of Iran. Both leaders were venerated by their countrymen, and each demanded the total sacrifice of their respective populations. This devastating war—in human terms the most costly Middle East war in the twentieth century—consumed an estimated 1 million casualties. It was but the latest chapter in a long history of rivalry between the two states. Major points of contention included rival territorial claims, control of the Shatt al-Arab waterway to the Persian Gulf, religious differences between Shiite and Sunni Muslims (especially following the emergence of a Shiite theocracy in Iran under the leadership of Ayatollah Khomeini), and vying for the dominant position in the oil-rich Persian Gulf region. *See also* FOREIGN-POLICY PROCESS: CAPABILITY ANALYSIS (15); WAR (305).

Significance

Beyond its human costs, the war between Iraq and Iran was of worldwide concern because they represented two of the leading oil-producing countries. Launched by Saddam Hussein, the Iraqi ruler, the war was expected to achieve Iraqi control over oil-rich Iranian Khuzistan, which Iraq called Arabistan. Iraq believed that the country had been taken illegally from them by the Persian shah Reza Pahlavi following World War I. Given the overthrow of the Pahlavi dynasty in 1979, and observing the disarray in Iran following the shah's fall, as well as witnessing the Soviet penetration of neighboring Afghanistan in December 1979, Saddam Hussein sensed that the time was propitious to strike a blow for Iraq. However, the Iraqi dictator miscalculated his own capabilities, and especially those of his adversary. Despite internal weaknesses and a revolution that had not yet been consolidated, the Iranians more than held

their own against the Iraqi invaders. A stalemate soon developed between the opposed sides, but Ayatollah Khomeini was determined to sustain the conflict that Iraq had precipitated. Describing Saddam Hussein in satanic terms, he called upon the Iranian people to martyr themselves in the struggle against Iraq. The war was thus protracted and, indeed, did not end until the United States entered the arena, ostensibly to keep the oil flowing from the Gulf, but in point of fact to tilt the war in favor of Iraq. The accidental shootdown of an Iranian commercial airliner by a U.S. warship stationed in the Gulf followed several punishing attacks by U.S. forces against Iranian military and oil installations. Only after the loss of the commercial airliner, however, did the ayatollah agree to a cease-fire. The war between Iran and Iraq ground to a halt in 1988 with neither side reconciled and each still holding some of the other's territory. During the Gulf War, precipitated by Iraq's invasion and conquest of Kuwait in 1990, Baghdad returned Iranian prisoners of war and withdrew from captured Iranian territory as an act of good will, but the two countries remained significant adversaries. The "limited war" between Iran and Iraq was limited only in geographic terms. At all times it threatened to become a much larger conflict; if it was prevented from spreading, it was because the United States, the Soviet Union, and China did not confront one another. This conclusion was given greater emphasis when the United States led a coalition of forces against Iraq in 1991; neither Moscow nor Beijing did anything to assist Baghdad.

"Clash of Civilizations?" | 34 |

The question raised by Samuel Huntington in his article in the journal *Foreign Affairs* (Summer 1993). Huntington discusses the new conditions prevailing in international relations following the demise of the Soviet Union and the termination of the Cold War. The author laments the spawning of a new age of conflict that followed the initial euphoria. World politics, Huntington asserts, has entered a new phase, but not one heralding more cooperative and accommodative communities. He sees great divisions in the human family, divisions based on cultural distinctiveness and exclusive representations of purpose. Huntington believes the twenty-first century will be one of increasing hostility among cultural entities, and that religion, history, language, and tradition will overwhelm efforts at bridging differences and reconciling people and nations. The impulses that divide humanity, Huntington argues, are greater than the transcendent experiences that tie one group to another, one nation to the other. He claims that the civilizational fault lines can be observed in contemporary struggles ranging from Bosnia in the former Yugoslavia to the Arab-Israeli conflict, to Tajikistan in Central Asia, and eastward to Timor, the Philippines, etc. Huntington sees religious experience, née fundamentalism, in its various configurations, driving many of the cultural conflicts. In citing the dilemma this poses for the United States, Huntington stresses that neither ideology in its more secular context nor economics driven by technological innovation and interdependence explains the unfolding condition. More than a clash of states, civilizations are pitted against one another, and hence become rivals of one another. His advice to the United States is not to stand above the fray or aloof from it, but rather to forge alliances with cultures similar to its own and, where possible, spread the values of that civilization in ways that aim at moderating the intensity of the conflict. All civilizations must learn toleration, he concludes, but in the interim, during this time of uncertainty, confrontation should not be avoided. *See also* ETHNICITY (51); ISLAMIC FUNDAMENTALISM (132).

Significance
Samuel Huntington's article was received with considerable interest. Provocative in the extreme, heralded by *Foreign Affairs* as the "X" article of the post–Cold War generation (a reference to George Kennan's 1946 article in the same journal that focused world attention on the subject of containment), Huntington had taken a measure of the post–Cold War period and candidly (some would argue recklessly) declared open warfare between the world's major cultures, not the least of which was the clash between Christian European/U.S. civilization and the world of Islam. The overt lumping of people under religious-*cum*-cultural experience, and facing them off in mortal combat, was questionable in an age of cross-cultural and multicultural experience where paradigms are more given to the creation of global and regional systems based on genuine cooperation. But Huntington could point to areas of the world rocked by savage engagements between unreconciled cultural/ethnic groups. Bosnia illustrated the very fault line to which he alluded. So, too, the Arab-Israeli peace process, where cultural elements at variance with one another sow despair and division, bringing Israel to contemplate the permanent separation of Israeli Jews and Muslim Arabs.

Colonialism   35
The rule of an area and its people by an external sovereignty pursuing a policy of imperialism. Historically, two broad types of colonialism can be identified: (1) the transplanting of emigrants from the mother country to form a new political entity at a distant location and (2) the imposition of rule over the technologically less developed indigenous peoples of Asia and Africa. In either case, the colony was established to advance the military security, economic advantage, and international prestige of the imperial power. *See also* DEPENDENT TERRITORY: COLONY (36); IMPERIALISM (53).

Significance
Opposition to the superior-inferior relationship and the racialism inherent in colonialism gave rise to a nationalism among dependent peoples of Asia and

Africa that proved to be an irresistible force in world politics after World War II. The war demonstrated that Western imperialists possessed no inherent invincibility; witness the early victories of the Japanese forces. Many of the colonial powers in Asia were so exhausted by the war that they granted independence either voluntarily or because political disturbances proved too costly to suppress. Independence movements were encouraged by principles enunciated in the Declaration Regarding Non-Self-Governing Territories of the United Nations Charter, which served to legitimate their aspirations for nationhood. By 1960 the emergence of new nations had doubled the membership of the United Nations, which in turn strengthened the assault on colonialism. In that year, the assembly adopted the historic Declaration on the Granting of Independence to Colonial Countries and Peoples; the following year, the assembly established a special Committee on Decolonization to implement its principles. The wave of independence movements that began in Asia swept over Africa in the late 1950s and into the 1960s, adding many new nations to the state system. The Portuguese territories of Angola, Mozambique, and Portuguese Guinea, along with the League of Nations–mandated territory of South-West Africa (now the independent state of Namibia), were major objectives of UN decolonization efforts. With a numerical majority in the General Assembly, the former colonial states have directed the focus of UN attention to the problems of political, social, and economic development. The concept of neocolonialism, however, symbolizes their ambivalence when it comes to leading a truly independent life. Many of the former colonies remain dependent on their previous colonial masters, which continue to dominate these countries' economic lives. While rejecting interference in their national political affairs, the newly independent states generally welcome economic and technical aid, as well as private investment from abroad. Although this heavy dependence on foreign assistance some-

what compromises the new nations' sense of control, they nevertheless display considerable acumen in balancing external intervention with a profound understanding of their independent needs.

Dependent Territory: Colony | 36 |

A noncontiguous territorial possession of a sovereign state. Colonies have been established by settlement, cession, and conquest, and their acquisition marks the successful pursuit of a policy of imperialism. Early in the twentieth century, much of Asia and almost all of the continent of Africa had been carved up into colonies by Great Britain, France, Belgium, Germany, Italy, Spain, Portugal, and the Netherlands. Colonies differ from other dependent territories such as protectorates, spheres of influence, and leaseholds in that the imperial power possesses full sovereignty over a colony. *See also* COLONIALISM (35); IMPERIALISM (53).

Significance
Colonies served the imperial powers as markets for manufacturers, sources of raw materials and investment opportunities, strategic locations and sources of manpower for national defense, and as symbols of prestige and great-power status. In the process of holding and administering their colonies, however, the metropolitan powers brought dependent peoples literacy, education, an ability to compare their conditions with other societies of the world, and nationalism, which created increasing dissatisfaction with continued subordinate status. Since World War II, almost all colonies have become independent states by peaceful negotiation with the imperial power, by force, or by some combination of the two.

Dependent Territory: Leasehold | 37 |

An area used by a foreign state under a lease agreement with the territorial sovereign. Leaseholds may be of short or long duration, and the extent of authority exercised by the lessee is established by specific agreement in each instance. Such lease agreements have been concluded freely or under various degrees of duress. Major European powers acquired economic rights in China by the leasehold technique during the nineteenth century.

Significance
As concessions to a foreign power, leaseholds are sources of tension and conflict in this age of rampant nationalism. An illustration of a contemporary leasehold is the U.S. lease of Guantánamo Bay in Cuba. To nationalists, leaseholds restrict the free exercise of territorial sovereignty and thereby imply an unacceptable superior-inferior relationship.

Dependent Territory: Protectorate 38

A relationship between a strong state and a semisovereign state, or an area or people not recognized as a state. The term *protectorate* also applies to the country under protection. Protectorates have been established voluntarily and by force, normally either to thwart the interests of third states or to provide for the administration of law and order in territory over which no responsible government exists. The extent to which the alien government exercises sovereign powers in the protectorate is controlled by treaty between the parties.

Significance
The protectorate is a device whereby a powerful state exercises various degrees of control over another state without actually annexing it. At a minimum, the protector usually exercises control over foreign affairs and national defense of the "protected" state. In the late nineteenth and early twentieth centuries, for example, France established protectorates over Tunisia and portions of Morocco. Great Britain entered into a similar agreement with Egypt, Japan with Korea, and the United States with Cuba. To provide for the establishment of law and order, Great Britain created protectorates in the territories adjacent to her colonies in Gambia

and Sierra Leone. Protectorates have virtually disappeared in an age of self-determination that has seen the elimination of the colonial system and the proliferation of self-governing, sovereign states.

Dependent Territory: Sphere of Influence 39

An area dominated by the national interests of a foreign power. In a sphere of influence, the foreign power does not possess sovereignty but imposes an international servitude that restricts the free exercise of local territorial sovereignty. Such servitude may be positive, as when the dominant state is granted a monopoly of commercial exploitation, or negative, as when the weaker state is required to refrain from fortifying a common border. *See also* NEAR ABROAD STATES (175).

Significance
Created with or without the voluntary agreement of the territorial sovereign, spheres of influence have usually been conceded by third states on a quid pro quo basis. This has amounted to recognition of the paramountcy of one state in a region, and agreement not to interfere with its pursuit of national interest in that portion of the territory of the weaker state. Spheres of influence may be established and recognized formally, as in a treaty. In the entente of 1907, Great Britain and Russia agreed to recognize each other's sphere of influence in the southeastern and northern portions of Persia (Iran). During the nineteenth century, Great Britain, France, Germany, Japan, and Russia created spheres of influence in China. The term *sphere of influence* is also used more loosely and informally to describe the area over which the power of one state has been or could be extended over that of its near neighbors. Examples of contemporary spheres of influence may be found in Russia's designation of its immediate neighbors as the "near abroad states" and in India's claim to preeminence in the Indian Ocean. Iraq's attempt to seize Kuwait and intimidate the

Persian Gulf states in 1990 was an example of the aggressive use of the sphere of influence.

Divided State   **40**

The division of a state, generally as a consequence of a war, forming two distinct units, each claiming to be sovereign and independent, but with each of the two parts arguing its legitimate right to possess the other. Divided states can also occur as a result of a retreating imperialism, wherein a former colony is divided to form two or more states otherwise perceived to be one and indivisible.

Significance

As a consequence of World War II, and the almost immediate emergence of the Cold War, several states were divided to form separate entities. In almost every instance, the divided states became the focal points of the Cold War, e.g., Germany in Central Europe, Korea in Northeast Asia, Vietnam in Southeast Asia, and China. Other significant divided states were India and Pakistan (more a consequence of the British withdrawal from South Asia, but no less a consequence of World War II); Cyprus, another former British colony in the Mediterranean; and the British mandate of Palestine.

Divided State: Germany   **41**

A consequence of Germany's defeat in World War II and the ensuing Cold War between the Western alliance and the Soviet bloc states. At the close of World War II Germany was occupied by the armies of the Soviet Union, the United States, Great Britain, and France. Each army operated in a different zone until the U.S., British, and French zones were united to form the German Federal Republic, or West Germany. The Soviet zone was then re-formed as the German Democratic Republic, or East Germany. All the armies remained in place, and there was little contact between East and West except for Berlin (located in East Germany), where

the four powers maintained their headquarters. In the matter of unifying the two Germanys, West Germany made the loudest claim. In 1961, as a consequence of the flight of East Germans to the West, the Soviet occupation force constructed a wall dividing Berlin, which made it very difficult for any interaction to occur between the two parts of the city, let alone the two Germanys. The Berlin Wall came to symbolize not only a divided Germany but the division of Europe. When the Soviet Union allowed the wall to be torn down in 1989, the unification of Germany became inevitable. Germany was unified in 1990, and the Soviet Union pledged to withdraw all its troops from the eastern sector by 1994. That promise was kept. The four-nation occupation of Berlin also ended in 1994.

Significance

The division of Germany was not envisaged by the Allied powers during World War II, but there had been considerable discussion as to how Germany would be treated when the war was over. The policy of unconditional surrender prolonged the war, but Germany's total defeat placed it at the mercy of the victorious powers. Originally, the plan was to strip Germany of its industrial capacity, thus preventing it from ever again disturbing the peace of Europe. The Morgenthau Plan (1944–1945), as it was known (named after Henry Morgenthau, Franklin D. Roosevelt's secretary of the treasury) was intended to turn Germany into an agrarian state, thus denying it the opportunity to create another military establishment. The plan was ignored with the onset of the Cold War and the perceived threat posed by the Soviet Union in the heart of Europe, not too distant from France, the Low Countries, and the English Channel. In 1948–1949 the Soviets tried to force the Allies out of Berlin by closing off their overland supply route through East Germany. An Allied airlift to Berlin broke the Soviet blockade, but the region remained in a state of tension even after Stalin's death in 1953. That same year, East Berlin revolted against

Soviet occupation, but the resistance was crushed as the Western powers stood by. Given Moscow's decision not to reduce the Red Army, and the weakness of the West Europeans following the war, the United States took steps to revitalize West Germany. In 1954–1955, West Germany was rearmed and made an integral member of the North Atlantic Treaty Organization (NATO). The Soviet response to this action was the creation of the Warsaw Pact, also in 1955. West Germany also developed the Halstein Doctrine (1955), which warned nations wishing to do business with the Federal Republic that their recognition of the East German state would deny them that possibility. The Halstein Doctrine remained in place until West German foreign minister and later chancellor Willy Brandt developed his Ostpolitik policy, his opening to the East (1967–1970). Relations between the two Germanys and with the East bloc were a bit easier after this action, but the lines remained fast between East and West. No one really anticipated a change in the division of the two Germanys, especially after the West Germans themselves recognized the Eastern regime. The fall of the Berlin Wall, therefore, was less the work of the Germans and more a consequence of the Gorbachev reforms, which impacted international relations as well as domestic Soviet affairs. It can also be traced to acts of defiance in Eastern Europe, beginning with the Hungarian uprising of 1956, the Czechoslovakian deviation of 1968, the massive demonstrations organized by the Polish labor movement Solidarity in the early 1980s, and, finally, to the intellectual ferment in Hungary, Czechoslovakia, and Poland in 1987–1988. The most dramatic chapter came in November 1989 when the Germans, energized by popular demonstrations in Eastern Europe, assaulted and broke open the Berlin Wall. As the German Democratic Republic merged with the German Federal Republic, the government of unified Germany acknowledged the "permanency" of the Oder-Niesse line with Poland. An expanded, more in-dependent Germany became the most powerful state in Europe west of Russia.

Divided State: Korea and Vietnam   42

States divided as a consequence of World War II, but more so by rival external powers during the Cold War. Korea was annexed by Japan in 1910 and remained an extension of the Japanese Empire until Japan's defeat in World War II. Indochina, which included Cambodia, Laos, and Vietnam, was a French colony dating back to the early part of the nineteenth century and under French administration through most of World War II. Korea was occupied by Soviet and U.S. forces when the war ended. The country was divided at the 38th parallel, with the U.S. forces in the south and the Soviets in the north. The United States organized a South Korean government under the leadership of an autocrat named Syngman Rhee; in North Korea, the Soviets installed Kim il Sung, a young Soviet protégé who had been trained in Moscow for a leadership role. Vietnam was occupied by Nationalist China and Great Britain, but with their withdrawal the French returned to reclaim the colony. The Vietnam question was initially more complex. A Vietnamese liberation force had supported the Allied cause during the war, and with the defeat of Japan, these Vietnamese, led by Ho Chi Minh, a much renowned nationalist and Communist leader, declared their independence. The return of the French colonialists was a most unwelcome event in Vietnam, and when the two sides failed to resolve their differences, the French launched a war aimed at destroying Ho's forces and reestablishing the original colony. The Vietnamese resisted the French, and finally defeated them at the epic battle of Dien Bien Phu in 1953. France was forced to retreat from Southeast Asia, and a peace conference was arranged in Geneva to work out the details of the surrender. While the French were pressing their colonial war in Indochina against the Vietnamese Communists, still another conflict between divided states erupted on the Korean peninsula. Taking advantage of a U.S. decision to remove its forces from the area, North Korea attacked South Korea. North Korean troops crossed the 38th parallel in June 1950 with the objective of destroying the U.S.-installed government in the South; their ultimate goal was the unifying of the peninsula under a single Communist government. U.S. forces, which had been redeployed in Japan, were ordered back to the peninsula. A long, difficult war commenced, with the U.S. command becoming the UN command, initially under General Douglas MacArthur, and raged on between 1950 and 1953. Communist China, the successor state to Nationalist China on the mainland, joined the fray against the UN forces. When a cease-fire was declared in 1953, neither side had defeated the other, and the two Koreas remained divided along a modified 38th parallel. Given the character of the Cold War and its spread to Northeast and Southeast Asia, the French surrender in Indochina was seen as a major threat to U.S. strategy, which aspired to contain the spread of international communism. The United States refused to accept North Vietnam's claim to represent all of the country, and it insisted on dividing Vietnam along the 17th parallel, with the Communists in the north under the leadership of Ho Chi Minh, and a U.S.-created government in the south under a confirmed anti-Communist, Ngo Dinh Diem. A popular plebiscite was agreed to at the 1954 Geneva peace conference, and was slated to be conducted in 1956 to determine which side, north or south, was more popular with the Vietnamese population, and therefore would prevail. It was never held. The United States realized that Ngo Dinh Diem would not receive the necessary support, and that an election would only confirm Ho Chi Minh as the ruler of an undivided Vietnam. When the United States attempted to reinforce the government of Ngo Dinh Diem in South Vietnam, the Vietnamese under Ho resumed the fight they had won earlier from the French. This first phase of the Second Indochina War began as an insurgency, and later, during the second phase, when the United States committed substantial forces to the defense of South Vietnam, North Vietnam sent its regular forces into the struggle. Whereas the war in Korea had ground to a stalemate, with the two sides poised to resume at any time, the North Vietnamese pressed the war against the South and the United States escalated its troop commitment. The Second Indochina War commenced in earnest in 1964 and was not brought to an end until North Vietnam eventually overran the South in 1975, unifying the two segments of the country. Only two years earlier (1973), the United States and North Vietnam had agreed to a peace settlement in which the United States believed that South Vietnam would be allowed to stand as an independent sovereign state in return for a U.S. troop withdrawal. But after the U.S. departure, the North Vietnamese overwhelmed South Vietnam's defenders and a unified Vietnam became a reality. *See also* NUCLEAR DIPLOMACY: NORTH KOREA–UNITED STATES (433).

Significance

The divided states of Korea and Vietnam, unlike Germany, were lethal experiences that tested the commitment of the parties to unify the two segments of their country. In Korea, an unpopular Syngman Rhee was ousted from power, but the South Koreans were determined to avoid the grasp of the North under Kim il Sung, and thus, despite the aggressive actions of the Communists, the two Koreas remained distinct entities. Moreover, the contest between two diametrically opposed ideologies was more apparent in Korea than in Vietnam. Korea had been liberated from its imperial yoke by the Allied armies of World War II, but its internecine conflict prevented a future as an independent state. North Korea remained a centralized ideological state under the charismatic leadership of Kim il Sung, and even his death in 1994 did not point to a shift away from this design. South Korea was subjected to long periods of military rule, but with a continued U.S. presence it made significant economic progress. Although the two Koreas discussed the question of their unification, they remained, even with Kim's passing, far from that goal. In Vietnam, the French did not yield their colony until forced to do so by the Vietnamese. In effect, the Vietnamese liberated themselves. That first liberation, however, remained inchoate due to U.S. actions; the United States refused to acknowledge an act of self-determination in Vietnam because after the takeover of China in 1949 by Mao's Communist legions, a shadow of international communism seemed to hover over all of Southeast Asia. Even the assassination of Ngo Dinh Diem by disgruntled members of the U.S.-organized South Vietnamese army did not deflect U.S. purpose in the region. The United States was convinced of the necessity of holding the line on the rimland of Asia. The all-consuming fear that the Communists were on the march, and if not stopped in Vietnam would seize virtually the entire Asian continent, seemed to require denying the Vietnamese a unified state. These fears proved to be unfounded in the years that followed the forceful unification of Vietnam by the Communists. Moreover, the end of the Cold War caused the United States to begin normalizing its relations with Vietnam. The Clinton administration formally recognized Vietnam in July 1995, and in August 1995, Secretary of State Warren Christopher officially opened the U.S. Embassy in Hanoi. On the Korean peninsula, however, the division and suspicion remained. The death of Kim il Sung in 1994 hinted at a changed diplomatic climate in the region, but with North Korea seemingly intent on establishing its bona fides as a nuclear power, the future of this divided state and the surrounding region remains uncertain.

Divided State: Partition of British India   43

The division of their Indian colony into two independent states, India and Pakistan. Although the British were accused of a "divide and rule" policy, there is little evidence that they were eager to see the division of British India. The inability of the major political movements—the Indian National Congress and the Muslim League—to reconcile their differences led to partition of the subcontinent. The weaker of the two entities was Pakistan, two geographic regions separated by a thousand miles of Indian territory. Neither the British nor the leaders of the Indian National Congress believed Pakistan would survive the first year of independence, but it defied all the doom-filled predictions and became a prominent Muslim state. Nevertheless, militant Indians, notably Hindus, never gave up the goal of reacquiring Pakistan and fusing it with the Indian Union. "*Akhand Bharat*," or "United India," was a cry heard during the India-Pakistan War of 1971 when the Indian army midwifed the creation of an independent Bangladesh from territory that had been East Pakistan. Not content with the dismemberment of Pakistan, Indian extremists insisted on the state's total destruction. *See also* WAR TYPE: REGIONAL WAR—KASHMIR (345).

Significance
This partition used religious preference as a guide in creating the states. Predominantly Muslim areas formed Pakistan, and the remainder of the former British India became the Indian dominion, later the Indian Republic. The partition scheme was flawed in several instances, however. Tens of millions of Muslims remained in India, and a substantial number of Hindus continued to reside in Pakistan. But perhaps the most notable flaw was the British provision that allowed approximately 600 princely states to opt for independence rather than join either India or Pakistan. Although most of the princes were forced to yield to India, some insisted on going it alone. The problem of Kashmir stemmed from just such a situation. Partition enabled the British to withdraw from India in peaceful fashion, but it produced the carnage of communal warfare, the death of approximately 3 mil-

lion people, and the flight of 20 million refugees; it denied the Sikhs the right of self-determination; and it planted the seeds of India-Pakistan hostility, which degenerated into warfare in 1947–1948, 1965, and 1971. No less important, partition gave rise to still other potential partitions that threatened the breakup of both the Indian and Pakistani federations. The formation of Bangladesh by India only fueled numerous separatist movements in both countries. India and Pakistan's unresolved differences, especially over Kashmir in the 1990s, threatens to develop into a wider and deeper conflict. Elevating the level of threat, by 1995 both countries were judged to be nuclear-weapons powers.

Divided State: Two China Policy | 44

The problem that has arisen with two states claiming the right to be identified as China by the world community. The Chinese Communist victory over the Nationalist Chinese, or Kuomintang, in October 1949 was not entirely successful in that the latter government, under the leadership of Chiang Kai-shek, fled to the island of Taiwan, where it established itself as the only legitimate government of all of China. The Chinese Communists under Mao Zedong created the People's Republic of China (PRC) and dominated the Chinese mainland, but the Republic of China (ROC) survived on Taiwan. The United States continued to recognize the ROC as the only genuine government of China and denied recognition to the PRC. The Soviets acted in reverse fashion, and each superpower did what it could to support the claims of its client. The ROC held the seat reserved for China in the United Nations for years after its defeat, and Communist China was confined to secondary status in the Communist world until the split between Beijing and Moscow in the late 1950s and early 1960s. The growing independence of the PRC was not exploited by the United States until 1971, when the United States agreed to support the PRC's claim for the right to represent China in the United Nations. In 1979 the United States formally recognized the PRC as the legitimate government of China; as a price for its new relationship with the Communist state, the United States was compelled to sever its official relations with the ROC. Neither the PRC nor the ROC have given up their claim to represent all of China. Beijing insists that it will one day take control of Taiwan, while the ROC sustains a counterclaim (though weaker in the 1990s) that it will again rule over the Chinese mainland. *See also* TAIWAN RELATIONS ACT, 1979 (675).

Significance
The Two China Policy would have permitted the bestowing of official recognition on two separate Chinas, but the Chinese Communists pressed a hard bargain and demanded that, in exchange for their normalization of relations with the United States, the U.S. government had to drop official relations with the ROC. The United States agreed to this demand, but did not break its security commitments with the ROC. Nor did the agreement prevent the United States from doing business with the ROC. In fact, the ROC on Taiwan became a major economic power, and its principal trading partner was the United States. Interestingly, the PRC also developed major commercial interests with the United States. The PRC established itself as a most favored nation in U.S. business ventures, and also enjoyed a surplus of trade with the United States. Thus, although the Two China Policy was not sustained in official terms, it nevertheless became the *de facto* and practical outcome of U.S. activities in East Asia. Even in its unofficial form, this policy highlighted the importance of sustaining two separate Chinas until such time as their governments are able to find a peaceful solution to their unification dilemma.

Ethnic Cleansing | 45

Unofficial Serbian policy (notably Bosnian Serb) specifying the elimination of non-Serbs by any necessary means such as forced migration, or even extermination, in territories conquered by Serbs and thus identified as Serbian. The term *ethnic cleansing* gained prominence with the onset of the war in Bosnia in 1991–1992; however, the term is not isolated to Serbs; Croatians and Bosnian Muslims also engaged in campaigns aimed at "purifying" some of the regions under their control. The heavy responsibility for ethnic cleansing fell upon the Serbs because their more aggressive behavior was often couched in ethnically exclusive terms. Charges emanated from a variety of sources that acts of indiscriminate violence against noncombatants were perpetrated by the Serbs, including the authorized rape of defenseless women. *See also* ETHNIC WARS (48–50); ETHNICITY (51); PEACEMAKING: VANCE-OWEN PLAN (456); POPULATION EXCHANGE (180).

Significance
Ethnic-cleansing programs and their accompanying atrocities made resolving the war in Bosnia difficult. The fear generated and the hatred harbored made reconciliation a tedious and often meaningless exercise. Numerous peace proposals were put forth by UN peacekeeping teams, the European Union, the Conference on Security and Cooperation in Europe, the Contact Group (which included both the United States and Russia), and private mediators. A well-publicized event by the latter group was the December 1994 attempt at peacemaking by former U.S. president Jimmy Carter. Numerous cease-fires, however, proved to be far removed from peace settlements, and the fighting continued. The protracted nature of the conflict exposed the population of the former Yugoslavia to relentless civil strife. It appeared doubtful that the ethnic conflict could be resolved short of an exchange of populations in agreed-to territorial zones, each of which would represent a distinct sovereignty. The 1995 effort led by Richard Holbrooke, a U.S. assistant secretary of state, appeared to involve such a solution, given the tentative agreement of the par-

ties to a Bosnian state divided between Serbs and Bosnian Muslims.

Ethnic Cleansing: Rwanda   46

The forced removal from a territory or state of one ethnic or tribal group by another, largely associated with genocidal behavior. Located in the heart of Africa, Rwanda and Burundi are products of Belgian colonialism. Two dominant ethnic or tribal groups, the Hutu and the Tutsi, are represented. Burundi's government, with a predominantly Hutu population, was managed by the Tutsi, a minority seldom at peace with the majority. Rwanda, also primarily Hutu, was led in 1994 by a Tutsi president, Juvenal Habyarimana, who included in his government members of the majority community. Habyarimana was instrumental in stabilizing a difficult situation between Rwanda and Burundi after communal violence caused the deaths of 5,000 Hutu and forced another 60,000 to flee to Rwanda in 1988. Later, Zaire authorities offered neutral ground for President Pierre Buyoya of Burundi and President Habyarimana to work out their differences. When these efforts failed, conflict between Hutu and Tutsi continued. Significant supplies of arms, some purchased by the respective governments, others smuggled into the country by clandestine bands, signaled that a still greater upheaval was in the offing. In 1994 disaster struck with genocidal impact. Sparked by the violent death of Habyarimana (believed perpetrated by the Hutu), armed Hutu began the indiscriminate and systematic slaughter of the Tutsi of Rwanda. Estimates of the dead ran into the hundreds of thousands, mainly Tutsi, who insisted that the Hutu ethnic-cleansing campaign was a well-planned, calculated move to eliminate all semblance of Tutsi power. The carnage drew a mixed reaction from the outside world, marked by considerable indifference. Virtually alone, the French sent a military contingent to Rwanda with the objective of stabilizing the situation so that relief agencies could funnel assistance to the desperate and displaced populations. Although the Hutu initially held the advantage, the Tutsi fought back, and a Tutsi Liberation Front eventually invaded the country, drove the Hutu from the capital, and forced the flight of the larger Hutu population, many of whom had participated in random violence against the Tutsi. Hutu refugee camps were established in Burundi, Zaire, and Uganda. The Tutsi reestablished a government in the Rwandan capital and urged the refugees to return to their homes. The government also called for the punishment of those judged responsible for the genocide.

Significance
The futility in reconciling ethnicities in cases such as the Hutu and Tutsi is observed in the carnage that continues to stalk their lives. Herded into refugee camps, totally dependent on external assistance and charity agencies, the Hutu are at the mercy of the more militarily accomplished Tutsi. Moreover, the campaign of mass slaughter perpetrated by the Hutu cannot be ignored by the Tutsi. It is difficult to imagine a scenario in which the Tutsi and Hutu can cooperate, pool their talents, and join together to build integrated societies. Ethnic strife will undoubtedly continue well into the twenty-first century, and it appears ever more remote that foreign governments will be disposed to involve themselves in the misery of the area. Only the relief agencies, the minimal efforts directed by the Organization of African Unity (OAU), or the United Nations can be expected to extend humanitarian aid to a people overwhelmed by events they have perpetrated upon themselves.

Ethnic Conflict | 47 |
Conflict between culturally distinctive groups inhabiting the same or contiguous territory. The potential for widespread ethnic conflict stalks contemporary Europe. Europe is not neatly divided into territorial units that are representative of distinct peoples. Minorities abound in all the European states and, in an age of heightened exclusivity, nations within larger nations are not easily accommodated. Often denied appropriate representations of their heritage, the several hundred thousand Turks of Bulgaria look to their brethren in the Turkish republic, just as the half million Hungarians of Slovakia seek solace and support from their relatives in Hungary. The northern Italian province of Trentino-Aldo Adige encloses the South Tyrol, which has a population of 300,000 ethnic Germans whose ancestors were subjects of the Austro-Hungarian monarchy prior to World War I. Neither the Bulgarization pursued by the Communists nor the Italianization schemes of Benito Mussolini altered the historic character of these people. The South Tyrol retained German cultural status following World War II, but the Suedtrioler Volkspartei continued to press for political autonomy, and terrorist incidents between 1956 and 1981 multiplied. Austria pressured the Italian government to declare a new autonomy statute in 1972, and the German population in northern Italy gained control over many of its local affairs. Still, the minority Germans were dissatisfied, and Austria again intervened, bringing the issue before the United Nations. More autonomy was granted to the South Tyrol in 1988, and again in 1991 by weak Italian governments. In fact, the rise of the new fascism in Italy is traced to the South Tyrol; anger with government capitulation to the German minority is expressed in demands for stronger, centralized Roman government. Moreover, divisions between northern and southern Italy are increasingly more difficult to manage. The emergence of the Northern or Lombardy League calls for special status for the northern areas, which are more sophisticated, and certainly more developed, than the south. Although not yet as potent a political force as the South Tyrol Germans, the Lombardy League won 9 of 47 mayoral races in northern Italy in 1993.

Significance
Historically, Europe has been a congeries of ethnicities—a veritable seedbed for ethnic conflict. Empires, nation-states, and regional unions have sought to quell or mollify culturally different people, neutralize their antipathy toward one another, and blend them into a single polity. Some of these efforts have succeeded, while others have failed despite herculean efforts by those pressing for larger community. Perhaps the most ambitious experiment during the twentieth century was the Union of Soviet Socialist Republics, a federal model constructed around a formidable center. The engineering of "Soviet man" was intended to replace narrowly expressed nationalistic yearnings. The nationalities that found themselves linked to one another through the ideologically driven doctrine of Marxism-Leninism were believed to have transcended their historic identities and embraced a higher form of psychocultural expression. Those perceptions, influenced by a fascination with and for dictatorship, were nurtured by the Soviet Union's success in defeating Nazi Germany and Moscow's role as one of the world's two vaunted and feared superpowers. But this image had little to do with reality; rather, it obscured the aggressive and often brutal suppression of the different nationalities in the Caucasus and Central Asia in the 1920s. It ignored the Stalinist Great Purge of the 1930s, and it overlooked the harsh treatment inflicted on certain nationalities accused of collaborating with the Nazis during World War II. But if all this was obscured through the years of the Cold War, the Soviet Union's many ethnic divisions could not be concealed, let alone neutralized. Immediately following the Cold War's passing, the fissures in Soviet society proved to be so deep, and had so undermined the centralized structure, that the entire Communist enterprise collapsed with virtually the first call for secession. Moreover, this disintegration proved merely a prelude to further unraveling of the Soviet-inspired republics that now assumed independence. Russia's dilemma in Chechnya is only one illustration of a broader problem. The Western Europeans adopted the nation-state as their model, hoping thereby to sustain unity of purpose among distinct ethnicities through notions of representation founded on pluralism and the building of voluntary consensus. The nation-state, however, fared only a shade better than the uniquely inclusive Soviet multinational model. The nation-states also sought to obscure the ethnic conflicts within their different domains. Whether it was the Waloons and Flemings of Belgium; the Basques of Spain; the South Tyrol, Lombardy, Piedmont and Vento Italians; or the Scots and Welsh of the United Kingdom—all elicited an aspiration for separation from the larger unit. Nevertheless, only a few of the West European states have experienced violent ethnic expression since World War II. In Eastern Europe, however, there is the tragedy of Bosnia, which threatens to spread to Kosovo and Montenegro, where the paramilitary Serb White Eagles terrorize the Muslim population of Sandzak (Novi Pazar). In October 1991 the Muslims of Sandzak overwhelmingly supported a referendum that would have fused them with a then Muslim-dominant Bosnian state. By 1995 that likelihood had become mere fantasy. The potential for wider conflict is apparent in the larger Balkans. Macedonia would not be left untouched if fighting spread from Bosnia to the neighboring region, and indeed, the small U.S. army force located there would be impacted; so too the bordering states of Albania, Greece, Bulgaria, and probably Turkey as well. The ethnic conflicts in the Balkans of the late twentieth century mirror events of a century ago. Once again the Balkans threaten to assume the dubious role of the powder keg of greater Europe.

Ethnic Wars: Abkhazia and Georgia   48

Contemporary conflict between culturally distinctive groups in the Caucasus Mountains. Abkhazia was an autonomous region of Georgia when the latter was a republic within the Soviet Union. Following the breakup of the USSR, Georgia gained its independence; almost immediately, Abkhazia demanded separation from Georgia and union with similar ethnic minorities inhabiting the Caucasus Mountains. In 1810 Russia seized Abkhazia from the Ottoman Turks, and in 1864 formally annexed it. With the collapse of Russian czardom and the emergence of the Bolsheviks as the dominant authority in Moscow, Abkhazia became an independent Soviet republic; however, shortly thereafter, Abkhazia was merged with a newly designed Soviet Georgian republic. During the Stalin epoch, Abkhazia remained a silent appendage of Georgia, but in 1978 it again publicized its desire for independent status. Although held in check, Abkhazian claims to self-determination remained; in 1990, gaining advantage from a weakened central government in Moscow, it again declared its independence from Georgia, which had declared its sovereign independence from Moscow a year earlier. In 1992 Abkhazia discarded its operative constitution and readopted its independent constitution of 1921. Georgia's independence in the wake of the Soviet dissolution brought the Abkhazians and the Georgians into close combat. Georgia resisted the Abkhaz secession, and in the fall of 1992 a major war resulted. Georgian president Zviad Gamsakhurdia was forcibly ousted from office by the Abkhaz and their supporters, but his successor, Eduard Shevardnadze, the Soviet Union's last foreign minister, was no less intent on preserving the integrity of the Georgian republic. Shevardnadze was thwarted in his effort to sustain the Georgian union by Russian troops who entered the war in support of the Abkhazians. Shevardnadze was forced to accept President Boris Yeltsin's demands that Georgia join the Commonwealth of Independent States in order to achieve a cessation of hostilities. The Abkhaz, however, sustained the fighting and took control of the Abkhaz capital of Sukhumi in 1993. The United Nations dispatched an observer mission to the region after another cease-fire was arranged, and Georgia proved unable to reclaim the territory. Georgia was then faced with still another rebellion, this time in South Ossetia, which sought unification with its counterpart in North Ossetia.

Significance

The arbitrary drawing of political frontiers has complicated the ethnic question in a host of states, particularly in the former Soviet Union. Soviet policy operated on the imperial premise of divide-and-rule, in which one ethnicity was balanced by another. By heightening the antagonism of one group to another, the central authority, a third party to the relationship, exploited their mutual hostility by intruding itself into their affairs. The Soviets posed as neutral bystanders when they were actually orchestrating the conflict. This legacy of intrigue and manipulation carried over into the new period of independent states, but these were states that the Soviet Union itself had created, and the Soviet Union no longer existed. The Soviet Union's breakup into independent states was a time for reassessing past associations and claims. Unfortunately, the successor states were not inclined to yield to negotiations that would further diminish their already limited role in domestic and regional affairs, and this ensured even more ethnic conflict. Considering that as many as 200 different ethnic groups inhabited the former Soviet Union, the likelihood for spreading ethnic conflict is not so much a question of whether, but when. The Soviets' drawing of frontiers to satisfy and complement certain political and military needs raise critical issues now that the USSR has passed from the scene. Russia's current claim to the Ukrainian-administered Crimean peninsula is a case in point. The Crimea is predominantly ethnic Russian, but Soviet policy placed the Crimea under the jurisdiction of Ukraine. Russia's desire to sustain a major presence on the Black Sea would seem to require its controlling the Crimea, but Ukraine is disinclined to bargain away the territory.

Ethnic Wars: Armenia and Azerbaijan $\boxed{49}$

Contemporay conflict between culturally distinctive groups in the Caucasus Mountains. Armenians, founders of the first Christian nation in A.D. 301, and Turks, conquerors of the Caucasus region of Armenia in 1390, have long been mortal enemies. The Armenian plight at the hands of the Ottoman Turks culminated in the genocide of an estimated 1 million Armenians during World War I because of the latter's alleged collaboration with the Russians during that conflict. With the demise of the Ottoman Empire after World War I came the reemergence of an independent Armenian state, but in 1920 Armenia was forcibly included within the Soviet empire. Supposedly protectors of the Armenian nation, the Soviets took advantage of Armenian-Turk hostility by playing one against the other. The key issue centered on the disposition of Nagorno-Karabakh, an Armenian enclave in an Azeri Turkic region. In 1923 Nagorno-Karabakh was made an autonomous oblast (province), and the Soviets permitted Azerbaijanis (Azeris) to live in districts that effectively severed Nagorno-Karabakh from any link to Armenia. Both Armenia and Azerbaijan became formal republics within the Soviet Union in 1936, and Nagorno-Karabakh, otherwise an extension of Armenia, was made an integral member of the latter. The Nagorno-Karabakh issue remained somewhat dormant until 1988, when reforms within the Soviet Union provided the Armenians with an opportunity to raise their claim to the territory. Moscow refused to alter the Stalinist design of the 1920s, provoking an uprising in Nagorno-Karabakh that echoed in the Armenian capital of Yervan. Russian troops were called to restore order to the region, and Moscow generally sided with the Azerbaijanis in their effort to retain the territory, as well as the border region of Nakhichevan, which also had been taken from the Armenians in the 1920s. Armenia accused Moscow of betrayal, and in 1990 declared its independence. The Russians stepped up their military action against Armenia, but the Soviet Union was crumbling from the center. In 1991 an Armenian referendum found 99.3 percent of the population in favor of secession. The Soviet Union collapsed later that year, and in January 1992 Nagorno-Karabakh declared its independence as the Mountainous State of Karabakh. Armenians then attacked in Nakhichevan and opened a corridor to the enclave. The failure of the Azerbaijanis to ward off the Armenian assault and the spreading of the conflict to other areas of Azerbaijan ultimately brought down the Azerbaijani government of Abulfez Elchibey; he was succeeded by Geidar Aliyev, a former KGB head in the Soviet Politburo. Under pressure from Turkey, in 1993 the UN Security Council called for an end to hostilities and for Armenian withdrawal from Azeri territory, including Nagorno-Karabakh. Armenia ignored the Security Council resolution and continued to perpetrate the war against Azerbaijan. Neighboring Turkey and Iran declared their concern with Armenian actions, and the threat of a wider war could not be ignored.

Significance

The Armenian-Turk antagonism is deep-seated, part of a larger arena of conflict between Greek Orthodox Christians and Muslim Turks. The disappearance of the Soviet Union left Muslim Turkey the most prominent power in the region south of the Balkans, west of the Caucasus, north of the Arab world, and east of Greece. The Ottoman Empire ranged over the broader region from the fourteenth to the nineteenth centuries, and the fault lines between Islam and Christianity were established during that extended period. In time, imperial Russia became the most significant threat to Ottoman power, with Moscow, the Third Rome, claiming the right to protect Eastern Orthodox and Armenian Christians from the machinations of the Ottoman Turks. Russia fought 13 wars with the Ottomans between 1774 and the outbreak of World War I in 1914. In almost every engagement the Russians forced the Ottomans to retreat from previously held territory. But this clash did not alter the division of Europe between Eastern and Western states and civilizations. Developments in the West did not have significant influence on the Eastern Europeans, or for that matter on the Russians, who were more intertwined with the world of Islam. The Armenian struggle against the Azerbaijani Turks, therefore, must be viewed against a larger backdrop involving far more than the enclave of Nagorno-Karabakh and its ultimate disposition. Indeed, the strife in Bosnia and the ethnic wars that rage there and threaten to spread throughout the Balkans are but another incident in this more comprehensive scenario. The alacrity with which Germany and Austria officially recognized and hence reinforced Roman Catholic Slovenia and Croatia in 1991 not only provoked the Orthodox Serbs, it also doomed the Bosnian Muslim attempt to create an independent, cosmopolitan—but nevertheless Muslim-dominant—state in the heart of the Balkans. The Greek decision to support Serbia in its attempt to assist the Bosnian Serbs, and Bulgaria's similar posture, was aimed at neutralizing a perceived Muslim Turk threat. Although the Armenian-Azerbaijani conflict has local ethnic features, it also is part of this larger configuration of cultural forces.

Ethnic Wars: Bosnia and Chechnya $\boxed{50}$

Contemporary conflict between culturally distinctive groups in the Balkans and the Russian Federation. In the aftermath of the Cold War, and following the breakup of both the Soviet and Yugoslav Socialist Federations, nationalism among their long-dormant ethnic groups assumed significant importance. Insisting on the establishment of self-governing states, ethnic groups (nations) within larger nations began to break away. Prominent among these initial demands for self-determination was Bosnia-Herzegovina in the former Yugoslavia and Chechnya in the new Russian Federation. Bosnia-Herzegovina declared its independence in 1992 under a Muslim-led government operating out of Sarajevo. Chechnya, a Muslim region, did likewise that same year. In the Bosnian case, hostilities erupted immediately. In Chechnya, the Russians did not move to crush the would-be independent state until 1995—three years after its declaration of independence. The savage ethnic war launched by the Bosnian Serbs, who were determined to carve their own state from the Bosnian territory, brought the United Nations into the conflict. The United Nations called for an embargo on arms, which fell most heavily on the Muslim Bosnian government, and UNPROFOR (United Nations Protection Force in Bosnia) was dispatched to provide humanitarian assistance and persuade the parties to the conflict to resolve their dispute at the conference table. After numerous cease-fires and a number of UN-offered plans failed, the Bosnian Serbs took control of almost three-fourths of the state, and the war dragged on. The Chechens, on the other hand, could anticipate only volunteers from Muslim countries in their struggle with the Russian army. The Russians were determined to retain the territory for fear its successful secession would precipitate other breakaway movements. Boris Yeltsin faced stiff opposition at home and abroad, but the Russian forces systematically destroyed Grozny, the Chechen capital, and threatened to do the same to the rest of the country if the resistance did not cease. A joint offensive by Croats and Bosnian Muslims in the summer of 1995 forced the Bosnian Serbs to relinquish a portion of their gains. This maneuver followed another Croat campaign that cleared the Serbs from the Croatian Krajina region. Given Croatian support, the Bosnian Muslims were encouraged to press their attack on the Serbs, which reduced their holdings in Bosnia-Herzegovina to about 50 percent of the territory. Croatia also took advantage of Serb weaknesses to pressure Eastern Slovonia, a Serb-initiated area of Croatia. *See also* ETHNICITY (51); PEACEKEEPING: SAFE HAVENS (448); PEACEKEEPING: UNPROFOR (451); PEACEMAKING: CONTACT GROUP

(452); PEACEMAKING: VANCE-OWEN PLAN (456).

Significance
The ethnic wars in Bosnia and Chechnya have also been identified as wars of religion. In each instance a seemingly Christian orthodoxy was at war with regional Muslims. However, the clashes were precipitated more by territorial demands and nationality differences, as well as the seemingly irrational need of the different groups to define their unique cultures. The post–Cold War world appears to be more inclined toward exclusive rather than inclusive societies, and the violent, protracted actions in Bosnia and Chechnya are only the more horrific examples of a resurgence in nationalistic fervor fed from the wellsprings of narrowly expressed political ethnicity. Post–Cold War ethnicity and nationalism are not entirely destructive. Where compromise and reasonableness remain operative, peaceful solutions can be found. The "velvet divorce" between the Czechs and Slovaks and the dissolution of the Czechoslovakian federation, or even the quiet disassembly of the Soviet Union and the formation of the 15 independent republics of the Commonwealth of Independent States, are cases in point. Ethnicity and nationalism can not only inspire the breakup of states but their peaceful merger as well. A prime example of this is the unification of Germany in 1990. It must be noted, however, that whereas the German unification is a success story, its very achievement may have provoked the conflict in Bosnia and the Greater Balkans. Germany's unification was perceived as a threat to Serbia at a time when the latter was losing control over the Yugoslav Federation. When Germany hastily recognized the independence of Croatia and Slovenia in 1991, the Serbs believed that Germany was again moving to impose its influence over Austria and the northern Balkans. A greater Germany was a declared Serbian concern, and the Serb attack on Croatia at Bukovar and Dubrovnik began almost immediately after the German recognition of Yugoslavia's more Roman Catholic populations.

The complexities of ethnicity are discerned in the Chechen retreat during imperial Russia's eighteenth- and nineteenth-century advance into the Caucasus. Historic memory, both distant and more recent, fuels the Chechen desire to be free of Russian rule. Like Abkhazia or Ossetia, Moldova, or Georgia, the Chechens seek their independence or, at the very least, autonomy, from Moscow. Indeed, the peaceful dissolution of the Soviet Union did not signal the tranquil dismemberment of the Russian state. Paradoxes abound in the ethnic dilemmas of the post–Cold War world, and they are no more apparent than in Bosnia and Chechnya.

Ethnicity $\boxed{51}$

Appearing in its modern form in the twentieth century, the term has been used since the 1960s to connote minority issues and aspects of relationships between groups that consider themselves to be and/or are regarded by others as being culturally distinctive. Ethnicity in contemporary international relations has been defined in several ways. One of the more prominent definitions describes ethnicity as an ethnic group comprised of persons sharing the same language, folk art, myths, religious experience, history, and territory. This explanation addresses the manner in which people live among one another, develop different mechanisms of cohesiveness (e.g., economic community), think about their territorial borders, and consciously or subconsciously accept collective identity and display their solidarity. Another definition places more emphasis on the imagined community, the importance of psychological factors, and the relevance of the temporal dimension of ethnicity. In this latter definition, the observer is more cognizant of ethnicity forged by the existing nation-state. Nation-state ethnicity gives a broader conception to distinctive culture, and emphasizes economic life and national identity. The language in managing solidarity is more politicized, and promotes supreme loyalty to the nation-state. The ethno-nation, by contrast, is no less abstract in its own way. The stirring of ethnic identity, the order to kill those possessing a different ethnicity (though they be one's neighbors), is only a more extreme representation of the nation-state. While the latter reveals attachments that are more intuitive and primeval, both the generalized notion of the nation-state as a melting pot or mosaic of peoples and the more narrowly conceived ethno-nation can each call upon their citizenry to blindly kill (or be killed) in defense of a common heritage, and as an act of self-preservation. *See also* ETHNIC WARS (48–50).

Significance

Ethnicity has assumed greater significance in the aftermath of the Cold War. Diverse peoples long held in check by political conditions that neutralized their individuality now clamor for recognition. At a time when the world of nation-states is inclined toward more significant interdependent relationships, peoples heretofore subordinated to the rule of those different from themselves now demand independent existence. The exclusive rather than inclusive character of nationalism influences the course of international relations at the dawn of the twenty-first century. In effect, the different definitional descriptions of ethnicity noted above reveal the dialectical aspects of ethnicity in the world today. With the world a closed political system—that is, with all the world's territory having been discovered and distributed among existing territorial states—within these same states some peoples are unreconciled to the established territorial configurations, contrived unions requiring or forcing people to share geographic space, or consolidations imposing an artificial identity. The concept of nations within larger nations frames two definitions. The first insists on secession, the claim to self-determination as a matter of right, or the right to fuse a territory with another (e.g., a greater Germany or a greater Serbia). The second reveals efforts made to sustain the territorial integrity of the nation-state irrespective of the human di-

versity within it, indeed, regardless of the means required—violent, if necessary— to justify the nation-state (e.g., the denial of Biafran independence from Nigeria in 1968). In the second definition, the use of force to meld otherwise different peoples into a unitary community is a common theme in current international relations. The first definition therefore addresses the more primeval aspects of human association and identity; the second, the more contrived national association and identity. Hence, ethnicity focuses attention on both the breakup and expansion of the contemporary territorial state.

Ethnocentrism ⟦52⟧

The belief that one's own group and culture is superior to all others. Ethnocentrism is a universal social phenomenon that distinguishes "we" from "they." The phenomenon emphasizes the differences between societies and their values, and the states that symbolize those values. The values of the "we" group are the standards by which "they" are evaluated, and since "they" are different, "they" are, by definition, inferior. Ethnocentrism is the stuff of patriotism and as such is nurtured by the nation-state, the primary political organization that defines but also divides humanity. Although all states require degrees of patriotism to generate national unity, exaggerated patriotism (often described as ultrapatriotism) is more divisive than inclusive, and linked with problems that are both domestically and internationally damaging. *See also* ETHNIC CLEANSING; ETHNIC WARS (48–50); ETHNICITY (51); NATIONALISM (57); NATIONALISM: XENOPHOBIA (61).

Significance

Ultrapatriotism, or ultranationalism, is the dominant and potentially most dangerous form of ethnocentrism in the modern world. This expression of ethnocentrism ascribes to national values a monopoly on truth, beauty, morality, and justice, and assumes the universal validity of a particular representation of national values. It neglects the fact that people and nations are the products of different circumstances and historical experiences, and that by beginning with a different set of premises they may with equal logic arrive at a different set of values or "self-evident truths." Because of different historical experiences, the word *democracy*, for example, may suggest individualism to a U.S. citizen and collectivism to a Japanese citizen. The central domestic problem in ethnocentrism is that specific groups within a given society will be judged as outside the larger cultural majority–associated experience, resulting in the out-group being made the object of the majority's hatred, e.g., the conflict between Bosnian Serbs or Muslims and Croats. The chief international danger in ethnocentric nationalism lies in its incapacity to understand what motivates other societies, and consequently a tendency to interpret differences in terms that are menacing, and therefore threatening.

Imperialism $\boxed{53}$

A superior-inferior relationship in which an area and its people are subordinated to the will of a foreign state. Imperialism can be traced through several chronological stages of development in the modern world. The first stage, which dates approximately from the voyages of Columbus to the end of the Seven Years' War in 1763, was a consequence of the emergence of the European nation-state system, the economic philosophy of mercantilism, and, in some cases, religious fanaticism and missionary ardor. During this period, much of the Western Hemisphere was brought under European control by conquest and colonization, and the first imperial forays into Asia were launched by trading companies chartered by European states. In the second stage, from 1763 to about 1870, the Europeans were preoccupied with the excesses of monarchy at home as well as with the emergence of the national state. The Industrial Revolution also consumed much of their energies, but the British nonetheless consolidated their gains in India and the French did likewise in Indochina. The

third stage, from 1870 to World War I, saw the last great wave of imperial expansion sweep across Africa and much of the Far East. In this period the industrial states reacted to increasing competition in international trade by seeking to create protected markets and sources of supply. By World War I, imperialism had reached its zenith and began slowly to recede. Following World War II, the process of liquidating empires accelerated as the policy of imperialism fell into disrepute. Moreover, the economic costs of imperialism had become too large to sustain, and the wave of nationalism enveloping Asia and Africa spawned scores of new independent states. The last of the imperial states with roots in the colonial tradition was the Soviet Union. Its fall and breakup in 1991, although unanticipated, released many of the territories and peoples heretofore connected to Moscow. By the last decade of the twentieth century, imperialism as it had been understood in the beginning of the century had ceased to be. The motives for imperialism have varied over time and with the nations involved, but major arguments have included (1) economic necessity—markets, raw materials, gold, "trade follows the flag"; (2) national security—strategic location, materials, manpower; (3) prestige—"manifest destiny," a "place in the sun," "the sun never sets on the British Empire;" and (4) humanitarianism—missionary activity, the "white man's burden," civilizing missions. *See also* COMMUNIST THEORY: IMPERIALISM AND COLONIALISM (102); COLONIALISM (35).

Significance
Imperialism spread the ideas, ideals, and material civilization of the Western world to all parts of the globe. The imperialists took much out of their territories, but they left behind assorted attitudes about such things as education, health, law, and government that are associated today with nation-building programs. Currently, the term *imperialism* is an emotion-laden concept used in a variety of circumstances, and therefore difficult to define and apply. Since World War II, it has become a

term with pejorative meaning. To argue, however, that imperialism has had positive as well as negative consequences is to acknowledge the character of the state system, citing those attributes that enhance the human experience and those that retard human development and transform otherwise accommodative peoples into archrivals with aggressive intentions. The reality of imperialism is the reality of human relationships in which the strong seek to dominate the weak. Classical European imperialism can now be considered a chapter in human history, but it is doubtful that the world is free of imperialistic ventures. The difficulties encountered in attempting to form a more perfect European Union, or in modifying the United Nations so that it can more effectively neutralize the aggressive intentions of rogue states, speaks volumes for people's concerns that new forms of imperialism are just around the corner, and that the strong still intend to dominate the weak.

Imperialism, Cultural   54

Imposing an alien ideology or civilization on an unwilling society. Cultural imperialism as a calculated policy by which a government imposes its values on others should be distinguished from the increasing spread of alien cultural influences resulting from trade, travel, and communication. National leaders who resent or fear foreign influences may brand them as cultural imperialism, but in doing so they are using the term as a propaganda device and not as an objective tool of analysis (unless the intent of the foreign government can be demonstrated).

Significance

Cultural imperialism may provide for an effective and long-lasting form of domination in that much of the original culture is destroyed and in time will cease to exist as an alternative. Because language is a fundamental vehicle for the expression of a culture and its "self-evident truths," it has been a primary weapon of cultural imperialism. When a subject people is forced to learn a new language to secure employment or education, for example, gradually and subconsciously the people accept the ideas and values expressed in the new tongue. At the same time, dependence on their original language as a carrier of their culture diminishes, and cultural attributes that can be expressed only in the original language are changed or disappear. However, if the recipients voluntarily adopt certain foreign values, as in the cases of Japan in the nineteenth century or Turkey after World War I, it would be inaccurate to describe such decisions as forms of cultural imperialism. On the other hand, people within a given society who adopt foreign manners and customs of their own volition may become the target of those within the society who aim to return it to its historic roots. Contemporary religious fundamentalism is a worldwide phenomenon, found in developed as well as developing nations. Fundamentalists seek to purify their societies and free them from all forms of foreign influence; their actions are often characterized by the violent methods they employ to press their objectives. The carnage in Algeria and Egypt, for example, perpetrated by extremists in the garb of fundamentalists, targets members of their Westernized intelligentsia. The self-righteous character of this form of bloodletting highlights the intensity of the argument that surrounds the subject of cultural imperialism at the close of the twentieth century.

Imperialism, Economic   55

Involvement of one country in the economy of another to such a degree that the sovereignty of the latter is impaired. Economic imperialism may result from a conscious policy or from the capital flow of private foreign investment. Suggestive of indirect control, economic imperialism is illustrated by the "dollar diplomacy" of the United States in the Caribbean area earlier in the century. A relationship between economics and imperialism has always been present, and much of its functionality can be traced to the period of mercantilism. The first well-developed modern theory concerned with economic imperialism was formulated in *Imperialism: A Study*, a 1902 book examining imperialism and authored by British economist J. A. Hobson. Hobson explained imperialism in terms of the search for new markets and capital investment opportunities. Hobson's ideas also influenced V. I. Lenin in developing his Communist theory of capitalist imperialism. In his *Imperialism: The Highest Stage of Capitalism* (1917) Lenin presented imperialism as the result of the "monopoly stage of capitalism." He asserted that excess capital accumulated in the home country because of underconsumption. The competitive search for new markets and investment opportunities, he concluded, led to imperialism and to imperialist wars that would hasten the inevitable downfall of capitalism. *See also* COMMUNIST DOCTRINE: LENINISM (85); COMMUNIST THEORY: IMPERIALISM AND COLONIALISM (102).

Significance
Economic imperialism implies a more subtle form of relationship than exists in traditional imperialism since economic imperialism does not involve actual political rule. The results may be similar, however, because the more economically dependent the weaker state, the more difficult it may be to resist political demands by the stronger power. Yet, where the rights of expropriation and expulsion exist, the charge of economic imperialism is more difficult to sustain. Developing countries require large amounts of investment capital from foreign sources, but because of their former colonial status they are extremely fearful of any semblance of foreign economic control or exploitation. In many instances they have sought to avoid the strings attached to bilateral grants and loans and any consequent derogation of sovereignty by seeking economic assistance through international financial agencies, particularly those of the United Nations.

Nation　　　　　　　　　 |56|
A social group that shares a common ideology, institutions, and customs, and a sense of homogeneity. The term *nation* is difficult to define because other groups exhibit some of the same characteristics. In the nation, however, there is a strong sense of belonging associated with a particular territory considered to be peculiarly its own. A nation may comprise part of a state, be coterminous with a state, or extend beyond the borders of a single state. *See also* INTERNATIONAL LAW: STATE (488); NATIONALISM (57).

Significance
The concept of the nation emphasizes the people and their oneness; this aspect is also implied in such derivative terms as nationality and nationalism. In common parlance the words *country, state,* and *nation* are often used synonymously, but they do not mean exactly the same thing. *Country* has geographical connotations, *state* expresses the legal organization of a society, and the term *nation* involves a sociocultural perception of the group. The hyphenated term *nation-state* aptly describes a socially and culturally homogeneous group possessing the legal organization to participate in international politics.

Nationalism　　　　　　 |57|
The spirit of belonging together, or the popular will that seeks to preserve the identity of a group by institutionalizing it in the form of a state. Nationalism can be intensified by common racial, linguistic, historical, and religious ties. It is usually associated with a particular territory. The concept may also be thought of as a function of the ability of a particular group to communicate among themselves more effectively than with outsiders. However the phenomenon of nationalism is explained, its essential characteristic is an active sense of the uniqueness of the group vis-à-vis the rest of the world. Nationalism developed first in western Europe through the consolidation of individual feudal units into kingdoms. It was not until the French Revolution and the wars of Napoleon that nationalism came to be identified with the commoner. *See*

also ETHNOCENTRISM (52); NATIONALISM: SELF-DETERMINATION (60).

Significance

Nationalism as a mass emotion is possibly the most powerful operative political force in the world. It makes the state the ultimate focus of the individual's loyalty, which is kept alive by the manipulation of a variety of symbols: national heroes, national uniforms, national pledges of allegiance, national holidays, and holy days. As a mass social phenomenon, nationalism can promote solidarity and a sense of belonging. It can also engender hostility, divisiveness, tension, and war between rival nationalist groups or states. Originally a European concept, since World War II nationalism has energized millions of dependent peoples in Asia and Africa in their transformation to independence. In Western Europe, the revitalization of nationalism following the end of the Cold War threatens to weaken NATO and stymie the movement toward a more integrated European community.

Nationalism: Chauvinism 58

Extravagant, demonstrative superpatriotism. Chauvinism implies uncritical devotion to the state, extreme jealousy of its honor, and an exaggerated sense of its glory. The term is derived from the name of Nicolas Chauvin, a Napoleonic soldier notorious for his unrestrained devotion to his leader and the empire. Chauvinism can be described as an extreme form of nationalism that holds that the state can do no wrong. *See also* ETHNOCENTRISM (52); NATIONALISM (57).

Significance

Chauvinism is particularly dangerous in an age of weapons of mass destruction. Superpatriotism, or ultrapatriotism, by excessive concern with and glorification of one nation-state, tends to become myopic. It can unnecessarily intensify international problems by failing to take into account the rights and interests of other states, or by riding roughshod over them. Chauvinism may also involve an unreal-istic fear for the security of the state, particularly in a time of profound domestic and/or international stress. States making war against one another—as in the case of Iraq and Iran in the 1980s—may use a form of chauvinism to unite the people and secure the sacrifices needed to gird the nation for battle.

Nationalism: Flemish-Walloon Issue 59

The conflict between approximately 5.5 million Dutch-speaking Flemings and 4 million French-speaking Walloons of Belgium. The Flemings occupy the agricultural northern section of the country, while the Walloons predominate in the more industrialized southern regions. These ethnic groups clashed in the 1830s after French was made the national language of the kingdom. The advantages derived by the Walloons and their more significant role in the country's political and economic life caused friction between the communities that spilled over into the twentieth century. Knowledge of the French language continues to be a key to success in contemporary Belgium, but the Fleming population is reluctant to part with its historic culture. The Egmont Pact of the 1970s attempted to bridge some of the differences by moving Belgium from its emphasis on a centralized government to one calling for a federal structure. Egmont divided Belgium into three autonomous regions (Flanders, Wallonia, and Brussels), but when the Flemings objected to this plan, which they believed gave the Walloons two of the three regions, it failed to carry sufficient support. A modified Egmont was implemented in 1980, establishing separate assemblies and executives for Flanders and Wallonia, each managing their own public health matters, urban needs, economic activity, and cultural events. The federal government retained its power over foreign affairs, defense, finance, justice, and education.

Significance

Belgium's ethnicity problem has endured since the formation of the nation-state, and it shows no sign of abating. Government action in addressing the issue has been enlightened on the whole, with a view toward reconciling the parties along lines that seem to best preserve the country's unity. The role of the monarchy, more symbolic than operational, centers on the need to bridge the Fleming-Walloon controversy without doing great damage to the state. But symbolic unity is no substitute for the real experience. The devolution of some power to local authorities while the central government clings to its critical responsibilities purchases time, but in no way assures the solidarity of the union. On the other hand, the movement toward greater European integration and Belgium's prominent place in the European Union suggest the possibility of reducing the ethnic dilemma. The emphasis on Europeanization may yet influence competing ethnic groups to modify their more parochial interests.

Nationalism, Integral   60

An intolerant, ethnocentric form of nationalism that glorifies the state as the highest focus of individual loyalties. Integral or totalitarian, nationalism aggressively concentrates on the security of the state, the augmentation of its power at the expense of other states, and the pursuit of national policies motivated by narrow self-interest. Liberal nationalism began to give way to integral nationalism by the end of the nineteenth century under the impact of industrial, trade, imperial, and military rivalries and as a result of increasing popular pressures for the state to protect economic and social interests against foreign competition. Historically, integral nationalism developed with the rise of absolute monarchy (dynastic nationalism), but is best typified by the Fascist totalitarianism of the 1930s and 1940s. Various manifestations of the same phenomenon are also observable in the ideological rivalries and national power struggles of the post–World War II period as well as the post–Cold War era. *See also* FASCISM (117).

Significance

The emphasis of integral nationalism begins where that of liberal nationalism leaves off. Liberal nationalism is concerned with the creation of the nation-state. Integral nationalism speaks of the state as an organic whole in mortal competition with other states. Integral nationalists believe all states are similarly motivated, and that only the most unified, determined, and aggressive will survive. Whereas the state is considered the servant of the people by liberal nationalists, integral nationalists demand near total conformity and blind obedience to authority. Integral nationalism is a pessimistic as well as messianic vision of the world. It is hostile, belligerent, and bombastic, and those representing the phenomenon do not consider compromise an option in the relations of nations.

Nationalism, Liberal   61

The aspirations of a group to achieve statehood and establish government based on popular sovereignty. Liberal nationalism was philosophically connected through the American and French revolutions with the decline of absolute monarchy as a legitimate form of government. It is closely associated with the democratic concepts of self-determination, individualism, constitutionalism, natural rights, and popular sovereignty. *See also* DEMOCRACY (108); NATIONALISM: SELF-DETERMINATION (60).

Significance

Liberal nationalism emphasizes self-rule, middle-class democracy, and freedom from foreign domination. Following the popularization of these principles the Spanish empire disintegrated, Italy and Germany were unified as national states, and, ultimately, monarchy survived only where it adopted the constitutional form. The state was regarded as the servant of the people, and it was hoped that the frequency of war would decline since it would not serve the best interests of the new sovereigns. The principles of liberal nationalism have also inspired the elites of the national independence movements in the post–World War II period.

Nationalism: Self-Determination $\boxed{62}$

The doctrine that postulates the right of a group of people who consider themselves separate and distinct from others to determine for themselves the state in which they will live and the form of government it will have. National self-determination is closely linked with the concept of liberal nationalism and is implicit in the American Declaration of Independence and the French Declaration of the Rights of Man and Citizen. It is the vehicle through which national groups seek to ensure their identity by institutionalizing it in the form of an independent sovereign state. The name most frequently associated with national self-determination is that of President Woodrow Wilson. The doctrine can be found in his 1918 peace aims, known as Fourteen Points. In the 1919 peace settlements it was instrumental in establishing the independence of Albania, Austria, Czechoslovakia, Estonia, Finland, Hungary, Latvia, Lithuania, Poland, Romania, and Yugoslavia. It also figured in the creation of the mandates system and its successor, the trusteeship system. The principle of self-determination has also been associated with the technique of the plebiscite as a basis for solving problems relating to boundaries and territorial sovereignty. The termination of the Cold War, however, caused thinkers to reexamine the principle of self-determination. Citing the many nationalities, ethnic groups, and tribal peoples arguing the right to establish independent states, and acknowledging that they cannot be accommodated without dividing and subdividing existing sovereign states, attention is now riveted on the need to provide assistance for minorities who may be at risk in established states but for whom the right of self-determination cannot be honored. Finding a formula that would allow for the physical protection of such peoples and that would provide them with the socioeconomic opportunities otherwise denied them is the task of scholars, if not statesmen. Studies that address the passing of the colonial age argue against the further fracturing of the geopolitical world, but nevertheless cite the necessity for recognizing humanitarian questions of considerable urgency. The ethnic wars raging in the former Yugoslavia and the republics of the late Soviet Union, as well as the dire plight of whole populations in places like Rwanda and Burundi, demand a new understanding of the problem of self-determination. *See also* ETHNIC WARS (48–50); ETHNICITY (51); NATIONALISM (57); PEACEFUL SETTLEMENT: PLEBISCITE (442).

Significance
National self-determination is frequently asserted as a right by national minorities and has often served as a rationalization for rebellion and secession when demands for separate government have not been met. As an expression of nationalism, the doctrine contributed to the vast increase in the number of states since the beginning of the nineteenth century, particularly after World War II. Combined with nationalism and carried to its ultimate conclusion, it is also an invitation to ongoing political fragmentation. It has already progressed to the point that the word *mini-state* has entered the vocabulary of international relations. International law, however, recognizes no such absolute right. Consequently, national self-determination is more a political than a legal phenomenon, and succeeds or fails on the basis of internal and external power considerations.

Nationalism: Xenophobia $\boxed{63}$

Fear or distrust of foreigners and of the policies and objectives of other states. Xenophobia is related to the mass emotions of ethnocentrism and nationalism in that they all involve a relationship between an in-group and outsiders that creates distinctions favorable to the in-group. Xenophobia involves perceptions of other people not as individuals but as stereotypes of something feared or hated. *See also* NATIONALISM (57).

Significance
Xenophobia may be manifested in attitudes of superiority to outsiders, but usually is a cloak for feelings of suspicion and resentment. It is particularly observable among people who have suffered from real or imagined exploitations by the peoples of other countries. China, for example, stereotyped all foreigners as barbarians, and for centuries refused to deal with them as equals. China was later subjected to humiliating treatment by European powers, and Chinese xenophobia took the form of intense anti-Westernism. Such feelings of mixed pride and inadequacy can be exploited for a variety of purposes. Foreigners are made scapegoats for the difficulties faced by newly independent countries, and frustrations are thus channeled away from rather than against the domestic regime. In much of the developing world, xenophobic charges such as neocolonialism are aimed at separating a country from what may or may not be exploitative foreign economic interests. Xenophobia can also occur among segments of the population of a single country, as in the antipathy against the large Chinese populations found in many countries of Southeast Asia.

Nationalist Movement: African National Congress (ANC) | 64 |

South African political organization founded in 1912 in reaction to the seizure of land from the black African population by the white-dominated Afrikaner government. The Afrikaners also imposed employment restrictions and curtailed freedom of movement by South African blacks within their own country. These restrictions were enshrined in the policy of apartheid (the forced separation of South Africa's races) that framed South African life following World War II. The ANC assumed responsibility for representing the larger community of black Africans; because the organization challenged the apartheid system, it was outlawed and its leaders arrested, often tortured and killed, or forced into exile. Many ANC leaders were tried and convicted of treasonous acts, among them Nelson Mandela, who spent 28 years in South African jails. Despite Mandela's incarceration, he remained the *de facto* leader of the ANC, and from his prison cell he symbolically represented the continuing and determined opposition of the ANC to all aspects of apartheid. Nelson Mandela's release from prison in the changed environment created by the termination of the Cold War brought an official end to the apartheid system. The open mingling of the races in South Africa led to the legalization of the ANC in 1991, and in 1994 Nelson Mandela, running on an ANC platform, was elected president of South Africa in a mixed black-white government. *See also* APARTHEID (31).

Significance
The ANC was chiefly responsible for the breaking of the apartheid system that was originally established in 1948 to provide the white minority in South Africa with absolute power in virtually all matters. But even ANC leaders acknowledged that their long struggle was crowned with success because of the enlightened leadership provided by South African president F. W. de Klerk, whose vision and courage overcame significant white resistance to the abolition of the apartheid system. De Klerk dismantled the monopoly of power constructed by the South African white elite. He also undermined elements within the black elite that had actually benefited from the apartheid system. In fact, the most critical resistance to the ANC came from some of the leaders of the black homelands that had been created by the apartheid system. The ANC had to counter stiff, often violent opposition from the Zulu community and its leader, Chief Mangosuthu Buthelezi, more than from the white supremacist *volkstaat* of Constand Viljoen. Buthelezi's Inkatha Movement, determined to resist a change in the country's political status that apparently threatened Zulu aspirations, tried to prevent the holding of the 1994 elections. Only a last-minute settlement between ANC and Inkatha permitted the smooth holding of

elections in April 1994, and the passing of the South African presidency from de Klerk to Mandela shortly thereafter.

Nationalist Movement: Basque Separatism | 65 |

A demand for self-determination by a culturally distinctive group in Spain. The Basque population was forced into the Pyrenees between France and Spain by the Visigoths in the sixth century. Long an isolated people, Basques differ from the general population of Spain by language and customs. The industrialization in Spain's northern regions brought southern migrants to the region, and the interaction between the indigenous Basques and the more Spanish settler population caused friction and ultimately conflict. The Basque population of approximately 2 million perceived a threat to their way of life from the newcomers. They also reacted adversely to the policies of the dictator, General Francisco Franco, whose representation of integral nationalism was resisted by the Basque population. The Spanish Fascists, however, were uncompromising, and Franco's draconian methods, e.g., his arbitrary arrest and torture policy, were comparable only to those of Mussolini in Italy and Hitler in Germany. Not until Spain's defeat in World War II was Franco's harsh rule eased. The Basque Homeland and Liberty Party, or Euzkadi ta Askatasuna (ETA), was formed in 1959, and almost immediately became active in terrorist assaults on Spanish officials and installations. Franco's death in 1975 cleared the way for even more dramatic ETA attacks on Spanish property and lives. Nevertheless, a new Spain emerged with the passing of the dictator. Spain introduced democratic reforms in the 1970s and 1980s; it established a constitutional monarchy and promised autonomy for the provinces and regions. But the ETA still insisted on self-determination and independence. By the 1990s the Basque region had gained virtual control over local government, taxation, and education; even the police force was exclusively Basque. Nevertheless, the ETA continued to pressure for inde-pendence. The 1978 constitution divided the country into 17 regional autonomies, but the ETA refused to accept the compromise. Madrid's policy then turned toward the general Basque population, and appealed to them, hoping to separate the common citizens from the ETA. Terrorist bombings in Madrid and Barcelona in 1993, attributed to the ETA, continued to take a toll of the innocent and did little to elevate the role of the party or its cause. To that extent, government strategy, which also included reform measures, resulted in alienating most Basques from the ETA. Spanish authorities became better placed to arrest ETA leaders, and the movement, though far from neutralized, assumed less of a threat in 1995.

Significance

The ethno-nationalist violence perpetrated by the Basques of Spain has prevented the country from attaining genuine stability. In major part, the ETA's purpose is to provoke the Spanish government into using excessive counterforce, thereby justifying the ETA's argument that the Madrid authorities are a mortal threat to the Basque nation. These tactics limit other Basque organizations and their leaders in finding acceptable solutions to the nationalities problem. Nevertheless, the Spanish government is determined to maintain the territorial integrity of the state, and its entreaties to Basque moderates continue, as does its attempt to neutralize the ETA.

Nationalist Movement: Chiapas Problem | 66 |

A demand for greater autonomy by a culturally distinctive group in Mexico. Chiapas, Mexico's southernmost state, has been the scene of an armed rebellion against the Mexican government since 1993. Chiapas is Mexico's most neglected state. Its indigenous population is by some estimates the most disadvantaged group in a nation of extreme wealth and extreme poverty. An armed group known as the Zapatista National Liberation Army, led by an obscure non-Chiapan known as Subcomandante Marcos, emerged in the 1990s to publicize the grievances of the peasantry, and its violent actions provoked a brutal counterresponse from the Mexican army. The central government indicated that it was interested in a diplomatic solution to the Chiapan problem, but its real objective was to isolate the general population from the Zapatistas.

Significance
The Chiapas problem in Mexico can be compared with numerous ethnic issues that surfaced in the aftermath of the Cold War. Much like the Chechens of Russia, the Chiapans express frustration with the majority community, which seldom takes their particular needs into account when making public policy. The worsening economic situation in Mexico could only fuel an already bitter dispute. A March 1994 plan offered by the government in return for a condition of normalcy was overwhelmingly rejected by the indigenous communities in the southern state even though the plan aimed at increasing social spending in rural areas and also promised increased political representation. Given the weakness of the Mexican center, the Zapatistas claimed the right to represent all of Mexico's impoverished people. The Zapatistas elevated their demands, and called for national reforms, which they hoped would bring an end to Mexico's longstanding one-party rule.

Nationalist Movement: Irredentism | 67 |

The desire of the people of a state to annex those contiguous territories of another country inhabited largely by linguistic or cultural minorities of the first state. Irredentism is a term of Italian origin and comes from the expression *Italia irredenta*, meaning "Italy unredeemed," or Italians not liberated from foreign control. After the creation of the Kingdom of Italy, the slogan was widely used by nationalists working for the annexation of bordering Italian-speaking communities, particularly those under Austrian rule in Trentino and the Tyrol. *See also* NATIONALISM: SELF-DETERMINATION (60).

Significance
Irredentism is an aspect of nationalism closely related to self-determination and is a source of international tension and conflict. It can occur wherever a political boundary does not coincide with linguistic or ethnic boundaries. Even with the best of intentions, in areas of mixed populations boundaries are difficult to draw with a precision that satisfies all parties concerned. Irredentism can also be used as a rationalization for territorial aggrandizement. Illustrations of irredentas include Alsace and Lorraine for France after 1870, the Sudetenland of Czechoslovakia for Germany after the Treaty of Versailles, and Iraq claiming Kuwait as its nineteenth province in 1990. Irredentism among the states of Africa and Asia, if not of Europe, will remain a potential source of conflict for years to come because the former imperial powers mapped their boundary lines with little reference to the linguistic, cultural, or communal integrity of the people inhabiting those states.

Nationalist Movement: Kurdistan Problem | 68 |

The futile quest for self-determination by culturally distinctive group in the Middle East. The Kurdistan problem concerns efforts since the end of World War I to create an independent state for the Kurdish nation. The Kurds, estimated at 15 to 20 million, are a non-Arab, non-Persian, marginally Turkic, Sunni Muslim people who inhabit a mountainous area straddling the borders of Iraq, Turkey, Iran, Azerbaijan, and Syria. These states have firmly resisted all efforts by the Kurds to achieve their stated objective. The Kurds have never quite represented a united front, and the divisive nature of the Kurdish nation is exaggerated by their domicile in the several countries noted above. The largest Kurdish population is found in Turkey, where approximately 12 million Kurds are generally described as Turks, and indeed many Turkish Kurds cannot be distinguished from the majority Turkish population. Nevertheless, a militant Kurdish organization, the Kurdish Worker's Party (PKK), has organized a terror war against Turkey, and since 1984 has pressured Ankara to yield a portion of the country to form a separate Kurdish state. Turkey has not hesitated to use significant counterviolence in an effort to destroy the PKK. The Iraqi Kurds have been similarly troublesome to Baghdad, but matters were brought to a head during and immediately following the Gulf War of 1991 when two Iraqi Kurdish factions launched a rebellion against Baghdad from their bases in northern Iraq. Iraq successfully beat back this attack, and to prevent a reoccurrence of the Kurdish threat it forced hundreds of thousands of Kurds into the barren mountains bordering Turkey and Iran. Allied forces acknowledged the desperate plight of the Iraqi Kurds, and they compelled Iraq to accept an autonomous Kurdish region in its northernmost territory. NATO command warned Iraqi planes to avoid flying over the area, and humanitarian aid was rushed to the refugees. The inability of the Kurdish Democratic Party and the Patriotic Union of Kurdistan, both Iraqi-based organizations, to unify their factions, however, prevented them from successfully policing their frontier with Turkey. This weakness was later exploited by the Turkish PKK, which sustained its war against Ankara. The PKK also found the Kurdish sanctuary in Iraq conveniently placed for their activities. *See also* WAR TYPE: INSURGENCY, KURDISH (340).

Significance
The Kurdish problem emerged with the collapse of the Ottoman Empire in World War I. Although Kurdistan was slated for inclusion in the mandates system supervised by the League of Nations, none of the major wartime victors wished to assume the role of mandatory power. Kurdistan was thus divided by the consequences of the war, and the problem of its independence was left to future generations. The Turkish army's 1995 incursion into the Iraqi security zone established by the United Nations and NATO was another indication that Kurdish independence remained a remote possibility.

In the post–Cold War era, cries for self-determination have diminishing appeal. Once considered to be a right of a people to self-government, and hence a separate political experience, self-determination is more and more judged a threat to national, regional, and even global stability. The argument pressed by established states is that the colonial era has passed and there is no longer justification for outright, notably militant demands for self-determination.

Nationalist Movement: Namibia   69

The successful achievement of self-determination by the majority population in Southwest Africa. Namibia is somewhat unique in that it was originally created as the German colony of Southwest Africa, occupied by British and South African forces in World War I, redesignated as a Class C mandated territory by the League of Nations, and placed under South African supervision when the mandates system was formally established. Due to the intransigence of South Africa it remained a mandate under the League of Nations long after the league ceased to exist. South Africa refused to transfer the mandate to the UN Trusteeship Council following World War II, and the region was a trouble zone until the 1980s, when the South African authorities finally acknowledged that the people of the territory had a claim to self-determination. After ignoring two advisory opinions from the International Court of Justice, and a 1966 resolution by the UN General Assembly declaring that the mandate had been terminated, South Africa was finally forced to accept the idea that Southwest Africa (Namibia) could not be denied its independence indefinitely. The UN decision to establish a council for Namibia and a UN commissioner to act as a government-in-exile finally impacted on the South Africans. Negotiations toward self-rule began in 1978, but the Southwest African People's Organization (SWAPO) engaged in armed rebellion, complicating the work of the diplomats. Nevertheless, in 1988 a plan was signed at UN

Headquarters by South Africa, Angola, and Cuba that called for the withdrawal of South African forces from the territory and Cuban troops from Angola. Elections were forecast and a government for an independent Namibia was projected. The UN Security Council set April 1989 for the beginning of the transition process, and a United Nations Transition Assistance Group (UNTAG) was assembled to assist the special representative of the UN secretary-general in Namibia. The United Nations also sent a mission to Angola, the United Nations Angola Verification Mission (UNAVEM), to assure Cuban compliance with the 1988 agreement. After all the stages were complied with, elections were held in Namibia in November 1989, and a constituent assembly was sworn in on 21 March 1990 under the presidency of Sam Nujoma, a SWAPO leader. In April 1990 Namibia became the 160th member of the United Nations.

Significance
Namibia not only illustrates the positive success of nationalism and the honoring of a persistent claim to self-determination, it also represents the most successful UN peacekeeping mission yet undertaken by the world body. The UN effort required a force of 8,000 and a budget of $373 million, approximately 10 percent less than the amount authorized by the UN General Assembly. The force of administrators, technicians, and soldiers faced many adversities, but their efficient performance prevented untoward events from disrupting the transformation of Namibia from a mandated territory to a sovereign, independent state. Although SWAPO's nationalistic purpose seldom faltered, it is acknowledged that independent Namibia was as much a consequence of effective UN intervention as it was the determination of the Namibians to gain their freedom.

Nationalist Movement:
Palestine Liberation $\boxed{70}$
Organization (PLO)
The political-military organization that since the 1960s has purported to represent the interests of the Palestinian people

in their struggle for independence and nationhood. Headed by Yasir Arafat, the PLO is a coalition of nationalistic groups, unified only by their hostility to Israel and their common aspirations for a Palestinian homeland. The liberation movement has only a tenuous stability because the various factions that comprise the PLO have continuing disputes over strategy and tactics to be used in seeking their common objectives. The PLO's primary motivation has long been the destruction of the state of Israel, but Arafat's decision in September 1993 to enter into an agreement with Yitzhak Rabin, the Israeli prime minister, dramatically altered the course and character of the organization. In this agreement, Rabin turned over the administration of the Gaza Strip to Yasir Arafat. Israel also gave the PLO control over the West Bank city of Jericho and promised to make still more concessions in the territory in return for a PLO pledge that its violence against the Jewish state would cease. Arafat declared his intention to open an era of peaceful exchange and dialogue with Israel, but still another Arab organization—Hamas, claiming no affiliation with the PLO—refused to accept the plan and sustained its assaults on Israeli targets in the West Bank, Gaza, and Israel itself. Suicide bombers ostensibly from the Hamas organization attacked Israelis at random, but singled out Israeli members of the armed forces whenever possible. At the same time, the Shiite Hezbollah organization, based in southern Lebanon, continued its attacks on Israeli military positions and settlements in the region. The sustained conflict, apparently beyond Arafat's ability to control, led observers to conclude that the peace process between Israel and the PLO could not succeed. Despite efforts at normalizing relationships in the area (Israel entered into a treaty of peace with Jordan in 1994), the inability of the PLO to quell acts of terror threatened to undo what little had been accomplished. But the peace process between Israeli and PLO officials continued, with the two sides pressing for a settlement that would give the entire West Bank territory (except for Israeli settlements there) to the PLO. Thus, another major PLO-Israeli accord was agreed upon in September 1995. This agreement announced the withdrawal of Israeli military forces from six additional West Bank cities, i.e. Jenin, Nablus, Tukarem, Qalqilya, Ramallah, and Bethlehem, as well as 450 towns and villages. Israeli troops, however, were to remain in Itebron to guard the small contingent of Jewish settlers. The agreement also called for the election of an 82-member self-rule council, and Palestinians were granted control over 30 percent of the West Bank, comprising 2,270 square miles. The holy sites in the region, with the exception of the tomb of the Patriarchs in Hebron, were to be turned over to Palestinian control, but special arrangements were made for Rachel's Tomb in Bethlehem and for Joseph's Tomb in Nablus. Free access and the right to worship at the holy sites was guaranteed. Finally an understanding was reached on joint PLO-Israeli patrols in the protection of Jewish settlers, and Israel declared its intention to release Palestinian prisoners in three phases. In return, the PLO pledged to revoke articles of the Palestinian Covenant that called for the destruction of the State of Israel. *See also* NATIONALISM: SELF-DETERMINATION (60); WAR TYPE: TERRORISM, STATE-SPONSORED (347).

Significance
The Palestine Liberation Organization has long held claim to a legitimacy usually reserved for sovereign states. The organization has been recognized by scores of governments, and Yasir Arafat has often been accorded the status of a head of state or government. The PLO has enjoyed observer status in the United Nations and the International Labour Organization (ILO), as well as membership in the Group of Seventy-Seven (G-77). The Third World Caucus and the Nonaligned Movement (NAM) have also given official attention to the organization. Although the PLO was driven out of Lebanon in 1982 by Israeli invasion forces, by the late 1980s it had reestablished its power base in northern Lebanon and received financial backing from

a number of wealthy Arab states. PLO successes were sidetracked in 1990–1991 when Arafat joined forces with Saddam Hussein and justified the Iraqi invasion and seizure of Kuwait. Following Iraq's defeat by an international coalition led by the United States, Kuwait, Saudi Arabia, and other Gulf states demanded the exodus of Palestinians working within their states. Kuwait and Saudi Arabia also suspended financial payments to the PLO. Acknowledging the flagging influence of the PLO, Yasir Arafat decided to satisfy a long-term U.S. demand that the PLO sit down with the Israelis and negotiate an end to their hostilities. Arafat's calculated gamble was not received enthusiastically in most of the Arab states or, for that matter, throughout the Islamic world. But with few options left to his PLO, and with younger, more determined terrorist organizations emerging in the guise of Islamic fundamentalism, it appeared to be the only plausible action.

Nationalist Movement: Sri Lanka $\boxed{71}$
The ethnic violence that erupted in Sri Lanka in the early 1980s has passed through several stages, but the end is not in sight despite efforts made by domestic and foreign actors, including India's military intervention in 1987. India's involvement was arranged by a peace-and-reconciliation accord negotiated between the principal Sri Lankan actors: the Hindu Tamil guerrilla group known as the Liberation Tigers of Tamil Eelam, located in the northern and eastern provinces of the island state, and the government dominated by Sinhalese Buddhists. The Indian army was called to act as a neutralizing force, but by February 1988 it was engaged in a tedious campaign aimed at eliminating the Tigers. In the end, India's intervention only escalated the level of violence. New Delhi terminated its operations and withdrew from the scene, hoping the disputants could find common ground for a peace settlement. Intermittent periods of tranquility followed, punctuated by violent assaults on government installations and officials as well as on the

general public. Cease-fires came and went, one in 1995 lasting only four months before the fighting resumed. By April 1995 more than 40,000 lives had been lost, and no one in Sri Lanka believed that true reconciliation was possible between the Tamils and Sinhalese—that is, short of Sri Lanka's partition into two independent states.

Significance
The ethnic turbulence and savagery in Sri Lanka continues to take its toll on both sides. Ethnic cleansing has been an unwritten policy of the Tamil Tigers; they claim a homeland in Sri Lanka, and seek to eliminate the habitations of all non-Tamils from those regions. The clash between Tamils and Sinhalese has colonial roots. During the period of British occupation, Tamils were brought to Sri Lanka from southern India to work the vast tea plantations managed by British companies. The swelling of the Tamil population also provided the British with opportunities for recruiting the Tamils to assist in administering the island, then known as Ceylon. In time, the Tamils enjoyed greater influence than the more indigenous and more numerous Sinhalese Buddhists. When the British withdrew from Sri Lanka in 1947, the majority community insisted on its right to control the new nation's future. Tamils were displaced by Sinhalese, and the Tamil "liberation" movement was sparked by their perception of second-class status. Cultural differences between Tamils and Sinhalese were significant, and national unity yielded to distinctiveness. Communal riots, notably in Colombo, targeted the minority Tamils. To defend their brethren, the Tigers organized clandestine military units, which ultimately assumed the capability to assault the government and lay claim to a right of self-determination. The Tamil population of southern India provided a source of strength and support for the Tigers, and for a while the Indian government seemed sympathetic to the movement. In time, however, the Tamil Tigers were judged a threat to the stability of the region, and despite sympathy for their cause, the Indian government was constrained from supporting them. Sri Lanka remains a country torn by violence; assassination, wanton destruction, and the killing of the innocent have become commonplace.

Nationalist Movement: Zionism   72

A form of nineteenth-century nationalism developed by European Jews who believed that the Jewish people would find true peace only in a sovereign state of their own choosing. The claim of self-determination was realized in 1948 when the sovereign state of Israel was carved from a portion of the Palestine mandate administered by Great Britain. Originally the dream of Theodor Herzl, the Jewish state opened its doors to Jews everywhere, but especially to that remnant of European Jewry who survived the Holocaust. The Jewish migration to Israel was assisted by the International Zionist Committee, which moved its headquarters from Europe to the United States during World War II. Non-Israeli Zionists also have labored to support the state of Israel, especially in time of conflict. Unfortunately, Israel has known little but conflict since its establishment. Zionism remains the guiding principle in Israeli life, but the country is also home to ultraorthodox Jews who do not acknowledge Zionism because they deem it to be a secular ideology. Nevertheless, Israeli Zionists try to coexist with the variety of Jews among them, and attempt to develop the same live-and-let-live attitude with their Arab population, also citizens of Israel. Israeli Zionism has not impeded democratic development in Israel; in fact, some observers believe that Israel is the only democratic state in the Middle East, in no small part because of the leveling character of Zionism.

Significance
Zionist groups are more active outside Israel than within the nation, particularly in the United States, which has substantial Jewish communities. Zionists encourage American Jews to influence political-party programs, and the Ameri-

can government has been most responsive to Israeli needs. Following the 1967
war between Israel and its Arab neighbors, the U.S. government believed it
would find Israel a staunch ally in the
Middle East. Since then, the United States
has been Israel's principal benefactor,
and the small Jewish state is the primary
recipient of American military assistance.
American Zionists recognize the importance of the American connection and
they strive to sustain the positive aspects
of the relationship, particularly when Israeli actions are questioned in government circles. American Zionists also
believe it necessary to counter Arab lobbying interests, which have developed
greater sophistication in recent years.

Neostructuralism   73

The formative processes of state behavior
in relationship to other states, as well as
the interaction between subnational, national and international, and supranational systems. Reacting to structuralist
approaches, which they define as too narrow in scope, the neostructuralists apply structuralism to a global concept of
politics. Citing advances in science and
technology that have altered global perceptions as well as communications,
neostructuralists address the increasing
complexity of a world influenced by external and internal factors of incredible
variety. The expansion of domestic economic interests that embrace global economic demands and movements is
unprecedented, and, therefore, according
to the neostructuralists, makes the study
of international relations more com-
pellingly holistic. For one school of
neostructuralism, the structure of the
global economy is a closed system, with the
dominance of the center driving the weaker
regions into still greater dependence, and
hence more intense poverty. The world
thus becomes increasingly polarized,
generating higher levels of cultural and
ethnic conflict, with flagrant acts of belligerency. Another school, arguing from a
somewhat different perspective, cites the
dysfunctional, often obsolete character of

the nation-state in a world driven by the
growth in transnational social relations.
Not only is the nation-state judged less
able to cope with the demands of its citizens, it is also confronted with contradictory options: It must cooperate with
efforts aimed at conserving the planet's
resources, while at the same time pressing its particular and exclusive interests.
Therefore, neostructural theory focuses
on either those processes promoting state
cooperation or those sustaining the sovereign isolation of the independent state
actor. *See also* "CLASH OF CIVILIZATIONS?"
(34); DEMOCRATIC PATTERN: SUBSIDIARITY
(705); STRUCTURALISM (77).

Significance
The post–Cold War era calls for a redefinition of the rationalistic positivism that elevated the omnicompetent nation-states
and their total concern with military and
economic prowess. The ideological division that sustained the rivalry between East
and West since the end of World War II is
a much-reduced factor in the current game
of nations. The contemporary interest in
paradigmatic pluralism in the social sci-
ences shifts attention away from the exclusive nation-state to international and
supranational arrangements that address
the need for more deliberately inclusive
regional and global accommodations. This
awareness leads to neostructuralist exege-
sis. Neostructuralism searches for systematic links integrating subnational, national,
and transnational politics, and a definitive
response has yet to emerge. The fact that
such international relations theory examines both the durability of the nation-state
and its obsolescence demonstrates the incomplete nature of the exercise. The concern with both the "culturist" and
"structuralist" perspective has given rise
to a "disciplined eclecticism" that demands synthesis, a goal likely to occupy
the interests of scholars well into the next
generation.

Neutralism   74

An attitude or policy of independence
and nonalignment. Neutralism describes

the political position of states that have decided not to support either side in a particular dispute or conflict. Because neutralism implies determination to maintain freedom to maneuver according to the dictates of national interest, it should not be considered a new phenomenon in international politics. Nor should it be confused with the legal concept of neutrality, which implies a policy of impartiality toward belligerents in a war. *See also* INTERNATIONAL LAW: NEUTRALITY (483); THIRD WORLD: NONALIGNED MOVEMENT (NAM) (28).

Significance
The policy of neutralism, or noncommitment, coupled with the great increase in the number of states, helped undermine the rigid bipolarity of the Cold War. Neutralism also restored freedom of action in the international balance of power. By pursuing an independent course, nonaligned countries were free to define their own national interests and to devote primary attention to the pressing problems of modernization and national integration. The neutralists thus placed themselves in positions where they could take aid from any source and, to some extent, force the opposed blocs to compete for their support. The impact of neutralism was particularly evident in the UN General Assembly, where the Afro-Asian countries gained an absolute majority. Many times during the Cold War years they forced the major actors to relax international tensions and concentrate their attention on the economic and social concerns of the new majority.

Polyarchy   75

A world devoid of a dominant structure that adequately frames both conflict and cooperation. Polyarchy exists when nation-states, subnational groups (nongovernmental organizations), and transnational interests (commercial and financial) and communities (custom unions, free-trade blocs, and security systems) vie for the loyalty of individuals. In a polyarchic system, international politics is no longer confined to nation-state rivalry; the international system is perceived as simply one subsystem among others in an expanded and much more complex structure of human relationships. *See also* NEOSTRUCTURALISM (73); STRUCTURALISM (77).

Significance
The complex global relationships accelerated by advances in science and technology challenged Marxist systems rooted in the smokestack era of the industrial revolution, and ultimately eroded their foundations and hastened their collapse. The assaults on the centers of state power from the periphery were engineered by subnational and transnational forces, the contemporary symbol of which was the crumbling of the Berlin Wall in November 1989. Polyarchal developments explain the failed efforts at reforming Soviet structure, process, and performance. Nor could market forces be accommodated within the framework of the Soviet Union's command economy. The state succumbed to its own dysfunction as disadvantaged groups, e.g., coal miners and farm workers, increased tensions and promoted societal conflict. The breakup of the Soviet Union, and the rise within the different republics of subnational and national elements with individualized agendas, addressed the extent to which polyarchic forces accrue leverage in spatial circumstances. In a broader context, the high unpredictability of polyarchy in international relations suggests a shift away from the limited constraints developed by nation-states to conditions that hint at even greater displays of international anarchy. Definable jurisdictions based on sovereignty provide a degree of stability when compared with unregulated polyarchy. This dangerous variant of polyarchy compels scholars to examine the circumstances under which self-interested actors in a world polity, lacking central mechanisms for lawmaking and law enforcement, struggle to establish and maintain international regimes of positive coordination and collaboration.

Population Exchange $\boxed{76}$

The systematic exchange of populations between states in which ethnic compatriots domiciled in those states are placed in jeopardy and the only recourse is their physical removal from territories where they are threatened and transference to territories where they can find asylum or refuge. Population exchanges are substantial undertakings, usually involving tens of thousands of people, possibly hundreds of thousands. The countries directly involved acknowledge the need to peaceably accept the secure and orderly movement of large numbers of people at risk, coordinated by external parties and institutions.

Significance

Population exchange is a diplomatic response to the problem of threatened minorities. It is distinguished from the haphazard, often chaotic flight of refugees from war zones, or situations in which people are no longer confident that their future can be managed in their places of birth. Population exchange strives to avoid the chaos that flows from the disorganized displacement of people, usually as a consequence war. The process involves the agreement of the sending state to permit the safe passage of minorities and the willingness of the accepting state to admit and resettle that population. Because population exchange is a two-way affair, each state both sends and receives population in a relatively orderly manner. The matter of population exchange was raised during the Greek-Turkish War of 1919–1922. At the conclusion of those hostilities, the international community assisted the Turks and the Greeks in removing significant numbers of their brethren from the respective countries. The war in Bosnia in the 1990s again gave substance to the issue of population exchange. The inability of Bosnian Serbs, Muslims, and Croats to share a common destiny pointed to the need to employ population exchange. The war in the former Yugoslavia that began in 1991 brought an end to the cosmopolitan character of the region and destroyed the ca-

pacity of the three groups to live freely with one another. The "ethnic cleansing" policy pursued by the Bosnian Serbs during the conflict forced the anarchic scattering of tens of thousands of refugees to other parts of Bosnia, the larger region, and the world. Population exchange, although a painful exercise, aims at regulating the safe passage of people, their resettlement, and ultimately the reestablishment of their normal way of life.

Structuralism $\boxed{77}$

Marxian interpretations of the state as primarily responsive to, as well as influenced by, social relations that emanate from the structure of the economy. The functions of the state are judged to be determined by the structures of the society, e.g., classes, material need, and monopoly capital, rather than by the individuals occupying the important positions of state power. Thus capitalism is observed as shaping the normative and behavioral features of a state, and it is the structure of society and the pursuit of material interest that is most compelling. The nexus between those who benefit and those who lose out in the economic process creates the dynamics in the formation of those social structures that perpetuate the distances between groups. More significantly, the beneficiaries of the process are the ones seeking to reinforce and preserve the status quo. Structuralism relies heavily on the concept of the state as a totality, not simply the state as a political instrument; thus, structuralists are more inclined to use the term *state* for its holistic meaning, rather than surrogate terms such as *government* or *political system*. In so doing, stress is applied to the entire network of social relations that define society, and the greater concern is with the arrangement of structures rather than with the myriad of particular activities. *See also* NEOSTRUCTURALISM (73).

Significance

Structuralism deviates from the more traditional approach to the study of international relations that centers attention exclusively on the independent state. Rather than consider the state a distinct and organic entity, the structuralists prefer to examine the state from the inside out, hence their indifference to the more conventional approach that emphasized the external factors influencing state behavior. The structuralists also focused on each state as single and isolated from the others, but their emphasis was not so much on the state as with the society that it represented. Thus, structuralism influenced the formulation of modernization and development theory, as well as the forays into dependency and world-system theory. In this way, the structuralists moved international-relations theory from its single-nation orientation to phenomena that were deemed as transforming the global condition. The structuralists argue that the larger world is changing in response to compelling forces at lower levels. Critics of structuralism not only find fault with the ideological character of the theory, they decry the failure to include in the analysis the impact of global processes on state/societal transformation. Claiming to represent a more complete theory, these critics have posited a neostructural approach to the study of international relations.

Transnationalism $\boxed{78}$

An open international environment exposing people in one state to ideas, values, customs, traditions, institutions, tastes, and behavior of others. The term *transnationalism* refers to the porous condition of frontiers in contemporary world society, and the overriding need of independent, sovereign states to mingle and commingle with other politically defined territories. No state can isolate itself completely from the external world of states, and virtually all have recognized the necessity for cooperation and accommodation. Transnationalism is evident primarily in economic and financial matters, but it is also observed in open, formal security systems, as well as in cultural interaction. Transnationalism has focused attention on the requirements of

people for legal protection extending beyond the borders of state citizenship. Transnationalism has also been experienced negatively, especially in contemporary political terrorism, where politically inspired individuals and groups seek psychological leverage in states unable to completely defend themselves against random assaults on their installations and people. *See also* "CLASH OF CIVILIZATIONS?" (34); ISLAMIC FUNDAMENTALISM (132).

Significance
Transnationalism, whether positive or negative, thrives when boundary barriers between sovereign states are reduced or eliminated. In a world of improved communication and transport, states find it virtually impossible to isolate themselves from the larger world. Closing borders is not only impractical, it is a self-defeating policy in a world of interdependent nations. Transnationalism is both a curse and promise. The greater openness—a product of accelerated technological, economic and political change—allows deviant and generally belligerent individuals and groups, if not states, to perpetrate aggressive acts that terrify and paralyze international intercourse. The bombing of the New York Trade Center in 1993 and the repeated attacks on Israelis by Palestinian members of fundamentalist organizations such as Hamas demonstrate the difficulties modern societies face in trying to protect themselves from transnational terrorists. On the more positive side, however, transnationalism promises a more compatible and congenial world community, with major benefits accruing to persons as well as states. Transnationalism describes the success of Europeanization in Western Europe, where the states of the European Union have eliminated their armed frontiers and opened their societies to one another. Transnationalism also defines efforts by students and practitioners of international law who are determined to expand the realm of international jurisprudence so that it applies more broadly to persons as well as to states.

Ideology
and
Communication

Atlantic Charter | 79 |

The joint declaration issued by President Franklin Roosevelt and Prime Minister Winston Churchill in August 1941, following their historic meeting aboard a ship in the mid-Atlantic. The Atlantic Charter proclaimed the principles that were to guide the two countries in their search for a just peace and a stable world after the destruction of the Nazi regime. These included (1) the Four Freedoms—freedom from fear and want, and freedom of speech and religion; (2) the application of the principle of self-determination in all territorial changes; (3) the right of all peoples to choose the form of government under which they live; (4) equal access to trade and the raw materials essential to prosperity, and economic collaboration among all nations; (5) peace with security for all states; (6) freedom of the seas; and (7) renunciation of the use of force, establishment of a permanent system of general security, and disarmament of all nations that threaten the peace. *See also* PROPAGANDA (137); WAR TYPE: PSYCHOLOGICAL WARFARE (343).

Significance

The Atlantic Charter, like the Fourteen Points enunciated by President Woodrow Wilson during World War I, was a major propaganda instrument aimed at sparking mass support for the Allied cause in World War II. It was particularly focused on overcoming isolationist sentiment in the United States (the charter was proclaimed four months before the Japanese attack on Pearl Harbor and the U.S. entry into the war). Charter principles, especially the Four Freedoms, gained broad support as war aims, but their influence became even greater in the postwar period. Many of the principles of the Atlantic Charter have been implemented. The principle of self-determination, for example, served to legitimate the aspirations of millions of colonial peoples for independence and statehood. The "permanent system of general security" took shape in the form of the United Nations, and economic collaboration has been fostered on an unprecedented scale. The Atlantic Charter continues to be invoked by those who pursue idealistic approaches to foreign policy issues.

Brainwashing `80`

A psychological technique for reorienting the individual's thinking to conform to a predetermined mode. The term *brainwashing* is derived from the Chinese colloquialism *hsi nao* (wash-brain). Brainwashing is carried out by obtaining a confession of wrongdoing, followed by a process of reeducation. The means used to brainwash an individual include combining extremely harsh and lenient treatment, interspersed with physical and psychological punishments and rewards designed to break traditional patterns of thought and substitute new ones. *See also* WAR TYPE: PSYCHOLOGICAL WARFARE (343).

Significance
The technique of brainwashing was used on a massive scale by the Chinese to inculcate new thought patterns in the years following the 1949 victory of the Communists in the civil war. During the Korean conflict, the Chinese attempted—successfully in some cases—to brainwash U.S. prisoners of war. Some prisoners renounced their allegiance to the United States, confessed to having committed war crimes such as waging germ warfare, and chose exile in China to repatriation. The effect of brainwashing as a technique for reshaping the individual's values and changing allegiance remains difficult to evaluate. Some psychological warfare experts believe it can be used more effectively to change ideological values than to change national allegiances.

Capitalism `81`

An economic theory and system based on the principles of laissez-faire free enterprise. The capitalist theory calls for private ownership of property and the means of production; a competitive profit-incentive system; individual initiative; an absence of governmental restraints on ownership, production, and trade; and a market economy that provides order to the system by means of the law of supply and demand. The theory also assumes the free movement of labor, capital, and trade, both domestically and in foreign markets, which should result in an international division of labor and national specialization. Although some forms of capitalism have always existed in human society, the sophisticated theories underlying modern capitalism were initially developed by the classical economists, beginning with Adam Smith's publication of *Wealth of Nations* in 1776. *See also* ECONOMIC THEORY: KEYNESIANISM (226); TRADE POLICY: FREE TRADE (244).

Significance
In the late eighteenth and nineteenth centuries, the new doctrine and practice of capitalism, together with the democratic concepts of political liberalism, began to replace the established order of mercantilism and monarchy. Mercantilism's stringent governmental controls over internal and foreign economic activity and trade progressively gave way to an individual- and freedom-centered system of entrepreneurship and trade. The resulting burst of economic activity helped to produce the Industrial Revolution. The twentieth century has witnessed the fruition of capitalism and, in turn, its substantial modification. In some states the change took the form of an expanding role for government in economic affairs, with private ownership and initiative combined with governmental promotion and regulation in a new "mixed economy." In others, capitalism was challenged by socialism or communism, which were based on rigid state control over the economy and trade. In the contemporary world, some observers believe that the basic nature of individualistic, free-enterprise capitalism has been perverted in some democratic states by a warfare economy and the vast power linkage between giant industrial corporations and the government. The failure of the Soviet Union's command economy, however, appeared to establish the merits of capitalism over those of socialism/communism, and in fact the self-destruction of the Soviet Union was considered evidence of the strength of capitalism, irrespective of its faults.

Moreover, the remaining Communist states, i.e., China, Vietnam, North Korea, and Cuba, all acknowledge the power of the capitalist system, its deepening appeal among Third World nations, and their own need to adjust their economies to the dominant global enterprise. China stands out as the Communist country that has made the most remarkable progress in opening its economy to market forces. Observers believe that it is only a matter of time until its Communist political system will also be reformed out of existence.

Communism 82

An ideology that calls for the elimination of capitalist institutions and the establishment of a collectivist society in which land and capital are socially owned and in which class conflict and the coercive power of the state no longer exist. Although numerous political philosophers since Plato have developed theories embracing diverse forms of communism, modern Communist doctrines were first postulated in the nineteenth century by socialists and other reformers, such as François Fourier, Robert Owen, and Claude Saint-Simon. Dismissing this group as well as church communalists as "Utopians," Karl Marx and Friedrich Engels fashioned a doctrine of "scientific socialism" that became the basis for the contemporary ideology of communism. Numerous Communist theoreticians and political leaders since the mid-nineteenth century have interpreted, modified, and added to these theories. The most important contributors to Communist ideology were Vladimir Ilyich Lenin, Josef Stalin, Leon Trotsky, Mao Zedong, and Josip Broz Tito. Because Lenin was also an action-oriented revolutionary and was credited with managing the Bolshevik Revolution that took control of Russia during World War I, his revisions of Marxism and his overall contributions to Communist doctrine were considered the most important. Marxism-Leninism (that is, Lenin's embellishment and restructuring of Marxism) became holy writ for Communists everywhere. Lenin, combined with Marx, espoused a philosophy of history that cited an inevitable progression from capitalism to socialism that would result from internal contradictions in capitalism. According to Communist doctrine, the contradictions within capitalism, notably the manifestation of the inevitable class struggle between the "haves" and the "have nots" (the property holders and the workers) will provoke an epoch-making struggle culminating in the destruction of capitalism. Replacing the repudiated economic system would be a "dictatorship of the proletariat," which was projected in time as being free of class warfare, state controls, or selfish interests. *See also* COMMUNIST DOCTRINE (83–90); COMMUNIST THEORY (91–105).

Significance

From the publication of the *Communist Manifesto* of 1848 up to World War I, Marxian communism served only as a topic of intellectual debate and a rallying doctrine for unsuccessful agitators in many countries. The Russian military and social collapse in 1917 provided the historical opportunity for the Bolshevik Revolution and for Communists to "build socialism in one country." Following World War II, in the years 1945–1949, occupation by the Red Army brought Communist regimes to power in Eastern European countries and North Korea, while indigenous Communist forces won power by their own efforts in Yugoslavia and Mainland China. The Communist world, considered to be a monolithic entity by many Western observers during the 1950s, was rent by a major Sino-Soviet schism in the 1960s and a growing independence of Communist states in Eastern Europe based on the Yugoslav model of Titoism or national communism. Lenin's adaptation of Marxism to Russia, and its spread and forced imposition on other nations following World War II, revealed that it too had major contradictions. Moreover, these contradictions proved more significant than those afflicting capitalism. Capitalism displayed greater flexibility and adaptability than Marxism-Leninism, Maoism, or any of the other major versions of twentieth-century communism. Efforts at reforming the Communist system, especially in the relationship between politics and economics, did not succeed. The Gorbachev reforms in the Soviet Union in the late 1980s were undertaken to modernize communism and make it more germane for the twenty-first century. The failure of those reforms was also the failure of the ideological system underpinning it and the command economy that was supposed to ensure the well-being of the citizenry. They did none of these, and when authority lost its grip on the institutions of coercion, the whole edifice collapsed. The flight from communism by the states of Eastern and Central Europe was followed by the self-destruction of the Soviet Union. Communist systems prevail in China, North Korea, Vietnam, and Cuba, but Communists are no longer doctrinaire devotees of Marx and Lenin, or even Mao and Ho Chi Minh.

Communist Doctrine: Gorbachevism | 83 |

A significant revision of Marxism-Leninism made under the leadership of Mikhail Gorbachev. In 1985, through a policy of liberalization, Gorbachev instituted a vast array of economic and political reforms, which he regarded as more accurately reflecting the fundamental ideas of true Marxism-Leninism. Economic changes included an attempt to increase worker productivity by reducing alcoholism and absenteeism in the workplace, the limited use of "joint ventures" with foreign private companies, greater autonomy for economic and commercial units to make decisions free from political controls and compatible with efficient operations, encouragement of some measures of private enterprise, and, in some fields, the workings of a supply-demand market economy. Gorbachev's revisions of Marxism-Leninism were framed by the Russian words glasnost (openness) and perestroika (restructuring of the economy and the administrative/political system). Gorbachev's style, similar to that of Western politicians, involved frequent media reports to the people and mingling with Soviet citizens to sound out grassroots sentiment on current issues. His approach also involved the freeing of many political prisoners, permitting publication of previously banned works, and encouraging competitive, democratic elections for political and economic leadership positions. *See also* COMMUNIST THEORY: GLASNOST (100).

Significance
Although Gorbachev's liberalization program was mainly domestic, he also introduced a number of serious reforms in Soviet foreign policy that included new arms-control and disarmament proposals and programs aimed at normalizing relations with the United States. Moreover, Gorbachev did not interfere, and in fact appeared to support, the U.S.-led action against Iraq, a Soviet ally, when that Mesopotamian nation invaded Kuwait. Gorbachev's behavior and policies caused a weakening in the ideological argument that undergirded Soviet actions. Its growing irrelevance, coupled with Gorbachev's assault on the Soviet bureaucracy, ultimately provoked the effort to overthrow him in 1990. The coup failed, but the event proved to be the denouement of the Soviet state. Although Gorbachev tried to retrieve what he could in preserving the Soviet Union, his call for a new, more loosely arranged federation fell on deaf ears. When the dust settled following the aborted coup, it was Boris Yeltsin, not Mikhail Gorbachev, who commanded the popular will. Gorbachev was ousted from his office in the Kremlin, and Yeltsin proceeded to dismantle the Soviet empire. Gorbachevism proved to be the last breath of Communist doctrine in the state that Lenin had built almost eight decades earlier.

Communist Doctrine: Khrushchevism | 84 |

Contributions to Marxist-Leninist theory and applications of Communist doctrine in the Soviet Union made by Nikita S. Khrushchev. Khrushchevism developed from 1956, when Khrushchev emerged as the dominant leader in the post-Stalin power struggle, to 1964, when he was deposed from power by a party faction headed by Leonid I. Brezhnev and Aleksei N. Kosygin. Khrushchev began his rise to power when he replaced Josef Stalin as first secretary of the Communist party after Stalin's death in 1953. He consolidated his control in 1958 when he removed Nikolai A. Bulganin as chairman of the Council of Ministers and assumed that post also. Khrushchev's main contributions to Communist doctrine include (1) repudiation of Stalin's "cult of the individual" and the restoration of the "true" Marxist-Leninist approach of collective leadership; (2) enunciation of the doctrine and policy of "peaceful coexistence" between Communist and capitalist states, while calling for "wars of national liberation" in the underdeveloped world; (3) denunciation of Stalinist totalitarianism and the institution of less tyrannical policies within the Soviet state; (4) establishment for the first time in any Communist country of a specific timetable (within 20 years) for a socialist state to complete the historical transition to pure communism; (5) a declaration that although classes and the state will wither away, the Communist party will remain as a directing force in the future society; and (6) development of the tactical position that communism would defeat capitalism in peaceful competition in the world by proving itself to be a superior social and productive system. *See also* PEACE POLICY: PEACEFUL COEXISTENCE (436); WAR TYPE: WARS OF NATIONAL LIBERATION (349).

Significance

Khrushchevism was less a contribution to Communist doctrine than an attempt to consolidate and legitimate power following the death of the country's supreme ruler, Josef Stalin. Khrushchev denounced Stalin's great purge, which caused the deaths of millions of Soviet citizens in the 1930s, as well as the dictator's all-consuming "cult of personality." In the foreign-affairs arena, Khrushchev recognized that the potential devastation

in a nuclear war had to be given first consideration in the contest with capitalism's most powerful states. Although acknowledging the need for "peaceful coexistence" between the superpowers, Khrushchev nevertheless believed that the Soviet Union had ample justification for supporting "wars of national liberation" occurring in Asia, Africa, and Latin America. Khrushchev also argued that Soviet communism would overtake and pass U.S.-driven capitalism. On one historic occasion, he insisted that the Communists would be around to "bury capitalism." Khrushchev is cited as having introduced incentives into the Soviet economy to stimulate workers to higher levels of productivity. He was also the first Soviet leader to be invited to visit the United States, a distinction conferred on him by President Dwight Eisenhower. For all his earthy, somewhat primitive charm, Khrushchev could not avoid the intrigue of his colleagues, who succeeded in ousting him from office in 1964. The coup marked the end of Khrushchevism, but it is interesting to note that Mikhail Gorbachev adopted some of the same reforms more than a score of years later. Between the two of them, the Soviet Communist state was eventually dismantled, not reformed.

Communist Doctrine: Leninism

$\boxed{85}$

Theoretical interpretations and practical applications of Marxist doctrine contributed to the ideology of communism by the Russian revolutionary leader Vladimir Ilyich Lenin. The main contributions of Leninism include (1) the theory that imperialism, the highest stage of monopoly capitalism, results from the contradictions of capitalism that force trusts and cartels to seek outlets abroad for surplus capital and production and to bring world sources of raw materials under their control; (2) the theory that imperialist competition between capitalist states generates war; (3) the theory that revolution can take place in a precapitalist colonial society no matter how primitive; (4) a redefinition of the Marxist conception of revolution to include such non-Marxist opportunities as a national disaster that the ruling class cannot handle or general public discontent with the government; and (5) the role of the Communist party, guided by a small, dedicated elite, to lead the revolution and serve as the instrument for implementing Marx's "dictatorship of the proletariat." A prolific author, Lenin's main ideas are found in his works *What Is To Be Done?* (1902), *Imperialism: The Highest Stage of Capitalism* (1917), and *State and Revolution* (1918).

Significance
Leninist contributions in theory and practice to the doctrines of Marx were so substantial that Communists have since called their basic ideological framework Marxism-Leninism. As a theoretician, Lenin foresaw the contemporary revolution of self-determination that swept Asia and Africa, and he predicted the struggles in the underdeveloped lands that Nikita Khrushchev called "wars of national liberation." As a revolutionary practitioner, Lenin conducted a continuous revolution and rejected all appeals for gradualism from Communists and others. His most important contribution, however, was as a practical political leader. He rallied the Russian people after the disasters of World War I and the subsequent period of War Communism, which was a form of civil war. He also initiated the political, economic, and social reorganization of the nation, and charted a course for socialism that transformed the Soviet Union into a superpower following World War II.

Communist Doctrine: Maoism $\boxed{86}$

The interpretations of Marxism-Leninism and the policies developed and actions taken by the Chinese Communist party under the leadership of Chairman Mao Zedong. Maoism's theoretical base was popularized by the aphorisms included in the widely distributed "Quotations from Chairman Mao Tse-tung." Mao's main theoretical contributions include (1) a theory for fighting guerrilla wars in agrarian colonial and semicolonial coun-

tries with the active support of the peasants; (2) a definition of democratic centralism in the Chinese context that the people should enjoy a measure of freedom and democracy while at the same time submitting themselves to "socialist discipline"; (3) a definition of Marx's "dictatorship of the proletariat" in the Chinese situation as "a people's democratic dictatorship, led by the working class and based on the worker-peasant alliance"; (4) a theory that recognizes contradictions within the people's socialist system as well as between it and the capitalist enemy; (5) rejection of Soviet doctrinal appeals for "peaceful coexistence" in favor of "permanent revolution" throughout the world against the remaining bastions of capitalism; and (6) rejection of the primacy of economic development and material betterment in favor of maintaining the purity of the revolution and the creation of the "new Chinese man" and a new society freed of all contradictions.

Significance
Maoism evolved as a peculiarly Chinese interpretation and application of the principles of Marxism-Leninism by that nation's Communist leaders during Mao's 35 years as undisputed head of the Chinese Communist party. The central events of the long struggle for power that shaped the nature of Maoism include the early civil war period, 1928–1934; the Long March of 1934–1935; the struggle against the Japanese and the alliance with Chiang Kai-shek, 1937–1945; the resumption of the civil war in 1946; and the victory of the Communists in 1949. Maoist policy after 1949 relates to Communist theory in the following ways: (1) the brief "hundred flowers" campaign for free discussion in the mid-1950s; (2) the Great Leap Forward development program and the establishment of communes in 1958; (3) the struggle with the Soviet Union for leadership of world communism, and the resulting schism in the international movement during the early 1960s; (4) the violent and costly Cultural Revolution, which began in 1967 as a contest between technocrats on the one hand and Maoist

ideologues on the other, and did not end until Chinese society was itself torn apart; and (5) the emergence of a period of détente in the 1970s between China and the West, leading to China's admission into the United Nations, and President Richard Nixon's visit to China and his meeting with Mao and other high-ranking Chinese leaders. Indeed, the later diplomatic recognition extended to China by the United States (during the presidency of Jimmy Carter) can be traced to the later stages of Maoism. Although most Maoist principles can be traced to Marx, Engels, Lenin, and Trotsky, Chinese leaders have claimed that interpretations, adaptations, and applications of Marxist-Leninist doctrines undertaken under Chairman Mao's direction add up to an original contribution. Following Mao's death in 1976, many of his ideological convictions as well as strategies and tactics were rejected by his successors.

Communist Doctrine: Marxism | 87 |

The body of economic, political, and social theories developed by Karl Marx and his collaborator Friedrich Engels in the nineteenth century. Marxism offers a comprehensive "scientific" philosophy of history that explains humankind's development dialectically as a series of class struggles that have produced new social orders. Marx viewed capitalism as a system suffering from irremediable internal contradictions with an intensifying class struggle that would culminate in a revolution carried out by the proletariat against the bourgeoisie. A period of "dictatorship of the proletariat" would follow in which capitalists would be stripped of their wealth and power, land and the means of production would become nationalized, and class distinctions would be abolished. According to Marx the state would then "wither away," a final stage of pure communism would be ushered in, and people would live in a perfect classless, stateless society of spontaneous cooperation in which each individual would contribute according to his or her ability and receive according to his or her

needs. Marx's ideas were developed in the *Communist Manifesto* of 1848 and in his principal work, *Das Kapital*, the first volume of which was published in 1867. *See also* COMMUNIST THEORY (91–105).

Significance
Although a nineteenth-century phenomenon, Marxism has had a profound impact on twentieth-century history. The development of Communist and Socialist parties espousing Marxist doctrines presented an open challenge to older, more established orders. The success of the Marxist-inspired Russian Revolution of 1917 and the emergence of Communist regimes in Eastern Europe, China, North Korea, Cuba, Vietnam, and several other Third World states after World War II split the world into rival ideological and military camps and affected the international relations of all states. The Cold War framed the relations of nations for more than four decades following World War II, impacting most directly on the Third World nations that achieved their independence during the period. Although the period demanded the utilization of resources for human development, nation-building plans were largely bypassed for military preparedness. Third World states either committed themselves to one of the blocs developed during the Cold War or opted for nonalignment. But whatever their "choice," their development programs were distorted or neglected. Like their competitors in the West, the Marxists addressed the need to service a desperate humanity, but their confrontation prevented serious efforts to modernize long-stagnant societies. Marxism had the same general effect on the major Communist states. The Cold War proved costly in human and material terms to the Marxist states, while capitalism continued to reform itself and even to thrive, as noted by the developments in West Germany, Japan, and along the Pacific Rim. Marxism could not hope to match these experiences, and in the final analysis it was repudiated by those who had earlier embraced it.

Communist Doctrine: Stalinism | 88 |

The theoretical interpretations and practical applications of Marxist doctrine contributed by Josef Stalin, who dominated the party and governmental machinery in the Soviet Union from the mid-1920s until his death in 1953. The main contributions of Stalinism include (1) his methods of organizing the Soviet people for achieving industrialization, (2) collectivizing agriculture, (3) defending the nation against Nazi attack, and (4) reconstructing the war-devastated nation. Stalin showed that, in addition to the Marxist and Leninist prescriptions for the victory of communism, military occupation by a Communist great power (as demonstrated in Eastern Europe after World War II) could also accomplish the goal if circumstances were favorable. Stalin contributed little to Communist doctrine, but in developing his "cult of personality," he restored the historic institution of the great and awesome leader chronicled in Russian history. In his almost 30-year reign, Stalin outdid the inhumanities committed in the name of Ivan the Terrible and rivaled Adolf Hitler in his savagery and brutality. The irony in this depiction is that Stalin was a Georgian (others would say an Ossetian), not a Russian.

Significance
As a result of the de-Stalinization campaign carried on by some of his successors, Stalinism was condemned as fostering dictatorial rule, personal infallibility, the establishment of a totalitarian state, the execution of former colleagues deemed opponents, the unleashing of the secret police against the citizenry, the imprisonment of millions of people in slave labor camps, and the torturing and murder of political dissenters. Concepts Stalin developed and applied in the Soviet Union with an impact on Communist doctrine include his idea of "socialism in one country," the Five Year Plans for fostering economic development, the collectivization of agriculture, and the 1936 Soviet constitution, which replaced the 1924 Lenin constitution. Despite the repudiation of Stalin, many of his theoretical and practical contributions survived to the last days of the Soviet state.

Communist Doctrine: Titoism | 89 |

The theory and practice of national communism espoused by Josip Broz Tito, Communist leader of Yugoslavia. Titoism emerged as a new Communist doctrine in 1948 when President Tito rejected Stalin's call for a monolithic approach to world communism and refused to accept the direction and control demanded by the Soviet Union. Tito saw nationalism and communism as complementary doctrines that called upon each Communist state to retain full political independence and to choose its own "road to socialism."

Significance
Titoism exposed the disunity within the Communist world, but at the same time unified the different ethnicities of Yugoslavia. By 1948 Yugoslavia followed a policy of nonalignment in foreign affairs, and did business with and accepted aid from both Communist and capitalist states. Tito envisaged a Yugoslav economy and political system that was pragmatically ordered and essentially free from external ideological or political controls. Although Stalin attempted to break the Titoist revolt, Nikita Khrushchev denounced Stalin's heavy hand. He reached a rapprochement with Tito in 1955, and this Soviet-Yugoslav understanding was sustained by Khrushchev's successors. Titoism was generally accepted throughout the Communist world, and most importantly, by Communist parties in non-Communist states. Karl Marx would not have recognized this development of national communism, but it suited the character of communism in the post–World War II era; Communists could argue that their loyalties to their nation-state took precedence over their loyalties to international communism. Titoism was even more important in cementing the disparate nationalities comprising the Yugoslav state. The Yugo-

slav federation prevailed during Tito's lifetime, in no small measure a testimony to his visionary leadership. But the state could not be sustained after the great leader's death, and especially following the crumbling of the Berlin Wall and the decommunizing of Eastern and Central Europe. The demise of the Soviet Union was the final event that undid Titoism, and the Yugoslav federation as well. Titoism fractured the Communist world in order to sustain the union of Yugoslavians. When the Communist world lost its most important member, Titoism could not prevent the fracturing of the Yugoslav state itself.

Communist Doctrine: Trotskyism | 90 |

The theories of Leon Trotsky, a leading Communist revolutionary who challenged Josef Stalin for the leadership of the Soviet Union following Lenin's death in 1924. After the Bolshevik Revolution of 1917 and the Civil War period, Trotsky argued for using the Communist base in Russia to achieve world revolution. Stalin, on the other hand, called for building socialism in one country to give communism a sound base, impregnable to capitalist counterrevolution. Stalin won the power struggle in the late 1920s, ousted Trotsky from the Communist party of the Soviet Union, and forced him to seek exile in Mexico City. Trotsky continued his opposition to Stalin, and in 1940 the Soviet dictator had him assassinated. Trotskyism as an ideology called for the unity of the proletariat of all countries. His goal was the establishment of a worldwide Communist commonwealth. Trotsky believed that the Russian Revolution failed because it had created a bureaucratic ruling class that exploited the workers and betrayed their interests.

Significance

Trotskyism became a synonym for deviationism and revisionism, long before Khrushchevism and Gorbachevism. Trotsky was a brilliant Marxist theoretician and author, as well as a military tac-

tician who had saved the Bolshevik Revolution by forging the Red Army into a first-class fighting force. But he was outmaneuvered in the post-Lenin power struggle by Stalin, who held the crucial party post of secretary-general. Trotskyism continues to find adherents, especially in the Third World, where the idea of a socialist commonwealth of peoples is still nurtured.

Communist Theory: Class Struggle | 91 |

The conflict between the proletariat and bourgeoisie that, under capitalism, results from the increasing impoverishment of the workers and a polarization engendered by a growing class consciousness. Karl Marx believed that the class struggle emerged out of the basic contradictions identified by the dialectical process as inherent in capitalism as well as in primitive, slave, and feudal social systems. Communists perceive it to be the means by which the transition from capitalism to socialism will occur. Although many revolutionaries antedating Marx based their doctrines on the class-struggle theme, Marx was the first to accord it the central role in a philosophy of historical evolution.

Significance

The Communist doctrine of class struggle assumes that there are only two social classes in capitalist society, that the two have contradictory interests, and that each will become implacably hostile toward the other. To encourage these developments, Communist agitators in many countries endeavored to develop a militant class consciousness among the proletariat. Critics of communism reject the idea that class struggle is predetermined and inescapable; they point out that in the United States, for example, the great majority of people consider themselves to be "middle class." Marx's predictions that the workers' lives would grow increasingly harsh and that poverty and unemployment would increase, leading to a sharpening of class interests, still have validity for post–Cold War socialists, but the movement toward more inclusive capitalistic activities appears to have neutralized the fervor of their argument.

Communist Theory: Communism | 92 |

The final stage of the dialectical process in which the "new Communist man" lives in a classless, stateless society, accepts a new and higher morality, and spontaneously cooperates with his fellow man. Marx anticipated that pure communism would follow the transitional stage of socialism under a proletarian dictatorship because the proletarian state would simply "wither away" as the classless society was achieved. Communism would constitute the final and highest stage of social development because the energizing force of class conflict would no longer exist, nor would there be a need for further evolutionary progress. According to Marx, the production and distribution of material wealth under communism would change from a socialist basis of "from each according to his ability, to each according to his work" to a system based on the Communist principle of "from each according to his ability, to each according to his needs."

Significance
The ultimate objective of pure communism linked Marx with Mikhail Bakunin and the philosophical anarchists of his day who also considered the state an instrument of oppression and sought its elimination. While never repudiating the ideal of pure communism, Communist theorists and national leaders have often rationalized it as a distant objective that cannot be achieved as long as hostile capitalist states threaten the socialist states. In the early 1960s, however, Premier Nikita Khrushchev announced to the representatives of 81 Communist parties convened in Moscow that the Soviet Union was completing the building of socialism and would be the vanguard in the movement to communism. The Communist vision of building a pure society—a

veritable heaven on earth—in the beginning attracted intellectuals, moralists, and others to the cause. Most, however, became disillusioned by the harsh discipline, rigid thought control, police-state methods, and especially the victimization of millions of innocent people within the Communist states.

Communist Theory: Contradictions of Capitalism | 93 |

The fundamental irreconcilable conflicts inherent in the nature of capitalism that, according to Communist dogma, will be instrumental in bringing about its collapse. Marx's theory is that the contradictions of capitalism begin at the production stage when the worker receives (in wages) only a small portion of the value of the article produced; the remainder, in the form of surplus value or profits, is kept by the capitalist. The result is insufficient purchasing power to buy the goods that are produced. According to Marx, this underconsumption produces increasingly severe economic depressions within nations, an increasing impoverishment of the working class, growing unemployment, a class struggle, and, ultimately, the collapse of the capitalist system and its replacement by socialism.

Significance
Communists believe that their theory of the contradictions of capitalism demonstrates that capitalism contains the seeds of its own destruction and will fall, not from attack by outside forces, but because of its own self-generated weaknesses and conflicts. Increasingly severe economic slumps culminating in the Great Depression of the 1930s appeared to Communists to be the denouement of the Marx-predicted apocalypse of capitalism. Critics of Communist dogma, however, point out that economic slumps have become less serious since the 1930s, that through trade unions and other means workers have been able to win a bigger slice of the economic pie, and that governmental fiscal and monetary policies permit adjustments within each nation's

economy to avoid the pitfalls Marx predicted. The applications of Keynesian economic doctrines and the development of mass consumer credit are viewed by some observers as the key ingredients to modifying and strengthening the capitalist system.

Communist Theory: Cultural Revolution | 94 |

The name given by the followers of Mao Zedong to their chaotic struggle in the mid-1960s against revisionism and betrayal of the revolutionary cause. The Cultural Revolution, according to Maoists, was a mass proletarian movement against either a Western or Soviet type of capitalist restoration. Constant struggle was held to be necessary because capitalist resistance increases as its end draws near.

Significance
In the Cultural Revolution, the real power struggle is not between communism and capitalism, but between the old revolutionaries and the succeeding generation of bureaucrats and technocrats. This struggle pits the spirit of revolution against the imperatives of nation building. The clash between the two contending forces split Chinese society and prepared the foundation for the quasi–free-market economic reforms that followed the death of Mao Zedong. The ultimate goal of communism—the changing of human nature to create "the new Communist man"—may have provided the inspiration for the Cultural Revolution, but its legacy is a China that is more realistic, more nationalistic, and more demanding of the creature comforts associated with the Western world.

Communist Theory: Democratic Centralism | 95 |

The doctrinally sanctioned method for making and implementing decisions within Communist parties. Democratic centralism, as developed by Lenin, calls for democratic participation through free discussion and deliberation on the devel-

opment of party policies by all Communist party members. Once decisions have been made, however, further dissent and debate are no longer tolerated, and well-disciplined party members are expected to lend their full support to the execution of policies by the centrally directed party organization. In other words, diversity during the formative stages of policy development must give way to monolithic unity in support of the party elite in implementing policy.

Significance
The working principle of democratic centralism was developed by Lenin to fuse the practical and psychological advantages of rank-and-file participation with the need for ideological unity and bureaucratic efficiency stemming from central control. Lenin saw this approach as necessary to provide the internal cohesion and efficiency needed both in waging the struggle to achieve power and in implementing the socialist program after the revolution had succeeded. The principle of democratic centralism was abandoned under the dictatorial rule of Josef Stalin, and for almost a quarter-century, decisions were made and enforced by a small oligarchy under Stalin's control. It continued to follow the Stalinesque formula until the administration of Mikhail Gorbachev, but his comparatively "democratic" style may have contributed to the failure of his reform program, and ultimately to his fall from power.

Communist Theory: Dialectical Materialism | 96 |

The concept that explains how the union of opposites produces social development. The dialectic, which Marx borrowed from the philosophy of Hegel, postulates a process by which each idea (thesis) produces a contradictory idea (antithesis), leading to a conflict out of which a new, higher idea (synthesis) emerges. Marx adapted the dialectical method to his materialist outlook and used it to describe the process in which the dominant economic classes in each society engage in struggle and produce new economic systems, culminating in the creation of a final, pure, classless, stateless society of communism. Lenin described dialectics as "the study of the contradiction within the very essence of things."

Significance
Dialectical materialism is vital to the philosophy of communism because Marxists believe that it constitutes a science of society that reveals the laws of social change. By inverting Hegel's philosophy, ideas for Marx became merely a reflection of material reality rather than the dominant factor in history. Embracing dialectical materialism as prescribed by Marx, the dedicated Communist accepts the historical inevitability of the transition from capitalism to socialism because all aspects of human society are controlled by material forces that govern individual choice and define man as a socially determined product. Critics reject the dialectical method developed by Marx on the grounds that it is unscientific, rooted in ideological faith, and pretentiously deterministic as a monistic causal interpretation of history.

Communist Theory: Dictatorship of the Proletariat $\boxed{97}$

The transitional stage following a proletarian revolution in which Communist power is consolidated, the bourgeoisie eliminated as a class, and socialism established. According to Marx, the dictatorship of the proletariat meant that the workers would control the machinery of the state and would use it to reorganize society and convert the means of production from private to public ownership, providing for the transformation of society into its final stage of pure communism. Lenin and Stalin saw the dictatorship as being vested in the Communist party, and its leaders as representatives of the proletariat. Its primary function was to defend the state and the revolution against a renaissance of the bourgeois class, which, they believed, had increased

rather than decreased its resistance following the overthrow of its power.

Significance
The dictatorship of the proletariat provides the means in Communist theory for the realization of the goals of communism. Although Marx believed that the historical transition of society from capitalism to socialism was inevitable, he designated the proletarian class as the means for effecting the transformation. Since Communist theory postulates that all states rest on force, and that law is merely the expression of the will of the dominant class, the proletarian class is assigned the role of using the state machinery to carry out its objectives. Critics of communism note that the intended dictatorship *of* the proletariat has been applied, in all Communist states, in the form of a dictatorship *over* the proletariat carried on by a single party leader or group of oligarchs. In the Soviet Union the term *proletarian democracy* was substituted in state and party propaganda for the less-appealing *dictatorship of the proletariat*.

Communist Theory: Economic Interpretation of History $\boxed{98}$

The assumption that the basic economic system or "mode of production" of a society determines its political, moral, legal, cultural, and religious superstructure and provides the motivating force that guides the development of society from lower to higher stages. Marx's "materialist conception of history" starts with the proposition that humankind's basic activity relates to the production and acquisition of their means of subsistence. The system for the organization, ownership, and operation of these productive forces and the distribution of food and material wealth produced by them determines the nature of society, and through class conflict provides the inner motivating power for the society's evolution. The three factors of production identified by Marx as most directly related to social change and historical development are labor, raw materials, and the instruments of production.

Significance

Marx's emphasis on the fundamental role of the economic system in societal development and in shaping other human institutions has led observers to characterize him as an economic determinist. Under capitalism, the dialectically inspired contradiction between modern productive techniques and bourgeois ownership leads, according to Marx, to an inescapable conflict in the form of class struggle. Marx and Engels, as well as contemporary Communists, denied the allegation of determinism, preferring to regard the struggle as an evolutionary historical process rather than a simple cause-and-effect relationship. Nevertheless, Marx and Marxists have always focused on the central theme that economic forces produce class struggle, which will inevitably result in the collapse of capitalism.

Communist Theory: Eurocommunism　99

The special role, policies, and programs of national Communist parties in Western European democratic countries. Eurocommunism evolved in the 1960s and 1970s as the monolithic control by the Soviet Union over European Communist parties ended. It remained intact after the Cold War, and is still a force to be reckoned with. Eurocommunism implies a renunciation of revolution as a means of gaining political power. In addition, Communist leaders in Western Europe continue to espouse nationalism, good government that is free from corruption, administrative efficiency, and effectiveness in dealing with economic problems. In Italy, France, Portugal, and Spain, which have relatively large Communist parties, the Communists also accept a role for the Catholic church.

Significance

Eurocommunism developed as an ideological appeal aimed at winning over the voters of Western Europe. Communist leaders and their organizations in Western Europe rejected violence and offered a viable alternative to the center, right-wing, and other left-wing parties. As a result, Communist parties in Western Europe still receive a respectable portion of the vote in national elections and in direct elections to the European Parliament.

Communist Theory: Glasnost　100

A Russian term defined as "openness." The policy of *glasnost*, along with that of *perestroika* (restructuring), became Soviet state policy during the rule of Mikhail Gorbachev. Gorbachev began his reform program with a heavy emphasis on modernizing and streamlining the Soviet economy. The program included a crackdown on corruption, alcoholism, and sloth. He called for increased decision-making freedom for small enterprise, and permitted a measure of competition in the economy. On the political level, Gorbachev freed a number of political prisoners, allowed persons wishing to emigrate to do so, and advocated filling political and economic posts by competitive elections. Gorbachev reduced censorship and sanctioned the publishing of works formerly banned from public view. He also encouraged truthfulness in reporting the news, and personally mingled with Soviet citizens in order to obtain their views on current topics. In addition to these revolutionary domestic changes, Gorbachev called for new relationships with the Western countries, and to prove the sincerity of his intentions, he offered to expand the arms-control negotiations on nuclear and conventional weapons. *See also* COMMUNIST DOCTRINE: GORBACHEVISM (83).

Significance

Although the Western world had reason to be skeptical when Gorbachev's reforms were first made public, time showed that he was genuinely interested in not only reducing tensions between the two camps, but also in dissolving those tensions. The summit meetings between Gorbachev and President Ronald Reagan were dramatically productive, in major part, because the Soviet leader was ready to reconcile differences with his country's chief nemesis. Reagan began his presidency in 1981 by describing the Soviet Union as the "evil empire" and closed out his tenure in 1988 walking arm-in-arm with Gorbachev in Moscow's Red Square. Always suspicious of Soviet desires for peace, and fearful that *glasnost* and *perestroika* (restructuring) were just the latest propaganda efforts by the Soviet behemoth, the United States trod cautiously. But ultimately, it could only acknowledge that Mikhail Gorbachev had changed the course of history and that future international relations would be sharply different.

Communist Theory: Historical Inevitability | 101 |

A philosophy of history in which Marx posited the preordained necessity and scientific certainty of the replacement of capitalism by socialism. Historical inevitability, according to Marx, results from the contradictions embedded in a society's mode of production wherein one class is made subservient for the sole benefit of the other, and therefore is exploited by that other, as exemplified in the respective relationships between the Greek freeman and the slave, the feudal lord and the serf, the aristocrat and the subject, and the bourgeoisie and the laboring masses. The inevitable clash between these juxtaposed classes creates the dynamics of history, and leads to the next stage, the next encounter—until the final stage is reached and the proletariat (labor) overwhelms the propertyholders and establishes their utopian community. To an orthodox Marxist, free will and individual initiative are insignificant in this broad sweep of history.

Significance
The doctrine of the historically inevitable triumph of the underclass gave communism a mystical aura with the anticipatory quality of a religious faith. Marx believed that the means for achieving socialism might initially be evolutionary and democratic (or if necessary, violently revolutionary), with the proletariat arrayed against the bourgeois ruling class. Marx forcefully argued the inevitability of the violent clash because he did not envisage the bourgeoisie yielding voluntarily to the demands of the proletariat. This preordained movement of history postulated still another Marxist dogma—that in the end, with the triumph of communism, all political structures including the state itself would wither away, and class conflict would at long last terminate. The prevailing belief that this revolutionary doctrine was buried with the Soviet Union needs to be reexamined. The home-grown extremist groups that surfaced in the United States after the bombing of the Federal Building in Oklahoma City in April 1995 espouse a similar argument. While not necessarily drawing their doctrines from Marx directly, they bitterly denounce established government and the order it oversees as tyrannical and antipeople. These alienated, disenchanted but nevertheless determined elements in U.S. society are replicated all over the planet—wherever government is found wanting in meeting the needs of complex societies. In industrial democracies such as Japan, Britain, France, and Germany, significant segments of the population are calling for revolutionary changes that would diminish government's role and allow them greater license in the pursuit of their particular objectives. Associated with the radical right rather than the left, they exhibit considerable confidence in addressing the inevitability of the final clash—and their ultimate victory.

Communist Theory: Imperialism and Colonialism | 102 |

An assumption that economic contradictions created by the nature of capitalism lead states into policies of overseas imperialism and colonialism. Capitalist imperialism and colonialism have been explained by Communists since Lenin's time. They are seen as the means for opening new outlets for investments, finding new markets for the excess production that cannot be sold on the home market, and securing cheap raw materials for domestic factories. The need to pursue overseas policies of conquest and control, according to Lenin, grows out of the changing nature of capitalism and its movement from an early competitive stage to a later "monopoly stage" dominated by cartels and trusts. According to Communist dogma, imperialist rivalry, aggravated by monopoly capital, causes destructive wars among capitalist states, ultimately weakening them to the point of collapse.

Significance
The theory that imperialism and colonialism are produced by the contradictions of capitalism can be inferred from Marx's writings, but it was not fully developed as an essential feature of Communist dogma until Lenin expounded it in his *Imperialism: The Highest Stage of Capitalism* in 1917. In developing the theory, Lenin borrowed heavily from the views expressed by English economist J. A. Hobson. In his book *Imperialism* (1902), Hobson developed the thesis that Western policies of imperialism and colonialism could be attributed to the propensity of the capitalist system to oversave, thereby creating the need to supplement the underconsuming domestic market by exploiting overseas outlets. Lenin's doctrine altered Marx's by predicting that proletarian revolutions might not occur in the advanced industrial nations, but they certainly would in the undeveloped societies of Asia and Africa where monopoly capitalism was totally exploitive. Historical developments have only partially disproved this theory. Lenin's forecast that upheavals in the colonial world (today's Third World) would impact adversely on the industrial world may still hold validity. The spread of politically inspired religious fundamentalism following the end of the Cold War is symptomatic of deeper ills than those diagnosed during the era of Soviet-U.S. confrontation. It is now generally believed that the Cold War obscured, submerged, or preempted developments that were much more salient than those dramatized by the struggle to prevent the spread of international communism.

Communist Theory: Revolution | 103 |

The use of force by the masses to win and hold power in the violent climax to the class struggle anticipated by Communist doctrine. Marx believed that in democratic states the proletariat could conceivably take power initially by winning the battle of the ballot box, but he forecast that when the proletariat sought to dislodge the bourgeoisie from its control of economic institutions, a counterrevolution would likely result. Lenin modified Marxism by postulating that the bourgeoisie would never relinquish its dominant role until its power was smashed by a violent proletarian revolution. In enunciating a policy of peaceful coexistence, Nikita Khrushchev declared in 1961 that communism does not need war to spread its ideals, that its weapon "is its superiority over the old system in social organization, political system, economy, the improvement of the standard of living and spiritual culture." Wars of national liberation fought by the masses in the underdeveloped lands of the world, however, were viewed by Khrushchev and later Soviet leaders as necessary and just.

Significance
Much of the Communist literature in the nineteenth and twentieth centuries was concerned with the nature of the Marxist-predicted revolution. The central question of debate has been whether the culmination of the class struggle would require a violent overthrow of the established government or could be accomplished peacefully through democratic processes. Most Communist theorists considered violent revolution as the legitimate and necessary means for achieving socialism, but none advocated war by Communist states against capitalist states as a proper or useful strategy. Communist leaders from V. I. Lenin to Mikhail Gorbachev expounded the idea that "revolution cannot be exported," that it must "result from indigenous conditions," and that the internal situation within societies must, in the Marxist sense, be "ripe for

revolution." Soviet leaders, however, justified support for revolutionary groups in other states on the ground that, when advanced capitalist states export counter-revolution to prevent the natural outcome of the class struggle, Communists are duty bound to provide support for the "progressive" forces involved in the struggle. Violating their own doctrine, however, in 1979 the Soviets invaded Afghanistan to suppress indigenous forces seeking to protect a particular way of life, and opened themselves to attack from the same counterforces they otherwise claimed to represent. The Soviet failure in Afghanistan proved the bankruptcy of their revolutionary doctrine, and exacerbated the disarray within the Kremlin and the nation at large. Ironically, the Soviet Union succumbed to its own theory of revolution.

Communist Theory: Socialist Program | 104 |

The basic changes to be undertaken, following a Communist revolution, that would transform society from capitalism to socialism and prepare the way for transition into the final classless, stateless stage of pure communism. The main objectives of the socialist program set forth by Marx in the *Communist Manifesto* of 1848 include (1) abolition of all private ownership of land, (2) a sharply progressive income tax, (3) abrogation of all inheritance rights, (4) state control of all banking and credit, (5) state ownership and operation of all communication and transport, (6) collectivization of agriculture and creation of industrial armies, (7) equal obligation for all to work, (8) abolition of child labor, and (9) free education for all children in public schools. The socialist program, according to Communist theorists, is to be implemented during the period of transition under the dictatorship of the proletariat.

Significance

The socialist program offered by Marx resembles a party platform aimed at gaining support for a set of governmental policy proposals. Although Communist

states espoused such goals, their realization proved elusive, and in most instances unreachable. State control of all property and infrastructure, and a command economy that seldom made decisions on the basis of fundamental issues, enabled the Soviets to assemble a formidable war machine and a relatively successful space program, but it could do little to meet the needs and aspirations of the general public. Moreover, wide-scale government waste and corruption, neglect of the environment, a reluctance to introduce the larger public to innovative technologies that were transforming neighboring regions of the world, and a propensity to reduce all activities, both domestic and international, to propaganda prevented the pursuit of stated objectives. Gorbachev's reforms were promoted with the purpose of bringing practice into balance with theory, but events show that it was too late for a simple course correction. Curiously, the transformation was not from capitalism to communism, but from communism to capitalism, not only in the Soviet Union but virtually throughout the Communist world.

Communist Theory: Surplus Value | 105 |

The Marxian postulate that the price of any product includes not only the "socially necessary" labor cost of production but also a "surplus value," which takes the form of profit for the capitalist. Marx's theory of surplus value meant that the worker who contributes all the value to a product is cheated out of just compensation, while the capitalist profits by exploiting another's labor. Marx developed the surplus-value concept by combining the classical labor theory of value expounded by John Locke, Adam Smith, and David Ricardo with the mercantilist doctrine of subsistence wages. The labor theory propounded the idea that all value is based on mixing one's labor with the raw materials of the earth, and the mercantilist doctrine articulates the philosophy that workers should be paid extremely low wages to provide them with an incentive to work by making their lives a struggle for sustenance.

Significance

The theory of surplus value developed by Marx constitutes the starting point in Communist doctrine for explaining the contradictions of capitalism. The natural tendency for capitalists to try to expand surplus value or profits, according to Marx and Lenin, creates an increasing impoverishment of the workers, underconsumption, and surplus production that results in economic depressions, imperialism, and colonialism. A class struggle between the exploited and exploiters follows as a necessary consequence. Defenders of capitalism had long challenged this Marxist argument, asserting that profits reward entrepreneurial ability and that such profits are essential in the creation of risk capital, which in turn encourages expansion and innovation. By the 1980s it had become apparent that workers in capitalist states enjoyed a standard of living far beyond that of workers in Communist societies. If surplus value was a relevant Communist argument, then apparently too much of it went to the state and very little was placed at the disposal of the worker. The alacrity with which Russia and the other republics of the former Soviet Union, as well as the states of Eastern Europe, adopted entrepreneurial systems, the free market, and a host of capitalist programs seemed to demonstrate the failure of surplus-value theory.

Consensus of Values   106

Mutual attitudes, beliefs, and aspirations among human beings. When a consensus of values exists, political action may be both motivated by and directed toward the achievement of common goals. When a group possesses a high level of value consensus, it is often described as a "community." *See also* DEMOCRATIC PATTERN: SUBSIDIARITY (705); MAASTRICHT TREATY (432); POLITICAL COMMUNITY (535); REGIONAL POLITICAL GROUP: EUROPEAN UNION (EU) (566); VALUES (144).

Significance

The degree of value consensus helps to determine the actual or potential level of political, economic, and social integration and the degree of stability within a social group. When rival social groups within a state are unable to agree on basic policy matters, revolution or civil war may erupt. Among nations, the creation of international institutions and the development of international law can proceed only as rapidly as a consensus of values evolves, and disagreement on basics may result in international conflict. On the regional level, an apparent Cold War consensus among Western Europeans, spurred by functional integration programs, helped to develop the European Community. However, following the Cold War, a return to narrower expressions of community is occurring. Although considerable momentum remains toward the development of an integrated European Union, the somewhat unified Western nations are again more keenly aware of national needs and national purpose. Value change shows itself to be more difficult to achieve than material or physical change. Social development is proving a greater challenge than either political or economic development, and the latter two are simply not possible without the former.

Cultural Exchange   107

International programs carried on by states or private groups to foster intercultural appreciation of artistic and scientific achievements and understanding of political, economic, and social institutions. Cultural exchange programs are often instruments of foreign policy employed by states to strengthen relations with friendly nations and to contribute to a relaxation of tension between peoples of potentially hostile countries. *See also* "CLASH OF CIVILIZATIONS?" (34).

Significance

Major governmental efforts to influence foreign peoples through cultural exchange activities date back at least to the period of the French Revolution. Since World War II, cultural exchange programs have often been directed more toward achieving national-interest objectives than toward improving international understanding. During the Cold War period such programs were carried on by both East and West. The United States, for example, fostered two-way exchanges of students and professors under the Fulbright Act of 1946; participated in a broad leadership exchange program under the Smith-Mundt Act of 1948; financed diverse overseas cultural programs under the surplus agricultural disposal program of Public Law 480; promoted exchange tours of artists, musical groups, authors, poets, and other cultural leaders; and sent thousands of Peace Corps volunteers to underdeveloped countries. The Soviet Union also sponsored Youth Festivals, sent its top performing and creative artists abroad, established a Friendship of Nations University in Moscow for the youth of the underdeveloped countries, and posted educational and scientific groups to special cultural missions. Both sides tried to convey the image of a highly cultured society that foreign peoples might well emulate in their own development. In addition to those programs motivated by foreign-policy objectives, the United Nations Educational, Scientific, and Cultural Organization (UNESCO) encouraged and sponsored national and international programs aimed at improving cultural cooperation and international understanding. These efforts were all significant in relating peoples to one another across great distances and cultural divides, but unfortunately, so much of the cultural exchange activity was committed to Cold War objectives that the real value of the exercises was lost. In other circumstances, the significant movement of people with alien traditions and experiences was judged too intrusive by people impacted by these visitations. The post–Cold War period exaggerates the differences among civilizations, the continued lack of understanding among cultures, and the alacrity with which people do violence to one another simply because others' motives or lifestyles are not understood. Fundamentalism as terrorism, in all its forms, centers its attack on alien cultures perceived as threats to tradition and self-image. Cultural exchange is a very weak tool in dealing with the deep-seated aspects of this most contemporary clash of civilizations.

Democracy 108

An ideology constructed around the liberal values of individual freedom, equality, human dignity and brotherhood, limited government, the rule of law, and the democratic political process. Although numerous political philosophers since Aristotle have contributed to the ideology of democracy, the foundations for modern democratic doctrines were fashioned by eighteenth- and nineteenth-century liberals, who transformed it from a theoretical formulation into a working system of government. Major contributors to democratic theory during this period include James Harrington, John Locke, Jean Jacques Rousseau, Thomas Jefferson, Thomas Paine, Jeremy Bentham, James Mill, John Stuart Mill, and Alexis de Tocqueville. The twentieth century has seen the further transformation of democratic doctrines from their earlier legal forms and principles to a full-blown ideology that postulates concepts for the "best" society rooted in individual freedom, social concern, and human dignity. Since the latter part of the eighteenth century, democracy had been associated with the economic freedoms of laissez-faire capitalism, but during the twentieth century it was reoriented toward the assumption of responsibility by government to deal with some of the economic and social maladjustments arising out of the Industrial Revolution. Individual theorists whose writings support a positive governmental role include L. T. Hobhouse, John Dewey, and Joseph Schumpeter. Democratic theory, however, remains a loose-knit congeries of theories, concepts, and practices, diversely interpreted and pragmatically applied, rejecting both dogma and the belief that the social good can be objectively or scientifically determined. It presupposes that the individual can make social-policy judgments and that a free society provides the best environment for constructing social institutions and ordering human relations. Political democracy, with its emphases on constitutionalism, sovereignty vested in the people, the accountability of public officials, civil liberty guarantees, the rule of law, and majority rule, remains the core of the ideology. Even these fundamental concepts, however, find diverse application among democratic states, and few contemporary theorists have sought to expand them. *See also* DEMOCRATIC THEORY (109–116).

Significance
Since the American and French Revolutions, democratic ideology has been pitted competitively against many rival political systems. Among these have been monarchy and the divine right of kings, aristocracy and oligarchy, fascism and the creed of the omnipotent state, and communism and its dogmatic creed of violence. Though often rejected after being tried by societies that misunderstood its principles, abused its freedoms, or sought quick-and-easy solutions to problems, democracy nevertheless continues to be an attractive ideal for both intellectuals and the masses. It has prospered most in the Atlantic community, the English-speaking Commonwealth countries and the Western European environment, which nurtured it through its Greco-Roman and Judeo-Christian roots and refined it through almost two centuries of speculative theorizing and pragmatic trial and error. Its particular effectiveness in these regions may also relate to the special conditions that encourage its development, including considerable degrees of social cohesion and consensus of basic values, a stable economic base, and educated and responsible peoples. The effort to spread democracy beyond the Atlantic community of West European and North American peoples was undertaken during the Cold War. The success of that endeavor is attributed to the collapse of the Soviet Union, but it is too early to conclude that it was the triumph of democracy that brought the Soviet Union down. It is unrealistic to assume that the demise of the Soviet state ushered in a new era of democracy everywhere. Democracy is not a permanent experience. Not only can democracy be lost, it is a very difficult system to operationalize in contemporary times. Democracy unleashes individual expression in all its diversity, while demanding social responsibility. It also seems to promise all things to all men, and that is a critical dilemma. In a world of enormous diversity, with population increasing at exponential rates, with people seeking the good life, with governments hard put (and essentially unable) to satisfy heightened popular expectations, with gross imbalances between the "haves" and the "have nots," and with more traditional cultural expressions in the ascendant, the future of political democracy as a preferred form of human organization in the twenty-first century is in considerable jeopardy.

Democratic Theory: Accountability | 109 |

A fundamental tenet of democratic theory that establishes the ultimate responsibility of all public officials to the people. Accountability is maintained through elections; constitutional controls; initiative, referendum, and recall; public-opinion surveys and polls; the activities of political parties; public meetings; freedoms of assembly, petition, speech, and press; and roll-call voting in legislative bodies.

Significance
All democratic systems accept the principle of accountability, but the institutions and procedures for implementation vary from country to country. In practice, the main lines of accountability run from the lowest bureaucratic levels up to the ministerial or cabinet levels, to the chief executive and legislative bodies, and finally, through elections, to the voters.

The lines of authority, consequently, run in the opposite direction. A responsible political-party system enhances the ability of the people to keep government accountable in policy matters as well as in decision-making and administrative areas. A working system of accountability distinguishes democratic systems of government from those based on absolutism and from those "guided" or "façade" democratic systems that use the forms and institutions of democracy but in fact exercise authoritarian powers over the people. As a rule, political systems that incorporate the highest levels of accountability and responsibility to the people—such as the British system—can be regarded as the most democratic.

Democratic Theory: Civil Liberties | 110 |

Guarantees that, in a democratic system, the individual's freedom will not be arbitrarily curtailed by government. Civil liberties are usually incorporated in a bill of rights or constitution that enumerates specific limitations on the authority of public officials. Major rights typically protected include freedoms of assembly, association, press, religion, speech, property, and due process and fair trial for those accused of crime. In the modern era, democratic governments increasingly assume a positive role in offering protection for the civil rights of individuals and groups from arbitrary interference by others in the society.

Significance
Protection of the individual's civil liberties and freedom to dissent is a key ingredient of the democratic creed. No right, however, can be absolute; all rights are limited by the need for protecting and advancing the legitimate interests of society. In a democracy, interference with the individual's freedom must not be arbitrary but reasonable and just, meeting the requirements of due process and the rule of law. The main problem in any democratic system is that of establishing an equilibrium between freedom and authority. If freedom is abused on a mass scale, resulting in deprivations of the rights of individuals and groups by others, the consensus that permits free expression and dissent may break down and give way to anarchy or authoritarian control over the society. A viable democratic society provides for as great a measure of individual freedom as is consistent with the requirements of an orderly democratic society.

Democratic Theory: Constitutionalism | 111 |

The basic concept that democratic government is limited in the scope of its authority, allowing government officials to exercise only those powers and perform those functions permitted by law. The major limitations of constitutionalism are incorporated in the fundamental charter or contract, whether written or unwritten, which is given formal or tacit approval by the people of the state.

Significance
The principle of constitutionalism applied to a working system of government provides one of the basic attributes that distinguishes a democratic system from those based on a form of absolutism. In a state in which many fundamental constitutional principles remain largely unwritten, as in Great Britain, the government is limited by custom, tradition, and acceptance by the people of political innovation and policy development through the many facets of the political process. In the United States and many other democratic countries, a written constitution serves as a contract between the people and the government. Through the process of judicial review, legislation and governmental actions that exceed constitutional limitations can be struck down by the courts, thus buttressing the principle of limited government and supplementing the role of the people in controlling their government through elections and other political techniques. Yet the limitations on government in modern democratic states have proved to be extremely flexible, permitting governments, through public acquiescence in broad interpretations of

fundamental laws, to become regulatory and service institutions. More recent efforts at reducing the size and role of government, and notably its centrality, comes at a time when societies have become more diverse yet interdependent. The loss of individual action, long a central feature of democratic societies, looms as a major threat to constitutionalism. Balancing individual rights with societal obligations continues to influence and hence challenge the relationship between citizen and government. The debate over more or less, or even no, government is destined to carry into the twenty-first century. Arriving at consensus decision making is more tedious, while pluralism (the belief in successful multicultural policies and programs) is under severe attack from elements that see only losses in yielding to such aspects of the constitutional experience.

Democratic Theory: Individualism   112
The concept underlying democratic systems of government that the chief purpose of government is to foster the well-being of the individual and permit each person to realize his or her full capabilities. The doctrine of individualism posits that government has an obligation to respect and protect each person's rights and to safeguard them from trespass by other individuals or groups.

Significance
Historically, the democratic doctrine of individualism has been based on the ideas that the people exercise supreme political power, that government authority is limited, and that each individual possesses certain inalienable natural rights. Economic individualism emerged in the Western state system during the eighteenth century, when the individual-centered doctrine and practices of laissez-faire capitalism began to replace the state-oriented systems of mercantilism. The American and French Revolutions of the latter part of the eighteenth century complemented the new economic liberalism by building working political systems based on the importance of the

individual. The United States' Declaration of Independence and France's Declaration of the Rights of Man and Citizen, for example, placed their main emphasis on providing freedom for the individual to enjoy in full measure the exercise of natural rights endowed from birth. The main ideological conflict in recent times pitted the democratic concept of individualism against the collectivist theories expounded in Socialist and Communist doctrine. That conflict apparently has been replaced by still another, far more complicated, in that the forces of extreme individualism, i.e., survivalists and white separatists, are arrayed against those representing social responsibility, the former verging on anarchy and the latter requiring heightened social consciousness and compassion. Constitutionalism has come to mean the protection of the weakest or most fragile members/institutions in society. Individualists, some verging on the anarchic extreme, claim that this is an incorrect application of constitutionalism; they argue that not only are their constitutional rights adversely affected by this use of constitutionalism, but that the constitution itself has been subverted. In a murky period that demands an updated definition of constitutionalism, simple answers are not sufficient.

Democratic Theory: Majority Rule   113
The principle that decisions in a democracy should be made by the greater number of citizens in any political unit. Although the majority possesses the right and the power to govern, democratic theory also demands that minority rights be protected and that the minority be permitted to criticize and offer alternatives to the policies of the majority and seek, through the electoral process, to become the majority.

Significance
The principle of majority rule has been accepted by most democratic theorists as the sine qua non of the doctrines and practices of democracy. If the majority does not rule, power must then be exercised by

an elite group selected on the basis of wealth, status, ability, or other criteria. Typically, if the will of the majority does not prevail, the governing system takes the form of absolutism or authoritarian control. Although rule by the majority is facilitated in a working two-party system—as in Great Britain—coalition governments based on groups of parties that join to form a majority and establish a government are most common in democratic states. Some democratic theorists reject majority rule in favor of government by consensus or by a concurrent majority, which offers minority groups a veto over major policies. Antidemocratic theorists regard majority rule as "mobocracy" or government by the untrained, unfit, and emotionally unstable masses. The application of the principle of majority rule to a working system of government, however, tends to encourage stability through widespread participation of citizens in public affairs.

Democratic Theory: Natural Law | 114 |

The concept of an unchanging, universally applicable set of laws governing human relationships that provides a moral standard by which to judge the actions of citizens and governments. The principle of *jus naturale* incorporated in democratic theory limits the powers of government, establishes the concept of natural justice, and propounds the idea of equality of all humankind in a universal society governed by the law of nature.

Significance

The theory of natural law was first expounded by early Greek philosophers, then postulated as the main guidepost in the development of a universal society by the Stoics, later modified by the Romans and by church philosophers during the Middle Ages, and finally brought to flower as the central theme in the eighteenth-century natural-rights doctrine underlying the ideology of democracy. In the latter case, the concept's transformation from "law" to "rights" reflected the new

emphases on individualism, popular sovereignty, and limited government that were embodied in the United States' Declaration of Independence and France's Declaration of the Rights of Man and Citizen. For the first time, working systems of government based on the democratic principles that recognized the natural and inalienable rights of citizens were established and flourished. The concept of natural law has also been influential in the development of legal, moral, ethical, and religious systems, but its main function has been to serve as a standard for individual and governmental conduct and to limit the powers exercised by the state over the individual. The ambiguous nature of the natural-law concept, however, has made it subject to conflicting interpretations and to challenge by those who reject it as a subjective metaphysical idea. Positivist legal scholars, for example, challenge the validity of the concept of natural law with their doctrine that law constitutes the sovereign will of the state and therefore can only be promulgated by government.

Democratic Theory: Popular Sovereignty | 115 |

The basic democratic principle that the people are the ultimate source of all legitimate political authority. The concept of popular sovereignty was enunciated in the eighteenth-century natural-rights philosophy, which served as the intellectual base for modern democratic theory. The doctrine of popular sovereignty holds that the people of a political unit or society possess supreme authority, that they establish government and delegate powers to public officials through a social contract or constitution, and that the government so created remains accountable to the people, who retain the supreme authority.

Significance

The theory of popular sovereignty seeks to explain the origins and location of power in democratic societies. It has also served as a justification for revolution against established civil authority when government has deprived the people of their rights. This doctrine was expounded by the American and French revolutionaries in 1776 and 1789. Although political power is ordinarily exercised indirectly by the people through representative institutions, under the doctrine of popular sovereignty the people retain the right to alter, abolish, and create new forms of government. In the final analysis, popular sovereignty expounds the idea of government by consent—an idea alien to any form of authoritarian or absolutist system. In the contemporary world, the idea that government in democratic states can be changed in free elections and basic laws altered or abolished by the action of the people has encouraged a wide variety of groups to assert themselves for a range of purposes that appear to run counter to government policies and intentions. In the United States, for example, advocates of gun ownership cite their constitutional right to bear arms, whereas others argue the need to restrict the availability of weapons, ostensibly as a technique in combating crime. Some reject a woman's right to abort a pregnancy, while others argue the matter of privacy and the woman's (individual's) right to control her own body. Issues such as these raise questions concerning the purpose of sovereign power and how it relates to the rights of the individual citizen on the one side, and the larger society on the other. In the two examples cited, a citizen might opt for the liberal position in the one case and the conservative position in the other, or vice versa. Determining the true sovereign will, therefore, is often an exercise in futility.

Democratic Theory: Rule of Law | 116

A fundamental principle of democratic government that proclaims the supremacy of law, establishing limits for public officials in the exercise of their powers. The concept of the rule of law buttresses the doctrine of limited government by protecting the rights of individuals from arbitrary interference by officials.

Significance
The rule of law in a democratic system contrasts sharply with the unlimited personal power and authority of rulers in an authoritarian state. Under the rule of law, all individuals are equal before the law and none can be convicted of a crime except through procedures guaranteed to ensure due process, fair trial, and punishment provided by law. However, protest movements that encourage mass violations of "unjust laws" as a means for attacking the established rules, particularly in civil rights and Selective Service arenas, have seriously challenged the rule of law in the United States and several other democratic countries. Many protesters view the law as a device used by "the establishment" to enhance and protect its own interests while those of minority groups remain unrecognized and unprotected. The rule of law can flourish in a democratic state only when a general consensus prevails among diverse groups that unjust laws and practices will be challenged through legitimate channels of the political process.

Fascism | 117

The ideology of the extreme right that fosters an authoritarian society based on rule by an elite, headed by a supreme leader or dictator. Roger Griffen, a contemporary student of fascism defines it as "a genus of political ideology whose mythic core in its various permutations is a palingenetic form of populist ultranationalism" (*The Nature of Fascism,* 1993). Fascists usually win power in a state through a coup d'état or during a turbulent revolutionary period when real or imaginary fears fueled by ideas or actions generally held to be alien lead large numbers of people to accept a radical transformation of democratic institutions to meet the problem of governmental instability. Fascism is often based on an exaggerated adulation of the nation, rejecting individualism and democratic concepts of limited government in favor of a system in which a disciplined people gives its full loyalty to an organic, monolithic, and reborn state. Dissent is eliminated and unity is fostered by secret police terror, extensive propaganda programs, the curtailment of civil liberties, and a single-party monopoly of power. An aura of xenophobia and militarism often pervades a Fascist state. Under fascism, private ownership of land and capital is retained, but all private businesses and organizations are regimented and directed by the state in pursuit of national objectives. *See also* FASCIST THEORY (188–122).

Significance
Modern fascism emerged out of the social, economic, and political crises of the interwar period of the 1920s and 1930s. The prototype of the Fascist state was forged by Benito Mussolini in the years following his coming to power in Italy in 1922, in the wake of World War I, and as a reaction to the Bolshevik Revolution in Russia. Fascist regimes were established subsequently by Adolf Hitler and the Nazi party in Germany, by Francisco Franco and the Falangist party in Spain, by Juan Perón and his Peronista party in Argentina, and in several Eastern European countries during the 1930s and 1940s. Although fascism as an ideology came into general disrepute following the defeat of the Axis Powers in World War II, neofascism has made gains in many developing countries where military juntas have seized power following the breakdown of fledgling democratic institutions. Fascist systems face serious problems of succession because the stability of the regime is often based on the glorification of the supreme leader, a charismatic personality who dominates the nation either by capturing the emotional support of its people or by using force and terror to rule. Fascism as an ideology contemptuously rejects the democratic political process based on freedom, fair elections, and accountability. Its appearance in Italy, a victor in World War I, and Germany, operating under a democratic Weimar constitution, illustrates its suitability, under specific circumstances, to established states as well as newer nation-

states. The fall of the Soviet Union in 1991, and the emergence of a democratic experiment in its successor, the Russian Federation, did not prevent Russian Fascists from winning considerable support among the voting public. By the same token, the increasing strength of the Fascist right in France, Italy, Germany, and Spain addresses the resiliency of post–Cold War fascism. In the United States as well, the forces of the extreme right confidently speak of a growing majority, and express views that mirror Fascist theory and practice.

Fascist Theory: $\boxed{118}$
Anticommunism
The belief and widely applied propaganda technique of fascism that only a united totalitarian state headed by a supreme leader (dictator) can master the threat posed by the conspiratorial tactics of communism. The anticommunism of fascism exploits the fear of communism prevalent in all classes in the advanced states, and Fascists use it to both win and hold power. Fascist regimes often dispose of political enemies by labeling them "Communists" or "agents of international communism." Fascist theory promises to defeat communism by establishing a "true" socialism that eliminates class struggle by reconciling the interests of all groups in common support for and service to the nation.

Significance
Fascism, possessing no extensive or coherent body of theory, has gained adherents and won power mainly by offering unity and stability to societies during times of crisis when Communist-inspired revolutions—real or imagined—have threatened the established order. Germany in the early 1930s, for example, was beset with mass frustrations growing out of economic malaise, severe unemployment, and social disintegration. By promising to save the country from communism, Adolf Hitler and the Nazi party gained the financial backing of wealthy industrialists and the voting support of a substantial portion of the middle and working

classes to win power in 1933. In recent years, military cliques in many developing countries have seized power through coups d'état, establishing Fascist-type regimes with the support of local power elites to protect the nation from actual or alleged Communist threats. More economically developed countries are not immune to the political blandishments, nationalistic appeals, and base instincts of those representing Fascist causes. The free use of the term "patriotism" at times when society is divided by political indecision, economic dislocation, and social confusion has enormous attraction. People with otherwise individually addressed grievances find satisfaction in the articulation of complaints by those artful in translating their sentiments into positive action. Fascists are mobilizers, and societies under stress, divided over passionate issues and debilitated by economic strain, are maneuvered, cajoled, and mesmerized by chants promising relief for their stress and easy remedies for their psychological depression. Fascism did not die with the destruction of Nazi Germany because the demagogues who prey on the torment of people, who promise deliverance from hopelessness, are found in every location, in every time, and in every place.

Fascist Theory: Elitism   119

The principle that state power should be exercised by a single hierarchically structured party headed by a supreme leader or small group of oligarchs. Fascist elitism rejects democratic processes, constitutional limitations on state power, and pluralism in favor of an organic state in which every group and individual plays a role assigned by the governing elite. Opposition to the elite group's rule is not tolerated, and the power of the state is used to destroy all resistance to the regime.

Significance

Rule by a highly centralized, nationalistically inspired elite group is one of the most common characteristics of fascism. In Germany during the 1930s, for example, Adolf Hitler and the Nazi party ruthlessly liquidated all opposition parties and individuals through the establishment of a totalitarian dictatorship. Similar tactics were pursued by Benito Mussolini's Fascist party in Italy, Francisco Franco's Falangist party in Spain, and Juan Perón's Peronista party in Argentina. Although Fascist elites usually seek support from the masses through propaganda, nationalistic fervor, and military ventures, they look with contempt upon any meaningful role for the average citizen in the political process. Vladimir Zhirinovsky was catapulted onto the world stage when his Fascist party won more seats than any other single organization in the Russian parliamentary elections of 1993–1994. Zhirinovsky's wild claims and charges, his revisionist and highly distorted historical accounts, and his appeal to Russian chauvinism bore all the marks of a devotee of hate and calumny. Nevertheless, he captured the support of those with similar thoughts as well as those sensing strength and purpose in his diatribe. Fascists are known by their exaggerated speech and personal remonstrations; nothing is too bizarre if it draws an attentive following. Truth has never been an objective of the most extreme radical right, but portrayals of power—invincible power—gathers support from those who find strength in elite manifestations, as well as among those intimidated by the spectacle.

Fascist Theory: Militarism   120

The emphasis placed by Fascists on military organization and discipline to strengthen the single national party and provide order and security for the state. Under fascism, militaristic values are inculcated in the young at school and in youth organizations, military heroes are revered, and spectacular ceremonies and parades extolling the virtues of the soldier are used to cultivate an honored role for the military as the defenders of the nation and to encourage acceptance of a well-disciplined social order.

Significance
Most Fascist dictatorships have come to power and have maintained their rule with the active support of the military. Adolf Hitler and Benito Mussolini, for example, donned uniforms and became the commanders in chief of their nations' armed forces, thus dominating the military rather than permitting it to dominate them. Francisco Franco of Spain and Juan Perón of Argentina also functioned as both military and civilian chiefs of their states. In the contemporary world, right-wing, Fascist-type takeovers of power in many underdeveloped countries of Asia, Africa, and Latin America have brought military cliques into power because of a lack of experience with institutions of self-government, and because of political cultures that both honor and fear men with guns. In former Communist nations of Eastern Europe, Communist leaders have assumed new roles as supreme nationalists, with extreme views that center on the glories of folk and nation. Given their popular acceptance, they too have found their way back into the halls of power. The shift to the right in Western Europe, often to the far right, is illustrated by the election of Jacques Chirac to the French presidency in 1995. Chirac's success was attributed to an unemployment figure approaching 14 percent, and to a pervading social and psychological malaise caused by more than a decade of failed socialism under François Mitterand. Not insignificantly, the new French president hints at a more active role for the French military than that projected by his predecessor.

Fascist Theory: Statism |121|
The concept that sovereignty is vested not in the people but in the national state, and that individuals and associations exist to enhance the power, prestige, and well-being of the state. The Fascist concept of statism repudiates individualism and exalts the nation as an organic body headed by a supreme leader and nurtured by unity, force, and discipline. Under this doctrine, the state creates worthy individuals who realize their destiny by contributing to the glory of the state.

Significance
The Fascist concept of statism is a modern adaptation of earlier forms of autocratic rule in which the individual offered complete obedience to the ruler, who personified the state. Nationalism, militarism, and, in some Fascist states, racism have been used to inculcate values that exist and assume importance because the state decrees them. In a Fascist state, no other loyalty than that to the state is permitted. The entire ideology of fascism in pre–World War II Italy and Germany was dominated by the dogmas of individual subjection to and immersion in the mystical entity of the nation.

Fascist Theory: Totalitarianism |122|
Authoritarian control by the state over individuals and organizations so that all activity is harmonized with the policies and goals of the regime. Fascist totalitarian tactics include using secret police and terrorist operations, eliminating dissent, denying civil rights, and carrying on an all-pervasive propaganda program through state-controlled communications media. A single political party inspired by the ideology of fascism monopolizes power and uses the machinery of the state to carry out its objectives.

Significance
Fascist systems of government vary in the extent of totalitarian control each extends over the people of its state. Each tends to be pragmatic about the amount of autocratic control that its leaders believe to be necessary or expedient to impose. For Fascists, totalitarianism is aimed at uniting the people in a highly integrated nation so that the public interest always takes precedence over private interests. Of the Fascist states, Germany achieved the highest level of totalitarian control during the 1930s and 1940s under the leadership of Adolf Hitler and the Nazi party.

Fourteen Points $\boxed{123}$

A statement of idealistic principles issued by President Woodrow Wilson in 1918 to frame the United States' reasons for entering World War I, as well as the intended purpose in winning the war and maintaining the peace that followed it. In his Fourteen Points, Wilson called for open diplomacy, freedom of the seas, disarmament, removal of economic barriers, international supervision of colonies, peaceful change based on self-determination, and the creation of an association of nations that would guarantee the political independence and territorial integrity of great and small states alike. *See also* LEAGUE OF NATIONS (532); WAR TYPE: PSYCHOLOGICAL WARFARE (343).

Significance

The Fourteen Points statement illustrates the powerful impact that an idealistic program can have on the thinking and actions of millions of human beings. The Fourteen Points were directed at the construction of a new world order from the debris of the Great War. Wilson was opposed to imperialism in all its forms, and he saw in the tragedy of World War I a need for peoples to reorganize their lives in keeping with the principles of open democracy, self-determination, and popular self-government. Wilson envisaged the freeing of the nationalities, not only those liberated from the conquered states, but those remaining within the grip of the established, victorious members of the entente. More immediately, the proclamation served to buttress morale in the last phase of World War I. The declaration received a positive response from the war-weary European publics, and Wilson expected to use this popularity to convince the other Allied leaders—David Lloyd George of Great Britain, Georges Clemenceau of France, and Vittorio Orlando of Italy—to forgo their designs for territorial aggrandizement. He also endeavored to obtain less harsh surrender terms for Germany. Although unsuccessful on both counts (the victorious Europeans used the creation of the man-

dates system to extend their imperial holdings, and imposed heavy reparations on Germany), Wilson nevertheless persuaded the European leaders to create the League of Nations, and his call for "open covenants, openly arrived at" encouraged the development of conference diplomacy. Wilson's major failures occurred at home: His own Senate refused to ratify the Versailles Treaty, and the United States never joined the League of Nations. Wilson died trying to sell his vision of a better, more peaceful world to the American people without success. Wilson's Fourteen Points and his vision lived after him, but they were not enough to prevent World War II.

Gaullism $\boxed{124}$

The political philosophy of Charles de Gaulle and its impact on French national life since World War II. The essence of Gaullism is the idea of national interest above self-interest, as interpreted by de Gaulle. He altered the emphasis in French politics by downgrading traditionally organized party politics and making the presidency the dominant feature of the government. He shaped the concept of an effective national administration run by an apolitical technocracy motivated by his idea of "the reality of an objective national interest." He insisted upon an almost selfless loyalty from his subordinates, and earned deep and lasting opposition from those who challenged the philosophy of his regime. Though he demonstrated a readiness to crush obstruction, he also showed a dedication to French constitutionalism. Through dramatic public appearances and masterful domination of the mass media he sought to convey an awesome impression of the president of France standing alone above politics, the symbol of sovereignty and the guarantor of national independence and integrity.

Significance

The history of the Fifth Republic until 1969 was dominated by the personality of

Charles de Gaulle. From a condition of external weakness and internal disarray he achieved the restoration of France's international prestige and national pride. The present style of French government seems to represent a lasting change in governmental technique and is not the mirror and vehicle of one man. The problem of succession was resolved in 1969 when Georges Pompidou was elected president. By the 1980s Gaullism had lost its appeal with the French population and François Mitterand, a bona fide Socialist, was elected president, then reelected even with the country in severe economic difficulty. Because of his health failing, Mitterand stepped aside in 1995, and although his Socialist candidate did better than expected at the polls, the conservative, Jacques Chirac, became president of France in May. Chirac succeeded on a platform calling for national renewal, and his elevation to the highest executive position in France indicated a return to Gaullist policies.

Human Dimension | 125 |

Post–Cold War Europe's attempt at building democratic orders using a humanity-centered paradigm. The concept of the Human Dimension (HD) was introduced in the Conference on Security and Cooperation in Europe (CSCE) process by the 1989 Vienna Concluding Document. The document was the outcome of three years of negotiations designed to remodel East-West cooperation in the wake of systemic reforms introduced by Soviet leader Mikhail Gorbachev. HD includes two main components: (1) a set of obligations flowing from Principle VII of the Helsinki Decalogue, entitled "Respect for Human Rights and Fundamental Freedoms;" and (2) guidelines for cooperation to implement those principles contained in the so-called "third basket" of CSCE documents. This dual structure of the HD applies to all CSCE documents from the Helsinki Final Act of 1975 to the 1989 Vienna Concluding Document. Since the demise of the Soviet Union, the HD concept has evolved to encompass an

even broader set of commitments. A radical change was introduced at the Copenhagen meeting of June 1990, and the ensuing Copenhagen Document went beyond listing the rights to be respected by participating CSCE states to the political and institutional conditions required to fulfill these rights. The conditions necessary to assure human rights as fundamental guarantees were described as "pluralistic democracy" and the "rule of law." The commitment of all CSCE states to these values was consecrated a few months later in the "Charter of Paris for a New Europe." According to the Copenhagen Document, pluralistic democracy includes political pluralism, i.e., the right of individuals and groups to establish political parties and other political organizations, and the right of those parties and organizations to compete with one another on the basis of equal treatment before the law. The document also requires unimpeded access to the media on a nondiscriminatory basis for all political groupings and individuals wishing to participate in the political process. Fair and free elections are also considered essential elements of a pluralist democracy. The rule of law covers the relations between the individual and the state as well as the structure of government, the political system, and the interaction between governmental institutions. *See also* ARMS CONTROL: HELSINKI ACCORD (359); ETHNICITY (51); MUTUAL-SECURITY ORGANIZATION: CONFERENCE ON SECURITY AND COOPERATION IN EUROPE (CSCE) (297).

Significance
The Human Dimension concept has become a prominent agenda item in almost all international forums following the termination of the Cold War. The breakup of the Soviet Union and Yugoslavia released nationalistic expressions that stressed sociopolitical representations of exclusivity at a time when economic forces were more likely to emphasize interdependence and cooperation across national frontiers and among peoples of diverse culture and tradition. In this struggle between centrifugal and centripetal forces, the human

condition appears to be most vulnerable. The ethnic wars involving Serbia and Croatia, Serbia and Bosnia, Russia and Chechnya, Georgia and Abkhazia, and Armenia and Azerbaijan are only some of the more attention-gathering. In each of these civil conflicts it is the Human Dimension that is most at risk and more than likely the target of aggressive nationalism. Although the former Communist world is not alone in confronting this problem, it is in this segment of the world that the success or failure of Human Dimension programs such as those emanating from CSCE will be determined.

Ideocracy   126

A concept describing political systems that are centered on an all-encompassing ideology, with no other expression countenanced or permitted. Such political systems dominate all aspects of human endeavor—social, economic, political, artistic, and philosophical—and are generally referred to as totalitarian systems. Totalitarian representations of ideocracy combine interest in the past, present, and future of people, their societies, and political experiences. Totalitarians view everything as unitary and indivisible; therefore, they not only demand absolute obedience and blind faith, they insist that society embrace the comprehensive truths articulated for them by their leaders. The virtual mindless obedience demanded of the people by their governors distinguishes ideocracy from mere ideology, which is always subject to interpretation and challenge. The subordination of all spheres of society to the government addresses the preeminence of the state over the people, and places a Fascist character on the political system. Only those thoughts and actions sanctioned and deemed important by authority are permissible. *See also* FASCISM (117); FASCIST THEORY: TOTALITARIANISM (122).

Significance

The post–World War I period brought to the fore the full character of ideocratic political systems. Ideocracy in the form of fascism emerged in Italy in the 1920s under the leadership of Benito Mussolini, the Italian Il Duce. A more complete version of ideocracy, however, was developed in Nazi Germany under the tutelage of Adolf Hitler, who was acclaimed the Führer of the German nation. Terms like *Il Duce* and *Führer* are synonymous with *Caesar* or *Great Leader*. Germany's total submission to Hitler was orchestrated by the Fuhrer's henchmen, who adopted fear as their principal tactic. Nothing in Hitler's Germany escaped the attention of the Nazis, and everything was subordinated to the needs of the German state— that is, the Third Reich—which Hitler declared would endure for a thousand years. The intoxicating nature of ideocracy, given the appropriate circumstances, is dramatically illustrated in the total mobilization of the German nation for the sole purpose of making war. Marxism-Leninism, the defining ideology in the Soviet Union, acted as the cementing force in that Eurasian nation. The coerced fusion of a multitude of nationalities and cultures offered a different representation of ideocracy from that found in Italy or Germany. Under Stalinism, the Soviet Union utilized similar instruments of control to assure the solidarity of the nation, but in World War II the pitting of one version (the Soviet) of totalitarianism against another (the Nazi) somewhat neutralized ideocracy as an organizational device. Only the Stalinistic form of totalitarianism survived World War II, and Soviet leaders had considerable difficulty in pressing their monistic beliefs. Moreover, they were rejected altogether when Mikhail Gorbachev called for glasnost (openness) and perestroika (restructuring). The crumbling of the Soviet Union in 1991 should have terminated political systems represented by ideocracy, but the phenomenon persists. The breakup of the Soviet Union and Yugoslavia in fact revitalized ideocratic expressions, and neo-Fascist movements resurfaced in Russia and other republics of the former Soviet Union. They also reappeared in Serbia and Croatia, as well as in Germany, France, and Italy.

The Cold War had ended, but ideocracy remained to challenge efforts aimed at promoting pluralistic democracy and global accommodation.

Ideocracy: Croatia | 127 |

An illustration of ultranationalism. At the end of World War I, Croat nationalists called for a "Greater Croatia" that would extend from the Swiss Alps to Bulgaria. However, acknowledging Serb claims, the major victors in the war—especially France, Britain, and Italy—pressed for and achieved a Kingdom of Serbia, Croatia, and Slovenia in December 1918. The kingdom was renamed Yugoslavia in 1929. The forced merger of these ethnic groups was a formula for continuing strife. The Catholic Croatians were repressed by the Orthodox Serbs, who gained control of the government and army. When the Croatian parliamentary leader was murdered by a Serb official, the Croats organized the Ustashi, a militant right-wing organization. The Croat Ustashi reacted to the Serbs' demonstration of violent behavior by showing their own capacity for terror. Members of the organization were responsible for the assassination of the Serbian king and for the aggressive campaign that secured territory from the polyglot empire. Ustashi assumed Fascist credentials and identified with Hitler and Nazi Germany. In World War II the Ustashi, assisted by Germany, engaged their local adversary in even bloodier encounters, and reputedly killed some 500,000 Serbs. Driven by a totalitarian notion of destiny, the Croat Ustashi systematically eliminated not only their immediate enemy, but Balkan minorities targeted by Hitler for extermination. Germany's defeat weakened the Ustashi, who were locked in mortal struggle with the Serb Chetniks, a guerrilla army led by Colonel Draza Mihailovic. Later, the Chetniks fought the Yugoslav Communists or partisans under the leadership of Josip Broz Tito, who gained the upper hand when Britain withdrew support from the Chetniks. Tito's success meant the termination of both Ustashi and Chetnik operations, but it also meant sustaining a unified Yugoslavia, i.e., the creation of the Communist federation of Yugoslavia. Nevertheless, the separate national causes represented by the Croats and Serbs remained, if in a dormant state. Tito held the federation together until his death in 1980, after which all the old wounds were again opened. The collapse of communism in Eastern Europe in 1989 precipitated the Croat secession from Yugoslavia in 1990 and its official declaration of independence in 1991. Significantly, the former Communist leader and now the Croat president, Franjo Tudjman, announced intentions to extend Croat sovereignty over the Croat regions of Bosnia-Herzegovina. The Serb response was predictable. Serbs in Croatia joined with elements of the Yugoslav national army, driven by their own call for a "Greater Serbia"; the civil war in Yugoslavia commenced in earnest on 25 June 1991. *See also* IDEOCRACY (126); IDEOLOGY (129); FASCISM (117).

Significance
Ideocracy frames the character of political behavior and organization in the Balkans, and it is most obvious in the historic conflict between Croats and Serbs. Each has developed similar visions of reality and the political systems corresponding with those mindsets. Both have demonstrated a capacity for ruthlessness that seems to know no limits. The group identified as Bosnian Muslims became the foil for both Serbs and Croats. Each resisted identifying an independent, sovereign Bosnia-Herzegovina because each found its destiny and the logic of its ideocracy inextricably intertwined with the most cosmopolitan and developed region of the former Yugoslavia, and perhaps with the entire Balkans. Croat association with the Bosnian Muslims in 1995 was nothing more than a marriage of convenience, given earlier Serbian success against both Croats and Bosnian Muslims in the ensuing and spreading conflict. But it is important to note that the Yugoslav civil war began in the struggle between

Croats and Serbs, and was precipitated by the Croatian declaration of independence and the almost immediate recognition it received from a very recently unified German government. Serbia's Communist-*cum*-Fascist leader, Slobodan Milosevic, was quick to cite the threat in the German action, joined in by Austria, that Serbian destiny in the new post–Cold War Europe would be determined by the strength of its ideocratic system vis-à-vis that of the other ideocrats in Croatia and the Germanic countries to the north.

Ideological Warfare | 128 |

A type of conflict between rival value systems or "ways of life" that involve efforts to gain mass conversions. Ideological warfare involves the utilization of propaganda; cultural programs; educational, artistic, and scientific exchange projects; foreign aid; and other activities aimed at winning or maintaining allegiance. The major ideological confrontations in the contemporary world are between the Communist and "free world" states, and between Soviet and Chinese communism. *See also* IDEOLOGY (129); PUBLIC OPINION (138).

Significance
Ideological warfare has become a major factor affecting international relations in the twentieth century. It is both a unifying force, pulling together people of diverse national backgrounds in a common cause, and a disintegrative force that tends to pit "true believers" against one another in holy wars fired by fanatical zeal. Each side in the contemporary ideological struggles tries to convince uncommitted millions of the strength of its position, the superiority of its social system, and the rightness of its cause as opposed to the warlike, decadent, and cruel nature of the rival system. The deep-rooted hatred for the ideology of the other camp inculcated in the minds of the people renders tolerance and compromise elusive. As a consequence, ideological

warfare increases the possibilities of an eventual open military clash between supporters of the rival systems.

Ideology | 129 |

The articulation of basic political, economic, and social values as a body of ideas that serve as the basis for an ideal social system or "way of life." An ideology is concerned with the nature of the political system, the exercise of power, the role of the individual, the nature of the economic and social system, and the objectives of society. As a fundamental belief system, an ideology not only incorporates a society's basic values but itself becomes the major value to be defended and, in many cases, spread to other societies. *See also* IDEOLOGICAL WARFARE (128); PROPAGANDA (137).

Significance
An ideology is a dynamic force in the power equation since the unity and vitality it creates can be directed against other states or groups. A set of ideas can win over human minds without using organized power, but ideologies are seldom spread without ideological-warfare campaigns supported by organized power. Typically, ideological convictions are closely intertwined with religious or nationalistic sentiments, and each tends to identify with and support the other. Most ideologies tend to focus on the basic nature of either individualism or collectivism. Historically, ideology has constituted a divisive force in international and national affairs when rival systems and their adherents have sought to achieve victory over others.

Internet | 130 |

The global, interconnected group of computer networks. Internally it is composed of heterogeneous networks that use different means to transmit and receive information. Through the use of special connections between networks, the Internet appears externally to be a single network. It offers electronic mail, network news, file transfers and information browsing. *See also* WORLDWIDE WEB (WWW) (146).

Significance

Anyone with a computer and the correct software can gain access to the Internet and hence to an unquantifiable wealth of information. The Internet permits users to communicate with any online office, school, living room, or government facility. The Internet has been referred to as the "information highway" and is publicized to be the most significant, all-encompassing avenue for information transfer and exchange on a worldwide scale. Just as the Internet is said to be good for business, education, and everyday general use, it also has negative influences, given its capacity for anyone to enter the system. Misinformation therefore also is linked with the Internet, and just as doctors can treat patients on the other side of the world, so too persons determined to spread hate and fear can network with similar members of their breed to sow dissension and plot violent acts. The development of the Internet coincided with the end of the Cold War, and negative as well as positive forces were released by the changing character of international relations. The resurfacing of ultranationalism in the form of neo- and protofascism is a case in point. Clandestine as well as overt movements seeking radical political change have revealed capacities for adaptation to shifting post–Cold War realities. Technologically-based fascists in the United States have spread computer games such as "Concentration Camp Manager II" to German teenagers, and anti-Semitic tracts have been transmitted using desk-top publishing software from Britain to anyone in the world wishing to access them. Neo-Nazi propaganda has moved into the mainstream of contemporary discourse by penetrating a wide variety of organizations, including environmentally based Green groups in Germany, Britain, Italy, Spain, and France. The principal outcome of all this activity is organizational internationalization on a scale that addresses the creation of still another "New world order." It was

only after the Oklahoma City bombing in April 1995 that authorities as well as the general public in the United States became aware of the use of the Internet by neo-Nazi organizations in the United States, or how the militias that sprung up in the 1990s utilized the electronic message board to promote their activities. The inability of governments, especially democratic governments, to effectively regulate the Internet makes it certain that domestic as well as international politics in the twenty-first century will be heavily influenced by this most intrusive new technology.

Iron Curtain   131

A phrase coined by Winston Churchill in 1946 to describe the Soviet policy of isolating the Communist states of Eastern Europe from Western Europe. The term *Iron Curtain* described as well as symbolized the barrier between East and West established by the Communist nations under Soviet direction, the secrecy and censorship imposed within the Soviet-dominated region, and the stunting of communication, leading to heightened suspicion, between the opposed blocs. *See also* WAR TYPE: COLD WAR (336).

Significance

The Iron Curtain was rigidly maintained immediately following World War II. Although a relaxation occurred following Josef Stalin's death in 1953, some of the harsh controls were restored because of the abortive Hungarian uprising of 1956. The flight to the West of Germans living in the Soviet occupation zone led to the erection of the Berlin Wall in 1961, and a more formidable barrier between Eastern and Western Europe. Acknowledging the difficulty in relating the Eastern region to the West, Chancellor Willy Brandt of the Federal Republic of Germany called for a relaxation of tension. His "Ostpolitik Policy" won the interest of the Communist bloc, and with West Germany's recognition of a sovereign East Germany, the Iron Curtain opened some significant windows. Even the 1968 events in Czechoslovakia did not prevent further improvement in the relations between East and West. By the late 1970s, the Iron Curtain had been lifted to the point where several million Western tourists visited Eastern Europe each year, numerous educational and cultural exchanges took place, diplomatic and consular relations were restored to near normalcy, and restrictions on communication and travel were also relaxed. Nevertheless, many of the Communist states retained travel restrictions, depriving their citizens of movement to "enemy" territory—until 1989. Several popular demonstrations occurred in Poland, Hungary, and Czechoslovakia, and East Germany also felt the impact. Huge throngs of enthusiastic and defiant young people tore down the Berlin Wall. The wall had symbolized the Iron Curtain, and its destruction precipitated the general repudiation of the Communist governments of Eastern Europe. By 1990 most of the major states of Eastern Europe had abandoned communism, thus setting the scene for its demise in the Soviet Union as well. The abortive coup in the Soviet Union in 1991 brought down the last remnant of the Iron Curtain, and with it the USSR.

Islamic Fundamentalism $\boxed{132}$

A term coined by the Western world to describe political terrorist movements led by Muslims who claim justification for their behavior in Islamic practice, if not scripture. Fundamentalism is linked to the French term *integrisme,* which refers to the experience of Catholic fundamentalism, rooted in the 1860s' Syllabus of Errors. The origins of the English word *fundamentalism* are found in the United States in the 1920s. It is linked to religious movements that interpret scripture literally and maintain the myth of an idealized past, based on a selective reading of history. The temptation to resort to this literal interpretation of scripture, however, is stronger in Islam than in other religions in the contemporary world, in part because Muslims believe the Koran was dictated directly by Allah (God) to

Muhammad through the voice of the archangel Gabriel. Even more important are their views that temporal and spiritual realms merge in the Islamic world and that religious and political matters are inextricably intertwined. Political matters therefore have religious importance, and political objectives are linked to theological beliefs. It follows that political actions, no matter how violent or arbitrary, are spiritually justifiable. Thus the term *Islamic fundamentalism* is widely used, loosely and somewhat indiscriminately, to denote the ideologies of numerous radical Islamic groups, as well as the regimes of some Muslim countries prone to commit acts of terror. *See also* "CLASH OF CIVILIZATIONS?" (34).

Significance

Muslim fundamentalists can be found in antiquity. What is new, however, is the development of movements today that advance a political project on the basis of Islam. By contrast, more traditional Islamic fundamentalists are more concerned with personal ethics and spirituality. Various terms are used to describe the rise of Islamic political movements: Islamic revivalism, political Islam, Islamic renaissance, Islamism, etc. The term *Islamic fundamentalism* has been widely adopted, but it fails to entertain the broader search for a form of social and political organization that best represents Islamic values and is not burdened with the Western biases associated with the word *fundamentalist.* North Africa illustrates the nature of the problem. Two primary Islamic political movements are found there. The first speaks for the vast majority of those Muslim organizations seeking to reform their political systems to bring them into conformity with Koranic values that embrace personal behavior as well as socioeconomic activity; the second represents a far smaller percentage of the Muslim population whose violent actions and inflammatory rhetoric bring it greater attention. The violent actions of these extremists affect the popular mood in Western publics toward Islam in general. In turn, moderate and radical Islamists are often united in their criticism that official corruption in their countries is a consequence of Western influence; therefore, they both reject Western values, whether socialist or liberal. To a large extent, Islamic fundamentalism serves as an ideological substitute for failed pan-Arabism or the Marxist-Socialist development model that some Muslim countries had adopted earlier.

Lustration   133
A term generally used in Eastern and Central Europe to emphasize the programs developed to decommunize societies long subject to Marxist rule. Such programs were aimed at rejecting Communist leadership as well as ideology and were supposed to prevent the revitalization and/or return to power and prominence of European Communists. In practice, lustration policies did little more than forbid high-ranking Communist party officials from holding office under new regimes. The most successful lustration laws were those passed by the Czechs and the Germans. In the new age of nationalism following the demise of internationalist and multinational communism, however, only these states in Central and Eastern Europe appear to be weathering the surge of narrow patriotism that has permitted former Communists to don nationalist mantles. By contrast, in countries like Slovakia, nationalist declarations have become commonplace among former Marxists. Even Slobodan Milosevic, the ruler of Serbia, has used his base in the Communist party of Yugoslavia to monopolize power.

Significance
Lustration has missed its mark in removing the key representatives of the former Communist governments of Eastern and Central Europe from power. The fruits of newly opened markets and privatization have fallen to members of the old regime, along with the political power that undergirds economic policy. The former Com-

munists have demonstrated considerable acumen in running with the tides of nationalism, and former Communist leaders have again coalesced with businessmen, financiers, military officials, and members of the literati who only a few years before identified and associated with the old Marxist governments. While there appears virtually no chance of ideological Marxism returning, lustration policies raise the question: What are the likely outcomes of democratic reforms in countries that are notably more capitalist, but nevertheless under the heavy influence, if not control, of a *nomenklatura* and ruling class that reflects little interest in open competition or free economic debate? More and more it is revealed that the former Communists have been the major financial beneficiaries of the economic reforms launched by the states of the former Communist bloc.

Mass Media   134
The technical apparatus for communicating with millions of people. The mass media include radio, television, newspapers, magazines, books, motion pictures, and official publications. *See also* PUBLIC OPINION (138).

Significance
Scientific and technical improvements in mass communication have made the world a battleground in the war of ideas. Within democratic states, the mass media play a vital role in helping to inform and interest the citizenry in public affairs. In dictatorial or oligarchic states, the governing elite monopolizes the mass media to control the thinking and actions of their people, insist on their legitimacy, eliminate opposition, assist in the creation of unity, and channel the energies of their people toward state-determined objectives. In the international arena, many states employ various technical means of communication for spreading propaganda and waging ideological warfare in their efforts to gain support for their policies and programs and discredit their rivals. The

mass media are also effective when directed at national opinion elites because such elites help to shape the attitudes of the mass publics. Some studies of the role of the mass media indicate that they are more useful in reinforcing than in creating or destroying mass views.

National Front | 135 |

Alliance with non-Communist groups, used by a Communist party to achieve its goals. The national-front approach is often employed in underdeveloped countries, where the Communists team up with nationalist elements in independence movements or undertake leftist-inspired revolutions against indigenous elites. *See also* WAR TYPE: WARS OF NATIONAL LIBERATION (349).

Significance

The national-front approach dates back to the 1930s when the Communists pursued a policy of encouraging the formation of anti-Fascist "popular front" party coalitions in the democratic states of Europe. Chinese Communists still make use of national-front tactics, but since the disappearance of the Soviet Union, there is declining interest in supporting wars of national liberation. The National Liberation Front (NLF) of South Vietnam was successful in enlisting non-Communist nationalist elements in their coalition against South Vietnam, especially when the government of South Vietnam targeted the Buddhist organizations shortly after coming to power in 1954–1955. The Buddhists of South Vietnam ultimately saw the Communists as the lesser of two evils, and the North Vietnamese victory in 1975 was in good part a consequence of their greater popular appeal.

New World Information and Communication Order (NWICO) | 136 |

A Third World proposal to provide international guidelines for the gathering and dissemination of news. The NWICO was proposed because of the belief that, internationally, news is controlled by Western press agencies, which provide insufficient, negative, or distorted coverage of Third World needs and achievements. The campaign began in the mid-1970s in the United Nations Educational, Scientific, and Cultural Organization (UNESCO), which proclaimed a set of 12 principles to guide nations. One of these was greater governmental control of the media, including the licensing of journalists. In the 1980s, the campaign moved from UNESCO to the UN General Assembly, which appointed a special 69-member UN Committee on Information to work on the proposal. But leading Third World countries such as India have proceeded with their own plans. In the 1990s, acknowledging the information revolution, India moved to develop a worldwide information net. *See also* UN SPECIALIZED AGENCY: UNITED NATIONS EDUCATIONAL, SCIENTIFIC, AND CULTURAL ORGANIZATION (UNESCO) (612).

Significance

The proposal to establish a New World Information and Communication Order has been highly controversial. Western states, with their basic ideas concerning freedom of the press and unregulated news gathering, have staunchly opposed the idea of establishing international media standards. One of the reasons for U.S. and British withdrawal from UNESCO membership was opposition to NWICO. The proposal is kept alive and active because of the majority voting power and strong support for NWICO by the Third World bloc in UNESCO, the General Assembly, and the Committee on Information.

Propaganda | 137 |

Any form of communication aimed at implanting data, ideas, or images in human minds to influence the thinking, emotions, or actions of individuals or groups. The objectives of propaganda include: (1) to win or strengthen friendly support, (2) to shape or alter attitudes and perceptions of ideas or events, (3) to weaken or undermine unfriendly foreign governments or their policies and programs, and (4) to counteract the unfriendly propaganda of other groups or countries. To be effective, propaganda must be relevant, credible to the recipients, repeated often, simple, consistent, interesting, identifiable with a local or national situation, and disguised so as not to be recognizable as propaganda by those for whom it is intended. Propaganda may take the form of an appeal to the idealism of the recipients, it may be factual but distorted through careful selection, or it may be based on outright falsehoods. Propaganda activities are instruments of psychological warfare aimed at influencing the actions of human beings in ways that are compatible with the national-interest objectives of the purveying state. *See also* IDEOLOGICAL WARFARE (128); PUBLIC OPINION (138); WAR TYPE: PSYCHOLOGICAL WARFARE (343).

Significance
Technological developments in the science of communication through the mass media and refinements in the art of psychological persuasion have given added impetus to the use of propaganda to pursue national objectives. Since the term *propaganda* often connotes an evil intent to deceive, state leaders commonly dismiss the communications efforts of other governments as nothing more than "propaganda," presenting their own official publications, news reports, and analyses as the unvarnished truth based on "straight news" and objective analysis. Once a government acquires a domestic or foreign reputation for having a credibility gap in its communications to various publics, its effectiveness in using propaganda to support its policies or programs is seriously weakened. Although most countries devote some efforts to international propaganda activities, during the Cold War the United States and the Soviet Union carried on the most intensive and extensive operations. The United States operates a vast network—radio and television broadcasting (Voice of America [VOA]), information centers, reading rooms, book and pamphlet distribution, and exhibits and displays of various kinds—under the United States Information Agency (USIA) programs, but the U.S. Congress senses less need for such an elaborate information organization. Moreover, the enterprise is expensive, and Congress believes information dissemination can be better accomplished by the private media. Consideration is therefore being given to dissolving the USIA and instead opening a small unit within the State Department to address specific government information needs. In addition, Radio Free Europe has been folded into a smaller Radio Liberty, but Radio Marti, beamed to Cuba, still has support in the U.S. Congress. Named after Cuban patriot José Marti, Radio Marti sustains elements of the Cold War, at least in the broadcast of news and opinion to Cuba.

Public Opinion | 138 |
Views and attitudes on domestic or foreign actions and issues held by the people of a nation, community, or group. Public opinion often fluctuates in response to independent or controlled stimuli in the political and social environment. In turn, public opinion may have a considerable impact on the environment by giving direction to the decisionmakers or by influencing or controlling their actions. In a totalitarian state, public opinion is shaped, manipulated, and controlled by the ruling elite using mass media, censorship, elimination of opposition, rigged elections, and nationalistic propaganda. In a democracy, no single public opinion prevails; there are, rather, many publics in a pluralistic society holding diverse views on a variety of subjects. Public opinion can be identified and measured with varying degrees of accuracy through elections; plebiscites; the initiative, referendum, and recall procedures; pressure-group activities; polls; public demonstrations; and elected officials who secure the views of constituents by various means of inquiry. *See also* IDEOLOGICAL WARFARE (128); MASS MEDIA (134); PROPAGANDA (137).

Significance
Public opinion is a crucial element in the field of international affairs, both in the development of domestic support for a state's foreign policies and in its efforts to influence publics in other states. No major foreign program carried out by a democratic or totalitarian state is likely to succeed unless a majority of its people give it their active or, at the very least, passive support. In addition, world opinion, consisting of the diverse views of many governments and peoples, can be developed into a powerful restraining force on state action in the General Assembly of the United Nations. Prestige, an element and objective of state power, is closely related to the views held by publics in both friendly and unfriendly countries. Some efforts to influence public opinion are directed at mass publics, whereas others are aimed more selectively at opinion elites. Although many studies have been carried out to gain a better understanding of the nature, role, and measurement of public opinion, it remains a vague yet powerful component of the political process because people act not necessarily on the basis of what is true but on what they believe to be true.

Public Opinion: Mass Public | 139 |

The general public as it relates to the making of governmental decisions. Far from being a cohesive unity with common attitudes, prejudices, and views, the mass public consists of many publics holding diverse and often conflicting opinions. The views of the mass public on specific issues may be expressed or divulged in various ways, but they are usually most effectively presented in democratic states through the electoral process or in polls. Mass opinion goes through three stages in the process of influencing governmental actions: formulation, expression, and direct effect upon or embodiment in policy decisions. *See also* MASS MEDIA (134).

Significance
The role of mass public opinion in influencing the policy-making process is typically more effective in domestic matters than in foreign affairs. Still, no political leader—certainly not in a democratic state—can ignore the attitudes of the general public if these are clearly and actively hostile toward the means or objectives of a long-range foreign-policy program. Although foreign-policy initiatives do not normally emerge from mass views, the latter often set the limits for policy experimentation. A leading example of a situation in which the views of the mass public played a decisive role in controlling policy leaders was the restraining force of American isolationist and neutral sentiment during World War II on efforts of the Roosevelt administration to expand aid to the Allies, especially Great Britain, prior to the Japanese attack on Pearl Harbor and the United States' entry into the war. Mass opinion also contributed substantially to the resignation of President Richard M. Nixon in 1974, the first resignation of a president in U.S. history.

Public Opinion: Opinion Elites | 140 |

Leadership elements influential in developing and shaping public opinion as a force in the political process. Opinion elites who influence foreign-policy decisions include business, professional, educational, labor, farm, religious, patriotic, and other interest-group leaders and persons active in upper-echelon political, administrative, and communications areas. Opinion elites compete to interest and influence both official decisionmakers and the mass public on contemporary issues of concern to the elites.

Significance
The influence of opinion elites on the political process depends mainly on the interest and receptivity of the mass public to the issues and on the degree of intra- and interelite competition. The countervailing theory of pressure politics, for example, postulates that a semblance of equilibrium will be maintained among elites and the interest groups they represent since they tend to line up on different sides of major issues and reduce each

other's power to influence foreign-policy decisions. Although students of the policy process generally agree that opinion elites play a part in making most foreign-policy decisions, their exact role and the degree to which they can influence governmental actions by shaping public opinion remains vague.

Social Cohesion | 141 |

The degree of unity within a national society. Social cohesion depends on the relationships among economic, social, and religious groups; the extent to which basic values are shared; common nationalistic and ideological impulses; and the nature of social organization. *See also* CONSENSUS OF VALUES (106).

Significance

Social cohesion helps to stabilize a national group or political community challenged by external enemies or internal problems. Traditional societies tend to be the most stable (prior to their exposure to external influences), because their members generally accept the rigid stratification of social classes and rule by a small, powerful elite as their unchanging way of life. The traditional society is village-oriented; daily actions are guided by long-accepted customs and traditions, and religion and conservative values provide the guidelines for most human actions. The social fabric of such societies, however, loses its resiliency and stability when outside forces bring change and aspirations for a new and better life to the people. A transitional society is characterized by disunity and instability as some members reject the old values and grope for new ones in the drive to achieve modernization. A "revolution of rising expectations" has swept over most of the centuries-old traditional societies, producing internal unrest and conflict on an unprecedented scale. Modern democratic, industrially advanced societies, on the other hand, generally enjoy a high degree of stability and social cohesion as a result of a widely shared consensus of values that permits and encourages diversity in a pluralistic society. Signs that pluralism is not revered to the extent found during the Cold War, however, points to difficulties of social cohesion in developed countries as well. Nevertheless, the prevailing view is that the established societies will master these challenges. On the other hand, authoritarian societies, both those oriented toward the right (Fascist) and toward the left (Communist), build social cohesion through such techniques as one-party systems, strict discipline, widespread propaganda, nationalism, and ideological dedication. In each type of society—traditional, democratic, and authoritarian—social cohesion depends on the extent to which the masses of people accept and are motivated by the basic values of that society.

Socialism | 142 |

An ideology that rejects individualism, private ownership, and private profits in favor of a system based on economic collectivism; governmental, societal, or industrial-group ownership of the means of production and distribution of goods; and social responsibility. The doctrines of socialism vary from those espousing democratic values to those calling for forms of absolutism and dictatorship. Advocates of socialism include utopians, Christians and other religious groups, political parties, welfare statists, leaders of developing countries, esoteric sects and societies, Communists, and anarchists. Major differences among groups professing the ideology involve the means for winning power and instituting socialism (democratic or revolutionary) and the nature of the socialist system to be established (state-controlled, syndicalist, or merely "cooperative"). In strategy, Socialists fall into either of two categories: Democratic Socialists, who strive to use the political machinery of the state to achieve their goals by democratically winning power and peacefully modifying the existing system; or radical Marxian Socialists, who believe their objectives can be achieved only through violence and the destruction of existing capitalist and democratic institutions. Socialists are also divided, in terms of objectives, between those who wish to establish a centrally organized system, using the power of the state, and the syndicalists, who aim for a decentralized system with groups of workers owning and controlling all industries. *See also* COMMUNIST THEORY: SOCIALIST PROGRAM (104).

Significance
Various Socialist doctrines were developed in Europe during the nineteenth century by reform groups, political parties, and intellectuals who were appalled by the suffering of the masses resulting from the factory system ushered in by the Industrial Revolution and from the early abuses of the capitalist system. In the twentieth century, limited systems of democratic socialism have been established in some of the advanced industrial democratic states, such as Sweden and Great Britain, in the form of extensive welfare-state programs and some governmental ownership of basic industries and services. Social democratic parties espousing Socialist programs also constitute powerful political forces in many continental European states. The former Soviet Union and the Communist systems imposed on Eastern Europe regarded themselves as Socialist systems in transition toward a final stage of pure communism. In addition, the leaders of many developing countries at one time described their diverse techniques of governmental planning and direction in economic development as "Third World socialism." The repudiation of the form of socialism represented by the Soviet Union has caused many of the experimenters in socialism to reexamine capitalism, mixed economies, and privatization as perhaps a better approach to their mundane needs. Even the Russian Federation seems to believe that the market economy is preferable to the command economy. China, still a Communist country, has deemphasized socialism in its economic sector as it too seeks to adapt capitalist experience to its development schemes.

Stereotype | 143 |
A generalized, fixed mental picture or image of a group or society based on limited experience, hearsay, or emotion. A stereotype as a generalization may either accurately or inaccurately describe the characteristics of a group or its individual members. Stereotypes are often created as a result of predispositions or expectations dominating perception. They exist because of a limited knowledge of the facts, and because each person's ability to perceive reality is limited by his or her preconceptions and prejudices. *See also* NATIONALISM: XENOPHOBIA (61).

Significance
Stereotypes affect the policy process in the field of foreign affairs because individual decisionmakers, opinion elites, and the general public may be unaware that the mental images they hold of other governments or peoples are inaccurate or biased. Governments also may seek to gain public support for their policies by creating a false public image of another nation that tends to support their decisions or programs. By stereotyping a nationality or an ideological group—for example, all Communists are aggression-minded, or the Chinese are cunning and treacherous—serious errors of judgment in policy development and hostile people-to-people relations may result. Policies based on stereotyped images reinforce the "pictures in our minds" because they evoke reactions from the stereotyped nation or group that tend to confirm the images.

Values | 144 |
Normative standards or goals that an individual, a group, a society, or a nation professes and strives to achieve. Values serve as guideposts for things or actions people consider to be just and desirable—the kind

of society that ought to exist. A society's values tend to become embodied within the broad framework of an ideology and are articulated in the form of an ideal or preferred "way of life" for that society—and for others as well. Values may also relate to power, prestige, and the pursuit of status by a state. *See also* CONSENSUS OF VALUES (106); SOCIAL COHESION (141).

Significance
The unity and strength of a society or group depends to a considerable extent on the degree of consensus on values. Values tend to become more numerous and diffused within a pluralistic society of a democratic state, although certain basic standards concerning the nature of the political, economic, and social system remain fundamental to its harmony. Authoritarian societies, on the other hand, attempt to foster a limited, highly integrated set of values directly related to the domestic and foreign goals of the nation. Value conflict within or between societies has been a major contributing factor to internal revolutions and civil wars and to struggles between nations. A conflict over fundamental values between the Hindu and Muslim communities, for example, led in 1947 to the partitioning of British India into two independent states—India and Pakistan.

Velvet Divorce | 145 |
A term used to describe the breakup of the Czechoslovakian Federation, forming the two independent states of the Czech Republic and Slovakia, on 1 January 1993. Czechoslovakia was formed after World War I from a segment of the Austro-Hungarian Empire, which ceased to exist following the hostilities. The federation survived through World War II, but was one of the key states occupied by Adolf Hitler's Nazi legions prior to the outbreak of that conflict. The Cold War placed Czechoslovakia behind the Iron Curtain, and as a Communist state it both tolerated and resisted Sovietization. In 1968 Czechoslovakia demonstrated a rare act

of defiance in what came to be known as the "Prague Spring" when the Czech reformist Communist party secretary, Alexander Dubcek, demanded liberal reforms and greater independence. The Soviet Red Army led other Warsaw Pact countries in a swift military campaign that destroyed this initiative, but Prague Spring adherents remained a thorn in the Soviet side. The movement continued to gather supporters through the 1970s and 1980s, and in 1989 it was instrumental in provoking the popular demonstrations that climaxed with the tearing down of the Berlin Wall, and the general rejection of communism throughout Eastern and Central Europe. The collapse of the Soviet Union in 1991, and its breakup into 15 independent republics, impacted Czechoslovakia. A year later it too split into separate states.

Significance
The Velvet Divorce conveys the peaceful nature of the Czechoslovakian separation into the Czech Republic and Slovakia. Unlike the breakup of Yugoslavia, there was no resistance to the tearing of federal bonds. The term Velvet Divorce was in fact borrowed from the 1989 Czechoslovakian decision to peacefully break the grip of Communist leadership. But behind the otherwise tranquil separation were two distinct peoples, the Czechs and the Slovaks, each representing a different cultural experience and each insistent on the elevation of its peculiar character. In fact, it was the more developed Czechs who had dominated Czechoslovakia in all areas, and it was the Slovakians who were most interested in establishing a sovereign homeland of their own choosing. Although last-minute efforts were made to sustain the union, the desire for separation was too strong to overcome. Rather than cause more stress and possibly high tragedy, the statesmanlike decision that called for the formation of two independent republics was peacefully executed.

World Wide Web (WWW) | 146 |
An information space on the Internet unified by a common addressing system and

distinguished by its capacity to link information from one computer to another. It is a hypertext-based, multimedia service used for browsing Internet resources. WWW spans most of the Internet and grows daily as network users and Web servers are added. WWW was created in 1989 at CERN, the European Center for Particle Physics in Switzerland, as a means of distributing research information. WWW today covers every imaginable subject and is made up of Web servers, which are computer programs providing service across a network. The hypertext represents text materials organized in nonlinear ways so that the reader can jump from one topic to related topics without having to read sequentially through all the material provided. *See also* INTERNET (130).

Significance
The World Wide Web is the easy-to-use portion of the Internet that allows anyone to roam the cyberspace world and point and click their way to words, pictures, sounds, and videos on virtually any sub-

ject. Until the WWW was developed in 1989, the Internet was primarily the bastion of computer specialists and cyberspace pioneers. Users currently are anyone, from young children to aged shut-ins who have access to the WWW through browser programs or online services such as Prodigy, America On-Line, Compuserv, or Microsoft. The international implications of the WWW are only now being addressed, but it is generally acknowledged that the information highway can be utilized by anyone for almost any purpose, that very substantial benefits are derived from the system, but that the WWW can also be used by political elements with violent agendas. It need only be noted what the audiotape technology meant to the revolution against the shah of Iran in 1979 or how the cellular phone aided and abetted the 1989 revolution against the Communist order in Eastern Europe and the Soviet Union. Indeed, the WWW and the Internet point to still greater importance for computer-generated technology in the information age.

Geography, Environment, and Population

Acid Rain

| 147 |

Rain, snow, or fog vapor that mixes with sulfur oxides and nitrogen oxides, forming an acidic compound that ultimately interferes with the earth's reproductive processes. Acid rain is a direct outcome of automobile emissions, oil-refinery processes, smelter exhaust, and a host of industrial operations. Finding its way into freshwater lakes, it is known to deplete the calcium in the bone structure of fish. It also causes chemical reactions in the subsoil of lakes, resulting in the injection of aluminum and other heavy metals into the water, which clogs the gills of fish and suffocates them. On land, acid rain damages the foliage of crops and arrests the growth of trees. It can corrode steel bridges and railroad tracks, and eat away the marble and limestone surfaces of buildings. *See also* GLOBAL COMMONS (168).

Significance

Although individual countries have taken some initiatives in dealing with the problem of acid rain, some of the remedies, such as the construction of high smokestacks, have merely dispersed the effluent over wider areas, and a generally local concern has become a national and even international issue. The higher altitude emissions remain suspended in the air long enough to be carried thousands of miles with moving weather fronts. Eastern Canada, for example, suffers heavily from emissions originating in the midwestern United States. By the same token, Scandinavian countries absorb substantial amounts of acid rain from sources originating in Germany, France, and notably Great Britain. Transboundary pollution responsibilities have been acknowledged in numerous environmental conferences, beginning with the Stockholm Declaration of the 1972 United Nations Conference on the Environment. An International Treaty on Long-Range Transboundary Air Pollution entered into force in 1983. The United Nations Conference on the Environment and Development (UNCED) convened in Rio de Janeiro in June 1992, attended by a majority of the world's heads of states and governments, and that conference again noted the importance of controlling the problem of acid rain.

Boundaries | 148

The limits within which a state exercises territorial jurisdiction. As delimitations of jurisdiction, boundaries relate not only to a specific portion of the earth's surface but to territorial waters, airspace, and subsurface resources as well. Boundaries may be fixed by negotiation, arbitration, adjudication, plebiscite, allocation by an international body such as the United Nations, and cession through purchase or war. Various types of, and reasons for, particular boundaries include (1) natural separators, such as rivers and mountains; (2) cultural differences, such as religious-majority areas that served as the basis for drawing the boundaries between India and Pakistan; (3) historical and political considerations, as in the case of many of the African states, whose boundaries were originally drawn by European colonial powers; and (4) those established by military equilibrium, as between Israel and her Arab neighbors, or between North and South Korea. *See also* ODER-NEISSE LINE (176).

Significance
Boundaries are symbols of national independence and power; they are also traditional sources of international tension and conflict. Illustrations of boundaries involving contemporary international tensions and conflict are those between Iraq and Iran, China and India, Israel and Syria, and Armenia and Azerbaijan. The importance of national boundaries in terms of national defense varies with the level of military technology involved. Boundaries involving terrain features such as mountains, rivers, swamps, or deserts may be important considerations in conventional warfare, of more limited significance when air operations are considered, and almost irrelevant in terms of nuclear missiles.

Buffer States | 149

Weak states, located between or on the borders of strong states, that serve the security interests of the latter. Buffer states often exist only at the sufferance of their more powerful neighbors, who desire a "crush zone" between themselves and their rivals.

Significance
Serving, as they do, the economic and military interests of their dominant neighbors, buffer states contribute to the maintenance of local and general power balances by reducing the chances of direct confrontation and conflict. Afghanistan, Tibet, and Persia (Iran) were used as buffers between British India and Russia prior to World War I. After World War I, the states of Central Europe were viewed as forming a buffer zone between Germany and Russia (then the Soviet Union). When Germany was geographically and politically divided at the end of World War II, it became something resembling a modified buffer between the NATO force on the one side and the Warsaw Pact forces on the other. Although West Germany was inducted into NATO in 1954, and East Germany became a member of the Warsaw alliance in 1955, war in Europe was avoided so long as the two Germanys were not interfered with. As a consequence of the successful operation of the German buffer, peace in Europe was sustained throughout the more than 40 years of the Cold War.

Central Asia | 150

An area identified with major power rivalry in the late nineteenth and early twentieth centuries, a crossroads for external influence and activity. Among the former Central Asian republics of the Soviet Union, Tajikistan, Kyrgyzstan, Uzbekistan, and Turkmenistan, all in close proximity to Afghanistan, have experienced considerable unrest and civil strife since gaining their independence in 1991–1992. Continuing internecine violence in Afghanistan has spilled over into these states, and large populations of ethnic Tajiks, Uzbeks, and Turkmen also inhabit the northern areas of Afghanistan, with its predominant but tribally divided Pashtun population. All the Central

Asian republics are ruled by former Soviet strongmen who must now contain militant Islamic fundamentalist movements emanating from Afghanistan. Tajikistan was plunged into a wide-scale and brutal civil war shortly after achieving its independence, and a Communist government struggles to survive against concerted pro-Islamic Tajik opposition. Elements of Islamic extremism are also found in Uzbekistan, where the Farghana Valley is host to a pro–Saudi Arabian Wahhabi Islamic insurrection. Samarkand and Bokhara, cradle of ancient Islamic civilizations, are largely inhabited by Tajiks who follow the call of a warlord from northern Afghanistan and draw assistance from Iran. Kabul, ravaged by civil war among competing factions and tribes since the Soviet withdrawal in 1988–1989, represents the strategic divide between landlocked Central Asia and the ports of Pakistan, and between secular governments and their religious opposition. The Central Asian states have cause to think about economic development; they all want road and rail links through Afghanistan to Pakistan in order to reduce their dependence on Russia for the export of their oil, gas, and mineral resources, or for the import of much-desired consumer goods. But until Afghanistan becomes stable, there can be no meaningful business between Pakistan and Central Asia, or vice versa. In the meantime, all the countries of the region are threatened by virulent forms of Islamic militancy that seek to eliminate secular political experiences. *See also* ISLAMIC FUNDAMENTALISM (132).

Significance
As long as Afghanistan remains in a state of high conflict between rival tribal and religious orders, Pakistan on the one side and the Central Asian states on the other cannot find workable equilibrium. Pakistan, the more mature of the actors in the region, may be better prepared to ward off assaults on its domestic institutions, but the Central Asian states have had little or no experience with self-government, and the Afghan-based religious militants,

supported by both Iranian and Saudi agencies, have fueled protracted struggle. Afghanistan is the key to the problem, and given the enormous stockpile of weapons in that country (an arsenal assembled during eight years of war with the Soviet Union), Central Asia is likely to be a center of conflict well into the twenty-first century.

Demographic Cycle   151
The series of changes in births and deaths that affect the size and composition of a society as it experiences technological change. The demographic cycle proceeds in three stages: from a preindustrial base of relative population stability, through a transitional stage of population explosion, to a final stage in which the rate of population growth slows down, stabilizes, and, in some countries, declines.

Significance
Historically, the various stages in the demographic cycle have been causally related to levels of economic development. The countries that first experienced the Industrial Revolution sustained larger populations at higher standards of living, but improved economic well-being ultimately resulted in lower birthrates. This experience accounts for much of the emphasis placed on economic—particularly industrial—development by the countries presently in the midst of the population explosion. Uncontrolled population growth overwhelms the state's capacity to satisfy popular demand for basic needs, while material improvements are neutralized by the same dilemma. International efforts aimed at moderating growth are complicated by both the would-be donor countries' predispositions about birth control and family planning, and the prevailing views in the target countries that insidious forces seek to weaken them or tamper with their fundamental beliefs. International agencies, both governmental and nongovernmental, that address the problem of overpopulation encounter impediments that complicate their already difficult tasks.

Observing the functioning of the demographic cycle, world demographers forecast dire consequences if current demographic trends remain unchecked. Whether national and international policies can be developed to relate populations to their environment is perhaps the major long-range problem facing the world today.

Demographic Cycle: Stage One | 152 |

The preindustrial demographic pattern, characterized by high birthrates and death rates. In stage one, life expectancy is low (approximately 30 years), infant mortality is high, and population increase is steady but slow. This preindustrial population pattern typified the Western societies in the period before the Industrial Revolution and the traditional societies of Asia, Africa, and Latin America prior to the 1930s.

Significance

Stage one societies experienced a slow rate of population growth for a number of reasons. The living standard was low, the economy was geared to subsistence agriculture, and nutritional standards were poor. Resistance to disease was low, and modern medicine and public sanitation facilities and standards were unknown. Large families were desirable because of the work children could contribute to the family, because having many children was a form of social security for aged parents, and because disease could be expected to kill off a number of children before they reached maturity. Such societies were also characterized by an early marriage age, the inferior status of women, and a low level of literacy. Stage one societies have virtually disappeared in the contemporary world; they have moved into the second demographic stage as a result of their own as well as international efforts.

Demographic Cycle: Stage Two | 153 |

The demographic pattern characterized by a population explosion. In stage two, the birthrate remains high, but the death rate declines sharply, resulting in rapid population growth. A dramatic decrease in infant mortality results in more young adults, who in turn produce additional children, so the rate of increase also rises. Since longevity has not yet increased substantially, the society tends to be biologically young. However, the same technology that makes industrialization possible—for example, improved medicine and sanitation—eventually brings about an additional population increase by reducing the death rate still further.

Significance

The population explosion, or the second stage of the demographic cycle, when coupled with the revolution of rising expectations, presents serious national and international problems. Not only are the people in these countries demanding more out of life than they did previously, but there are also more people in these countries to demand better living standards at an increasing rate of improvement. Because their expectation curve rises faster than their achievement curve, the distance between the two lines increases and may be described as a frustration gap. Thus, rising populations and expectations strain the resources and ingenuity of governments, many of which are relatively young and inexperienced. Some of the resulting problems and frustrations involve (1) increasing internal tensions, disorders, and frequency of coups d'état; (2) increasing irresponsible international actions designed to divert the masses (if only temporarily) from domestic problems; and (3) growing pressure on developed countries to provide vast amounts of development assistance in ways that will not offend self-conscious young nationalism. Meanwhile, the gap between developed and developing countries is growing wider, increasing the international ferment. Because the size of the active population relative to the total population initially decreases, the burdens on the workforce to produce higher living standards are substantially greater than at either of the other two stages of the demographic cycle. In addition, the large proportion of unemployed young people in such societies increases the level of tension and the propensity for revolution.

Demographic Cycle: Stage Three

155 | 154 |

The demographic pattern characterized by the declining rate of natural increase in the population. In contrast to the preceding stage, in which the birthrate remains high while the death rate falls sharply, in the third stage the death rate continues to fall, but more gradually, while the birthrate declines rapidly. The result is a marked increase in the average age of the population. The decline in the birthrate is usually ascribed to a complex set of changes in social attitudes and institutions that makes large families less desirable, particularly for economic reasons. Stage three of the demographic cycle is associated with such industrialized societies as the United States, Japan, and those of Western Europe.

Significance

The industrial countries of stage three of the demographic cycle are characterized by high standards of living, which entail increased costs for luxuries, education, and child rearing, and soaring public expenditures for welfare-state programs. In such countries, the costs for young dependents can still be considered an investment in the future, but the costs for old dependents are increasing and represent a social debt. Countries in the third stage have a larger portion of their societies in the active working population (ages 15–65) than countries in either of the first two stages. Yet despite high labor productivity, technological developments—particularly automation—threaten large-scale unemployment, increased tensions, and social dislocations that tax the creative capabilities of social and governmental leaders. A continued trend of declining birthrates could also have a serious impact on power relationships if the industrialized countries experience a population decline at the very time when the populations of most of the countries of the world are growing rapidly and competing with increasing vigor for a larger share of world resources.

Earth Summit

| 155 |

The term used to describe the 1992 United Nations Conference on Environment and Development convened in Rio de Janeiro. Prompted by the worldwide concern for environmental issues that developed in the 1980s, a World Commission on Environment and Development was formed in 1987 under the leadership of Gro Harlem Bruntland, Norway's prime minister. The commission published a lengthy document known as the Bruntland Report, which served as the stimulus for the Earth Summit. The Earth Summit represented the most ambitious undertaking in history, bringing together representatives of 172 countries, including 100 heads of state and government. In addition there were 1,500 accredited observers and 30,000 participants in parallel forum sessions. The Earth Summit approved the Rio Declaration on Environment and Development, establishing 27 principles for sustainable development; Agenda 21, a plan for achieving the broad goals of the conference; and a separate set of principles aimed at conserving and preserving the world's diminishing forests. Conventions on biodiversity and climate change were also signed. The Earth Summit set up a Commission on Sustainable Development, and a Department for Policy Coordination and Sustainable Development in the UN Secretariat. *See also* DEVELOPMENT: AGENDA 21 (187); SUSTAINABLE DEVELOPMENT (182).

Significance

The Earth Summit was a historic event, prompting the holding of the International Conference on Population and Development in Cairo in 1994, and the Copenhagen Conference on Poverty in 1995. But the Rio, Cairo, and Copenhagen Conferences were not enthusiastically received in all political circles. The United

States was a less-than-enthralled participant in all the conferences. Despite the overwhelming support offered by its scientific community and environmental groups, the U.S. government, confronted by substantial opposition from within the U.S. Congress and from a variety of private- and public-interest groups, resisted the international effort to influence U.S. domestic policy. Overall, cleavages between developed and developing nations over questions of development and environment could not be bridged. President Bush attended the Earth Summit reluctantly, and his administration refused to sign the Biodiversity Treaty at Rio. Despite the Clinton administration's heavier emphasis on the environment, the Bush performance was not reversed. Sustained opposition to programs geared to protect the global environment have generally paralyzed governmental actions. Moreover, the U.S. government ceased support for family-planning programs in Third World nations in the 1980s, and the strength of pressure groups opposed to birth control (let alone legalized abortion) prevented the United States from playing a prominent role at the Cairo Conference on Population and Development. The Copenhagen Conference on Poverty extended an invitation to President Clinton, but his decision to avoid the meeting despite the attendance of many world leaders was another example of U.S. reluctance to follow through on Earth Summit programs. Indeed, the Berlin Conference on World Climate Change in March 1995 again failed to draw the attention of the president of the United States. Without the presence of the U.S. president, and the cooperation of the United States, the Earth Summit remains a symbol rather than a reality of global cooperation.

Ecologism | 156 |
The term coined in the 1970s by Richard Falk in his book *The Endangered Planet*. Falk suggested the development of a new world order that centered on transnational, nonterritorial actors and the di-

minishing role played by the territorial nation-states. Falk stressed the interdependence of the world's populations struggling to survive and progress in conditions of increasing scarcity. The "limits of growth" established the basis for this new world order, he argued, and the physical nature of the planet and its declining ecological resources, along with uncontrolled population growth, necessitated new levels of cooperation. Falk framed his thesis in the concept "nonterritorial central guidance," that is, the development of values transcending the nation-state. *See also* POLITICAL COMMUNITY: NONGOVERNMENTAL ORGANIZATION (NGO) (540).

Significance
Ecologism called for a recognition that anticolonialism, antiracialism, genuine equality between human beings, and the pressing need for ecological balance would produce new majorities in international organizations, notably the United Nations. Falk anticipated the development of populist movements less tied to national states and more intimately associated with world peace, justice for all, and the preservation of the planet's scarce resources. Transnational contacts in the form of the nongovernmental organization (NGO) were seen as multiplying, their combined weight eventually shifting the balance away from the exclusive nation-state to a more inclusive humanity. The Falk vision was at best futuristic; at worst it suffered from its heavy dependence on the limits of growth and scarcity, which have been challenged by modern science and technology. It also ignored conflict within and between interdependent movements, and the enormous problems confronting those responsible for not only coordinating humanity, burdened as well with the operationalizing of new, more embracing aspects of democracy and egalitarianism. In a world still highly parochial, Falk's stress on ecologism was well-intentioned, but nevertheless far removed from reality. Despite its idealistic character, Falk's thesis is valuable in describing the

phenomenal growth of the nongovernmental organizations.

Ecosystem 157

The intertwining and interdependence of all the earth's living species with the global environment that nourishes, sustains, and reproduces life. The twentieth-century proliferation of the human species and the expansion of new technologies to service their needs and desires has put increasing strain on the earth's resources and environment, undermining the assumption that the earth has self-equilibrating mechanisms enabling it to adapt and rebound to normal conditions no matter what is done to them. Scientists and environmentalists cite the danger in such assumptions, and demand immediate attention to ecosystem matters before the problems caused by overpopulation and humanity's insatiable appetite for creature comforts becomes unmanageable. *See also* GLOBAL COMMONS (168); SUSTAINABLE DEVELOPMENT (182).

Significance
According to members of the world's scientific community, the global ecosystem is at serious risk, from mountain streams down to the farther reaches of the continental shelf and out to the high seas beyond national jurisdiction, from the airspace above the water and land, through the land and water, to the subsoil in the oceans and the riverbeds and lakebeds of great water systems. They argue that living and nonliving resources of great value to much of the world's population are being abused and exhausted and that, no less significantly, the imbalances in the natural order address a bleaker future global environment. As a consequence of increased publicity, a global consciousness has emerged, sparked in part by Rachel Carson's *Silent Spring* (1962) and subsequent reports of the widespread death of aquatic animals and plants from oil spills and the unregulated dumping of waste materials. Ridding the world of nuclear waste material is high on the agenda of many nations, but it nevertheless remains an unanswered dilemma. The magnitude of the ecosystem problem is downgraded by political and economic interests, especially in the more industrialized states, but international efforts are not without a modicum of success. Examples of how the world is coping with the dilemma are seen in the Law of the Sea Treaty (1982); in the Convention on Long-Range Transboundary Air Pollution, which went into force in 1983; the Convention for the Protection of the Ozone Layer, which went into force in 1988; the Basel Convention on the Control of Transboundary Movements of Hazardous Wastes and Their Disposal, which went into force in 1992; and the Rio Declaration of 1992.

Geographic Power Factor: Climate 158

The effect of weather conditions on national power. The climatic conditions of a state are determined mainly by its characteristic wind, precipitation, and temperature pattern. Historically, the greatest national power developments have taken place in those regions marked by temperate climate conditions. Adverse climatic conditions are not impossible to overcome, but extremes of heat and cold demand a greater expenditure of human energy and resources to sustain life than is the case in regions of moderate climate.

Significance
Climate is probably the most important of the geographic power factors because of its direct effect on society's ability to grow food and perform work. The effects of climate can be altered to some degree, but usually at the expense of increased production costs. Within limits, arid lands can be irrigated, and seawater can be desalinated to overcome insufficient rainfall. Advanced technology can improve working conditions in the colder regions of the world. New strains of seed and food animals capable of withstanding greater extremes of temperature are being developed. Disease control, improved

nutrition, new technological skills, and development capital are enhancing human energy in tropical countries where the climate was once considered too enervating to increase productivity much beyond the subsistence level. The most favorable climates for human activity are those of the temperate zones, which range between 20 and 60 degrees north and south of the equator. Approximately 85 percent of the world's land area, 75 percent of the habitable land, and about 90 percent of the population are located north of the equator, which helps to explain why the North Temperate Zone continues to dominate the international political stage.

Geographic Power Factor: Location | 159 |

The relationship between physical position on the globe and national power. The location of a state is related to national power through climate; access to and from the sea; control over river, sea, and land transportation routes; and the availability of natural resources. The presence or absence of powerful neighbors is also a function of location.

Significance
Location is a factor in the national power equation in both geographic and strategic terms. Historically, the states having the greatest impact on human affairs have been located in the Northern Hemisphere, particularly in its temperate zone. The strategic connection between location and foreign policy has been obvious from ancient times, and more recently has given rise to geopolitics as a field of study. Attention has often been drawn, for example, to a connection between the absence of obstacles to invasion across the northern European plain from the Rhine to the Urals, and the militarism of German and Russian regimes. Water barriers, on the other hand, have made Great Britain, Japan, and the United States relatively secure from invasion during most of their history. The security and, consequently, the foreign policies of Canada

and Latin America continue to be affected by their proximity to the United States and their distance from other centers of world power. Switzerland's traditional neutrality is perhaps the classic illustration of the impact of location on domestic and foreign policy. But location does not grant power; it can only facilitate its acquisition and use. The contribution of location to national power can also be changed by developments elsewhere in the national power spectrum. Changes in the locations of markets and in the commodities traded have altered trade routes, and the development of air travel has increased the importance of locations previously less accessible by land or water.

Geographic Power Factor: Raw Materials | 160 |

The resources of water and soil, their products, and the minerals of the subsoil in relation to national power. Access to raw materials is essential to the standard of living and the security of the state, and dependence on them relates to the technological developments that create demands for them either at home or abroad. Iron and coal have long been the basis for industrialization, but increasing technological sophistication is creating new demands for other materials, such as uranium as an energy source and titanium for jet engines. The advanced technologies of such fields as space exploration, medicine, and warfare depend on high levels of industrialization, which in turn requires a diversity of raw materials. Developing countries seeking ways to sustain growing populations at improved standards of living add to the pressures on diminishing supplies of world resources.

Significance
National power and well-being are directly dependent on the possession and availability of—and capacity to use—raw materials. The uneven distribution of raw materials around the world is a prime reason for international trade and the de-

velopment of transportation facilities. The need for secure sources of supply is both a historic cause of imperialism and war and a reason for the drive to liberalize trade policies that has occurred since World War II. The increasing demand for and shrinkage of raw materials occasioned by advancing industrialization and the population explosion is also speeding the search for new supplies, new uses, and the development of substitutes. One approach has been to develop synthetics from raw materials available in relatively large quantities, such as the petrochemical derivatives of petroleum. Although total reserves of raw materials are diminishing, the available supply of many on the world market exceeds demand, resulting in price instability and worsening terms of trade for the supplying countries.

Geographic Power Factor: Size | 161 |

The effect on the power equation of the relationship between the surface areas of states. Enormous variations in size exist among the more than 180 states of the world, ranging from Russia with approximately 6 million square miles (17 million sq km), to the Vatican with 108.7 acres (44 hectares). China, Canada, and the United States range from 3.6 to 3.8 million square miles (9.3 to 9.8 million sq km). Brazil, Australia, India, and Argentina each have over 1 million square miles (2.6 million sq km). There are almost 60 states in the range from 100,000 to 1,000,000 square miles (260,000 to 2.6 million sq km), 30 from 40,000 to 100,000 (100,000 to 200,000 sq km), more than 30 from 3,000 to 40,000 (7,800 to 100,000 sq km), and over 30 with less than 3,000 square miles (7,800 sq km).

Significance

Size alone does not guarantee national power (the state of Israel is one of the world's smallest), and it is necessary to examine additional elements such as population, natural resources, technological levels, social cohesion, and leader-

ship. However, size is related to a state's ability to develop its power. A greater diversity and quantity of raw materials are likely to be found in large states than in small ones, increasing the opportunities of supporting a growing population. On the other hand, at current technological levels, raw materials from local sources may be inaccessible or unusable, and not all of a state's territory may be capable of supporting life. Human ingenuity may be able to overcome deficiencies in size to some degree, but given the same ingenuity, the larger the country the greater the power advantage it is likely to enjoy.

Geographic Power Factor: Topography | 162 |

The effect on national power of the physical features of a state. Topography includes such elements as altitude, river systems, mountain ranges, plains, and marshlands. Other factors such as size, location, raw materials, and climate, when considered with topography, constitute the geographic element of national power.

Significance

Topography affects both the social and political life of a state and its relations with other states. For example, altitude and the direction of slopes in relation to sun and wind are determinants of the kind of agriculture that can be practiced. Mountains, plains, and river systems are related to the concentration of population. Historically, cultural differences have been long-lasting in regions where topographic features have impeded communication. The configuration of the land in terms of the ease or difficulty of ingress and egress has helped to determine the stability of political boundaries as well. Topography is thus an inescapable power factor, but its importance in a given place and time is determined by its relationship to other elements of power, such as the level of technology applicable in the same situation. The relative importance of topography is demonstrated by the differing impact of mountain ranges or defenses in depth across wide plains on conventional military ground operations as compared with aerial or rocket warfare. Modern communications, on the other hand, can overcome virtually any topographic obstacle.

Geopolitics   163

An approach to foreign policy that attempts to explain and predict political behavior and military capabilities in terms of the physical environment. Geopolitics involves varying degrees of historical determinism based on geography. Friedrich Ratzel (1724–1804) compared the state to a living organism that must expand or die. His disciple Rudolf Kjellen (1864–1922) carried on this process of anthropomorphism, by which the state became more than a legal concept. He developed a body of "laws" on the state as a "geographic organism in space," and gave them the name "geopolitics" in his book *The State as a Form of Life* (1916). Much geopolitical theorizing, although presented in terms of scientific analysis, contains large elements of propaganda. The reputation of geopolitics has suffered because geopoliticians like Karl Haushofer (1869–1946) have frequently been the advocates of particular political ideologies or national policies, which they have sought to explain or justify in terms of geographical causation. The term *geopolitics* may also be used to describe political geography considered in terms of the structure of the world and its component states, or to refer to those aspects of foreign-policy planning that must take into account various geographic factors.

Significance

Political events always occur in a geographic setting, and geographic factors may influence the course of events, but it is always humankind and not geography that makes political events. Geography is a complex of such factors as size, location, climate, and topography. In addition, geography is an important element, but not the only factor, of national power; its importance is relative to such considerations as economics, technology, human power, and morale. An evaluation of all these elements, considered together as the national power equation, is meaningful only in relation to the power equations of other states studied in the context of some specific time, place, and situation. Geographic facts are persistent concerns of the foreign-policy practitioner, but they are not absolutely constant. For example, open borders facilitate contact, but they do not make conflict inevitable. The polar ice cap means one thing in terms of sea power, and another in terms of air power. Thus, geographic theories, like such monistic causal interpretations of history as economic determinism, are unsatisfactory as complete explanations of human behavior. Nevertheless, they are useful approaches to more widely ranging studies of the complexities of international politics.

Geopolitics: Haushofer   164
Geopolitik

The German branch of geopolitics developed by Karl Haushofer (1869–1946), army general, geographer, geologist, historian, and Far Eastern traveler. The *geopolitik* of General Haushofer began with the heartland theory of British geographer Sir Halford J. Mackinder, and with Friedrich Ratzel and Rudolf Kjellen's concepts of space and the organic state. Haushofer and his disciples at the Institute of Geopolitics in Munich used these ideas to explain the German defeat in World War I and to plan future German conquests. As a major general in the German army, Haushofer no doubt viewed Adolf Hitler and the Nazi party as upstarts to be used for the realization of Germany's destiny. Hitler, on the other hand, used the Haushofer *geopolitik*, particularly ideas like *lebensraum* (living space), to suit his own purpose. In line with the heartland theory, Haushofer and his army followers advocated a German-Russian-Japanese bloc, with Germany destined to emerge as the dominant partner. Haushofer also saw that German power would be dissipated in the vastness of Russia should Hitler go through with his plan to invade the Soviet Union. When he tried to dissuade Hitler from this course, he fell from favor. His son Albrecht was later implicated in the failed plot to kill Hitler, and was executed. Haushofer himself was imprisoned in the concentration camp at Dachau in 1944; he was released after Germany's defeat in 1945, and committed suicide within a year.

Significance

The Haushofer *geopolitik* was a pseudo-scientific conglomeration of geographical metaphysics, economics, anthropology, and racism. It was important, however, because it was accepted by many Germans caught in the psychological doldrums of their World War I defeat. The major precepts of the Haushofer geopolitik include the ideas that (1) the military objectives of the state require policies of economic self-sufficiency; (2) the German master race is destined to bring peace to the world through domination, and thus other states must acquiesce in granting Germany her required *lebensraum*; (3) German rule must be extended first to all territories German by language, race, or economic interest, and then to the entire world; (4) German domination of the Afro-Eurasian island could be accomplished by overcoming sea power through long land marches, which would make Germany economically and militarily secure, and would provide the base for complete world domination; and (5) all territorial boundaries are useful starting points for war and are subject to change according to the dictates of German national interest. All geopolitical study has suffered to some extent from the disrepute thrust upon it by the Haushofer *geopolitik* as a rationalization for German territorial expansion.

Geopolitics: Heartland Theory

| 165 |

The theory that the state that could control the human and physical resources of

the Eurasian landmass between Germany and central Siberia would be in a position to control the world. The heartland theory was developed by British geographer Sir Halford J. Mackinder (1869–1947) in his paper "The Geographical Pivot of History" (1904) and in his best-known work, *Democratic Ideals and Reality: A Study in the Politics of Reconstruction* (1919). The heartland theory emerged from Mackinder's detailed study of the global relationship between land and sea power.

Significance

Mackinder postulated the dominating influence of certain geographic "realities" on the course of world politics. His realities included (1) a "world island" (Europe, Asia, and Africa) surrounding the Eurasian "heartland" or "pivot area," which is inaccessible from the sea; (2) its coastlands, called the "inner crescent" or "marginal crescent," made up of maritime powers; and (3) insular power bases composed of North and South America and Australia, called the "insular crescent" or "outer crescent." Based on his assumption of the growing ascendancy of land power over sea power, Mackinder warned that "who rules East Europe commands the Heartland; who rules the Heartland commands the World Island; who rules the World Island commands the World." Mackinder advocated policies aimed at creating an equilibrium of power between the land and sea powers so that no single country would be in a position to dominate the pivot area. By the time of World War II he had refined his theory so that it also took into account the development of air power and the growing national power of the United States, located outside the world island. In 1919 Mackinder warned of the consequences should Germany ever gain control of the Soviet Union. He was considered one of the architects of the buffer-state strategy, which saw the breakup of the Austrian-Hungarian Empire into the states of eastern and central Europe. In 1943, sensing Germany's eventual defeat in World War II, Mac-kinder warned of the consequences should the Soviet Union take control of Germany. Mackinder's analyses were also used in the post–World War II period to explain the rationale of the U.S. policy of containing the Soviet Union (Truman Doctrine), and spell out the even greater consequences deriving from a close union of the Soviet Union and China.

Geopolitics: Rimland Theory   166

The theory that emphasizes the rimlands of Europe—the Middle East, Africa, South Asia, and the Far East—as the keys to the security of the United States. The rimland theory was developed by U.S. geographer and geopolitician Nicholas J. Spykman (1893–1943). In his book *The Geography of the Peace* (1944), Spykman developed his theory around the concept of the rimlands, which corresponded to the inner crescent of British geographer Sir Halford J. Mackinder, modified and renamed. Spykman postulated that domination of any of these areas by a hostile power threatened the security of the United States, because from such a position the encirclement of the New World became a possibility. Spykman's revision of Mackinder's famous dictum became "who controls the Rimland rules Eurasia; who rules Eurasia controls the destinies of the world."

Significance
In developing the rimland theory, Spykman was concerned that the United States recognize (1) the ultimate responsibility of each state for its own security, (2) the importance of a world balance of power, and (3) the necessity of using U.S. power to stabilize such a balance. His analysis of the security needs of the United States took into account these worldwide factors: (1) geographic—location, size, topography; (2) economic—agricultural and industrial resources, the people, industrial production; and (3) political—national morale, political stability, social integration. Spykman was not a geographic monist, but he stressed geography as the "most fundamentally conditioning factor of foreign policy."

Geopolitics: Sea Power Theory   167

The theory that posits naval power as the key to world power. Sea power as the basis for a geopolitical theory was first developed by a U.S. naval officer. Admiral Alfred Thayer Mahan (1840–1914) perceived that the seas of the world connected landmasses rather than separated them. The acquisition and defense of overseas empires, therefore, were dependent on the ability to control the sea. Central features of Mahan's work include (1) a scholarly analysis of British naval history that explained Great Britain's role as a world power, (2) a dedication to the idea of a U.S. world mission to be carried out through overseas expansion, and (3) a rationalization of imperialism on the assumption that countries cannot stand still spatially, but must expand or decline.

Significance
The application of the sea-power theory to the United States was based on Admiral Mahan's view that the United States' geographic position was analogous to that of Great Britain. Mahan argued that European land powers with strong neighbors could not challenge the maritime supremacy of Great Britain or the United States because of the necessity of supporting large land forces. He concluded that British naval supremacy was not permanent and that the United States could establish its supremacy in the Caribbean and the Pacific. Mahan's book *The Influence of Sea Power upon History 1660–1783* (1890) was read by a generation of expansionists, particularly in the United States and Germany. Mahan's thinking remains relevant in that states with worldwide interests must be capable of projecting and using their power effectively at great distances from their homeland.

Global Commons   168

A term referring to the interdependent nature of humankind and its combined utilization of the world's resources. The term is derived from a nineteenth-century English view that village life was made more manageable when open cattle-grazing land was shared by all the inhabitants. The land was held in common, and therefore the cattle of all were free to draw their sustenance from it. In contemporary international relations, *global commons* has come to mean resource areas and ecosystems that are shared across national frontiers, in effect held in common for all to enjoy. The cited international or global commons are: outer space; the moon and other celestial bodies; the oceans and the seabed; Antarctica; internationally used seas, lakes, and rivers; and plant and animal ecologies. The purpose in identifying the global commons involves not only the fair sharing of resources but also their conservation and preservation. *See also* ECOSYSTEM (157).

Significance
The overgrazing of the English commons led to their destruction, so those promoting a global commons are ever mindful of the misuse of new technologies that would allow humankind to exploit the world's resources to a point of utter depletion. The fouling of the environment and the breakdown of ecosystems by rampant economic development have received considerable attention in contemporary times. Nevertheless, independent states are reluctant to address the larger issues, preferring to emphasize their narrower national interests. Indeed, whether it is the destruction of the Amazon rain forest, or the elimination of valuable wetlands in North America, individual states are reluctant to buy the global-commons argument. The difficulty confronting the implementation of the Law of the Sea Treaty stems from the refusal of the United States to acknowledge the global-commons concept that the larger world community wishes to apply to the exploitation of minerals in the deep seabed lying beneath the oceans of the world.

Green Revolution   169

A dramatic change in agricultural production begun in the 1960s through development of new high-yielding wheat and rice seeds and the application of large quantities of water and fertilizer. Led by Nobel Prize–winning geneticist Norman E. Borlaug, who pioneered in the experiments that led to the new seeds, the Green Revolution was aimed at providing the food needed to break the famine cycles of Third World countries, especially those of Asia and Africa. *See also* POPULATION CONTROL (179).

Significance
Early successes of the Green Revolution led to a doubling and even tripling of food production in many countries of Asia and Africa during the 1960s. In the 1970s and 1980s, despite the high cost of energy needed to make fertilizer and pump water, a great increase in production occurred. However, drought in some regions led to production losses, and by the late 1980s, African harvests were lagging far behind the explosion in population. Scientists around the world are attempting to launch a second Green Revolution that would be more attuned to an energy-short world. For example, they are developing new seeds that produce two annual harvests instead of one, and looking for grasses and other plants that can be sown with wheat and rice to provide these grains with the necessary nitrogen. The second Green Revolution efforts are part of the global race to develop the means to support a population explosion of massive proportions.

Greenhouse Effect   170

The heating of the earth as a consequence of the injection of industrially produced fluorocarbons into the atmosphere. The earth's temperate climate is dependent on a balance between the heat obtained from the sun that is absorbed by the earth's surface and the heat that is reflected back out of the atmosphere. The buildup of an atmospheric belt of concentrations of chemical substances, predominantly carbon dioxide (from the burning of fossil fuels on earth) and methane, is judged to be changing the planet's basic temperature balance by blocking the escape of heat back into space. This is called the

"Greenhouse Effect." The 1995 Berlin Conference on Climate Change represented the first worldwide effort to combat the Greenhouse Effect. A 1995 University of Colorado study from the Alpine Institute of Arctic and Alpine Research reported, after studying hundreds of the more than 500,000 small glaciers around the world, that their mass had diminished by approximately 11 percent in the last 100 years. Moreover, the reduction was spectacular in the European Alps, which lost more than 50 percent of their ice since 1896. Much of this loss is attributed to industrial and automobile emissions in the crowded environment of the European continent. The study concluded by noting that the earth has warmed by 1 degree Fahrenheit over the past two centuries, and that this degree of change was convincing evidence of global warming. *See also* GLOBAL COMMONS (168); OZONE LAYER (178).

Significance
Scientists fear that continued warming of the biosphere, even by a few degrees, will have catastrophic effects by melting the polar ice caps. The resulting rise of the world's oceans would inundate continental regions, swallowing major cities and ultimately swamping large as well as small islands. Numerous frightening scenarios have been developed, but the greater attention is on preventive measures. Scientists and environmentalists argue the need to cease large-scale deforestation because tree foliage absorbs carbon dioxide. Protection of the world's rain forests has become an international concern, but as with most environmental issues, it can be addressed only by individual nation-states. Material progress is thwarted by environmental schemes, so the issue of economic advancement must be weighed alongside scientific fears that may appear too long-term or—to many who remain skeptical—even problematical.

International Frontiers | 171 |
The political if not the legal separation of countries from one another. The more common frontier is the land boundary between one state and another. The less common is the maritime boundary, especially those emanating from the territories of states open to extensive bodies of water, whether seas or oceans. International frontiers center on the importance of the territorial imperatives that sovereign states extend over specific locations, and the manner and character of jurisdiction they impose in and over them. International frontiers are observed in four distinct settings: (1) alienated frontiers, where the boundaries between state actors are made most difficult due to war, political disputes, ethnic rivalry, or a host of psychological, cultural, and economic issues; (2) coexistent frontiers, where minimal border stability is assured through agreements, understandings, and exchanges; (3) interdependent frontiers, where considerable interstate rapport and movement enhances cooperation and promotes the well-being of the adjoined states; and (4) integrated frontiers, where economic activity and social interaction have significantly reduced the importance of international borders and thus induced a higher degree of integration and stability.

Significance
International frontiers focus attention on the geopolitical and geoeconomic dimensions of interstate behavior. The four models of international frontiers identified above describe prevailing conditions in the contemporary international state system, and lead from the most determined national rivalry (alienated frontiers) to the least demonstrated state rivalry (integrated frontiers). The simultaneous existence of each of these models portrays the character of extreme geopolitical behavior in alienated frontiers, moderated political rivalry in coexistent frontiers, more genuine economic cooperation in interdependent frontiers, and more compelling international community building in integrated frontiers. The Middle East could be examined from the vantage point of alienated frontiers, East Asia in coexistent frontiers, Southeast

Asia with regard to interdependent frontiers, and Western Europe where integrated frontiers have produced the European Union.

International Fund for Agricultural Development (IFAD) | 172 |

An agency that began in 1977 to offer grants and loans to help increase food production in needy Third World countries. IFAD is a specialized agency of the United Nations and functions under the oversight of the Economic and Social Council and the General Assembly. IFAD financing was set up mainly on the basis of contributions from OPEC and the West. IFAD's governing council has a three-way balanced representation that includes donor-developed countries (mainly the West and Japan), donor-developing countries (mainly OPEC), and recipient-developing countries (the Third and Fourth Worlds). *See also* GREEN REVOLUTION (169).

Significance

The International Fund for Agricultural Development was created largely in response to serious famine and malnutrition problems in developing countries resulting from exploding populations, bad weather, lack of seeds and fertilizer, and other conditions that limited crop production. The idea of a special agency to fund agricultural development emerged from the World Food Conference that met in Rome in 1974. The financing system worked well at first by providing several billions of dollars for agricultural development, but the collapse in world oil prices led to the refusal of OPEC nations to contribute sizable amounts as they had in the past. Disagreements over financing have seriously jeopardized the future operations of IFAD.

Malthusianism | 173 |

The theory that postulates that population increases geometrically (2, 4, 8, 16, 32, . . .) while the means of subsistence increase only arithmetically (2, 4, 6, 8, 10, . . .). Therefore, Malthusianism asserts that improvement in the standard of living is not possible, and that a livable ratio between population and food supply can be maintained only through the corrective intervention of recurring wars, pestilence, disease, and famine. Named for its formulator, economist Thomas Malthus (1776–1834), Malthusianism went out of vogue when the Industrial Revolution made it possible for the countries of Western Europe to have both a rising standard of living and a substantial increase in population. *See also* DEMOGRAPHIC CYCLE (151); GREEN REVOLUTION (169).

Significance

In the contemporary world, Malthusianism is frequently called neo-Malthusianism because the old concept is being applied to a new environment. The terms symbolize growing concern with the worldwide worsening relationship between population and food supply. In the industrialized countries, standards of living continue to rise. However, in many of the developing countries, which contain most of the world's population, the standard of living is barely holding its own, and many food exporters have become net importers. The result is a progressively widening gap between rich and poor societies. Neo-Malthusians warn that unless the population explosion is brought under a measure of control, natural resources are used less wastefully, and food production is increased substantially, humanity's future may well be one of recurring disasters as Malthus had predicted.

Migration | 174 |

Population movements from one state or region to another. Immigration is the movement viewed from the receiving state, while population movements out of a country are called emigration. The record of human migration is as old as recorded history, but perhaps the greatest wave involved the emigration of over 25 million people from Europe between the 1870s and

World War I. In Asia, during the same period, Chinese emigration averaged 70,000–80,000 annually, although civil war in central China caused this figure to go above 200,000 in 1926 and 1927. Most Chinese migrants went to countries of Southeast Asia, where their communal culture created problems of national integration. Heavy migration declined after World War I, and by the 1930s virtually stopped. The greatest single migration after World War II involved well over 1 million Jews from all over the world—mainly Europe, North Africa, and the Middle East—who flocked to the new state of Israel. The term *migration* indicates voluntary displacement from one country to another, and does not refer to populations forcibly removed or transferred by treaty. *See also* OVERSEAS CHINESE (177); POPULATION EXCHANGE (180); WAR: REFUGEE (313).

Significance
Migration has advantages and disadvantages for both sending and receiving states. For the country of origin, the migration of its citizens relieves some social pressures, such as peasant poverty; emigrant remittances are economically helpful; and the departure of numbers of malcontents or national minorities aids political stability. The disadvantages of emigration involve the loss of the energies and potential skills of young and vigorous migrants, the economic loss of those already trained, and a loss of military power. For the receiving country, immigrants provide necessary skills and human power, fill up empty lands, and speed economic development. On the other hand, immigrants create problems of assimilation, cause increased pressure on job markets, and frequently complicate political relations between sending and receiving countries. Policies of unrestricted immigration generally ended after World War I, so migration is no more than a theoretical answer to the problems of overcrowding in some countries. Calculations on the basis of comparative population density indicate that countries such as Australia, Canada, Brazil,

Russia, and the United States have room for a large number of immigrants. Space, however, is not the problem. Although some immigration does take place, ethnocentrism, nationalism, fear of economic competition, and other psychological and social prejudices cause immigration policies to be highly selective. Nevertheless, migration is offered—along with birth control and expansion of food and other resources—as a potential means for reducing some of the pressures resulting from the population explosion. The end of the Cold War brought new waves of emigration from Eastern and Central Europe, much of it moving in the direction of unified Germany. As a consequence of unlimited flows, Germany took actions restricting the numbers entering the country. Similar problems troubled France as the North African community in that country began to swell, causing strain within French society. Conservative politicians used the issue of emigration to criticize the French government, and the shift to the right of a large segment of the French electorate was a direct outcome of these developments. Similar fears concerning unlimited emigration from neighboring overpopulated nations impacted the United States and encouraged Californians to support a ballot proposal (Proposition 187) that called upon the government to deny services to illegal emigrants, especially those streaming into the state from Mexico. Such fears also prompted the U.S. Congress to make legislation restricting entry into the United States of extended family members of immigrants already resident in the country. The U.S. government sent troops to Haiti in 1994, officially to restore an elected president to the office he had been forced to yield by the Haitian military, but no less important, to thwart the flow of Haitians wishing to resettle in the United States. The United States accepted hundreds of thousands of Cubans fleeing Communist Cuba, but in 1994 the Clinton administration tried to deny admission to yet another stream of Cuban refugees. By 1995, after quartering several thousand Cubans in the U.S. base at Guantánamo, the Clinton administration announced that those housed in the makeshift refugee camp would be taken in, but that future emigration would be handled according to immigration laws and procedures, not (as in the past) on the basis of a political condition.

Near Abroad States | 175 |

The former republics of the Soviet Union—Latvia, Estonia, Lithuania, Belarus, Ukraine, Moldova, Georgia, Armenia, Azerbaijan, Uzbekistan, Turkmenistan, Kazakhistan, Tajikistan, and Kyrgyzstan. The Russian use of the term *near abroad states* signals the importance of these states to the security of the Russian state. The phrase describes a Russian-dominated region that borders the Eurasian state and signals to the outside world that, while the Soviet Union has succumbed to the forces of history, Russian interests are constant, and Moscow's primary concern continues to be the protection of its strategic frontier.

Significance
The near abroad designation for Russia's immediate neighbors hints at Moscow's right to intervene in the internal affairs of those states if Russia's security is threatened from without. The term *near abroad* is judged a more palatable description than older geopolitical expressions such as sphere of interest or pan-region. Russian hegemony in the Eurasian landmass that includes these 14 republics is historic, and Moscow has indicated by its actions as well as its words that it intends to secure its extended borders by sustaining a near presence in the states of the former Soviet Union. The term also signals to any powers with an interest in rearranging political relationships following the demise of the USSR that the successor Russian Federation will not permit actions that seek to isolate it from its neighbors. The extension of Russian influence in the near abroad states is also meant to demonstrate the Russian claim that it remains a major actor in international affairs.

Oder-Neisse Line | 176 |

The *de facto* boundary established between East Germany and Poland at the end of World War II, and now the boundary between unified Germany and post-Communist Poland. The Oder-Neisse line is named for the two rivers that form the boundary from the Baltic Sea south to the border of Czechoslovakia. Following victory in World War II, representatives of the Allied Powers met at Potsdam in 1945 to consider, *inter alia,* a provisional German settlement and procedures for drawing up final peace treaties. They agreed that northern East Prussia was to be annexed "in principle" by the Soviet Union, and that, pending a final boundary determination, southern East Prussia and German territory east of the river line were to be "under the administration of the Polish State." The Allies also agreed to an "orderly and humane" transfer of resident ethnic Germans out of Poland, Czechoslovakia, and Hungary. The Oder-Neisse boundary line was recognized by both sides for the first time in the Helsinki Accord of 1975, by which the East and West accepted the post–World War II status quo in Europe. With the unification of Germany in 1990–1991, questions arose concerning the official border between Germany and Poland. The German government had hinted at redrawing the boundary, but when Poland indicated its distress, and both the Soviet Union and the United States insisted that the border was nonnegotiable, the Germans did not press the idea. In fact, Poland and Germany entered into an agreement reaffirming their frontier at the Oder-Neisse line, and the issue was officially but not enthusiastically laid to rest. *See also* ARMS CONTROL: HELSINKI ACCORD (359); BOUNDARIES (148).

Significance
The Oder-Neisse line will remain an issue in German-Polish relations because the demarcation line cuts across historical claims and nourishes national emotion. Central Europe and Eastern Europe have experienced so many politically-inspired

divisions and are so diverse and mixed in population that no plan can be designed that will satisfy everyone. Every national/ethnic group argues that its claim to territory is the correct one, and there are often too many unreconciled elements in every society to permit a rational approach to the dilemma. The German-Polish claim on territory is an important illustration of the larger problem. Historic enemies, Germany and Poland have seldom found common ground. The Cold War muted their differences for almost five decades because of the *de facto* division of Germany into the Federal Republic (West Germany) and the Democratic Republic (East Germany). German territory east of the Oder and Neisse Rivers was annexed by the Soviet Union and Poland, and approximately 10 million Germans were forced to emigrate to East Germany; ultimately, many fled to the Federal Republic. The Helsinki Accord reaffirming the boundary between East Germany and Poland may not have constituted binding international law, but it nevertheless reinforced the postwar arrangement. While the unification of the two Germanys was not believed possible even in the late 1980s, its sudden occurrence in the 1990s required immediate attention to the frontier question. The German government recognized that external opinion was decidedly opposed to any unilateral alteration of the Oder-Neisse line.

Overseas Chinese   177

People of Chinese ancestry and culture living outside the borders of mainland China and Formosa. Millions of overseas Chinese living in the countries of Southeast Asia represent a major problem of cultural assimilation.

Significance
The overseas Chinese are distinct among the minorities of Southeast Asia because of their numbers, their tendency to live in segregated communities, their economic drive, and their cultural and political ties to Beijing and Taipei. These qualities

often alienate them from local populations, threaten political stability, and hamper the process of nation building. Ethnic minorities are found in all the countries of the area, but the Chinese minority represents a special problem in Vietnam, Indonesia, Thailand, Burma, and Malaysia, where their rejection of assimilation and their economic strength make them a potent political force. Overseas Chinese are found in smaller numbers in the United States and Europe, where they have contributed to the growth and economic development of their adopted countries. With the improvement in relations with the United States, Communist China has allowed more of its citizens to travel abroad, and many have come to the United States, ostensibly for education, but often with the expectation that they will be allowed to remain in the country. Other Chinese have washed up on U.S. shores in less-than-seaworthy vessels, and have tried to enter the United States illegally in search of greater opportunity. Efforts by U.S. immigration authorities to return such emigrants to China have not been very successful, in major part because the majority of illegals escape notice and quickly melt into the established Chinese communities scattered throughout the country.

Ozone Layer   178

Concentrated region of the atmosphere that encloses the planet 9 to 30 miles above the earth. The purpose of the ozone layer is to shield the planet's living organisms from harmful ultraviolet radiation. Ozone gas is needed to screen out most of the sun's biologically damaging rays. *See also* GLOBAL COMMONS (168); GREENHOUSE EFFECT (170).

Significance
The ozone layer became an issue of international concern in the 1980s when atmospheric scientists noticed holes in the ozone layer, which they determined were caused by industrially produced chlorofluorocarbons (CFCs). A hole of alarming proportions was identified over

Antarctica. Fears were registered that the ozone hole was spreading and would eventually reach populated areas in the Southern Hemisphere. Similar concerns were raised over the development of ozone holes in the north polar region, which would cause a detrimental effect on life in the Northern Hemisphere. Damage to DNA cells and increased incidences of skin cancer were linked to the thinning of the ozone layer. No less significant, the food chain was judged to be under threat, given the fear that plankton and fish larvae floating near the ocean surface could be wiped out by unfiltered radiation from the sun. Still another dilemma was lower crop yields. With no individual state capable of addressing the problem, the issue demanded the cooperation of all nations. The first objective was the need to alter human behavior, particularly humanity's growing dependence on industrial and high-tech products. The United States, Canada, and the Scandinavian countries banned aerosol propellants that rely on CFC gases, and in 1987 delegates of 40 countries convened under the auspices of the UN Environmental Program to promote a treaty freezing the production of all CFCs at 1986 levels, and promising to cut production by 50 percent before the year 2000. The Earth Summit convened in Rio de Janeiro in 1992 addressed the problem of global warming, and an International Conference on Climate Change was held in Berlin in 1995 to review the consequences of climate change and the impact on the global ecosystem. Nevertheless, interest groups opposed to restrictions or limitations on development continued to lobby their respective governments, calling upon them to refrain from ratifying programs that would curtail their activities. Acknowledged to be a matter for each state's legislative process, the issue remains a subject of considerable debate in the more industrialized nations.

Population Control | 179 |

Adjustments in population size resulting from national policies and individual birth-control practices. Historically, government measures involve efforts to influence the quantity and quality of population by various techniques, including (1) encouraging or discouraging immigration and emigration, (2) fostering or discouraging large families, and (3) carrying out a policy of mass extermination, as in the case of Nazi Germany. The availability of improved contraceptive methods, especially in Western societies, has made family size increasingly a matter of individual choice. At the beginning of the twentieth century there were approximately 2 billion human beings on the planet. In 1995, with a global population approaching 6 billion, the world's birthrate continues to rise. Given greater opposition to birth-control practices in the developed as well as many of the developing countries, world population is projected to increase to more than 10 billion in the twenty-first century. One reason for the gain in world population is the increase in population growth in China as a result of the government's easing of restrictions on family size. China's 1.2-billion population in 1995 is expected to increase to 1.5 billion by 2025, but in all likelihood that figure is a low estimate. Perhaps more compelling is the demographers' belief that India, with a much higher birthrate than China's and far less control over the size of families, will surpass the population of China by 2025. By the third decade of the twenty-first century, even Pakistan will more than likely have a population greater than 250 million. The same forecast is given for Indonesia and Brazil, and Iran and Mexico are projected to have well in excess of 100 million early in the next century. *See also* DEMOGRAPHIC CYCLE (151); MALTHUSIANISM (173).

Significance
The problem of population control is particularly acute in the developing countries and transitional societies of the Third World in the second stage of the demographic cycle. Their societies are attempting to change from a preindustrial to an industrial orientation

while simultaneously experiencing a population explosion. Characteristics related to the size and condition of population include (1) death rates falling faster than birthrates, (2) a large number of young people, and (3) a relatively small workforce under pressure to produce rapid improvements in economic conditions. Governments in such countries are cross-pressured to preserve old values and foster new ones while population growth consumes the added increments of economic development. The sheer magnitude of the problem forced some traditionally hostile attitudes toward population control fostered by many of the world's religions to give way to policies and programs designed to reduce the birthrate. These included efforts to (1) eliminate illiteracy as a barrier to the communication of new values, (2) improve health and sanitation so that producing large families will not be needed to ensure the survival of some children, (3) emphasize the economic advantages of smaller families, and (4) provide information and resources to encourage widespread birth-control practices. Governments interested in developing birth-control programs received assistance from public and private sources in some developed countries, especially Sweden. Modern science also facilitated birth control by developing increasingly simple and effective methods involving oral contraceptives ("the pill") and economical intrauterine devices (the IUD). But the problem was complicated immeasurably by opposition to any form of birth control in countries such as the United States. U.S. population-control assistance to Third World nations was suspended during the Reagan administration. Moreover, the papal encyclical of 1995 continued to admonish those engaged in restricting births by artificial means.

Population Transfer

180

The peaceful, systematic two-way exchange of large groups of people between states. Population transfer is a possible solution when ethnic compatriots domi-

ciled in another state are placed in jeopardy, and the only recourse is their transference to territories where they can find asylum or refuge. Population transfers are substantial undertakings, usually involving tens of thousands of people, or even hundreds of thousands. Once the countries directly involved acknowledge the need to peaceably accept the secure and orderly movement of large numbers of people at risk, the population transfers are arranged in coordination with external parties and institutions. *See also* ODER-NEISSE LINE (176).

Significance
Population transfer is a diplomatic response to the problem of threatened minorities. It is distinguished from the haphazard, often chaotic flight of refugees from war zones or areas where people are no longer confident that their future can be managed in their places of birth. Population transfer attempts to avoid the chaos that stems from the disorganized displacement of people, usually as a consequence of war. It involves the sending state permitting the safe passage of minorities, and the accepting state admitting and resettling the population. Because population transfer is a two-way affair, both states send and receive population in a relatively orderly manner. The war in Bosnia in the 1990s gave substance to the issue of population transfer. The inability of Bosnian Serbs, Muslims, and Croats to share a common destiny pointed to the need to employ population transfer. The war in the former Yugoslavia that began in 1991 brought an end to the cosmopolitan character of the region and destroyed the capacity of the three groups to live freely among one another. The "ethnic cleansing" policy pursued by the Bosnian Serbs during the conflict forced the anarchic scattering of tens of thousands of refugees to other parts of Bosnia, the larger region, and the world. Although a painful exercise, population transfer regulates the safe passage of people, assists their resettlement, and ultimately helps reestablish their normal way of life.

Spratly Islands | 181 |

A remote island group in the South China Sea and a source of international conflict. Officially referred to as the Paracel and Spratly Islands, they represent a considerable number of essentially uninhabited archipelagic islets, atolls, and reefs in the South China Sea, lying within the 200-mile exclusive economic zone of the Philippines. In addition to the Philippines, the islands are also claimed by China, Vietnam, Malaysia, Taiwan, and, to some extent, Indonesia. The Spratlys have been an arena of conflict since the 1970s, when mineral deposits and especially petroleum were detected in their offshore waters. China and Vietnam clash periodically as both nations pursue aggressive claims. Malaysia and the Philippines, and, to some extent, Indonesia—all members of the Association of Southeast Asian Nations (ASEAN)—have elevated tensions among one another, and with China and Vietnam, over the disposition of the Spratlys, but the dispute has yet to yield to diplomatic negotiations.

Significance
The Spratly Island dispute has disrupted ASEAN efforts to engender greater cooperation among its members. More ominous is the ongoing feud between China and Vietnam, each of which has declared its intention to control the archipelago. International agreements calling for moderation and negotiation have been largely ignored by the parties, notably China, which dispatched a naval force to the South China Sea in February 1995 and proceeded to construct a symbolic base on Mischief Reef, one of the principal atolls in the chain. China's action was intended to establish that nation's claim to the Spratlys, but it was also a violation of the 1982 Law of the Sea Convention. The Spratly Island dispute, if not resolved by the parties involved, will continue to threaten the peace of the region and, more immediately, if violence between the states intensifies, the economic vitality of the region will be seriously affected.

Sustainable Development | 182 |

Economic growth that conserves global resources and avoids destruction of world ecosystems. The concept emerged from the United Nations Conference on Environmental Protection, convened in Rio de Janeiro in 1992, in which more heads of state and government participated than in any other conference in history. Sustainable development was the major theme of this conference, known as the Earth Summit, which saw economic progress as necessary and predetermined, but not to the degree that growth should ignore costs to the environment. The conference recognized that sustainable development applies to developed and developing states, advanced industrial regions, and those lagging behind in the Third World. The conference agreed to place limits on economic growth to protect the global environment as well as to husband the world's exhaustible resources. The conferees discussed the "carrying capacity" of the earth and the anticipated breakdown of the planetary ecosystem if unlimited and unrestricted development was not brought under control. Species depletion, global warming, and the exhaustion of irreplaceable resources were problems receiving attention. Those advocating sustainable development programs emphasized the need for "steady-state" economies that balanced population growth and needs with existing and accessible resources. The Earth Summit produced an overall plan known as Agenda 21, wherein Third World nations agreed to limit their industrialization to environmental needs, and the more industrialized states agreed to provide the necessary technological assistance to help them meet their goals and moderate the economic losses. Finally, the Earth Summit created the Sustainable Development Commission to monitor compliance with the pledges made at the conference. Comprised of 53 members, the commission allocated 19 seats from industrialized regions, 12 from Africa, 12 from Asia, and 10 from Latin America. *See also* EARTH SUMMIT (155).

Significance
Sustainable development centers attention on the fouling of the environment and the depletion of the earth's resources by unrestricted economic development. Sustainable development lies at the heart of the environmental problem, that is, too many people and too many nations consuming too much of the world's available resources without significant concern for the consequences. The Earth Summit at Rio placed the United States in the embarrassing position of appearing to oppose many of the limitations called for by the conferees. President Bush's presence demonstrated the conference's importance, but his reluctance to accept restrictions on U.S. economic growth raised the question of who among the world's nations would actually comply with the principles cited by the conferees. In the absence of an enforcement mechanism (the Sustainable Development Commission has no such authority), the course charted by the Earth Summit will be followed only if the participating states voluntarily and individually agree to the restrictions discussed at the meeting. Despite the cynicism reflected in the behavior, actions, and statements of the different sovereign states, sustainable development is a recognized necessity. A positive example of cooperation is the NATO Advanced Research Workshop, which examined sustainable development of the Lake Baikal region, a model project for working the concept.

Third World: Urban Crisis | 183 |

The movement of hundreds of millions of people in Latin America, Asia, and Africa from their rural habitat to the large cities and urban complexes. The urban crisis in the Third World is largely a product of exploding population growth, the inability of many to survive in the rural areas or to enjoy a minimal standard of living, and the dream of many to change their lives for the better by migrating to urban areas and finding employment. Although the urban centers are not in a position to absorb the great influx, they are incapable

of stopping it. The sudden population growth in Third World cities poses serious problems for urban governments, not only in unemployment but also in such areas as waste disposal, transportation, environmental protection, health, and supplying basic necessities such as water and food for millions. *See also* MIGRATION (174).

Significance
The slow but steady movement of rural peoples into urban centers over several centuries has become a mad rush for survival in some Third World countries. Whereas in 1987 only 29 cities in the world had populations of more than 5 million, demographic experts project 59 such cities by the year 2000. During this time span the number of people living in urban centers will increase by 77 percent (from 1.8 billion in 1987 to 3.2 billion in 2000), and an estimated 2 billion people will live in Third World cities by the latter date. In 2000, Mexico City is projected to be the largest urban area in the world, with a population of 31 million. While these estimates may prove to be too liberal or too conservative, the massive trek to the urban centers in Third World countries will likely continue at an unprecedented pace far into the future.

Visegrad States | 184 |

Poland, the Czech Republic, Slovakia, and Hungary. These four states are located between Germany and Russia and, from a security standpoint, are historically the more insecure of the European states. The Visegrad four have the closest working association with the 16-nation NATO organization, and were the first states to accept NATO's arrangement under the Partnership for Peace (PFP) in 1994. They have pledged to dedicate themselves to peaceful processes, democratic principles, human rights, and military reform and restructuring. Although officially outside both NATO and the European Union, the Visegrad four have established themselves in NATO headquarters and have been pledged assistance in the protection of their territorial integrity.

Significance

The Visegrad four were noticeably distressed by NATO's reluctance to grant them full membership in the alliance. Fearful of a resurgent Russian nationalism, they voiced their concerns in Washington and other NATO capitals. The Clinton administration, however, firmly believed that Russia's experiment with democracy would be seriously undermined if NATO established itself on Russia's borders. Nevertheless, the Visegrad four were poised for admission to the European Union, and sustained debate in the United States, notably within the U.S. Congress in 1995, called for the admission of the Visegrad states into NATO over the opposition of the president. The uncertainties caused by these public discussions slowed the Russian government's acceptance of the Partnership for Peace, which it had agreed to join a year before. In May 1995, however, Russian fears were apparently ameliorated, and Russia acknowledged its NATO association through the PFP. The Visegrad states, especially Poland, were quick to indicate their relief that Russia accepted close liaison with the Western alliance.

International Economics and Development

Asia-Pacific Economic Cooperation (APEC) | 185 |

The linking of nations on both sides of the Pacific Rim. The Asia-Pacific Economic Cooperation forum was launched in Australia in 1989 with 12 participants: the six members of ASEAN (Thailand, Malaysia, Singapore, Indonesia, Brunei, and the Philippines), and the United States, Canada, Japan, South Korea, Australia, and New Zealand. China, Hong Kong, and Taiwan joined in 1991, followed by Mexico and Papua New Guinea shortly thereafter, and Chile in 1994. The combined economies of the APEC nations represent more than half of the world gross domestic product (GDP) and approximately 40 percent of world trade. Moreover, some 65 percent of their exports are with one another, a figure significantly higher than the corresponding share for the European Union. The foundation for APEC's guiding principles was laid by the Pacific Economic Cooperation Conference (PECC), formed to engender cooperation and advanced thinking on a variety of economic issues. APEC covers similar ground; previously an intellectual exercise, it now seeks more practical avenues of interac-tion among some of the world's most dynamic trading nations. Because of its already great size, APEC struggles with the problem of its broadening and deepening experience. Expansion of membership beyond the current 18 states has been delayed as the group investigates its purposes and capabilities. APEC claims not to be a copy of the European Union, nor is it focused on becoming an expanded NAFTA (North American Free Trade Agreement). Rather, APEC's objective appears to be support for the GATT (General Agreement on Tariffs and Trade) agreements, and regional agreement on issues that cannot be solved in other organizations or through the use of other instruments. Essentially, APEC sees its role in limited perspective, that is, as a catalyst for new global trade negotiations promoting further liberalization. APEC contemplates a new model of regional cooperation that emphasizes "open regionalism." *See also* TRADE POLICY ORGANIZATION: GENERAL AGREEMENT ON TARIFFS AND TRADE (GATT) (268); TRADE POLICY ORGANIZATION: WORLD TRADE ORGANIZATION (WTO) (275).

Significance

Asia-Pacific Economic Cooperation is a forum for the exploration of ideas, not an organization concerned with the creation of a customs union or free-trade area. Its "open regionalism" strategy would avoid preferential treatment on a variety of issues, particularly in competition policy and new industrial standards. APEC can act in areas in which it possesses a monopoly, e.g., computer technology. In general, APEC strategy is to open its particular arrangements to nonmember countries that undertake corresponding obligations. Such approaches are to be found in GATT, and APEC is most responsive to that set of international agreements arrived at in 1994. But APEC also ensures that there will be no free rides by outsiders, including large trading entities like the European Union, that could disturb domestic conditions within the societies of APEC members. It is significant that the ASEAN Free Trade Area, which like NAFTA came into operation in January 1994, has limited benefits to member countries only and has not offered to extend them to outsiders. However, APEC has a positive purpose, and its success would counter the view that different civilizations are more likely to confront one another than to cooperate. APEC reminds the world that cooperation through multicultural experience is indeed possible.

Development | 186 |

The generally held process of improving the quality of life for all or at least a majority of human beings. Development centers attention on (1) raising the level of living standards from the bottom up by increasing employment, and therefore income and consumption levels of food, education, medical care, etc., and by encouraging and operationalizing economic growth processes available in given societies; (2) promoting a positive attitude about progress, that is, increasing confidence in the future by creating and successfully managing political, economic, and social systems and institu-

tions that promote community and the value and dignity of each person; and (3) expanding opportunities for growth by increasing people's freedom to access information and make rational choices.

Significance

Development is often equated with economic improvement, especially when attributed to national development in individual countries. Development tends to focus on increasing the capabilities of the state, not only in the construction of infrastructure—roads, bridges, airports, etc.—but also in the state's determination to assemble substantial military forces and complexes. This fascination with state power and state building often leads to the neglect of real development, the purpose of which is to enhance the lives of the citizenry. The heavy expenditures on armed forces by Third World countries, for example, drains scarce resources—capital, technical expertise, material, etc.—from the real goal of development—the psychological and physical well-being of all the people. As a consequence, political systems and institutions remain in an underdeveloped state and tend to cater to elite groups and to the military establishment, which in many African, Asian, and Latin American countries has become the political authority by coup and/or martial law. If scholars have learned anything about development, it is the fact that development is more than an economic phenomenon, more than gains in the growth of GDP and per capita income, and more than "trickle-down" policies and benefits.

Development: Agenda 21 | 187 |

The primary document discussed at the United Nations Conference on Environment and Development in June 1992. Agenda 21, an 800-page nonbinding blueprint, outlined the areas for international cooperation in promoting internationally sustainable growth and development in the twenty-first century. The agenda was adopted by consensus and emphasized the following six areas of international action: (1) allocating resources for poverty alleviation and environmental health, e.g., clean water and sanitation; (2) investments in research and extension services to reduce soil erosion; (3) the allocation of more resources to family planning, and assisting women in expanded education and job programs aimed at reducing population growth; (4) lending technical assistance to governments in poor countries with the goal of reducing environmental harm; (5) providing funds to protect natural habitats and biodiversity; and (6) investing in research and development on noncarbon energy alternatives with a view toward dealing with climate changes and the need to reduce greenhouse gases. *See also* EARTH SUMMIT (155); SUSTAINABLE DEVELOPMENT (182).

Significance
Agenda 21 emerged from the Rio Summit, or Earth Summit, of 1992. It focused on the worldwide environmental dilemmas but gave special attention to the role played by the less developed nations, whose traditional practices, lack of environmental awareness, and concerns with development complicate the problems challenging the global ecosystem. Global environmental concerns were heightened in the 1990s with the recognition that the gap between rich and poor nations was increasing, and that to prevent falling even farther behind the developed nations, the less developed were ignoring the negative impact their projects and operations had on their environment. Schemes developed by these poor nations to improve living standards were not only accelerating the degradation of the environment, but also driving their populations deeper into poverty. The focus of development thus required a shift from simple economic growth to one of sustainable development. If these key issues were not dramatically attacked on a global scale, Agenda 21 concluded, not only would the poor countries increase their suffering, but the developed world would also be impacted negatively. Agenda 21 thus represented a new ex-pression of global interdependence. The less developed countries exerted leverage on international economic and political decisions, and it was in the interest of all nations to work toward a cleaner, more livable world. Rich and poor nations alike were responsible for reducing the damage that each caused the earth's common heritage of land, water, and air, and all needed to link forces in confronting their common dilemma.

Development: Appropriate Technology | 188 |
Technology that is proper and adequate for existing conditions and factor endowments. Appropriate technology is also described as intermediate technology because it is concerned with the utilization of existing resources in more productive and efficient ways, but always in a manner that can be readily comprehended and adapted by the local population. Appropriate technology therefore employs a higher percentage of labor rather than machinery, especially where workers are abundant and capable, and machinery is expensive and the socioeconomic benefits questionable. Appropriate technology seeks to avoid factor-price distortions, or situations in which the factors of production are paid prices that do not reflect their true scarcity value.

Significance
In many less developed countries the prices paid for capital and intermediate-producer goods are artificially low because of special capital-depreciation allowances, tax rebates, investment subsidies, etc., while labor is paid a wage above its competitive value partly because of trade unions and political pressures. Factor-price distortions can lead to the use of inappropriate technology or techniques of production and its concomitant, the underutilization of available labor. The inappropriate use of technology also results in grandiose, eye-catching projects to the neglect of more fundamental programs that would elevate the general public's standard of living. For example, scarce funds are spent

on technologies requiring high energy use, e.g., nuclear reactors, when fossil fuel–burning stations would be more appropriate.

Development: "Big Push" Theory | 189 |

The theory stating that the only thing less developed countries require to accelerate their development, indeed to take off into a period of self-sustaining economic growth, is a massive investment program designed to promote rapid industrialization and the building of economic infrastructure. *See also* DEVELOPMENT: APPROPRIATE TECHNOLOGY (188).

Significance
Despite relatively impressive rates of industrial output, in many less developed countries growth has not occurred. In fact, industrial growth has done little to alleviate the problem of underemployment and unemployment in Third World countries. Experts studying the dilemma cite the increased productivity of the industrial sector as a key problem: A specified increase in national output is not generally accompanied by a similar increase in employment (fewer industrial workers are needed to produce a given level of total output). On the other hand, more employment means more income for the poor and lower-middle class, followed by a greater demand for locally produced basic consumption goods. The solution appears to be labor-intensive projects rather than those that cater to large-scale industry and limit employment possibilities. The general rule of thumb negating the "big push" theory is that more jobs and income lead to higher growth rates of both national output and aggregate employment, and concomitantly, to more politically stable societies.

Development: Brady Plan | 190 |

A plan to reduce the size of outstanding commercial debt burdening the less developed countries (LDCs). Named after U.S. Treasury Secretary Nicholas Brady, this 1989 plan centered on debt forgiveness procured in exchange for International Monetary Fund (IMF) and World Bank guarantees. These guarantees were in turn tied to assurances from the targeted countries that they would adhere to an IMF requirement to undertake fiscal, monetary, and international commercial reforms as a condition to receiving a loan for their balance-of-payment difficulties. This arrangement is also known as "conditionality." The announcement by the Bush administration in June 1990 of the Enterprise for the Americas Initiative was described as an extension of the Brady Plan. The initiative sought to forgive Latin American debts owed to the United States in return for economic reform, the stimulation of foreign investment, and more intensive action on environmental problems. *See also* DEVELOPMENT: THIRD WORLD DEBT CRISIS (196).

Significance
The Brady Plan enabled LDCs to make debt-for-equity swaps, but the problem with such arrangements was that they required private international banks to initiate or endorse the policies, and most were unwilling to take steps that would harm their short-run balance sheets. In the absence of unilateral debt repudiation by LDCs—a policy that would profit no one—most plans do not begin to solve the debt problem; they merely postpone the day of reckoning when the debts again come due, and cause further and perhaps more intense disruptions in the economic and political condition of Third World nations. Of course, the burden of debt consumes any progress made toward development, a case in point being the debt crisis in Mexico in 1995, with its broader implications for the global financial community. To acquire international financial assistance from the United States, Mexico was required to use as collateral its domestic real assets in the form of petroleum reserves. Moreover, critics of the 1990 Enterprise for the Americas Initiative were proved correct in their assessment of the policy—that it was

largely symbolic, and merely aimed at overcoming adverse Latin American reaction to Bush's 1989 Panama invasion.

Development: Capital $\boxed{191}$

A factor of production—along with land and labor—that is expressed in terms of money and producer goods. The application of capital to the expansion of productive capacities depends upon profits, the amount of profits saved, and the extent to which savings are channeled into investments in the form of capital goods. Advanced capitalist states encourage capital formation through security markets, extensive banking systems, and governmental fiscal and monetary policies. Communist state planning directs a large portion of national income into capital goods development. Sources of capital for underdeveloped states include local savings, private investment from abroad, trade, and foreign aid. Capital provides such essential elements in the economic equation as buildings, machines, tools, supplies, power, and transportation facilities.

Significance
The accumulation of capital is the key ingredient in promoting economic growth in advanced states and economic development in underdeveloped countries. Actual capital investment, however, depends on the size of the market and the demand for goods. Modern economic theories and practices provide for government to encourage transfers from savings into investments when the nation suffers from a dearth of capital or when economic stagnation threatens. In the underdeveloped world, capital accumulation through foreign trade (its major source) is seriously jeopardized by deteriorating terms of trade, protectionism in advanced states, and the development of synthetic substitutes to replace primary commodities. Private investment in underdeveloped states has failed to measure up to expectations because investors in advanced states fear expropriation and are attracted by vast opportunities for safe investment in industrialized countries. Moreover, most foreign-aid programs focus on technical assistance and infrastructure development, providing only meager amounts of capital. International institutions such as the World Bank Group and the African, Asian, and Inter-American Development Banks supply capital mainly on a "hard loan" basis.

Development: Economic Growth $\boxed{192}$

The increase in a nation's net national product. Economic growth rates may be measured on an absolute basis in contemporary currency values or may be adjusted to take into account population changes and inflationary or deflationary factors. Economists regard an annual growth rate of 5 percent as satisfactory for most nations. Some substantially exceed this rate, but most do not achieve it. Although many developing countries have been able to increase gross national income at a high rate, when the figure is adjusted for population growth the net per capita rate seldom exceeds 1 or 2 percent. Some have suffered per capita income losses despite gains in national income. *See also* ECONOMIC THEORY: GROSS NATIONAL PRODUCT (GNP) (225).

Significance
Competition among states—especially those having different economic, political, and social systems—is keen as each strives to achieve a higher rate of economic growth than its rivals. As a rule, poorer underdeveloped states can, in two senses, achieve higher percentages of annual increase than the more advanced: The poorer states have labor and resource surpluses and, since their base is much smaller, minor increments are reflected in high rates of increase. Both sides in the capitalist-Communist ideological struggle consistently claimed superiority for their system in promoting economic growth, but the repudiation of socialism/communism as a device promoting economic growth in the 1990s caused even those states remaining communistic to

proclaim the superiority of the capitalist market system over that of the Marxist command economy. Developing nations that adopted or considered adopting the Socialist model are also turning their economies in the direction of free competition and privatization. Today these techniques are considered more appropriate, and hence more likely to provide the needed economic stimulus. Finally, economic growth is a crucial element in the power equation because it provides the basic support for foreign and domestic programs.

Development: Infrastructure | 193

The economic, political, and social base to support a society's drive to achieve modernization. Infrastructure development involves institutional change to support a national effort to develop such facilities as roads, dams, power plants, and communication, irrigation, and transportation systems. Once the infrastructure base has been created, a nation's economy may—if capital for industrialization is available—move to the stage of self-sustaining economic growth.

Significance
Infrastructure development is an essential forerunner to industrialization and receives a high priority in the modernization plans of underdeveloped states. Foreign-aid programs of advanced Western states, including the United States, are based on the assumption that building an infrastructure foundation and developing technical skills in the underdeveloped states would result in the attraction of private investment capital to give impetus to the process of modernization. In many states, surplus labor in agriculture is taken off the land and organized to undertake construction projects requiring a mass effort in the absence of modern machines. Societies in states that have made progress in infrastructure development, but lack capital to utilize the base effectively, often suffer from a mass frustration that produces social unrest and political instability.

Development: Revolution of Rising Expectations | 194

A change in attitude—prevalent among millions in the poor nations of the world—from a fatalistic resignation and acceptance of poverty to an optimism that living conditions can be substantially improved. The revolution of rising expectations is engendered by improved communications, which have brought an awareness to underdeveloped societies that advanced nations have better living conditions, and a recognition that they too can improve life by altering the environment.

Significance
The revolution of rising expectations has helped to produce an increasingly dangerous "frustration gap" in the form of a gross disparity between expectations and achievements. Visible signs of economic development exist in most countries, leading to ever greater aspirations for improvement. Yet the population explosion tends to negate these advances and keep standards of living depressed. As the gap widens between the rich and poor societies of the world, nationalistic fervor, demands for self-determination, and violent changes of governments have come to typify the poorer states. During the Cold War, the Communists provided aid to help poor states develop, but simultaneously exploited their frustrations by promoting the overthrow of established governments. The West's policy was to offer economic aid to encourage progress while providing military assistance to governments in the poorer states to combat radical groups trying to achieve social change by violent means. Although a residual of Cold War aid-giving remains in the matter of sales and transfers of weapons, the demise of the Soviet Union caused developed countries such as the United States to reconsider its aid-giving program. Americans are less prone to offer assistance to developing countries confronting rising expectations. Rising expectations within Third World nations

are no longer framed by ideological rivalry between the First and Second Worlds. It is becoming more apparent that Third World nations have been left to find their own way through the thicket of rising expectations.

Development: Technology 195

The application of scientific knowledge and human skills to the solution of problems in the practical or industrial arts. The level of technology depends mainly on research and development—that is, the acquiring of new basic knowledge and its application to innovation. The process of modernization in the contemporary world involves the transfer of skills from technically advanced to underdeveloped societies. *See also* DEVELOPMENT STRATEGY: TECHNICAL ASSISTANCE (215).

Significance
Improved technology has produced revolutionary changes in military weaponry, industrial production, communication, transportation, and medicine. These changes have in turn produced such results as the danger of nuclear war, a revolution of rising expectations, a worldwide ideological-propaganda-economic conflict, and the threat of a massive population explosion. Technological advances are outstripping society's ability to adapt to or deal with the social consequences of progress. The level of technology used by a nation relative to that of other countries (especially potential enemies) is a major determinant in the evaluation of national power.

Development: Third World Debt Crisis 196

The critical condition of the international economy as a result of the huge Third World debt owed mainly to Western private banks and the inability of these countries to make installment payments. The world debt crisis involves overextended loans made by both private and public capital-supplying institutions, overextended debt accumulation by Third World countries and several former Communist states, and the failure of many debtor countries to make regular payments to loan agencies. Increasing numbers of defaults on debt payments during the latter part of the 1980s produced a growing crisis in the world financial markets. As a result of interest charges and new loans, by 1997 the size of the debt will have grown to more than $2 trillion. The debt crisis stems largely from the world oil crisis of the 1970s and early 1980s, massive inflation in many Third World countries, and the overwhelming desire of such countries to secure the capital needed to develop and modernize their economies. Major debtor countries are Argentina, Bolivia, Brazil, Chile, Colombia, Ecuador, Ivory Coast, Mexico, Morocco, Nigeria, Peru, and the Philippines, with Brazil and Mexico owing the largest amounts. *See also* DEVELOPMENT: CAPITAL (191).

Significance
The massive world debt has created a serious national and international crisis for lenders and borrowers alike. Payment defaults and the threat of defaults usually result in a rescheduling of the defaulting nation's debt payments, and new loans from the International Monetary Fund (IMF) and, more recently, the World Bank (IBRD) to provide the means for resuming payments. Typically, when such desperation loans are made, the recipient country must agree to changes in its national economy, including substantial reductions in government spending and general austerity for the entire population. Such conditions in countries with exploding populations and widespread poverty encourage protests, rioting, and rebellion. In the 1980s, IMF desperation loans were supplemented by loans from the IBRD, and this was repeated in the 1990s, notably in Mexico's debt crisis in 1995. Along with pledges of assistance from some of the leading financial countries, the United States in particular moved promptly to relieve the anxiety in international financial circles caused by the Mexican debt crisis. In general, major nations

attempted remedies that would expand the economies of debtor countries so they would be capable of making payments on their huge debts in the future. The creditor countries most directly involved in the debt crisis—the United States, Japan, Germany, France, Great Britain, and Canada, known as the Group of Six—cooperated in developing approaches and policies to avoid a general default. A worst-case scenario envisaged chaotic conditions in the world money market if payments on debts were stopped altogether, causing Western banks to fail and ushering in a worldwide depression.

Development: Unbalanced Growth 197

The argument made by some economists that the most effective means of generating and sustaining high levels of economic growth is to invest heavily in a single sector of the economy or a select zone of a developing country. In the first instance, it was a matter of choosing where to concentrate—the industrial sector or the agricultural. Some experts believed it better to emphasize housing and consumer sectors rather than industrialization or improved agriculture because the development of these areas would more likely provoke and increase mass demand for items produced in the other sectors. In the second part of the theory, an area of a particular country would be chosen in which to concentrate technical assistance, investment, and new construction. Albert Hirschman, author of *The Strategy of Economic Development* (1959) and a leader in the theory of unbalanced growth, argued that it made little difference which sector was stimulated because a concentration in one would impact the others, raising the level of overall economic output. Public investments in directly productive or social-overhead activities would lower costs, increase demand, and promote investment of private capital. Hirschman wrote that "unbalanced growth would generate and enlist resources and abilities for develop-

ment that had been previously hidden, scattered or badly utilized." Hirschman believed that growth was automatic at that point, and that economic policymakers could sit back and "watch the proceedings from the sidelines." *See also* DEVELOPMENT: "BIG PUSH" THEORY (189).

Significance
This overly optimistic approach to development was countered by other economists who insisted on the "big push" theory, which involved heavy doses of foreign aid in all sectors of the economy simultaneously. They felt that the unbalanced-growth theory would create a top-heavy situation in one sector or region at the expense of another sector or region. Balanced investment, in their view, would prove to be a better utilization of national resources, promote high employment, and eventually wean countries from their dependence on foreign aid. The problem with unbalanced-growth thinking, as with the "Big Push" enthusiasts, was that they did not address the question of mass poverty in developing countries. The approaches and strategies recommended by the experts simply widened the gap between the affluent and the impoverished. Social conditions for the many were neglected in the drive toward material economic improvement for (it turned out) the very few. As a consequence, political and administrative systems were confronted by organized demands for the alleviation of mass misery. The emergence of groups and movements, especially fundamentalist nongovernmental organizations antithetical to government and government policy, to champion the neglected sectors of society explains the present volatility of the less developed societies and the obstacles they face in promoting genuine political as well as economic development.

Development: Underdevelopment 198

A condition characterized by economic, social, and political backwardness measured by the standards of the advanced societies. Typical features of underdevelopment include (1) low national and per capita income and productivity; (2) high rates of illiteracy; (3) high birthrates with decreasing death rates, leading to a virtual "population explosion;" (4) a heavy dependence upon subsistence-level agriculture; (5) extensive use of child labor and few educational facilities and opportunities; (6) decentralized political institutions; (7) a rigid class structure with a minimum of social mobility; and (8) rudimentary communication and transportation facilities. *See also* DEVELOPMENT: ECONOMIC GROWTH (192).

Significance
Underdevelopment, the accepted way of life for millions of peoples over the centuries, is under attack within most such societies today. The process of modernization to overcome underdevelopment involves fundamental economic, social, and political changes to replace economic stagnation with self-sustaining economic growth. The failure of most states to make substantial headway has produced a dangerous "frustration gap" within societies no longer willing to accept their poverty as a normal and continuing state of affairs. Lack of savings and investment capital, the refusal to undertake basic economic and social changes, and the population surge are the main stumbling blocks to progress. Help to overcome underdevelopment has been offered by the advanced states and by various regional and global international organizations, but little progress—especially when measured on a per capita basis—has occurred.

Development Agency: International Bank for Reconstruction and Development (IBRD) | 199 |

A specialized agency of the United Nations established by the Bretton Woods Agreement of 1944 to help nations recover from World War II and to promote economic development in underdeveloped lands. The World Bank, as it is called, has more than 150 members. It is headed by a president and a board of governors, who meet annually to determine basic policies. Loan decisions are made by executive directors meeting monthly in Washington, D.C., the World Bank's headquarters. Decisions are made through a weighted voting system based on the amount of subscribed capital stock each director represents. The bank operates from a capital base estimated to be approximately $40 billion, with U.S. subscriptions totaling more than one-fifth. The capital stock represents both a guarantee fund to enable the bank to obtain working funds from private sources in world capital markets (90 percent) and a paid-up contribution to the loan fund by member governments (10 percent). In 1956 the International Finance Corporation (IFC) was established to help finance private investment, and in 1960 the International Development Association (IDA) became an affiliate, offering no-interest, long-term loans, These three public lending agencies function jointly as the World Bank Group. Most loans are made to member governments, but may be made to private firms if repayment is guaranteed by a member. Loans for major development projects are primarily made by consortiums in which various international and national lending agencies join with private banks to finance the projects. *See also* DEVELOPMENT: CAPITAL (191); UN SPECIALIZED AGENCY (605).

Significance
The World Bank's initial role in aiding the recovery of war-devastated areas was replaced in 1949 by a new focus on lending to foster economic development. By 1992 the total amount of loans made by the World Bank exceeded $200 billion, spread over more than 3,000 projects. The volume of lending has increased steadily since 1946, and currently exceeds $20 billion annually. Terms of the loans have varied, with interest rates running close to those in private capital markets and with payment periods ranging from 10 to 35 years. Loans have been granted for such projects as irrigation, mining, agriculture, transport and communications, and

general industrial development. The bank has also undertaken a broad infra-structure-development and technical-assistance program to help prepare the ground for useful loans and to help recipients make effective use of the loans once granted. Although the bank has progressively increased the pace of its lending operations, it is severely limited in its ability to supply the capital needs of developing states. The main drawback is the inability of many prospective developing-state clients to finance repayment of loans in hard currency because their debt-servicing capacities are already overly strained. Nevertheless, new loans have been made that relate mainly to the role played by the World Bank and the International Monetary Fund (IMF) to alleviate the Third World debt crisis. Conditions for the loans included the requirements that major debtors change their state-managed economies through market-oriented economic reforms and that they pursue drastic austerity programs.

Development Agency: International Development Association (IDA) | 200 |

An affiliate of the World Bank established in 1960 as a specialized agency of the United Nations to grant members "soft loans" to promote economic development. Between 1960 and 1993 the IDA committed approximately $70 billion for projects in the world's 55 least developed countries. Although IDA is a separate institution, its management and staff are the same as those of the World Bank (IBRD). Working funds are obtained from contributions made by capital-surplus states and from loans made to IDA by the IBRD. Soft-loan features of IDA include the low cost of a loan (no interest, but a small annual service charge), a long repayment period (50 years), and a slow amortization rate (10-year grace period, then 1 percent of the loan repayable annually for the next 10 years, and 3 percent repayable annually for the next 30 years). *See also* UN SPECIALIZED AGENCY (605).

Significance
The International Development Association was set up as a result of criticism of the World Bank's conservative lending policies and because of growing U.S. apprehension over the Soviet Union's aid-trade offensive of the late 1950s. The idea of a soft-loan affiliate of the World Bank was first discussed in the U.S. Congress, emphasizing the key role of the United States in its creation. Support for IDA comes mainly from recipient countries, which regard it as the next best thing to capital grants from the United Nations. Whether aid-receiving countries will be able to pay off IDA loans on schedule once the ten-year grace period expires depends on their progress in economic development and their ability to earn foreign exchange.

Development Agency: International Finance Corporation (IFC) | 201 |

A specialized agency of the United Nations established in 1956. The IFC supplements the role of the World Bank (IBRD) in stimulating economic development by making loans to and direct investments in private companies in developing countries. The IFC's members have subscribed to capital stock in the corporation at the same ratio as their capital investments in the IBRD. Working funds are secured from the sale of securities in world capital markets and from loans made to the IFC by the World Bank. *See also* UN SPECIALIZED AGENCY (605).

Significance
The International Finance Corporation has made commitments totaling billions of dollars to many developing countries. However, given the magnitude of the problem of economic development, the IFC has barely scratched the surface of world capital needs. Critics charge that the agency has never gained acceptance among either donor or recipient states, as evidenced by its modest funding and lending activities. Its objective of encouraging the private sector of the economy in

developing states by meshing capital from both private and public sources has failed to overcome the basic incompatibilities inherent in such a mixture.

Development Agency: Multinational Corporations | 202 |

Businesses that have a home base in one country and carry on operations through subsidiaries in other countries. Also known as transnational corporations, multinational corporations typically expand their operations to take advantage of economies of scale (i.e., reductions in the average costs of products as a result of growth and an increased level of output). In some cases, multinationals enjoy oligopoly or near-monopoly conditions in the marketplace. *See also* DEVELOPMENT: ECONOMIC GROWTH (192); IMPERIALISM, ECONOMIC (55).

Significance
Multinational corporations operate under advantageous conditions in the Third World because of the stronger demand for industrial goods over primary commodities and because of the price-fixing and market-controlling abilities of many giant business operations. In attempting to cope with the growing role of multinationals, since 1976 Third World countries have pushed in the United Nations for International Codes of Conduct for Transnational Corporations. The need for such codes was dramatized in 1984 when nearly 2,000 people were killed in Bhopal, India, as a result of a gas leak at a plant owned by the U.S. firm Union Carbide. Matters provided for in the codes include general behavior of multinationals, worker safety, ownership and control, taxation, transfer pricing, and the impact of the multinational's operations on the host country's balance of payments. Although Western nations participated in the drafting of such codes, they remain cool toward the idea of limiting multinational operations in a global economy. Multinationals have often been criticized because of their involvement in the political affairs of Third World nations. In ex-

treme cases, some have been instrumental in overthrowing unsympathetic or left-leaning regimes or in lending strong support to a friendly government.

Development Agency: Regional Banks | 203 |

Public lending institutions created by governments to foster regional and subregional economic development. Regional development banks have been established in Europe, Latin America, Africa, and Asia. The European Investment Bank, formed in 1958, is an institution of the industrially developed states of the European Economic Community (EEC). Its headquarters are located in Luxembourg, and it received an initial capitalization of $1 billion. The membership of the Inter-American Development Bank, operational in 1960, is composed of 21 Western Hemisphere republics. Headquartered in Washington, D.C., the bank was authorized capitalization of $3.15 billion. The African Development Bank, organized in 1965 with headquarters in Abidjan, Ivory Coast, has a membership that includes most African countries and an authorized capital of $250 million. To supplement meager capital allotments from its African members, an African Development Fund was created in 1972 to encourage capital contributions from capital-surplus states outside the region. The Asian Development Bank was organized in 1967, with headquarters at Manila, and had an initial capitalization of $1.1 billion. In addition to its Asian and Pacific regional participants, the bank's members include the United States, Great Britain, West Germany, Belgium, the Netherlands, Italy, and Switzerland. *See also* DEVELOPMENT: CAPITAL (191).

Significance
The establishment of regional development banks resulted from the dimensions of the problem of economic development, which necessitated pooling of scarce capital resources. Most bilateral and multilateral aid programs focus on technical

assistance and infrastructure development, with little provided to support industrialization. The primary function of the regional banks is to fill this need. Membership in the regional banks follows no set pattern. The European Bank is composed exclusively of industrially advanced states, the African bank was organized by the underdeveloped countries of that continent exclusively, the Inter-American bank has only one highly industrialized member (the United States), and participation in the Asian bank is divided between developed and less developed countries. Capital is supplied to the regional development banks by governments and through the proceeds of the public sales of bonds. The banks are part of the worldwide movement to attack economic problems through the establishment of functional international organizations. Their effectiveness in contributing to modernization and nation building in the less developed countries will continue to be tested into the twenty-first century.

Development Agency: United Nations Conference on Trade and Development (UNCTAD) | 204 |

An organ of the UN General Assembly established to develop world trade policies. UNCTAD began in 1964 as a special trade conference attended by 122 states in Geneva, and was given permanent status by the General Assembly that same year. The underdeveloped states of the world pushed for its creation as a forum where they could apply pressures on the advanced industrial states to lower their trade barriers to permit expanded trade in primary commodities. Their main objective is to increase foreign-exchange earnings to support development programs. With a current membership that spans the planet, UNCTAD is convened in plenary session every three or four years to serve as a center for harmonizing trade and development policies. A Trade and Development Board initiates policy proposals between UNCTAD sessions,

and a secretariat is located at UNCTAD's Geneva headquarters. *See also* DEVELOPMENT STRATEGY: NEW INTERNATIONAL ECONOMIC ORDER (NIEO) (212).

Significance
The United Nations Conference on Trade and Development represents a political victory, but not necessarily an economic one, for the underdeveloped states in their efforts to secure capital through increased trade. The industrial states that resisted UNCTAD's creation as a duplication of the role of the General Agreement on Tariffs and Trade (GATT) were consistently outmaneuvered at the initial session in 1964 by the underdeveloped bloc's "caucus of the seventy-seven." Economic gains, however, will depend on whether the advanced states will agree to UNCTAD's objectives of stabilizing commodity prices and extending most-favored-nation treatment to the underdeveloped states without reciprocity. In recent years the Third World has carried on a vigorous campaign at UNCTAD meetings to establish a New International Economic Order (NIEO) involving a redistribution of the world's wealth.

Development Agency: United Nations Industrial Development Organization (UNIDO) | 205 |

An agency established by the UN General Assembly "to promote industrial development . . . and accelerate the industrialization of the developing countries, with particular emphasis on the manufacturing sector." UNIDO began its operations as an "autonomous" organization within the United Nations in 1967. Its responsibilities include intensifying, coordinating, and expediting the efforts of the United Nations in the field of industrial development. An Industrial Development Board, elected by the General Assembly, functions as UNIDO's principal organ, developing principles and policies to guide its program. The board also supervises activities, creates subsidiary organs when needed, and reports annually to the General Assembly. A secretariat functions at UNIDO's headquarters in Vienna.

Significance

The establishment of the United Nations Industrial Development Organization resulted from the emphasis developing states place on industrialization and their voting power in the General Assembly. This emphasis on industrialization as the best route to modernization is not always shared by the industrialized states, which fear low-cost competition and the loss of markets and investment opportunities. African, Asian, and Latin American states also hold a majority of the seats on the Industrial Development Board, which enables them to apply continual pressures on the advanced-state members to offer greater help to achieve industrialization. UNIDO has sponsored an international symposium on industrial development and conducts a Special Industrial Services (SIS) program to provide practical industrial/technical assistance to members that request help. Examples of projects aided by UNIDO include a steel-rolling plant in Jordan, textile manufacturing in the Sudan, and the production of raw materials from sugarcane wastes in Trinidad.

Development Agency: United Nations Institute for Training and Research (UNITAR) | 206

An autonomous agency established by the UN General Assembly in 1963 to train individuals for work in economic and social development, and particularly for technical-assistance programs. UNITAR programs include: granting fellowships to enable individuals from developing countries to upgrade their skills for national or international services, providing experts to teach special courses at colleges and universities in these states, and conducting research on subjects related to economic development. Its governing body consists of a Board of Trustees, who serve as individuals rather than as representatives of states. Trustees are appointed by the secretary-general in consultation with the presidents of the General Assembly and the Economic and Social Council.

Significance

The United Nations Institute for Training and Research attempts to serve as a bridge between the United Nations and the international academic community. One of UNITAR's unique programs involves special training for young people from Asia, Africa, and Latin America in preparation for careers as foreign-service officers or secretariat officials. The voluntary participation of eminent scholars and statesmen as lecturers sponsored by UNITAR has aided the development of diverse academic programs in several countries. Research projects include studies on strengthening the United Nations' capabilities and procedures, development and modernization, and communication and information.

Development Strategy: Colombo Plan | 207

A regional economic-aid program providing multilateral consultative machinery to encourage and coordinate bilateral assistance programs among its members. The Colombo Plan was established in 1950 at a Commonwealth Conference at Colombo, Ceylon. Initially it provided for a $5 billion, six-year development program, with capital furnished equally by developed and developing states. Over 25 states have participated in the program, including Commonwealth countries (Australia, Canada, Ceylon, Great Britain, India, Malaysia, New Zealand, Pakistan, and Singapore), other Asian countries and protectorates (Bhutan, British Borneo, Burma, Cambodia, Indonesia, Japan, South Korea, Laos, Nepal, the Philippines, South Vietnam, and Thailand), and the United States. A Consultative Committee for Economic Development in South and Southeast Asia, with all participating states represented, meets annually to review old programs, plan new ones, and discuss the problems of economic development. A Council for

Technical Cooperation functions as a secretariat at the Colombo headquarters to facilitate the exchange of technical experts among members. *See also* DEVELOPMENT STRATEGY: FOREIGN AID (210); REGIONAL POLITICAL GROUP: COMMONWEALTH OF NATIONS (562).

Significance
Although started as a Commonwealth program, the Colombo Plan now includes the United States as a major aid-giver and most of non-Communist Asia as aid recipients. Because the administration of all aid programs is bilateral, each donor state retains full control over the size and nature of its contributions. The Consultative Committee also serves as a forum, however, in which a developing state can present its case for larger or more appropriate projects. Since 1950 more than $25 billion in loans and grants has been supplied to Asian nations for developmental purposes, and many thousands of people have received technical training.

Development Strategy: Dependency Theory | 208

An economic and political explanation of the historical and contemporary processes that have contributed to Third World underdevelopment and political conflict. The dependency theory focuses on the many years of imperial/colonial relationships between the industrialized countries of Western Europe, Japan, and the United States and the areas of Africa, Asia, and Latin America that were subjected to their dominance. Dependency theory has received many contributions from Latin American scholars such as Fernando Henrique Cardoso, Theotonio dos Santos, and Ruy M. Marini, who have tried to explain the contemporary dependent relationship of Latin states to the industrial capitalistic states of the West, particularly the United States. Other scholars—Samir Amin, Clive Thomas, and Walter Rodney, for example—have examined dependency in other areas of the world. In their view, the world trading system tends to keep most developing states in a condition of economic and political bondage, resulting in a neoimperial and neocolonial relationship between rich and poor countries. *See also* DEVELOPMENT: UNDERDEVELOPMENT (198); DEVELOPMENT AGENCY: MULTINATIONAL CORPORATIONS (202); THIRD WORLD (27).

Significance
Scholars and others use dependency theory mainly to explain the lack of substantial developmental progress in Third World countries. In the view of dependency theorists, the economic life of such countries is dominated through exploitation by powerful capitalist states from outside the Third World. Accurate or not, the theory has gained the support of many scholars and Third World leaders, who regard it as the main reason for the failure of so many African, Asian, and Latin American states to make substantial economic progress. Also, they believe that giant multinational corporations control many of the Third World economies and lend political support to local elites. The inflow of foreign capital produces industrial enclaves in many developing states, yet the rest of the country often exists in conditions of dire poverty. For many supporters of dependency theory, neoimperialism and neocolonialism must be destroyed and replaced with a new international economic order that ends the dependent status of Third World states.

Development Strategy: False Paradigm Model | 209

The scholarly proposition that Third World countries have failed in their development schemes because their development strategies were formed from erroneous data and nonapplicable models of development. The False Paradigm Model addresses the failure of development programs, especially those prepared and imposed on the less developed countries by outsiders (foreign experts who did not understand the social complexities or conditions prevailing within these states). The argument is validated by the instability of political institutions in the developing countries, as well as the unbalanced growth generated by models of development catering to the advantaged members of society at the expense of the disadvantaged. *See also* DEVELOPMENT (186).

Significance

On one side, the False Paradigm Model is an accurate depiction of the failure of those developmental models generated in the Western world and utilized in the less developed world. On the other side, however, the criticism leveled against international development experts obscures the roles played by the development actors within the Third World nations. These indigenous "experts" also bear responsibility for the failure of developmental schemes. Indeed, if the foreign model stressed capital accumulation and neglected social and psychological needs, it was the on-the-scene expert who pressed the program, believing that the benefits accrued by the state would also, in time, improve the well-being of the general public. Both sets of experts, foreign and domestic, failed or neglected to take into account the social needs and the social condition prevailing within the particular society. In their concerted effort to elevate the role of the state, they planted the seeds for sustained unrest, and hence continuing underdevelopment.

Development Strategy: Foreign Aid · 210

Economic, social, or military assistance rendered to a country by another government or international institution. Foreign aid is offered bilaterally, by regional organizations, and by global agencies under the United Nations system. Economic aid includes categories such as technical assistance, capital grants, development loans, surplus food disposal, public guarantees for private investments, and trade credits. Military aid involves transfers of military hardware, advisory groups, defense support (e.g., paying for civilian projects to make up for funds the aid-receiving country spent on its own defense), and payments to support friendly military establishments. Objectives of foreign aid include supporting allies, rebuilding war-shattered economies, promoting economic development, gaining ideological support, obtaining strategic materials, and rescuing nations from economic collapse or natural disaster. Bilateral programs of major economic and military aid are carried on by the United States, Russia, Communist China, France, Germany, Japan, the Scandinavian countries, and Great Britain. Regional programs of economic aid include those carried on through the Alliance for Progress, the Colombo Plan, the European Development Fund of the EEC, the Organization for Economic Cooperation and Development (OECD), and by the African, Asian, and Inter-American Development Banks. Global programs carried on under UN auspices include the United Nations Development Program, the International Monetary Fund (IMF), the World Bank Group (IBRD, IFC, and IDA) and other specialized agencies, the United Nations Conference on Trade and Development (UNCTAD), and special autonomous bodies such as the United Nations Industrial Development Organization and the United Nations Institute for Training and Research. (*For specific institutions and programs, see* Index.)

Significance

The first large-scale foreign-aid program was that of U.S. aid to its allies during and following World War I; more than $14 billion in principal and interest remains unpaid. During World War II, the Allies used a Lend-Lease program that provided for mutual military and economic aid. The postwar period saw the development of several U.S. aid programs including the Marshall Plan to foster the rebuilding of Western Europe, the Truman Doctrine to provide military and economic assistance to states threatened by Communist aggression, and the Mutual Security Program to strengthen the defenses of the North Atlantic Treaty Organization (NATO) in Western Europe.

U.S. aid to underdeveloped countries started with the Point IV program of technical assistance in 1949 and was expanded to include development grants and loans and military aid during the 1950s and 1960s. Other industrialized countries of Western and Eastern Europe and Japan inaugurated major aid programs to the developing states in the 1960s. All aid-giving nations utilize bilateral, regional, and global channels, although key decisions concerning most economic and military assistance are made unilaterally by the donor country. Most donor countries prefer to give technical-assistance and infrastructure-development aid because they believe that the capital for industrial development should come from private sources, typically multinational corporations. Recipient countries, however, are most earnest in their quest for capital aid in the form of grants or low-interest, long-term loans because they want to maintain control over their development programs and their nation's economic future. Financing for specific capital-development projects by Western nations usually takes the form of loans supplied by the World Bank Group or by the African, Asian, or Inter-American Development Banks. Grantors of bilateral aid make their decisions mainly on the basis of political and security factors rather than recipient country needs. In the 1980s and 1990s, for example, much U.S. aid went to a few key countries, such as Israel and Egypt, with the remainder distributed among almost 100 developing countries.

Development Strategy: Group of Seventy-Seven (G-77)

211

A Third World caucusing group active mainly in dealing with economic issues in the UN General Assembly and at international conferences. G-77 began to function in global decision-making processes in 1964 at the first United Nations Conference on Trade and Development (UNCTAD) with its original 77 members from Asia, Africa, and Latin America. In the 1990s, G-77 included the vast majority of Third World nations, including representatives from North and South Korea, Tonga, and the Palestine Liberation Organization (PLO), although none of the latter four is a member of the United Nations. The major focus of G-77 is to develop a common approach to global economic and trade problems. Another large caucusing group, the Non-Aligned Movement (NAM), supplemented the efforts of G-77 by focusing attention on anticolonialism, human rights, and regional issues, but its relevance in the aftermath of the Cold War is a matter of conjecture. *See also* DEVELOPMENT AGENCY: UNITED NATIONS CONFERENCE ON TRADE AND DEVELOPMENT (UNCTAD) (204); THIRD WORLD (27).

Significance
The Group of Seventy-Seven has played a major role in promoting the interests of developing countries and in pressuring the industrialized countries to provide foreign aid, technical cooperation, and better trade conditions, as well as other matters of interest to the Third World bloc. Voting victories, however, have not always been followed by tangible advances in the conditions that relate to trade or to development and modernization. Therefore, the Third World nations increasingly attempt to negotiate consensus decisions with the industrialized states. G-77 has proved ineffectual in some issue areas because of conflicting interests of its members. In the negotiation of the Law of the Sea Treaty, for example, the Third World broke up into rival coalitions because of conflicting positions resulting from the fact that some are coastal states or islands whereas others are landlocked, and some are exporters and others importers of minerals found in the ocean seabed. In general, however, G-77 functions on many issues as an unofficial but very effective decision-making body in the General Assembly.

Development Strategy: New International Economic Order (NIEO) | 212 |

A major campaign fought mainly in the UN General Assembly and the United Nations Conference on Trade and Development (UNCTAD) by the less developed countries (LDCs) to liquidate the existing world economy and replace it with a new system more favorable to the interests of the poor countries. NIEO was first proclaimed at the Sixth Special Session of the General Assembly in 1974 when that body adopted a Declaration on the Establishment of a New International Economic Order. Later that same year, the General Assembly followed up its proclamation with approval of the Charter of Economic Rights and Duties of States, which spelled out in detail the principles and practices needed to implement NIEO. Operating politically through its Group of Seventy-Seven (G-77), the NIEO issue produced a confrontation between the relatively rich industrialized countries of the First World and the numerous but largely poor and less developed countries of Africa, Asia, and Latin America. *See also* DEVELOPMENT AGENCY: UNITED NATIONS CONFERENCE ON TRADE AND DEVELOPMENT (UNCTAD) (204); THIRD WORLD (27).

Significance

The drive to establish a New International Economic Order is in effect a demand by the developing countries that the international economic system be restructured and the world's wealth be redistributed. From the perspective of the Third World, the international economy is rigged against the poorer, developing countries, thus frustrating their desperate efforts to develop and modernize. They believe that prices for their primary commodities and other products have been kept artificially low in world trade channels for many years as a result of colonialism and neocolonialism. NIEO is one more political effort by the LDCs to achieve economic goals, and the drive appears to have been another failure. Previous efforts to obtain the capital needed for development include the Special United Nations Fund for Economic Development (SUNFED) proposal, the United Nations Capital Development Fund (UNCDF), the United Nations Conference on Trade and Development (UNCTAD), the creation of the International Development Association (IDA), and efforts to use the International Monetary Fund (IMF) and World Bank to promote developmental goals. In their efforts to finance development, the LDCs have demanded increased foreign aid from rich to poor nations, transfers of technology, a greater share of decision-making power in global economic institutions (such as the World Bank and the IMF), higher and more stable prices for raw materials, and improved access to markets in the developed countries. The mission to sell the rich countries on the idea of creating a New International Economic Order took on the aspects of a holy crusade. But the developed countries, led by the United States, have either rejected specific proposals or permitted them to remain in limbo, a natural development because the existing economic order obviously benefits the industrialized countries. One of the by-products of Third World efforts from the 1970s into the 1990s was the creation of a new order in the global economy that included a large role for the United Nations as a central meetinghouse where major economic issues could be discussed and debated. Some LDCs, frustrated by their unsuccessful efforts to change the global economy, have begun to seek economic improvement by following the lead of the Organization of Petroleum Exporting Countries (OPEC) and its cartel policies as a more appropriate means for coping with the economic strength of the First World.

Development Strategy: Privatization | 213 |

The control of the means of production by private corporations and business. In contemporary conditions, privatization emphasizes decisions by governments to sell off their public assets or corporations to private business groups and interests. During the Great Depression of the 1930s and following World War II, non-Marxist governments assumed greater responsibility in managing the economy, and in some ways replaced private-sector activity or assumed those activities in which the private sector would not engage because they did not promise a profit. In the developing nations gaining independence following World War II, governments developed public corporations to serve a broad line of activities from the construction and management of power plants, to the development of textile industries and steel mills, to running agro-business complexes. These public ventures proved to be more costly and less efficient than similar private operations; hence the decisions in recent years to sell public facilities to private entrepreneurs, who were expected to produce better products more cheaply.

Significance
Western governments such as the United States developed public corporations to serve the needs of the public where private organizations were hesitant or disinterested. The development of the Public Broadcasting System (PBS) in the United States in 1970 was an effort by government to provide the public with radio and television programs that were not considered commercially viable by private broadcasting systems. In 1995, however, a majority in the U.S. Congress argued that PBS should not be funded from public revenues and ought therefore to be privatized. More significantly, the disappearance of the Soviet Union, and the repudiation of Marxist models of economic decision making in Central and Eastern Europe, as well as in Russia, shifted the spotlight away from public management of the economy to private-sector free-enterprise activity. The perception that the private sector was more efficient, more cost-conscious, and more productive and inventive drove the decisions to transfer public holdings to private hands. Moreover, nations seeking

U.S. aid found that they would be better served if they demonstrated their own shift toward the private sector and away from anything that resembled the command economy of the Socialist world.

Development Strategy: Stages of Growth Model of Development | 214 |

A 1960s theory of development associated with economic historian Walt W. Rostow, author of *The Stages of Growth: A Non-Communist Manifesto* (1960). Rostow argued that development would be achieved in the course of five phases or stages of growth, each necessary to the one following. These stages are: (1) the stagnant or traditional low per capita stage; (2) a transitional stage in which the necessary preconditions for growth are created; (3) the takeoff stage, signifying the beginning of economic development; (4) the stage in which experience, industry, and achievement develop positive payoffs, the drive to maturity; and (5) the development stage, the realization of goals, industrialization, mass production, and high consumption. *See also* DEVELOPMENT STRATEGY: FALSE PARADIGM MODEL (209).

Significance
The thesis on stages of growth described by Rostow was very popular in the 1960s and early 1970s, but lost support in the later 1970s and into the 1980s. By the 1990s few scholars or developmental practitioners found utility in the formulation. Too simplistic a formula, too much a reflection of the American scene, too heavily influenced by Western culture and development, Rostow's approach to development, when applied in the Third World, simply did not generate the anticipated results. The thesis proved to be too general and too abstract for the complexities associated with individual Third World nations. His theory did not take into account cultural circumstances or historic conditions at variance with his own experience, nor did it examine the agents of change in the less developed countries who would be called upon to operationalize the program's stages. Linked with the notion of

"people's capitalism," the stages of growth said more about Third World fears of neocolonialism than how to achieve material benefits for impoverished societies. Nevertheless, the Rostow formula influenced U.S. thinking, and to some extent policy, especially in Vietnam in the 1960s. The belief that capitalism was the popular choice over socialism was an underlying feature of U.S. involvement in Vietnam. Moreover, from scholarly criticism of the stages-of-growth model emerged a shift to structural-change theory. This theory acknowledges the difficulties Third World countries have in fully utilizing their resources, and the obstacles they encounter from institutional factors that have their origins in often contradictory domestic and international situations.

Development Strategy: Technical Assistance | 215 |

The teaching of new technological skills. Technical-assistance programs of foreign aid are offered by the advanced states to the underdeveloped states to help them progress toward the goal of modernization. Technical assistance includes the transference of skills ranging from the most rudimentary to the highly complex—from teaching simple farming skills to the operation and maintenance of a modern industrial plant. Technical-assistance programs seek to develop industrial, managerial, educational, public health, agricultural, mining, and administrative skills. *See also* DEVELOPMENT: TECHNOLOGY (195); DEVELOPMENT AGENCY: UNITED NATIONS INSTITUTE FOR TRAINING AND RESEARCH (UNITAR) (206).

Significance
The transference of technical skills to the peoples of the underdeveloped areas of the world was begun on a small scale during the era of colonialism by missionaries, colonial business enterprises, and philanthropic organizations. Since World War II, major programs have been carried out through bilateral aid, regional organizations, and the United Nations. UN technical assistance has been offered mainly through its Expanded Program of Technical Assis-

tance (EPTA) and its Special Fund. These two programs were combined into the United Nations Development Program (UNDP) in 1965 to provide a unified approach to the granting of technical assistance. Regional programs that offer substantial training in modern skills include the Alliance for Progress, the Colombo Plan, the European Development Fund of the European Economic Community, and the Organization for Economic Cooperation and Development (OECD). Western states generally emphasize technical assistance in their foreign-aid programs rather than capital grants, with the expectation that the acquiring of skills and their application to infrastructure development would attract private investment from the capital-surplus states to give impetus to the developmental process.

Economic Integration: Customs Union | 216 |

An agreement among states that provides for free trade among members and for a common external tariff on imports from outside the union. A customs union arrangement usually provides for the central collection of import duties and their division among the members of the union according to a formula. The common external tariff rates are typically based on an average of preunion rates. *See also* REGIONAL ECONOMIC GROUP: BENELUX (549); REGIONAL POLITICAL GROUP: EUROPEAN COMMUNITY (EC) (565); REGIONAL POLITICAL GROUP: EUROPEAN UNION (EU) (566).

Significance
A customs union encourages an expansion of trade among its members through the elimination of barriers to trade, specialization in production, and creation of a favorable climate of public opinion supporting intraunion trade. Progress toward further economic unity, involving free movement of capital and labor and the establishment of common fiscal and monetary policies, may be encouraged by the customs union. A customs union may also be a forerunner of political union, as

in the cases of Germany and Austria-Hungary in the nineteenth century. The Benelux Customs Union (Belgium, the Netherlands, and Luxembourg) and the European Economic Community, now the European Union, have functioned as economic unions since 1948 and 1958, respectively. Many nations have also established customs unions with their dependent territories, as, for example, in the U.S. arrangement with Puerto Rico.

Economic Integration: Economic Union | 217

The integration of their economies by two or more states through development of common economic policies. An economic union establishes a common market and a common external tariff, provides for the free movement of labor and capital, harmonizes taxes and subsidies that affect trade within the region, and works toward a general consonance of fiscal and monetary policies. Political institutions for joint economic decision making are essential to an economic union. The European Union (EU), for example, functions as an economic union through its joint political organs. *See also* MAASTRICHT TREATY (432); REGIONAL POLITICAL GROUP: EUROPEAN COMMUNITY (EC) (565); REGIONAL POLITICAL GROUP: EUROPEAN UNION (EU) (566).

Significance
An economic union provides for the highest level of economic integration short of that which results from full political union. Although it contains features similar to those of a free-trade area and a customs union, an economic union differs mainly in the extent to which the members' domestic fiscal and monetary policies are harmonized. The level of integration in an economic union is not fixed; it may broaden as the development of community consensus supports additional fields of cooperation. The objective of economic union is to encourage a broader market, greater specialization, and generally higher standards of living through the increased competition that results when

the mantle of government protectionism is withdrawn.

Economic Integration: Free-Trade Area | 218

A region consisting of two or more states in which tariffs and other barriers to trade have been eliminated. A free-trade area is more than a preferential system that retains tariffs and provides for more favorable rates for members, but it does not go as far as a customs union that, in addition to establishing a free-trade area provides for a common external tariff applicable to nonmembers. In a free-trade-area agreement, members retain full freedom to develop their individual trade policies with the rest of the world. Examples of free-trade areas include the European Free Trade Association (EFTA) and the Latin American Integration Association (LAIA). *See also* REGIONAL ECONOMIC GROUP: EUROPEAN FREE TRADE ASSOCIATION (EFTA) (552); REGIONAL ECONOMIC GROUP: LATIN AMERICAN INTEGRATION ASSOCIATION (LAIA) (553).

Significance
A free-trade-area arrangement aims at maximizing trade among its members while leaving their trade relations with other states unchanged. As with all preferential systems, however, "outside" nations tend to view the system as discriminatory because their exports to the free-trade area become more expensive and less competitive when compared with those of the "inside" members. EFTA was the first multilateral free-trade area to succeed in achieving its basic objective of removing all industrial tariffs among its members.

Economic Integration: Marshall Plan | 219

A proposal made by Secretary of State George C. Marshall in 1947 that the United States undertake a vast program of economic aid to help rebuild the war-shattered economies of Western Europe. The U.S. Congress accepted the plan in 1948 when it established the European Recovery Program (ERP) to provide grants and loans for European nations that agreed to participate. At U.S. urging, the 16 countries sharing in the program established a regional Organization for European Economic Cooperation (OEEC) to encourage cooperation in reconstruction projects and draw up a collective inventory of resources and requirements. The Soviet Union and other Communist countries of East Europe were invited to join the program, but declined. From 1948 to 1952, the United States provided $15 billion in loans and grants-in-aid under the Marshall Plan program. *See also* DEVELOPMENT STRATEGY: FOREIGN AID (210); MARSHALL PLAN (655).

Significance
The success of the Marshall Plan, the first major post–World War II aid program, encouraged U.S. policymakers and the U.S. Congress to use foreign aid as a tactic for combating instability and thwarting Communist aims in the developing countries. By 1952 the plan had sparked a general recovery in Europe that saw prewar production levels surpassed in participating countries. U.S. efforts under the Marshall Plan to encourage the integration of European economies in achieving the objective of a single common market for all of Western Europe came close to fruition with the expansion of the European community. In 1961 the Organization for Economic Cooperation and Development (OECD) replaced the OEEC. The OECD elicits common action on economic matters from its 24 members through a consultative structure; its decisions are influential, but not binding. Economic cooperation fostered by the Marshall Plan was supplemented in 1949 by the Atlantic Community's military-security approach to integration embodied in the North Atlantic Treaty Organization (NATO).

Economic Integration: Preferential Trade Arrangement | 220 |
An agreement among several states to grant one another favorable trade treatment. Members of a preferential system mutually reduce their tariffs or other trade barriers to an agreed-upon level. The difference between tariff levels for members and those applied to other states is referred to as the "margin of preference." A preferential system may be multilateral (for example, the Commonwealth of Nations system of preferences) or bilateral (as in the case of United States–Philippines economic agreement). Any trade agreement between two or more nations that reduces barriers to trade but does not incorporate the most-favored-nation clause to apply those reductions to nonsignatory states is preferential in nature. *See also* REGIONAL POLITICAL GROUP: COMMONWEALTH OF NATIONS (562); TRADE POLICY ORGANIZATION: IMPERIAL PREFERENCES (270).

Significance
A preferential trade arrangement may evoke retaliation from other states or trading blocs and lead to a trade war because it tends to discriminate against all trading partners not party to the agreement. For example, under its rules for trade conduct, the General Agreement on Tariffs and Trade (GATT) group prohibits the creation of any new preferential systems or increases in the margin of preference by existing systems. The states' main objective in establishing preferential trade arrangements is to encourage more extensive trade with some of their trading partners while maintaining their general levels of protection vis-à-vis other states. Political and security objectives may also figure prominently in a decision to establish a preferential system. One of the most persistent demands for preferential trade treatment comes from the underdeveloped countries in their efforts to secure lower tariff rates for primary commodities without reciprocity. Free-trade areas, customs unions, and economic unions are widely used contemporary types of preferential arrangements.

Economic Theory: Depression | 221 |
The business-cycle period of economic stagnation. A depression or slump is characterized by business retrenchment,

weakened purchasing power, mass unemployment, deflation, and a substantially reduced gross national product. In a complex modern economy, the failure of one segment to perform adequately may trigger depressive events in other sectors, leading to a general economic malaise. Historically, in capitalist countries depressions follow periods of peak expansion in the nation's productive facilities and overexpansion of credit, resulting in a boom-bust cycle. The interdependence of the international economy leads almost inevitably to the spread of depression beyond a state's boundaries. An economic downturn of lesser proportions and shorter duration than a depression is termed a recession. *See also* MONETARY POLICY: DEFLATION (231).

Significance

Economic depressions have always had serious consequences in terms of economic dislocation and social and political unrest. The Great Depression of the 1930s helped to usher in a period of economic nationalism, dictatorship, and war on a scale previously unknown. At a time of competitive ideological struggle, a major depression in the West could have equally serious consequences by making communism appear more attractive. Classical economic theory held that depressions were a natural phenomenon that would be overcome by self-correcting economic forces inherent in the capitalist system. Today, economic theory and practice are used in governmental fiscal and monetary policies to prevent the nation's economy from sliding into a depression. During a period of recession, for example, government actions discourage savings, stimulate investment and purchasing, reduce taxes, provide employment, and give a psychological lift so that the slide into a full depression can be avoided. Leading trading nations work out common international monetary and investment policies to help stabilize the world economy when a depression threatens. Through such policies, serious economic recessions in the post–World War II period have been arrested and reversed before a major depression could materialize.

Economic Theory: Economic Nationalism |222|

Governmental direction and control of external economic matters. A policy of economic nationalism endeavors to achieve a state's economic, political, or security objectives by protecting the domestic market and/or increasing trade opportunities abroad. Economic nationalism is the opposite of a free-trade system, in which economic actions are liberated from governmental regulations and controls. Policies of economic nationalism may range from partial manipulation of a basically free economy by government to the all-embracing control of economic policy and practice and its direction toward the achievement of national objectives, typical of state-trading countries and most nations at war. Techniques of economic nationalism include (1) directed trade, (2) tariffs and quotas, (3) barter arrangements, (4) exchange controls, (5) currency manipulation, (6) export subsidies and controls, (7) embargos and boycotts, (8) preferential trading systems, (9) expropriation and nationalization, and (10) dumping. *See also* TRADE POLICY: AUTARKY (239).

Significance

Economic nationalism became common state policy during World Wars I and II and the interwar period of the 1920s and 1930s. During the 1930s, most states tried to escape the mass unemployment and general economic stagnation brought on by the worldwide depression through discriminatory and restrictive external economic policies. Some, such as Germany and Italy, sought to develop their war-making potentials through economic policies of autarky (national self-sufficiency) and by directing trade toward the enhancement of national power. Policies of economic nationalism tend to incite retaliatory actions by aggrieved states, often negating any initial advantages. The result is a cumulative buildup of restrictions that reduces trade, investment, and other international economic activities and depresses general economic well-being. Post–World War II efforts have been steered toward preventing a resurgence of economic nationalism by constructing a multilateral trading and payments system through collective actions undertaken by international institutions such as General Agreement on Tariffs and Trade (GATT) and the International Monetary Fund (IMF). In 1994–1995 differences over trade practices between the United States and Japan, two of the world's three leading commercial nations, threatened a breakdown in these efforts, as each appeared determined to hold to its own national policy. Demanding that Japan level the playing field and allow more American consumer items (notably automobiles and automotive spare parts) to enter the country, in 1995 the United States ordered higher tariffs on Japanese luxury cars that virtually prevented their sale in the United States. Japan publicized its indignation and suggested that it would retaliate against any U.S. action. At the same time, Japan insisted on taking the matter to the World Trade Organization, established barely six months earlier and not yet fully operational. Whether these were simply tactics and pressures in a game of psychological warfare, the world's major trading nations yielded some ground and thus averted a crisis.

Economic Theory: Expropriation   223

Government seizure of foreign-owned property and transfer of ownership to the state. Although recognized as a rightful exercise of sovereign power, under international law expropriation can be neither retaliatory nor discriminatory and is conditional on payment of prompt and fair compensation. The United States also stipulates that expropriated property be taken only for a public purpose and in accordance with due process of law. Expropriation is a form of nationalization, although the latter term refers more broadly to the purchase or expropriation of either foreign or domestically owned

private property. A declaration of war leads to the expropriation of all properties owned by enemy aliens.

Significance

The threat of expropriation undermines the flow of capital from capital-surplus states to the developing states. Prompt compensation may be beyond the capabilities of expropriating states, and "fair payment" for properties is a matter of controversy and protracted negotiations. One of the first acts undertaken by a Communist government after taking power is often the expropriation of foreign-owned property and the nationalization of privately owned basic industries. Retaliation by a state for the expropriation of property owned by its nationals may take the form of diplomatic protest, severance of diplomatic relations, economic reprisal, or military sanctions. Expropriation of over $1 billion of U.S.-owned assets by the Castro regime in Cuba led to the severance of diplomatic relations. To increase the flow of private capital, some supporters of economic development call for massive government insurance programs in the capital-surplus states to encourage private investment abroad by guaranteeing it against expropriation. The United States is currently involved in over 100 cases of expropriation of property owned by U.S. nationals in foreign countries.

Economic Theory: Gross Domestic Product (GDP)   224

The total value of output produced by an economy of a state, by both residents and nonresidents. GDP represents the total output of goods and services produced within a country's economy and within its territory regardless of its allocation between domestic and foreign claims. *See also* ECONOMIC THEORY: GROSS NATIONAL PRODUCT (GNP) (225).

Significance

Economists use gross domestic product to gauge the level of a country's economic activity. GDP includes the role played by nonresidents in a domestic economy because nonresidents such as foreigncorporations can have significant impact on an economy. The figures on GDP combined with GNP (gross national product) indicate that in 1990 the total national product of all nations was valued at $20 trillion, and $16.6 trillion originated in the economically developed regions. Thus, approximately 83 percent of the world's total income was produced by 23 percent of the world's population. The Third World, with almost 77 percent of the world's population, existed on less than 20 percent of the world's income. For example, in 1990 tiny Switzerland had a per capita income 93 times that of India.

Economic Theory: Gross National Product (GNP)   225

The gross national income of a nation measured in terms of the value of goods and services produced by its economy. The GNP is expressed in terms of the total market value of all consumer and capital goods and services produced over a specific time period, usually one year. *See also* DEVELOPMENT: ECONOMIC GROWTH (192); ECONOMIC THEORY: GROSS DOMESTIC PRODUCT (GDP) (224).

Significance

When carefully computed to avoid duplication in adding value at different stages of production, gross national product serves as a useful indicator of economic growth. GNP can be used as an analytical tool to compare the current performance of a nation's economy with that of preceding years, or it can be used to compare performance with other countries. It is often used to compare the economic progress of different economic and social systems. In comparing economic growth rates, however, the GNP should be adjusted to constant currency values to avoid distortion by inflationary or deflationary price changes, and capital goods figures should be adjusted to exclude any portion of new investment that merely replaces worn-out or discarded productive capacity. To compare standards of living in different countries, population-growth factors must also be used to adjust GNP figures to a per capita income basis.

Economic Theory: Keynesianism   226

A philosophy and practice of utilizing the machinery of government, through fiscal and monetary policies, to guide and direct a free enterprise economy. Keynesianism, based on the principles and analyses originally propounded by British economist John Maynard Keynes, seeks to improve rather than replace capitalism by providing an orderly, predictable pattern of economic activity based on economic indicators used by policymakers. Techniques used by Keynesians to manage a state's economy include government control and direction of such matters as budgeting, spending, tax policy, interest rates, and credit availability. Instead of allowing the undirected free interplay of market forces that characterizes a laissez-faire approach, Keynesianism substitutes rational decisions made by state leaders in pursuit of specific social goals. Keynes believed that the key problem of a capitalist system is oversaving, and he prescribed various kinds of governmental action to encourage the transfer of savings into investment and consumption. Keynes focused on the role of government fiscal policy to correct the imbalance between potential output (controlled by supply factors) and actual output (controlled by the aggregate demand of consumers, investors, and government). *See also* CAPITALISM (81).

Significance

The "new economics" approach based on Keynesian principles that emerged out of the Great Depression and World War II experiences has been generally adopted as state policy in most of the advanced industrial states of the world. Political leaders increasingly make decisions concerning their states' economies on the basis of recommendations offered by economic advisers who accept the Keynesian approach. By managing a nation's economy, Keynesians endeavor to avoid cyclical movements, unemployment, and inflation, while at the same time encourage economic growth and general economic well-being. Keynesianism has functioned effectively since World War II to alleviate downturns in the economies of the industrialized countries. However, weakened by large governmental and consumer debt and heavy inflation, it is challenged today by two new approaches: (1) monetarism, which emphasizes a free market with government policy focused on controlling the money supply; and (2) supply-side economics, which emphasizes favorable tax and economic policies for business and industry as a means for achieving general economic well-being.

Economic Theory: Mercantilism | 227

The economic philosophy and practice of government regulation of a nation's economic life to increase state power and security. Mercantilism provided the economic model followed by European states from the sixteenth through the eighteenth centuries. Each state sought to build up its treasury by maintaining a surplus of exports over imports, so that the favorable trade balance would result in inflows of gold and silver. Cottage industries were encouraged by government policies in agriculture and mining, since finished goods offered lower shipping costs and higher prices. Colonies were used as sources of cheap raw materials and as markets for expensive manufactured goods. Governmental regulation and control permeated all sectors of each nation's economy. Wages were kept low to add to the profit for the nation's treasury and to stimulate industriousness among the masses who were otherwise, it was believed, too lazy to work. *See also* DEPENDENT TERRITORY: COLONY (36).

Significance

The system of mercantilism dominated the international economy until gradually replaced by the individualistic laissez-faire theories of capitalism during the late eighteenth and early nineteenth centuries. Although later discredited, mercantilist theories were practical applications of state power in an age of war and plunder when a state's survival depended on its financial ability to hire and maintain professional armies. Some "neomercantilist" practices, such as emphasis on a favorable trade balance and extensive governmental regulations and promotion of the economy, are followed by many states today. Some nations continue to strive to build up their gold reserves, believing, like the mercantilists, that the precious metal will increase state power. Communist states most closely approximated the mercantilist ideal in subordinating economic policies to the political objectives of the state.

Monetary Policy: Bretton Woods Conference | 228

The United Nations Monetary and Financial Conference that drafted the Articles of Agreement for the International Bank for Reconstruction and Development (IBRD) and the International Monetary Fund (IMF). Called at the initiative of President Franklin Roosevelt, the conference met at Bretton Woods, New Hampshire, on 1–22 July 1944, with 44 nations represented. *See also* DEVELOPMENT AGENCY: INTERNATIONAL BANK FOR RECONSTRUCTION AND DEVELOPMENT (IBRD) (199); MONETARY POLICY: INTERNATIONAL MONETARY FUND (IMF) (238).

Significance

The Bretton Woods Conference represented the initial attack on the problems of postwar economic reconstruction. The IBRD and IMF are part of the cooperative base for building a sound international monetary and investment system to replace the chaotic conditions fostered by the economic nationalism of the 1930s. The bank and the fund were established on 27 December 1945 when the necessary number of nations accepted the articles of agreement for each; in November 1947, both were brought into a specialized-agency relationship with the United

Nations. The bank and the fund represent the application of Keynesian economic principles and policies to the international economic system.

Monetary Policy: Convertibility 229

The free interchange of a national currency into units of foreign currency by private individuals or businesses, without government control. A convertible currency, therefore, is one that is not regulated in value or amounts exchanged by a national system of exchange control. *See also* MONETARY POLICY: EXCHANGE CONTROL; (233) MONETARY POLICY: FOREIGN EXCHANGE (235).

Significance
The convertibility of a currency is most commonly restricted when a government seeks to protect the nation from a serious disequilibrium in its balance of payments, when it maintains an artificially high or low exchange value for its currency, or when it tries to control currency exchanges to achieve national political or military goals. In developing countries, for example, dollars and other hard currencies are often conserved for purchases of capital goods to promote economic growth. The national currency cannot be freely exchanged for hard currency to purchase foreign consumer goods. World currencies can be divided into three basic categories: (1) "hard" currencies of the industrialized nations, (2) "soft" currencies of the developing countries, and (3) "controlled" currencies of the Communist and state-trading countries. Whereas the currencies in the first group are freely convertible, those in the last two categories may legally be converted into foreign currencies only with government approval. This often results in a foreign-currency black market with unofficial exchange rates.

Monetary Policy: Counterpart Funds 230

Local currencies paid by an aid-receiving country to a donor country for military,

developmental, or technical-assistance loans. Under grant programs, a recipient country may also be required to establish a special fund of national currency to match the amount provided in foreign exchange. *See also* DEVELOPMENT STRATEGY: FOREIGN AID (210).

Significance
Because counterpart funds are not freely convertible into hard currency, they are frequently ploughed back into local infrastructure programs or expended on educational exchange and other noninflationary projects by the aid-giving government. Donor countries carrying on extensive foreign-aid programs, such as the United States, hold vast amounts of local currencies in counterpart funds, which increasingly gives them a voice in the determination of national policies in recipient countries. In some cases, this situation has given rise to charges of imperialism by groups within the aid-receiving country.

Monetary Policy: Deflation 231

A decrease in the price level of goods in a nation's economy. Deflation results from a decrease in the supply of money and credit or from the overproduction or underconsumption of consumer goods. Deflation is usually associated with a serious economic decline, whereas inflation is typically a problem during an economic boom. *See also* MONETARY POLICY: INFLATION (237).

Significance
Economic tacticians regard substantial deflation as a serious threat to a nation's economy because it fosters unemployment, reduces investment, diminishes consumption, and generally contributes to economic stagnation. In an economy based on credit, deflation makes debt reduction more difficult and discourages individuals and businesses from incurring new loans. Proponents of a stable monetary policy call for vigorous governmental actions to avoid or correct deflationary swings before they produce serious

substantive and psychological damage to the nation's economy. All modern states use monetary and fiscal policies as corrective actions when deflation threatens. In some cases, however, a government may pursue a deliberate deflationary policy to check inflationary dangers or to correct a balance-of-payments disequilibrium by making exports more attractive.

Monetary Policy: Devaluation | 232 |

A reduction in the exchange value of a nation's monetary unit. Devaluation is usually a deliberate policy undertaken by a state to depreciate the value of its national currency in terms of gold or other national currencies. *See also* MONETARY POLICY: FLEXIBLE EXCHANGE RATES (234).

Significance
Devaluation is often used as an instrument of trade policy by a nation suffering from a serious deficit in its balance of payments. By devaluing its national currency, a state lowers the prices for its products in world markets and stimulates its export trade. At the same time, imports become more costly to its own consumers, resulting in a reduction in the state's import trade. Thus, a state may use devaluation to correct a fundamental disequilibrium in its balance of payments. If other states follow this lead and devalue their currencies, however, all will be back on pretty much the same level of currency relationship. During the Great Depression of the 1930s, for example, the international monetary system was in disarray because of successive competitive rounds of depreciations as many states sought to solve their domestic economic problems by capturing a larger share of the world market. To regain international monetary stability, the International Monetary Fund (IMF) was established after World War II to regulate currency values and to permit members to draw foreign exchange to tide them over periods of financial hardship. The leading industrial countries have also organized pool arrangements, which provide additional monetary resources to fight any threatened devaluation during a financial crisis. Numerous devaluations of national currencies have occurred since World War II, but the most significant have been limited to cases involving necessary adjustments approved by the IMF; competitive devaluations have been avoided. A flexible exchange-rate system with relatively free-floating currencies established in 1973 helped stabilize currency values. In the 1980s, however, the United States implemented policies to devalue the dollar by more than 30 percent in an effort to correct its massive balance-of-trade and balance-of-payments deficits. By 1994–1995, the value of the dollar against other major world currencies, e.g., the Japanese yen and the German mark, fell to all-time lows. Repeated efforts by governments to shore up the value of the dollar were not successful, thus bringing into question the dollar's usefulness as a worldwide gauge for financial transactions. In May 1995 some petroleum-exporting countries, financially hurt by the drop in dollar values, insisted that oil be paid for in yen or marks rather than dollars. Moreover, the 1980s devaluation policy failed to achieve its objective; U.S. trade deficit continued to grow through the 1990s.

Monetary Policy: Exchange Control | 233 |

Government regulation of the exchange of national and foreign currencies. Exchange control substitutes arbitrary decisions of administrative officials for free market forces in the buying and selling of currencies. Control is usually directed toward two objectives: (1) maintaining an arbitrary exchange ratio between national and foreign currencies and (2) permitting exchanges of national into foreign currencies only when national-interest considerations are satisfied. Exchange control may range from full regulation over all monetary transactions to limited supervision over certain types of activities to correct temporary monetary difficulties. *See also* MONETARY POLICY: CONVERTIBILITY (229); MONETARY POLICY: FLEXIBLE EXCHANGE RATES (234).

Significance
Exchange control is a technique of economic nationalism. Its main objectives are the correction of a serious balance-of-payments problem or the withholding of scarce foreign exchange from unnecessary imports in favor of capital projects to produce economic growth. In industrialized states, currency exchange has often been regulated to check exports. When war threatened during the 1930s, many European states used exchange control to prevent capital flight to the United States. Exchange control is most extensive when a nation is at war and all foreign economic activities must be directed toward the achievement of victory. Although Western European states maintained exchange control for some years after World War II, their rebuilding of substantial dollar and gold reserves brought about the elimination or moderation of control. State-trading countries, however, maintain full control over currency exchange, and most of the developing nations use it to conserve foreign exchange for economic development projects. A flexible exchange-rate system emerged in the 1970s when the United States ended fixed convertibility between gold and the dollar. Since that action, currencies of the industrial countries have been permitted to "float," with their exchange values determined mainly by market conditions.

Monetary Policy: Flexible Exchange Rates | 234 |

An international monetary system in which the value of each national currency is determined by the free interplay of market forces. In a flexible exchange-rate system, the values of national currencies change regularly as a result of the impact of supply and demand for each currency. Flexible exchange rates were instituted in 1973 by the Western bloc of nations headed by the United States. The fixed-rate exchange system, in which all leading currencies were tied to the dollar and their exchange values were set by agreement through the International Monetary Fund (IMF), prevailed until 1971. Because the dollar was tied to gold at the fixed rate

of $35 per ounce, all other currencies in that system were also tied to gold. In 1971 the United States was unable to meet the demands of foreigners to turn their dollars into gold, and the system collapsed. A temporary "adjustable peg" exchange-rate system replaced the gold-exchange-standard system, but by 1973 a flexible exchange-rate system was operational. *See also* MONETARY POLICY: EXCHANGE CONTROL (233); MONETARY POLICY: FOREIGN EXCHANGE (235); MONETARY POLICY: GOLD STANDARD (236).

Significance
Flexible exchange rates have helped to construct a stable international monetary-value system since 1973 because national currency values are largely set by supply/demand market forces rather than by governmental fiat. When critically necessary, the value of a national currency can be affected by governmental policies. The system has helped countries in their balance-of-payments adjustments by giving early indications of a weakening or strengthening of national currency values. Therefore, exchange rates are generally reliable indicators of the overall economic condition of each nation. The system managed to endure the shocks of the 1970s and 1980s, in which tremendous increases followed by dramatic decreases in world oil prices occurred, and in which a great expansion in trade and international liquidity with high inflation rates challenged its survival. At times the system has been weakened by great market turbulence—sometimes occasioned by the actions of powerful speculators—and by heavy unemployment and other adverse economic conditions in leading industrial countries. Nevertheless, the flexible exchange-rate system has prevailed and is likely to survive all but a cataclysmic world depression or a period of severe economic nationalism such as occurred in the 1930s.

Monetary Policy: Foreign Exchange | 235 |

National currencies used to make purchases of foreign goods or settle accounts. The price or exchange ratio for national currencies is determined by supply and demand in the international money market or by an arbitrary fixing of the rate of exchange through a national system of exchange control. *See also* MONETARY POLICY: CONVERTIBILITY (229); MONETARY POLICY: EXCHANGE CONTROL (233); MONETARY POLICY: FLEXIBLE EXCHANGE RATES (234).

Significance

A businessperson wishing to purchase foreign goods must convert his or her domestic money into foreign currency. When heavy spending abroad jeopardizes the value of a nation's currency, the government may take action. Exchanges may be made subject to approval by government officials (exchange control), foreign products may be made more or less desirable by altering the exchange ratio between the two currencies (currency appreciation or depreciation), or tariffs and other trade barriers may be raised or lowered to reduce or increase foreign imports. Such governmental actions, however, usually result in retaliatory measures by affected countries. To avoid resorting to restrictive devices, major countries of the West have entered into "pooling" arrangements whereby currency values on the international market may be protected by large-scale countertrend buying and selling of major currencies by the pool to maintain exchange stability.

Monetary Policy: Gold Standard | 236

An international monetary system that uses gold as the common standard of value. Under a gold-standard system, each nation's currency is backed by gold, has a value measured in gold, and can be freely converted into gold or any national currency operating within the system. Deficits and surpluses in the balance of payments are settled by gold flows from one country to another. Under a modified gold-exchange standard, central banks buy and sell national currencies backed by gold at a fixed price. *See also* MONETARY POLICY: INTERNATIONAL MONETARY FUND (IMF) (238).

Significance

The gold standard was established as the basic international monetary system from the middle of the nineteenth century to 1914, was restored briefly from 1925 to 1931, and from 1958 to 1971 functioned in a gold-exchange-standard form. In 1971 the Nixon administration was forced to cut the tie between gold and the dollar at a fixed rate of exchange because of the excessive number of dollars in the world that constituted claims against a dwindling supply of U.S. gold. Although the gold standard had the advantage of ensuring free convertibility of all currencies in a truly multilateral payments system, the limited supply of gold made it difficult to build adequate reserves during periods of increasing trade. Flows of gold in and out of countries produced unwanted deflations and inflations because the value of a national currency was based on the quantity of gold held by the nation. When governments established national goals of price stability, full employment, and rapid economic growth, the automatic adjusting mechanism of the gold-standard system became incompatible and was replaced by "managed" paper currencies. The gold-exchange-standard system that existed until 1971 was weakened by a world gold shortage, perennial U.S. balance-of-payments deficits, and the rapid conversion of dollar balances into gold by several countries, especially France. In 1967, however, the Group of Ten—the leading industrial powers—agreed to bolster the world monetary system by creating "paper gold" in the form of Special Drawing Rights (SDRs) for all members of the International Monetary Fund (IMF). Through the additional credits thus made available, the major trading nations attempt to manage the international monetary supply in somewhat the same way that governments manage their domestic currencies through their central banks. The price of gold, which had remained fixed at $35 an ounce for many years, soared in world markets as a result of heavy inflation affecting most currencies.

Monetary Policy: Inflation 237

An increase in the general price level of goods in a nation's economy. Inflation may result from an increase in money and credit, the absence of competitive conditions in the marketplace, or a decrease in the supply of goods available. Inflationary conditions are often created by government actions such as deficit spending or by ill-timed monetary policies. Whatever the trigger, economists believe that mass psychological factors are responsible for increasing its impact and scope. For example, fear of continued price increases may stimulate installment buying, which in turn may contribute to further inflation. *See also* MONETARY POLICY: DEFLATION (231).

Significance

A monetary inflation may constitute a serious threat to a nation's economy. Low-income groups usually bear the greatest hardship from a serious inflation, with the result that political stability may be threatened. Progress toward the objectives of economic development may be thwarted by a runaway inflationary spiral, which eats up savings that could have been channeled into investment. Foreign trade may suffer because the nation's exports may be priced out of the highly competitive world market. Yet a moderate, controlled inflation of less than 3 percent annually may provide a stimulus to the economy and help reduce private and public debts. For many years, inflation in the United States was kept within an average of less than 7 percent annually, one of the lowest in the world. The 1970s and early 1980s, however, saw annual inflation rates for most countries, including the United States, soar to 15–20 percent. By the mid-1980s, the United States brought inflation under control through a rigorous monetary policy. In 1995, inflation in the United States was pegged at 2 percent. But in developing countries, rates soared to over 100 percent annually. Several countries, such as Israel, Chile, and Argentina, suffered from hyperinflation that exceeded 1,000 percent annually. On the other hand, those countries with the strongest economies—Japan and Germany, for example—have maintained strong currencies with low inflation rates.

Monetary Policy: International Monetary Fund (IMF) 238

A specialized agency of the United Nations established by the Bretton Woods Monetary and Financial Conference of 1944 to promote international monetary cooperation. The major objectives of the IMF include (1) promotion of exchange stability, (2) establishment of a worldwide multilateral payments system, and (3) provision of monetary reserves to help member nations overcome short-run disequilibrium in their balance of payments. By 1996 more than 150 members joined the fund. The two major stabilizing functions performed by the IMF are (1) regulating currency values by controlling exchange rates and (2) providing a pooling arrangement whereby members may purchase foreign currencies with their own domestic currencies to tide them over periods of serious financial hardship. When a member is able to do so, it repurchases its own currency with foreign exchange, thus replenishing the fund's available resources. Voting power in the IMF is determined by the size of a member's contribution; the United States casts about one-fifth of the total. IMF decisions are usually reached initially by the Group of Ten, a caucus of the major industrial powers, which casts most of the votes in the fund. *See also* MONETARY POLICY: GOLD STANDARD (236); UN SPECIALIZED AGENCY (605).

Significance

The International Monetary Fund was established to avoid a return in the post–World War II era to the anarchic financial conditions of the 1930s, with wildly fluctuating exchange rates and competitive depreciations. Major exchange depreciations, with the exception of those of the sterling bloc in 1949 and 1967, have been avoided, and the IMF has generally been successful in promoting stable currency values. The main problems facing the fund are the persistent deficit in the U.S. balance of payments, the shortage of international reserves at a time when trade has expanded at a rapid rate, and demands for a return to the gold-standard system. Because of the limited supply of gold and dollars available as reserves, in 1969 the IMF began to issue Special Drawing Rights (SDRs) to supplement existing reserves, with an initial issue of $3 billion. SDRs are no more than bookkeeping entries in the IMF accounting system, leading the media to refer to them as "paper gold." Because of the Third World debt crisis, the IMF has had to function as a lender-of-last-resort by providing new loans for debtor countries to use in making loan payments, thus avoiding major defaults. In the 1980s, and again in the 1990s, the IMF joined with the World Bank in an effort to avoid a general default by Third World countries. Most such loans were earmarked for making payments on outstanding debts owed to public and private financial institutions.

Trade Policy: Autarky | 239 |

National economic self-sufficiency. Since such a policy lessens dependence on other states, a state may adopt a policy of autarky in anticipation of war or to correct a serious deficit in its balance of payments. A government that adopts a policy of autarky typically will curtail imports, encourage the development of substitutes and synthetics to replace imports, and subsidize production for the domestic market. *See also* WAR MEASURES: STOCKPILING (329).

Significance

By adopting a policy of autarky, a state substitutes national economic, political, or military considerations for the free interplay of supply and demand in the international marketplace. During the 1930s, for example, Germany placed major emphasis on developing a self-sufficiency based on synthetics and stockpiling, which would make the nation blockade-proof when war came. The autarky plan failed during

World War II mainly because of the insufficiency of oil and food reserves. After World War II, the United States followed a policy of stockpiling large quantities of commodities essential to fighting a nonnuclear war, but nevertheless did not adopt a policy of autarky.

Trade Policy: Competitiveness | 240 |

The necessity, in a free global market, to be able to compete effectively with producers in many other nations in the production and sale of goods and services. The idea of competitiveness assumes that a nation's economic problems, such as unemployment, inflation, and slow growth, can be overcome by substantial increases in productivity. When a nation suffers from a large deficit in its balance of trade and its national currency loses exchange value, it can be assumed, according to the protagonists of the competitiveness doctrine, that the nation's economy needs to improve its competitive position. This means that its businesses and industries, along with labor, must undertake policies that will make its products desirable in foreign markets. *See also* TRADE POLICY ANALYSIS: BALANCE OF TRADE (248).

Significance

Competitiveness has become a political buzzword to describe the need for the United States to develop a more favorable trade and investment position in the world economy. Other nations are also caught up in the competitive battle to outproduce, outsell, and earn greater profits than their rivals. The most competitive countries in the 1990s include Japan, Germany, South Korea, Singapore, Taiwan, and Hong Kong. Problems arise when a nation that has enjoyed unparalleled superiority in trade and finance discovers that in a few brief years it has changed from being the world's largest creditor nation to the world's largest debtor. The United States has tried to deal with the problem of mammoth trade deficits and extensive borrowing by depreciating the value of the dollar. In this way,

U.S. exports were made cheaper and supposedly more competitive in foreign markets, while foreign products became more expensive (but not necessarily less competitive) in the U.S. market. The fall in the value of the dollar against other established and competitive currencies did not have the anticipated effect. In the 1990s, Americans continued to purchase foreign goods at levels that sustained and actually increased the U.S. trade deficit, while nations with a surplus of trade in their commercial dealings with the United States continued to make it difficult for U.S. products to be sold in their countries. The United States threatened specific economic sanctions, such as the imposition of Super 401 restrictive trade policies, in their negotiations with trade officials in Japan, but it did not impose them. Moreover, in 1994, and again in 1995, the Japanese amassed huge trade surpluses in their dealings with the United States. Not to be outdone, Communist China, South Korea, and Taiwan all enjoyed similar advantages, if not as substantial, in their trade with the United States—despite acknowledged increases in U.S. productivity.

Trade Policy: Directed Trade　　241

The determination of trade policies by a government in pursuit of a state's economic, political, or security objectives. Directed trade differs from free trade, which permits the supply and demand of the marketplace to determine the flow of trade.

Significance
All states direct their trade, ranging from the moderate intervention of liberal democratic states to the totally controlled systems of state-trading nations. A state may direct its trade in order to bolster its system of alliances, strengthen its colonial ties, expand its political influence, spread its ideology, or maximize its economic gain. Techniques for directing trade include preferential agreements, boycotts and embargoes, barter, currency regulations, tariffs and quotas, special credits, price manipulation, and bilateral trade agreements. Since World War II, most nations have joined in collective efforts through UN agencies to encourage freer trade by the establishment of a multilateral trade and payments system.

Trade Policy: Export Control　　242

Governmental restrictions on the sales of certain materials, commodities, products, or weapons in foreign trade. Certain types of weapons, for example, may be excluded from foreign sales through export controls. States possessing nuclear weapons generally prohibit the export of nuclear devices, weapons-grade uranium or plutonium, and technical information. In the economic area, states may restrict the export of certain materials or products that are in short supply within the country, usually for the duration of the shortage. For many years, the United States sought to weaken Communist states through the Battle Act (Mutual Defense Assistance Control Act of 1951), which prohibited trade in strategic materials with "any nation threatening the security of the United States." Under the Export Administration Act of 1979, the United States extended controls over the export of strategic goods and technology having both civil and military uses. Export controls that limit or prohibit shipments going out of a state supplement exchange controls that limit or prohibit imports of certain products, especially in state-trading countries. *See also* MONETARY POLICY: EXCHANGE CONTROL (233).

Significance
Export controls are one of the major means by which nations try to safeguard their national security and economic interests in the field of trade. Advocates of free trade reject most export controls as unnecessary encumbrances on the free flow of goods; they advocate eliminating controls in favor of free market conditions. In the United States, export control powers vested in the president by Congress are very extensive. Articles of commerce subject to presidential control in

the 1980s included nuclear materials, crime control and detection equipment, computers, aircraft, large tractors, and petroleum equipment. In addition, the president was empowered to forbid all exports to North Korea, Vietnam, Cambodia, and Cuba except for a few innocuous educational, gift, and travel materials. Changing world conditions in the 1990s, however, required modification of this policy. The UN role in Cambodia opened that country to U.S. trading possibilities. Vietnam and the United States normalized their relationship, and commercial relations were encouraged. Faced with a nuclear-weapons program in North Korea, the United States entered into an agreement with Pyongyang that promised economic and financial assistance in return for a North Korean agreement that would freeze its nuclear-weapons program. Generally speaking, the Battle Act did not live up to expectations, although the policy was not without some early successes. If anything, it was U.S. allies who undermined the policy by freely selling their economic and strategic products to Communist and other targeted states. As a result, the U.S. business community was compelled to bring pressure on Congress to alter the act so they too could compete with the European countries and Japan in the otherwise off-limits markets.

Trade Policy: Fordism   243

A term describing a regime of intensive accumulation and mass consumption under monopolistic regulation. It is based on an organization of labor that combines the distribution and standardization of tasks with mechanization. The consequence is a process of rapid growth in the productivity of labor and fixed capital. Regulation of this regime of accumulation is based on controlling wage labor through coercive institutional forms. Fordism dominated the Northern and Western regions of the world following World War II, but began yielding to greater displays of internationalism in the 1970s. By the 1990s the developed West-

ern regions were inextricably intertwined with regions in the larger world, notably in Pacific-Asia, where interdependencies and/or joint and overlapping enterprises had created new demands for cooperation and accommodation.

Significance
Contemporary Fordism addresses the interregional division of world labor, heretofore centered on the exclusive nation-state. The classical spatial division of labor between primary-goods producers (developing nations) and manufactured-products producers (developed nations) ran out of steam in the 1960s following a decline in productivity and a steady increase in the technical composition of capital. The result was a fall in profitability that diminished the capacity of the developed nations to monopolize the market and sustain their economic preeminence. Ultimately, the collapse of classic Fordism plunged the narrowly based entrepreneurial states into financial crisis. Efforts to counter the crisis only accelerated the internationalization of production and markets, thus bypassing more nationalistic expressions of regulation and control.

Trade Policy: Free Trade   244

The flow of trade based on supply and demand, free from governmental regulations, controls, and promotional activities. Free trade was espoused by Adam Smith in his *Wealth of Nations* (1776) to foster an international division of labor based on national specialization in production that would raise productivity and standards of living in all countries. The absolute advantage posited by Adam Smith was later modified by David Ricardo's theory of comparative advantage. The comparative-advantage theory recognized that many countries would not have an absolute advantage in the production of any goods and should, therefore, specialize in those products that they would be able to produce with comparative efficiency, trading these for their other needs. Under capitalism, a laissez-faire (hands-off) policy by government in domestic- and foreign-trade matters permits the forces of the marketplace to determine economic actions. *See also* CAPITALISM (81); TRADE POLICY: DIRECTED TRADE (241).

Significance
Free trade was developed in theory and practice as a reaction to enterprise-stifling policies of mercantilism. Relatively free trade flourished in many countries during the nineteenth and early twentieth centuries, but after World War I most countries instituted protectionist policies. The main thrust of international economic relations since World War II involves a collective effort to remove trade barriers erected during the period of economic nationalism in the 1920s and 1930s. Although free trade may be unassailable in theory, practical political and military considerations and the attraction of short-run economic gain tend to override it in the councils of governments. The trend since 1945, however, has been toward freer trade among most nations and toward free trade among members of the common markets established by regional groups. In the 1990s, despite approving the General Agreement on Tariffs and Trade (GATT) agreements, the United States, faced with a huge annual trade deficit, threatened to use protectionist measures that could precipitate a trade war and move the world away from the ideal of freer trade.

Trade Policy: Protectionism | 245 |
The theory and practice of using governmental regulation to control or limit the volume or types of imports entering a state. Protectionism involves the use of tariffs, quotas, licensing, exchange control, and other devices to reduce or eliminate imports, or to increase consumer cost of foreign-trade commodities that compete with domestically produced articles of commerce. The degree of protection afforded domestic producers varies from state to state, but every country employs some protective measures. *See also* ECONOMIC THEORY: ECONOMIC NATIONALISM (222).

Significance
Trade protectionism has been used by governments since the earliest development of international commerce, but the extent to which the principle is applied varies among states and different historical epochs. Most democratic countries have witnessed continuing political battles between the advocates of free trade and protectionism. Proponents of governmental protection for domestic producers argue that (1) infant industries must be protected until strong enough to compete with mature, efficient foreign producers; (2) developing states, by excluding finished products, may force manufacturing companies to establish branch plants, thus encouraging modernization; (3) natural resources, especially those subject to depletion, should be protected from foreign exploitation; (4) production costs should be equalized between domestic and foreign producers to protect domestic labor from low-wage foreign competition; (5) protectionist devices can be used in trade negotiations to secure quid pro quo (reciprocal) concessions from other states; (6) tariff duties can be a sizable source of income for a poor state; (7) national defense requires that essential industries such as steel, machine tools, and shipbuilding be protected so that they are available for fighting a modern war; and (8) nations suffering from serious disequilibrium in their balances of payments may use protectionist devices to correct the deficits and protect their international currency reserves. Opponents of protectionism argue that it tends to vitiate the international division of labor and specialization encouraged by the forces of the marketplace in a free-trade environment. The result is that protectionism defends inefficient producers, raises the price of goods for the consumer, and permits governments to direct trade to achieve national goals at the consumer's expense. In the 1990s, with a more conservative U.S. Congress driving legislation, the intensity of world economic competition divided the country between those advocating protectionism and those calling for competitiveness and freer trade.

Trade Policy: Reciprocity 246

A quid pro quo (something for something) basis for international bargaining on tariff rates. While reciprocity is the basis for negotiating mutual trade concessions, it can also imply retaliation for tariff increases by other nations. Tariff rates may be raised unilaterally, but they are seldom if ever lowered without reciprocal reductions. *See also* TRADE POLICY INSTRUMENT: TARIFF (264).

Significance
In the United States, the principle of retaliatory commercial reciprocity was introduced by the McKinley Tariff of 1890, which authorized the president to raise certain tariff rates if other countries placed unreasonable duties on U.S. exports. Reciprocity as a tool for direct bilateral negotiations in lowering tariff barriers came into general application with the inauguration of the U.S.-inspired Reciprocal Trade Agreements Program in 1934. Hundreds of trade agreements based on quid pro quo concessions were concluded over the next 30 years. The inclusion of the most-favored-nation clause in each bilateral agreement broadened the impact of reciprocity to include all other nations involved in the program. Reciprocal reductions in tariffs have been accelerated since 1947 through the multilateral bargaining encouraged by General Agreement on Tariffs and Trade (GATT) machinery. GATT's Kennedy Round negotiations from 1963 to 1967, the Tokyo Round from 1973 to 1979, and the Uruguay Round completed in 1994 culminated in the removal of most tariffs as serious impediments to trade by the twenty-first century.

Trade Policy Analysis: Balance of Payments 247

The net balance between the total income and expenditures of a nation, both public and private, in its trade and financial transactions with the rest of the world. A nation's balance of payments resembles an accounting sheet for a private business in reflecting credits (earnings) and debits (spendings). Since a nation's accounts must balance, a surplus or deficit must be offset—for example, by using reserves or by short-term borrowing. Included in the accounting are such credit categories as exports, foreign-tourist spending, profits from investments, and shipping and banking income. Debits include imports, tourist spending abroad, foreign investments, interest payments on loans, and payments for services. Typically, the major factors in calculating a nation's balance of payments are its export and import categories. *See also* TRADE POLICY ANALYSIS: BALANCE OF TRADE (248).

Significance
A nation's balance of payments is an indicator that shows its economic strength or weakness in the international economy. If a country runs up a sizable deficit in its transactions with the rest of the world, steps must be taken to correct the imbalance. A temporary disequilibrium may not be serious and can usually be carried through short-term borrowing. A long-term—or fundamental—disequilibrium, on the other hand, reflects a basic weakness in the economy, and government action to correct the deficit is in order. Corrective policies may include higher tariffs, export controls, quotas, exchange control, currency depreciation, austerity programs, export subsidies, or other actions designed to reduce imports, increase export earnings, or both. States generally strive to maintain a favorable (surplus) balance so that reserves of foreign currencies and gold can be built up to carry them over future payment crises. Surpluses for some states, however, produce deficits for others. Because corrective actions may substantially reduce international trade, the International Monetary Fund (IMF) was established to provide loans to tide nations over temporary payment crises. The United States has had a deficit in its balance of payments for most years since World War II, resulting in an accumulation of huge dollar balances as international reserves by other countries. These are often referred to as "Eurodollars" and "petrodollars,"

reflecting the weak trade position of the United States vis-à-vis some European countries, and the importation of huge quantities of oil. From the 1970s through the 1990s, much of the U.S. deficit related to the huge surpluses Japan acquired in its trade with the United States.

Trade Policy Analysis: Balance of Trade   248

A nation's annual net trade surplus or deficit, based on the difference in the values of its total imports and exports. The balance of trade is distinguished from the balance of payments; the trade balance is only one part of the many debits and credits that comprise a nation's balance of payments. In a carryover from the days of mercantilism, a surplus of exports over imports is often called a "favorable" balance of trade, and imports over exports an "unfavorable" balance of trade. *See also* TRADE POLICY ANALYSIS: BALANCE OF PAYMENTS (247).

Significance
The balance of trade comprises the major part of a nation's balance of payments. A heavy surplus of merchandise exports over imports, for example, will enable a state to pay for activities such as foreign aid and military actions abroad, whereas a substantial trade deficit will often force a nation to cut back on these or other international programs. In an effort to secure a favorable trade balance, a nation's leaders may subsidize exports, depreciate the currency, raise tariffs and other impediments to imports, join other countries in an OPEC-type cartel arrangement, cut back on foreign purchases, or undertake other actions aimed at expanding sales and income from abroad. U.S. policy in the 1990s, for example, became more protectionist as a result of a trade deficit that exceeded $200 billion annually.

Trade Policy Analysis: Terms of Trade   249

The relationship between the prices a country receives for its exports and the prices it pays for its imports. The terms of trade serve as a means for measuring the trend of a nation's gains or losses from trade compared to a previous base period by determining the barter or exchange value of commodities bought from and sold to other countries. If, on the average, export prices rise or import prices fall, or both occur, the nation's terms of trade have improved; if, on average, export prices fall or import prices rise, or both, its terms of trade have worsened. *See also* TRADE POLICY ANALYSIS: BALANCE OF TRADE (248); TRADE POLICY INSTRUMENT: COMMODITY AGREEMENT (254).

Significance
Over the past 50 years, the terms of trade between the First and Third Worlds improved for the industrially advanced countries and worsened for the underdeveloped nations. The trend toward higher prices for manufactures reflects the stronger demand for industrial goods and the price-fixing and market-controlling propensities among the multinational corporations that are the prime suppliers. The trend toward lower prices for primary commodities results from the competition among numerous suppliers; this supply exceeds demand, and depresses world market prices. Primary-commodity prices have increased substantially only during those years when the industrial nations have been at war. The developing nations seek to improve their terms of trade through barter arrangements, the use of tariffs and other trade control techniques, and commodity agreements that limit supply and maintain price levels. A shift in a nation's terms of trade may have a significant impact on its balance of payments.

Trade Policy Instrument: Barter   250

An arrangement between governments for the exchange of goods. Under a barter agreement, quantities of goods are exchanged at an agreed ratio without any monetary transactions. Barter arrangements typically are entered into by nations to overcome foreign-exchange problems that hinder trade between them. *See also* TRADE POLICY INSTRUMENT: BILATERAL TRADE (251).

Significance

Barter agreements to foster trade became commonplace during the Great Depression of the 1930s and during World War II, when normal trade practices suffered from monetary restrictions imposed by exchange control, blocked accounts, and competitive depreciations. Since World War II, the Communist countries have made wide use of barter arrangements to open up trade with many developing countries. Soviet foreign aid, for example, usually takes the form of trade credits, which are paid off in commodities over a period of years by the recipient country according to the terms provided by a barter agreement. Barter systems are advantageous not only in promoting trade but for avoiding balance-of-payments problems as well. The main disadvantage of barter is that it promotes bilateral rather than multilateral trade. State-trading countries are more likely to utilize barter in their trade because the government holds a monopoly over all foreign commercial transactions. Barter arrangements are of limited use in systems based on private enterprise because individual firms are unlikely to exchange their products for foreign goods rather than for foreign exchange.

Trade Policy Instrument: Bilateral Trade | 251 |

An understanding between two states to foster cooperation in trade and related economic matters. A bilateral economic agreement may take the form of a clearing arrangement in which payments for imports and exports are paid through a single central bank account, or of a payments agreement that includes all financial transactions between the two countries. In its simplest form, a bilateral agreement may provide for a barter arrangement whereby two countries exchange goods in specified amounts with no payments in foreign exchange. The most common use of economic bilateralism is in trade agreements providing for a mutual reduction in tariffs or other trade barriers. *See also* TRADE POLICY INSTRUMENT: BARTER (250).

Significance

Bilateral agreements play a major role in promoting trade between nations during periods of economic nationalism. They are useful in overcoming restrictive national policies that involve exchange control, tariffs, and quotas, and in directing trade to achieve political objectives. However, they also tend to be preferential arrangements, which by their very nature discriminate against other nations and frequently evoke retaliation. The inclusion of most-favored-nation treatment in bilateral agreements—as in those concluded within the framework of the General Agreement on Tariffs and Trade (GATT)—eliminates their discriminatory impact. In this way they may contribute to the growth of a freer multilateral trading system rather than encourage trade discrimination. Communist states have used bilateral agreements in granting foreign aid to developing countries. They generally extended long-term credits for technical assistance, capital goods, and military equipment, which were paid for by the receiving state in shipments of commodities over a period of many years. The remaining Communist states in the 1990s, however, display little interest in the barter of long-term credit agreements. More concerned with the market value of their products, they seek advantages—hence, quick profits—much as the capitalist states do.

Trade Policy Instrument: Boycott | 252 |

Refusal to buy products from a particular country or group of countries. A boycott may be government-sponsored or may be initiated by private groups that seek to influence consumers against making purchases of goods from the boycotted nation. *See also* TRADE POLICY INSTRUMENT: EMBARGO (257).

Significance

A boycott is an instrument of trade policy that may be motivated by economic, political, security, or ideological factors. The general U.S. boycott of Japanese imports before World War II was directed mainly at protecting U.S. jobs and industries from low-wage competition. Although such purchases were not prohibited by law, the private boycott substantially reduced imports from Japan and worsened political relations between the two nations. Efforts by American patriotic groups to promote a general boycott of goods made in Communist countries had little impact on foreign trade. Government purchasing policies, such as those promoted by the "Buy American" Act, may constitute a partial but indirect boycott of foreign suppliers. In the 1980s and 1990s, heavy Japanese exports into the United States created public outcry for protection of domestic industries and jobs, especially in the automobile industry.

Trade Policy Instrument: Cartel 253

An agreement among independent businesspersons or countries to restrict competition. A cartel agreement is based on a contractual understanding typically involving prices, production, and the division of the market. The term *cartel* originated in Germany during the 1870s (from the Latin *charta*, meaning "contract"). Cartels are employed mainly in mass-production industries where exclusiveness is protected by patents or quality differences are minor, and in the energy field, especially in oil and gas. The market for most primary commodities, especially agricultural products, is highly competitive and does not lend itself to cartelization, resulting in deterioration of commodity prices relative to prices of manufactured products. *See also* TRADE POLICY ORGANIZATION: ORGANIZATION OF PETROLEUM EXPORTING COUNTRIES (OPEC) (273).

Significance
Up to one-half of world trade during the Great Depression of the 1930s was subject to cartel control. Cartelization of the market diminished after World War II, owing to the establishment of antimonopoly legislation in Great Britain and joint anti-cartel action by members of the European Community. Although Germany was the center for cartel activity for many years, Japan is now the most active of the industrial countries. In the United States, cartels have been illegal since the passage of the Sherman Antitrust Act of 1890 although, under the Webb-Pomerene Act of 1918, business associations competing with foreign cartels for world trade are exempted from the provisions of the antitrust laws. The Organization of Petroleum Exporting Countries (OPEC), the most effective contemporary cartel, was established in 1961.

Trade Policy Instrument: Commodity Agreement 254

An international contract by which signatory states strive to establish an orderly world marketing system for a primary commodity. Commodity agreements are sought mainly by producer states to overcome the destructive competition that emerges from gross overproduction and results in a world "buyers' market." Through a commodity agreement, states establish production controls, regulate exports, establish minimum and maximum world export prices, and provide for reserve stocks of the commodity. States heavily dependent on imports of the commodity may also join in an agreement. The most successful commodity agreement is the Organization of Petroleum Exporting Countries (OPEC), established in 1961. Because oil-importing states are not represented in OPEC, the commodity agreement has been converted into a cartel, which attempts to control production, pricing, and marketing. Encouraged by OPEC's success with oil, commodity agreements have been concluded for such products as coffee, olive oil, sugar, wheat, tea, cotton, rubber, tin, and beef. *See also* TRADE POLICY ANALYSIS: TERMS OF TRADE (249).

Significance
Commodity agreements may be particularly useful when many developing states competing for scarce foreign exchange produce large surpluses of a commodity,

saturating the market and driving prices down. Under conditions of free competition, each producer would increase production to make up for the loss caused by lower prices, with the result that prices are driven even lower. But through agreement, states can establish near-monopoly marketing conditions for their producers by rigorously controlling private actions. Major conflicts may arise, however, when the commodities regulated are produced in the advanced states as well as in the developing states, resulting in a significant difference between world export price levels and domestic prices. The difficulty of reaching agreement on production and marketing quotas among primary commodity–producing states, some of which depend almost entirely on the commodity for their foreign-exchange earnings, is illustrated by the years of intensive but fruitless negotiations to conclude a cocoa agreement. OPEC's occasional successes encourage other primary commodity–exporting states to follow OPEC's lead, but most raw materials and foodstuffs suffer from a weak demand in the world market compared to the strong demand for oil.

Trade Policy Instrument: Countervailing Duty | 255 |

A special assessment levied on imports to offset an advantage or discount provided by a foreign seller or government. A countervailing duty is applied against those products that might provide unfair competition for locally produced articles of commerce as a result of foreign governmental subsidies or other special advantages. The duty levied is in addition to the normal tariff charge. *See also* TRADE POLICY INSTRUMENT: TARIFF (264).

Significance
Countervailing duties are aimed mainly at nullifying the special market advantage of foreign producers when government subsidies permit them to sell below the normal market price. In the United States, the secretary of the treasury has discretionary authority to levy counter-

vailing duties when it is believed that such conditions exist. This type of duty is one of many retaliatory weapons used in trade warfare to protect the home market from unfair competition.

Trade Policy Instrument: Dumping | 256 |

Sales of goods in foreign markets at net unit prices lower than those charged domestic consumers. Dumping may involve below-cost sales as a means of reducing large inventories, or the sales may be an attempt to drive competitive firms out of the market. Dumping may be carried on by private companies, subsidized and encouraged by the state, or directly by state-owned enterprises. State-trading countries may use it as an economic weapon in pursuit of political or ideological objectives. *See also* TRADE POLICY INSTRUMENT: COUNTERVAILING DUTY (255).

Significance
The technique of dumping has been an international trade practice since the nineteenth century, when trusts and cartels used it to fight for markets. Dumping constitutes a threat to an orderly market system. Although consumers may benefit initially, if competitive firms are driven from the market by the practice, ultimately the consumer will pay higher prices for the product. State policy has often supported dumping with export bounties during times of weakness in domestic economies, especially during the Great Depression of the 1930s. The Soviet Union occasionally disrupted orderly marketing by dumping large quantities of primary commodities received in payment of foreign aid, such as tin and cotton, at below world market prices. In the 1980s, foreign competitors charged that the United States engaged in dumping by subsidizing the sale of large quantities of wheat to the Soviet Union at lower than domestic prices. Similarly, in 1987 the United States raised its tariff with Japan on some electronic products that were being dumped in the United States and other markets. The Japanese generally sell all

their products in the United States at prices lower than those found in Japan. Considering the precipitous fall in the value of the dollar against the yen in 1995, some of these Japanese dumping practices may have to be curtailed.

Trade Policy Instrument: Embargo | 257 |

A government edict prohibiting citizens from trading with one or several countries. The embargo may apply only to certain types of products, or it may be a total prohibition of trade. *See also* TRADE POLICY INSTRUMENT: BOYCOTT (252).

Significance

An embargo is a weapon of national economic policy levied for the achievement of strategic or political objectives. Partial embargoes, such as the U.S. prohibition of trade in strategic goods with Communist countries, may be aimed at weakening the military capabilities of potential enemies. The total embargo forbidding Americans to ship any kind of material or product to Iran in 1995 was intended to pressure the Tehran government to cancel its nuclear-weapons program and end its support and sponsorship of international terrorism. U.S. efforts to pressure allied nations to reduce or eliminate their trade with Iran is another matter in the post–Cold War era, when commerce looms larger than political affiliation. Trade embargoes may be circumvented through illegal trade or by channeling it through a third country for transshipment to the embargoed nation. The embargoed nation may also increase its trade in prohibited articles with third countries and develop its own industries to overcome the impact of the embargo.

Trade Policy Instrument: Escape Clause | 258 |

A provision inserted in a trade agreement that permits a party to terminate or alter a tariff concession. An escape clause can be invoked only after a specified period of notice has elapsed. In the United States, tariff concessions may be withdrawn if imports substantially threaten or injure a domestic producer. The United States

International Trade Commission has established "peril points" at which, when imports reach such levels, the president and Congress are informed of the danger to U.S. producers. The president may then invoke the escape clause provision in the agreement to reduce the threat of injury. *See also* TRADE POLICY INSTRUMENT: TARIFF (264).

Significance

The escape clause and peril point provisions were introduced by the United States as amendments to the Reciprocal Trade Agreements Act in 1951, and were continued in subsequent trade acts. Other states have accepted—usually reluctantly—the escape clause provisions when entering into a trade agreement with the United States. The president has invoked them to restore higher tariff rates on a number of occasions, usually to offer protection demanded by powerful domestic pressure groups. Insistence on inclusion of an escape clause in a trade agreement weakens the hand of the negotiator because it implies a lack of sincerity in achieving a maximal expansion of trade.

Trade Policy Instrument: Licensing | 259 |

A trade control device whereby a government grants permission to certain private individuals and companies to engage in importing or exporting commodities, and regulates their activities by the conditions of the license. Under a trade licensing system, administrative officials determine which companies shall be permitted to engage in certain types of trading activity. Licensed companies must comply with state policy and administrative directives or their licenses may be suspended, revoked, or not renewed. Licensing systems are used primarily to allocate import quotas among several companies. Licensing thus seeks to avoid the rush-to-import characteristic of a global quota system, which permits any importer to purchase goods up to the limit of the quota. *See also* ECONOMIC THEORY: ECONOMIC NATIONALISM (222); TRADE POLICY INSTRUMENT: QUOTA (261).

Significance

State licensing of private trading companies is aimed at controlling the direction, nature, and quantities of exports or imports, or both. It substitutes the economic, political, or military objectives of state policy for the free interplay of the marketplace. Many states adopted extensive licensing systems during the period of economic nationalism in the 1930s in an attempt to improve domestic economic conditions through control over foreign trade. State licensing is also used as a technique for waging economic warfare to limit or proscribe shipments of goods to enemy or potential enemy states. The use of licensing by the industrial nations to control trade flows has been reduced in the post–World War II era.

Trade Policy Instrument: Most-Favored-Nation Clause $\boxed{260}$

A provision inserted in a trade agreement that extends tariff concessions agreed to by the signatories to all nations participating in the reciprocal system. The most-favored-nation clause avoids trade discrimination against third states by granting equal treatment to all. Likewise, more favorable tariff arrangements extended to other states by any signatory will automatically apply to the original parties. *See also* TRADE POLICY ORGANIZATION: GENERAL AGREEMENT ON TARIFFS AND TRADE (GATT) (268).

Significance

The insertion of the most-favored-nation clause in a trade agreement means that the parties are not attempting to establish a bilateral preferential arrangement that would discriminate against other trading partners. The clause can turn an otherwise discriminatory series of bilateral agreements into an outward-looking program for the general reduction of trade barriers. It has been used since 1934, for example, to rebuild a liberal trading system out of the maze of discriminatory barriers established during the early years of the Great Depression. Both the Reciprocal Trade Agreements Program and the General Agreement on Tariffs and Trade (GATT) provide for the incorporation of the most-favored-nation principle in all trade agreements. In the United States, the president may withhold the application of the clause from trade with nations that discriminate against U.S. exports. This discretionary power was used to withhold most-favored-nation treatment from the Soviet Union, but not from Communist China. Moreover, China retained most-favored-nation treatment even after the 1989 Tiananmen Square massacre, and the heavy criticism directed against it by the U.S. Congress.

Trade Policy Instrument: Quota $\boxed{261}$

A quantitative restriction established by a state to control the importation of certain commodities. Variations of the quota system used in different countries provide for (1) increasing customs duties as larger numbers of items are imported, up to the limit of the quota (customs quota), (2) individual quotas for specific countries (allocated quota), (3) a general limit on imports, applicable to all countries (global quota), (4) individual quotas for specific companies (import licensing), (5) reciprocal arrangements for limiting trade (bilateral quota), and (6) import limits determined by the relationship of the articles to domestic production (mixing quota). *See also* TRADE POLICY: PROTECTIONISM (245).

Significance

Quotas have been used to limit foreign competition in the domestic market, correct balance-of-payments deficits, buttress protective tariff systems, provide a tool for governmental direction of trade, and wage economic warfare. A quota is a more effective weapon than a tariff for domestic protection or economic warfare because it provides for an absolute limitation on imports, whereas a tariff is a tax that, if the consumer is willing to pay the additional cost for the article, merely increases prices but does not bar goods. Most countries use quota systems to supplement their tariff policies, applying the quotas to protect their least-competitive industries or those having the most political influence. In the advanced industrial states, this usually means quota protection for farmers and other primary-commodity suppliers and for automobile makers.

Trade Policy Instrument: Smoot-Hawley Tariff Act of 1930 | 262 |

An act that imposed extremely high tariff duties on agricultural and industrial imports to the United States. Passage of the bill in Congress resulted from the political pressures exerted by numerous special-interest groups seeking protection. President Herbert Hoover, petitioned by leading economists to veto the bill, permitted it to become law without his signature although he was personally opposed to it. *See also* TRADE POLICY: PROTECTIONISM (245).

Significance
The Smoot-Hawley Tariff imposed the highest rates on imports in U.S. history and helped to "export" the U.S. depression to the rest of the world. Most countries swiftly retaliated by raising their tariffs, severely depressing world trade and deepening the effects of the economic malaise. The high rates established by the act have been progressively whittled down through negotiations and agreements concluded under the Reciprocal Trade Agreements Program since 1934 and the General Agreement on Tariffs and Trade (GATT) since 1947. Many of the high Smoot-Hawley rates, however, still apply to those countries that are not members of GATT and do not receive most-favored-nation treatment. The tragic results of the Smoot-Hawley Tariff Act emphasize the interdependence of nations in the world economy, and the threat posed by resurgent protectionism.

Trade Policy Instrument: Subsidy | 263 |

Direct or indirect aid offered by government to private individuals or industries to increase their economic well-being. A direct subsidy may take the form of a sharing of construction costs, an export bounty, or governmental purchases of a portion of production at a guaranteed price. An indirect subsidy may involve protection of the home market through quotas, tariffs, or other restrictionist devices that permit higher prices for domestic business and industry by reducing foreign competition.

Significance
Every state has adopted subsidy policies for sectors of the economy, policies that vary in their directness, size, and objectives. Subsidies for particular industries often result from political influence. The most extensive subsidies are those aimed at stabilizing an important domestic industry, such as agriculture in the United States, and those used to encourage exports to correct a deficit balance of payments. Export subsidies are often regarded as an offensive instrument of trade policy by other states, especially when they permit dumping (selling a product abroad for less than in the domestic market). Subsidies that benefit one industry may have a harmful economic impact on others that are in direct or indirect competition with the subsidized products.

Trade Policy Instrument: Tariff | 264 |

A tax levied on imports or exports. Tariffs are commonly applied to imports to protect domestic business, agriculture, and labor from foreign competition in the home market. In some countries, the primary objective of a tariff is either to raise revenue or to retaliate against the restrictive trade policies of other nations. A tariff is discriminatory if rates vary on similar products from different countries. Tariffs on imports are paid by domestic businesses, which pass on the cost to the consumer. Most tariff rates are based on an ad valorem duty (i.e., on a percentage of the value of the imported articles) although some are based on weight, quantity, and fixed duties. Unlike specific duties that remain constant despite price changes, ad valorem tariff rates fluctuate with the price variations on imports, rising during periods of inflation. *See also* TRADE POLICY: FREE TRADE (244); TRADE POLICY: PROTECTIONISM (245).

Significance

Tariffs are almost universally applied to imports, whereas tariffs on exports are seldom used because of their adverse effect on foreign sales. States justify their tariff systems as a means to correct deficits in their balances of payments, protect infant industry, equalize costs, attract investment capital, improve the terms of trade, raise revenue, reduce unemployment, safeguard national defense industries, retaliate against the discriminatory trade policies of other states, or serve as a bargaining tool for obtaining trade concessions. Like other restrictionist devices, tariffs tend to reduce standards of living in all countries because they limit the flow of trade and reduce the international division of labor and national specialization. The high tariff walls set up during the 1920s and early 1930s have been progressively attacked through almost continuous negotiations over a period of more than 50 years. Numerous trade agreements concluded bilaterally under the Reciprocal Trade Agreements Program initiated in 1934, and through the multilateral negotiations carried on within the General Agreement on Tariffs and Trade (GATT) organization since 1947, have reduced tariff barriers to their lowest point in years. Tariffs have also been attacked through regional preferential systems, such as the common-market arrangements established by the European Union (EU) and the European Free Trade Association (EFTA). The history of international trade, however, demonstrates that low-tariff periods are typically followed by a return to protectionism when national economies are depressed.

Trade Policy Organization: Economic Community of West African States (ECOWAS) | 265 |

An economic community of 15 West African states, formed in 1975 for the purpose of pooling the resources of the member states in order to make them collectively more competitive with the economic unions developed in other areas of the world. ECOWAS brought together nine formerly French colonies, five formerly British, and one formerly Portuguese to comprise the largest example of economic integration on the continent. With a total population of approximately 150 million people, and with a land area roughly more than twice that of the contiguous United States, ECOWAS's principal participants are Nigeria, Ghana, Burkina Faso, Senegal, Niger, and Chad.

Significance

ECOWAS was apparently established well before its time. In theory, its organization and purpose suggests the course taken by the West Europeans in establishing their European Union. ECOWAS promised to reduce trade barriers between member states, remove restrictions on the movement of labor, and center attention on joint projects and regional development. But the intentions and declarations did not compensate for national endeavor, national purpose, or national exclusivities. Moreover, ECOWAS was fashioned in the early years of the oil boom. Nigeria, a principal promoter of the organization, anticipated making great strides in its development program as a consequence of its own important reserves of high-grade petroleum. Provoked by OPEC and OAPEC's influence and power in the 1970s, Nigeria believed that its leadership of ECOWAS would give Sub-Saharan Africa a significant place in international circles, accelerate the development of the region, and open up new possibilities for African (especially West African) integration. The fall in the world market price of oil, therefore, was a blow to ECOWAS and Nigerian aspirations. The organization could not promote the envisaged regional development in a condition of limited resources, and without the material justification for pressing ECOWAS objectives, it faltered. Although it remains in the 1990s to remind West Africans of their collective interests, its gains are modest at best.

Trade Policy Organization: Economic Summit   266

An annual conference of the leaders of the seven major economic Western powers to develop common approaches to current economic and political problems. The economic summits are not aimed at writing treaties or agreements but rather at harmonizing and coordinating the national policies of the participants. By 1995, 21 annual economic summits had been held. Most of these included the representatives of five nations, but in the 1980s Italy and Canada were invited to join, and it became the Group of Seven (G-7). Russia, the successor state to the Soviet Union, was invited to attend the summit meetings in 1993–1994 in recognition of its efforts at developing a market economy, but its feeble financial status did not entitle it to membership in the G-7. *See also* DIPLOMACY, SUMMIT (414).

Significance
The economic summit brings together the heads of state/government on an annual basis for the purpose of discussing world economic problems. The agenda generally includes confronting growing protectionism, abrasive trading practices, the international debt crisis, currency stability (especially of the dollar), the need to boost economic growth, and the persistent dangers inherent in spiraling inflation, unemployment, and the ever-increasing gap between rich and poor nations. The summit also has discussed such political issues as the spread of nuclear weapons, transnational terrorism, and the escalation of ethnic and tribal wars. Combating AIDS (Acquired Immune Deficiency Syndrome) also has been an agenda item. Typically, each summit meeting results in the issuance of one or more economic as well as political declarations.

Trade Policy Organization: Export-Import Bank   267

A U.S. government corporation that makes direct loans to foreign and domestic businesses to promote international trade, and provides financing for social and economic infrastructure projects in developing states. Chartered in 1934, the Export-Import Bank's operations are governed by a five-member bipartisan board appointed by the president with Senate approval. Loans to foreign companies must be guaranteed by their governments, a requirement that has led to governmental control of or involvement in most development projects financed by the bank. The loans generally cover purchases in the United States of capital equipment necessary to supplement local labor and materials for the projects. The loans must be repaid in dollars. *See also* FOREIGN AID (643).

Significance
The Export-Import Bank was originally established to extend credit to private U.S. exporters in order to encourage foreign trade, especially with the Soviet Union and Latin America. In more recent years, its lending policies have been aimed mainly at helping developing states. Since 1934 the bank has made loans totaling billions of dollars to Latin America, Europe, Asia, Africa, and Oceania. Substantial profits earned by the bank go into reserves against future losses and to the U.S. government as dividends. Loans from the bank have aided developing states in the construction of dams, irrigation projects, canals, roads, processing plants, mines, and manufacturing industries.

Trade Policy Organization: General Agreement on Tariffs and Trade (GATT)—Origins   268

An international organization that promotes trade among its members by serving as a forum for negotiating agreements to reduce tariffs and other barriers. GATT first met in Geneva in 1947 to function as an interim arrangement until the proposed International Trade Organization (ITO) could be established as a specialized agency of the United Nations to provide for orderly world trade. When the United States rejected ITO, GATT was developed as the main instrument to encourage freer trade. (Unlike ITO, which was based on a treaty, GATT was based on executive agreements and, consequently, did not have to be approved by the Senate.) GATT's membership increased from the original 23 participants to more than 100 associate members, who together carry on more than 80 percent of world trade. In 1971 GATT approved a General System of Preferences (GSP), authorizing the developed countries to give preferential tariff treatment to developing countries. In 1976 the United States joined many countries of Europe and Asia in adopting the GSP approach, resulting in the lowering of hundreds of tariff rates for the imports of developing countries. GATT's functions include (1) negotiating the reduction of tariffs and other impediments to trade, (2) developing new trade policies, (3) adjusting, or moderating, trade disputes, and (4) establishing rules to govern the trade policies of its members. Members are mandated to negotiate bilaterally and multilaterally at periodic meetings. The most-favored-nation clause incorporated in all agreements and concluded at GATT sessions ensures that trade concessions will be made applicable to every member. A nondiscrimination rule prohibits members from using quantitative restrictions, quotas, export subsidies, special taxes, or other devices to circumvent the concessions granted. GATT operates under the direction of its steering committee, the Consultative Group of Eighteen (CG-18), with a membership of nine developed and nine developing countries. Parity of the two blocs reflects efforts of the industrialized nations to escape Third World charges that GATT functions largely as a "rich man's club." Its headquarters are located in Geneva. *See also* TRADE POLICY INSTRUMENT: MOST-FAVORED-NATION CLAUSE (260); TRADE POLICY INSTRUMENT: TARIFF (264); TRADE POLICY ORGANIZATION: GENERAL AGREEMENT ON TARIFFS AND TRADE (GATT) (269); TRADE POLICY ORGANIZATION: WORLD TRADE ORGANIZATION (WTO) (275).

Significance

In its formative years, members of the General Agreement on Tariffs and Trade more or less successfully negotiated substantial reductions in trade barriers, but progress was slow and tedious. The Tokyo Round of negotiations in 1979, which reciprocally reduced tariffs by an average of 33 percent, chiefly benefited the industrial countries. Most developing countries boycotted the signing ceremony because the sessions had not responded to their demands, such as the need to liberalize tariff rates on primary commodities and processed goods. Numerous disputes among members, however, were resolved, and some major trade wars were avoided. GATT represented the serious intentions of nations to set comprehensive rules for the guidance of its members in their trade relations, and consequently nontariff barriers were kept in relative equilibrium through the Uruguay Round of negotiations, which commenced in 1986. Many developing countries still regard GATT as the "rich man's club," and a central issue of GATT is to address demands of the developing countries for the creation of a new international economic order, with a fairer trading system as a central part of that new order. The Uruguay Round of negotiations, which involved more developing countries than at any other time in GATT history, was completed in 1994.

Trade Policy Organization: General Agreement on Tariffs and Trade (GATT) | 269 |

International organization established in 1948 to lower tariff barriers in order to stimulate worldwide economic and financial growth. From GATT's inception to the 1990s, tariffs fell from an average 40 percent to 4.7 percent. However, its most important role was the creation of forums for countries to resolve their trade disputes through arbitration, thus avoiding costly trade wars. In September 1986 the eighth general renegotiation of GATT rules began in Punte del Este, Uruguay. Known as the Uruguay Round, these renegotiations were not completed until

December 1993, when 123 governments agreed to comply with new rules of trade in areas never before subject to multilateral agreements. These agreements were intended to prevent discrimination in trade services, transnational investments, agricultural trade, textiles, and clothing. They also revised and tightened trade rules in such areas as intellectual property, government procurement, antidumping enforcement, and subsidies. GATT passed through a major transition in 1994. On 15 April 1994 the United States signed the Final Act of the Uruguay Round, and it only remained for the U.S. Congress to approve the trade bills implementing the agreement. With U.S. approval of the new GATT agreement, other nations such as Japan were quick to follow the U.S. example. The new GATT agreement cuts average tariffs worldwide by one-third and eliminates tariffs for many items. Of significant importance, the 1994 GATT agreement officially established the World Trade Organization (WTO), which replaced the GATT secretariat. WTO will administer the system of trade law, and thus become the key institution to enforce the rules of trade. WTO's Trade Policy Review Body will supervise trade practices of member governments, identify problems, and make recommendations to address practices in restraint of trade. A permanent process for revising international trade rules replaces the periodic rounds that formerly characterized GATT operations. The new GATT came into force 1 January 1995. *See also* TRADE POLICY ORGANIZATION: GENERAL AGREEMENT ON TARIFFS AND TRADE (GATT)—ORIGINS (268); TRADE POLICY ORGANIZATION: URUGUAY ROUND (274); TRADE POLICY ORGANIZATION: WORLD TRADE ORGANIZATION (WTO) (275).

Significance
GATT is a complicated and elaborate set of rules and procedures to ensure the free and equitable distribution of trade among the member states. Trade protection is no longer judged a "best" interest of individual states, and through GATT, the member states have declared their intention to avoid the economic nationalism of the 1930s, which contributed to the conditions leading to World War II. GATT's most important benefit is the discouraging of trade practices by its member governments that discriminate against foreign producers. GATT requires equality of treatment, and at its core is the operation of most-favored-nation principles, which prevent governments from favoring some foreign producers over others. By the same token, GATT forbids governments to favor its own nationals over foreigners. Moreover, the creation of the World Trade Organization as a permanent rule-enforcing assembly for nations eager to expand exports is a historic achievement. It gives consumers in all nations better access to the most technologically and scientifically advanced goods and services, and allows them to benefit from the free movement of capital investment. Critics in member countries believe that too much sovereignty has been sacrificed to the WTO; proponents argue that a minimum price has been paid in bringing the world economy to accept a system of law vital to economic growth and progress.

Trade Policy Organization: Imperial Preferences   270

A system by which Great Britain and other Commonwealth countries reciprocally grant preferential trade treatment to one another. Imperial preferences originated in 1919, when Great Britain had no general tariff, as an arrangement whereby members of the empire granted Great Britain economic preferences in exchange for protection by the British fleet. The system was expanded in 1932 when Great Britain adopted a general tariff and, in the Ottawa Agreement, granted special treatment for the Dominions to sell their primary commodities in the British market in exchange for continued preference for British manufactures in their markets. To protect infant industry in the Dominions, tariffs were raised on all entering manufactured goods, but rates that applied to Great Britain were kept much lower, though still protective. *See also* ECONOMIC INTEGRATION: PREFERENTIAL TRADE AR-RANGEMENT (220); REGIONAL POLITICAL GROUP: COMMONWEALTH OF NATIONS (562).

Significance
The system of imperial or Commonwealth preferences was a key factor in attracting members and developing unity in the multiracial Commonwealth of Nations. Many formerly colonial Third World states such as India, Guyana, and Nigeria were attracted to joining the Commonwealth to retain their sizable market in the British Isles. Imperial preferences, however, were a major stumbling block in Great Britain's efforts to achieve membership in the European Economic Community (EEC). France demanded that Great Britain relinquish such preferential arrangements as a condition of membership, a situation that could have jeopardized the stability of the Commonwealth, yet Great Britain yielded to the demands and, following its entry into the EEC in 1973, special trade arrangements with many Commonwealth countries were concluded by the EEC.

Trade Policy Organization: Lomé Convention | 271 |

A special trade treaty concluded at Lomé, Togo, in 1975 between the European Economic Community (EEC) and 46 developing countries of Africa, Asia and the Pacific, and the Caribbean. The Lomé Convention superseded the Yaoundé Conventions of 1963 and 1969, signed by the EEC and 18 African countries. The main purpose of the Yaoundé and Lomé Conventions was to provide for trade preferences for the Third World signatory countries. Since 1971 these preferential arrangements have been administered in accordance with the Generalized System of Preferences established by the General Agreement on Tariffs and Trade (GATT). In addition, they provided for an export revenue stabilization system (STABEX) that includes price supports for a stipulated list of raw materials. *See also* REGIONAL POLITICAL GROUP: EUROPEAN COMMUNITY (EC) (565).

Significance
The Lomé Convention has proven so successful that over 60 countries of the Third World are currently members. Affiliation in the convention provides benefits for all parties, but mainly for the developing-state members, which were at one time colonies of the European Economic Community countries. The value of the trade arrangements included in the Lomé Convention relates mainly to the need of Third World countries to expand their trade so as to earn the hard currency needed for achieving developmental objectives.

Trade Policy Organization: North American Free Trade Agreement (NAFTA) | 272 |

Free-trade-area agreement negotiated by the United States, Canada, and Mexico in 1991–1993. NAFTA was approved by the three countries, in individual legislative sessions, in 1993–1994, and desiring the opening of NAFTA to additional Latin American states, Chile was admitted in 1994. Initiated by the Bush administration because of developments in the European Union, NAFTA set up a trading bloc of approximately 440 million consumers with a total output of $6 trillion (approximately 25 percent more than the European Union). Canada and Mexico represented the United States' chief trading partners before NAFTA, and the creation of a free-trade area among them appeared to guarantee expansion of that commerce. Nevertheless, the primary opposition to NAFTA arose in the United States, where its critics argued that Mexico, a poor economy in contrast to that of the United States, would reap benefits paid for through the loss of U.S. jobs. Proponents of NAFTA countered this argument, insisting that the agreement would improve cooperation within the North American region and, in the long term, enhance the U.S. economy by opening a still larger market to U.S. goods and services. In point of fact, NAFTA called for significant trade liberalization in all three countries, and Mexico, with its more protectionist policies, was the most affected. Acceptance of NAFTA meant the lowering and sometimes the elimination of tariff barriers heretofore imposed on goods of the member states. Mexico's average tariff rate was about 9.4 percent, and it also maintained licenses on 198 products from beans to trucks to dairy products. But just as Mexican agricultural production would be affected by the influx of U.S. products, U.S. labor saw pressure from a cheaper Mexican labor market. On balance, however, NAFTA appeared to promise mutual benefits for all the states. *See also* ASIA-PACIFIC ECONOMIC COOPERATION (APEC) (185); REGIONAL ECONOMIC GROUP: CARRIBEAN COMMUNITY AND COMMON MARKET (CARICOM) (550); REGIONAL ECONOMIC GROUP: CENTRAL AMERICAN COMMON MARKET (CACM) (551); REGIONAL ECONOMIC GROUP: LATIN AMERICAN INTEGRATION ASSOCIATION (LAIA) (553); REGIONAL MILITARY GROUP: INTER-AMERICAN SYSTEM (556); REGIONAL POLITICAL GROUP: EUROPEAN UNION (EU) (566).

Significance
Free-trade areas in the Western Hemisphere are not new. The Latin American Free Trade Area (LAFTA) was created in 1960. It focused attention on the integration of the region's economies, but was most effective when world economic conditions were poor. When world economic growth accelerated in the late 1970s and 1980s, LAFTA proved to be an obstacle to national development schemes. Moreover, global economic pressures, more than regional pressures, influenced national and international economic policy. The shadow of LAFTA's limited achievement looms over NAFTA, which is described as a trading bloc for the twenty-first century. NAFTA's critics in the three North American countries are articulate and unyielding in their claim that the arrangement stunts rather than promotes the growth of their individual nations. Mexico's significant debt crisis in 1995 provided more ammunition to those who would destroy NAFTA even before it was adequately tested. Mexico's political system was jolted by the assassination of the leading party's presidential candidate in 1994, by an armed rebellion in Chiapas province, and by the general ineptness of its new government. In addition, government corruption (after several decades of one-party rule), the widespread use of bribes and kickbacks for goods sold and services rendered, and the enormous black market fueled by the country's elites and generally sanctioned by the ruling party raised important questions about Mexico's role in the overall NAFTA scheme.

Trade Policy Organization: Organization of Petroleum Exporting Countries (OPEC) | 273 |

A group of 13 oil-exporting countries that established an intergovernmental cartel to regulate production and agree on oil pricing in the world market. OPEC's membership includes seven Middle East Arab states (Algeria, Iraq, Kuwait, Libya, Qatar, Saudi Arabia, and the United Arab Emirates), two African states (Gabon and Nigeria), two Asian states (Indonesia and Iran), and two Latin American countries (Ecuador and Venezuela). OPEC was established by treaty in 1961, but it was not until the Middle East War of 1973 that its cartel arrangements became effective. A somewhat more politicized organization—the Organization of Arab Petroleum Exporting Countries (OAPEC)—was established in Beirut in 1968 by Saudi Arabia, Kuwait, and Libya. Other Arab countries that joined the new group include Iraq, Egypt, Syria, Qatar, Dubai, Bahrain, the United Arab Emirates, and Algeria. OAPEC planned and carried out a major oil boycott during the 1973 Arab-Israeli War. After the war ended, greatly increased demands for oil in the industrialized countries of the West and in the Third World led to vastly increased prices for oil and a drain of monetary resources to OPEC members. But the increase in oil prices also impacted the world's major oil corporations in positive ways. The high price of petroleum made it possible for oil companies to prospect for the resource in fields and regions heretofore considered too costly. The further exploitation of older fields, which once again became financially profitable due to high prices, as well as the opening of new ones for more or less the same reasons, caused oil company profits to soar. The production of more oil elsewhere also prompted the OPEC states to produce more themselves, and caused divisions within the organization that have been difficult to reconcile. OPEC unity has always been a relative phenomenon, and in the 1990s the organization pulled in different directions. This OPEC divisiveness, coupled with more sophisticated technologies such as the improved mileage of new automobiles, led to increased oil stores and plummeting prices. The world market glut in oil reduced the price of petroleum products markedly, with the United States as a major beneficiary: Gasoline prices at the pump in the 1990s dropped to almost pre-1973 levels. *See also* TRADE POLICY INSTRUMENT: CARTEL (253).

Significance
From 1973 to 1975, the Organization of Petroleum Exporting Countries' price-setting mechanism essentially quadrupled world oil prices. These increases were responsible for major rounds of inflation in importing countries, reduced productivity, the threat of a major depression, growing unemployment, and frantic efforts to develop alternative sources of energy. The flow of oil produced a reverse flow of money, creating major balance-of-payments problems for many countries, including the United States. Third World developing countries were especially affected by the high energy costs, leading many to acquire huge debts and cut back severely on their modernization programs. The United States and other industrialized countries sought to counter OPEC's cartel pricing by creating an importing countries' organization to develop common policy approaches, and by applying diplomatic and economic pressures on OPEC countries. Other actions undertaken to counteract OPEC's economic power have been the storage of huge quantities of oil underground, the encouragement by governments of the development of alternate energy sources, major conservation programs, and special price and policy inducements to produce more oil within nations to reduce dependence on imports. These measures, added to the inability of some OPEC members to limit production and maintain prices, resulted in a great glut of oil in the world market in the 1980s that continued into the 1990s, with a consequent near collapse in oil prices. However, if the OPEC countries were to again cut off oil shipments to the industrial countries as they did in the 1970s, the industrialized countries would be faced with a major dilemma. Neither OPEC nor OAPEC is the perceived problem; political instability, especially in the oil-rich Middle East, is considered the real challenge. Iraq's decision to invade Kuwait in 1990, and the response to that invasion by the UN coalition led by the United States, centered on the oil reserves of the area. The United States in particular was concerned that Iraq intended to control the petroleum resources of the Arabian peninsula, and that its thrust into Kuwait was also directed against Saudi Arabia, Bahrain, Qatar, Oman, and the United Arab Emirates. The Gulf War of 1991 centered on liberating Kuwait, but it also aimed at safeguarding the interests of the oil-producing states. The United States was less concerned with OPEC or OAPEC than it was with "rogue states" like Iraq that were intent on changing the power equation in the region and, where oil is concerned, in the larger world as well.

Trade Policy Organization: Uruguay Round | 274 |

A series of negotiations on reductions of impediments to international trade conducted by the General Agreement on Tariffs and Trade (GATT). The Uruguay Round began in 1986 when ministers from member states launched a new round of multilateral trade negotiations at Punta del Este, Uruguay. Reduction of tariff rates on both goods and services was high on the agenda. Following the opening discussions at Punta del Este, negotiations continued at

GATT'sheadquarters in Geneva. *See also* TRADE POLICY ORGANIZATION: GENERAL AGREEMENT ON TARIFFS AND TRADE (GATT) (269); TRADE POLICY ORGANIZATION: WORLD TRADE ORGANIZATION (WTO) (275).

Significance
The Uruguay Round was the eighth major series of multilateral trade negotiations conducted by GATT since its creation as a negotiating body. Several of these had major economic consequences. The Kennedy Round (1964–1967) reduced the level of world tariffs by one-third and opened up the European Community (EC) to trade from outside, and the Tokyo Round (1973–1978) emphasized the export needs of developing countries and the problem of coping with nontariff barriers to trade. The Uruguay Round was particularly important because it was directed at keeping world markets open and fighting protectionism. The Uruguay Round negotiations were completed in 1994; not only were all its objectives met, but the World Trade Organization was created.

Trade Policy Organization: World Trade Organization (WTO) | 275 |

The Geneva-based organization created on 1 January 1995 at the close of the Uruguay Round to replace the General Agreement on Tariffs and Trade (GATT) secretariat as the final arbiter in commercial disputes between member nations. Under WTO procedures, two sides to a dispute have 60 days for bilateral talks, after which they can ask for a neutral adjudication panel to assess which side is violating trade rules established by GATT. WTO is more stringent than the older GATT in that it allows fewer options for countries wishing to evade unfavorable rulings on violations of trade agreements. An adjudication panel has six months to issue its report, and the losing party can appeal the finding before a seven-judge court, which has 90 days to consider the appeal. The ruling of the WTO court is final, however. If a country ignores the decision of the court, other WTO members are authorized to retaliate by raising duties on its exports. The United States was a major actor in establishing these rules, but because the Clinton administration had difficulty in steering the agreement through the U.S. Congress, a provision was inserted in the agreement permitting the United States to withdraw from the organization if three "unfair" judgments were passed against it. The first WTO chief was Renato Ruggiero, a former Italian trade minister, who assumed office on 1 May 1995.

Significance
The World Trade Organization was created to facilitate international trade, smooth commercial relations between the member states, and enhance individual economic pursuits by encouraging collective measures based on accommodation and fairness doctrines. Hardly six months after its creation, WTO was burdened with a major dispute that threatened to destroy the young organization. Trade differences between the United States and Japan brought a warning from the Clinton administration that it would unilaterally impose $5.9 billion of punitive tariffs on Japanese automobiles if Tokyo did not open its market to U.S. auto manufactures. Japan filed a letter with U.S. trade officials requesting bilateral consultations. Tokyo insisted on urgent talks, thus triggering WTO adjudication procedures. The action prompted the WTO chief to urge the two sides to abide by the trade group's negotiating systems, but the Clinton administration pressed ahead with its plan to pressure Japan to either yield ground in the dispute or face the imposition of the higher tariffs. Although the United States received some sympathy for its position vis-à-vis Japan, the U.S. move angered most WTO members because the unilateral action threatened to destroy the WTO rules the United States had been prominent in creating.

War and Military Policy

Alliance
276

An agreement by states to support one another militarily in the event of an attack against any member, or to advance their mutual interests. Alliances may be bilateral or multilateral, secret or open, simple or highly organized, of short or long duration, and may be directed at preventing or winning a war. Balance-of-power systems tend to encourage the conclusion of military pacts to offset shifts in the power equation. The United Nations Charter recognizes the right to "collective self defense" in Article 51. *See also* ALLIANCE: NORTH ATLANTIC TREATY ORGANIZATION (NATO)—COLD WAR (284); ALLIANCE: NORTH ATLANTIC TREATY ORGANIZATION (NATO), COLD WAR (285); ALLIANCE: PARTNERSHIP FOR PEACE (PFP) (286); BALANCE OF POWER (1); PATTERNS OF POWER: ALLIANCES (21); PATTERNS OF POWER: COLLECTIVE SECURITY (22); PATTERNS OF POWER: MUTUAL SECURITY (23).

Significance
Most post–World War II alliances did not survive the Cold War. The only significant alliance remaining from that period is the North Atlantic Treaty Organization (NATO). The Warsaw Treaty Organization (WTO) was dissolved with the collapse of communism in Eastern Europe and the Soviet Union. Russia, the successor state to the Soviet Union, has not indicated an interest in organizing alliances; it has joined NATO's Partnership for Peace and, if the opportunity arises, might consider membership in NATO. NATO has displayed interest in the Visegrad states (Poland, Hungary, the Czech Republic, and Slovakia), which want to become full members of NATO, but it hesitates to take action that might disturb the relationship with Russia. Some other continuing alliances are the Arab League, the Organization of African Unity (OAU), and the Organization of American States (OAS). Although these organizations include some measure of commitment to mutual security, they are politically rather than militarily oriented. Alliances may contribute to a sense of security and provide a deterrent to aggression, but they may also contribute to international tension and the formation of counteralliances. Alliance rivalries tend to produce arms races, frequent crises, and,

on occasion, wars. Alliance systems as a function of the balance-of-power mechanism are likely to exist until an effective universal collective-security system or sustainable mutual-security system is established.

Alliance: Act of Chapultepec | 277 |

A resolution adopted by American states that an attack against any of them by a hemispheric or nonhemispheric state would be considered an act of aggression against all. The Act of Chapultepec was signed in Mexico City on 6 March 1945 by the representatives of 21 American republics. This declaration was the forerunner of the Rio Treaty of Reciprocal Assistance of 1947. It provided for sanctions and regional action if an American or non-American state committed aggression against an American state. *See also* ALLIANCE: RIO TREATY (INTER-AMERICAN TREATY OF RECIPROCAL ASSISTANCE) (288); REGIONAL MILITARY GROUP: INTER-AMERICAN SYSTEM (556).

Significance
The Act of Chapultepec had the effect of expanding the Monroe Doctrine's unilateral guarantee against intervention in the Americas to a system providing for a collective response to aggression from outside or within the Western Hemisphere. The act resulted from a U.S. initiative to ensure that the Security Council of the proposed United Nations organization would not prohibit American states from taking collective action on hemispheric security matters.

Alliance: ANZUS Pact | 278 |

A tripartite treaty of alliance concluded in 1951 by Australia, New Zealand, and the United States to safeguard the security of the Pacific area. The treaty, which remains in force indefinitely, provides that an attack on any of the three signatories would be dangerous to all, and that each should act to meet the common danger according to its constitutional processes. The parties further agreed to increase their defense capabilities by self-help and mutual aid. *See also* ALLIANCE: SOUTHEAST ASIA COLLECTIVE DEFENSE TREATY (SEATO) (289); ARMS CONTROL: RAROTONGA TREATY (1987) (370).

Significance
The ANZUS Pact was designed to overcome Australian and New Zealand objections to a Japanese peace treaty. After the French military defeat in Indochina in 1954, the U.S. secretary of state, John Foster Dulles, sought to widen the treaty and provide for the defense of southern Asia from communism through the creation of the wider Southeast Asia Treaty Organization (SEATO). Although SEATO was dissolved in 1977, ANZUS remains in force. ANZUS has been supplemented by numerous bilateral pacts between the United States and several Asian nations, including the Philippines, Japan, Taiwan, and South Korea. The ANZUS Pact was also a recognition that the United States had assumed Great Britain's role in providing security for these two Commonwealth members. In 1986, however, the viability of ANZUS as a defensive alliance was impaired by a disagreement involving New Zealand's protest over the introduction of U.S. nuclear weapons into the region.

Alliance: Baghdad Pact | 279 |

An alliance to safeguard peace and security in the Middle East that served as a base for the development of the Central Treaty Organization. The Baghdad Pact was concluded in 1955 by Iraq and Turkey and acceded to by Great Britain, Pakistan, and Iran in the same year. Although the United States promoted the organization and served on its key committees, it never became a signatory to the pact. All members of the Arab League and major Western powers concerned with the maintenance of security in the Middle East were invited to join the pact, but none did. In 1959 the Baghdad Pact was renamed the Central Treaty Organization (CENTO), following the formal withdrawal of Iraq in the wake of its 1958 revolutionary change of government. Pakistan withdrew from SEATO following the loss of East Pakistan and the formation of Bangladesh in 1971–1972, but it remained a member of CENTO because of its ties to Turkey and Iran. The Iranian Revolution of 1979, however, eliminated the Iranian monarchy, and the new revolutionary government broke its ties to the United States and hence to CENTO. Iran's departure heralded the collapse of CENTO. Pakistan's subsequent departure from the organization caused its formal dissolution in the 1980s. *See also* REGIONAL MILITARY GROUP: CENTRAL TREATY ORGANIZATION (CENTO) (555).

Significance
The Baghdad Pact was developed under U.S. encouragement and represented the Middle Eastern "northern tier" in a global series of alliances encouraged by Secretary of State John Foster Dulles to "contain" Communist expansionism. Although the United States never joined, its representatives participated in CENTO committee sessions and it concluded bilateral security pacts with Iran, Pakistan, and Turkey. The United States also underwrote the pact by supplying military and defense support aid to the parties. The Soviet Union condemned the Baghdad Pact and its CENTO successor as imperialist instruments with aggressive designs. From the start, the security alliance was weakened by the reluctance of the United States to become a signatory member, France's unwillingness to join, the absence of Arab states in its membership, the evolving neutralism in Pakistani policies, political instability in Iran, and the virtual disappearance of British military power in the Middle East.

Alliance: Bilateral Security Pact | 280

A treaty between two nations pledging military support for each other in case of an attack by a third state. Bilateral security pacts may provide for immediate and unconditional assistance in case of an attack upon one of the parties, or they may merely call for consultation between the parties. The pacts may apply against any third state that attacks either party, or they may be limited to attacks launched by specific states named in the pact. *See also* ALLIANCE: JAPANESE-AMERICAN SECURITY TREATY (283).

Significance
Most bilateral security pacts are guarantees offered by great-power states to stand by weaker states when they are in danger. A powerful state pursuing a foreign policy of defending the status quo may enter into security pacts as a means of justifying an intervention if the security or territorial integrity of any of the weaker states is threatened. In the Middle East, for example, the United States entered into bilateral arrangements with Iran, Pakistan, and Turkey during the 1950s. Other U.S. bilateral security pacts were concluded with the Philippines, Japan, Korea, Taiwan, and Spain.

Alliance: Dunkirk Treaty | 281

A 50-year security pact concluded by Great Britain and France in 1947 calling for consultation and joint action against any renewal of German aggression. The Dunkirk Treaty of Alliance and Mutual Assistance provides for continual consultation on economic as well as military matters. *See also* ALLIANCE: BILATERAL SECURITY PACT (280); ALLIANCE: EUROCORPS (282); REGIONAL MILITARY GROUP: WESTERN EUROPEAN UNION (WEU) (559).

Significance
The Dunkirk Treaty was based on fears engendered by historic German domination of the European continent. The treaty symbolized the reemergence of France as a great power after the French catastrophe in World War II. In 1948 the Dunkirk Treaty served as a nucleus for the creation of the Brussels Treaty Organization, which expanded the bilateral security guarantee to include Belgium, the Netherlands, and Luxembourg. In 1955 the Brussels Treaty Organization was renamed the Western European Union (WEU), Germany and Italy were added as

members, and the objective of the pact was changed from deterring German aggression to providing for joint action in the event of an attack by the Soviet Union. WEU in turn led to the expansion of NATO through the admission of West Germany. The Dunkirk Treaty remains in force following the Cold War, but it has less importance in light of developments expanding the mission of the WEU and the creation of Eurocorps by Germany and France.

Alliance: Eurocorps

282

A German and French effort to establish their own defense structures independent of NATO and the Western European Union (WEU). Organized in 1988 by the Federal Republic of Germany and France, the two countries created a Joint Security Council as well as a joint Franco-German Army Brigade. The brigade, consisting of approximately 4,000 troops, became operational in October 1990. The basis for the Eurocorps was established in October 1991 following a decision by the two governments to take further steps to increase their military cooperation. The mission of the Eurocorps is framed within the structure of the European Union and centers on common defense, peacekeeping and peace enforcement, and the providing of humanitarian aid. Other European countries were invited to participate, and a formational agreement on 22 May 1992 made Strasbourg its provisional headquarters. Belgium announced its participation in the Eurocorps in June 1993, and in May 1994 Luxembourg announced that it too would join. The Netherlands and Spain also expressed an interest in participating. The Eurocorps became operational in 1995, and in its initial stage consisted of a Franco-German brigade and a number of smaller permanent elements. German, French, and Belgian formations of divisional size have been considered for possible assignment to Eurocorps. *See also* ALLIANCE: NORTH ATLANTIC TREATY ORGANIZATION (NATO)—COLD WAR (284); ALLIANCE: NORTH ATLANTIC TREATY ORGANIZATION

(NATO)—POST–COLD WAR (285); ALLIANCE: WESTERN EUROPEAN UNION (WEU) (291).

Significance
The formation of Eurocorps represents both negative and positive aspects of European integration and broader Atlantic cooperation. On its face, Eurocorps appears to emphasize the need for a European security system commensurate with developments driving the European Union. An agreement was concluded between French and German authorities and NATO's Supreme Allied Commander in Europe (SACEUR) on the relationship between Eurocorps and NATO and the employment of the corps for operations under NATO command. In May 1993 Eurocorp's role as a multinational force under the auspices of the WEU was confirmed by the governments involved, and in November 1993 an agreement was reached on the manner of its future employment. But the French and the Germans are clearly the dominant actors in the European Union, and as such impact the smaller states of Western Europe. Britain is disturbed by the formation of Eurocorps, preferring to link its security interests with the WEU and NATO. Britain fears a U.S. withdrawal from the continent, and the new emphasis given to the WEU—and now, too, to Eurocorps—suggests a maneuver that might cause the United States to reconsider its role in Europe. NATO may yet prove to be a superfluous organization, bypassed by a Europeanized security system. Although the French have publicly stated that their objective is a separate but not separated security system (from NATO), there appear to be other motives behind the formation of Eurocorps. France has reason to be concerned with a unified Germany, and is particularly interested in tying Germany to arrangements that give Paris an equal voice in a future Europe. Sensing that the United States will grow more distant from Europe and prefer to focus its attention on the Pacific Rim nations, Paris and Bonn have set the scene for a future transition that momentarily appears redundant, but in the long term

may address the Europe of the twenty-first century.

Alliance: Japanese-American Security Treaty $\boxed{283}$

A bilateral defense pact that provides for joint consultations if the security of Japan is threatened. The original Japanese-American Security Treaty was signed in 1951, and a revised Mutual Security Treaty was signed in Washington in 1960 and reaffirmed in 1995. Under the treaty, the United States retains the right to maintain land, sea, and air forces in Japan, which may be used (1) without prior consultation, to maintain peace and security in the Far East, or (2) following consultation, to defend Japan against an armed attack. The treaty specifies that military operations conducted from Japanese bases outside Japan "shall be subject to prior consultation with the Government of Japan." *See also* ALLIANCE: BILATERAL SECURITY PACT (280).

Significance
The Japanese-American Security Treaty, along with Japanese rearmament and the special rights granted to U.S. military units to use Japan as a base, produced political controversy in that nation. When the security treaty was being considered for ratification in 1960, large-scale rioting forced President Eisenhower to cancel his trip to Japan. Although the Japanese Diet approved the treaty, periodic demonstrations and outbreaks of violence by left-wing student groups kept the issue of the security arrangement alive. Questions concerning the future of the alliance were again raised in September 1995 by the reported rape of a Japanese girl on Okinawa, where the bulk of U.S. forces are based. Okinawan demands for closure of U.S. bases were sidestepped by the Japanese government, which insisted that Japanese law apply in the prosecution proceedings. The character of the incident raised the issue of a continuing U.S. military presence in Japan, but neither Tokyo nor Washington was prepared for a change in alliance commitments. U.S. ac-ceptance of primary responsibility for the security of Japan in the 1954 pact was necessitated by the Japanese constitution of 1947, which provided for a renunciation of war and militarism. The 1960 treaty, however, encouraged Japanese rearmament for defense and sought to encourage cooperation between the two nations toward that objective. Today, Japan has a powerful self-defense force—an army, navy, and air force.

Alliance: North Atlantic Treaty Organization (NATO)—Cold War $\boxed{284}$

A mutual-security treaty, signed 4 April 1949, to provide peace and security in the North Atlantic area through joint defense. The 16 North Atlantic Treaty signatories include 12 original parties (Belgium, Great Britain, Canada, Denmark, France, Iceland, Italy, Luxembourg, the Netherlands, Norway, Portugal, and the United States), and 4 that subsequently ratified (Greece and Turkey in 1952, West Germany in 1955, and Spain in 1982). To implement treaty provisions, the extensive military-political-administrative structure of the North Atlantic Treaty Organization (NATO) was created. Major NATO organs include (1) the North Atlantic Council, composed of the foreign, economic, and defense ministers, who decide important political-military policy questions; (2) the military committee, composed of the chiefs of staff of member countries, who formulate policies of military strategy for consideration by the council; and (3) a staff secretariat headed by a secretary-general. The heart of the treaty is Article 5, which states: "The Parties agree that an armed attack against one or more of them in Europe or North America shall be considered an attack against them all; and . . . each of them . . . will assist the Party or Parties so attacked." Since 1969 Article 13 has permitted any signatory to "cease to be a Party one year after its notice of denunciation." None, however, has denounced the treaty. *See also* ALLIANCE: NORTH ATLANTIC TREATY ORGANIZATION (NATO)—POST–COLD WAR (285).

Significance
The North Atlantic Treaty served as the basic military alliance for the West in countering the perceived threat posed by the Soviet military establishment. The treaty represented a departure for the United States from its historic policy of avoiding peacetime military alliances. Although there is no evidence that the Soviets planned a military attack on the North Atlantic area, the treaty was a product of the fear and apprehension prevalent in signatory states that such an attack might come. The parties to the treaty considered it to be a defensive alliance, but the Soviet Union viewed NATO as an offensive threat, especially after West Germany was made a member. As a counterweight to the treaty and NATO, the Communist states signed the Warsaw Pact in 1955 and established the Warsaw Treaty Organization (WTO). The main challenges to the concept of North Atlantic unity embodied in the treaty, however, came from within, and they involved a struggle for leadership between France and the United States. France forced the departure of NATO headquarters from Paris and its relocation in Brussels. France also refused to participate in NATO exercises or share in its responsibilities, but it nevertheless reiterated its continuing commitment to the principles of the alliance.

Alliance: North Atlantic Treaty Organization (NATO)—Post–Cold War | 285 |

The transformation of NATO in the post–Cold War era. NATO was organized with the specific mission of defending Western Europe against a possible attack launched by the Soviet Union. The United States committed itself to European defense, acknowledging that the European states could not, without U.S. involvement, prevent the Soviets from overrunning Western Europe. From its inception, therefore, NATO has been an Atlantic alliance, tying North America in intimate embrace with Western Europe. Moreover, U.S. army officers have commanded the alliance from its inception, and the United States agreed to judge any attack on a member state as an attack on itself. The original member states were: Belgium, Canada, Denmark, France, Iceland, Italy, Luxembourg, Netherlands, Norway, Portugal, the United Kingdom, and the United States. Turkey and Greece, later Germany, and finally Spain joined in subsequent years. As a consequence of NATO solidarity, following World War II Europe enjoyed its longest period of peace in centuries, and in 1989 the Cold War that had pitted NATO forces against those organized by the Soviet Union suddenly ended without a NATO shot having been fired. The signal for the end of the Cold War was the fall of the Berlin Wall in November 1989, the symbol of East-West rivalry. Shortly thereafter, in 1991, the Soviet Union itself crumbled, leaving in its place 15 new republics, the principal one being the new Russian Federation, which emphasized its desire to work with the United States and Europe in promoting worldwide peace and security, as well as democracy. The end of the Cold War and the Soviet Union raised new questions about NATO purpose, and indeed, if it was necessary to retain an organization that appeared to have completed its mission. This latter question was answered in the affirmative at Copenhagen in June 1991 when the member states agreed that future European peace and security was dependent on the maintenance of trans-Atlantic solidarity. At the Rome Summit in November 1991, the NATO members declared their intention to transform the alliance but not to diminish its operational coherence. NATO authorities cited the importance of bolstering the security responsibilities of the Western European Union (WEU), as well as the European Community. In the Brussels Summit of January 1994, the NATO heads of state and government welcomed the entry into force of the Maastricht Treaty and the official launching of the European Union. They cited NATO's supportive role as the Europeans move to formulate a common foreign and security policy. *See also* ALLIANCE: EUROCORPS (282); ALLIANCE: NORTH ATLANTIC TREATY ORGANIZATION

(NATO)—COLD WAR (284); ALLIANCE: PARTNERSHIP FOR PEACE (PFP) (286); ALLIANCE: WESTERN EUROPEAN UNION (WEU) (291); REGIONAL POLITICAL GROUP: EUROPEAN COMMUNITY (EC) (565); REGIONAL POLITICAL GROUP: EUROPEAN UNION (EU) (566).

Significance

Instead of dissolving itself, NATO has gained still more supporters. The states of Eastern and Central Europe have registered their desire to become NATO members, but cognizant of Russian sensitivity to a plan extending NATO to the very borders of Russia, the alliance has worked out another formula that, while not adding to NATO membership, addresses the security concerns of the East European states. The Partnership for Peace (PFP) was created in 1994 as an initiative of the Clinton administration. The PFP was only a second-best option for those wanting full membership in NATO, but viewing the original NATO mission in defending Western Europe, the PFP expands NATO's role to Europe proper, to Eurasia, and indeed to the Pacific Rim. New dimensions of the NATO mission were observed in the alliance's support role during the Gulf War of 1990–1991 when NATO air, sea, and land units were despatched to the Middle East to counter Iraqi aggression against Kuwait. More direct NATO involvement, however, occurred when the alliance intervened in the Bosnian conflict in support of United Nations peacekeeping efforts there. After initial minor demonstrations of force, NATO airpower unleashed a full-scale attack on Bosnian Serb military positions and installations, command centers, communication facilities, and supply depots, in late August 1995. This NATO military action, the first of its kind in NATO history, hinted at NATO's future role, perhaps as a "balancer" in critical areas of international affairs.

Alliance: Partnership for Peace (PFP) | 286 |

An association proposed by the heads of state and government participating in the meeting of the North Atlantic Council held at NATO headquarters in Brussels on 10–11 January 1994. The partnership invited former Warsaw Pact states, including the former republics of the Soviet Union, to engage in military exercises and generally cooperate with the North Atlantic Treaty Organization (NATO). The partnership was prompted by efforts made by Eastern and Central European states to gain full membership in NATO. NATO was not yet prepared to admit these states to its official membership, so the partnership was geared to promote cooperation and collective action between NATO and the partner members in matters of peace and security. The plan emphasized the need to avoid interstate rivalry and unending mutual insecurity. The partnership was designed to tie partner institutions to the North Atlantic Council (NAC), the North Atlantic Cooperation Council (NACC), and the various civil and military subordinate structures of NATO. In so doing, NATO shifted its operations into an enlarged institution, while retaining for its 16 full members those specialized functions related to Article V, i.e., common defense against actual attack. The partnership came under annual NATO review, and NATO provided physical space for the partners in the alliance's supreme headquarters, subordinate headquarters, military committee, etc. The new partners also were brought into NATO air defense and air traffic control systems, AWACS (airborne radar) operations, communications systems (including the crypto system), and the common infrastructure system (airfields, pipelines, and logistics depots). *See also* ALLIANCE: PARTNERSHIP FOR PEACE SIGNATORIES (287).

Significance

The Partnership for Peace did not fully meet the demands of the East and Central European states favoring NATO membership as a security measure. The overriding concern in Eastern and Central Europe was the potential emergence of an aggressive Russian state managed by ultranationalists determined to restore the old empire. NATO acknowledged these apprehensions, but it was also confronted with the complexities involved in adding new members to the alliance. Concerned that the inclusion of Poland, Hungary, the Czech Republic, and others would send the wrong signal to Moscow, NATO opted in favor of its working relationship with the Russian Federation. An alliance arrangement that Moscow could accept had to take into account Russian fears of a revitalized, aggressive Western containment policy or a new encirclement program. Thus, the NATO powers saw the necessity for inducing Russia to join the partnership, along with the near abroad states or former republics of the Soviet Union. Not inclined toward fueling a new Cold War, NATO encouraged Russian democratic reforms, and promoted the scaling back of the Russian military establishment. Moreover, the

United States, Russia, and Ukraine entered into an agreement on the reduction and disposal of nuclear weapons. Always suspicious of NATO's real intentions, Moscow delayed the official announcement of its membership in the PFP until May 1995.

Alliance: Partnership for Peace Signatories   287

Number and order of membership in the Partnership for Peace. The Partnership for Peace was guardedly accepted by the states of Eastern and Central Europe as well as the European and Asian states of the former Soviet Union soon after its announcement. The following states and their official signatories affirmed their membership in the NATO-related scheme in 1994–1995:

1994

26 January	Romania	Teodar Melescanu, Foreign Affairs
27 January	Lithuania	Algirdas Brazauskas, President
2 February	Poland	Waldemar Pawlak, Prime Minister
3 February	Estonia	Juri Luik, Foreign Affairs
8 February	Hungary	Geza Jeszenszky, Foreign Affairs
8 February	Ukraine	Anatoly Zlenko, Foreign Affairs
9 February	Slovakia	Vladimir Meciar, Prime Minister
14 February	Bulgaria	Jelu Jelev, President
14 February	Latvia	Valdis Birkavs, President
23 February	Albania	Sali Berisha, President
10 March	Czech Republic	Vaclav Klaus, Prime Minister
16 March	Moldova	Mircea Snegur, President
23 March	Georgia	Alex Chikvaidze, Foreign Minister
30 March	Slovenia	Janez Drnovsek, Prime Minister
4 May	Azerbaijan	Geidar Aliyev, President
9 May	Sweden	Baroness of Ugglas, Foreign Minister
9 May	Finland	Heikki Haavisto, Foreign Minister
10 May	Turkmenistan	Boris Shikmuradov, Deputy Prime Minister
27 May	Kazakhstan	Kanat Saudabaev, Foreign Minister
1 June	Kyrgyzstan	Askar Akayev, President
22 June	Russia	Andrei Kozorev, Foreign Minister
13 July	Uzbekistan	Saidmukhtar Saidkasimov, Foreign Minister

1995

11 January	Belarus	Uladzmir Syanko, Foreign Minister
10 February	Austria	Alois Mack, Foreign Minister
26 April	Malta	Guido de Marco, Deputy Prime Minister
5 October	Armenia	Vahan Papazian, Foreign Affairs

Significance

Although the former Warsaw Pact states preferred full membership in the North Atlantic Treaty Organization, President Bill Clinton convinced them that the Partnership for Peace was the next-best arrangement for ensuring Eastern Europe's security and territorial integrity. From the perspective of the NATO countries, the acceptance of the PFP by the Russian Federation seemed to assure the success of the plan. The East and Central European states, however, were less sanguine over Moscow's inclusion as a partner, in major part because it intertwined them with their old mentor and hence seemed to provide the Russians, rather than NATO, with the dominant role in shaping and directing the partnership. Thus, after Russia's initial signing of the agreement in June 1994 there was continued pressure to include Poland, Hungary, and the Czech Republic in NATO. Moreover, the Republican leadership in the U.S. Congress called for the formal membership of the Visegrad states in the alliance. Sensing American duplicity, Russia held up its entry into the PFP. Not until May 1995—during an emergency NATO meeting in Brussels concerning Bosnia—did the Russians indicate their acceptance of the PFP.

Alliance: Rio Treaty (Inter-American Treaty of Reciprocal Assistance) | 288 |

Regional defense pact providing for a mutual-security system to counter acts of aggression committed in the Western Hemisphere, signed in Rio de Janeiro on 2 September 1947. The signatories include 21 American republics, although one of these—the Castro government of Cuba—has been excluded from participation in the inter-American system since 1962. Implementation of treaty provisions is handled by the Meeting of Consultation of Ministers of Foreign Affairs of the Organization of American States (OAS) or, provisionally, by the OAS Council. The treaty applies to the entire Western Hemisphere, an area stretching from the North Pole to the South Pole, and pertains not only to a direct attack against an American state, but indirect aggression that is "not an armed attack." In the case of a direct attack, each signatory agrees to undertake action against the aggressor, although each may determine the nature of its response until collective measures can be agreed on. In cases of aggression not involving a direct attack, such as the support of revolution in one state by another, the signatories agree only to "consult," but a two-thirds vote of alliance members may invoke compulsory sanctions ranging from diplomatic and economic to military measures. *See also* REGIONAL POLITICAL GROUP: ORGANIZATION OF AMERICAN STATES (OAS) (571).

Significance

The Rio Treaty climaxed a half-century of efforts to secure a hemispheric arrangement for cooperation in defense matters and served to multilateralize U.S. opposition to foreign intervention originally proclaimed in the Monroe Doctrine of 1823. The Rio Treaty was the first general-security pact entered into by the United States, and its basic commitment that "an armed attack by any State against an American state shall be considered as an attack against all" became a model for the NATO and SEATO treaties. The treaty was invoked against the threat of international communism in the cases of the Castro government of Cuba in 1962 and the Dominican revolution in 1965. Economic sanctions and a collective rupture of diplomatic relations with the Castro government were instituted against Cuba, and a specially created Inter-American Peace Force provided the means for a collective intervention in the Dominican Republic. The main problem of applying the Rio Treaty to deal with revolutions, civil wars, and subversion within signatory countries is that it is likely to reopen old questions concerning "Yankee interventionism," and may stifle social revolutions essential for modernization. For example, because most Latin American members did not support U.S. actions in Grenada (1983), or the actions against the Sandinista government in Nicaragua during the 1980s, the Rio Treaty was not invoked and the OAS did not undertake collective action. Nor did the OAS become involved in the Falklands (Malvinas) War (1982) between Great Britain and Argentina, or in the U.S. intervention in Haiti in 1994, which was aimed at restoring President Jean-Bertrand Aristide to the office from which he was ousted by the Haitian military. It is interesting to note that the United States called upon the United Nations, not the OAS, to oversee the restoration of democracy in Haiti.

Alliance: Southeast Asia Collective Defense Treaty (SEATO) | 289 |

A mutual-security pact signed in Manila in 1954 that called on the signatories to consult and to meet the common danger in accordance with their constitutional processes. The treaty applied to both external aggression and internal subversion in Southeast Asia and the Southwest Pacific. Parties to the Southeast Asia Collective Defense Treaty were Australia, Great Britain, France, New Zealand, Pakistan, the Philippines, Thailand, and the United States. To implement the treaty's guarantees, in 1955 its signatories established the Southeast Asia Treaty Organization (SEATO), which functioned through a council and a secretariat located at SEATO headquarters in Bangkok. By a special protocol to the treaty, the covered security area was extended to include Cambodia, Laos, and South Vietnam, but the treaty excluded Hong Kong, South Korea, and Taiwan because the Asian signatories

were unwilling to assume responsibility for their defense. SEATO was dissolved in 1977, but the treaty was never abrogated.

Significance
The Southeast Asia Collective Defense Treaty, intended to be the Asian counterpart of the North Atlantic Treaty, was concluded under U.S. leadership as part of a worldwide alliance system to "contain" communism within its existing boundaries. Although all non-Communist countries of South and Southeast Asia were invited to join the pact, only three nations (heavily dependent on U.S. aid at the time)—Pakistan, the Philippines, and Thailand—opted to do so. The treaty never quite served the interests of the parties. U.S. assistance to India, and the latter's intervention in Pakistan's civil war in 1971, led to the creation of independent Bangladesh. Because Pakistan lost its southeast Asian province, SEATO ceased to have relevance for that nation. French demands for the neutralization of Southeast Asia also contributed to the growing disarray within the alliance. The refusal of Great Britain, France, and Pakistan to support the U.S. effort in the Vietnam War, and the minimal contributions made by other signatories, left the main burden of providing security in Asia to the United States. The dissolution of the alliance in 1977 merely reinforced what the members had known all along—that the alliance had been developed in haste, and without considering its internal contradictions.

Alliance: Warsaw Pact | 290 |

The 20-year Eastern European Mutual Assistance Treaty established by the Communist bloc in 1955, and extended for a similar term despite the security arrangements agreed to at Helsinki in 1975 at the Conference on Security and Cooperation in Europe. Members of the Warsaw Pact originally included Albania, Bulgaria, Czechoslovakia, the German Democratic Republic, Hungary, Poland, Romania, and the Soviet Union. The treaty of "friendship, cooperation, and mutual assistance" established a unified military command for the armed forces of the eight members, with headquarters in Moscow, and provided that each give immediate aid by all means considered necessary, including the use of armed force, to any signatory attacked in Eastern Europe. Following the tearing down of the Berlin Wall on 9 November 1989, the East European states discarded their Communist systems and separated themselves from prior Warsaw Pact commitments. The Warsaw Pact was officially dissolved in 1991. *See also* REGIONAL MILITARY GROUP: WARSAW TREATY ORGANIZATION (WTO) (558).

Significance
The Warsaw Pact was a Soviet reaction to the creation of the Western European Union, the decision to permit the rearmament of West Germany, and West Germany's inclusion in NATO. The pact served as the basis for the establishment of the Warsaw Treaty Organization (WTO), a military-political structure that functioned as a counterweight to NATO. The text of the Warsaw Pact, in fact, nearly duplicated the wording of the action clauses of the North Atlantic Treaty. The Warsaw Pact countries also committed themselves to stand in defense of the gains of socialism. Basically, however, the Warsaw Pact created a political and military structure that merely changed the form but not the substance of Soviet hegemonic policy in Eastern Europe. Like France in NATO, Albania left the pact in 1962 and never again participated in its decisions or joint maneuvers. The alliance was plagued by a number of deep-seated dilemmas, some of which surfaced in the Hungarian uprising in 1956 and the Czechoslovakian deviation in 1968. In both these instances, the Red Army was used to crush rebellions against its authority, which Moscow believed to be Western-inspired. The Warsaw Pact was always considered a questionable alliance in the West, and observers long believed that, in the event of hostilities, many of the East European forces would have refused to fight alongside the Soviets.

Alliance: Western European Union (WEU) | 291 |

The first European military alliance following World War II. The Western European Union dates back to 1948, and the modified Brussels Treaty of 1954, when the West European states noted the need to defend themselves against a perceived Soviet threat. NATO's formation in 1949 overrode the organization, as its member states were included in that more formidable alliance. Nevertheless, the Hague platform on European security interests convened in October 1987 by WEU member states expressed the intention to develop a more cohesive European defense identity. A declaration on the role of the WEU and its relations with the European Union and the Atlantic Alliance (NATO) was included in the Maastricht agreement on European union in December 1991. It was then stated that WEU's objective was the creation and strengthening of a European pillar for the Atlantic alliance. The WEU full member states are Belgium, France, Germany, Greece, Italy, Luxembourg, the Netherlands, Portugal, Spain, and the United Kingdom. Seventeen associate, associate-partner, and observer members bring the total membership to 27. With the Maastricht endorsement, and its inclusion in the European Union, WEU headquarters was moved from London to Brussels. The Maastricht Treaty that revived WEU avoids the "Europeanizing" of the alliance, but stresses common defense. Cooperation between Eurocorps and WEU was demonstrated when France, Italy, Spain, and Portugal agreed to the organization of a land force (EUROFOR), designed as a rapid reaction force in Europe's southern region, and a Maritime force (EUROMARFOR) in the Mediterranean. Both forces were open to all WEU members. The latter was also made available to NATO. WEU centers on the establishment of a European pole of security based on links to the European Union, and complementing but not replacing NATO's role. Together the WEU and NATO reaffirm European unity and transatlantic solidarity. A declaration by the heads of state and government meeting at NATO headquarters in January 1994 clearly spelled out the need to support "separable but not separate capabilities" that could respond to European requirements and thus contribute to alliance security. NATO appears to welcome the close and growing cooperation between itself and WEU because the WEU is said to be based on agreed principles of complementarity and transparency. *See also* ALLIANCE: EUROCORPS (282); REGIONAL MILITARY GROUP: NORTH ATLANTIC TREATY ORGANIZATION (NATO) (557); REGIONAL MILITARY GROUP: WESTERN EUROPEAN UNION (559); REGIONAL POLITICAL GROUP: EUROPEAN COMMUNITY (EC) (565); REGIONAL POLITICAL GROUP: EUROPEAN UNION (EU) (566); TRANSPARENCY (461).

Significance
The objective of the Western European Union (WEU) is to strengthen the European pillar of the Atlantic alliance and to serve as the defense component of the European Union. At the May 1995 Lisbon Ministerial meeting, steps were taken to enhance WEU's operational development. WEU's definitive role was addressed at the 1996 Inter-Governmental Conference, while links between the WEU and the European Union were strengthened with regard to NATO's overall role in the defense of the Atlantic community. It is clear that WEU does not intend becoming a subsidiary of NATO. It claims singular responsibility for the defense of Europe, but welcomes defining the modalities for the use of the total alliance's collective assets—from command facilities to joint task forces to communications networks. But cooperation between WEU and NATO does not exempt the Europeans from making their own defense effort. Although duplication is to be avoided, the European states insist on having individually available military assets for their own key functions. Thus, the WEU of the future will be far more proactive than its Cold War original. Moreover, WEU is not intended to be a carbon copy of NATO. The NATO principle of "an attack on one is an attack on all" does not carry over to WEU; it will not commit its members to actions engaged in by other members if the individual states believe their national interests are not directly involved. WEU appears to have opted for cooperation, not integration, and the building of the organization's permanent structures will be tempered by the member states' national interests. National flexibility, and less than total commitment, reflects WEU's association with the European Union.

Armistice | 292 |

A temporary cessation of hostilities agreed to by belligerents. Sometimes called a truce, an armistice may be general in scope or may apply only to specific areas. Under international law, an armistice does not affect the legal status of the war, which may be continued in all respects other than those provided for in the truce agreement.

Significance
An armistice may provide a pause in hostilities to encourage negotiations for peace between belligerents, or provide an opportunity for a third party or an international organization to undertake mediatory activity. In the Arab-Israeli Wars of 1948–1949, 1956, 1967, and 1973, for example, armistice agreements stopped the fighting and, in each case, were followed by vigorous but unsuccessful efforts by the United Nations to work out a permanent peace settlement. A truce agreement may also serve as a means for halting the fighting before one side suffers complete defeat or is forced to surrender unconditionally. In World War I, for example, Germany accepted an armistice agreement so that surrender terms could be considered before its armies collapsed and its homeland was opened to invasion.

Dual Key | 293 |

Arrangements between the North Atlantic Treaty Organization (NATO) and the United Nations to ensure that decisions on air-strike targeting and execution will be taken jointly by UN and NATO military commanders. The principle of proportionality in response to a violation of UN resolutions continues to be respected, as is the need to avoid unacceptable casualties, especially among UN peacekeeping forces. The secretaries-general of the United Nations and NATO confirmed the cooperation between their two organizations in the implementation of the relevant UN Security Council resolutions at UN Headquarters in New York City in October 1994. They also reaffirmed the effective use of air power, under the authority of the Security Council and in accordance with relevant North Atlantic Council (NAC) decisions. *See also* PEACEKEEPING: UNPROFOR (451).

Significance
The dual key arrangements between NATO and the United Nations were necessitated by the protracted war in Bosnia. UNPROFOR (United Nations Protection Force), a peacekeeping force dispatched to the region in 1991–1992, found itself a target of the belligerents, notably the Bosnian Serbs. To protect UNPROFOR, the UN Security Council called upon NATO for assistance, and particularly NATO air power, which was described as a deterrent force, not a participant in the conflict. NATO hoped to assure the protection of the UN peacekeepers by threatening retaliatory air strikes against forces deemed to be targeting UN troops. According to agreements arrived at in New York extending the NATO mission in this regard, air strikes, if needed, would be authorized on a timely basis, after general warning had been given the offending party. The agreement noted that neither NATO nor the United Nations would be required to give tactical warning of impending air strikes. Moreover, NATO command noted that three or four targets would be authorized for each strike, and that the action would be undertaken by NATO command in close coordination with UNPROFOR. Despite the elaborate arrangements for deterring aggressive activity in Bosnia and Herzegovina, and the occasional NATO air strikes against Bosnian Serb positions, the plan did not protect the peacekeeping forces, nor did it deter the aggressive behavior of the belligerents, especially the Serbs, who were the principal target for NATO strikes. NATO also hesitated to carry out its threat for fear of escalating and spreading the conflict. The French and the British, with peacekeepers on the ground, believed that their troops would be more exposed to attack if NATO raised the ante. It is important to note that the United States refused to put troops on the ground in Bosnia, but was willing to supply the air power. Following an escalation of Serb shelling of Sarajevo and Bosnian "safe havens" in May–June 1995, NATO attacked Bosnian Serb ammunition depots near Pale. In retaliation, the Serbs seized more than 300 UN peacekeepers, threatening their lives if the bombing continued. At that point NATO halted the air action. Britain and France again cited the tenuous nature of the peacekeeping mission and, with the Netherlands, they agreed to organize a 10,000-member combat-ready Rapid Reaction Force (RRF) to protect the peacekeepers. Considering the layers of NATO and UN involvement, each capable of neutralizing or complicating the role of the other, it was not surprising that the Bosnian Serbs maintained the more active hand in this high-stakes conflict. Following an escalation in fighting, however, NATO airpower was again introduced. NATO air attacks targeted Serb command and control installations as well as munitions depots and infrastructure, and after more than 2,000 sorties, the Bosnian Serbs agreed to find a formula for peace. Another U.S.-engineered cease-fire was arranged in October 1995.

Limited War | 294 |

An armed conflict fought for objectives less than the total destruction of the enemy and his unconditional surrender. Limited war may be restricted with regard to the level of destructive power used, the number of participants, the territory involved, or the substitution of political considerations for military strategy, individually or in any combination. Situations of limited war may include (1) conflicts between nuclear powers in which neither side employs its weapons of mass destruction nor attacks the population centers of the other; (2) hostilities between small states with no direct intervention by the great powers; (3) conflicts between small states aided directly or indirectly by nuclear powers, fought within a restricted geographical area and without using nuclear or atomic weapons; (4) military actions undertaken by a nuclear power against a small state without interference by other great powers; (5) domestic uprisings against a colonial power or established government in which both sides use conventional weapons and receive logistic or manpower support, or both, from rival nuclear powers; (6) collective actions undertaken by police units of an international organization to prevent territorial conquest or to achieve political goals; and (7) the theoretical possibility of limited nuclear wars in which the great powers employ only tactical atomic weapons against strictly military targets. *See also* WAR TYPE: TOTAL WAR (348).

Significance
The development of nuclear and other weapons of mass destruction by the great powers forced them to keep war limited in scope and intensity and to work for political settlement as a matter of sheer survival. The limited-war concept in the nuclear era emerged during the Korean conflict of 1950–1953, when neither U.S. nor Communist Chinese forces attacked the main base of the other, located outside the immediate theater of combat. In the Vietnam War during the 1960s and early 1970s, the United States, the Soviet Union, and Communist China intervened in attempts to affect the outcome of the struggle; yet each, to varying degrees, exercised restraint to avoid escalation into total war. Similar restraint was used in the Soviet-Afghan War from 1979 to 1988. Although the United States supplied the Afghan mujahiddin resistance with modern

weapons, the United States and its Pakistani ally avoided direct involvement. In a limited war neither major power is likely to win a victory in the traditional sense, since efforts by either to employ greater force are balanced by counteractions from the other. Therefore, the Korean War ended in a stalemate. North Korea continues to pursue an independent foreign policy, and its military program involves the development of nuclear weapons. North Vietnam emerged the triumphant party from both its wars with the French and the Americans, ultimately unifying the two segments of a country divided in the aftermath of World War II. A successful Afghan resistance to Soviet Red Army aggression not only forced the more substantial army to retreat behind its own frontier in February 1989, it also had a role in the Soviet Union's demise in 1991. Considering that these were the three major wars of the Cold War era, it can be concluded that limited-war policies actually weaken major powers and add to the strength of the lesser ones. Limited wars prevent the spread and escalation of the conflicts, but their political consequences are yet to be fully understood.

Limited War: Afghan-USSR | 295 |
Soviet efforts aimed at sustaining influence throughout Central Asia. Hostilities commenced with the Soviet invasion of Afghanistan in December 1979. The objective seemed to be the creation of a submissive Marxist state on the Soviet border in a strategic region of Central Asia. The result, however, was a protracted, almost ten-year guerrilla war between the Afghan resistance (the mujahiddin) and approximately 125,000 Soviet troops. The Soviets seemed inclined to secure military positions on the Persian Gulf and Indian Ocean following the collapse of the U.S.-sponsored government in Iran. Afghanistan was seen as the gateway to open warm water (a historic interest of czarist Russia as well as the USSR), and Iran was the next possible objective. The Soviets also marched their forces into Af-

ghanistan to neutralize what they perceived to be increasing Muslim militancy, emanating not only from Afghanistan but from Iran and Pakistan as well. Afghanistan was located in close proximity to the Soviet Union's Central Asian Muslim republics, and Moscow feared the influence on them by resurgent Islamic movements. The determination of the Afghan resistance, despite their heavy casualties, eventually convinced the Soviets, under the leadership of Mikhail Gorbachev, that it would be unwise to sustain the conflict in that mountainous state. At that time, Gorbachev was intent on reforming the Soviet economy and bureaucratic system, as well as altering his relationship with the United States. To accomplish these goals, Gorbachev believed he needed to end the conflict in Afghanistan, and in April 1988 he accepted the agreement worked out by the UN mediator, Diego Cordovez. In February 1989, the last Soviet soldier departed Afghanistan. *See also* CENTRAL ASIA (150); WAR (305).

Significance

Historically, Afghanistan has served as a buffer against czarist and Soviet ambitions in the Persian Gulf and Indian Ocean regions. The positioning of Soviet forces just a few hundred miles from the mouth of the Persian Gulf provoked the Carter Doctrine in January 1980. President Jimmy Carter warned the Soviet Union that any Soviet attempt to control the Gulf would threaten U.S. vital interests, and that the United States was prepared to meet such a threat with force if necessary (the next president, Ronald Reagan, later concurred). The face-off between the superpowers was obvious, but direct confrontation was studiously avoided. With the Reagan Doctrine, the United States declared its support for wars of national liberation that were directed against the forces of international communism, and arms were funneled into Afghanistan by way of Pakistan. Pakistan agreed to play the role of a front-line state, and thus was assured of heavy U.S. military aid. With the additional arms, the mujahiddin were not only able

to defend themselves, they could take the war to the Soviets; on occasion, they even struck Soviet installations across the Oxus River frontier. The sustained conflict was reminiscent of the war in Indochina, only this time it was the Soviets who were mired in a limited war they could not win, either on the battlefield or at the conference table. Therefore, the UN-authorized mediation was the only option in resolving the dilemma. UN diplomacy was carried forward with patience and skill by Diego Cordovez, who finally won Moscow's favor. After years of haggling in "proximity talks" (so-called because the parties to the talks—the Afghan Marxist government in Kabul, and officials from the Pakistan government—never met at the same table), a formula was arrived at that allowed the Soviets to withdraw from the country. The departure of Soviet forces, however, did not terminate the conflict in Afghanistan. The mujahiddin continued to assault the Marxist government in Kabul; after they finally succeeded in destroying it, they turned on one another. The several factions that made up the resistance could not agree on either the form of government or the personnel who would lead it, protracting their own civil war. That civil war assumed an even more deadly form in 1993–1995. Groups identified as Islamic fundamentalists battled others described as more secular in orientation. In reality it was tribal warfare at its worst. The continuing Afghan war spilled over into the new republics of Central Asia, notably into neighboring Tajikistan, mirroring the bloodletting in Afghanistan. What had been a limited war in the years of the Cold War suddenly was not so limited anymore.

Limited War: Falklands $\boxed{296}$

The limited war between Argentina and Great Britain in April–June 1982. At issue was the question of sovereignty over the Falkland Islands, known in Latin America as the Malvinas. Located some 300 miles offshore from Argentina, the territory comprises approximately 4,700 square miles of territory with about 1,800 inhabitants, mainly of British origin. Argentine claim was based on the claims of succession from Spain following Argentine independence in 1816. The islands have been a British dependency since 1833, and the inhabitants demonstrate a preference for continuing the British connection. When protracted efforts at negotiation failed, Argentina resorted to military force. *See also* FOREIGN-POLICY PROCESS: CAPABILITY ANALYSIS (15); WAR (305).

Significance
The Falklands War, like many, seems to have been the result of serious errors in capability analysis and assessment of situational factors. Argentina appears to have assumed that Great Britain would not or could not respond so massively so far from home. It is also likely that the Argentine government wanted to divert its Argentine citizenry from worsening domestic political, social, and economic problems. Resolute efforts at mediation by U.S. Secretary of State Alexander Haig and UN Secretary-General Javier Pérez de Cuéllar were unsuccessful. Since the end of hostilities, the General Assembly's call for renewed negotiation has gone largely unheeded.

Mutual-Security Organization: Conference on Security and Cooperation in Europe (CSCE)   297

The security organization that emphasized diplomacy and avoided military confrontation. The Conference on Security and Cooperation in Europe emerged from the Helsinki Accords in 1975 as an East-West collection of 35 states that included both the United States and the Soviet Union, as well as all the states of the North Atlantic Treaty Organization (NATO) and the Warsaw Pact. Beginning as an amorphous process, it moved from conference to conference with no fixed address or schedule. For 15 years, however, its review conferences and experts meetings succeeded in focusing attention on a range of interrelated problems from

human rights to the environment to threatening military maneuvers. Operating on the principle that these and other elements of security could not be treated separately, the deliberations were not without fruit. Mutual-security agreements between the United States and the USSR complemented and in some ways went beyond what could be achieved with collective-security arrangements. Confidences were established that ultimately led to a normalization of relations between the two superpowers in the era of Mikhail Gorbachev. However, the end of the bipolarity "system" that characterized the Europe in which CSCE was created led many of its participants to look to the CSCE as a new overarching "system" within which its members could improve both their security and cooperation. As such, they pleaded for more structure and permanence for CSCE's activities. The Paris Summit of November 1990 endowed CSCE with its first permanent institutions: the CSCE Secretariat, the Conflict Prevention Center, and the Office of Free Elections, later expanded to the Office for Democratic Institutions and Human Rights. Meetings of heads of state or government were envisaged every two years. Foreign ministers, along with other ministers, were expected to meet annually, and senior officials were scheduled to meet three to four times each year. The CSCE Secretariat was established in Prague, the Conflict Prevention Center in Vienna, and the Office of Free Elections in Warsaw. In April 1991, parliamentarians from the participating states formed the CSCE Parliamentary Assembly, which meets once each year to review the organization's activities. CSCE assumed a higher profile with the collapse of communism in Eastern Europe and the demise and breakup of the Soviet Union. Its membership swelled to 52 states in 1992 (53 if Yugoslavia, i.e., Serbia, is reinstated). No longer a timid, behind-the-scenes operation, CSCE is given credence as a peacemaking body with a membership dwarfed only by the United Nations. More extensive procedures were developed to allow CSCE bodies to send missions to a state without that state's participation in the decision-making process, engage in conciliation or other forms of peaceful settlements, exclude a participating state from membership (e.g., Yugoslavia and Chechnya), and even deploy CSCE peacekeeping forces. *See also* PATTERNS OF POWER: MUTUAL SECURITY (23).

Significance
The origins of CSCE are traced to the Soviet proposal introduced in 1954 that called for the convening of a pan-European security conference. Resistance to this concept was rooted in many of the realities of the Cold War. The United States believed that the proposal, which excluded it and Canada, constituted a Soviet-sponsored attempt to divide the North Atlantic alliance. Moreover, the Federal Republic of Germany refused to undertake any action that could cause it to relinquish its aspirations for a united Germany or limit its ability to participate in NATO. The West European countries were reluctant to take up the Soviet offer because the proposal seemed to limit the possibility of reducing East-West friction. These concerns were somewhat alleviated at the 1975 meetings in Helsinki when the Soviet Union professed interest in promoting civil rights and encouraged the formation of an East-West organization that included the United States. The CSCE of that period was described by diplomats as little more than a "floating crap game," moving from city to city with no fixed beginning or end. The membership (then 35 states) focused its attention on discussion of national practices and finding areas of common agreement. The ten fundamental principles of the 1975 Helsinki Final Act and subsequent documents inspired private citizens and non-governmental organizations as well as governments to identify with CSCE and forcefully champion human rights in their respective states through that organization. It is generally believed that these practices, and the pressure exerted by them, contributed to the collapse of communism in East-Central Europe, and

ultimately in the Soviet Union. Since the end of the Cold War, the structure for CSCE has moved only slightly from its east-of-the-Elbe orientation, but the fall of the Berlin Wall in 1989 and the 1990 Paris Charter substantially transformed the organization. It is now recognized as an important security organization in Europe as a whole, and even the opposition registered in the U.S. Congress has been somewhat muted. Today, CSCE is balanced between human rights and military issues, but it has been plagued by conflict in the successor states to the Soviet Union and Yugoslavia. It is also concerned with the general problem of minorities at risk in countries professing a virulent form of nationalism. CSCE has achieved greater visibility and considerably more responsibility, but its capacity to address the problems of security and cooperation in a Europe that stretches from the Atlantic to the Pacific, from the frozen Nordic regions to the arid conditions of Central Asia, is recognizably limited. However, CSCE provides another forum for diplomatic exchange at official and private levels. Its tasks are far more complex than those envisaged in 1975, or even in 1990, but the dedication of its professional members is acknowledged, and the body is destined to play an important role in a newly configured but nevertheless troubled Europe.

Nuclear Arms Race | 298 |

Insecurity in the nuclear age. During the Cold War, the nuclear arms race was confined to the major world powers, i.e., the United States, the USSR, Great Britain, France, and China. India detonated a nuclear device in 1974, but no other country was detected exploding atomic bombs; if others possessed such weapons, they did not test them, let alone publicize their capabilities. With the passing of the Cold War, however, the development of nuclear weapons in numerous other countries has been acknowledged. Among these states are those cited as potential threats to international peace, and others who are generally judged to be more responsible members of the international community, and hence whose possession of nuclear weapons is not considered a menace to the larger world. Iraq, Iran, Libya, Syria, Algeria, Pakistan, and North Korea are perceived to be in the former category, while Israel, India, and Sweden are placed in the latter. Belarus, Ukraine, and Kazakhstan, nuclear-weapons powers because of their earlier role as republics within the Soviet Union, entered into formal agreements to transfer their weapons to Russia or destroy them, and these states are not judged to be nuclear-weapons threats. Nevertheless, their material capabilities and know-how could pass to other states, thus making their nuclear status a sustained, if not direct threat. Germany and Japan, both nuclear weapons–capable, have ignored the temptation to develop these weapons of mass destruction, and do not seem inclined to produce them in the future. The indefinite extension of the nuclear Non-Proliferation Treaty (NPT) in May 1995 calls upon these states to forgo any distant decision aimed at making them nuclear-weapons powers. The NPT, however, does not force other states to follow the German and Japanese example. Given the continuing reluctance of states such as India and Israel to sign the treaty, it is expected that nuclear weapons will spread to other states. *See also* ARMS CONTROL: NUCLEAR NON-PROLIFERATION TREATY CONFERENCE, 1995 (364); ROGUE STATES (304).

Significance
The nuclear arms race generally focuses attention on states often described as "rogue states." Such states are perceived differently by the established nuclear powers. For example, the United States believes that Iran and North Korea are the two most threatening states in the world today. Iran is considered the most aggressive state in sponsoring terrorism around the world. North Korea is acknowledged to possess one of the world's largest standing armies, and its missile technology has improved to the extent of placing the larger region, including Japan, within range of its nuclear weapons. Because of

the closed nature of many of these societies and their facilities, the international community is left with the science of monitoring techniques that chemically test minute quantities of water, air, and dust near nuclear facilities to determine what kinds of uranium and plutonium are being produced. Secret work on nuclear weapons can be detected by comparing nuclear exports and imports with the various technologies of weapons-making to identify combinations of components incompatible with a country's known nuclear-power program. Nothing, however, can substitute for on-site inspections by International Atomic Energy Agency (IAEA) experts, who must be able to move freely within the targeted country. But even such inspections only provide marginal protection. In the absence of absolute safeguards, nuclear-weapons states are anticipated to grow exponentially. Even poor, isolated states like North Korea can develop nuclear weapons. Moreover, given the inadequate accounting system in the former Soviet Union's successor states, it is believed that thousands of kilograms of nuclear weapons–grade materials have found their way into other countries. The sting operation in New York City in June 1995 that uncovered a Ukrainian smuggling ring engaged in the sale of nuclear materials already secreted in U.S. warehouses is a major case in point. Unfortunately, the IAEA still spends 60 percent of its safeguards budget monitoring stockpiles in Japan, Germany, and Canada. The failure to successfully address the nuclear-weapons programs in North Korea, despite an agreement entered into in the fall of 1994, and the difficulty in guaranteeing the termination of Iraq's nuclear program even with IAEA members on the ground in that country, illustrate the difficulty of preventing the spread of nuclear weapons. Finally, the spread of nuclear weapons is fueled by states' perception of security threats from their neighbors, both near and distant. Egypt declared in 1995 that it could not countenance a continuation of its support for the NPT until such time as Israel destroys its nuclear arsenal. Israel, in turn, is not prepared to yield to Egypt's demand so long as it confronts hostile neighbors. Similar problems arise for those seeking to curtail Pakistan's nuclear-weapons program. The Muslim country insists that it cannot avoid developing nuclear capabilities so long as it perceives India as doing so. India has ignored Islamabad's call for a nuclear-free South Asia, citing its fear of nuclear-armed China. Iran has contracted with the Russian Federation to build ten nuclear reactors, which raises the question of why an oil-rich state would need so many nuclear facilities simply for the generation of power. Iran, it must be assumed, is interested in establishing itself as a nuclear-weapons power, and U.S. entreaties to Russia to reconsider the reactor deal have fallen on deaf ears in Moscow. Clearly, there is no simple way of stopping nations determined to add nuclear weapons to their arsenals. Barring more satisfactory political solutions among contending states, the nuclear arms race is bound to continue well into the twenty-first century.

Nuclear Strategy: Balance of Terror | 299

The equilibrium of power among nuclear states stemming from common fear of annihilation in a nuclear war. The balance of terror between the United States and the Soviet Union rested on the mutual understanding that each side possessed various types of delivery systems armed with massively destructive power that defensive actions could not prevent from wreaking mass destruction upon the other's population centers. The knowledge that a surprise first strike could not destroy the other's protected and widely dispersed retaliatory capability reinforced the deterrence created by the balance of terror. The balance-of-terror standoff was in fact strengthened rather than altered by the efforts of both sides to produce deadlier weapons and more dependable delivery systems. Together, the two superpowers were estimated to have about 60,000 nuclear warheads, with a variety of bomber, missile, submarine, and naval delivery systems. The balance of terror was based on the doctrine of mutual assured destruction (MAD).

Significance
The vast arsenal of destructive power underlying the balance of terror eliminated total war as a rational instrument of state policy, but grossly increased the dangers of accidental war. The early post–World War II balance of terror based on atomic weapons had been buttressed by the development of thermonuclear bombs and warheads thousands of times greater in magnitude than the atomic bomb dropped on Hiroshima. For the first time in history, but only in some circles, war, but only some wars, became an unattractive instrument for securing political objectives of the state. A gain in relative power in the arms race no longer conferred a significant advantage, only greater "overkill" capacity, which did not upset the balance of terror. However, the development of a perfect defense against all delivery systems (regarded as an unlikely if not impossible undertaking by most scientists and military experts) would upset the balance of terror and increase the danger of war. Nevertheless, U.S. president Ronald Reagan initiated a major attempt called Strategic Defense Initiative (SDI), or "Star Wars," to develop an impregnable shield that would destroy incoming missiles. The threat of mutual annihilation did not prevent limited wars, such as those fought in Korea, Vietnam, or Afghanistan, but it did restrict the participants' means and objectives. With the disappearance of the Soviet Union, it seemed that the balance of terror had passed into history. Although the Russian Federation maintains a substantial nuclear-weapons capability, it agrees with the United States that they should no longer target each other. But Ukraine, Belarus, and Kazakhstan also possess nuclear capability, and even though they agreed to transfer their nuclear warheads to Russia and dismantle their delivery systems, the availability of nuclear devices, technology, and know-how from these countries is of interest to

other states not yet nuclear weapons–capable. With North Korea and Pakistan already believed to possess nuclear weapons, and with Iran, Iraq, and perhaps additional countries planning to become nuclear powers, the concern over nuclear terror has risen to new levels in the 1990s.

Nuclear Strategy: Deterrence | 300

Activities undertaken by a state or group of states to discourage other states from pursuing policies objectionable to the deterring state or states. Deterrence involves a strategy of threatened punishment or denial to convince others that the costs of their anticipated action will outweigh the gains. The means by which states pursue policies of deterrence include increasing their general military capabilities, developing superweapons of mass destruction, concluding alliances, and threatening reprisals. To be effective, a deterrent threat must be fully credible to the parties at which it is directed. *See also* NUCLEAR STRATEGY: BALANCE OF TERROR (299); NUCLEAR STRATEGY: MASSIVE RETALIATION (302).

Significance
During the Cold War, balance-of-power, collective-security, and mutual-security approaches to peace were built around the concept of deterrence. A potential war-maker was threatened by the retaliatory action of the rival military bloc in the balance system, the collective police action of the international community, and/or the individual resolve of the other superpower in a mutual-security arrangement. The development by the United States and the Soviet Union of unprecedented nuclear-striking power (also known as MAD, mutual assured destruction) created a near-perfect system of mutual deterrence because neither side could attack the other without suffering unbearable losses and destruction. The key to nuclear deterrence was found in each side's "hardened" and dispersed delivery systems, providing retaliatory capabilities that could survive a surprise first strike by the other and reciprocate massively. The nuclear standoff was compared to the situation of two scorpions in a bottle, each having the capability of stinging the other to death but itself certain to be destroyed in the fatal embrace. Mutual deterrence, however, was considered alterable by the development of new offensive or defensive weapons by one of the parties, or by an accidental war caused by human error or technical failure, which could destroy the system's inherent stability, along with its participants.

Nuclear Strategy: First Strike | 301

The strategy of launching a surprise nuclear attack to destroy or decisively weaken the enemy's capacity to retaliate. The first-strike theory assumes that one side could deliver a paralyzing and devastating blow of such magnitude that it could win a nuclear war before the enemy could recover from the blow. A nation's first-strike capability depends on its arsenal of nuclear warheads and delivery systems, but its employment of a first-strike attack is limited by the potential enemy's second-strike or retaliatory capability. *See also* NUCLEAR STRATEGY: PREEMPTIVE STRIKE (303).

Significance
A nation's security from attack in the nuclear age may depend on the ability of its retaliatory force to deter a first strike by offering the certainty of massive nuclear retribution. If its capacity to retaliate massively is not credible, a nuclear power may be placed in a dangerously vulnerable position. To avoid destruction of second-strike capability, the United States and the Soviet Union placed intercontinental missiles in silos and other "hardened" sites, dispersed their delivery systems by arming submarines with multiple-warhead missile-launching devices, and kept some of their nuclear-armed bombers in the air at all times. In addition to protecting their offensive weapons, both countries tried to develop antiballistic missile (ABM) systems to

avert a first strike by providing a measure of defense against incoming missiles and other delivery systems. If either side ever came to believe it had an effective defense system, it might have risked a first-strike attack. On the other hand, if one believed that the other was planning an imminent attack, it might have launched a preemptive first strike. This policy of deterrence suggests just how precariously the world teetered at the edge of oblivion during the era of the Cold War.

Nuclear Strategy: Massive Retaliation | 302 |

The threat of nuclear response to restrain the actions of another state. After the Korean War, U.S. president Dwight D. Eisenhower's administration adopted a policy of massive retaliation to cope with the threat of limited peripheral wars fostered by the Communists. The policy was aimed at preventing such wars by announcing in advance that the United States reserved the right to meet any new peripheral aggression not only at the point of outbreak but by a "massive retaliation at places and times" of the nation's own choosing. The concept of massive retaliation framed U.S. and Soviet contemporary policies of deterrence during the years of the Cold War; both sides accepted the premise that neither could destroy the other's retaliatory capability in a surprise first strike and that a massive retaliation would follow. *See also* NUCLEAR STRATEGY: BALANCE OF TERROR (299); NUCLEAR STRATEGY: DETERRENCE (300).

Significance

The Eisenhower administration's policy of massive retaliation, according to Secretary of State John Foster Dulles, brought the United States and the Soviet Union to the brink of nuclear war on several occasions during the 1950s. Each time, according to Dulles, the Soviets backed down. With Soviet development of long-range nuclear-striking power, however, the U.S. threat lost its credibility. As a result, the Kennedy and Johnson administrations adopted a policy of building "bal-anced forces" to meet aggression through a system of "graduated deterrence," which would use only that level of force needed to meet the specific threat or act of aggression. U.S. and Soviet development of "hardened" missile sites, missile-firing submarines, and other nuclear forces that could survive a surprise attack established an equilibrium of power based on their mutual ability to retaliate massively. The Reagan administration's Strategic Defense Initiative (SDI), or "Star Wars," policy proposed to install a screen of laser and particle-beam weapons in the expectation that Soviet missiles could be destroyed before reaching their U.S. targets. However, critics maintained that the SDI system's protective shield was not scientifically and technically feasible.

Nuclear Strategy: Preemptive Strike | 303 |

A first-strike nuclear attack undertaken on the assumption that an enemy state is planning an imminent nuclear attack. The concept of a preemptive attack was developed by Soviet military tacticians during the 1950s as a defense measure to transform an enemy's planned first strike into a less dangerous counterblow. The purpose of a preemptive attack would be to seize the initiative and gain the advantage of surprise while a state's offensive power remained undamaged. Also known as a "spoiling" or "blunting" attack, it would be undertaken only after state leaders received intelligence data clearly indicating that the rival state was preparing a nuclear strike. *See also* NUCLEAR STRATEGY: FIRST STRIKE (301); WAR TYPE: PREVENTIVE WAR (342).

Significance

The concept of preemptive attack evolved during a period when considerable time was needed to ready bombers and liquid-fueled rockets, which then comprised the main striking forces for nuclear states. However, the development of push-button warfare, and the emplacement of solid-fuel intercontinental ballistic missiles, meant that a nuclear attack could be launched with such speed that the victim of the attack would be unaware of the preparations. Moreover, the dispersal of nuclear delivery systems and the steps taken to protect them from destruction during a surprise attack set up the possibility of a devastating retaliatory strike against the preempting state. Military analysts also recognized that a preemptive strike could be triggered by false or misleading intelligence data. During a crisis, for example, precautionary activities undertaken by each side to guard against a surprise attack by the other could be interpreted as preparations for an attack. Developments in nuclear technology have all but eliminated the preemptive attack as a rational, credible instrument of military policy.

Rogue States $\boxed{304}$

Countries judged by the United States to be outside the circle of civilized nations. Civilized states are those deemed to play by the rules of international law, and willing to acknowledge their responsibilities in the creation of international equilibrium. Rogue states are perceived as engaging in or sponsoring transnational terrorism, clandestinely or brazenly thwarting world public opinion by developing nuclear and other weapons of mass destruction, and/or representative of illegitimate governments that sustain their authority through intimidation, repression, and isolation of its citizenry. Rogue states are thus held to be untrustworthy, and diplomatic arrangements with such states can proceed only under clearly drawn safeguards.

Significance

The rogue states identified by the United States are generally those actors deemed to be the chief sponsors of international terrorism. Such states are Libya, particularly because of its alleged role in the Pan Am 103 incident; Iraq, because it is led by Saddam Hussein; Syria, because it has a long record of terrorist assistance against Israel; Iran, because it created and nourishes the Hezbollah terrorist organization; and North Korea, because it has

sponsored attacks on South Korean government officials. In one way or another, all the rogue states represent potential nuclear threats, and although attempts have been made to deal with some of these matters through normal diplomatic channels, the larger question of rogue states playing outside the rules of acceptable state behavior appears to obviate the possibility of real progress. Nevertheless, the United States has developed a diplomatic relationship with Syria through its effort to broker a peace treaty between Damascus and Israel. The Syrian leader, Hafiz al-Assad, sees the opportunity not only to regain control of the Golan Height but also to win the favor of the United States. If a deal is finalized, it would more than likely remove Syria from the list of rogue states. North Korea also entertains U.S. diplomacy, and in return for a scaling down of its nuclear program, Pyongyang anticipates receiving substantial technical and material aid, as well as an opening to the world's trading community.

War $\boxed{305}$

Hostilities between states or within a state or territory undertaken by means of armed force. A state of war exists in the legal sense when two or more states declare officially that a condition of hostilities exists between them. Beyond this, international jurists disagree as to the kinds of conditions, intentions, or actions that constitute war by legal definition. De facto war exists whenever one organized group undertakes the use of force against another group. The level of hostilities may range from total war, utilizing nuclear, chemical, bacteriological, and radiological weapons of mass destruction, to limited war, confined to the use of conventional land, sea, and air forces. The objectives of war may range from the total destruction of a state or group to more limited purposes such as securing a piece of territory or determining a boundary line. It may be fought by well-organized armies or by guerrilla bands ranging through the countryside. The causes of war are many and complex, but unquestionably include political, ideological, economic, religious, and psychological factors. Under international law, the conduct of the belligerents during a war is governed by the rules of warfare developed through custom and broad multilateral treaties. (*For specific aspects of war, see* Index.)

Significance

Historically, international law accepted war as a normal function of sovereign states in pursuit of their national objectives. Modern efforts to restrain nations in their resort to war and to civilize their conduct during hostilities were begun during the nineteenth century through large multilateral conferences. Restraints on the use and techniques of warfare that were embodied in nineteenth-century conventions, culminating in those that emerged from the Hague Conferences of 1899 and 1907, helped to build the League of Nations system and eventually contributed to the development of the United Nations. The United Nations was set up to maintain peace through three complementary approaches: (1) peaceful settlement of disputes, (2) collective security against aggression, and (3) building an orderly world through economic, social, and humanitarian programs. Although a world war has been avoided since 1945, more than 40 major wars have broken out, ranging from the Korean and Vietnam conflicts to internal revolts in many Third World countries. War among the great powers has become dysfunctional with the development of arsenals of weapons of mass destruction that could result in the annihilation of the attacking states as well as those attacked.

War: Belligerency | 306

The recognition by foreign states that a condition of civil war exists within a state. The determination of the point at which an armed rebellion is accorded the legal status of belligerency is a political rather than legal question. The effect of such recognition is to confer on the insurgents a *de facto* international status with regard to the rights and duties of legal warfare. Recognition of belligerency also acknowledges that the antigovernment forces have a right to govern those areas of the state that are under their *de facto* control. *See also* WAR TYPE: INSURGENCY (339).

Significance

A determination that a state of belligerency exists within a nation may have profound consequences because it permits the states that recognize its existence to give material, political, and moral support to the forces in rebellion. French recognition of the American belligerency during the War for Independence, for example, provided the legitimacy for supplying the rebelling colonists with aid to help win the struggle. The *de facto* recognition of the National Liberation Front of South Vietnam by several states helped accord it a measure of legitimacy otherwise lacking. Premature recognition of antigovernment forces, however, may be considered an unfriendly act and may lead to a diplomatic rupture, the threat of war, or a declaration of war against the recognizing state.

War: Contraband | 307

War materials that may not be sold to belligerents by neutrals. International law recognizes the right of belligerents to deny shipments of contraband materials to the enemy, but the international community has never been able to agree on exactly which goods are contraband and which are unrelated to the war effort. Goods shipped to a neutral port, if ultimately destined for shipment to the enemy, may be seized as contraband under the doctrine of continuous voyage or ultimate destination. A category of "conditional contraband" consists of goods normally for peacetime consumption but that may be useful for military purposes. *See also* INTERNATIONAL LAW: NEUTRALITY (483); WAR MEASURES: BLOCKADE (319).

Significance

Modern war, with its emphasis on breaking civilian morale, tends to obliterate the difference between contraband and permissible goods shipped by neutrals to belligerents. Most goods, even foodstuffs, are recognized in the contemporary world as significant contributions to a nation's war effort. The right of belligerents to stop and search neutral ships and to seize contraband destined for the enemy conflicts with the general principle of the freedom of the seas. During World Wars I and II, for example, relations between neutral nations and belligerents were frequently embittered by such actions.

War: Enemy Alien | 308 |

A citizen of a foreign state living in a state at war with his or her homeland. The regulation of enemy aliens is covered primarily by customary law, which leaves much discretion to government officials in the state in which they reside, subject to the general requirement of humane treatment. *See also* CITIZENSHIP: ALIEN (463).

Significance
When war was declared prior to World War I, enemy aliens were generally permitted to either return to their own country or remain in residence subject to their good behavior and avoidance of any actions that might give aid or comfort to the enemy. During World Wars I and II, enemy aliens were subjected to various degrees of control including registration, denial of freedom of movement, restriction of occupation, and, in some instances, detention in relocation centers.

War: Escalation | 309 |

Increasing the intensity or geographical extent of hostilities in a war. Escalation may involve an increase in the number of troops engaged in a limited war; participation in hostilities by additional countries; an expansion in the area of operations; a resort to the use of deadlier, more powerful weapons; or a change in the goals sought by the military action. The objective underlying escalation of hostilities in a limited-war situation may be the defeat

and surrender of the enemy, or the meting out of increased punishment to force the enemy to negotiate or cease an activity that was the initial *casus belli* (cause or reason for war). *See also* LIMITED WAR (294); WAR TYPE: TOTAL WAR (348).

Significance
The escalation of hostilities by one side almost inevitably results in counterescalation by the other if it is within its capabilities. In Vietnam, for example, the U.S. application of graduated deterrence by a progressive buildup in troop strength, growing intensity of the war effort, extension of the bombing to North Vietnam, and the gradual addition of new bombing targets produced counteractions by the Vietcong and North Vietnamese, and increased their support from the Soviet Union and Communist China. This made further escalations dangerous because they could have resulted in a major nuclear war. In the nuclear age, escalation poses the grave danger that the process of raising the ante in the search for victory may get out of control and result in a total war of mutual annihilation. Since escalation is rationally limited to the employment of "conventional" weapons only, many analysts believe that in the contemporary world, limited wars in which nuclear-weapons states are directly or indirectly involved can end only in stalemate and political negotiations.

War: Martial Law | 310 |

Establishment of military authority over a civilian population in time of war or during an emergency. Under martial law, rule by decree replaces civil laws, and military tribunals supersede civil courts. *See also* WAR: MILITARY GOVERNMENT (312); WAR TYPE: COUP D'ÉTAT (337).

Significance
Military officers exercise vast discretionary power under martial law. To avoid abuse of this power, most nations circumscribe its application by the military, permitting only political leaders to decide when, where, and for how long it should

be invoked. In the United States, only the president nationally and the governors within their states are empowered to declare a state of martial law. Martial law is commonly applied by military government officials of a victorious state in the occupied territory of the defeated state. In the Third World, military coups are typically followed by a declaration of martial law.

War:
Measures Short of War   311

Actions undertaken by one state against another to protect its legal rights or punish a wrongdoer, without a formal declaration of war. Measures short of war may involve such unilateral state actions as (1) breaking diplomatic relations, (2) retortion (a legal but unfriendly action taken against a state that had acted in an equally unfriendly but legal way), (3) reprisal (undertaking a normally illegal action to retaliate against a state that had perpetrated a wrong), (4) an embargo or boycott, (5) a blockade, or (6) the occupation of foreign territory. *See also* WAR MEASURES: BLOCKADE (319); WAR MEASURES: REPRISAL (327).

Significance
Measures short of war have been recognized for several centuries under customary international law as legitimate exercises of a state's retaliatory power to redress wrongs committed against it. In the absence of a central world authority to punish wrongdoing and protect rights, each state could only resort to self-help to obtain justice. Yet, the use of measures short of war may deepen international controversies and lead to declarations of war. Under the League of Nations Covenant and the United Nations Charter, members in effect renounced resort to self-help measures short of war to settle their controversies with other states. Each member of the United Nations has agreed to settle its international disputes peacefully by using traditional settlement procedures, by resort to regional agencies or arrangements, or by submitting the dispute to the Security Council, the General Assembly, or the International Court of Justice (ICJ).

War: Military Government   312

Military rule imposed on the civilian population of conquered territory. The authority of military government stems from the military necessities of the invading army and the obligation of civilized treatment of the population of the occupied territory. Although military government cannot compel civilians to take an oath of allegiance, it can demand temporary obedience. A military government may also function in liberated areas within a military theater of operations pending the reestablishment of civil government. *See also* WAR: MARTIAL LAW (310).

Significance
The application of military government over the peoples of conquered territory is as old as the history of warfare, but its role has been expanded, which requires more sophisticated methods in the contemporary era. Efforts are made not only to control hostile populations but to win them over politically and ideologically. During and following World War II, for example, the Allies helped the Axis nations reestablish acceptable political, economic, and social institutions and prodded them into restructuring those not acceptable. Their successes are illustrated by the fact that, without exception, territories occupied by the Western Allies established governments patterned on the democratic model.

War: Refugee   313

A person who is expelled or deported, or flees from his or her country of nationality or residence. Since refugees have no legal or political rights, their welfare has become a matter of concern and action by international bodies. Refugees may be repatriated to their homeland or resettled and assimilated into other societies when governments agree to accept them. The 1951 United Nations Convention Relating to the Status of Refugees, as amended by a 1967 protocol, defines a refugee as a person who "owing to well-founded fear of being persecuted for reason of race, religion, nationality, membership of a particular social group, or political opinion, is outside the country of his nationality and is unable or, owing to such fear, is unwilling to avail himself to the protection of that country." *See also* UNITED NATIONS HIGH COMMISSIONER FOR REFUGEES (UNHCR) (597); UNITED NATIONS RELIEF AND WORKS AGENCY (UNRWA) (604).

Significance
The tactic in modern war of terrorizing civilian populations, along with the deeply rooted ideological and nationalistic hatreds engendered by revolutions and civil wars, has produced millions of refugees in the twentieth century. Large-scale international action to aid refugees began when the League of Nations created the office of High Commissioner for Refugees in 1921 to provide help for 2 million people who fled Russia during the Bolshevik Revolution. A notable accomplishment in helping refugees during the interwar period occurred with the introduction of the Nansen passport, a certificate issued by a state on recommendation of the high commissioner that substituted for a regular passport and enabled refugees to travel across national boundaries in Europe. World War II produced additional millions of displaced persons who fled their homelands, were expelled, or were deported as prisoners of war or for forced labor. From 1943 to 1947, the United Nations Relief and Rehabilitation Administration (UNRRA) carried on a massive relief and repatriation program for 8 million refugees. UNRRA was succeeded by the International Refugee Organization (IRO), which, during its years of existence from 1947 to 1952, helped to resettle and repatriate almost 2 million refugees from Africa, Asia, Europe, and the Americas. Since 1952 general responsibility for dealing with refugee problems has been vested in the office of the United Nations High Commissioner for Refugees (UNHCR), which is charged with finding permanent solutions through resettlement and assimilation.

War: Rules of Warfare　314

Principles and practices set forth in international law to govern the conduct of nations engaged in hostilities. The rules of warfare initially took the form of customary law, but since the latter half of the nineteenth century they have been based on major multilateral international conventions. Major instruments that set forth the "laws of war" and their main fields of application include (1) the Declaration of Paris of 1856, which limited sea warfare by abolishing privateering and specifying that a blockade had to be effective to be legally binding; (2) the Geneva Convention of 1864 (revised in 1906), which provided for humane treatment for the wounded in the field; (3) the Hague Convention of 1899, which codified many of the accepted practices of land warfare; (4) the Hague Convention of 1907, which revised the 1899 convention concerning the rights and duties of belligerents and of neutral states and persons, and proclaimed rules governing such new weapons as dumdum bullets, poisonous gas, and the use of balloons for bombing; (5) the Geneva Convention of 1929, which provided for decent treatment of prisoners of war and the sick and wounded; (6) the London Protocol of 1936, which limited the use of submarines against merchant ships; and (7) the Geneva Convention of 1949, which updated rules concerning the treatment of prisoners, including the sick and wounded, and the protection of civilians. In addition to these and other minor conventions and regional treaties, belligerents in the contemporary world are bound by customary international law and a "law of humanity" forbidding unwarranted cruelty or other actions affronting public morality but not covered by either customary or treaty law. *See also* INTERNATIONAL LAW (480); INTERNATIONAL LAWMAKING: INTERNATIONAL CRIMINAL COURT PROPOSAL (493).

Significance

The development of rules of warfare is based on the assumption that it is unlikely that war will be completely abolished and therefore should be made as humane as possible. The thrust of international law limiting conduct during fighting is to establish minimum standards of civilized behavior that will be reciprocally respected and mutually beneficial to all belligerents. The rules of warfare are often violated in the heat of battle, in fierce ideological or nationalistic struggles, in civil wars and revolutions, and in those wars where national survival is believed to be at stake. Modern strategic warfare involves a total effort to break the morale of whole populations through indiscriminate destruction of the enemy's industrial potential and population centers as well as its forces in the field. Yet, states at war make an effort to observe most of the rules; flagrant violations are more publicized than lawful behavior. The outbreak of politically and ideologically motivated guerrilla, ethnic, and fundamentalist warfare in many countries through the 1990s, however, threatens to destroy the ideal of civilized conduct underlying the historical development of the rules of warfare.

War: World War I   315

The first total war. The outbreak of World War I began with the assassination of Archduke Francis Ferdinand, heir to the Austro-Hungarian throne, by a Serbian anarchist in the summer of 1914. Austria's ultimatum to Serbia on 23 July 1914 elicited a bellicose response from imperial Russia, a protector of Serbia, declaring that it had mobilized its forces. In effect the Austrian ultimatum to Serbia was read as a direct assault on the sovereignty of Russia, Austria-Hungary's rival in the Balkans. Serbia's reply to the Austrians failed to mollify them, and the latter began to shell Belgrade, the Serbian capital. General war became inevitable. Germany supported Austria, and seemed almost eager to take on not only the Serbs,

but the Russians as well. Britain and France were more guarded in their reaction to the crisis, but nevertheless determined to shape the course of events as well as protect and satisfy their own ambitious undertakings. By 1914 Europe's extended period of tranquility, founded on a balance of power beneficial to the major actors of the day, came to an end. The events in the summer of 1914 revealed a definite impatience with the status quo throughout the continent, and as the old equilibrium crumbled, the Great War commenced. The nations of the Triple Entente—France, Britain, and Italy—confronted the Central Powers, composed of Germany, Austria-Hungary, and the Ottoman Empire. Before the war ran its course four years later, virtually all the major nations, most of the minor ones, and numerous colonial possessions would be consumed in history's most atrocious bloodletting to date. Japan in the East and the United States in the West were drawn into the contest, and when the opposed sides finally put down their arms in November 1918, approximately 30 million lives had been lost. Described in more graphic terms, France lost 7.7 percent of its population and Germany had sacrificed 8 percent (adding indirect losses) to the gods of war. Behind these figures was the stark reality that war takes the young and spares the old, thus leaving not only a ravaged European continent, but also a Europe that lost its vitality and could not recover its past. It was a Europe that would have even greater difficulty charting its future. World War I began at the highest moment of Western imperialism; when it ended, the imperial age was marked for extinction. The general prevailing civility of the European scene prior to World War I also was shattered by a war of attrition that knew no limits and involved the use of the period's most deadly technologies.

Significance

Citing the consequences of World War I is to set the scene for all that has happened in the twentieth century. The long age of European imperialism reached its closing stage in the great conflict. Nationalism was unleashed with more fervor than that experienced in the Napoleonic revolution and generally through the nineteenth century. The nation-state replaced the imperial state as the preferred form of political organization. World War I also began the unleashing of the colonial people from their subordination to alien rulers. It destroyed the German, Austro-Hungarian, and Ottoman Empires. It precipitated the Bolshevik Revolution in Russia, and spawned a host of new independent states in Eastern and Central Europe. It whetted the appetite of the Japanese for a larger sphere of influence in the Pacific, and it awakened the United States to major power status. No less important, World War I harnessed the Industrial Revolution and focused it on the modernization of warfare. New technologies and scientific discoveries led to the invention and production of war machines that were more murderous than anything ever encountered. The Great War—World War I—drew new frontiers, elevated some nations and humiliated others, promised change and promoted stagnation, but it left nothing resolved. Victorious statesmen envisaged a different future involving closer cooperation and more intimate connections, but the past proved more influential than tomorrow's vision. World War I solved nothing; in the end it would be remembered as the prelude to a still more catastrophic encounter—World War II.

War: World War II $\boxed{316}$

The second total war. World War I was to be "the war to end wars," but only 20 years after that first global conflict, World War II demonstrated that few if any nations were really ready for peace. World War II was in fact an extension of the Great War. Developments set in train by the initial struggle continued to evolve during the interwar period, propelled forward by whole societies alienated from established governments and seeking solace, as well as direction, in the mendacious oratory of minor but nonetheless popular personalities. Economic deprivation, social unrest, and political weakness nourished the expositors of hateful fascism, and demoralized peoples eagerly and enthusiastically succumbed to the ministrations and promises of history's most rapacious demagogues. Germany's defeat in World War I meant more than the loss of empire; the German soul was pierced and bleeding, and only an Adolf Hitler emerged to treat the wound. Earlier, Benito Mussolini, pledging to restore Roman power, forced the Italian government to submit to his will, and a romantic people heeled to his call for service and unity. Similar currents moved through the Balkans and washed up against the states of Western Europe. In the midst of the Great Depression, the millions of Europe's unemployed, the destitute, and the disillusioned saw in the new statist movements and their leaders a salvation from their common predicament. Still another form of popular demagoguery arose, this time in the Soviet Union. Marxist-Leninist communism also promised release from life's tribulations and the eternal hope for a better future. Josef Stalin, the heir to Lenin, mobilized nationalities that were once oppressed subjects of the czars, and focused their energies on the creation of a new world order, in which the worker would reign supreme and history would have a new beginning. Even distant Japan could not avoid the force of the changes sweeping Eurasia. Dissatisfied with its spoils from World War I, the Japanese government came under the influence of a military establishment that centered the country's energy on territorial expansion in East and Southeast Asia. Having already seized Manchuria, Japan joined forces with Nazi Germany and Fascist Italy to form the Axis Alliance, and commenced the invasion of the Chinese heartland. World War II, in effect, began in East Asia. It added dimension when Italy seized Ethiopia and the Soviet Union invaded Finland. It was propelled forward by the merger of Austria with Germany, and the latter's occupation of Czechoslovakia. But it did not officially commence until Hitler's legions invaded Poland in 1939. Poland's plight forced France and Great Britain into the war. France, weakened by unrecovered losses in World War I and undermined by domestic Fascists, quickly yielded to the Germans. That left Britain to face the Axis Powers alone—not only in Europe but also the Pacific, where Japan was busy swallowing British colonial possessions. Because of its policy of isolationism, the United States avoided the spreading conflict, but nevertheless attempted to help the beleaguered British with war supplies. In violation of its nonaggression pact with the Soviet Union, Nazi Germany invaded that country in June 1941, and its forces moved quickly to the gates of Moscow. The Japanese attacked the Americans in December of that year, sinking a substantial portion of the U.S. fleet at its moorings in Pearl Harbor. World War II was now a worldwide conflagration, with more areas directly affected than in World War I. It would wreak greater devastation and cause more deaths than the earlier Great War. Between 40 and 50 million lives would be lost in World War II, more than half of them in the Soviet Union. Only the Western Hemisphere would emerge unscathed. The most costly war in human history was also the stage for the world's and history's most heinous act of genocidal villainy—the Holocaust—launched by Adolf Hitler against European Jewry but consuming millions of others as well. An Allied policy of unconditional surrender brought Germany to its knees in May 1945, and when the Americans exploded the world's first and second atomic bombs over Hiroshima and Nagasaki, the Japanese also capitulated. By August 1945, World War II ground to a halt.

Significance

The tools of war reached a level of destructiveness in World War II that could only be understood in terms that addressed the extinction of life on the planet. The failure of the League of Nations to prevent World War II caused its dissolution, but not until another world body was constructed to replace it. The

United Nations alliance had defeated the forces of totalitarianism, and it was anticipated that its members would continue their collaboration in building the peace. Acknowledging the changes wrought by the atomic age, and with two global wars within scarcely more than 30 years ravaging the earth and brutalizing humanity, the victors of World War II were expected to pool their efforts and establish a permanent peace. The United Nations alliance was perpetuated after the conflict by lending its name to the creation of a new world body, and indeed the United Nations was formed in 1945 with primary responsibility for ensuring the peace. The major victors of World War II were given the major obligation to realize that responsibility. However, only the United States emerged from the war more powerful than when it had entered the contest. Britain and France were weak and unable to manage their own affairs. China was beset by civil war and the Soviet Union was confronted with the enormous challenge of reconstruction. Only the United States seemed able to guarantee the peace, and it was eager only to return to normalcy and savor its success. The breakup of the remaining colonial empires followed the end of hostilities. Although the French, Portuguese, Dutch, and Belgians tried to retain their possessions, their efforts proved futile and their empires crumbled. The British were more generous, but also too infirm to cling to empire, and they transferred power to their colonial successors without a struggle. In these circumstances the United States found itself confronting a determined Soviet Union, led by the last of the master dictators, Josef Stalin. Stalin noted the weakness of the West Europeans, the humbling and occupation of Germany, and the disappearance of Japanese power in the Pacific, and moved quickly to fill the vacuum on both his West European and Pacific frontiers. He harbored deep suspicions of the Americans with their atomic monopoly, and in the American hatred for Marxism he saw a plot to destroy the Soviet Union's Communist system. Stalin therefore consolidated his hold on Eastern Europe and refused to accept common arrangements for the occupation of Germany. The Cold War began before the embers of World War II had even cooled. Winston Churchill's "Iron Curtain" speech in Fulton, Missouri, in 1946 brought an end to one historic epoch and opened still another.

War Measures: Arms Transfers

317

The sale or outright gift of military equipment to states by others as a commercial arrangement or for the purpose of assisting a particular state whose defense is in the interest of the transferring party. Most military transfers take place between states, but there is considerable movement of weapons, generally by sale, from private weapons and munitions dealers to interested client-governments or political movements seeking political power. Generally speaking, the trade in conventional arms is unregulated and made more complicated by clandestine shipments, secret technology transfers, sales of dual-use technologies (technologies that can be used for both peaceful and warlike purposes), and military support and training agreements that are linked with educational programs. Following the Cold War, some effort has been made by the G-7 (the major financial and economic states—the United States, Great Britain, France, Japan, Canada, Germany, and Italy) countries and the United Nations to slow the transfer of weapons worldwide. The Register of Conventional Arms transfers arranged through the United Nations aim at establishing legally binding norms for transfers, as well as verification, and a ban on the transfer of some specific weapons such as land mines. But the attack on illicit trade in arms is still a casual endeavor because the market in arms is so great, the demand so universal, and the profits so huge. It is estimated that the nations of the world spend 30 to 50 percent of available public revenues on arms procurement. With weapons systems more sophisticated than in the past, and hence more costly, that figure is likely to increase before it

diminishes. Although the traffic in nuclear materials, know-how, and weapons is still restricted, and no state claims an active business in this area of unconventional weapons, some of the states of the former Soviet Union, or their citizens, allegedly engage in the unpublicized sale of services and/or weapons-grade plutonium and uranium. Moreover, other weapons of mass destruction, e.g., chemical and bacteriological, have been produced in countries such as Libya and Iraq with assistance from German firms and technicians.

Significance

While states continue to recognize the legitimate right of self-defense, modern war, even in limited context, has devastating consequences. So deadly are the weapons of the current era that it becomes more doubtful that war can ever again be considered a rational choice in solving political, economic, or social problems. States need to safeguard their security, but the question remains: How much and which arms are required for a coherent defense posture? The principle of sufficiency is a guide, but too abstract to answer the conundrum. In an ideal world, both importing and exporting states must be able to justify the need for arms. But given deep-seated suspicions harbored by virtually all nation-states, justification is more a reaction to perception than to existing realities. On the other side of the arms-transfer equation is the commercial opportunity in the arms market. It may be argued that there is no economic interest that can of itself justify either the production or the transfer of weapons. Certainly, pacifists and idealists make a case for the absence of moral legitimacy in using reduced costs of national production, or the maintenance of a technological base, or the need for jobs in the arms industry to justify arms sales. But a radical transformation is not in the offing. Cynically, states continue to judge and weigh their interests in what they consider an anarchical world; that is, the many sovereign actors seek to advantage themselves and maximize their opportunities in conditions that do not yet elevate the community of nations over the individual state. Real security may well lie in the development of regional cooperation and in international guarantees, but no state is yet prepared to take the risk of unilaterally denying itself defensive measures, and hence states and entrepreneurs engaged in the sale and transfer of weapons will continue to exploit a lucrative market.

War Measures: Asia-Pacific Arms Production   318

The arms race on the Pacific Rim. The Asia-Pacific region, according to defense analysts, generates 35 percent of the global demand for weapons systems in the post–Cold War era. So intense is the quest for state-of-the-art weapons capability in Asia-Pacific that the pattern of demand has shifted from completed weapons systems to production technology. Between 1970 and 1990, South Korea, Taiwan, Singapore, and Indonesia achieved remarkable growth in weapons procurement as well as manufacture. The production and research and development capabilities of these countries have been made possible primarily through licensed production agreements and other forms of military-technology transfers from the West and the former Soviet Union. During the 1980s the defense industrialization programs pursued in East and Southeast Asia were actively encouraged by the United States. The Americans wanted to reduce their commitment of military forces in the region, and assumed they could maintain control over the disposition of defense forces by the several states of the area. The United States believed that it was constructing a web of interrelated dependencies among the Asian states; it did not envisage them striking out on their own, or acting aggressively. Indeed, the U.S. government believed that its defense-oriented program was foolproof. But the end of the Cold War brought a realignment of arms sourcing, and countries such as Taiwan and South Korea moved away from their dependence on U.S. weapons transfers.

Moreover, the United States displayed a clear reluctance to share its more sophisticated weapons capability with the Asian nations, thus opening a path for the Europeans, who were eager to invade the market and had no compunctions about the types of weapons technology they transferred.

Significance

The decision by Taiwan and South Korea to concentrate resources on developing new, more offensive technologies independent of U.S. leverage has had the effect of raising regional tensions on the Pacific Rim. The U.S. conflict with North Korea over its reprocessing of plutonium, and the North's apparent intention to stockpile nuclear weapons as well as their delivery systems, can be traced in part to developments in Asia-Pacific that may not appear threatening on the surface, but when seen from Pyongyang, must be judged mortal threats. North Korea has not enjoyed the opportunity to access the larger international industrial market, and it perceives South Korea's collaboration with other technologically based states in the Pacific Rim and Europe as more than securing strategic business alliances. North Korea could not be oblivious to the reality that between 1970 and 1990, South Korea, Taiwan, Singapore, and Indonesia achieved remarkable growth in the sophistication of their military hardware (fighter aircraft, tanks, armored personnel carriers, missiles, and naval craft). Therefore, the tendency in Asia-Pacific to pursue more independent technological capabilities in defense production has consequences far beyond those involving commercial transactions between the actors.

War Measures: Blockade   319

A naval action aimed at preventing supplies from reaching an enemy. A blockade may be directed against troops in the field or at denying resources and food to an entire civilian population. A pacific blockade, considered not an act of war but a reprisal for a legal wrong, may be levied by one state on another during peacetime to deny the offending nation's ships (but not those of other nations) access to another nation's ports. A land "blockade" to deny transit across a nation's territory may also be established during peacetime. In the case of the Berlin Blockade, for example, during the Cold War ground access across East Germany to Berlin was denied to Allied forces, necessitating an airlift in 1948. Blockade enforcement under international law permits confiscation of ships and cargoes of belligerent and neutral registry seized in the act of attempting to run the blockade. *See also* WAR: MEASURES SHORT OF WAR (311).

Significance
International law forbids "paper blockades" by requiring that a blockade be maintained by a force of sufficient size to make it effective; otherwise, neutral ships are not legally required to respect the blockade. In addition, advance warning must be supplied to neutrals, and their ships must be given a reasonable amount of time to leave the blockaded state unmolested. A blockade serves as an effective weapon for fighting modern war because of the extensive economic interdependency of states. Examples of wars in which blockades played important roles in bringing war to an end include the North's blockade of Southern ports during the American Civil War and Great Britain's blockade of Germany during World Wars I and II.

War Measures: Civil Defense |320|
Government programs to protect civilians, maintain essential services, preserve law and order, and provide support for the nation's war effort in the event of an enemy attack. Civil defense preparatory activities include construction and designation of shelters, stocking of food and medicines, disaster planning, providing for emergency communication and transport facilities, and operating warning and radiation-detection systems. Defense for civilians in the contemporary world in-

volves the development of programs to protect against nuclear, chemical, bacteriological, and radiological weapons of mass destruction as well as conventional weapons.

Significance
Civil defense in the preatomic era mainly involved protecting a nation's major population centers so that they might function as postattack mobilization bases. In the nuclear age, however, development of support for the nation's military effort following a major attack on its cities is no longer the primary objective. Some security analysts now conceive of civil defense as a means to ensure the survival of at least a portion of a state's population to facilitate recuperation of the nation after the war. Others regard the civil defense efforts of various nations as useless exercises in self-delusion, believing that there is no practical defense against nuclear war. Although none of the nuclear powers has undertaken a major civilian defense effort—preferring to seek security in the development of weapons to deter an attack—two neutral countries, Sweden and Switzerland, devote sizable portions of their national budgets to civil defense programs.

War Measures: Curfew |321|
An emergency or wartime order restricting the freedom of movement of the civilian population in a danger zone to specified time periods. Curfews are frequently established to proscribe movement during hours of darkness. They are widely used in fighting insurgencies that use guerrilla warfare. *See also* WAR: MARTIAL LAW (310).

Significance
Curfews are usually imposed by a local military commander when freedom of movement might jeopardize security. They are considered essential because of the increased vulnerability of utilities, communications facilities, and supply lines during the hours of darkness. Following the outbreak of war with Japan,

for example, President Franklin D. Roosevelt declared the West Coast area of the United States to be a military zone, and all enemy aliens and natural-born U.S. citizens of Japanese ancestry were ordered to be in their homes from 8 P.M. to 6 A.M. The validity of this action was upheld by the U.S. Supreme Court on the grounds that the threat of a Japanese invasion and the large numbers of persons of Japanese ancestry in the area justified the curfew (*Hirabayashi v. United States,* 320 U.S. 81 [1942]).

War Measures: Declaration of War | 322 |

A formal proclamation issued by a nation to announce that a legal state of hostilities exists with another nation. The requirement that a declaration of war precede the commencement of hostilities was established as an international obligation by the 1907 Hague Convention Relative to the Opening of Hostilities, but many of the ratifying states have ignored the obligation, and most of the hundred-plus nations created since 1907 have never accepted it. A declaration of war is directed not only at enemy nations, it also notifies neutral states of the new situation and provides for certain domestic changes, such as the government's assumption of special emergency powers.

Significance

The legal concept of requiring a declaration of war before the opening of hostilities destroys the advantage of surprise attack. Increasingly, as the state system has sought to outlaw war or aggression, states avoid making formal declarations of war against their enemies, preferring to regard them as defensive operations or police actions. Although war has been quite common since the end of World War II, not one has been formally declared. The increased incidence of ideologically based internal strife in the form of insurgencies, revolutions, and civil wars has likewise reduced the applicability of formal declarations because a declaration would accord full rights of belligerency to the antigovernment

forces. The revolution in warfare technology has also added urgency in keeping local limited wars from escalating through successive declarations of war to the ultimate stage of a total war of mass destruction. The Korean conflict, the Vietnam War, and the Afghan War are examples of hostilities carried on by a number of states without any formal declaration of war. In the United States, Congress (by joint resolution) must approve the president's request that war be declared. This action has been taken only five times in U.S. history.

War Measures: Fifth Column | 323 |

A subversive movement to weaken a government's defensive efforts during a civil war or an attack by another nation. The term *fifth column* originated during the Spanish Civil War when the rebel forces of Francisco Franco attacked the Loyalists in Madrid with four columns and proclaimed that a fifth existed within the city to aid their cause. *See also* WAR MEASURES: SABOTAGE (328).

Significance

Fifth-column adherents may be motivated in their support for antigovernment forces by ideological, ethnic, political, or religious attachments to the cause proclaimed by the rebels. Others may merely be pragmatic in their belief that they are standing with the side destined to win the war. The actions of the Quisling group of traitors in Norway during the Nazi attack in 1940 offers an example of the decisive role that a fifth column may play in sabotaging government resistance.

War Measures: Intervention | 324 |

Coercive interference in the affairs of a state by another state or group of states to affect the internal or external policies of that state. Under international law, intervention may be legally justified if (1) the intervening state has been granted such a right by treaty, (2) a state violates an agreement for joint policy determination by acting unilaterally, (3) intervention is necessary to protect a state's citizens, (4) it is necessary for self-defense, or (5) a state violates international law. Intervention is also justified by the United Nations Charter when it involves a collective action by the international community against a state that threatens or breaks the peace or commits an act of aggression. *See also* DOLLAR DIPLOMACY (639); MONROE DOCTRINE (657); WAR TYPE: INSURGENCY (339).

Significance
Most interventions have involved the actions of great powers in extending or maintaining hegemony over weaker states. Other reasons include undertaking reprisals against weaker states to protect the rights of their nationals, securing payment of debts, obtaining trade concessions, and protecting property. Since World War I, ideological factors have constituted the main basis for interventions as major powers have sought to determine the outcome of rebellions and civil wars in other states. After 1917, for example, the Allied Powers sent troops to Russia in an effort to quash the Bolshevik Revolution. The suppression of the Hungarian Revolution by the Soviet Union in 1956 and U.S. intervention in the Dominican Republic in 1965 were motivated by fears that important states would be lost to the rival ideological camp. Soviet intervention in Afghanistan in the 1980s was also motivated by a belief that, without intervening, the country and its people would reject communism and Soviet hegemony. Politically and ideologically motivated interventions are most likely to occur when a great power's hegemonic role is threatened within its sphere of influence. The passing of the Cold War has in part also meant the passing of ideological struggles and the reemergence of conflicts involving the lesser powers and otherwise remote peoples. Ethnic wars such as those in the former Yugoslavia, Russia, and some of the other former republics of the Soviet Union are cases in point. Moreover, these latter-day, nonideological struggles are in some re-

spects more savage than those witnessed during the Cold War, if only because they occur in more highly concentrated environs and pit against one another peoples who, not too long before, considered themselves neighbors and fellow countrymen. The savage conflict in Bosnia, the awesome violence in Chechnya, and the mass murder of hundreds of thousands of innocents in Rwanda are but a few of the most recent examples of still another form of intervention. Nor can the world ignore the deaths of perhaps millions in Cambodia by other Cambodians, or the unleashing of otherwise restricted chemical agents by Iraq on its Kurdish citizenry.

War Measures: Lend-Lease | 325 |

A program of mutual assistance carried on among the nations fighting the Axis Powers during World War II. The United States initiated the program in March 1941 with the passage of the Lend-Lease Act, which canceled the "cash and carry" provisions of the Neutrality Act of 1937. The Lend-Lease Act empowered the president to sell, transfer, exchange, lease, lend, or otherwise dispose of any item related to support of the Allied cause, including weapons, food, raw materials, machine tools, and other strategic goods. Under the act, executive agreements concluded by the president with Allied nations provided for a mutual balancing of accounts for services rendered to encourage a common war effort and facilitate postwar settlements. *See also* DEVELOPMENT STRATEGY: FOREIGN AID (210); FOREIGN AID (643).

Significance
The Lend-Lease program, undertaken by the United States nine months prior to its entry into World War II, constituted the turning point from neutrality to active U.S. support for the Allies. It proved to be a decisive factor in bolstering morale, supporting hard-pressed Allies threatened with exhaustion of their economic and military resources, and cultivating a

common cause in the war effort. Under the program, the United States became the "arsenal for democracy," providing more than $50 billion worth of goods and munitions (over $11 billion of them to the Soviet Union) from 1941 to 1945. After the war, controversy over payment of Lend-Lease debts owed to the United States by the Soviet Union became a source of conflict that contributed to the emergence of the Cold War. Long after the war, some recipient countries continue to make annual installment payments to the United States on their Lend-Lease accounts.

War Measures: Mobilization 326

Actions undertaken by a state to place it in a condition of readiness for war. Mobilization may include placing the armed forces on alert, calling up reserves for duty, closing frontiers, expelling or controlling enemy aliens, safeguarding against sabotage, establishing curfews, and invoking emergency powers for management of the nation's economy. *See also* WAR (305).

Significance
Every modern nation has developed mobilization plans and standby arrangements to be implemented when war threatens. Often, mobilization indicates that diplomatic negotiations have broken down and the outbreak of fighting may be imminent. The act of mobilizing a nation's strength will inevitably result in countermobilizations by other states and may in itself incite a potential enemy into taking military action. When Russia began to mobilize its reserves on the eve of World War I, for example, German leaders decided they could no longer await the outcome of negotiations, and launched an attack. Conversely, mobilization at a critical time may help to avoid war by calling a potential aggressor's bluff. Mobilization for a nuclear war in the contemporary world can be accomplished in a matter of minutes by placing delivery systems on instant alert.

War Measures: Reprisal 327

A coercive measure short of war, undertaken by one state against another as a means of redressing a wrong or punishing an international delinquency. Reprisals may include a show of force, boycott, embargo, pacific blockade, freezing of assets, or seizure of property belonging to the offending state. *See also* WAR: MEASURES SHORT OF WAR (311).

Significance
Reprisals have been used primarily by powerful states against weaker ones to exact payment or retribution for illegal acts. Before engaging in reprisal action, a state has an obligation to attempt to secure redress through peaceful settlement of the dispute. Acts of reprisal are forbidden if they injure third parties or if the punishment is excessive when compared to the injury suffered. Reprisals taking the form of military action against an offending state are no longer legally permissible under the peaceful-settlement and collective-security provisions of the United Nations Charter, but they occur anyway. The United States attacked Libya in 1986 when that country was implicated in a terrorist bombing in Germany that caused American deaths. Israel has repeatedly attacked Hezbollah targets in southern Lebanon because the terrorist organization sustains a relentless assault on Israeli soldiers and citizens.

War Measures: Sabotage 328

Destruction of military, industrial, communication, and transportation facilities in an enemy's homeland or in enemy-occupied territory, carried on by fifth-column elements, guerrillas, or professional agents. Acts of sabotage are aimed at reducing production of military equipment, cutting lines of communication, weakening enemy morale, and forcing the enemy to divert large numbers of troops from the fighting fronts to deal with the saboteurs. The term derives from the *sabot* (wooden shoe) that, during the early part of the Industrial Revolution, French workers threw into the new machines to wreck them so as to avoid unemployment. *See also* WAR MEASURES: FIFTH COLUMN (323); WAR TYPE: GUERRILLA WAR (338).

Significance
Sabotage has become a key factor in fighting modern wars. Because wars increasingly involve ideological conflict, any citizen having a strong attachment to the enemy's philosophy may be a potential saboteur. Efforts to inhibit sabotage in an occupied territory by committing atrocities against the civilian population—as attempted by the Nazis in occupied Europe during World War II—tend to be counterproductive because they inspire greater hatred toward the enemy and encourage others to undertake acts of sabotage. In a guerrilla action, such as the Vietnam War, it becomes extremely difficult to undertake preventive action against potential saboteurs because most of the enemy force functions in that capacity, is widely dispersed throughout the country, and is often indistinguishable from other members of the population. Guerrilla sabotage was combated in Vietnam (often unsuccessfully) by such means as clearing the entire population from large tracts of land, requiring fingerprint identification cards for all citizens, and subjecting thousands of potential saboteurs to intensive interrogation.

War Measures: Stockpiling | 329 |

The accumulation of reserve supplies of raw materials and finished products for use in the event of war, when supply sources might be cut off. Stockpiling may enable a nation to overcome a blockade, control of the seas, or disruption of supply sources. Modern nonnuclear war produces an unparalleled demand for critical commodities to feed the factories and foodstuffs to maintain the armed forces, the civilian population, and, often, allies as well. *See also* WAR MEASURES: STRATEGIC MATERIALS (330).

Significance
Stockpiling of critical materials may mean the difference between a military collapse and the capability of fighting a long war. During the 1930s, Germany stockpiled large quantities of strategic materials in preparation for war to avoid a repetition of their World War I experience, when the Allied blockade helped to produce a German defeat. However, in 1945 shortages of certain critical materials—especially oil and foodstuffs—again contributed to the German military debacle. During the Cold War era, the United States amassed the world's largest stockpile of over 75 strategic materials. Such programs carried on by the advanced nations tend to aid the underdeveloped countries because stockpiling increases demand for primary commodities (raw materials and foodstuffs), raises the prices of their exports, and provides them with food from overstocked reserves in the advanced countries, as in the United States' Food for Peace program. Stockpiling also enhances a nation's ability to carry on economic warfare during peacetime by either curbing imports or affecting the flow of trade and market prices through dumping practices.

War Measures: Strategic Materials | 330 |

Raw materials and semifinished and finished products essential for fighting a modern war. The availability of strategic materials is a significant component in the determination of national power. The number of materials considered to be strategic has increased rapidly with the technological revolution in warfare since 1940. Some of the most critical strategic materials include foodstuffs, aluminum, cadmium, copper, magnesium, tin, tungsten, mercury, cobalt, uranium, diamonds, petroleum, antimony, and lead. *See also* WAR MEASURES: STOCKPILING (329).

Significance
Access to strategic materials may prove to be a decisive factor in national power when a nation is engaged in a long war of

attrition. To bolster its defensive posture, a country may pursue policies of stockpiling strategic materials, developing synthetics to reduce or eliminate dependence on such materials, subsidizing their domestic production during peacetime, cultivating close political ties with major supplier nations, and preemptive buying to deny strategic materials to the enemy. Using these approaches, the United States has built up a huge stockpile of strategic materials, developed synthetic industrial diamonds, subsidized domestic production of petroleum and uranium, and sought to maintain good relations with Latin American countries that supply many strategic materials.

War Policy: Strategic Defense Initiative (SDI) | 331

A major research and development program initiated by President Ronald Reagan's administration to establish a defensive screen that would protect the United States from a Soviet missile attack. Popularly known as "Star Wars," SDI involved a massive effort to develop new defensive weapons, such as lasers and particle beams, that could destroy Soviet missiles either in their boost phase after launching or in outer space. The program was expected to cost hundreds of billions of dollars, and perhaps several trillion dollars when the cost of deployment was included. According to President Reagan, the main purpose of SDI was to switch from a policy of mutual assured destruction (MAD) to one of "mutual assured survival." *See also* NUCLEAR STRATEGY: BALANCE OF TERROR (299); NUCLEAR STRATEGY: DETERRENCE (300).

Significance
The Strategic Defense Initiative (SDI) was immersed in controversy from its inception. Its supporters included the Reagan administration, scientists working on SDI research projects, corporations that were awarded research and development contracts, and members of Congress and the general public who believed the system would work. Opposition to SDI came mainly from scientists who rejected claims that the system could work as projected, analysts who believed that SDI actually increased the risk of nuclear war, and members of Congress and the general public who believed SDI would make it more difficult to solve the budget deficit problem and would divert badly needed funds from social problem areas. The Soviets were particularly opposed to SDI, claiming that it violated the SALT I ABM treaty and would increase the dangers of a major nuclear war. The Soviets offered greater flexibility in arms-control and disarmament negotiations as a quid pro quo for ending SDI development and deployment. Although President Reagan and some SDI advocates regarded SDI as the creation of a perfect defense, other supporters questioned whether it could ever be made "leakproof" against Soviet missiles. Their support was based on the notion that SDI would provide an effective defense of the U.S. capacity to retaliate, thus ensuring continued deterrence in the nuclear arms race. SDI was sidelined with the dissolution of the Soviet Union in 1991, but it was resurrected in 1995 when the new Republican-dominated Congress continued its funding for research and development purposes.

War Policy: Unconditional Surrender | 332

Termination of hostilities without stipulation of terms. In an unconditional surrender, the vanquished nation places itself fully under the discretionary authority of the victor nation or nations, which may legally impose any terms or conditions considered appropriate. An unconditional surrender is likely to involve, as a minimum, occupation of the defeated state's territory, punishment of "war criminals," imposition of reparations, and a basic change in political, economic, and social institutions in line with the wishes of the victors.

Significance
The promulgation of a policy of unconditional surrender by one or both sides during a war is likely to prolong the hostilities until one side is completely exhausted

and its armies routed. The doctrine of unconditional surrender typifies the total-war concept of the twentieth century, which constitutes a significant departure from the limited wars fought for limited objectives during the nineteenth century. In World War II, for example, an Allied policy calling for the unconditional surrender of all Axis Powers was enunciated by President Franklin D. Roosevelt at the Casablanca Conference in 1943. Critics of the policy charged that it was unrealistic because it would deny the defeated great powers a continuing role in the postwar balance of power, it helped to prolong the war by giving the Axis states no choice but to fight to the finish, and it necessitated the dropping of atomic bombs on two Japanese cities. Unconditional surrender, however, was a very popular policy, one that the general public could rally round in a war fought with total means for total ends. Anything less than unconditional surrender would not be understood by the larger population, and indeed, Americans had great difficulty in understanding the character of limited war that was the touchstone for U.S. warmaking during the Cold War. General MacArthur's often quoted statement that "in war there is no substitute for victory" frames the U.S. view of war, and explains why President Roosevelt was obliged to pursue a policy of unconditional surrender during World War II.

War Type: Accidental War | 333 |

An unintended armed conflict touched off by incidents caused by human error or by electronic or mechanical failure. Accidental war in the nuclear age relates to the possibility that an all-out nuclear exchange between major powers could be triggered by a misinterpretation of intentions or by the accidental delivery of a weapon of mass destruction. Events that could precipitate a major war include the inadvertent destruction of a major population center, an error on a radar screen that leads to the belief that an attack is under way, or the actions of a demented military commander who orders a major attack. *See also* ARMS CONTROL: "HOT LINE" AGREEMENT (360).

Significance
The danger of accidental war between nuclear states has increased with advances in delivery-system technology and the proliferation of nuclear weapons among other states. The development of intercontinental missiles with nuclear warheads, for example, has greatly increased the danger of accidental destruction of a major city and the consequences of that act. Proliferation of nuclear weapons among additional states may increase the dangers more than proportionally because the newcomers to the nuclear club do not have equal experience or effective security systems to protect against human error and mechanical failure. To reduce the threat of accidental war, in 1963 the United States and the Soviet Union established a "hot line" teletype communication link between Washington and Moscow so that discussions could be initiated immediately during a crisis. In 1966 a similar communication link between Paris and Moscow was established, and in 1967 a hot line became operational between London and Moscow. In 1968 the Treaty on the Nonproliferation of Nuclear Weapons was opened for ratification. The danger of war by accident among the nuclear powers is emphasized by congressional reports disclosing that thousands of persons each year are removed from access to nuclear weapons because of drug abuse and physical and mental problems.

War Type: Civil War | 334 |

A war fought between different geographical areas, political divisions, ideological factions, or ethnic and/or religious groups within the same country. Civil war may involve a struggle between an established government and antigovernment forces, or it may develop during an interregnum period between groups contesting for power and legitimacy as the new government. *See also* ETHNIC WARS (48–50); WAR: BELLIGERENCY (306); WAR TYPE: INSURGENCY (339).

Significance

The outcome of civil wars is seldom decided solely by the struggle for power within a state. Other states are often prone to intervene, particularly when the struggle involves an ideological or religious contest for supremacy that duplicates the rivalry of the international balance-of-power conflict. The defeat of the Loyalist government in Spain during the 1930s, for example, was made possible by the infusion of troops and military equipment supplied to the rebel forces of Francisco Franco by Nazi Germany and Fascist Italy. A civil war is most likely to escalate into a broader conflict when states sympathetic to the rebel cause grant diplomatic recognition and provide open military support; premature recognition of a rebel government may be considered an unfriendly act by the established government and may lead to a declaration of war.

War Type: Civil War in Chad   335

Internationalized civil war in Central Africa. The civil war in Chad, like most postindependence conflicts in Africa, is rooted in the character of its geography, the stagnant nature of its economy, and ethnic quarrels that have often turned lethal. Chad is the world's largest landlocked country and is dependent on its six neighbors (Cameroon, the Central African Republic, Niger, Nigeria, Sudan, and Libya) for access to the sea and/or movement of its commerce. Chad's population is in excess of 5 million, divided between the Muslim pastoralists of the northern region and black Christians and animists of the southern region. The southern area supports agricultural production, while the north is essentially barren. Chad was formerly colonized by the French, who established their capital in the south; today, the capital also houses the country's major economic centers and educational institutions, and provides the administrative personnel who manage the state. Neglect of the northerners and mismanagement and corruption in government circles spawned several resistance movements, the principal one being FROLINAT, the Front for the National Liberation of Chad, formed in 1965. FROLINAT was sponsored by the Sudanese, who took a serious interest in Chad's Muslim population, in major part because the Sudanese (also Muslims) were engaged in violent actions against the non-Muslim black Africans in the southern part of the country. Libya also intervened in Chad in an attempt to seize the Aouzou Strip in the northernmost part of the country. During the Cold War, France, the United States, Nigeria, Egypt, and others involved themselves in the ill-defined struggle in Chad, all for different reasons, but nevertheless further complicating the situation. France and the United States were determined to prevent Libya from gaining control of northern Chad, or from influencing the course of Chadian government. After years of conflict that placed French forces in the region as well as some U.S. military units, the end of the Cold War seemed to rule out a continuation of this involvement. By May 1994 a semblance of peace was established in Chad when the different nations that had exploited Chad's political instability agreed to retire from the scene. In that same year the International Court of Justice returned the disputed Aouzou Strip to Chad, and Libya removed its forces from the area.

Significance

The Chadian civil war reveals how external actors such as France and the United States, in addition to a number of African states, especially Libya and Sudan, escalated an internal conflict, gave it an international dimension, and destroyed whatever chance Chad had to reconcile its different groups and work toward a common future. The numerous Chadian guerrilla factions each had their external sponsors, and as time passed, all of them shifted their alliances from one side to another, from one sponsor to another. In effect, national purpose was sacrificed to personal rivalry. Chad remains a ravaged country, not yet at real peace with itself, but at long last it may be allowed to find its own destiny.

War Type: Cold War | 336 |

The extreme state of tension and hostility that developed between the Western powers and the Communist bloc of Eastern Europe after World War II. The Cold War period was characterized by political maneuvering, diplomatic wrangling, psychological warfare, ideological hostility, economic warfare, a major arms race, peripheral wars, and other power contests falling short of an all-out "hot" war. The origins of the Cold War are found in the conflicts over the partition of Germany, the reconstruction of a new balance of power at the war's end, the communization of Eastern European states and their conversion into a Soviet sphere of influence, the development of an active anti-Communist philosophy and policy in the United States, and the building of alliances and counteralliances that created a pervasive atmosphere of fear and suspicion among the wartime allies. *See also* BALANCE OF POWER: BIPOLARITY (2); DIPLOMATIC TOOL: DÉTENTE (426).

Significance

The Cold War was an inevitable development in the complex postwar period of defeated and divided states, power vacuums, ideological rivalry, massive reconstruction programs, atomic weapons, and the political and power rivalry of two emerging superpowers. Forces unleashed by the early hostility in the Cold War gave it a self-generating impetus that sustained its intensity for 15 years. During the 1960s, however, the Cold War slowly began to moderate. The Soviet Union eased its "Iron Curtain" restrictions, growing polycentric nationalism in Eastern European states weakened Soviet

influence, and intense rivalry within the Communist camp (between the Soviets and Communist China) diverted Soviet concern from the Cold War and ushered in a period of détente. Coterminously, the progressive deterioration of U.S. leadership in the Western camp, a weakening of the bonds of unity within NATO, and a growing U.S. concern with Asian problems helped to erode some of the old bitterness of the Cold War. By the late 1970s, however, an escalating arms race and a bitter human rights conflict threatened to revitalize much of the Cold War antagonism. In the 1980s, as a result of Soviet aggression in Afghanistan, détente was replaced with a new series of escalations in the arms race, a boycott of the Olympic Games in Moscow and Los Angeles, and an increasing spirit of distrust and hostility between the superpowers. Mikhail Gorbachev's ascension to power in the Soviet Union in 1985 marked the beginning of the end of the Cold War. Gorbachev's reform policies produced internal and external changes that dramatically altered the character of the ongoing conflict. The Soviets normalized their relations with the United States by emphasizing genuine arms reductions, acknowledging the right of the Baltic states to self-determination, agreeing to withdraw their forces from Afghanistan, and pledging to operate through the aegis of the United Nations. Soviet support for the U.S.-led coalition against Iraq, a Soviet ally, in 1990–1991 signaled the relative sincerity of the Soviet Union's transformation from an archantagonist to a reasonable competitor. Gorbachev's policies did not please all the leaders in the Kremlin, however, and their attempt to remove him spoke volumes for the decline of the Soviet state. The coup against Gorbachev failed, but when the dust settled it was Gorbachev's rival, Boris Yeltsin, who controlled the weakened state forces. Separated from its ideological conviction Soviet society had come apart, and when the government could no longer press its internal reforms, the entire Communist apparatus collapsed. The end of the Soviet Union in

1991 also ended the long era of the Cold War.

d'état must acquire a degree of legitimacy in the eyes of the masses to be secure and govern effectively.

War Type: Coup d'État | 337 |

A swift, decisive seizure of government power by a political power or military group from within the existing system. A coup d'état differs from a revolution in that it is not based on a popular uprising and does not necessarily involve a trans-formation in the established political and social institutions of the society, although revolutionary changes may be instituted after a coup. The organizers of a coup d'état usually carry it out by capturing or killing top political and military leaders, seizing control of key government build-ings and public utilities, and using the mass media of communication to calm the masses and gain their acceptance of the new regime. *See also* WAR TYPE: REVO-LUTION (346).

War Type: Guerrilla War | 338 |

Irregular warfare fought by small bands against an invading army or in rebellion against an established government. Guerrilla war is fought mainly in the rural areas by indigenous elements who know the territory and are often indistinguish-able from the rest of the population. The success of a guerrilla movement depends largely on the support accorded the guer-rillas by the local population in supplying food and havens, giving aid by carrying supplies, and refusing to divulge infor-mation to the antiguerrilla forces. Many within the movement function as part-time farmers and part-time guerrillas. Be-cause an outside source of supply is often the key to the success of guerrilla war, the cutting of supply lines becomes a main strategy for the antiguerrilla units. Guer-rilla war in Third World countries is often one phase of a broad political-economic-social-ideological revolution fought against an established order. *See also* WAR TYPE: CIVIL WAR (334); WAR TYPE: IN-SURGENCY (339); WAR TYPE: WARS OF NA-TIONAL LIBERATION (349).

Significance

Throughout history, the coup d'état has been a frequently used device by factions or subordinate members within a soci-ety's power structure to elevate them-selves to top positions of leadership. A countercoup engineered by supporters of the ousted leaders or by personal enemies of the new leaders often follows a success-ful coup d'état. Numerous coups have occurred in the developing countries, many involving seizures of power by military cliques from constitutionally elected political leaders. Growing frustra-tions over the failure to realize economic development goals and the threat of revo-lution may encourage such coups in Third World countries. The 1980 military coup in Bolivia, for example, was a typi-cal military takeover following an elec-tion in which left-wing elements won political power. The Greek military coup d'état of 1967 demonstrated that even Western states with long traditions of democratic government are not immune from coups d'état. Eventually, a new re-gime that has achieved power by coup

Significance

Guerrilla war has proved to be an effec-tive means of harassing an invading army, as, for example, in its widespread use in the Soviet Union against German forces during World War II. In the con-temporary world, it was offered by the Communists to the peoples of underde-veloped countries as a basic tactic for un-dertaking the first phase of a "war of national liberation." Control of the rural areas, along with isolation of the cities, was regarded as the logical first step to-ward the victory of the masses over regular army forces with their more so-phisticated weapons. To accomplish this, according to Mao Zedong, the leading Communist tactician of guerrilla warfare, the guerrilla must be like a fish, swimming in the friendly sea of the rural population. Guerrillas were defeated in Malaya immediately following the end of World War II, but others were even more aggressively fought in countries of Latin America and Asia. A major test for guerrilla warfare was in Vietnam, where Vietcong guerrillas, later joined by regular forces from North Vietnam, eventually gained the advantage over the forces of the Republic of Vietnam, the United States, and several allied nations.

War Type: Insurgency | 339 |

A revolt against an established government that does not reach the proportions of a full-scale revolution. Under international law, an insurgency is a rebellion not recognized as a belligerency or civil war. An insurgency may result in the issuance of proclamations by other states warning their citizens to exercise caution in commercial and travel relations, but the international community regards insurgency as primarily a domestic matter. If the revolt is not quashed in due time by the lawful government, however, other states may accord belligerent status to the rebels. *See also* WAR: BELLIGERENCY (306); WAR TYPE: CIVIL WAR (334); WAR TYPE: REVOLUTION (346).

Significance
During revolutionary epochs the problem of insurgency has tended to become an international issue disrupting interstate relations between rival ideological groups. Insurgency was generally the form of warfare preferred by Communist forces during the Cold War era. These insurgencies exploited nationalistic and economic aspirations of the general population to challenge the established order in many underdeveloped states. Soviet and Chinese proclamations called for "wars of national liberation," which produced counterinsurgency policies and programs by Western states, especially the United States. To deal with Communist-inspired Third World insurgencies, the U.S. military created select

units such as the Green Beret special forces and the Rapid Deployment Force. Major insurgencies included the war in Indochina, uprisings in the formerly Portuguese territories of Angola and Mozambique in Africa, the antiapartheid struggle of the African National Congress (ANC) in South Africa, the guerrilla insurgency of the South-West African People's Organization (SWAPO) in Namibia, and several guerrilla wars waged in Latin American countries.

War Type: Insurgency, Kurdish | 340 |

Subnational conflict in the Turkish Republic. The Kurds represent the largest minority (approximately 12 million) in the Turkish Republic. They are also a prominent minority in Iran and Iraq. For more than a century, the Kurds have endeavored to carve out an independent state, without success. Their greatest opportunity arose after World War I with the formation of the mandates system, but given the events in the region they occupy, they could not compete with the formation of the Turkish republic, the Iraqi monarchy, or the new Iranian dynasty under the Pahlavi shah. The Kurds were divided among the three states, and separate attempts to achieve independence in each of them were beaten back by the respective governments. The struggle to gain Kurdish freedom continued after World War II with the same results. In Turkey, where the largest community of Kurds is found, a Marxist Kurdish Workers Party (PKK) was formed in the easternmost area of the republic. Although the PKK was not supported by the majority of the Kurdish population, the zealousness of its members had considerable impact on the general Kurdish condition. The PKK drew new strength from the Kurdish enclave created along the Turkish border in northern Iraq by the United States and other Western nations following Operation Desert Storm in 1991. Seeking to protect the Iraqi Kurds from Baghdad's aggressive activity, the Western-protected enclave became a marshaling area for the

PKK in its insurgency against the Turkish army and government. The situation on both sides of the Turkish frontier with Iraq became critical in the mid-1990s, and Turkey felt compelled to send its forces into the protected enclave with the objective of rooting out the PKK. The military operation in 1995, however, was no more successful than other ventures. Despite the magnitude of the campaign, the PKK demonstrated its capacity to take casualties while sustaining its determination to establish a Kurdish state.

Significance

Post–Cold War Turkey represents the most formidable power in the region, connecting the Balkans, the Middle East, and the Caucasus. Turkey is the only non-Christian country in NATO, and has long sought membership in the European Union (EU) as well. Rejected earlier by member EU states because of cultural disparities (but even more because its democratic political processes were suspect), in 1995, with U.S. assistance, Turkey won approval for membership in the EU Customs Union. In practical terms, Turkey's admission to the EU Customs Union was payment for services rendered during the Cold War as well as for its role in assisting the U.S.-led coalition against Iraq in 1990–1991. But the growing intensity of the Kurdish insurgency threatened to undo what had been achieved elsewhere. The Turkish incursion into northern Iraq in 1995 took a toll of Kurds not otherwise associated with the PKK, and although the PKK was generally considered a terrorist organization, Turkey's aggressive tactics did not play well among the Europeans and was a source of embarrassment for the United States. No formula has been found that satisfactorily addresses the Kurdish problem. It is clear, however, that Turkish power needs to be sustained, its secular experiment requires nurturing, its economic condition demands cooperative ventures, and its geopolitical dilemmas—including a spreading war in the Balkans, an estrangement with Greece over Cyprus, and instability on its eastern borders, i.e., in Georgia, Armenia, Azerbaijan, and Chechnya—require forbearance and understanding from the international community. The Kurdish insurgency impedes Turkey's management of national and international matters extending far beyond Asia Minor.

War Type: *Intifada*

| 341 |

Specifically, a series of minor clashes provoked by Arab Palestinian youth with Israeli occupation forces in the West Bank and Gaza Strip territories that in December 1987 escalated into a full-scale revolt. The term *intifada* can also apply to situations where a militarily weak civilian population challenges the authority and enforcement capabilities of what they judge to be an alien military force. *Intifada* is the Arabic term for resurgence, a form of violent resistance by civilian groups against a uniformed military establishment. The term also applies to the uprising in the 1990s of Kashmiri youth against Indian army and paramilitary occupiers. In both the West Bank/Gaza and Kashmir, the perpetrators of *intifada* have paid a high price for their assault on heavily equipped occupation forces. Almost 1,000 Palestinians died in the *intifada* prior to the Israeli-PLO Agreement of September 1993, and an estimated 11,500 Kashmiris are reported to have lost their lives between 1990 and 1995.

Significance

Intifada cannot be used to defeat an adversary, but it can make conditions so difficult that an occupying force might be more receptive to third-party efforts toward a political settlement. In some circumstances, it may provoke sympathetic nations to join the resurgence, thus expanding and intensifying the conflict. The *intifada* in the West Bank/Gaza was organized by the group known as Hamas, not the PLO. Thus, when the PLO reached its initial agreement with Israel, and Hamas insisted on sustaining the struggle, Hamas also had to contend with the new PLO enforcers of order. The *intifada* did not completely subside, but its character diminished significantly following the PLO takeover of the Gaza Strip in 1994. The Kashmir *intifada* has been more violent and more costly in lives, but less publicized. Inflexible when it comes to Kashmiri autonomy, let alone independence, India refuses to yield to the youthful Kashmiri protesters, who are supported by Pakistan, New Delhi claims. Another aspect of *intifada* as a form of warfare is the assault on targets that might otherwise be judged off-limits, even in more violent struggles. In Israel and the land under its administration, as in Kashmir, sites deemed to have high religious significance have not escaped the ravages of sustained struggle. The *intifada*, therefore, is more a form of symbolic warfare, aimed at influencing the psychology of people, than the attainment of physical objectives.

War Type: Preventive War   342

A military strategy that calls for an attack by a nation that enjoys a temporary advantage in striking power. The doctrine of preventive war calls for a surprise attack dedicated to the destruction of an enemy state that is developing a superior force for a crushing future attack. The theory assumes that the other side in an arms race is determined to undertake a future aggression, that time is on its side, and that an immediate decisive strike could destroy that future threat. *See also* NUCLEAR STRATEGY: PREEMPTIVE STRIKE (303).

Significance
The concept of preventive war is expounded mainly during a conventional arms race between nations of limited military and economic potentiality. In the Middle East in 1967, for example, an Israeli preventive war launched by a surprise attack destroyed several Arab armies arrayed against the state. Israeli leaders determined that superior Arab manpower resources and Soviet military aid would in time be combined to jeopardize the existence of the state of Israel. The possibility of a preventive war undertaken by the United States or the So-

viet Union was all but eliminated by revolutionary developments in nuclear and delivery-systems technology. The retaliatory capabilities of each side would make a preventive-war attack suicidal for both.

War Type: Psychological Warfare   343

Political, military, economic, and social activities carried on during war or Cold War periods aimed at influencing thoughts and actions. The major objectives of psychological warfare are to weaken an enemy's or potential enemy's will to fight, strengthen the resolve of a nation's people or its allies, and achieve diplomatic objectives. Psychological warfare is conducted mainly through propaganda or ideological campaigns based on carefully planned strategies and tactics directed toward the achievement of specific goals. The "weapons" employed include radio, television, films, public rallies, demonstrations, slogans, posters, books, newspapers and magazines, news conferences, and other means for reaching and affecting the thinking and emotions of opinion elites or mass publics. Psychological warfare may also be carried on at a more limited, sophisticated level in an effort to mislead or confuse policymakers or military commanders. *See also* FOURTEEN POINTS (123); IDEOLOGICAL WARFARE (128); PROPAGANDA (137).

Significance
As a technique for replacing or improving the use of military force for accomplishing military or diplomatic objectives, psychological warfare is as old as recorded history. Its broader use as an instrument of statecraft in the contemporary world has been facilitated by the technological revolution in mass communication, making it possible to reach the minds and influence the attitudes of millions of people in foreign lands. Psychological warfare directed at mass publics seeks to evoke such emotional responses as fear, hatred, horror, or fellowship, and often takes the form of building stereotyped images in the minds of recipients. The

first well-organized use of modern psychological warfare occurred during World War I in the form of massive Allied propaganda campaigns, which were remarkably successful in weakening the civilian and military morale of the Central Powers and winning the support of many neutrals to the Allied cause. The enunciation by President Woodrow Wilson of his "Fourteen Points," for example, provided a major psychological victory for the Allies by boosting their sagging morale and raising the hopes of the Central Powers for a just peace. In World War II and the Korean War, both sides engaged in extensive psychological programs, with varied results. The Allied demand for the unconditional surrender of Germany and Japan, for example, backfired by strengthening their will to resist and prolonging the war. The Vietnam War demonstrated the crucial role of psychological warfare in a guerrilla operation in which neither side is able to destroy the other militarily but each endeavors to win over the "hearts and minds" of the people. Since 1945 psychological warfare has increasingly taken the form of ideological competition under the assumption that, if the individual's loyalty to a belief system can be won over, the victory will be more lasting and meaningful than winning pieces of territory. Psychological warfare has become a major factor influencing a whole range of foreign policy and diplomatic activities carried on by the major powers, as, for example, in the fields of disarmament negotiations and foreign aid.

War Type: Regional War—Iraq and Kuwait | 344 |

Iraq's quest to dominate the Arabian peninsula and Persian Gulf. In August 1990 Iraq sent its forces into the sovereign state of Kuwait, quickly overran it, and almost immediately annexed the state. Baghdad justified its action by claiming that the kingdom was legally its nineteenth province. This invasion of Kuwait provoked an international response, monopolized by the United States but ultimately including a UN Security Council–sanctioned

force comprising troops from 36 nations. The UN coalition led by the United States forced the Iraqis to withdraw from Kuwait, and in 1991 the kingdom was restored to its original rulers. The Iraq-Kuwait dispute traces to a time in the nineteenth century when both countries were part of the Ottoman Empire. Iraq was then three provinces (Mosul, Baghdad, and Basra), administered by Turkish authorities. Kuwait was attached to the province (*vilayet*) of Basra, but the Turks never exercised jurisdiction over the region. Kuwait was then ruled by the al-Sabah family, and the leader of the clan was recognized as the prefect (*qaim-maqam*) by the Ottomans. In 1896 Shaykh Mubarak at-Sabah murdered his brothers and asked Great Britain to grant him protection from the Ottoman Empire. In 1899 Britain entered into a secret agreement with the al-Sabah chieftain, promising protection in return for British control over his foreign policy. Unable to reverse the condition, the Ottomans recognized Mubarak as the ruler of Kuwait, and the Kuwaiti shaykh, with British assistance, claimed and took control of the islands of Warba and Bubiyan at the mouth of the Shatt al-Arab River. At the outbreak of World War I, the Kuwaiti ruler renounced all ties to the Ottomans and supported British war efforts. The collapse of the Ottoman Empire after World War I allowed Britain to seize its territories and assemble Iraq from the Mesopotamian provinces of Mosul, Baghdad, and Basra. Iraq was established as a British mandate, and its Arab government, installed by the British, renounced all territorial claims. The boundary between Iraq and Kuwait was settled by the British in 1923. In 1932 Britain yielded its mandate, Iraq was declared an independent state, and the border between Iraq and Kuwait was reaffirmed. On 19 June 1961, however, British agreements with Kuwait expired, and Kuwait joined the United Nations as a fully sovereign state. Six days later, the Iraqi general who had seized control of Iraq in 1958 claimed sovereignty over the whole of Kuwait. British and (later) Arab League forces prevented Iraq from forcibly seizing the state. Two years later Iraq had another sudden change in government. The new government in Baghdad seemed inclined to improve relations with Kuwait, but Kuwait's retention of the strategic islands at the mouth of the Shatt al-Arab River had significant military, political, and economic implications. Thus, old matters were allowed to fester, and when Saddam Hussein gained control of the Baghdad government in 1979, they all contributed to the dramatic events of 1990. Iraq quickly overran Kuwait in August 1990, forced the monarch to flee, and annexed the territory. Kuwait's role as a major oil-producing country and its strategic proximity to the oil fields of Saudi Arabia galvanized the U.S.-led international response to Iraqi aggression. Justified in defending a sovereign UN member, the United States organized and executed the strategy that forced Iraq to retreat. The coalition succeeded in reestablishing the independence of Kuwait, but permitted Saddam Hussein and the bulk of his forces to survive, leaving the possibility that Iraq would try yet again to capture the territory.

Significance
The Iraq-Kuwait conflict did not end with the 1991 Gulf War. Although Iraq was defeated by a combined international force and Baghdad was again forced to acknowledge the independence of Kuwait, the Iraqi government led by Saddam Hussein remained in power. By 1994 Iraq had repaired the damage inflicted on its army and had moved some of its front-line forces to within a few miles of the Kuwait frontier. The Clinton administration responded with alacrity to the threat and dispatched U.S. military units to the region. Other U.S. contingents prepositioned in Saudi Arabia and in the regional seas were also alerted for possible action. When Saddam called his troops back, the crisis dissipated, but observers wondered how often the United States would have to perform its policing role in defense of Kuwait and the other oil producers. Iraq was placed under close

surveillance by the International Atomic Energy Agency, as well as by U.S. military and intelligence services. It nevertheless continued to rebuild its military strength and was still suspected of developing or seeking to acquire weapons systems of mass destruction. Although Iraq publicly declared Kuwait's right to an independent existence in 1994, few believed it had really dispensed with the idea of seizing Kuwait. Moreover, international economic sanctions imposed on Iraq in 1990–1991 were sustained despite feverish efforts by Russia and some West European states to have them lifted on humanitarian grounds.

War Type: Regional War—Kashmir $\boxed{345}$

Religious identity and national claims in South Asia. India and Pakistan engaged in their first regional war on the day of their independence in 1947. They went to war with one another again in 1965, and once more in 1971. Since that last encounter, both have threatened several times to make war on one another yet again, but have avoided such confrontation through last-minute diplomatic efforts. The central problem in the India-Pakistan relationship is the Himalayan state of Kashmir, which at the time of the British transfer of power was left under the authority of a Hindu maharajah who was determined to rule over an independent state of Jammu and Kashmir. Muslim tribesmen from Pakistan's northwestern frontier had other ideas, and they led an assault on the territory, which the maharajah's forces had difficulty in repelling. When the maharajah called for assistance from India, New Delhi demanded his opting for the Indian Union in return for their aid; he complied, and Indian forces entered the region. Pakistani troops also joined the conflict, and it did not subside until the United Nations arranged a cease-fire in 1949. That cease-fire was achieved with India holding Jammu and most of Kashmir, notably the predominantly Muslim Vale; Pakistan controlled the territory to the west, with which it shared a common border. When India refused to permit a UN-conducted plebiscite to determine the preference of the population on both sides of the cease-fire line, the dispute between the two occupied regions hardened. U.S. admiral Chester Nimitz and U.S. senator Frank Graham attempted to mediate the dispute, but in 1957 India unilaterally declared Jammu and Kashmir a state within the Indian Union, ending that effort at diplomacy. The Kashmir issue continued to plague the relations between the two countries, and in 1965 Pakistan tried to seize the territory by force. They were repelled by the Indian army, which struck Pakistan all along its frontier; the Indian air force bombed East Pakistan. The 1965 war was mediated by Soviet leaders, who invited the Indian prime minister and Pakistani president to Tashkent. However, the Tashkent Agreement between the parties did not resolve the Kashmir dispute, and it remained a major source of tension between the two countries. In 1971 Kashmir became a minor battlefield when Indian forces moved to liberate the Bengalis of East Pakistan from the authority of the Pakistani government housed in West Pakistan. In so doing, India dismembered Pakistan (creating Bangladesh), and confirmed Pakistan's worst fear that New Delhi was determined to destroy the Muslim state.

Significance
What remained of Pakistan after the 1971 war was the western region that joined with Kashmir to its north. Although Prime Minister Zulfikar Ali Bhutto appeared to yield to India on the Kashmir question during his summit meeting with Prime Minister Indira Gandhi at Simla in 1972, Kashmiri Muslims and their supporters in Pakistan did not give up their quest for an independent state. Kashmir remained somewhat dormant until the late 1980s when, encouraged by the *intifada* in Israel's West Bank territory, Kashmiri youth rebelled against Indian authority and looked to Pakistan and the extended Muslim world for support. Thus the 1990s brought an escalation of the struggle. In 1995 matters appeared to

reach a new level of hostility when Indian forces, already having taken a heavy toll of Kashmiri dissidents (an estimated 12,000 over a five-year period), attacked a broad section of the Kashmiri population. To demonstrate their resolve, they also destroyed a highly venerated Muslim mosque and shrine, the Char-e-Sharif. The Muslim population sought to avenge this action by launching attacks on and destroying Hindu temples. Although the human toll was heavy in Muslim communities, Hindu losses were light. Assaults on the Hindu population of Srinigar were minimized because the community had fled the Srinigar area at the first signs of the Kashmiri Muslim *intifada* in 1990. With an Indian security force of 500,000 members in the state, it was expected that order would be restored, but the long-festering problem still impacted negatively on Indian unity, secularism, and democracy. Moreover, India and Pakistan remain mortal enemies in a region where nuclear weapons are more and more accessible.

War Type: Revolution | 346 |

A basic transformation of the political, economic, or social principles and institutions in a state, resulting from the overthrow of an established governmental order. A revolution typically involves a popular uprising and the use of violence against the governing elite. If successful, the revolutionary leaders take control of the government and may then institute basic reforms in accord with revolutionary goals. A revolution differs from a coup d'état in that the latter involves a seizure of governmental power within the elite group without the support of the masses and, usually, with little or no basic political change. *See also* WAR TYPE: INSURGENCY (339); WAR TYPE: WARS OF NATIONAL LIBERATION (349).

Significance
Over several centuries of the state system's history, most revolutions have been motivated by ideological or religious principles. The three that have most

dramatically and profoundly affected the international system—the American, French, and Russian revolutions—were bitter ideological contests fought by protagonists of social change against the established order's vested interests. Because most governments in the contemporary world possess a monopoly of modern weapons, revolutions increasingly are taking the form of guerrilla actions supported by ideological sympathizers from outside the state's borders.

War Type: Terrorism, State-Sponsored   347

The sovereign state's role in promoting transnational terrorism. In 1995 the United States listed seven countries as prime sponsors of international terrorism: Cuba, Iran, Iraq, Libya, North Korea, Sudan, and Syria. The growing sophistication, mobility, technical competence, and ingenuity of the terrorists, combined with their use of modern communications, make them an increasingly dangerous threat to global equilibrium. The U.S. State Department has made itself the recordkeeper of politically inspired acts of violence against noncombatants involving citizens of more than one country, or the territory of more than one country. During 1994 the department cited 321 bombings, kidnappings, armed attacks, and other international terrorist acts. Not included in its recordkeeping are acts of violence judged to be strictly internal and domestic, such as the 1995 Oklahoma City bombing, or the random sectarian killings perpetrated daily in Karachi, Pakistan. The March 1995 assassination of U.S. diplomatic personnel in Pakistan, however, was considered an international terrorist action. The number of terrorist actions recorded in 1994 was down from the 431 cited in 1993 and the 665 committed in 1987. Nevertheless, the acts of international terror in 1994 were, on average, more deadly than those recorded in the previous five years. In effect, statistics demonstrate that terrorists currently kill and wound more people *per act* than ever before, and that much of the increase is due to the assistance the perpetrators receive from specific sovereign states. *See also* ROGUE STATES (304).

Significance
More terrorists are being arrested, prosecuted, and/or extradited as nations increasingly look to law enforcement as the best weapon against them. In the past there was a tendency to tolerate terrorism, to look the other way because of their political motivation, but given the increasing threat posed by these agents of violence against the fragile institutions of society, more resolute strategies have been adopted. Governments, especially the United States, are deeply concerned about the prospect that terrorists can gain possession of nuclear, biological, or chemical substances and use them for their nefarious purposes. Although many terrorist organizations lost their patron and refuge with the collapse of the Soviet Union, the less-than-perfect control over nuclear weapons, technologies, and know-how in the former Soviet republics makes accessing such devices by terrorists more credible. The New York World Trade Center bombing in 1993, which killed six people and injured approximately 1,000, illustrates the extent to which terrorists will go in pressing their cause. Although a direct link with a state sponsor was not identified in this incident, a number of those states appearing on the State Department list were connected in one way or another with the perpetrators of the crime. The destruction of Pan Am 103 over Lockerbie, Scotland, in 1988 caused 269 deaths, and that act of terror was traced to Libya. Muammar Qaddafi refused to yield the alleged perpetrators despite the imposition of international sanctions.

War Type: Total War   348

A modern war fought for unrestricted objectives with all means available for marshaling national power. Total war involves (1) participation of entire populations in the war effort; (2) terrorization of civilian populations to destroy their will to fight; (3) the use of modern weapons offering a vast range of destructive power; (4) participation of most nations in the war, with fighting carried on globally; (5) gross violations of the international rules of warfare; (6) intense mass emotional attachment to nationalistic or ideological ideals or goals that transform the war into a moral crusade for both sides; (7) demands for unconditional surrender; and (8) the political, economic, and social reconstruction of the defeated states according to the dictates of the victors. *See also* LIMITED WAR (294).

Significance
The twentieth century is truly the century of total war. In the beginning of World War I, participants believed that it would be another brief, limited war, but technical progress in weapons development and the commitment of whole populations turned it into a total war of attrition fought for national survival. World War II was fought for unconditional surrender, sought by almost unlimited means, resulting in the most destructive war in history. The threat of nuclear war in the contemporary world entails the risk of total extermination of belligerents and, conceivably, of the human race.

War Type: Wars of National Liberation | 349 |

A doctrine first expounded by the Communists, calling for anti-Western or anticapitalist uprisings by the developing world. Although Marx and Lenin alluded to national revolutions fought by Communists to win power, the broader contemporary definition was first expressed by Premier Nikita Khrushchev in 1961. In short, wars of national liberation are insurgencies undertaken against the established order in colonial territories and in the nations of Asia, Africa, and Latin America. Communists consider them to be "just wars" to liberate the masses from economic and political bondage imposed by Western-oriented elite groups. Communist Chinese leaders under Mao Zedong have also expounded the doctrine of national liberation wars, calling for a general uprising by the peasants in all

class-dominated societies. President Ronald Reagan saw the utility of the program supporting wars of national liberation and turned it against the Soviet Union in Afghanistan, Angola, and Mozambique. The Reagan Doctrine, as it came to be known, was also applied in Cambodia against the Khmer Rouge, and later the Vietnamese occupiers of the neighboring state. *See also* COMMUNIST DOCTRINE: KHRUSHCHEVISM (84); COMMUNIST DOCTRINE: MAOISM (86).

Significance
The doctrine of wars of national liberation was a basic tactic of Communists in pushing for their goal of the eventual triumph of communism. Recognizing that a nuclear war would be suicidal, Soviet leaders declared that all wars are unthinkable and unjust except for those fought by the masses for their own deliverance. While unwilling to become directly involved in the fighting of such wars, the Soviets nevertheless accepted responsibility for supporting them with arms and other forms of aid. Their view was that, so long as the West "exports counterrevolution," aid must be given to support indigenous revolutions. The Vietnam War, insurgencies in Ethiopia and Namibia, and guerrilla actions carried on in several states of Latin America, notably Nicaragua, were regarded by the Communists as wars of national liberation. When the Soviet Union crossed the line and invaded a Third World country—Afghanistan—the Reagan administration saw the opportunity to use the same doctrine and even the same tactics employed by the Communists. The success of this aspect of the Reagan Doctrine is demonstrated by the Soviet withdrawal from Afghanistan in 1989, the phasing out of the Cuban intervention in Angola and to a lesser extent in Ethiopia, and the neutralizing of the conflict in Mozambique. U.S. support for wars of liberation, however, has a negative side. Land mines provided to the belligerents continue to take hundreds of lives each day in various sectors of the world. Forces trained for guerrilla actions in Third World countries

are not necessarily prepared to lay down their arms after the initial enemy has been defeated or forced to withdraw. The continuing war in Afghanistan is a case in point. Finally, freedom fighters often transform into international terrorists, capable of selling their services, or opting for causes that are yet to be realized in the larger world. Some of the Trade Towers' bombers were traced to the Afghan resistance movement, and their likes are today spread across the planet.

Arms Control and Arms Reduction

Arms Control | 350

Measures taken unilaterally or through agreement among states to reduce the danger of war by such means as partial disarmament, security arrangements to avoid nuclear war, and the stabilization of force levels. Arms-control measures are aimed at restricting only certain aspects of the arms race, for example, prohibiting certain types of weapons, restricting nuclear testing, or demilitarizing geographical areas.

Significance

Although the terms are sometimes used interchangeably, arms control differs from disarmament in that its main objective is to stabilize rather than reduce or eliminate arms. A partial list of arms-control measures adopted to limit the arms race during the years of the Cold War include (1) the Antarctic Treaty of 1959, which demilitarizes that continent; (2) the Partial Nuclear Test Ban Treaty of 1963, which prohibits all but underground nuclear tests; (3) the Outer Space Treaty of 1967, which bars weapons from outer space and celestial bodies; (4) the establishment of direct communications links ("hot lines") in the 1960s between Moscow and Washington, Paris, and London; (5) the 1967 Treaty for the Prohibition of Nuclear Weapons in Latin America (Treaty of Tlatelolco), which created a nuclear weapons–free zone (NWFZ) in Latin America; (6) the Non-Proliferation Treaty of 1967, which seeks to limit the nuclear club to its existing membership; (7) the Seabed Treaty of 1970, which prohibits signatory states from placing nuclear weapons in the seabed outside the 12-mile territorial waters; and (8) Strategic Arms Limitation Treaties, referred to as SALT I and SALT II, which were efforts by the Soviet Union and the United States to restrain the arms race. Virtually all the agreements entered into with the Soviet Union, and in force when the Soviet state was dissolved, have been acceded to by the Russian Republic, the successor state to the USSR.

Arms Control: ABM Treaty, 1972 | 351

A treaty between the United States and the Union of Soviet Socialist Republics on the Limitation of Anti-Ballistic Missile

Systems. The treaty was signed 26 May 1972, and entered into force 3 October 1972. A Protocol on the Limitation of Anti-Ballistic Systems, further limiting each party to a single ABM system-deployment area, was signed on 3 July 1974; it entered into force on 24 May 1976. *See also* ARMS CONTROL: START II TREATY, 1993 (374); WAR POLICY: STRATEGIC DEFENSE INITIATIVE (SDI) (331).

Significance
The technological difficulties and financial costs of constructing and operating effective ABM systems influenced the Americans and Soviets to virtually scrap their development. The United States initially placed a primitive ABM system around one of its continental ICBM bases, but later dismantled it when it was judged unable to fulfill its mission. The Soviets deployed a system around Moscow, but its utility also was of questionable value. The later development of the Strategic Defense Initiative (SDI), or "Star Wars," project during the Reagan administration was a throwback to ABM. Although SDI was criticized heavily by substantial numbers of the U.S. scientific community, it disturbed the Soviet leaders, who declared that it was a violation of the ABM Treaty. By the 1980s, the Soviets were ever more impressed with the advances made in science and technology by U.S. scientists. Although SDI was never demonstrated as an operational antimissile weapon-defense system, it nevertheless left the Soviets believing they were falling farther and farther behind the Americans. It was anticipated, following the dissolution of the USSR, that the United States would halt its SDI program; however, the U.S. Congress continued to press for the development of the anti-ballistic system, and in 1995, over the president's objections, the legislators voted to sustain funding for the program. This unilateral action by the United States changed agreed upon understandings of the ABM Treaty and would permit the development of Theater Missile Defense (TMD) systems. The action not only raised questions concerning the ABM Treaty,

but it also complicated START II ratification actions in the Russian Duma (parliament). In response to U.S. maneuvering, Russian legislators demanded the unconditional implementation of the ABM Treaty as a precondition for START II ratification.

Arms Control: Antarctic Treaty of 1959 $\boxed{352}$
An agreement to prevent the militarization of the Antarctic continent and to remove it from Cold War conflicts. Signed in December 1959, the Antarctic Treaty came into force in June 1961, following ratification by its 12 signatories—Argentina, Australia, Belgium, Great Britain, Chile, France, Japan, New Zealand, Norway, South Africa, the Soviet Union, and the United States. Brazil, China, India, Uruguay, Poland, and West Germany became full parties to the treaty later. The major provisions of the treaty include (1) the prohibition of all military activity on the Antarctic continent, with each signatory accorded the right to aerial surveillance; (2) the prohibition of nuclear explosions or dumping of radioactive wastes on the continent; (3) the right to inspect one another's installations to safeguard against violations; (4) the nonrecognition of existing territorial claims, and agreement that no new claims may be made; and (5) the responsibility to settle disputes peacefully and cooperate in scientific investigations on the continent. *See also* REGIONAL POLITICAL GROUP: ANTARCTIC SYSTEM (ATS) (560).

Significance
The Antarctic Treaty was the first disarmament agreement concluded by the United States and the Soviet Union during the era of the Cold War. The treaty set a precedent for territorial disarmament, but efforts to apply its successful formula to the negotiation of additional demilitarization agreements failed. A treaty to prohibit nuclear weapons and nuclear testing on the South American continent, however, was signed in 1967 and has since been ratified by most Latin American states (Treaty of Tlatelolco).

Arms Control: Chemical/Biological Weapons (CBW) | 353 |

Weapons of mass destruction that utilize poisonous agents or toxins. Chemical and biological (bacteriological) weapons have been legally banned from use in warfare by the Geneva Protocol of 1925. That treaty, however, bans only the use of such weapons, not their production and stockpiling. The Convention on the Prohibition of the Development, Production and Stockpiling of Bacteriological (Biological) and Toxin Weapons and on Their Destruction was signed on 10 April 1972, and entered into force on 26 March 1975. It prohibited the possession of biological weapons and toxin weapons derived from natural poisons such as snake venom. Nearly 100 nations are now parties to both the Geneva Protocol and the Biological Weapons Convention, including the United States and Russia.

Significance
Chemical weapons remain a threat to world peace, in part because they are easier and cheaper to build than other weapons of mass destruction. Although prohibitions exist on the development, deployment, and use of chemical weapons, some states continue to develop them and some have used them. During the war between Iran and Iraq, the Iraqis used chemical agents against the Iranians as well as on their own Kurdish citizens, accused by the Iraqis of aiding the enemy. Libya has engaged in the production of chemical weapons, although it has not used them. German firms and technicians have been charged with assisting both countries by building chemical-weapons facilities and providing the necessary expertise in their manufacture. The U.S.-led coalition that forced Iraq to retreat from Kuwait in 1991 feared Iraq's use of chemical weapons. Although none were detected in the fighting, at the end of the conflict many members of the U.S. force claimed to be suffering from an unknown disease (Gulf War Syndrome), which they attributed to poisonous substances. Israel was attacked repeatedly by Iraqi missiles during the Gulf War of 1991 even though it was not a belligerent and did not retaliate. The Israelis also believed they would be hit by chemical weapons, but that fear proved unwarranted. The United States used chemical agents during the war in Indochina. Agent Orange was used to defoliate the jungles so that the troops and airmen would have a clearer field of fire. Agent Orange, however, proved to have lasting effects not only on the Vietnamese population but on the Americans who came in contact with it. The danger of chemical weapons was dramatized by the release of Sarin gas in a Tokyo subway in April 1995 by a religious cult-*cum*-terrorist organization identified as the Aum Shinri Kyo. Sarin was developed by the Nazis in World War II but never used because of fear of retaliation. The continued development and even use of chemical weapons by states and terrorists alike in the contemporary world suggests there is less fear of retaliation by those using the weapon. It also illustrates the frail character of treaties seeking to outlaw its use.

Arms Control: Chemical Weapons Convention, 1993 | 354 |

A convention prohibiting the development, production, stockpiling, and use of chemical weapons, and calling for the destruction of existing chemical weapons. Drafted by 39 nations of the Conference on Disarmament, the convention was intended to ban the development, manufacture, and use of chemical weapons worldwide. It was opened for signature in Paris on 13 January 1993, and by the end of 1994 had been signed by more than 150 nations. The convention is to enter into force 180 days after the deposit of the sixty-fifth instrument of ratification.

Significance
Chemical weapons, notably poison gas, were banned from use after World War I. Since that time, although chemical agents have been used in warfare (e.g., defoliants), their use has been significantly limited. Reports that Iraq had used chemical weapons in its war with Iran (and notably against its own citizens, who were deemed

to be aiding Iran) signaled a weakening of the prohibition. After the Gulf War, the United Nations demanded the destruction of Iraq's chemical-weapons facilities and took measures to monitor compliance. Reports that other countries are engaged in the manufacture of chemical weapons and are being aided by chemical industries in other countries (notably Germany) underline the need for still more effective enforcement measures. Libya and Iran have both been reported to be developing chemical weapons. The ease with which chemical weapons can be constructed was illustrated in the gassing of Tokyo subway riders by members of the religious cult Aum Shinri Kyo in 1995. Indeed, as a weapon of mass destruction, chemical weapons are the cheapest and easiest to produce. Although international conventions place restrictions on established states, there is little that can be done to constrain a rogue state, and even less to stop an extremist movement bent on wreaking havoc on a civilized population center.

Arms Control: Conventional Forces in Europe Treaty (CFE), 1990 | 355 |

A treaty that reduces key armaments and military forces in Europe. The Treaty on Conventional Armed Forces in Europe was agreed to prior to the dissolution of the Soviet Union, but its importance was acknowledged by the Russian Republic, the successor state to the USSR. Originally signed by the 22 NATO and Warsaw Pact states on 19 November 1990, in the aftermath of the Soviet demise, it was applied provisionally on 17 July 1992, and entered into force on 9 November 1992. Full implementation was slated within 40 months of its coming into force. *See also* ALLIANCE: PARTNERSHIP FOR PEACE (PFP) (286); ARMS CONTROL: OSLO FINAL DOCUMENT, 1992 (366).

Significance

The Conventional Forces in Europe Treaty reduces and sets ceilings from the Atlantic Ocean to the Ural Mountains on key armaments essential for launching

surprise attacks and initiating large-scale offensive operations. CFE scales back the number of combat-ready forces in both East and West Europe. Russia's withdrawal of its armed forces from the former East Germany in 1994 was reciprocated by the pullback of U.S. forces from the former West Germany. Berlin is no longer garrisoned by foreign troops, and U.S. long-range plans involve the removal of the bulk of U.S. troops from Germany and the transfer of their German military bases to German/NATO command. When fully implemented, CFE will reduce significantly the relative strength of U.S. and Russian military establishments deployed in the Central European region.

Arms Control: Conventional Forces in Europe Agreement | 356 | (CFE 1A), 1992

Follow-up to the CFE agreements initiated by the United States and the USSR in 1990. Cited as the concluding act, it focused attention on personnel strength of conventional forces and military equipment distribution in Europe from the Atlantic to the Urals. It was signed on 10 July 1992 and entered into force on 17 July 1992. The agreement called for its implementation within 40 months of its entry into force. *See also* ARMS CONTROL: CONVENTIONAL FORCES IN EUROPE TREATY (CFE), 1990 (355); ARMS CONTROL: OSLO FINAL DOCUMENT, 1992 (366).

Significance

As with previous Conventional Forces in Europe agreements, this final action was taken to reduce the threat of a recurrence of East-West military rivalry. The terms of the agreement called for drastic reductions in combat forces, as well as a pullback of forces from former Cold War positions; however, fundamental changes since the 1990 treaty was established have raised new questions in Russia. Moscow's compliance would mean Russia is limited to one-third the forces allowed NATO, and only one-fifth the forces allowed an expanded NATO. CFE would also limit Russia's internal deployment of forces on its northern and southern flanks. Similar restrictions apply only to the Ukraine. Russian military authorities argue the country's security is placed at risk, and in Chechnya alone Soviet troop levels far exceed those permitted by the treaty. Given Moscow's decision to ignore the limitation of forces deadline (17 November 1995), it appeared the CFE treaty will be renegotiated still another time. Final implementation of the CFE Treaty was jeopardized by a disagreement between the Russian Federation and the West over the "flank zone." Russian non-compliance with the treaty's restrictions on the area raised questions concerning the reliability of the Chemical Weapons Convention, the Biological Weapons Convention, and the Open Skies Treaty and jeopardized further arms control negotiations. The Russian minister of defense, Pavel Grachev called for all out war against the Chechens in October 1995, furthering tensions with Turkey and its NATO allies.

Arms Control: ENMOD Convention, 1977 | 357 |

Convention on the Prohibition of Military or Any Other Hostile Use of Environmental Modification Techniques. It was signed 18 May 1977 and entered into force 5 October 1978.

Significance
The treaty prohibits the hostile use of certain environmental modification techniques that are determined to have widespread, long-lasting, and severe effects, for example, destroying arable land or changing the weather.

Arms Control: Hague Peace Conferences (1899 and 1907) | 358 |

Special international conferences called at the initiative of Czar Nicholas of Russia to elicit agreement on arms control and other measures for maintaining peace and making war more humane. The Russian proposal at the first Hague Conference that all participants agree to restrict their armaments to existing levels failed to gain support. A vaguely worded resolution calling upon all states to consider

limiting their war budgets for "the welfare of mankind," however, was adopted unanimously. At the second Hague Conference, British efforts to secure agreement on arms limitation were discarded when the chief German delegate threatened to veto any arms-control proposal. *See also* INTERNATIONAL LAWMAKING: HAGUE PEACE CONFERENCES (1899 AND 1907) (492).

Significance
The Hague Peace Conferences produced no concrete arms-control measures but were an important milestone in the disarmament field because they were the first attempts by the international community to limit arms by general agreement. Considerable accord was achieved in collateral fields, however, with the establishment of a Permanent Court of Arbitration and by extensive codification of the laws of war and neutrality. The fruitless search at the Hague Conferences for means to halt the arms race was followed by the catastrophe of World War I. The conferences and the war contributed to the increased vigor with which officials pursued arms-control and disarmament goals during the 1920s and 1930s under the League of Nations system, but these efforts failed to prevent World War II.

Arms Control: Helsinki Accord | 359 |

A major diplomatic agreement aimed at providing peace and stability in Europe between the East and the West. Known as the Helsinki Final Act, the accord was signed in Helsinki by 35 nations on 1 August 1975 at the conclusion of the Conference on Security and Cooperation in Europe (CSCE). The participants included the NATO countries, the Warsaw Pact nations, and 13 neutral and nonaligned European nations. The accord was divided into four sections or "baskets." Basket I dealt with questions relating to security in Europe, including basic principles guiding relations among states and specific problems of security including the institution of confidence-building measures. In pursuit of the latter, the Final Act required notification of military maneuvers involving more than 25,000 troops. Basket II provided for cooperation in the fields of economics, science and technology, and the environment. Basket III encouraged cooperation in promoting humanitarian endeavors, including human rights, culture, education, and the free flow of people, ideas, and information throughout Europe. Sometimes referred to as Basket IV, the accord also provided for the holding of review conferences in which participating states were called upon "to continue the multilateral process initiated by the Conference." Major review conferences met in Belgrade (1977), Madrid (1980), and Vienna (1987). *See also* MUTUAL-SECURITY ORGANIZATION: CONFERENCE ON SECURITY AND COOPERATION IN EUROPE (CSCE) (297).

Significance
The Helsinki Accord was a major effort to reduce hostility between East and West by getting all European nations and the United States to accept the post–World War II status quo in Europe and promoting programs of cooperation and understanding among all European nations. Although the accord was merely a diplomatic agreement, and therefore did not constitute binding international law, it created certain expectations concerning the conduct of participating states and provided for periodic review conferences to goad states into meeting these expectations. Some beneficial results occurred following the signing of the Final Act. For example, Soviet authorities permitted increased Jewish emigration, and the German Democratic Republic declared an amnesty and released many political prisoners. In the field of environmental protection, participating European states signed a convention aimed at coping with problems of air pollution. Some observers point to the Helsinki Accord as the starting point for the decline of the Soviet Union. The softening of the Soviet position in human rights matters, as well as in East-West relations, also produced a diminution in ideological rhetoric, and set the scene for a normalization of relations with the United States. Mikhail Gor-

bachev's assumption of power in 1985 can be traced to Soviet efforts at realizing some of the positive aspects of the accords.

Arms Control: "Hot Line" Agreement   360

U.S.-Soviet agreement to establish official teletype communications link between Washington and Moscow. Known as the "hot line" agreement, Washington and Moscow signed the Memorandum of Understanding at Geneva on 20 June 1963 to permit direct contact between heads of government during a crisis. The agreement developed out of a fear that nuclear war might be initiated as a result of misunderstanding, miscalculation, accident, or failure to communicate. Similar teletype cable links were established between Paris and Moscow in 1966, and between London and Moscow in 1967.

Significance
The Cuban Missile Crisis of 1962 alerted U.S. and Soviet leaders to the grave danger of a nuclear attack. A communications failure forced President John F. Kennedy to use commercial facilities to communicate rapidly with Premier Nikita Khrushchev. The "hot line" arrangement only supplemented the slower, more cumbersome diplomatic channels of communication, but it was essential at a time of great crisis. During the brief Arab-Israeli War of 1967, for example, the teletype cable arrangement was used to communicate more than 20 messages between U.S. and Soviet leaders so that both sides could make it clear to each other that neither wanted an enlargement of the war. The communications-link idea was only one of a number of proposals discussed by the United States and the Soviet Union over the years as means for reducing the danger of nuclear war. Other proposals—to establish ground observation posts, give advance notice of major military movements, and permit aerial observation of each other's military facilities, for example—were dismissed by either the Soviets or the United States as instruments for espionage or as attempts to gain an advantage in the arms

race. These developments waited on the termination of the Cold War. Nevertheless, in 1987 a U.S.-Soviet agreement updated the hot line arrangement in a further effort to avoid an accidental nuclear holocaust. The agreement provided for the opening of "nuclear risk reduction centers" in both countries, the sharing of information about nuclear accidents, and joint action to prevent thefts of nuclear weapons.

Arms Control: Inhumane Weapons Convention, 1981 | 361 |

Restriction of the use of certain conventional weapons deemed to be excessively injurious or to have indiscriminate effects. The convention was signed on 10 April 1981 and entered into force on 2 December 1983.

Significance

Since the Hague peace conferences of 1899 and 1907, the world's major nations have sought to outlaw weapons regarded as unnecessarily damaging to humanity. As a consequence of such efforts, a variety of weapons are judged inappropriate in the conduct of formal warfare. Just as the crossbow was declared illegal in medieval times, and poison gas following World War I, serious attention has been given to outlawing chemical, biological, and nuclear agents. Although some progress has been made in banning the manufacture and use of chemical and biological weapons, on the matter of nuclear weapons no firm decision has yet been taken to declare such instruments illegal.

Arms Control: Intermediate Nuclear Forces (INF) Treaty, 1987 | 362 |

Bilateral treaty to partially denuclearize Eastern and Western Europe by eliminating intermediate-range and shorter range missiles. The INF treaty between the United States and the Union of Soviet Socialists Republics was signed 8 December 1987 and entered into force on 1 June 1988.

Significance

The Intermediate Nuclear Forces Treaty eliminated or banned all U.S. and Soviet ground-launched ballistic missiles and cruise missiles with a range capability of 300–3,400 miles (500–5,500 km). Emplacement of intermediate-range and cruise missiles in Western Europe provided the United States with a forward-strike capability to hit the Soviet Union with little if any warning. The United States used this strength to induce the Soviets to reduce their missile deployments aimed at Western Europe. In a somewhat similar maneuver, the Cuban Missile Crisis of 1962 led the Soviets to agree not to place nuclear armed missiles in Cuba in return for a U.S. agreement to remove its missiles from Turkey. This INF treaty resembled in outline that earlier agreement, but somewhat in reverse form.

Arms Control: Nuclear Non-Proliferation Treaty (NPT) | 363 |

An international agreement to prohibit the diffusion of nuclear weapons among nonnuclear states. The Treaty on the Non-Proliferation of Nuclear Weapons was hammered out during four years of intensive negotiations in the UN Eighteen Nation Disarmament Committee (ENDC) and in the UN General Assembly's Political and Security Committee, leading to assembly approval of the draft treaty in June. It was signed on 1 July 1968 and came into force on 5 March 1970. Under the terms of the treaty, each nuclear-weapon state agreed "not to transfer, . . . assist, encourage, or induce any nonnuclear weapon State to manufacture or otherwise acquire nuclear weapons." Each nonnuclear state agrees "not to receive . . . manufacture or otherwise acquire nuclear weapons." The 11-article treaty took effect after its ratification by three nuclear powers (Great Britain, the Soviet Union, and the United States) and 40 nonnuclear countries. More than 160 nations were signatories to the treaty, accepting its terms as a limitation on their freedom of action in the nuclear-weapons field. To counter the threat of future "nuclear blackmail," in a Security Council action the three nuclear powers offered to provide "immediate assistance, in accordance with the Charter, to any non–nuclear-weapon State that is the victim of an act or an object of a threat of aggression in which nuclear weapons are used." The original treaty was renegotiated in 1995. *See also* ARMS CONTROL: NUCLEAR NON-PROLIFERATION TREATY CONFERENCE, 1995 (364); ARMS CONTROL: PARTIAL TEST BAN TREATY (1963) (368); DISARMAMENT PROPOSAL: DENUCLEARIZATION (392); DISARMAMENT PROPOSAL: NUCLEAR PROLIFERATION SAFEGUARDS (396).

Significance
The Treaty on the Non-Proliferation of Nuclear Weapons represented a major breakthrough in the effort to control the threat of nuclear war. The long standoff in negotiations over the treaty resulted from conflict over Western efforts to establish a fleet of Polaris missile ships within NATO, based on the Multilateral Force (MLF) proposal. The Soviets, fearing in particular a German nuclear capability, took the position that such a system involved nuclear proliferation. When dissension within NATO forced the United States to give up the MLF project, subsequent negotiations with the Soviets led to agreement on the treaty. The major aims of the treaty were to reduce the threat of nuclear war, encourage progress in the search for nuclear disarmament, and contribute to the peaceful development of nuclear energy in all states. Its basic objective—to perpetuate the status quo of five nuclear states—is inherently discriminatory, but relates to the security of all states because each addition to the nuclear club increases the dangers of nuclear war through accident, miscalculation, or escalation. Often called the "nth nation" problem because of the unknown number of potential members of the nuclear club, proliferation is threatened by the 20 or more nations that have, or soon will, the scientific, technical, and industrial base for building nuclear weapons. Countries that possess nuclear-weapons potential in terms of technology and availability of fissionable materials include India, Pakistan, South Africa, Israel, Brazil, Egypt, Japan, Germany, North Korea, and Italy. A number of these states

have refused to sign or ratify the NPT. South Africa announced in May 1995 that it had produced several atomic bombs, but later decided to forgo stockpiling the weapon, and in fact had destroyed all those in its possession. However, other states, such as Iran and Iraq, were eager to possess nuclear weapons. Iraq's nuclear-weapons facility at Osirak was destroyed by an Israeli air attack in 1981. Following the Gulf War of 1990–1991, Iraq's nuclear program was monitored by the International Atomic Energy Agency (IAEA), but Iraq is believed to still be capable of clandestine operations. The United States launched strenuous efforts to prevent Iran from going nuclear. Indeed, a Russian decision in 1995 to supply Iran with ten nuclear reactors drew strong criticism from Washington. Moscow parried the American complaint, noting that the United States had entered into an agreement in 1994 to supply North Korea with the same light-water nuclear reactors that Russia would construct for Iran. Washington countered that argument by citing Russia's decision to assist Iran in constructing a gas centrifuge facility capable of converting nuclear-waste material into weapons-grade plutonium. Russia later announced that it would not proceed with the gas centrifuge project. Despite efforts extending the NPT indefinitely, major power differences in dealing with the dilemma of nuclear-weapons proliferation leaves global security in a precarious state.

Arms Control: Nuclear Non-Proliferation Treaty Conference, 1995   364

Conference to extend or terminate the Non-Proliferation Treaty. The NPT Conference was convened at UN headquarters in New York City in April 1995 and the work was completed on 10 May 1995. Unlike the Treaties of Tlatelolco and Rarotonga, which have permanent status, the NPT could not continue in force unless the nations subscribing to the 1970 agreement concurred on its extension. The Non-Proliferation Conference was called under Article X.2 of the treaty, and while the treaty did not provide the delegates with the option of terminating the treaty directly, its termination could have resulted from an inability of the conferees to find a formula for the treaty's extension. Review conferences, meeting every five years since 1975 to assess the treaty's implementation, had complicated rather than smoothed the task of the conferees. Under Article X.2 the members to the treaty were given three options: (1) Vote for the treaty to continue in force indefinitely, (2) vote to extend the treaty for an additional period, or (3) vote to extend the treaty for additional periods. In the end, no vote was taken, but the treaty was extended indefinitely by simply not opposing the decision to sustain the treaty. The 24 days of back-room deliberations that ultimately resulted in the acceptance of the U.S.-backed plan making the 25-year-old pact permanent were heated and full of controversy, but the power of the nuclear-weapons states and the support received from a majority of the delegates overcame the opposition. The plan perpetuated an international system in which only five nations legitimately possess nuclear weapons: the United States, Russia, Great Britain, France, and China. In order to placate nonweapons states who sought to pressure the nuclear powers into moving more quickly on nuclear arms control, a list of disarmament goals was attached to the extension decision. Those objectives, which included completion of a comprehensive nuclear test ban treaty by 1996, were paired with a plan for annual meetings to review progress toward the goals. In compliance with these objectives, in August 1995 President Clinton announced that the United States had terminated all nuclear testing. Some critics of the decision to indefinitely extend the NPT dismissed the scheme as meaningless because the goals were not binding on the nuclear powers. In sum, however, the conference believed it had succeeded in holding the line against the spread of nuclear weapons. *See also* ARMS CONTROL: NUCLEAR NON-PROLIFERATION TREATY (NPT) (363); NUCLEAR ARMS RACE (298).

Significance

The second of the three options before the Nuclear Non-Proliferation Conference proved to be the most challenging. Under the first or third, the treaty would continue in one form or another. If the second option had been adopted, it would have inferred the self-destruction of the treaty after a particular extension period because no mechanism existed under this option to extend the treaty beyond an additional term. Had the delegates not concurred on any of the three options, the 1970 treaty might have continued in force on a provisional basis, or it might have been ruled dead. Therefore, the task before the representatives of the 150 member states attending the New York conference was monumental, notably because the face of the nuclear club had changed during the 25-year period of the treaty. Israel, India, Pakistan, and North Korea were considered undeclared nuclear powers. South Africa declared publicly that it had built nuclear weapons but had decided to destroy them, and urged other new nuclear-weapons nations to follow its example. Considerable open and private debate centered on Israel's nuclear capability. The Arab states, especially Egypt, argued that they could not pledge themselves to nonnuclear status so long as Israel was allowed to possess the weapon. Fourteen Arab states held up the decision to extend the NPT by a last-minute resolution that called on Israel to adhere to the NPT without delay, and to dismantle their nuclear-weapons program. Israel responded that it would consider signing the treaty two years after it wins peace agreements with all the Middle East states. The success in getting the established nuclear powers to honor Article VI of the NPT, which requires them to pursue negotiations to end the nuclear arms race and work toward nuclear disarmament by agreeing to dramatically reduce their individual weapons stockpiles, was acknowledged. The Non-Nuclear Weapons States (NNWS) juxtaposed their compliance with the treaty against that of the nuclear states, and NNWS pressure forced the nuclear-weapons states to accept the comprehensive test ban agreement as a demonstration of good faith.

Arms Control: Oslo Final Document, 1992 | 365 |

Agreement by which the successor states to the Soviet Union assumed the rights and obligations of all arms treaties previously signed by the USSR. The Oslo Document was arrived at in the Extraordinary Conference of States. The parties adhered to the Treaty on Conventional Armed Forces in Europe (CFE), and the document was collectively entered into and deemed to be in force on 5 June 1992. The document sustained the CFE Treaty following the dissolution of the Warsaw Pact and the Soviet Union, and took into account the new international conditions caused by these events. *See also* ALLIANCE: PARTNERSHIP FOR PEACE (PFP) (286); ALLIANCE: PARTNERSHIP FOR PEACE SIGNATORIES (287); ARMS CONTROL: CONVENTIONAL FORCES IN EUROPE AGREEMENT (CFE 1A), 1992 (356).

Significance
The Oslo Document noted the 15 May 1992 agreement in Tashkent among the successor states of the USSR with territory within the area of application of the CFE Treaty, and apportioned among them the obligations and rights of the USSR, making them parties to the treaties. The question of succession in international law involved the assumption of international obligations entered into by the predecessor state that now impacted on its successors. Thus, this document enabled new republics like Ukraine, Belarus, etc., to adhere to and become signatories of the CFE Treaty. The acceptance of CFE arrangements set the stage for the 1994 development of the Partnership for Peace.

Arms Control: Open Skies Treaty, 1992 | 366 |

A treaty to allow unarmed overflights by observation aircraft. The Treaty on Open Skies emerged from the deliberations of the Conference on Security and Cooperation in Europe. Nations accepting the terms of the treaty committed themselves to the opening of their airspace, on a reciprocal basis, for overflights of their territory by unarmed observation aircraft. The treaty was signed and applied provisionally on 24 March 1992, but will not enter into force until 20 states have deposited their instruments of ratification.

Significance
The Open Skies Treaty represents a collective desire to enhance confidence-building measures from the North Atlantic states to much of Eurasia. A sensitive program, it has been accepted in principle, but the full implementation of the treaty awaits its operationalization by the major powers.

Arms Control: Outer Space Treaty | 367 |

The Treaty on Principles Governing Activities of States in the Exploration of Outer Space, Including the Moon and Other Celestial Bodies. This international convention restrains the arms race, seeks to elicit cooperation, and establishes rudimentary rules of international law for outer space. The Outer Space Treaty was approved by the UN General Assembly in 1966 without a dissenting vote. It was signed on 27 January 1967 and put into force by 84 signatory nations on 10 October 1967—a decade after the launching of the first Soviet Sputnik. Major provisions of the treaty (1) prohibit placing nuclear or other weapons of mass destruction in orbit or on the moon and other celestial bodies, (2) ban military bases and maneuvers on the moon and other planets, (3) provide that all explorations and uses of outer space be for the benefit and in the interests of all countries, (4) forbid claims of national sovereignty in outer space, and (5) encourage international cooperation in exploring space, assisting astronauts and space vehicles, and exchanging scientific information. *See also* JURISDICTION: OUTER SPACE (511).

Significance
The Outer Space Treaty culminated nearly ten years of negotiations and de-

bates in the United Nations and disarmament bodies to conclude an agreement that would limit the military space race and begin the process of internationalizing space. The treaty embodied principles that had been enunciated in six resolutions adopted by the General Assembly between 1958 and 1963, and those proclaimed in the assembly's broad 1963 Declaration of Legal Principles Governing the Activities of States in the Exploration and Use of Outer Space. The treaty dramatized the advances made in technology for exploring space and attempted to neutralize their use for warlike purposes.

Arms Control: Partial Test Ban Treaty (1963) | 368

A treaty banning nuclear-weapons tests in the atmosphere, in outer space, and under water. Signed in Moscow on 5 August 1963 by Great Britain, the Soviet Union, and the United States, the Test Ban Treaty permits underground nuclear tests so long as such explosions do not pollute the environment with radioactive debris outside the territorial limits of the state conducting the tests. Article IV of the treaty establishes the right of each party to withdraw from the treaty after giving three months' notice if "extraordinary events" jeopardize "the supreme interests of its country." The treaty entered into force and was registered with the United Nations on 10 October 1963. The Russian Republic, the successor state to the Soviet Union, assumed the obligations entered into by the Soviets.

Significance

The Partial Test Ban Treaty of 1963 was the first arms-control measure concluded in the nuclear-weapons field during the United Nations era, and the first between the United States and the USSR. Although most countries have acceded to the treaty, two critical nuclear powers— France and the People's Republic of China—have not become parties. The partial nature of the treaty overcame earlier demands for an effective inspection system because the three types of weapons tests it outlaws are capable of being

detected with existing scientific devices. Negotiations in the field of nuclear testing have continued, with the objective of concluding a comprehensive ban on all testing, but fears that underground tests could be carried on surreptitiously in the absence of on-site inspection, or that a comprehensive test ban treaty would favor a would-be adversary, have prevented agreement. This controversy was highlighted in June 1995 when the new Gaullist French president, Jacques Chirac, announced that his country would resume nuclear testing at its site in the South Pacific.

Arms Control: Peaceful Nuclear Explosions Treaty (PNET), 1976 | 369

A treaty between the United States and the Soviet Union limiting underground nuclear explosions. The Treaty on Underground Nuclear Explosions for Peaceful Purposes was signed 28 May 1976 and entered into force 11 December 1990.

Significance

The Peaceful Nuclear Explosions Treaty limited any individual nuclear explosion carried out by the parties outside United States and Soviet weapons test sites to 150 kilotons. In effect the PNET was brought into conformity with the Threshold Test Ban Treaty, and both treaties went into force on the same date.

Arms Control: Rarotonga Treaty (1987) | 370

A 1987 agreement that declares the South Pacific region to be a nuclear-free zone. The Treaty of Rarotonga prohibits the manufacturing, use, and testing of nuclear devices in the region. Rarotonga, where the treaty was signed, is located in the Cook Islands in the South Pacific. *See also* DISARMAMENT PROPOSAL: DENUCLEARIZATION (392).

Significance

The Treaty of Rarotonga was signed by a number of states, including Australia, New Zealand, Indonesia, Fiji, and the Soviet Union. Although the United States acceded to other treaties providing for nuclear-free zones in Latin America, Antarctica, and the seabed, it did not sign the Rarotonga treaty. Nor did France, which maintained a test site near Tahiti. The U.S. position resulted in the virtual breakup of the ANZUS Pact when New Zealand refused port calls by U.S. nuclear-armed ships. The French announcement in June 1995 that they would resume nuclear testing at their site in the South Pacific angered the nations of the region, notably Australia and New Zealand, who threatened Paris with economic and political retaliation. Moreover, the Rarotonga treaty was placed in jeopardy only a month following the indefinite extension of the Nuclear Non-Proliferation Treaty and the pledge made by the nuclear-weapons powers to scale back and eventually eliminate their weapons.

Arms Control: Rush-Bagot Agreement (1817) | 371 |

A treaty between Great Britain and the United States to demilitarize the U.S.-Canadian border and the Great Lakes in perpetuity. The Rush-Bagot Agreement was part of the peace settlement for the War of 1812. It permits each country to sail on the Great Lakes only those warships required for patrol duty and customs inspection. The agreement was concluded originally as an executive agreement in 1817 and approved the following year as a treaty.

Significance
The Rush-Bagot Agreement remains to date the oldest and most successful disarmament agreement ever negotiated. It avoided a naval race for supremacy on the Great Lakes and stabilized the boundary between Canada and the United States. The Rush-Bagot Agreement has also encouraged good political, economic, and social relations between those two nations of North America.

Arms Control: Seabed Treaty | 372 |

Treaty banning nuclear and other weapons of mass destruction from the seabed of the world's oceans outside each state's

12-mile territorial waters. The agreement was signed on 11 February 1971 and entered into force on 18 May 1972. Officially titled the Treaty on the Prohibition of the Emplacement of Nuclear Weapons and Other Weapons of Mass Destruction on the Seabed and the Ocean Floor and in the Subsoil Thereof, it was endorsed in 1970 by the Twenty-fifth General Assembly of the United Nations, signed 11 February 1971, and entered into force 18 May 1972. Most of the nations of the world have signed the treaty, including three nuclear powers—the United States, Russia, and Great Britain—which have also ratified it. *See also* ARMS CONTROL (350); JURISDICTION: TERRITORIAL WATERS (514).

Significance
The Seabed Treaty supplemented earlier treaties aimed at keeping nuclear weapons out of Antarctica (1959), outer space (1967), and Latin America (1967). However, the treaty is weakened by not prohibiting emplacement of nuclear weapons within a state's 12-mile contiguous zone off its coasts. By ratifying the Seabed Treaty, for the first time the United States officially agreed to set aside the traditional 3-mile limit and endorsed the 12-mile limit in an international treaty. The treaty was weakened by the failure of two nuclear-weapons states—France and China—to participate in the treaty process or sign the completed document. Although the treaty prohibits emplacement of nuclear weapons in the seabed of the world's oceans, submarines and other devices that use the sea but not the seabed are permitted to operate freely under its terms.

Arms Control: START I Treaty, 1991 | 373 |

A treaty entered into by the United States and the Union of Soviet Socialist Republics on the Reduction and Limitation of Strategic Offensive Arms. START establishes significantly reduced limits for intercontinental ballistic missiles and their associated launchers and warheads, as well as the deployment of heavy bombers and their armaments, including long-range nuclear air-launched cruise missiles. It was signed on 31 July 1991, but has not entered into force.

Significance
Following the dissolution of the USSR, the United States and Russia agreed to a protocol to the START Treaty. Known as the Lisbon START Protocol, it enables implementation of the START I Treaty in the conditions following the collapse of the Soviet Union. The protocol constitutes an amendment to, and is an integral part of, the START Treaty. It makes it possible for Russia, Belarus, Ukraine, and Kazakhstan to succeed to the Soviet Union's obligations under the original treaty. Also, Belarus, Ukraine, and Kazakhstan committed themselves to accede to the Nuclear Non-Proliferation Treaty (NPT) and to divest themselves of nuclear weapons in the shortest possible time. In accompanying letters, these states committed themselves to the removal of all nuclear weapons from their territory within seven years. The protocol was signed on 23 May 1992, and all signatory states later ratified the agreement through their respective legislatures. Belarus and Kazakhstan were the first to accede to the NPT. In 1994 the United States, Russia, and Ukraine announced the removal of weapons-grade plutonium from Ukraine to Russia. The United States also pledged substantial sums of money and technical know-how to Belarus, Kazakhstan, and Ukraine in dismantling and destroying their nuclear weapons.

Arms Control: START II Treaty, 1993   374

A treaty between the United States and the Russian Federation on the further reduction and limitation of strategic offensive arms. It was signed on 3 January 1993, and would enter into force with the ratification by the United States and Russia of the START I Treaty of 1991. Among other reductions, START would eliminate the Russian SS18 multiple-warhead and other intercontinental ballistic missiles, thus leaving the United States with a possible advantage in existing warheads. *See also* ARMS CONTROL: ABM

TREATY, 1972 (351); ARMS CONTROL: START I TREATY, 1991 (373).

Significance
The START II Treaty further reduced U.S. and Russian strategic offensive arms by eliminating all MIRVed (multiple independently targeted reentry vehicles) ICBMs (intercontinental ballistic missiles), including all "heavy" ICBMs. START II was slated to reduce the overall total of warheads for each side to between 3,000 and 3,500, but Russia registered concern that the United States would maintain an advantage in numbers if the terms of the treaty were complied with to the letter. START II also called for a number of bilateral safety, security, and disarmament agreements between NATO member states and the successor states to the Soviet Union with nuclear weapons on their territory (Belarus, Kazakhstan, Russia, Ukraine). These agreements would facilitate the safe storage, removal, or destruction of nuclear weapons under the terms of relevant arms-control agreements (START I and II and the Non-Proliferation Treaty). Apart from those nuclear weapons transferred to Russia from the other republics of the former USSR, the United States agreed to provide the funds and technical know-how for the dismantling and/or transfer of nuclear materials to the United States. Although President Boris Yeltsin submitted the START II Treaty to the Russian Duma (parliament) for ratification in late June 1995, Russian legislators have not been eager to approve the document because: (1) it imposes an unreasonable financial burden on Moscow, causing it to commit substantial funds to destroying heavy ICBMs and replacing them with single-warhead missiles at a time when military pay, housing, and other needs are more pressing (the high cost of safely removing nuclear weapons from the active force posture was not foreseen during START negotiations, and defense expenditure estimates did not include adequate funding for such purposes; (2) Russian leaders would like to see the START II time frame extended beyond 2003 so that nuclear

weapons need not be withdrawn before they reach the end of their designed life-cycle; and (3) Duma representatives were concerned that START II shifts the focus from land to sea-based weapons, in which U.S. forces are thought to be more capable.

Arms Control: Stockholm Document, 1986 | 375 |

The document of the Stockholm Conference on Confidence and Security-Building Measures, and Disarmament in Europe. The Stockholm Document contains six concrete and mutually complementary confidence-building measures, including mandatory ground or aerial inspection of military activities. The document was adopted on 19 September 1986 and entered into force on 1 January 1987.

Significance
The Stockholm Document was the first major breakthrough in altering relations between East and West during the Cold War. Its contents represent the success of Mikhail Gorbachev, who assumed authority in the Soviet Union in 1985, in beginning the process of normalizing relations with his major adversaries. The document improved on the safeguards written into the Helsinki Final Act, and proved to be the stepping-stone to more serious arms-reduction agreements with the United States.

Arms Control: Strategic Arms Limitation Talks (SALT) | 376 |

Negotiations carried on between the United States and the Soviet Union with the objective of reaching agreement on the control of strategic nuclear weapons, delivery systems, and related offensive and defensive weapons systems. SALT negotiations were first undertaken in Helsinki in 1969. The initial objective was to limit or eliminate construction of anti-ballistic missile (ABM) systems, which both countries were planning at that time.

Subsequent discussion covered the whole range of strategic weapons systems, including a comprehensive nuclear test ban, denuclearization of specific geographical areas, limitation on numbers of certain types of nuclear delivery systems, multiple independently targeted reentry vehicles (MIRVs), limits on the building of ABM sites, and avoidance of the escalation of limited war into a nuclear conflagration. In the first series of talks (SALT I, 1969–1972), an interim agreement was reached to limit the number of ABM defense systems in each country to two. It was signed by President Richard Nixon and President Leonid Brezhnev on 26 May 1972 and entered into force on 3 October 1972. In a second agreement, SALT I also limited the number of missile-delivery systems with nuclear warheads, but agreement could not be reached on the number of nuclear warheads in each missile (MIRVing). SALT II guidelines were worked out at the Nixon-Brezhnev Summit meeting in Washington in 1973. These called upon the two parties to reach agreement on (1) permanent ceilings on offensive strategic forces, that is, ICBM deployment; (2) controlling the qualitative factors in their offensive weapons arsenals, namely the number of warheads placed aboard strategic missiles; and (3) ultimately establishing a mutual reduction of strategic forces with an accompanying reliable verification system. On 18 June 1979, a SALT II Treaty, including arms-control provisions, was signed in Vienna by President Jimmy Carter and President Leonid Brezhnev, and was submitted by Carter to the Senate for its consent to ratification. However, SALT II came to naught. Carter withdrew it from Senate consideration following the Soviet invasion of Afghanistan, and it was never resubmitted by President Ronald Reagan. President Reagan renamed future negotiations as Strategic Arms Reduction Talks (START), and they bore fruit in 1991. Although SALT II was never formally ratified, both the United States and the Soviet Union informally agreed to be bound by the provisions of the treaty. *See also* ARMS CONTROL: START II TREATY,

1993 (374); DISARMAMENT STRATEGY: UNITED NATIONS DISARMAMENT FORUMS (402).

Significance

The SALT I agreements and the SALT II Treaty were products of a period of détente between the two superpowers. With the Soviet invasion of Afghanistan in 1979, its involvement in Africa and Asia, and its growing position of strength in the overall arms race, détente gave way to new U.S. initiatives. Examples of these included restoration of export controls for trade with the Soviets, a boycott of the Olympic Games in Moscow in 1980, and a new emphasis on rebuilding a position of U.S. military parity or superiority. As a result, chances that the Senate would approve ratification of the SALT II Treaty were greatly reduced. Although neither the SALT I agreements nor the SALT II Treaty could be regarded as major arms-control actions, they did provide for some potentially useful precedents for eventual control of what can only be described as dual systems of mutual assured destruction (MAD). The main objective—to avoid a runaway arms race by setting firm limits on major weapons systems of mass destruction—remained unrealized until the termination of the Cold War and the demise of the Soviet state promised more substantial progress.

Arms Control: Threshold Test Ban Treaty, 1974 | 377 |

Treaty between the United States and the Union of Soviet Socialist Republics on the Limitation of Underground Nuclear Weapons Tests. It was signed 3 July 1974 and entered into force on 11 December 1990.

Significance

This treaty prohibited underground nuclear weapons tests of more than 150 kilotons. It required more than 16 years from its signing to the time it came into force because both countries were determined

to complete their testing programs before agreeing to the ban.

Arms Control: Treaty for the Prohibition of Nuclear Weapons in Latin America | 378 |

An agreement, also called the Treaty of Tlatelolco, that created a nuclear weapons–free zone (NWFZ) in Latin America. The treaty was signed in Mexico City in 1967 by 21 Latin American countries. By 1980 the treaty had been signed by 25 Latin American countries, and was ratified and in force for 22 of them. Two protocols are part of the main treaty: Protocol I is applicable for states having territorial interests in the Americas, and Protocol II includes all nuclear-weapons states. The treaty prohibits all states from injecting nuclear weapons into the region, and includes a prohibition on foreign powers against bringing nuclear weapons into their bases in Latin America. Protocol II has been accepted by all the major nuclear powers—the United States, the Soviet Union, Great Britain, France, and China. The treaty set up operational machinery to oversee enforcement of its provisions, known as OPANAL (Agency for the Prohibition of Nuclear Weapons in Latin America). *See also* DISARMAMENT PROPOSAL: DENUCLEARIZATION (392); REGIONAL MILITARY GROUP: INTER-AMERICAN SYSTEM (556).

Significance

The Treaty for the Prohibition of Nuclear Weapons in Latin America is the first successful effort to denuclearize a geographical region carried out by countries in the region. Most of the nations involved have ratified the treaty and its protocols, but some key Latin countries with growing nuclear programs—Argentina, Brazil, and Chile—have not yet fully accepted the treaty. However, Cuba became a signatory in 1995. The procedures used in creating the denuclearized region may prove useful in other regions. For example, the Treaty of Rarotonga, modeled on the Latin American Treaty, declares the

South Pacific region to be a nuclear-free zone and prohibits the manufacture, use, and testing of nuclear weapons in the region.

Arms Control: Trilateral Nuclear Agreement, 1994   379

Agreement to transfer nuclear weapons from Ukraine to Russia for dismantling. This trilateral statement by the presidents of the United States, Russia, and Ukraine details procedures to transfer Ukrainian nuclear warheads to Russia with the associated compensation and security assurances to Ukraine from both the United States and Russia. The statement was signed in Moscow on 14 January 1994. *See also* ARMS CONTROL: START I TREATY, 1991 (373); ARMS CONTROL: START II TREATY, 1993 (374).

Significance
The Trilateral Nuclear Agreement sets out simultaneous actions to transfer SS19 and SS24 warheads from Ukraine to Russia for dismantling and provide financial compensation to Ukraine in the form of fuel assemblies for nuclear power stations, as well as security assurances to Ukraine, once START I enters into force and Ukraine becomes a nonnuclear-weapons-state party to the Nuclear Non-Proliferation Treaty (NPT).

Arms Control: UN Register of Conventional Arms Transfers   380

A device to monitor the flow of conventional weapons systems worldwide. On 10 December 1991 the UN General Assembly overwhelmingly approved the establishment of a register to record the import and export of specific major weapons systems, aircraft, armor, artillery, etc. Reports of such transactions were to be made by complying states to the register in the UN Secretariat by 1993.

Significance
Arms-control advocates viewed the establishment of the Register of Conven-

tional Arms Transfers as an important step in controlling the flow of conventional weapons systems worldwide. Its existence promised greater openness, and it was hoped that the register would simplify the monitoring of excessive arms buildup by any one country. In accordance with a UN General Assembly resolution, members adhering to the arrangement were to submit their information beginning with 30 April 1993. In the first year of its existence, the register recorded the import and export activities of more than one-third of the UN membership. By April 1995, 91 states had made submissions to the register, particularly major arms exporters. Compliance is also high among arms importers, although Saudi Arabia, North Korea, United Arab Emirates, Kuwait, Syria, Libya, Bangladesh, Algeria, and Myanmar (Burms) remain among those countries that have not submitted. Countries not members of the UN system, e.g., Taiwan, have not been asked to provide information on weapons sales and purchases.

Arms Control: Vienna Document, 1990   381

Measures designed to enhance East-West cooperation. This document centered on negotiations and confidence- and security-building measures in accordance with the relevant provisions of the concluding document of the Vienna meeting of the Conference on Security and Cooperation in Europe (CSCE). The Vienna Document formally adopted and incorporated the Stockholm Document of 1986, and added measures related to transparency (the open and mutual examination of military preparations) on military forces and activities. It emphasized the need for improved communications and contacts, as well as verification of military exercises and deployments. The document was adopted on 17 November 1990 and entered into force on 1 January 1991. *See also* ALLIANCE: PARTNERSHIP FOR PEACE (PFP) (286).

Significance

The Vienna Document entered into force barely a year before the collapse of the Soviet Union. Russia, the successor state to the Soviet Union, assumed responsibility for the perpetuation of the terms of the document. The former East-West adversaries not only opened their military installations to one another, they participated in joint exercises. The elimination of the Warsaw Pact left NATO intact, and in 1994 the Partnership for Peace associated former members of the Soviet bloc with NATO.

Arms Control: Vienna Document, 1992 | 382 |

Expansion of negotiations on the Vienna Document of 1990 following recommendations emanating from the Vienna meeting of the Conference of Security and Cooperation in Europe (CSCE). The document incorporated agreement on opening national military establishments to international scrutiny as well as the need to apply constraints on military activity. It was adopted 4 March 1992 and entered into force 1 May 1992. *See also* MUTUAL-SECURITY ORGANIZATION: CONFERENCE ON SECURITY AND COOPERATION IN EUROPE (CSCE) (297).

Significance

The Vienna Document of 1992 established the bona fides of the Conference on Security and Cooperation in Europe, and acknowledged that organization's role in enhancing confidence-building measures between former Cold War adversaries. The Vienna Document also expanded the zone of application for such state interaction, including virtually all the territory of the former Soviet Union. The extension of CSCE concerns to regions and countries beyond the traditional zone of Europe (Kazakhstan, Kyrgyzstan, Tajikistan, Turkmenistan, and Uzbekistan) signified a shift in security thinking to more broadly defined interests. It also brought NATO into more immediate proximity with greater Eurasia.

Arms Control: Washington Treaty for the Limitation of Naval Armaments (1922) | 383 |

An agreement reached at the Washington Naval Conference of 1921–1922 by the leading sea powers to limit the size and construction of their capital ships and establish an agreed power ratio in 20 years. The Washington Treaty stipulated that (1) battleships would be limited thereafter to 35,000 tons with 16-inch guns, and aircraft carriers to 27,000 tons; (2) new construction of vessels in this class was forbidden for ten years; (3) replacements of capital ships after 1931 should establish by 1942 a ratio of: Great Britain 5, the United States 5, Japan 3, France 1.67, and Italy 1.67; and (4) signatories would limit their naval bases and fortifications in the Pacific area. Efforts to reach agreement at the conference to limit other naval craft, such as submarines, cruisers, and destroyers, failed to achieve a consensus. *See also* DISARMAMENT PROBLEM: RATIO QUESTION (387).

Significance

The Washington Naval Treaty is a rare example of agreement by great powers to an arms-control measure. The treaty was prompted by the desire to avoid a costly post–World War I naval arms race among the victorious powers. The United States, for example, was committed to a policy of equality in capital ship tonnage with Great Britain, but instead of undertaking a highly competitive and expensive building program, the United States sought agreement for adjustments that would ultimately produce parity through the treaty. However, the treaty did not provide for inspection and enforcement, and all signatories were soon engaged in nullifying the spirit and, in some cases, the letter of the agreement by competitive naval building programs in related classes of vessels. By the 1930s the treaty was scrapped because of the resurgence of German military power and the evolution of a new world power balance. The Washington Naval Treaty experience indicates that great-power agreement on arms-control measures in a limited field is a tenuous matter that is unlikely to survive when a competitive arms race in other military fields and political conflict threaten the security of its signatories.

Arms Control Principle: Transparency and Nuclear Weapons | 384 |

Openness among states concerning nuclear weapons capabilities. Transparency in nuclear weapons is a sine qua non in nonproliferation programs. Without the capacity to inspect nuclear facilities, the international community can never be assured that countries complying with the Nuclear Weapons Non-Proliferation Treaty (NPT) are actually in compliance. Moreover, without transparency, those states that refuse to become signatories of the agreement but nevertheless publicize the peaceful purposes of their programs cannot be trusted. Transparency signifies an open window on a country's nuclear enterprise, its acceptance of specific safeguards, and more open reporting of verification results by international agencies such as the International Atomic Energy Agency (IAEA). More open programs allow a better opportunity to determine who is in compliance with treaty limitations and who is not. Therefore, confidence-building safeguards include (1) the organization of a system of total programmatic transparency consistent with legitimate industrial, commercial, or proprietary interests; (2) a system to report all significant transactions involving nuclear facilities, equipment, components, and use; (3) a system of flexible implementation of safeguards, such as unannounced inspections; and (4) the creation of a reporting system that publicizes verification, country by country, to the larger world community. *See also* DISARMAMENT PROPOSAL: NUCLEAR PROLIFERATION SAFEGUARDS (396); DISARMAMENT PROPOSAL: VERIFICATION—NUCLEAR WEAPONS (398).

Significance
Transparency is a subjective concept that remains suspect in a world of independent, sovereign states, each responsible for its own security and hence determined to maximize its advantages, often oblivious to its impact on the international system. The dilemma is one that can be successfully addressed only when the technical and policy communities of individual states work with others in constructing a more balanced and secure political environment. Changes in the international arena that have resulted in the proliferation of national sovereignties make more urgent, if not more difficult, the objective of nuclear-weapons transparency. A beginning has been made in agreements with Kazakhstan, Belarus, and Ukraine, but the problem has not been resolved. It is questionable whether the IAEA, an organization assembled during the Cold War, can adapt to these new conditions, which demand a greater degree of assertiveness. The agency has experienced restraints on its right of access, the frequency and intensity of its inspections, and the extent to which it may apply discretionary judgment in planning, scheduling, and conducting inspections. If transparency is to be assured in the matter of nuclear weapons, it appears essential that IAEA undergo its own transformation, and that the international community, which now looks to it for ensuring weapons safeguards, bestow upon it greater powers.

Disarmament Problem: Enforcement | 385 |

The establishment of machinery to provide and administer the sanctions required to implement a disarmament agreement. The enforcement function is related to inspection because any detection of a violation raises questions concerning its political and military consequences. Setting up an enforcement system would be likely to raise such questions as: (1) What should be the composition, powers, and procedures of the enforcement agency? (2) What specific actions would constitute violations? (3) What punishment or sanction would be applied against a violator? (4) Should a state placed at a security disadvantage by a violation be entitled to undertake unilateral measures to restore the power balance? (5) Would a veto power apply to the determination of sanctions against a violator? *See also* DISARMAMENT PROBLEM: INSPECTION (386); UNITED NATIONS: SANCTIONS (586).

Significance

A viable disarmament agreement must provide for enforcement action of unquestionable effectiveness during and following the process of disarming. No state could or would be likely to countenance a real or imagined violation that threatened its security without the existence of a dependable system for detecting and punishing violators. After 1962, Soviet and U.S. proposals for general and complete disarmament provided for the establishment of an International Disarmament Organization (IDO) to inspect and enforce the disarmament process.

Disarmament Problem: Inspection | 386 |

The establishment of machinery to verify compliance with or to detect violations of a disarmament treaty. In the negotiation of an inspection system, specific questions to be answered would likely include: (1) Should inspections be carried on by a national or international body? (2) What should be the extent of access to each country's territory? (3) What forms of inspection should be utilized? (4) How frequently should inspections be conducted? (5) What powers should be exercised by inspection teams? (6) What constitutes a violation of the disarmament agreement? *See also* DISARMAMENT PROBLEM: ENFORCEMENT (385).

Significance

Inspection is a key ingredient of any disarmament agreement because the security of each participant depends on the compliance of all to the terms of the accord. The ultimate failure of the Washington Naval Treaty of 1922 to limit naval armaments, for example, was at least partly the result of the absence of any inspection system when real or imagined

violations produced counterviolations. An effective system of national inspection of other states' activities was created by the Antarctic Treaty of 1959 to supervise the demilitarization of that continent. Both Eastern and Western disarmament plans during the years of the Cold War included provisions for international inspection. The United States placed major emphasis on inspection by its insistence that a workable, comprehensive international inspection system be set up before any disarmament was undertaken, a position the Soviets asserted was guided by U.S. espionage designs. In 1979, U.S. officials announced that the Soviet Union had agreed to permit ten seismic monitoring stations within its borders to make a comprehensive test ban (CTB) treaty feasible. Both the United States and the Soviet Union proposed the establishment of an International Disarmament Organization (IDO), which would function under UN control and have "unrestricted access without veto to all places as necessary for the purposes of effective verification." However, each side insisted on the fulfillment of different sets of prior conditions essential to the establishment of the IDO, and genuine inspection programs were not launched until the United States and Russia embraced one another following the demise of the Soviet Union. The long-term importance of that embrace, however, waits on future relationships between the two states.

Disarmament Problem: Ratio Question | 387 |

Issues that arise in disarmament negotiations over the schedule for disarming, the categories of forces, and other factors related to the future power relationships of participants. The ratio problem can be overcome only if all states involved in negotiating a disarmament agreement can be convinced that their security will not be jeopardized by an imbalance in weapons at any stage of the disarming process. *See also* ARMS CONTROL: CONVENTIONAL FORCES IN EUROPE TREATY (CFE), 1990 (355); ARMS CONTROL: CONVENTIONAL FORCES IN EUROPE AGREEMENT (CFE 1A), 1992 (356).

Significance
The ratio problem is typically one of the most difficult facing disarmament negotiators because it involves balancing different categories of forces (e.g., land versus air and naval, or nuclear versus conventional) and both arms destroyed and arms retained. During the years of their rivalry, for example, the United States and the Soviet Union searched unsuccessfully for a formula to determine the numbers and types of forces to be disarmed at specific stages and the ratio of forces remaining. The CFE agreements of 1990 and 1992 between the United States and Russia aimed at legitimating a ratio factor between the former adversaries, but difficulties encountered in weighing NATO forces against those of Russia in the absence of the Warsaw Pact raised new problems.

Disarmament Problem: Technology Diffusion   388

War and peace uses of technology. In the post–Cold War environment, questions relating to the diffusion of militarily relevant technology introduce new and contentious issues into the international security arena. Export controls and the sharing of technology have emerged as issues in arms-control forums. Concern is increasingly expressed about whether the international community can meet the challenge of managing the diffusion of military-related technology in a way that achieves arms-control objectives while securing other commercial and national goals. Appropriate modes for dealing with this dilemma remain mired in Cold War thinking, but the combination of changes in the way technology is developed, produced, and made available on the international level and the pattern of demands for military-relevant technology give rise to the need to examine the prospects for managing technology diffusion. *See also* ARMS CONTROL PRINCIPLE: TRANSPARENCY AND NUCLEAR WEAPONS (384).

Significance
Some significant trends in technology diffusion are (1) the increasing difficulty of distinguishing between military and civilian technology; (2) the global redistribution of technological capabilities, with more states increasingly competent in technological areas; (3) the shift toward technology rather than platforms as the medium of exchange in defense-related transfers; (4) the declining share of the technology market under government control; (5) the economic imperatives of industrial states confronting shrinking defense budgets; and (6) the increased pressure to provide military assistance. Generally speaking, the international community was awakened to the urgency of managing technology diffusion after the Gulf War of 1990–1991. Not only were Iraq's programs of weapons of mass destruction significantly more advanced than previously believed, but Iraqi Scud missiles brought the missile dimension into a regional conflict in a way not previously encountered. The international coalition against Iraq confronted weapons systems they had earlier sold and transferred to Iraq. These militarily challenging developments raised questions about the long-term viability of a system based on export controls and technology denial. Moreover, the Gulf War only whetted the appetites of other states to acquire advanced and state-of-the-art weapons. In another way, the Gulf War demonstrated that it may be cheaper for states to emphasize weapons of mass destruction ("equalizers") rather than expensive but beatable conventional weapons. The war also intensified the interest of states in securing advanced manufacturing processes and software development capabilities that lie at the heart of the military technical revolution.

Disarmament Proposal: Atoms for Peace Plan   389

A proposal presented by President Dwight D. Eisenhower to the eighth UN General Assembly in 1953 that would provide for cooperation among the nuclear states and other nations in the peaceful development and application of atomic energy. The Atoms for Peace plan called for the establishment of an international agency under the United Nations to promote cooperation in the atomic field, and it urged nuclear states to divert fissionable materials from their weapons stockpiles by contributing them for peaceful research and development projects. *See also* UN SPECIALIZED AGENCY: INTERNATIONAL ATOMIC ENERGY AGENCY (IAEA) (607).

Significance

The Atoms for Peace plan was offered by the United States as a dramatic new program that might help to restrain the nuclear arms race and break the disarmament deadlock. Although the objectives were not realized at the time, the proposal achieved its limited goal of fostering peaceful development of atomic energy with the creation of the International Atomic Energy Agency (IAEA) in 1957. The main objective of the IAEA was to prevent the proliferation of nuclear weapons by inspecting and regulating transfers of materials for peaceful nuclear-power development so as to prevent their conversion into weapons.

Disarmament Proposal: Baruch Plan | 390 |

A proposal for atomic control and disarmament submitted by the United States to the United Nations Atomic Energy Commission in 1946. Based on the recommendations of a special Board of Consultants (Acheson-Lilienthal Report), the plan was presented by elder statesman Bernard Baruch as the official proposal by the United States to give up its monopoly of atomic weapons under an international security system. Major points incorporated in the Baruch Plan included (1) establishing an International Atomic Development Authority to control all phases of the development and use of nuclear energy, (2) granting unlimited inspection powers to the authority to safeguard against violations, (3) applying stiff penalties for any violations related to the use of fissionable materials for weapons development, (4) terminating the manufacture of atomic weapons and destroying all existing stockpiles after the authority had estab-

lished control, and (5) changing the voting system in the Security Council so that the veto power could not be used to prevent the punishment of violators.

Significance

The Baruch Plan for atomic disarmament and control, although rejected by the Soviet Union in 1946, provided many of the essential features offered in subsequent nuclear disarmament proposals by the United States. Soviet rejection of the plan was based on a recognition that after its implementation the United States alone would retain the capability for making atomic weapons. The Soviets realized that the United States dominated the decision processes in the United Nations and, therefore, would probably control the authority as well. Moreover, at that time the Soviets were undertaking a crash program to develop an atomic weapons capability, which culminated in their first test explosion of an atomic device in 1949. U.S.-Soviet controversies over specific provisions of the Baruch Plan involved disagreements over timing in implementing inspection and control, national or international development of atomic energy, and the powers to be exercised by the inspection and control authorities.

Disarmament Proposal: Defense Conversion | 391 |

The disarmament programs that emerged as a consequence of the termination of the Cold War. The transforming of war-making capabilities and instruments to peacetime use was given high priority. The international community was in general agreement that military establishments could be reduced; implements of war could be cut back, if not eliminated; and installations producing weapons of war could be assigned other responsibilities. The matter of defense conversion has been most salient among NATO and former Warsaw Pact states. In that context, NATO organized the Allies and Cooperation Partners on Defense Conversion consultation group in 1992. The group is charged with exploring areas where concrete cooperation can be implemented through seminars, colloquiums, workshops, and regular meetings of the NATO Economics Committee with Cooperation Partners, now members of the Partnership for Peace. Cooperation Partners submit proposals for pilot projects to NATO, where they are assessed for their feasibility. Individual members of NATO act as "pilot" or "copilot" countries in relation to specific projects, and also contribute to their budgets in order to reduce the financial burden on Cooperation Partners. The NATO Economics Directorate acts as the clearinghouse for the projects. *See also* ALLIANCE: NORTH ATLANTIC TREATY ORGANIZATION (NATO)—POST–COLD WAR (285); ALLIANCE: PARTNERSHIP FOR PEACE (PFP) (286).

Significance
Although defense-conversion projects are in their early stages, they are being pressed in a number of countries. The NATO Economics Directorate collates information for a database to be used by defense-conversion experts. This database is now operational. A second database will bring together information on defense-sector firms in partner countries that are working on conversion projects and interested in establishing cooperation agreements with firms in allied (NATO) countries. Defense-conversion projects promise more intimate relationships between former adversaries. They also demonstrate the sincere desire of the parties to alter their industrial capacities from war to peacetime purposes. Moreover, the thrust of the program acknowledges the expertise and the financial and technical resources available in the West and lacking in the East. NATO therefore took the lead in advancing the idea of defense conversion in promoting social stability, privatizing industries, and restructuring armaments centers.

Disarmament Proposal: Denuclearization   392
An agreement to prohibit nuclear weapons in a specific zone, country, or region. The denuclearization of various areas was extensively discussed for more than

a decade in the UN General Assembly, disarmament commissions and committees, and other international and national bodies, but only five nuclear-free zones—Antarctica, the seabed, Latin America, the South Pacific, and outer space—have been established by treaty. Discussions in the United Nations concerning denuclearization have included such geographical areas as the Arctic, the Bering Strait, the Adriatic, the Balkans, the Mediterranean, the Indian Ocean region, the Middle East, and Scandinavia, but UN resolutions and formal plans and proposals have dealt chiefly with Africa, Central Europe, and Latin America. *See also* DISARMAMENT PROPOSAL: DISENGAGEMENT (393).

Significance
Denuclearization as a partial disarmament measure aimed at avoiding nuclear war is related to such other arms-control devices as nonproliferation treaties, a complete ban on nuclear testing, and limitations on the production of weapons-grade fissionable materials. The establishment of nuclear-free zones has been supported in principle by the United States, Russia, and the other nuclear and near-nuclear powers. Some general support was also shown for the proposals advanced by Foreign Minister Adam Rapacki of Poland in 1957, and by Polish premier Wladyslaw Gomulka in 1964, for the control of nuclear weapons in Central Europe. The Rapacki Plan called for denuclearization and simultaneous reduction in conventional forces in East and West Germany, Czechoslovakia, and Poland, while the Gomulka Plan endeavored to overcome Western objections to the earlier plan by providing only for the freezing at existing levels of all nuclear weapons in the region. States in two regions of the world—Africa and Latin America—have tried to exclude nuclear weapons from their areas by denuclearization treaties. A resolution calling upon all African states to agree to the denuclearization of that continent was adopted by the UN General Assembly in 1965, but implementation of the resolution's principles, which is the responsibil-

ity of the Organization of African Unity (OAU), has not occurred. The Latin American states, on the other hand, began the implementation of similar assembly resolutions adopted in 1962 and 1963 at a special conference in Mexico City in 1967. The Treaty of Tlatelolco was signed, banning all forms of nuclear weapons from the region. The principal nuclear-weapons states, including the United States, the Soviet Union, Great Britain, France, and China, ratified a protocol to the treaty agreeing not to bring nuclear weapons into the region. In 1987 the United States and the Soviet Union reached agreement to partially denuclearize Eastern and Western Europe by removing all Soviet and Western intermediate- and short-range missiles and their nuclear warheads from the region. Following the end of the Cold War and the fall of the Soviet Union, Russia and the United States agreed to cease targeting each other, opened their nuclear sites to mutual inspections, and labored to disarm many of their offensive missiles and destroy their nuclear warheads. U.S. resources were also directed at assisting Ukraine, Kazakhstan, and Belarus in dismantling their nuclear arsenals. From a technical as well as political point of view, Western Europe, Eurasian Russia, and the North Atlantic community are moving toward denuclearized-zone status. The same cannot be said for South Asia. Despite repeated efforts by Pakistan to establish a nuclear-free zone in the region, India has rejected all such propositions.

Disarmament Proposal: Disengagement

| 393 |

The withdrawal of two potentially hostile military forces from positions of direct confrontation. Almost 100 disengagement plans for demilitarizing and neutralizing central European areas or states were offered during the late 1950s and early 1960s by Western- and Eastern-bloc political leaders, scholars, and disarmament specialists. Most disengagement proposals called for the neutralization of West and East Germany and part or all of Czechoslovakia and Poland, the

acceptance of post–World War II boundary settlements, and the conclusion of a nonaggression pact between NATO and Warsaw Pact countries. *See also* ARMS CONTROL: CONVENTIONAL FORCES IN EUROPE TREATY, 1990 (355); ARMS CONTROL: CONVENTIONAL FORCES IN EUROPE AGREEMENT (CFE 1A), 1992 (356); DISARMAMENT PROPOSAL: DENUCLEARIZATION (392).

Significance

Proponents of the disengagement of Eastern and Western military forces during the years of the Cold War claimed that the establishment of a neutralized zone would reduce the danger of a major war growing out of border incidents or accidents, ameliorate tensions, and provide a start toward a general disarmament. Western opponents, especially U.S. and German political and military leaders, argued that disengagement would favor the Soviet bloc because it would weaken NATO defenses in Western Europe by nullifying the defense-in-depth strategy and by removing powerful German units from the NATO defense forces. The Soviet Union opposed most Western schemes out of fear that the neutralization of Eastern European states would result in loss of control and influence over them, and because it might weaken the hold of communism in the region. The most celebrated disengagement proposal during this period of extreme rivalry was one presented before the UN General Assembly in 1957 by Adam Rapacki, the Polish foreign minister. The Rapacki Plan called for an "atom-free, demilitarized zone composed of East and West Germany, Poland, and Czechoslovakia." Although periodically updated, the Rapacki Plan was consistently opposed by U.S. leaders because it contained no limitation on conventional forces. The Conventional Forces in Europe (CFE) Treaty of 1990 and the Conventional Forces in Europe Agreement (CFE 1A) of 1992 promised genuine disengagement, notably after the dissolution of the Warsaw Pact and the Termination of the Cold War. The Russian Federation, although originally adhering to the terms of the two treaties, in

1995 hesitated accepting arrangement that appeared to place it at a disadvantage vís à vis its former adversaries.

Disarmament Proposal: General and Complete Disarmament | 394 |

Proposals to eliminate all armed forces and armaments under a system of international control. The first official consideration of proposals for general and complete disarmament after the United Nations was formed occurred when Premier Nikita Khrushchev of the Soviet Union placed the question on the agenda of the Fourteenth General Assembly in 1959. The Soviet proposal and a combined British-U.S. plan constituted the substance of the Western- and Eastern-bloc proposals for general and complete disarmament. Both plans provided for complete disarmament in three stages, inspection and control functions vested in an International Disarmament Organization (IDO), and enforcement through the Security Council of the United Nations. *See also* ARMS CONTROL (350).

Significance
The subject of general and complete disarmament and specific proposals made by the rival Western and Eastern blocs following World War II were major items on the agenda of the General Assembly, its First Committee, the United Nations Disarmament Commission, and various negotiating committees. Although some areas of consensus were reached during the Cold War, the signing of a general and complete disarmament treaty never materialized. General and complete disarmament must be distinguished from arms-control efforts. Whereas numerous arms-control treaties were put into effect during the existence of the Soviet Union, no consensus on general and complete disarmament was possible, or indeed, even a realistic goal. General and complete disarmament perhaps remains an unrealistic goal in contemporary times. Nation-states are not prepared to yield their instruments of war, and in fact are

progressively sophisticating those weapons. Arms control is several steps removed from disarmament, and is the more realistic option in a world of nations given to accelerated arms races even after the Cold War.

Disarmament Proposal: International Disarmament Organization (IDO) | 395 |

A verification and control agency proposed by both U.S. and Soviet disarmament plans to supervise the three-stage process to achieve a general and complete disarmament. The Soviet-proposed IDO would have consisted of a conference and a control council, and the U.S. version would have included a general conference, a control council, and an administrator who would manage the IDO under the direction of the control council. Under both plans, the conference would operate as a general policy-making body, and the control council would be charged with carrying out the verification, inspection, and enforcement functions. IDO was to be established upon the entry into force of a disarmament treaty and would function within the framework of the United Nations. Although the disarmament treaty remains a distant goal, the Disarmament Commission established by the UN General Assembly in 1978 continues to perform its tasks. The commission was instrumental in negotiating the text for a chemical weapons convention in 1992. *See also* DISARMAMENT PROBLEM: INSPECTION (386).

Significance
Under both U.S. and Soviet proposals, the International Disarmament Organization would have wielded extensive investigative and control powers. It would have supervised the destruction or transfer of weapons in successively broader zones during the three stages of disarmament and would have checked on weapons retained until completion of general disarmament. Although all parties to the disarmament treaty were to be represented on the IDO control council under both

plans, the Soviet proposal further insisted that its composition "must ensure proper representation of the three principal groups of States existing in the world at that time" (Socialist, capitalist, and non-aligned). The U.S. plan, unlike the Soviet, provided that stage-two disarmament could proceed only after "all militarily significant states" (i.e., all nuclear-weapons states) adhered to the treaty and participated in the IDO. Although the United States and the Soviet Union agreed on proposals for the creation of an IDO as the central control body for administering a disarmament treaty, little progress occurred in the field of general and complete disarmament. Even with the collapse of the Soviet Union and improved relations between Russia and the United States, there was little indication that this objective could ever be realized.

Disarmament Proposal: Nuclear Proliferation Safeguards

396

Institutions and techniques employed at national and international levels to protect against surprise attack by a would-be aggressor state. Safeguards also describe the international regimes in place to thwart efforts contributing to nuclear proliferation. Safeguard effectiveness depends in large part on synergism among expectations, authority, resources, and implementation. This condition was essentially met during the first two decades of the Nuclear Non-Proliferation Treaty (NPT), despite limitations in providing the necessary funds for the work of the International Atomic Energy Agency (IAEA), the international instrument primarily responsible for implementing the safeguards. The IAEA is singularly responsible for overseeing national nuclear programs, and for promoting confidence among the states. The IAEA is charged with inspecting all source and special fissionable material in all peaceful nuclear activities. Material that is removed from safeguard verification follows agency-applied rules. To facilitate its mission, IAEA may invoke the right of special in-

spection, that is, scrutiny beyond routine or ad hoc inspections. *See also* ARMS CONTROL PRINCIPLE: TRANSPARENCY AND NUCLEAR WEAPONS (384); TRANSPARENCY (461).

Significance

The importance of safeguards in preventing the spread of nuclear weapons cannot be overstressed. But the capacity of the IAEA to meet its responsibilities, indeed to reassure a suspicious international community, remains dependent on the goodwill of the country under inspection. Iraq and North Korea have demonstrated abilities to avoid IAEA scrutiny, conceal nuclear-weapons programs, and even hide from public view the development of nuclear weapons. The system of safeguards has its limitations, and the mere attempt to account for weapons-grade materials is an awesome task. Moreover, in regard to nations that wish to conceal their activities, process weapons-grade materials, and produce nuclear devices, there is little the IAEA can do. Too many technical, legal, and resource limitations prevail for ironclad guarantees to be effective, or even to demonstrate that a state is not engaged in nuclear-weapons development/procurement. Clandestine activity aside, safeguards are a necessary building block in the establishment of an international environment free from the threat of accidental nuclear war.

Disarmament Proposal: "Open Sky"

397

A plan to reduce the fear of a surprise nuclear attack and break the deadlock in disarmament negotiations. Submitted by President Dwight D. Eisenhower to Soviet premier Nikita Khrushchev at their first summit conference in Geneva in 1955, the "open sky" proposal was developed by a panel of governmental and private experts who met at the U.S. Marine Base at Quantico, Virginia. It provided for the United States and the Soviet Union to exchange blueprints of their military establishments and to carry on continuous aerial surveillance of each other's territory. *See also* ARMS CONTROL: OPEN SKIES TREATY, 1992 (365).

Significance
The "open sky" proposal was a dramatic effort to break the stalemate in nuclear disarmament talks. It offered a first-step plan to overcome Soviet objections to U.S. demands for on-site inspections. Ultimately, the Soviet Union rejected the proposal on the ground that its main purpose was to permit U.S. espionage. U.S. initiation and Soviet rejection of the proposal, however, provided the United States with a propaganda victory that was widely exploited. With the passing of the Soviet Union, an open skies treaty was made manifest in 1992.

Disarmament Proposal: Verification—Nuclear Weapons | 398 |

Process of checking state compliance with nuclear arms treaties and agreements. Verification usually applies to matters of nuclear-weapons development and deployment. Verification is an important element in the Treaty of Tlatelolco in Latin America and the Treaty of Rarotonga in the South Pacific. Both treaties include provisions for dealing with special compliance problems, and in each, the major responsibility is given to regional institutions, not individual states. Assisting in this effort is the International Atomic Energy Agency (IAEA), which has particular responsibility to verify that nuclear material is not diverted to nuclear explosives. The two South American countries most inclined toward nuclear-weapons procurement are Brazil and Argentina, and their rivalry in this area is somewhat muted by the Treaty of Tlatalolco. Both countries have publicly proclaimed their commitment to nonproliferation, formally renounced nuclear testing, established a bilateral safeguards regime, and accepted the full scope of IAEA safeguards. Although Tlatalolco establishes an accounting and control agency, that agency operates in accordance with rules and guidelines established by IAEA. In 1992 North and South

Korea agreed to create a nuclear weapons–free zone and included provisions for procedures to verify compliance. Events in 1994, however, illustrated the frailties of the agreement. North Korea's hard line ultimately required still another arrangement, this time highlighted by an agreement between Pyongyang and Washington, with Seoul an active participant. *See also* DISARMAMENT PROPOSAL: NUCLEAR PROLIFERATION SAFEGUARDS (396); NUCLEAR DIPLOMACY: NORTH KOREA–UNITED STATES (433); TRANSPARENCY (461).

Significance
Regional verification of nuclear-weapons development, production, and deployment is a major concern of an international community anxious to dispel the fear of accidental or deliberate nuclear war. Tensions between the parties are a principal blockage to successful verification. Such is the case on the Korean peninsula where North Korea fears the United States more than it does its southern neighbor; the 1994 agreement between Pyongyang and Washington was aimed at addressing this fear. All arrangements are subject to monitoring, and the IAEA is given chief responsibility in guaranteeing the existing safeguards. In the meantime, it can only be hoped that the parties primarily concerned with the dilemma will agree to take the necessary steps in building confidence, and display a willingness to normalize their relationship. The crisis on the Korean peninsula demonstrates that a two-tier arrangement of verification is necessary. Regional verification is a starting point, but it is no substitute for international means to police delicate situations. Only an international authority can represent the interests of countries not immediately connected to the regional arrangement but nevertheless affected by its implementation or nonimplementation. International verification adds another degree of assurance in that out-of-region states otherwise inclined to support a state may reconsider its association in political, economic, and security matters if it is deter-

mined that an actor is in noncompliance of the agreement.

Disarmament Strategy: Direct Approach 399

A strategy for seeking agreement on disarmament that places primary emphasis on negotiations for securing arms reduction rather than on related problem areas. The direct approach is best described by its advocates' maxim: "The way to disarm is to disarm." It differs from the indirect approach, which regards armaments as a reflection of major political disagreements that must be resolved before disarmament can become a feasible objective. *See also* DISARMAMENT STRATEGY: INDIRECT APPROACH (400).

Significance

Advocates of the direct approach to disarmament assume that the arms race itself provides the main source of insecurity among its participants. The solution to bringing the arms race under control, therefore, involves reversing its upward-spiraling tendencies and reducing tensions through specific acts of disarmament. Once substantial confidence-building moves have been reciprocally undertaken, the solution of political issues will be facilitated and a general disarmament agreement may be possible.

Disarmament Strategy: Indirect Approach 400

A strategy for seeking agreement on disarmament that places primary emphasis on resolving major political and related issues as necessary antecedents to the development of a consensus on disarmament. Advocates of the indirect approach regard disarmament as a secondary rather than immediate objective because, in their view, armaments are a product of the deep insecurities of the state system fostered by conflicts of national interests. The indirect approach differs from the direct approach, which postulates that the arms race itself is responsible for world tensions and, consequently, must be ameliorated first. *See also* DISARMAMENT STRATEGY: DIRECT APPROACH (399).

Significance

Advocates of the indirect approach to disarmament assume that negotiations for arms limitations will be unproductive until the strained relations among the nations caught up in an arms race have been improved by a new climate of trust and mutual understanding. This might mean, for example, that in the contemporary world the resolution of the most divisive issues and the establishment of an effective UN peacekeeping system should be given a higher diplomatic priority than disarmament talks.

Disarmament Strategy: Unilateral Disarmament 401

A strategy advocated by some disarmament protagonists to overcome a continued deadlock in negotiations by undertaking one-sided initiatives. Unilateral disarmament schemes are predicated on the assumption that both sides in an arms race would prefer to disarm, but that the fear, tension, and mistrust generated by the search for security through increased armaments stymies the quest. Unilateral disarmament theorists believe that by demonstrating peaceful intentions rather than merely talking about them, one side could put the arms-race cycle into reverse by evoking reciprocation of its disarmament initiatives.

Significance

Advocates of unilateral disarmament range from pacifist groups to scholars and political leaders who view it as a national-interest policy rather than a moral question. Idealists in the pacifist group believe that a conquest induced by one side's unilateral disarmament should be met only by a continuing policy of passive resistance. The realists, on the other hand, believe that if one side undertakes a substantial unilateral initiative that is not reciprocated or is used by the other side to gain an advantage in the arms race, an immediate return to a hard-line policy of weapons building is called for. Both scholars and political leaders view unilateral disarmament as a "psychological primer" to encourage bilateral disarmament negotiations by demonstrating good intentions. In contemporary arms races, the massive array of weapons invalidates a unilateral initiative because the side undertaking it would retain the power to destroy the other. Although unilateral proposals provide an alternative to arms escalation, they are directed at a highly irrational arms-race environment and have not been accepted as policy approaches by national leaders, whose foremost concern is national security.

Disarmament Strategy: United Nations Disarmament Forums | 402

Various discussion and negotiating committees and commissions created by the United Nations to try to secure agreement on disarmament and arms-control measures. In 1946 the first UN disarmament forum—the United Nations Atomic Energy Commission, consisting of the permanent members of the Security Council plus Canada—was established to try to implement the Baruch Plan, which called for complete nuclear disarmament. In 1947 the Commission for Conventional Armaments was established by the Security Council to supplement the Atomic Energy Commission's efforts. In 1952 these two commissions were merged by the General Assembly into the United Nations Disarmament Commission, also composed of the permanent members of the Security Council plus Canada. The Disarmament Commission then created a Five-Power Sub-Committee, consisting of the United States, the Soviet Union, Great Britain, France, and Canada, which met in private from 1954 to 1957. In 1959 the East-West pattern of representation was established with the setting up of the Ten-Nation Committee on Disarmament, with Bulgaria, Czechoslovakia, Poland, Romania, and the Soviet Union on one side, and Great Britain, Canada, France, Italy, and the United States on the other. In 1961 the Ten-Nation body was enlarged into an Eighteen-Nation Disarmament Committee (ENDC), which was given re-

sponsibility to "undertake negotiations with a view to reaching . . . agreement on general and complete disarmament under effective international control." The East-West membership-parity arrangement was continued in the new forum, with eight nonaligned countries added to the membership. In 1969 the ENDC was converted into the Conference of the Committee on Disarmament (CCD). An expanded Third World membership brought the new forum to a total of 26 participants. In the same year, strategic arms limitation talks (SALT) between U.S. and Soviet negotiators to limit nuclear weapons were begun and have continued over the years. In 1978 the Tenth Special Session of the General Assembly (SSOD I) was devoted to breaking the disarmament logjam. At this session, the CCD was expanded into a new 40-member Committee on Disarmament (CD), and the United Nations Disarmament Commission, inactive since 1965, was reconstituted by action of the nonaligned countries, who wanted an active forum that was universal in membership. A second Special Session on Disarmament (SSOD II) was held in 1982. The most significant nuclear disarmament forum was the conference convened at UN headquarters in New York City in May 1995, which approved the indefinite extension of the Non-Proliferation Treaty. In addition to these forums, the United Nations encourages disarmament and arms-control talks in various regions of the world, and the Security Council and General Assembly continue to explore the possibilities of a breakthrough. *See also* DISARMAMENT PROPOSAL: BARUCH PLAN (390); DISARMAMENT PROPOSAL: GENERAL AND COMPLETE DISARMAMENT (394).

Significance

Throughout the history of the United Nations, various disarmament forums have met in protracted sessions on literally thousands of occasions. Many of their efforts have focused on the achievement of general and complete disarmament, an objective that continues to elude negotiators despite their professed interest in achieving it. On the other hand, efforts to secure more limited arms-control objectives have been fairly effective. These include the successful completion of the Antarctic Treaty, the "Hot Line" Agreement, the Partial Nuclear Test Ban Treaty, the Non-Proliferation Treaty, the Seabed Treaty, the Outer Space Treaty, and the Atoms for Peace Agreement. For many years, progress toward nuclear disarmament was limited by the refusal of two nuclear-weapons states—China and France—to participate in negotiations. The nonaligned states were somewhat involved in keeping disarmament issues alive in the United Nations when the great powers avoided coming to grips with them. In almost all disarmament forums, the nonaligned applied pressure on the nuclear powers to continue negotiations in the hope that some of the major disarmament deadlocks could be broken. Increasingly, however, Third World countries are caught up in arms races of their own making and elevated tensions with their neighbors, thus complicating the objective of securing a truly disarmed world. Curiously, in the post–Cold War era it is the major powers that endeavor, without much success, to pressure Third World rivals to settle their differences with one another peacefully. Nevertheless, these same major powers are primarily responsible for the sale and distribution of sophisticated weapons throughout the Third World.

Disarmament Strategy: World Disarmament Conference | 403 |

An international meeting of all states concerned with achieving world disarmament to draft a major treaty to accomplish that goal. The first World Disarmament Conference was called by the League of Nations and convened at Geneva from 1932 to 1934 with 61 states represented. The calling of a *de facto* second World Disarmament Conference occurred in 1978 when 149 member states and many nongovernmental organizations (NGOs)

met in a United Nations Special Session on Disarmament (SSOD I) to try to achieve a deadlock breakthrough in critical areas. A second United Nations Special Session on Disarmament (SSOD II) was held in 1982; participating were 19 heads of state and 50 foreign ministers, along with all members of the United Nations. All indicated a fervent belief in the need for disarmament, but no concrete actions to reduce armaments emerged. On 31 January 1992, however, for the first time the major powers, in a Security Council Summit Declaration, declared their intention to work toward the goal of disarmament.

Significance

The World Disarmament Conference approach is to break existing deadlocks in negotiations by encouraging most or all states to participate, marshaling world opinion to pressure the great powers into reaching agreement, and tackling all major problems of disarmament and security simultaneously. The first conference, however, failed to produce any tangible results when the great powers presented diverse proposals that could not be harmonized. The main conflict, between French demands for arms superiority over Germany and German insistence on arms equality with France, weakened the conference from the start. When Adolf Hitler came to power in 1933 and withdrew Germany from the conference, all hope for reaching agreement faded. The second conference, which was called in 1978 by the UN General Assembly, attacked the problem of how to bring the growing arms race in the less developed countries under control. The conference also adopted a Program of Action on Disarmament that would result in major progress by the nuclear states. Specific agreements (e.g., the SALT II Treaty, 1979; the Inhumane Weapons Convention, 1981; the Stockholm Document, 1986; the INF Treaty, 1987; the Vienna Document, 1990; the CFE Treaty, 1990; the START I Treaty, 1991; the Chemical Weapons Treaty, 1993; the START II

Treaty, 1993; and the Trilateral Nuclear Agreement, 1994) all developed from these earlier efforts.

Nuclear Winter   404

An apocalyptic vision of the total impact of a nuclear war on the earth and its human population. In the view of many scientists, nuclear winter would produce global environmental effects that would make it questionable as to whether human life could continue to exist. In a nuclear war, besides the direct effects of nuclear explosions—blast, heat, and local radioactivity—there would be secondary effects that include a general radioactive fallout and the destruction of the earth's ozone layer. Scientists now project the additional threat of nuclear winter, which would result from the smoke and dust in the atmosphere from a nuclear exchange. These particles would screen out much of the sunlight reaching the earth's surface, thereby producing a cooling of land areas, which, according to some scientists, would produce subfreezing temperatures. The result would be likely to approach the level of human extinction. *See also* DISARMAMENT PROPOSAL: GENERAL AND COMPLETE DISARMAMENT (394).

Significance

The hypothesis that nuclear war would produce a nuclear winter that would destroy human life on the planet remains unprovable and controversial. According to many scientists, much would depend on the level of intensity of the nuclear war. They believe that a threshold point exists below which nuclear war could be fought without total catastrophe. Others believe that the security of human beings demands a substantial reduction in nuclear weapons to a level that would eliminate the threat of nuclear winter by providing for a minimal deterrent. Because there is no certainty in the concept of nuclear winter, its threat has not served to alter the direction of those states determined to assemble nuclear-weapons arsenals.

Diplomacy, Peacekeeping, and Peacemaking

Diplomacy | 405 |

The practice of conducting relations between states through official representatives. Diplomacy may involve the entire foreign-relations process—policy formulation as well as execution. In this broad sense, a nation's diplomacy and foreign policy are the same. In the narrower, more traditional sense, however, diplomacy involves means and mechanisms, whereas foreign policy implies ends or objectives. In this more restricted meaning, diplomacy includes the operational techniques whereby a state pursues its interests beyond its jurisdiction. The increasing interdependence of states has steadily expanded the number of international meetings and the instances of multilateral conference and parliamentary diplomacy. States deal with one another on such a great number of occasions and topics, however, that the bulk of diplomatic activity remains bilateral and is conducted through the normal diplomatic channels of the foreign ministry and the resident diplomatic mission. Critical issues are sometimes negotiated at the highest level, involving heads of government in summit diplomacy. *See also* DIPLOMACY, SUMMIT (414); DIPLOMATIC TOOL: NEGOTIATION (427).

Significance
The type of diplomacy employed—open or secret, bilateral or multilateral, ministerial or summit—varies with the states, the situation, the political environment, and the interests involved. Diplomacy of every type contributes to an orderly system of international relations and is the most common political technique for the peaceful settlement of international disputes. Though aided by technology, diplomacy remains an art rather than a science, and supplies the indispensable element of personal contact in the relations of states.

Diplomacy: Contribution Principle | 406 |

Refers to the changing character of international relations in the post–Cold War era, and the shift from the model of international leadership, as exemplified by the United States since World War II, to another reflecting new patterns of international participation. The distinguishing feature of the contribution principle is cooperation, or the willingness of individual states to join together in order to perform urgent and important international tasks. Historically, the contribution principle has applied to the range of middle powers showing the greatest readiness to offer their international services in a forthcoming manner. Because Canada has led the field in this activity, the contribution principle is often referred to as the "Canadian model." *See also* PEACEKEEPING (443).

Significance
The contribution principle means adapting national military strategy and diplomacy to worldwide conditions. It is postulated on a set of assumptions that no one country in the contemporary world, including the United States, has the physical capacity, intellectual competence, or political will to attempt to manage the transition to a new world order by itself. The increasing complexity of international relations and the vast variety of problems to be confronted require broader participation from members of the global community, as well as a more cooperative attitude on the part of all states, both the more and the less powerful. The need for greater cooperation between the states, for posturing national assets for the greatest international benefit, comes at a time when the United States appears more inclined to practice incremental aloofness. In the absence of a primary threat, the U.S. Congress, driven by considerable popular resolve, seems more interested in reducing the nation's international commitment. More guarded of U.S. sovereignty today, the Congress, and perhaps the president, reflects the citizens' desire to return to a period of quasi-isolationism rather than be the "policeman of the world." Attacks on the United Nations from within Congress are echoed in the larger public. Congress has expressed particular disfavor with the UN secretary-general, and is opposed to any move that would place U.S. armed forces under his leadership. Moreover, a

growing reluctance to engage in foreign-aid programs or peacemaking assignments, indeed, in confidence-building measures, underlines American unwillingness to adopt the "contribution principle," that is, the Canadian model, as its own. The United States appears to be saying, "We have contributed enough!" The United States has been the largest financial contributor to UN operations, as well as the driving force behind the airlift of relief supplies to Bosnian forces. It has been the chief enforcer of sanctions against Serbia, Iraq, and Haiti, and was the key country to prepare a peacekeeping force to replace the French in Rwanda. Therefore, a diminished U.S. role raises difficult questions. Without continued U.S. support for international operations, it is doubtful that countries like Japan and Germany—long inclined to stand at a distance in peacekeeping situations—will abandon their comfortable positions. The success of the contributing principle, or its failure, will be determined by the role played by the United States. Moreover, the very survival of the United Nations as the organization primarily responsible for ensuring an accommodative world of nations is at stake in the American decision.

Diplomacy: Conversations | 407 |
A diplomatic exchange of views between governments. Conversations may be undertaken for information only, or may lead to more detailed negotiations. Conversations are a normal diplomatic activity carried on by an ambassador or members of his staff, but they may also take place through the use of specially appointed diplomatic agents.

Significance
Conversations are exploratory and do not involve definite commitments. However, continued contact, by probing and putting out feelers on topics of interest to either or both sides, enables a diplomat to determine when the time is right to launch a specific initiative. Sometimes

called "quiet diplomacy," conversations are carried on continuously, on both bilateral and multilateral levels, at UN headquarters, national capitals, and international conferences. All major international agreements are preceded by informal conversations, which begin the process of developing consensus.

Diplomacy: Fait Accompli   408

An act by one or several states that creates a new situation vis-à-vis another state or group. Following a fait accompli, the other side no longer shares in the power of decision, and finds its options reduced to doing nothing or reacting to the altered situation. *See also* DIPLOMACY (405).

Significance

In diplomacy the fait accompli, as a one-sided act, is the antithesis of negotiation and is frequently the result of a diplomatic deadlock. At other times, it represents an initiative that brings advantages and can be carried through in the hope that other parties will accept it. One example is Adolf Hitler's remilitarization of the Rhineland (1936) in defiance of the Versailles Treaty. Another is the building of the Berlin Wall, which presented the Western allies with a fait accompli. The determination to act in this fashion is always risky because the other side is also free to react unilaterally.

Diplomacy: Hegemony   409

The extension by one state of preponderant influence or control over another state or region. A policy of hegemony may result in a client-state or satellite relationship and the creation of a sphere of influence. *See also* DEPENDENT TERRITORY: SPHERE OF INFLUENCE (39).

Significance

Wide discrepancies in power may produce hegemonic relationships between otherwise sovereign and equal states. The preponderant power of one, even with the best intentions, represents at least a potential threat to the security of another. Hence, no sovereign state can be expected to endure such a relationship indefinitely without trying to change it. Several Latin American states, e.g., Panama and Colombia, have increasingly asserted their independence from U.S. hegemonial ambitions. In 1989 Panama suffered a U.S. invasion, and in the ensuing battle hundreds of innocent Panamanian citizens were killed. Moreover, the U.S. force seized the country's leader, Manuel Noriega, brought him to Florida, and tried and convicted him for drug trafficking. Colombia, the home of the world's largest drug cartel, accepted U.S. intervention in running down narcotics peddlers, but a heavy price was paid in the country's sovereignty; attempts to scale back U.S. operations in the country are now more in evidence.

Diplomacy: Middle East   410

Seeking a peaceful resolution to the Palestinian-Israeli conflict and the Arab-Israeli dispute. On 13 September 1993, Prime Minister Yitzhak Rabin of Israel and PLO Chairman Yasir Arafat signed an agreement aimed at ending almost half a century of conflict between Israelis and Palestinians. The agreement came after secret meetings in Norway that followed 11 rounds of public peace talks in several locations in Europe, Washington, and the Middle East, and more significantly, after five wars and legions of violent incidents within and outside the region. With this accord, both parties agreed to formally recognize the other; more importantly, the Israelis acknowledged the need to trade land for peace. Israel agreed to the immediate transfer to the PLO of its authority over the Gaza Strip and the West Bank city of Jericho. Transfer of the entire West Bank to PLO administration awaited further negotiations, and in September-October 1995 a follow-up agreement called for the withdrawal of

Israeli troops from six additional cities and several hundred towns and villages. The 1993 agreement, therefore, was a major step in the long and arduous set of discussions among the Israelis, PLO representatives, and other Arab governments whose domains bordered the Jewish state. Egypt's peace treaty with Israel in 1979 began a diplomatic process that the Arabs had resisted since Israel's independence in 1948. War, not diplomacy, had pervaded Arab-Israeli thinking and actions. It took Egypt's president, Anwar el-Sadat, to break the impasse and move the process from the battlefield to the negotiating table. Sadat's surprise 1977 visit to Jerusalem created an environment more conducive to diplomatic ventures. Moreover, it enlisted the United States in the proceedings, and President Jimmy Carter was encouraged to invite Menachem Begin and Sadat to Camp David, where the details of a peace settlement were developed. The 1979 Peace Treaty between Israel and Egypt was symbolically signed in Washington. Israel withdrew from the Sinai, and the two countries agreed to separate their forces in the region. A U.S. army contingent was interposed between Israeli and Egyptian forces to watchdog the peace. Although Sadat was assassinated in 1981 for bringing peace to the area, his successor, Hosni Mubarak, honored the agreement and labored to bring other Arab governments to the conference table. Although a 1983 agreement with Lebanon failed because of a raging civil war in that country, the diplomatic process was sustained. The defeat of the conservative Likud bloc and the return to power of the Israeli Labor party set the scene for more concerted diplomatic efforts following the Gulf War of 1990–1991. Indeed, the Gulf War opened up new diplomatic possibilities, and Rabin and Shimon Peres, the Israeli foreign minister, were determined to exploit the new conditions created by the successful war against Saddam Hussein. The PLO agreement followed from that initiative, and the Kingdom of Jordan entered into another in 1994–1995. Again Israel traded land for

peace when a minor piece of real estate was returned to Jordan, but more important was the acceptance of a plan that would link the two countries in an arrangement to assure a relatively peaceful West Bank under PLO authority. This settlement set the scene for more concerted diplomatic action on the Syrian front. Damascus had supported the U.S.-led coalition against Iraq and had taken advantage of the prevailing conditions to impose its writ (control) in Lebanon, ending a civil war that had begun in 1975. Syria used its developing relationship with the United States to pressure Israel to yield the Golan Heights, which Israel had captured in the 1967 war. After months of private talks, Israel's Labor party government declared its willingness to return the Golan in return for a firm peace agreement. U.S. Secretary of State Warren Christopher met repeatedly with the leaders of the two countries, and finally in June 1995, a breakthrough appeared possible. Israel acknowledged in principle the Golan as Syrian land and pledged its return so long as it was demilitarized and policed by a U.S. force similar to the one operating in the Egyptian Sinai, but Syria insisted on the unconditional withdrawal of Israeli forces before entering into a formal agreement. The building of confidences, the trading of land for peace, and the reduction of military forces opened vistas that only the most idealistic thought possible. Despite attempts by the opposition in both camps to derail the diplomatic process, the negotiators persisted. Jericho elected a Palestinian Council empowered to supervise the establishment of Palestinian rule in the city and make preparations for an Israeli military withdrawal. The agreement called for Palestinian elections and the formation of an 82-member self-rule council with executive and legislative authority over the West Bank. A fully sovereign Palestinian state was to become a reality before the end of the twentieth century. *See also* NATIONALIST MOVEMENT: PALESTINE LIBERATION ORGANIZATION (PLO) (70); NATIONALIST MOVEMENT: ZIONISM (72); PEACEKEEPING:

MULTINATIONAL FORCE AND OBSERVERS (MFO) (446).

Significance

The Israeli-Arab conflict had long been considered insoluble on both sides, but the 1979 Israeli-Egyptian Treaty proved to be a turning point in the matter of peaceful coexistence between Jews and Arabs in the Middle East. Moreover, subsequent events such as the Gulf War of 1990–1991, and the threat posed to traditional Arab governments by expanding Islamic fundamentalism, influenced the decision to tackle the Israeli-Palestinian problem as well as the larger, more complicated Israeli-Arab dilemma. Indeed, no sooner had the opposed sides agreed to their peace plan than extremists on both sides agitated for policies that would rescind it. On the Israeli side, Jewish settlers on the West Bank and Gaza condemned the action, and violent incidents were precipitated by settler determination to hold their ground. Islamic fundamentalists were equally resolute and even more violent in their condemnation of the agreement. They opposed any understanding that would permit Israel to sustain its presence in the region. The fundamentalist Hamas organization, the most popular opposition group in the West Bank and Gaza, pledged to continue the struggle and carry the fight to Israel proper. Acts of terror multiplied in the period following the PLO agreement, and when Hamas suicide warriors stepped up their operations against Israeli military units and urban targets, the viability of the agreement was brought into question. Even Israeli moderates were forced to conclude that the only peace possible between the two sides would be one in which there was strict separation between the Israeli and Arab communities. But Yitzhak Rabin refused to scale back his diplomatic initiative. Although Israel turned to Thailand and the Philippines for labor when Palestinians were denied entry to Israel, Rabin held to the peace process. In June 1995 he declared that the parties, but especially Israel, had passed "the point of no return," and that Israel would transfer the West Bank to the PLO and return the Golan Heights to Syria, only after an ironclad agreement had been reached. The assassination of Rabin by an Israeli extremist on 4 November 1995 illustrated both the strength and weakness of the Middle East peace process.

Diplomacy, Conference $\boxed{411}$

Large-scale multilateral diplomatic negotiation conducted at international meetings. Historically associated with the establishment of peace after a major war, conference diplomacy dates from the beginning of the Western state system at the Congress of Westphalia (1642–1648), which ended the Thirty Years' War. Used increasingly in the nineteenth century, conference diplomacy was institutionalized and systematized on a global scale with the creation of the League of Nations in 1919. As the successor to the league, the United Nations constitutes a world diplomatic conference in permanent session, theoretically capable of dealing with any international political, legal, social, economic, cultural, or technical problem. Regular conference diplomacy also occurs on a limited topical or geographical basis, as in the case of meetings held by the International Monetary Fund (IMF), the North Atlantic Treaty Organization (NATO), or the Organization of African Unity (OAU). Similarly, ad hoc conference diplomacy has been employed by the Third World countries since the Bandung Conference of 1955. The knowledge explosion and technological advances have produced a variety of both ad hoc and institutionalized conferences, many of them called by specialized agencies of the United Nations. The formal and quasi-parliamentary nature of conference diplomacy involves selection of a chairman, adoption of standard working procedures, the establishment of a committee structure to expedite the work, and a system for reaching decisions. *See also* DIPLOMACY (405); DIPLOMATIC TOOL: NEGOTIATION (427).

Significance
Conference diplomacy is a form of "open" as opposed to "secret" diplomacy, in the Wilsonian sense of "open covenants openly arrived at." The multilateral nature of conference diplomacy facilitates airing grievances, defining problems, exchanging views, and working cooperatively to find solutions to common problems. As a mechanism for the conduct of international relations, it does not, however, guarantee agreement. The records of both the League of Nations and the United Nations are replete with examples of "open disagreements openly arrived at." Nevertheless, the technique of conference diplomacy may encourage the solution of problems when national interests are not irreconcilable by providing a forum for discussion and bargaining.

Diplomacy, Machiavellian ⎡412⎤
The pursuit of national objectives by crafty, conspiratorial, and deceitful tactics motivated solely by narrow self-interest. The term derives from Niccolo Machiavelli (1469–1529), the Florentine diplomat and scholar who, in his celebrated book *The Prince* (1514), described and advocated unscrupulous tactics to win and hold political power. *See also* DIPLOMACY (405).

Significance
In the absence of absolute standards of diplomatic conduct, the distinction between cleverness and Machiavellianism may depend on "whose ox is gored." Diplomacy takes its nature more from the times and the international environment than from the personality of the negotiator or the characteristics of his or her country. At this juncture in world history, the characteristics of the diplomat resemble those of the scientist, technician, and economist. Covert operations carried on by many states in promoting subversion, revolutions, and coups d'état, however, are not dissimilar from the Machiavellian intrigues of the sixteenth century.

Diplomacy, Parliamentary ⎡413⎤
A form of conference diplomacy that emphasizes the search for agreement through the construction of majorities within continuing international institutions. The term, attributed to U.S. Secretary of State Dean Rusk, emphasizes similar political processes in the UN General Assembly and other international organs and in national parliaments. Parliamentary diplomacy calls attention to the maneuvering of the various regional and special-interest groups, which resembles legislative caucusing, pork barreling, and log rolling in national assemblies. *See also* DIPLOMACY (405).

Significance
Parliamentary diplomacy serves to define issues, focus attention, and consolidate points of view, but it does not automatically lead to problem solving at the international level. The participants are the diplomatic representatives of sovereign states who function as instructed delegates without the freedom exercised by national legislators in decision making. Numerical majorities do not automatically change national interests, but they may create an atmosphere conducive to negotiation. As a pressure tactic, however, steamroller majorities may solidify disagreement and produce discord instead of harmony.

Diplomacy, Summit ⎡414⎤
Personal diplomacy by heads of state or government as contrasted with diplomacy at the ambassadorial or ministerial level. Summit diplomacy emerged during the era of absolute monarchy and has continued sporadically. Summit diplomacy currently centers on the G-7 (i.e., the United States, Japan, Germany, Great Britain, France, Canada, and Italy) postindustrial states that dominate the world's financial markets. Meeting annually in what is described as an economic summit, the members attempt to coordinate their commercial actions; they also

address pressing political matters. Although Russia is not a member of the G-7, it is usually invited to attend some of the summit's deliberations as a gesture of recognition of its standing as a formidable military power. *See also* DIPLOMACY (405); TRADE POLICY ORGANIZATION: ECONOMIC SUMMIT (266).

Significance

Summit diplomacy as a mechanism for the conduct of international relations is highly dramatic, but has no greater inherent potential for success than other kinds of diplomacy. Summits were headline-makers during the years of the Cold War when U.S. presidents met face-to-face with leaders of the Soviet Union. Diplomacy at the summit may establish broad areas of agreement, leaving details to be worked out at lower levels, or it may break deadlocks at lower levels. The technique may also be employed to improve the climate of relations between states. In some cases, however, it may be too expeditious, for when heads of state negotiate, there is no fall-back authority to which matters may be referred to gain time for reflection. National leaders, moreover, are only rarely experienced diplomats. The drama of negotiations between heads of state or government may also make failure at the summit more spectacular, frustrating, and dangerous. Summit diplomacy is least controversial when it formalizes agreements worked out in advance at lower levels.

Diplomatic Exchange: Agrément | 415 |

The formal indication by one country of the acceptability of a diplomat to be sent to it by another. The *agrément* by the intended receiving state is a response to inquiries initiated by the sending state prior to the formal nomination of the diplomat under consideration. The procedure followed by the two states is called *agréation*. *See also* DIPLOMATIC EXCHANGE: *PERSONA GRATA* (419).

Significance

The *agrément* is a useful diplomatic device to facilitate good relations between countries. Since any state can refuse to receive a particular individual, advance inquiries as to whether the person is *persona grata* (acceptable) avoids embarrassment to both states. In the practice of the United States, for example, the secretary of state seeks the *agrément* from the head of the foreign government. When it is received, the secretary notifies the president, who then submits the name of his nominee for that post to the Senate for confirmation.

Diplomatic Exchange: Diplomatic Privileges and Immunities | 416 |

Exemptions of a diplomat from national and local civil and criminal jurisdictions of the state to which he or she is accredited. Diplomatic privileges and immunities include freedom from arrest, trial, civil suit, subpoena, and legal penalty. A diplomat's dwelling, offices, and archives may not be entered, searched, or appropriated, and his or her privileges and immunities also normally apply to members of the official staff and household. Consular officers do not have diplomatic status but, because of their functions, may by law, treaty, and usage enjoy privileges not granted to other aliens. Privileges and immunities enjoyed by UN delegates and personnel are governed by an agreement concluded between the organization and the United States as the host country.

Significance

Diplomatic privileges and immunities are exceptions to the general rule of international law that each sovereign state is supreme within its own boundaries and has jurisdiction over all persons and things found within its territory. Governments would be hampered in their foreign relations if their diplomatic agents could be prevented from enjoying full access to the host governments or were prevented from returning home upon the completion of their duties. In the interest of good relations between countries, the granting of privileges and immunities also implies the diplomat's responsibility to obey the laws and regulations of the host country. If the conduct of a diplomat is unacceptable, his or her own government may be requested to either recall the person or waive immunity so that the diplomat can be subjected to civil or criminal process. The receiving state may also declare a diplomat *persona non grata* and expel that individual from the country. Improper treatment of a diplomat may, however, lead to a serious rupture in relations between two countries, as in the Iranian-U.S. hostage crisis (1979–1981).

Diplomatic Exchange: Exequatur | 417 |

A formal act by which a receiving country recognizes the official status of a newly appointed consular officer and authorizes him or her to engage in those activities appropriate to the office. In those countries that issue no formal *exequatur* or similar document, the consul enters upon his or her duties when the receiving government publicly recognizes his or her status by announcement in the official gazette or some other formal act. *See also* DIPLOMATIC PERSONNEL: CONSUL (421).

Significance
Although not required by international law to receive foreign consuls, states issue *exequaturs*, which authorize the consul to exercise jurisdiction within the territory of the receiving state with all the privileges and immunities customarily granted to such officers. The revocation of the *exequatur* by the receiving government terminates the consular mission for the individual upon whom it was bestowed.

Diplomatic Exchange: Letter of Credence | 418 |

The formal document by which the head of the sending state introduces the diplomatic representative to the head of the receiving state. The letter of credence attests to the diplomat's representative character, expresses confidence in his or her ability, outlines the mission and the extent of his or her powers, and requests that full faith and credit be given to activities undertaken by the representative on behalf of his or her government. The letter of credence is usually presented to the chief of state in a formal audience. *See also* DIPLOMATIC PERSONNEL: DIPLOMAT (422).

Significance
The letter of credence certifies the diplomat's credentials. Through this document the sending country indicates its desire for normal diplomatic relations between the two states. Acceptance of the letter of credence by the receiving chief of state indicates that the diplomat is duly accredited and may enter upon his or her official duties.

Diplomatic Exchange: Persona Grata | 419 |

An expression used to indicate that a particular individual would be, or continues to be, acceptable as an official representative of a foreign state. The concept of *persona grata* implies that a state may also declare a diplomatic representative of another state to be unacceptable (*persona non grata*). *See also* DIPLOMATIC EXCHANGE: *AGRÉMENT* (415); DIPLOMATIC EXCHANGE: DIPLOMATIC PRIVILEGES AND IMMUNITIES (416).

Significance
The discretionary authority of a government to determine if a diplomat is *persona grata* occurs first at the appointment stage through the process of *agréation*, which enables the receiving country to express its willingness or unwillingness to receive the particular representative. After a diplomat has been received, the individual may be declared *persona non grata* if he or she violates local law, international law, or the canons of proper diplomatic behavior. The receiving state may then request the sending state to recall its diplomat or, more drastically, expel him or her from the country.

Diplomatic Personnel: Attaché   420

A technical specialist attached to a diplomatic mission to perform representational and reporting activities related to his special field. Attachés specialize in political, military, economic, agricultural, informational, labor, civil aviation, petroleum, and cultural fields. Some are recruited and hired by a state's foreign office, while others are attached to diplomatic missions from other governmental agencies. *See also* DIPLOMATIC PERSONNEL: DIPLOMAT (422).

Significance

The data and interpretations acquired through the technical expertise of diplomatic attachés constitute an essential part of the raw material for the formation of foreign policy. Although the use of technical specialists in the form of attachés departs from the diplomatic tradition of employing generalists capable of dealing with broad political and economic issues, technological developments require increasingly specialized knowledge. The expanded use of attachés from diverse fields often creates the problem of distinguishing between the collection of technical data and espionage. Many attachés have been accused of spying and have been expelled by the host country, followed typically by the sending state's retaliatory expulsion of an attaché of equal standing.

Diplomatic Personnel: Consul   421

Public agents sent abroad to promote the commercial and industrial interests of their state and its citizens and to offer protection to fellow nationals living or traveling in the second state. Consuls do not have diplomatic status, but by law, treaty, and usage may enjoy privileges and immunities not accorded to other aliens. Consular duties include services related to shipping and navigation, citizenship, passports and visas, protecting nationals accused of crimes, and opening new markets. Consulates are established in one or more of the major cities of other states, the choice depending on the volume of business. *See also* DIPLOMATIC EXCHANGE: *EXEQUATUR* (417).

Significance

Consular activities are the same or similar to those performed by the local sovereign, and no country is legally obligated to permit foreign consuls to operate within its jurisdiction. The consul's role is usually defined bilaterally, but may be augmented by use of the most-favored-nation clause in consular or commercial treaties, which aims at avoiding discriminatory treatment. The flow of international trade, travel, commerce, and shipping is substantially dependent on the exchange of consular missions.

Diplomatic Personnel: Diplomat   422

An accredited agent of a head of state who serves as the primary medium for the conduct of international relations. Diplomatic titles and order of rank were established by the Congresses of Vienna (1815) and Aix-la-Chapelle (1818) and include (1) ambassador extraordinary and plenipotentiary, and papal legate and nuncio; (2) envoy extraordinary, minister plenipotentiary, and papal internuncio; (3) minister resident; and (4) *chargé d'affaires* and *chargé d'affaires ad interim*. Though ambassador is the highest rank a diplomat can hold, both ambassadors and ministers may serve as chiefs of mission, are accredited to the head of the state to which they are sent, and are responsible for the conduct of their official families and staffs. The official quarters occupied by a mission are designated as an embassy when headed by an ambassador, and a legation if headed by a minister. Virtually all diplomatic missions are now embassies headed by ambassadors. A *chargé d'affaires* accredited to the minister of foreign affairs is the diplomat placed in charge of a mission before an ambassador or minister has been appointed, or from which the chief of mission has been withdrawn. The senior diplomatic officer temporarily responsible for a mission because of the absence, disability, or death of the ambassador or minister is designated *chargé d'affaires ad interim*. In the practice of the United States, the title "diplomatic agent" is used for a representative accredited to the foreign minister of a dependent state. Diplomats take precedence from the date of their arrival at a particular capital. The senior ambassador is the dean (or *doyen*) of the diplomatic corps at that capital, and on occasion represents the corps with the foreign office. *See also* DIPLOMATIC EXCHANGE: LETTER OF CREDENCE (418); DIPLOMATIC TOOL: NEGOTIATION (427).

Significance
Diplomats provide the personal link between governments for dealing with a great number of subjects of mutual concern. They serve as eyes and ears for their country by observing and reporting economic, political, military, social, and cultural developments. They represent their country both formally and informally as the official agent of communication and, in their personal conduct, as an example of the people of their country. While endeavoring to remain *persona grata* (acceptable to the host government), diplomats must stand ready at all times to protect and advance the interests of their own country and its citizens. The basic function of the diplomat, however, is one of continual negotiation in the search for accommodation and agreement.

Diplomatic Policy: Yalta Agreement | 423

A World War II executive agreement signed at a summit conference of the Big Three (President Franklin D. Roosevelt, Prime Minister Winston Churchill, and Premier Josef Stalin) held at Yalta in the Russian Crimea in February 1945, to reach agreement on the occupation of Germany, the future of Eastern Europe, a common strategy for the defeat of Japan, and major issues related to the proposed United Nations organization. Major war-related decisions included: (1) German surrender must be unconditional, (2) German war criminals should be swiftly

brought to justice, (3) reparations should be exacted, (4) liberated countries of Eastern Europe should hold free democratic elections, (5) Polish and Russian borders should be shifted westward to the Oder and Neisse Rivers at the expense of Germany, and (6) the Soviet Union would join in the war against Japan within three months after the end of the European war. Decisions concerning the proposed United Nations organization included agreement that (1) original membership in the new world organization would be open to all states that declared war on the Axis Powers by 1 March 1945, (2) the Soviet Union would receive three memberships in the United Nations (the Soviet Union, Ukraine, and Byelorussia) instead of the 16 demanded by Stalin, (3) a trusteeship system would be set up to replace the League of Nations mandates agreement, and (4) the veto power in the Security Council would not apply to procedural decisions and could not be used by a party to a dispute to block its consideration. *See also* EXECUTIVE AGREEMENT (640).

Significance
The Yalta Agreement helped to reshape the power structure and spheres of influence in Eastern Europe and Asia. Because no general peace treaty was signed at the close of World War II, the agreement became a basic instrument for attempting to harmonize the policies of the victorious Allied Powers toward the defeated Axis states. The main Anglo-American objective—to prevent Soviet domination and the communization of East European states occupied by the Red Army—failed when the Soviets manipulated the elections to secure Communist victories in the 1946–1948 postwar period.

Diplomatic Tool: Appeasement | 424

Surrender of a vital interest for a minor quid pro quo, or for no reciprocal concession at all. Such an agreement could result from weakness, or from confusion over which of a nation's interests are vital and which secondary. Appeasement is associated historically with the Munich Conference of 1938, where Prime Minister Neville Chamberlain of Britain and Premier Edouard Daladier of France accepted Adolf Hitler's demand for the Sudetenland in Czechoslovakia in return for an empty promise of peace. *See also* DIPLOMATIC TOOL: NEGOTIATION (427).

Significance
The charge of appeasement is often invoked as a term of opprobrium applied to any concession granted to a diplomatic opponent. The development of modern communication techniques, the glare of publicity, and the concept of "open diplomacy" have made genuine negotiation difficult. The general public often fails to appreciate that negotiation involves the search for agreement through compromises, and may view any concession as appeasement. Negotiation viewed mainly as a technique for achieving "diplomatic victory" may seriously limit the diplomat's room to maneuver and impair the development of a stable world community based on the solution of problems through mutual agreement.

Diplomatic Tool: Comity   425
Courtesies extended by one state to another. Comity is based on the concept of the equality of states, and is normally reciprocal. The idea of comity emerged during the monarchical era, when the relations of states involved the relations of personal sovereigns and their agents.

Significance
Practices based on comity are indispensable in promoting and maintaining friendly relations between countries. Comity is involved in such matters as (1) extradition, (2) execution by local courts of judgments handed down by foreign courts, (3) one state bringing a suit in the courts of another country, and (4) diplomatic immunity as an exemption from local jurisdiction. Customs and traditions based on comity have supplemented the development of international law in regularizing the relations of states.

Diplomatic Tool: Détente   426
A diplomatic term indicating a situation of lessened strain or tension in the relations between two or more countries. A period of détente may be established by formal treaty or may evolve out of changes in national strategies and tactics over several years. *See also* DIPLOMATIC TOOL: RAPPROCHEMENT (428).

Significance
The concept of détente describes an improved environment that may in time contribute to the amelioration of fundamental points of conflict between states. The Locarno Treaties of 1925, for example, ushered in an era of relative stability in Europe that helped strengthen the League of Nations' security system through conclusion of such treaties as the General Act of 1928 and the Kellogg-Briand Pact of Paris of 1928. Beginning in the 1960s, a détente in U.S.-Soviet relations, based on the idea of peaceful coexistence, evolved out of an awareness of the possibility of mutual destruction and because of a growing nationalism among alliance partners within each camp rather than from the conclusion of a major treaty. The term *détente* has not been used in the post–Cold War era, and more common descriptive terms tend to frame relationships between states at variance with each other.

Diplomatic Tool: Negotiation   427
A diplomatic technique for the peaceful settlement of differences and the advancement of national interests. The objectives of negotiation are accomplished by compromises and accommodations reached through direct personal contact.

See also DIPLOMACY (405); DIPLOMATIC TOOL: APPEASEMENT (424).

Significance
The essential nature of negotiation is frequently misunderstood by the general public, especially in times of great international tension, when it becomes difficult to offer any concession to an opponent. Yet, reaching agreement through negotiation implies a willingness on both sides to make mutually acceptable concessions (quid pro quo). Ultimatums, threatening speeches, boycotts and walkouts, and resort to force may be a part of diplomacy in the broadest sense, but they are not negotiation. Nevertheless, such actions are often related to negotiation and may affect its ultimate success or failure. Secondary interests may be sacrificed to secure agreement in negotiations, but primary or vital interests are rarely negotiable. Skillful negotiation involves obtaining agreement at the least cost to good future relations, while leaving the other side relatively satisfied.

Diplomatic Tool: Rapprochement $\boxed{428}$
A reconciliation of interests of rival states after a period of estrangement. In diplomatic parlance, rapprochement implies a policy of attempting to reestablish normal relations. *See also* DIPLOMATIC TOOL: DÉTENTE (426).

Significance
Rapprochement is a common diplomatic term of French origin that describes one of the critical changes that can take place in the relations of states. Following World War II, a rapprochement in Franco-German relations virtually ended more than a century of bitter rivalry.

Diplomatic Tool: Treaty $\boxed{429}$
A formal agreement or contractual obligation among sovereign states that establishes, defines, or modifies their mutual rights and obligations. Treaties are international law and, in the United States,

also domestic law by virtue of the "supreme law of the land" clause (Article VI) of the U.S. Constitution. A treaty and other types of international agreements—act, *aide mémoire*, charter, covenant, convention, entente, *modus vivendi*, protocol—may involve such topics as peace, territorial cession, alliance, friendship, commerce, or other matters of international concern. *See also* DIPLOMATIC TOOL: NEGOTIATION (427); INTERNATIONAL LAW: *PACTA SUNT SERVANDA* (484); INTERNATIONAL LAW: *REBUS SIC STANTIBUS* (486).

Significance
The juridical effect, or binding nature *(pacta sunt servanda)*, of a treaty is not dependent on the name of the instrument. A treaty may be multilateral or bilateral, and of specific or indefinite duration. Treaty making as a process involves negotiation, signature, ratification, exchange of ratifications, publication and proclamation, and execution. Ratification of treaties, an executive act by which the state finally accepts the terms of the agreement, is accomplished for each signatory in accordance with its constitutional processes. International contractual obligations may be terminated after specified conditions have been met, at the end of a stated time period, by mutual consent, by unilateral denunciation as during a state of war between the parties, or, theoretically, when conditions essential to the agreement have changed *(rebus sic stantibus)*. Since World War II, the relations of states have been regulated with increasing frequency by multilateral treaties on a variety of topics. Examples include the United Nations Charter, the North Atlantic Treaty, the Rome Treaties on European integration, the Nuclear Test Ban Treaty, and the Outer Space Treaty.

Diplomatic Tool: Treaty Ratification $\boxed{430}$
The act by which a state formally confirms and approves the terms of a treaty. Normally an executive act, ratification is accomplished for each signatory of a treaty in accordance with its constitu-

tional processes. This usually requires the consent of one or more houses of the national legislature. In some countries, legislative participation is *pro forma*, but in others, such as the United States, it is the critical stage in the treaty process. *See also* CONGRESS: TREATY POWER (634); PRESIDENT: TREATY POWER (670).

Significance
Internationally, treaties come into force when instruments of ratification have been exchanged (in the case of a bilateral treaty) or deposited with a particular government designated in the treaty (in the case of multilateral treaties). In the latter case, it may be stipulated that the treaty will enter into force when ratifications from specific states have been deposited or when a specific number of ratifications have been received, as illustrated in Article 110 of the Charter of the United Nations and Article 11 of the North Atlantic Treaty.

Diplomatic Tool: Ultimatum | 431 |
A formal, final communication from one government to another, requiring the receiving government to comply in some stated fashion with the wishes of the sender or be prepared to take the consequences, ultimately war. An ultimatum indicates that the diplomatic process is but one step short of a breakdown and that a sovereign state is willing to risk the use of force if necessary to impose its will upon another. *See also* DIPLOMATIC TOOL: NEGOTIATION (427).

Significance
Whether a bluff or in earnest, an ultimatum signifies a serious crisis in international relations. It indicates that one of the parties has decided to abandon negotiation and will seek its objectives by other means. In 1914 Germany sent an ultimatum to Belgium to permit the passage of German troops through Belgium to fight against France, or be treated as an enemy of Germany. Both the League of Nations and the United Nations were designed in part to provide meeting places and tech-

niques whereby settlements might be sought beyond the limits inherent in bilateral diplomacy, free from delivery of ultimatums.

Maastricht Treaty | 432 |
An agreement to form a European Union, based on the European Community, with common economic policies and currencies, signed on 7 February 1992. This agreement, better known as the Treaty on European Union, emanated from the Maastricht Conference of December 1991, and was drafted by the members of the European Community (EC). The Maastricht Treaty was the most important step in a four-decade-old plan to integrate the economies and ultimately the political systems of the Western European countries. The Maastricht Treaty created a new European Union on a foundation established by the European Community. Despite opposition to some of its provisions, Maastricht divides into three "pillars": The first amends the older European Economic Community (EEC), the European Coal and Steel Community (ECSC), and the Euratom treaties; the second centers on foreign and security policy (adopting the existing intergovernmental procedures of European Political Cooperation; and the third covers issues of justice and home affairs. The first and last sections of the treaty comprise a preamble and final provisions, and seek to bind the three pillars together into a European Union. The three-pillar structure has been complicated by some members emphasizing the separate nature of the pillars, with others preferring to cite their interrelationship. More nationalistic members, such as Great Britain and Denmark, were able to prevent the creation of a single federal structure (indeed, the term *federal* was expunged from the document), and the looser formulation of an "ever closer union" was ultimately adopted. By so doing, the way was open to gain the opposition's acceptance of "subsidiarity," a federal element that among other matters permits the European Court of Justice to fine member governments

who violate or breach EC law. The different, generally ambiguous interpretations given to the Maastricht Treaty bring into question the real character of the European Union. The language of the treaty is, on the whole, positive and forward-looking. It is also the longest of European Community documents, running to hundreds of pages. Nevertheless, the treaty falls far short of representing genuine union. The more immediate and central aim of the treaty, as well as its more positive accomplishment, is the formation of an Economic and Monetary Union (EMU). EMU seeks to promote a harmonious and balanced development of economic activities, sustainable and noninflationary growth respecting the environment, a high level of employment and social protection, the raising of living standards, a high degree of convergence in economic performance, and economic and social cohesion among member states. The Maastricht Treaty establishes the goal of a currency union, and toward this end the EC has been granted exclusive authority over money. Maastricht pools the monetary sovereignty of the member states, and supersedes any independent activity. EMU is managed by a new supranational institution, the European Central Bank, which is scheduled for inauguration in 1997, or 1999 at the latest. In the interim, the treaty creates a European Monetary Institute, and prescribes a single currency, a customs union, common trade policy, and a single market. In summary, the Maastricht Treaty spells out the requirement of member states to make their individual economies matters of common concern. *See also* ALLIANCE: EUROCORPS (282); DEMOCRATIC PATTERN: SUBSIDIARITY (705); REGIONAL POLITICAL GROUP: EUROPEAN UNION (EU) (566); REGIONAL MILITARY GROUP: WESTERN EUROPEAN UNION (WEU) (559).

Significance
Since the close of World War II in 1945, the West European nations have made remarkable progress toward the creation of a united Europe. In spite of many obstacles, they have moved toward more intimate union, and nowhere is this more obvious than in the area of economic cooperation. Western Europe has created an internal market of approximately 350 million people, providing for free movement within the community (with limited exceptions) of goods, capital, services, and citizens of member states. In January 1994 the West European Common Market was extended to include members of the European Free Trade Association (EFTA), i.e., Austria, Finland, Norway, Sweden, and Iceland, making it the world's largest free-trade zone, comprising almost 400 million people. Moreover, serious consideration has been given to Turkey's admission to the European Customs Union, which adds another 50 million people. This enormous achievement has been made in the face of stiff and difficult opposition from a variety of member states, especially Great Britain and France, who are major actors in the community. But for all its economic achievement, the European Community comes up short in political accomplishment. In an age of reinvigorated nationalism, member states are reluctant to yield aspects of individual sovereignty for more all-inclusive, centralized, supranational union. The catalyst for the creation of a unified Western Europe was the Cold War, and its passing, as well as the unification of Germany, raises new questions about the future of European integration. Whereas the benefits of economic cooperation in a world increasingly divided into major trade and commercial zones are obvious, the advantages and benefits of political union are less clear. The United States is not a player in the European Union, and Britain's reliance on the United States in the face of a more substantial Germany, as well as an uncertain Franco-German combination, raises old fears and new concerns. Britain displays ambivalence on the issue of European federalism, but it accepts the concept of subsidiarity, and thus does not reject all constraints on its national sovereignty. The future projects a continuing struggle to bring into balance both centripetal and centrifugal forces on the

European continent. After all the factors have been weighed, it would appear that Maastricht points to the anticipated formation of a more perfect European Union.

Nuclear Diplomacy: North Korea–United States | 433 |

Confronting nuclear proliferation on the Korean peninsula. The cease-fire that brought a close to hostilities on the Korean peninsula in 1953 did not end the rivalry of North and South, let alone reduce the international tension generated by the conflict. North Korea maintained a bellicose posture throughout the years of the Cold War. With its passing, Pyongyang appeared even more resolute in promoting its own version of political reality in the region. North Korea proceeded with its nuclear-weapons program despite its acceptance of the Nuclear Non-Proliferation Treaty (NPT). In 1993, when called to acknowledge its violation of the treaty, it withdrew its compliance. In 1992–1993, a CIA report revealed that the North Koreans had produced several nuclear weapons and had plans to make numerous others. In addition, North Korea's armament industry had produced missile-delivery systems capable of reaching Tokyo and more distant regional targets. Efforts by the International Atomic Energy Agency (IAEA) to monitor the North Korean nuclear program were stymied by a pugnacious North Korean government. Pyongyang's behavior disturbed the United States, which continued to station some 37,000 U.S. soldiers in South Korea. In an atmosphere of rising tension, the Clinton administration offered to enter into diplomatic discussions with the Korean government, but when the North Korean leader, Kim il Sung, agreed to a conference between the two countries, few observers registered optimism. Kim il Sung's death in August 1994, just before the negotiators were to meet, caused a temporary postponement, but the negotiations went forward several weeks later. Both sides were well prepared for the bargaining that ensued, and it took

only a few weeks to agree on a plan. A treaty was signed on 21 October 1994 that called for political and financial concessions to North Korea in return for its promise not to proceed with nuclear-weapons production. IAEA authorities also were promised open access to the North's extensive facilities. However, North Korea was permitted to retain its nuclear fuel enrichment facility until such time as the United States and its partners, namely Japan and South Korea, funded and constructed replacement light-water nuclear facilities that could be used only for the generation of electricity. The two 1,000-megawatt light-water reactors were to be constructed by South Korea with supervision from an international consortium that included Japan. The treaty also called for the delivery of up to 500,000 tons of heavy oil annually. The first shipment of 50,000 tons was made in January 1995. In return, North Korea pledged to halt development of its existing graphite-moderated reactors and "eventually dismantle these reactors and related facilities." Seoul and Tokyo agreed to pay the substantial portion of the aid package, slated to range between $3–$4 billion. Pyongyang also was led to believe that in due course diplomatic recognition would be granted by the United States, and that the trade embargo imposed on the country would be lifted. *See also* TRANSPARENCY (461).

Significance

The nuclear-proliferation dilemma is perhaps the most vexing problem confronting the international community. Although the Clinton administration's treaty with North Korea was sanctioned by South Korea and Japan, and received support from China and Russia, it proved very controversial in the United States. The Korean demilitarized zone is the most militarily fortified region on the planet, with almost 2 million troops poised for action at any time. For more than three decades, North and South Korean officials have discussed terminating their conflict and merging their interests, without positive results. Indeed, North and

South Korea entered into a Reconciliation and Denuclearization Agreement in 1992, which the North promptly ignored. The matter of trust and confidence-building therefore remains problematical and the peninsula continues to be a dangerous place. Nevertheless, the U.S.-North Korea agreement was a ray of sunshine in an otherwise gloomy environment. It is important to note that the agreement was not so much bilateral as it was multilateral, involving China, Russia, Japan, South Korea, and the United States. In addition, the negotiations shifted the focus from a short-term military crisis to a longer term political process at a critical time of transition in North Korea, given the passing of Kim il Sung and the somewhat ambiguous role played by his son and successor, Kim jong-il. If there was optimism in the period immediately following the agreement, pessimism again became the order of the day when the North Koreans rejected the plan to have South Korea construct the light-water reactors. Pyongyang insisted that the work had to be done by the Americans. Because the financial arrangements involved South Korea, the United States was reluctant to backtrack on the deal. The impasse led to still more negotiations between U.S. and North Korean officials, who met in Berlin, Germany, and Kuala Lumpur, Malaysia, in 1995.

Peace Policy: Japanese Constitution, Article Nine | 434

That part of the constitution adopted in 1947 in which the Japanese "forever renounce war as a sovereign right of the nation and the threat or use of force as means of settling international disputes." Article 9 also provides that, to implement the ideal of permanent peace, "land, sea, and air forces, as well as other war potential will never be maintained." The Japanese constitution was written under the direct supervision of the U.S. occupation forces commanded by General Douglas MacArthur. *See also* ALLIANCE: JAPANESE-AMERICAN SECURITY TREATY (283).

Significance

The Japanese constitution was approved by General MacArthur before the Cold War developed and prior to the enunciation of the "containment" doctrine by the United States. With the onset of the Cold War, however, the United States encouraged the Japanese to arm in self-defense. Since the end of the Cold War, the Japanese continue to add to their military capability and have assembled a credible arsenal that is described in defensive terms, but which can engage offensively under certain circumstances, if warranted. Although the Japanese remain fundamentally antiwar in their national philosophy, they joined with the United States in a bilateral security pact, established a National Police Reserve, and created a defense agency consisting of ground, maritime, and air self-defense forces. Article 9 has been interpreted by successive Japanese governments to prohibit offensive, but not defensive, armaments. This issue was hotly debated during the Gulf War of 1990–1991, when some Japanese opinion leaders believed it necessary for Japan to supply combat forces for the UN coalition led by the United States.

Peace Policy: Kellogg-Briand Pact | 435

A general treaty, concluded in 1928 and subsequently ratified by almost all nations, that sought to outlaw war as an instrument of national policy. Officially titled the General Treaty for the Renunciation of War, and also known as the Pact of Paris, it was drawn up by U.S. Secretary of State Frank B. Kellogg and Foreign Minister Aristide Briand of France. The two main articles provided, first, that signatories "condemn recourse to war for the solution of international controversies, and renounce it as an instrument of national policy in their relations with one another," and second, "the settlement or solution of all disputes or conflicts, of whatever nature or of whatever origin . . . shall never be sought except by pacific means." In ratifying the pact, however, many nations attached a reservation that proscribed only "offensive" military actions, not those of a defensive character. The United States, for example, stipulated that the pact did not impair the right of self-defense, including enforcement of the Monroe Doctrine, nor did it obligate the nation to participate in sanctions against an aggressor. *See also* INTERNATIONAL LAWMAKING: WAR CRIMES TRIALS (497); WAR (305).

Significance
The Kellogg-Briand Pact represented an attempt to strengthen the League of Nations peacekeeping system in two ways. First, it gave the United States, which had refused to join the league, an opportunity to participate in a general condemnation of war. Second, it was aimed at closing the gap in the league's security system, which, under its covenant, permitted states to go to war under certain circumstances. Because of the reservations attached to the pact's ratification, however, the intended restraint on state actions was largely nullified. Because states that go to war usually claim self-defense, and no definitions were provided in the treaty to distinguish a war of aggression from a war of national defense, the pact did little to discourage resort to war. Trumped-up border incidents, for example, were used by Japan in its attacks on China in 1931 and 1937, and by Italy in its aggression against Ethiopia in 1935, so that the attacking state could claim self-defense. Violations of the Pact of Paris, however, were among the charges levied against individual Nazi and Japanese war criminals convicted by Allied tribunals at Nuremberg and Tokyo after World War II.

doctrine called for both sides to avoid nuclear war and refrain from exporting revolution or counterrevolution. Competition between states with different social systems, according to Khrushchev, was to continue in all nonmilitary areas until communism proved itself superior and presided at the burial of capitalism. *See also* COMMUNIST DOCTRINE: KHRUSHCHEVISM (84).

Significance
The doctrine of peaceful coexistence was recognition that the threat of nuclear annihilation required the adoption of a new tactical approach for spreading communism. The doctrine did not espouse pacifism, however, since "just wars" of national liberation fought by indigenous peoples were designated as the means for achieving the goal of communism in the developing areas of the world. The right to "export" aid to revolutionary groups to offset capitalist support propping up reactionary regimes opposed by the masses became an integral part of the new Soviet dogma. Many of the ideas expounded in the doctrine were reiterations of Lenin and Stalin's interpretations of Marx, but the emphasis on avoiding a major war with the West was based on a realistic appraisal of the dangers of nuclear war. Although Chinese leaders in the 1950s and 1960s delivered scathing denunciations of the peaceful coexistence doctrine as a rejection of the principles of Marxism-Leninism and a mark of cowardice on the part of Soviet leaders, in the 1970s they adopted their own peaceful coexistence doctrine as a basis for a Chinese-American détente.

Peace Policy: Peaceful Coexistence | 436 |

A reinterpretation of Leninism that rejects the inevitability of a major war between the leading Western and Communist states. The Communist doctrine of peaceful coexistence was enunciated by Premier Nikita Khrushchev of the Soviet Union before the Twentieth Party Congress in 1956. As a basis for Soviet policy, the new

Peace Policy: Reparations | 437 |

Compensation demanded by victor nations from defeated states for wrongs committed by the latter before or during hostilities. Reparations often take the form of capital goods removed from the defeated nation's territory to replace those destroyed during the war, but may also involve monetary payments.

Significance
Reparations constitute both a punishment levied on the defeated states, aimed at reducing their war-making potential for a period of years, and a subsidy for the victor nations to aid in their reconstruction. At the end of World War I, the European allies, led by France, demanded huge reparations from Germany to compensate not only for war damage but also to cover disability pensions. In case of German default in payments, the allies retained the right to send punitive expeditions into Germany. German reparations payments, progressively scaled down, continued until 1931, when the Great Depression forced a suspension of most war-debt payments. After World War II, the Soviet Union carried out an extensive seizure of goods and industrial equipment in the countries occupied by the Red Army, particularly in Germany and Manchuria. Reparations taken by the Soviet Union from Germany alone amounted to an estimated $28 billion.

Peaceful (Pacific) Settlement | 438 |

The resolution of international disputes without resort to force. Pacific settlement involves the procedural techniques by which conflicts over substantive rights and duties of states can be resolved. The two categories of techniques for the peaceful settlement of international disputes are (1) legal, which involve the application of international law to the facts of the dispute, and (2) political, which involve diplomatic procedures. Arbitration and adjudication comprise the legal methods of pacific settlement, and the political techniques include diplomatic negotiation, good offices, mediation, inquiry, and conciliation. *See also* DIPLOMACY (405).

Significance
The increasing destructiveness of war, together with its social and economic costs, has been responsible for a profusion of efforts to establish and render obligatory a number of generally acceptable alternatives for the resolution of international disputes. The Hague Peace Conferences of 1899 and 1907 produced the first large-scale multilateral efforts to establish obligatory peaceful settlement procedures. These efforts and procedures have been supplemented in such treaties as the Covenant of the League of Nations, the Statute of the Permanent Court of International Justice, the General Act of Geneva (1928), the Kellogg-Briand Pact (Treaty for the Renunciation of War, 1928), and the Charter of the United Nations. Developments in the field of pacific settlement have been augmented by efforts in related fields such as disarmament, international organizational activity, economic development, and educational and cultural changes.

Peaceful Settlement: Conciliation | 439 |

A peaceful settlement procedure in which the representatives of a group of states establish the facts in a dispute and use them as the basis for recommending a solution. Conciliation, which is often linked with inquiry, can be viewed as group mediation. Commissions of conciliation may be established ad hoc and are also included in the peaceful-settlement provisions of many bilateral as well as multilateral treaties. Such provisions are included, for example, in the Pact of Bogotá of the Organization of American States (1948) and the Brussels Treaty, signed the same year by Belgium, Great Britain, France, Luxembourg, and the Netherlands. *See also* PEACEFUL (PACIFIC) SETTLEMENT (438).

Significance
As a peaceful-settlement device, conciliation has several advantageous characteristics. It involves formalized, even quasi-judicial procedures, and its recommendations carry the weight of group opinion. Under the Charter of the United Nations, the Security Council can appoint a conciliation commission or call on the parties to a dispute to do so. On many occasions, however, the Security Council itself acts as a conciliation body as it attempts to resolve international disputes

in fulfillment of its responsibility for the maintenance of international peace and security.

Peaceful Settlement: Good Offices and Inquiry | 440 |

Techniques for the peaceful settlement of international disputes whereby a third party acts as a go-between. The good offices of a third state involve diplomatic efforts to reestablish direct bilateral negotiations between the parties, aimed at bringing about a settlement by the disputants themselves. In the absence of treaty provisions to the contrary, the parties to a dispute are not obligated to accept an offer of good offices, nor is the third state entitled to enlarge a dispute through resentment at having its offer declined. Inquiry concerns the impartial determination of the facts involved in an international dispute. Inquiry procedure involves the establishment of a fact-finding commission by the parties to the dispute or by an international body. After conducting its investigation, the commission of inquiry issues a report of its findings to the disputants or to the international agency. Unless inquiry is followed by additional peaceful settlement procedures like mediation or conciliation, the parties to the dispute are free to determine the use to be made of the findings. *See also* PEACEFUL (PACIFIC) SETTLEMENT (438).

Significance
When bilateral diplomacy has become deadlocked or proves impossible in an international dispute, good offices is a peaceful settlement procedure that involves a minimum degree of friendly intervention by a third party. The third state or representative of an international organization acts only as a channel of communication and does not involve itself in the subject matter of the dispute. U.S. offers of good offices were refused by the disputants at the outset of both World Wars I and II. Hostilities between the United States and Japan were brought to an end in 1945 through the good offices of Switzerland. The rationale for using inquiry is that dispute settlement may be facilitated if the facts in the case can be precisely and impartially determined. Disputants may also be willing to submit to inquiry since this procedure does not involve suggestions from third parties on how to settle the controversy, as is the case in mediation and conciliation. Inquiry is provided for in many bilateral treaties and was first institutionalized in the Hague Convention for the Peaceful Settlement of International Disputes (1899). It was also among the peaceful settlement procedures included in the League of Nations Covenant and the Charter of the United Nations. The findings of an ad hoc commission of inquiry were instrumental in resolving the Dogger Bank incident (1904), which involved the accidental sinking of British fishing vessels by Russian warships. The League of Nations appointed a commission of inquiry (Lytton Commission) to determine the facts surrounding the Japanese invasion of Manchuria in 1931. Efforts at conciliation based on the facts obtained by the commission failed, however, and Japan withdrew from membership in the league.

Peaceful Settlement: Mediation | 441 |

A peaceful settlement procedure whereby a third party aids the disputants in finding a solution by offering substantive suggestions. Mediation may be requested by the parties to a dispute or volunteered by a third state. In international practice, the disputants are not entitled, even during the course of hostilities, to view an offer of mediation as an unfriendly act, nor are they obligated to accept an unsolicited offer of mediation. *See also* PEACEFUL (PACIFIC) SETTLEMENT (438).

Significance
Successful mediation involves reducing the tension between the disputants and reconciling their opposing claims. The former requires sensitivity and tact of a high order. The latter requires skill in finding a formula whereby the disputants can retreat from their extreme positions

and reach a compromise solution to their problems. President Theodore Roosevelt's effort in arranging the Treaty of Portsmouth to end the Russo-Japanese War in 1905 is a classic illustration of mediation. The direct mediation efforts of Secretary of State Henry Kissinger in the Middle East were described as "shuttle diplomacy" because of his frequent flights between Israel and Egypt. A successful act of mediation was that conducted by Diego Cordovez, the representative of the UN secretary-general, who engaged diplomats from Pakistan and Afghanistan in more than six years of "proximity talks," which avoided their meeting face-to-face but nonetheless produced a 1988 agreement for the withdrawal of the Soviet army from Afghanistan.

Peaceful Settlement: Plebiscite | 442

A vote to determine the will of an area's entire population on a matter of great public interest. Plebiscites have frequently been used in international relations in connection with territorial cessions. Although a specific treaty of cession may stipulate that a plebiscite must be held, there is no customary rule of international law that requires the approval of the inhabitants before sovereignty over a territory can be legally transferred. *See also* JURISDICTION: CESSION (503); NATIONALISM: SELF-DETERMINATION (62).

Significance
The practice of holding a plebiscite in connection with the cession of territory, though not generally required in international law, has been followed with increasing frequency since the second half of the nineteenth century. The rationale of the plebiscite in international relations can be traced to the democratic concept of popular sovereignty and the doctrine of the right of national self-determination. Some plebiscites were provided for in the peace treaties of 1919, but the device was not generally applied in the territorial transfers resulting from World War II. Although India and Pakistan agreed in 1949 to resolve the Kashmir issue by pleb-

iscite, the United Nations has been unsuccessful in arranging the conditions for its administration. Other recent examples of plebiscites include those conducted by the United Nations in several former African trust territories when they emerged as independent nations. The United Nations also secured the agreement of Indonesia to the holding of a plebiscite to determine whether the indigenous population of former Dutch New Guinea (West Irian) wished to remain under Indonesian rule. A plebiscite has also been suggested as a way of resolving the long-standing dispute between Great Britain and Spain on sovereignty over Gibraltar. A plebiscite was slated to be held in both North and South Vietnam in 1956 to determine which unit would be unified with the other, but the United States opposed it, and it was never conducted.

Peacekeeping | 443

Efforts made by the United Nations to neutralize civil and regional conflicts. The passing of the Soviet Union opened new opportunities for UN action in dealing with threats to the peace. Made a UN responsibility following the end of World War II, the maintenance of peace and security shifted to the member states when the world organization failed to act or proved ineffective. Article 51 addressed the right of collective self-defense, and the alliances forged during the Cold War (in particular NATO and the Warsaw Pact) represented the world's answer to the problems of war and peace. Because virtually all conflicts were subsumed under U.S.-Soviet rivalry, the United Nations was more likely to follow than lead in the attempts to cope with the great issues. The veto power enjoyed by the permanent powers (United States, Soviet Union, Britain, France, and China) in the Security Council, however, prevented that body from assuming its stated responsibilities. The Uniting for Peace Resolution of 1950 transferred major peacekeeping responsibilities to the UN General Assembly. The General Assembly authorized the creation of United Nations Emergency Forces, which were dispatched to numerous trouble spots, e.g., Congo, Cyprus, Papua New Guinea, the Sinai peninsula, Angola, and Cambodia. But the United Nation's peacekeeping record during the period of the Cold War was a limited one, represented more by rhetoric than actual accomplishment. The end of the Cold War, the reluctance of the United States to take unilateral action, and the expressed desire of major and lesser powers to give the United Nations a firmer hand in peacekeeping operations signaled a significant change: UN emergency forces were transformed into peacekeeping forces. The key feature was UN neutrality in the conflict, and its acceptance by the parties as a concerned intermediary, with responsibility for steering the belligerents to the negotiating table and providing humanitarian assistance to the affected civilian population. The United Nation's peacekeeping purpose was to be the creation of an international ambience in which order could be established and maintained, and most importantly, hostilities brought to an end. Given this larger role, UN peacekeeping forces increased from 15,000 to 80,000 between 1991 and 1994. The UN budget for this activity rose from $14 million to $3.6 billion in the same period, and by 1995 had topped $4 billion. The enormity of the responsibility was demonstrated by the 17 different UN peacekeeping and peacemaking missions in 1995. Moreover, the assumption of UN responsibility came at a time when individual states questioned the support they provided and, more importantly, the extent of their financial and general commitment to the United Nations. *See also* DIPLOMACY: CONTRIBUTION PRINCIPLE (406); PEACEKEEPING: PEACEKEEPERS (447); PEACEKEEPING: UN OPERATIONS (450).

Significance

UN peacekeeping operations following the end of the Cold War have increased, not diminished. The projected era of world peace following the demise of the Soviet Union did not materialize. Generally localized ethnic, religious, and nationalist wars have raised concerns among UN members, and members have, individually or collectively, authorized UN intervention to prevent these conflicts from igniting a broader, general war. The difficulties involved in taming a troubled area, however, are all too evident. The United Nations failed to complete its mission in Somalia, from which it was forced to retreat in March 1995. It failed to reconcile the parties in the former Yugoslavia, notably in Bosnia, where its actions appeared to enhance the power of more aggressive forces. Other missions were similarly distressed. The UN secretary-general was accused of failing to adequately use the prestige of his office to enhance diplomatic settlements. Moreover, the increasing cost of peacekeeping operations bankrupted the United Nations, a condition made worse by a U.S. congressional decision in 1995 to slash the U.S. contribution. The secretary-general's report on 1 June 1995 pessimistically called for an end to peacekeeping actions. Noting that the peacekeepers have not been received as neutrals, the secretary-general cited their being targeted, killed, and taken prisoner by the belligerents, notably in Bosnia. Arguing the futility of future peacekeeping missions in war zones, he declared that in the future only a well-armed international combat force should be sent into world trouble spots. Boutros Boutros-Ghali's report was not well received among the contributing nations, in part because it exposed the weaknesses of the world body. But the real issue was peacekeeping itself. The UN peacekeeping operation in Bosnia was doomed from the start because peacekeeping can only be effective after relative calm has come to a region and the principal belligerents are genuinely interested in finding a compromise formula. That means the combatants must be ready to lay down their arms and begin the process of reconciling their competing claims. A third force can then act as a neutral peacekeeper, at least until the parties to the dispute have resolved the main issues that divide them. But to send peacekeepers into a raging civil conflict is to invite exactly what occurred in Bosnia. Peacemakers and peacebuilders are a different matter. They supposedly have combat capability, and are ready to confront one or more of the parties engaged in the conflict. The more aggressive form of peacemaking and peacebuilding was attempted in Somalia, but there, too, the United Nations was found wanting, not because it was not ready to perform a difficult assignment, but because the member states, particularly the United States, were not inclined to expend lives in situations where their fundamental state interests could not be justified.

Peacekeeping: Cambodia   444

UN efforts at restoring equilibrium to Cambodia. In November 1991 the United Nations sent a force of 286 men to Cambodia to cover the withdrawal of Vietnamese military units from the country. That force was known as the United Nations Advance Mission in Cambodia (UNAMIC). A UN resolution on 28 February 1992 converted UNAMIC into the United Nations Transitional Authority (UNTAC), with a force of 21,900 men drawn from several UN member states, notably Japan, and led by Yasushi Akashi, who called for the disarming of the Khmer Rouge in order to assemble a Cambodian government of reconciliation. Originally designed to operate at least five of Cambodia's ministries, UNTAC confronted resistance from the major factions in divided Cambodia, especially from the extremist Khmer Rouge, who had no desire to relinquish their weapons or subordinate themselves to other authorities, whether national or international.

Significance

The presence of UNAMIC and UNTAC and the promise of international aid brought a semblance of stability to Cambodia, but the long period of strife preceding the UN intervention had so deeply divided the country that no formula existed for ameliorating the situation. Neighboring Vietnam, as well as the factions within Cambodia, ques-

tioned the long-term presence of UN personnel in the country. UNTAC agreed to a limited role, and has confined its activities to feeding and providing basic medical services to the more destitute members of the population. Attempts at re-creating a workable government that was representative of the many competing groups, however, was beyond the capabilities of the most determined UN force. It has been noted that the United Nations, like other well-intentioned groups in Cambodia, is no match for Phnom Penh's profiteers, or the Khmer Rouge and Chinese businessmen of Southeast Asia, let alone the country's annexationist neighbors in Vietnam and Thailand. Despite the money poured into the country by international sources, estimated at more than $2 billion between 1992–1994, the social condition has worsened, peasant displacement is unchecked, the gap between rich and poor continues to widen, and official corruption and criminal activity is on the ascendant. But the Khmer Rouge's genocidal actions and a ten-year Vietnamese occupation have ended, and the country is at last beginning to reassume a sense of itself. To that extent, UN peacekeeping has been a positive factor, even if far from an inspiring success.

Peacekeeping: Cyprus   445

Monitoring order in a divided island nation. The United Nations Force in Cyprus (UNFICYP) was deployed on the island in 1964 in order to separate warring Turkish and Greek Cypriot communities. Cyprus is the home of a population that is 80 percent Greek (approximately 400,000) and 20 percent Turk (approximately 100,000). A consequence of history, Cyprus was an extension of ancient Greek civilization, but the Ottoman Turks seized the island and overran Greece itself, dominating the Hellenic world for almost 400 years. The descendants of Greek and Turk communities on the island of Cyprus are representative of this earlier history. The British Empire took control of Cyprus in 1878, and it remained under colonial rule until after World War II. Cyprus insisted on independence from Britain in the postwar years, but difficulties in establishing a government that spoke for both communities produced the instabilities that provoked intervention from both Greece and Turkey. Athens initially sought to unify Cyprus with Greece, but this plan met with stiff resistance from the Turk community on the island, and Ankara reinforced their dissatisfaction. The UN peacekeeping operation in Cyprus tried to buy time for the negotiators, who were pressed to find a compromise solution that would leave the island a unified entity. However, increasing violence between the communities and a military coup, allegedly inspired from Athens, provoked Turkey to intervene. In the escalated fighting between Turkish and Greek Cypriot forces, the latter supported by Greece, the island was effectively partitioned in the 1970s and remains divided in the 1990s.

Significance

The historic hostility between Greeks and Turks plays out in contemporary life in Cyprus. The UN peacekeeping mission on the island can do little more than monitor conditions and interpose itself between the antagonists so that the two communities can find a semblance of tranquility within their respective zones. Plans to end the partition have failed, but the United Nations is reluctant to remove UNFICYP, believing that its continuing presence at the very least helps to bring a degree of calm to an otherwise tense environment. To measure the success of a UN peacekeeping mission, the historic character of the problem must be appreciated and assessed. No UN peacekeeping force is capable of reconciling centuries of conflict between Turks and Greeks, and although critics of UN peacekeeping point to the number of "failed" missions, it is also necessary to acknowledge the absence of answers to hard questions. The patience displayed by the peacekeepers in UNFICYP demonstrates that even in otherwise hopelessly insoluble situations, at least a modicum of peace is possible.

Peacekeeping: Multinational Force and Observers (MFO) | 446 |

Peacekeeping mission in the Sinai peninsula. The MFO is among the more successful peacekeeping missions operating in various sectors of the globe. Serving in the Sinai peninsula, a consequence of the Israeli-Egyptian Peace Treaty of 1979, MFO is drawn from 11 countries and represents a contingent of 2,000 lightly armed soldiers, at least half of whom are U.S. troops. Unlike other peacekeeping forces in places like Bosnia, Cyprus, Cambodia, Haiti, or Rawanda, MFO is not answerable to the United Nations or any other international body. Individual countries favorably disposed toward the peace treaty between Israel and Egypt supply units from their respective military establishments with the approval of the treaty principals. The contributing countries determine the force's commander, who need not be (and often has not been) an American. The non-UN character of the operation was insisted upon by Israel, which did not want a repeat of an earlier peacekeeping experience that triggered the 1967 war. That earlier mission placed UN forces in Sharm al-Shaykh, a strategic location in the Sinai at the entrance of the Strait of Tiran. Egypt's call in 1967 to the UN secretary-general to withdraw that force, and the United Nations' compliance, was perceived in Israel as a prelude to a renewal of hostilities, and Israel struck Egypt before the latter could launch its attack. Israel agreed to relinquish control of the Sinai (occupied during the 1967 war) in 1979, but it insisted that a third force be positioned on the peninsula, preferably American, and not affiliated with the United Nations. The outcome of extended deliberations was the MFO, which has monitored activities in the region on a self-perpetuating basis. Egypt would like to see MFO withdraw from its sovereign territory, but MFO remains to remind these nations of their pledges to avoid a return to the battlefield. *See also* PEACEKEEPING (443); PEACEKEEPING: UNPROFOR (451); PEACEMAKING: UNOSOM II (455).

Significance
The Sinai-positioned Multinational Force and Observers has been so successful that a similar operation was suggested for the Golan Heights, and may be an integral feature of a future Israeli-Syrian peace treaty. Israeli withdrawal from the Golan Heights would signify the demilitarization of the region and the interposition of an effective international monitoring force. Insofar as it is the United States that presses the settlement between Tel Aviv and Damascus, Washington may well assume major responsibility for enforcing peace. Israel's concern that a UN peacekeeping operation would be inadequate for the responsibility necessitates the creation of a peacekeeping operation that would not crumble in crisis or be subject to narrowly defined political pressures. Israel has sufficient reason to hold Hafiz al-Assad to a higher test and to demand a cessation of all Syrian-sponsored terrorist organizations, including Hezbollah and its Iranian connection. Syria's major presence in Lebanon, the seat of Hezbollah, places it in a position to neutralize the organization. The question is: Will it do so, and at what cost? Building confidence between Israel and Syria, therefore, is far more difficult than those relationships established with Egypt and Jordan. Observers are legitimately skeptical, and fear Israel's yielding of the Golan to Syria will precipitate more hostilities, not reduce them. U.S. critics of the plan also argue against placing U.S. soldiers in the Golan Heights because they could be caught in the middle of a conflict that might well be precipitated by the Israelis. In such circumstances, what would be the response of the United States, and are U.S. troops being placed needlessly at risk? Although the Sinai MFO has not been targeted by terrorist organizations, the fear persists that the Golan, more exposed to unreconciled fundamentalist/terrorist groups, would take advantage of the opportunity to destroy any peace process.

Peacekeeping: Peacekeepers | 447 |
The human toll in peacekeeping missions. In April 1995 the United Nations cited the number of peacekeepers lost while serving in programs authorized by the world organization. From June 1948, when the first peacekeeping (emergency) mission was dispatched to the Middle East in an effort to pacify the area disrupted by the Israeli-Arab conflict, to January 1995, 748 UN peacekeepers have lost their lives. Of this number, 299 were killed by hostile fire; the remaining 449 died from illnesses and accidents. By 1995 there had been 34 UN peacekeeping missions, and 17 were still in operation. The largest operation in the mid-1990s was the involvement in the former Yugoslavia, notably Bosnia, Croatia, and Macedonia. In a separate report issued in 1995, the UN Secretariat announced that compensation had been paid to the families of the soldiers lost in UN missions, but that such payments varied in accordance with national laws prevailing in the different countries. Thus a family of a soldier from the industrial nations could receive $85,300, while those from less developed countries received only $19,500. Given the discrepancy in death payments, a UN working committee was to be established by the General Assembly to standardize this procedure.

Significance
The UN report on losses suffered by UN peacekeepers in a variety of missions authorized by the Security Council or the General Assembly focuses attention on the great risks such forces assume when engaged in UN actions aimed at promoting peace. The difference in death payments to the families of those killed in the service of the United Nations also raises questions concerning the different missions because the majority of the peacekeepers are drawn from Third World or developing nations. Pakistan, India, and Bangladesh have provided the larger share of the forces, and these countries have suffered the higher losses. Although the level of training of the peacekeepers varies from

country to country, and the troops drawn from the developing nations are often judged to be lacking in expertise, without their service and the commitment of their nations, UN peacekeeping operations would be impossible. The Clinton administration, while rejecting the use of U.S. ground forces in the Bosnian civil war in September 1995 agreed, despite congressional objections, to send 25,000 members of the U.S. armed forces to police a peace settlement. That force comprised about 16,000 army personnel, 2,000 marines, 1,000 airmen, and 6,000 naval personnel. The administration made it clear that these servicemen would be used only to implement a peace settlement and would remain no more than one year. Clinton also reiterated that they would not be peacekeepers in the UN mold; they were not being sent to do combat, but nevertheless would be heavily armed to deter peace violators.

Peacekeeping: Safe Havens   448

Metropolitan centers identified by the UN peacekeeping force in Bosnia for special protection from Bosnian Serb guns. The safe haven cities were Srebrenica, Bihac, Goradze, Zepa, and Tuzla, all reputed to be Muslim-Bosnian, all coming under sustained heavy attack, and all confined to relatively small pockets of resistance. According to the 1992 census in Bosnia and Herzegovina, Muslims constituted 44 percent of the population, Serbs 31 percent, and Croats more than 17 percent. In the initial period of the war, the Bosnian Serbs drew support from Greater Serbia. Indeed, it was Serbia's policy to extend its rule over much of Bosnia, as it had in Croatia. By 1994 the Bosnian Serbs reportedly controlled almost 70 percent of Bosnia and Herzegovina. Thus, the Serbs could order the forced removal/liquidation of Bosnian Muslims from areas where the latter were previously in the majority. The Serb program of "ethnic cleansing" provoked the world's conscience, and UNPROFOR, the UN peacekeeping force in Bosnia, de-

clared its intention to protect some of the more threatened urban areas, hence the "safe haven" concept. UNPROFOR was authorized by the UN secretary-general to assist the people "trapped" in these "protected" areas, and if necessary to call upon NATO command for backup aid. Although the safe havens provided some sanctuary for their bloated refugee populations, Bosnian Serb violations were legion, especially in and around Bihac, Tuzla, Srebrenica, Zepa, and Goradze, which could not truly be protected by the United Nations or NATO, despite their designations as a "safe havens." In July 1995 both Srebrenica and Zepa were overrun by Serb forces while the UN protection force looked on and NATO refrained from taking action. *See also* ETHNIC CLEANSING (45); ETHNIC CONFLICT (47); ETHNICITY (51); PEACEKEEPING: UNPROFOR (451).

Significance
The safe haven policy established by UN forces in Bosnia provided little more than a brief respite from the continued fighting or the many atrocities that characterized the war in the former Yugoslavian state. Safe havens for Muslims also meant a prohibition on arms to the Bosnian Muslims. That same prohibition, however, had little if any effect on the Bosnian Serbs. Even after Serbia declared that it would cease providing weapons to the Serbs in Bosnia and Herzegovina, the Bosnian Serbs appeared quite capable of accessing the weapons needed to protract the conflict. Although the UN embargo on arms to the Muslims was sustained, clandestine shipments were received from a variety of sources, especially Iran. Safe havens did nothing to end the war, but they helped reduce the number of civilian casualties from more than 100,000 in 1993 to something under 10,000 in 1994. The seizure of Srebrenica and Zepa was followed by the forced separation of men and boys from women and female children, and the reported killing of many of the former by Serb forces. Given the feeble character of the UN response, 16 countries met in London

in July 1995 to determine a NATO response if the Serbs sustained their assaults on the "safe havens." As a result of those deliberations the United States, along with France and Britain, declared intentions to take aggressive action against Bosnian Serb forces if they intended to do likewise in Goradze and Bihac. In August, however, Croatian troops entered the war, ostensibly to recover the Krajina region of Croatia seized by the Serbs in 1991, but also to repulse the assault by Serb forces against Bihac. Croatian victories in the Krajina region spurred the Bosnian Muslims to join in the struggle against the Serbs thus breaking the siege of Bihac. The international community braced itself for the possible entry into the war of Serbia proper, and if such was the case, to the widening of the war. Whatever the outcome of the struggle, however, it was obvious that the UN safe haven policy was a failure and that NATO had been upstaged by Croatia. The failure of the "safe haven" program, however, galvanized the Americans and a punishing air attack by NATO in August-September 1995 against Bosnian Serb installations and command centers eventually lifted the siege of Sarajevo, and Assistant Secretary of State Richard Holbrooke led a diplomatic mission aimed at terminating the hostilities. Faced with heavy NATO airstrikes and the loss of territory to combined Croatian-Bosnian Muslim forces, in September the Holbrooke-engineered agreement was tentatively accepted by the Serbs and other warring parties. The agreement called for the creation of a single Bosnian state within which the Serbs would control 49 percent of the territory, and the Muslim-Croat Federation 51 percent. A weak central government was to be installed in Sarajevo, and Bosnia-Herzegovina would accommodate an entity to be known as Srpska (Serb-dominated). Confederal links would tie Srpska to Bosnia-Herzegovina. Because Serbia proper sanctioned the Holbrooke plan, UN sanctions imposed on Belgrade in 1992 were to be lifted. While the Holbrooke plan had achieved a modicum of success, it was acknowledged that the opposed sides had not yet made peace.

Peacekeeping: United Nations Mission in Haiti (UNMIH) | 449 |

United Nations peacekeeping and U.S. peacemaking responsibilities in Haiti. Initially an all-U.S. operation, UNMIH signaled the general success of the U.S. action in restoring President Jean-Bertrand Aristide to the office he had been forced to yield some years earlier. But reestablishing the Haitian president in his elected office was only the first of a number of still more challenging objectives. The U.S. forces were directed to disassemble the military/police organization that had terrorized the Haitian population and replace it with better-trained, more disciplined, professional law-enforcement institutions. Having created an ambience in which to build a more secure foundation for the Haitian nation, the United States urged the United Nations to take over the major chores that lay ahead. The affirmative response from the United Nations came on 30 January 1995 when the Security Council approved the transfer and called upon the secretary-general to create the mechanism. UNMIH was the result of this effort in March 1995. It was agreed that UNMIH would consist of 6,000 soldiers and police, 2,500 from the United States and the remaining 3,500 coming from Pakistan (the major contributor, with an initial force of 800), Bangladesh, Nepal, France, Canada, Honduras, Guatemala, and the Caribbean (CARICOM). The orders to UNMIH described a six-month peacekeeping operation and an extended program to assist Haiti in organizing a professional police agency, separate from a reconstituted army. *See also* PEACEKEEPING (443); PEACEMAKING (452–456).

Significance

The United Nations Mission in Haiti was assembled by the United Nations at the insistence of the Clinton administration, which was faced with considerable domestic pressure to withdraw all its troops from the island. UNMIH enabled the United States to maintain at least enough force in Haiti to sustain its protection of Aristide, as well as oversee the development of new military and police institutions. Although peacekeeping was judged less and less an activity for the U.S. armed forces, it was acknowledged that a total U.S. withdrawal would doom all the projects planned for the island nation. UNMIH was not given much chance of achieving its goals, and with UN peacekeeping operations under pressure all over the globe, some observers argued that UNMIH would do irreversible damage to the UN's peacekeeping/peacemaking role. The UN mission's initial success somewhat silenced the critics, but the elections of 1995 were seriously flawed and the discordant voices were again energized, notably in the U.S. Congress.

Peacekeeping: UN Operations | 450 |

A summary of some of the United Nation's most significant peacekeeping missions. UN peacekeeping operations began in 1948 when the first emergency force was dispatched to the Middle East. UN peacekeepers are drawn largely from Third World nations in Asia-Africa and from Canada and Eastern Europe. The major powers are generally but not necessarily excluded from the assembled forces, but they are most prominent in providing the logistic and financial support necessary for the operations. The principal UN peacekeeping forces are: United Nations Good Offices Mission in Afghanistan and Pakistan (UNGOMAP), United Nations India-Pakistan Observation Mission (UNIPOM), United Nations Interim Force in Lebanon (UNIFIL), United Nations Iran-Iraq Military Observer Group (UNIIMOG), United Nations Iraq-Kuwait Observation Mission (UNIKOM), United Nations Military Observer Group in India and Pakistan (UNMOGIP), United Nations Mission for the Referendum in Western Sahara (MINURSO), United Nations Mission in Haiti (UNMIH), United Nations Observation Group in Lebanon

(UNOGIL), United Nations Observer Group in Central America (ONUCA), United Nations Observer Mission in El Salvador (ONUSAL), United Nations Observer Mission in Georgia (UNMIG), United Nations Observer Mission in Liberia (UNOMIL), United Nations Observer Mission in Uganda and Rwanda (UNOMUR), United Nations Operation in Mozambique (UNOMOZ), United Nations Operations in Somalia (UNOSOM), United Nations Force in Cyprus (UNFICYP), United Nations Protection Force in the Former Yugoslavia (UNPROFOR), United Nations Transitional Authority in Cambodia (UNTAC), and United Nations Yemen Observation Mission (UNYOM). *See also* PEACEKEEPING: PEACEKEEPERS, (447); PEACEMAKING: PEACEBUILDING (454).

Significance

The number of UN peacekeeping missions has multiplied since the end of the Cold War, virtually bankrupting the world organization. Major donor countries such as the United States have registered a desire to scale back their contributions. Moreover, the diversity and complexity of the conflicts confronting the lightly armed and essentially noncombative peacekeepers present the United Nations with impossible choices. Primarily concerned with humanitarian assistance, the peacekeepers themselves are not involved in the conflicts, and too often the hostile parties ignore UN efforts to relieve populations under threat. The peacekeeping missions are dependent on the cooperation of all sides to a conflict, and in the absence of such assistance, their missions are judged little more than futile gestures. The future of the UN peacekeeping operations was placed in special jeopardy following the March 1995 withdrawal of UNOSOM from Somalia and the ineffectiveness of the UNPROFOR operation in Bosnia.

Peacekeeping: UNPROFOR | 451 |

United Nations Protection Force. Originally a 23,000-troop contingent, with some 21,000 stationed in Bosnia, the force was sent as peacekeepers to protect humanitarian agencies in the distribution of food and medicine to the innocent population victimized by the Bosnian civil war. The force was supported by air units from NATO, predominantly American, as well as a nightly airlift flying food and medicine to Sarajevo and other beleaguered Bosnian cities. The airlift, involving NATO aircraft, represented the largest effort of its kind in world history. UNPROFOR also had the mission of interposing itself between the belligerents with the anticipation that its noncombative presence would be respected by the warring factions and would provide, for those seeking a negotiated settlement, an appropriate climate in which to perform their duties, that is, to find a political settlement to the dilemma of Bosnia. UNPROFOR was not slated, nor was it directed, to participate in the fighting, let alone take sides. In June 1995 the UNPROFOR force comprised 3,493 French, 3,283 British, 2,973 Pakistani, 1,539 Malaysians, 1,485 Dutch, 1,468 Turks, 1,402 Spanish, 1,239 Bangladeshi, 995 Swedes, 801 Canadians, 712 Norwegians, 609 Ukrainians, 507 Russians, 430 Egyptians, 254 Danes, 253 New Zealanders, 100 Jordanians, and 96 Belgians. It also maintained a presence in Croatia. *See also* ASSERTIVE MULTILATERALISM (618); ETHNIC CLEANSING (45); ETHNIC WARS (48–50); PEACEKEEPING: PEACEKEEPERS (447); PEACEKEEPING: SAFE HAVENS (448); PEACE-MAKING: CONTACT GROUP (452); PEACE-MAKING: VANCE-OWEN PLAN (456); TRANSNATIONAL PATTERN: RAPID REACTION FORCE (RRF) (713).

Significance
The United Nations Protection Force represented the United Nations' most ambitious peacekeeping effort following the end of the Cold War. It also also proved to be its most difficult operation, and the failure of the peace mission, not the humanitarian effort, dealt a severe blow to UN peacekeeping activities. A nonbelligerent force, it was attacked militarily and politically, verbally and psychologically.

Lightly armed and spread over a vast area in many small units, UNPROFOR troops were easy targets for the belligerents, particularly the Serbs, who in May–June 1995 seized more than 300 UNPROFOR troops, declaring them to be prisoners of war. Operating in mountainous terrain, UNPROFOR could not defend itself, let alone provide physical protection for the victims of the savage ethnic war. Ultimately, the mission became one of the targets in the protracted conflict, suffering numerous casualties. The Security Council contemplated removing UNPROFOR in the fall of 1994, but the difficulties involved in extricating the force from the war scene, and the negative impact that such a withdrawal would have on the United Nations, overruled that option. The withdrawal option surfaced again in the spring of 1995 when both UNPROFOR troops and civilians were seized by defiant Bosnian Serbs who declared their intention to wreak a bloodbath on UN forces if NATO were to mount a rescue mission. In response to the hostage problem, France, Britain, and the Netherlands assembled a Rapid Reaction Force (RRF) of 10,000 troops, made up of army contingents more adequately armed for the conditions in Bosnia. By June 1995 some of these troops began arriving in the region. The sending countries declared that they had no intention of siding with one group or another, but that the RRF would be responsible for protecting the peacekeepers and would not be included in UNPROFOR (they were not being sent to protect the civilian population). This effort at salvaging the UN peacekeeping operation in Bosnia received the encouragement of the UN secretary-general and President Clinton, but Clinton made it clear that U.S. troops would not be used for the RRF. On the other hand, U.S. policy seemed to indicate that U.S. troops would be used if UNPROFOR required emergency evacuation or relocation. Conditions on the ground in Bosnia, however, were little changed. On the one side, the United Nations continued to deny arms to the Muslim Bosnians, while their Bosnian Serb adversaries had no difficulty in procuring their war materiel. On the other, even the bolstered UNPROFOR presence merely acted as a wedge for the Bosnian Serbs in Bosnian Muslim territory. Unwittingly, UNPROFOR made it possible for the Bosnian Serbs to press their objectives and consolidate their territorial gains. It appeared that the United Nations could not go forward nor retreat, and this ambiguity played into the hands of the Serbs, who believed they could operate with impunity where the international community was involved. In the end, UNPROFOR peacekeepers were mere hostages, left to the mercy of the aggressive Bosnian Serbs. Initial NATO air attacks proved to be little more than pinpricks that further incensed the Serbs and put the UN peacekeepers at greater risk. Cease-fires were arranged and broken, or only purchased time for the belligerents to catch their breath, store more weapons, and plan their next moves. So-called safe havens proved to be free-fire zones, and UNPROFOR postured a helplessness that did little for the war-weary civilian population. Diplomatic missions by the European Union, the Conference on Security and Cooperation in Europe, the UN special negotiators, the personal intervention of former President Jimmy Carter—all failed to produce the desired results. The Contact Group (made up of representatives from the United States, Russia, France, Great Britain, and Germany) also proved unsuccessful, although entreaties to the Serbian leader, Slobodan Milosevic, did from time to time result in some temporary arrangements that reduced immediate tensions. The Greek intervention with Milosevic in June 1995 over the taking of UNPROFOR hostages also bore some fruit. UNPROFOR members were released from captivity, but nothing had been accomplished in bringing a satisfactory end to conflict. Given the intractable nature of the Bosnian ethnic war, criticism of the UN operation was easy, but on closer analysis it is clear that no agency, institution, nation, or individual enjoyed any more success or gained any more respect than the

United Nations. Never were so many humiliated by so few—the reputations of a host of nations and international organizations suffered as a consequence of the Bosnian conflict. In what was described as a last attempt to find a diplomatic and political solution to the Bosnian civil war, the Clinton administration organized a negotiating team that was led by Assistant Secretary of State Richard Holbrooke. Prompted by Croatian military victories in Croatia's Krajina region in July–August 1995 and by successful joint Croatian–Bosnian Muslim actions in relieving the siege of Bihac, Holbrooke pressed the Serbs to accept a political settlement that would leave them with less than their Bosnian gains, but with almost half of all Bosnian territory. These negotiations were protracted due to Bosnian Serb reluctance to yield any territory. Three high-ranking American negotiators, key members of Holbrooke's team, were killed in a road accident outside of Sarajevo, but the assistant secretary pressed on with his mission. Further incidents on the ground, allegedly provoked by Bosnian Serbs, complicated the diplomatic effort. So too the NATO air campaign commenced on 30 August 1995 and was declared to be ongoing until the Bosnian Serbs removed their heavy artillery from positions around Sarajevo and other "safe havens." Serb leader Slobodan Milosevic used the occasion of the NATO air campaign to announce that he would negotiate in behalf of the Bosnian Serbs, hinting that the Holbrooke mission could be the long-awaited catalyst for a compromise solution to the Bosnian problem, and possibly to the larger question of peace in the region of the former Yugoslavia. By October 1995, continuing but sporadic NATO air attacks on Bosnian Serb targets and joint Croat-Bosnian Muslim successes on the battlefield forced the Bosnian Serbs to accept a U.S.-arranged cease-fire. Indications that the Bosnian civil war had entered a more concerted diplomatic phase included a U.S.-hosted peace conference, the planned phase out of UNPROFOR and their replacement by a heavily equipped 60,000-man NATO force (including a sizeable contingent of Americans), and the reassignment of Yasushi Akashi, the chief UN representative in Bosnia. Akashi had assumed his role in Bosnia following a successful tour in Cambodia in 1993. He departed Bosnia, however, under a cloud of controversy that centered on the weakness of the United Nations in aggressive situations.

Peacemaking: Contact Group   452

A group formed by the United States, Russia, France, Great Britain, and Germany to find a peaceful settlement for the war in Bosnia. Assembled by the great powers most concerned with the situation in the former Yugoslav republic (Italy registered its concern but was not invited to join the group), the Contact Group moved between the parties to the conflict, offering diplomatic solutions and sometimes threatening to use force against the recalcitrant parties, notably the Serbs. The Contact Group was divided in its thinking and decisionmaking because of the different positions taken by the United States and Russia (the United States supporting the Bosnian Muslims and the Russians, the Serbs). However, the Contact Group seemed to reach common agreement in May–June 1995 after the Bosnian Serbs took UN peacekeepers hostage and threatened their lives. Despite the Bosnian Serb seizure of the "safe havens" of Srebrenica and Zepa in July 1995 the Contact Group was still determined to press for a diplomatic solution to the problem of Bosnia. The successful Croat offensive in the Krajina region and the link-up of Croat and Bosnian Muslim forces to relieve the Serb seizure of Bihac (in August) was viewed as opening new possibilities for a new diplomatic solution. The Contact Group also saw the Croat victory over the Serbs in a negative light, that is, as the spreading of the conflict to include the Belgrade Serbs. *See also* ETHNIC CLEANSING (45); ETHNIC WARS (48–50); PEACEMAKING: VANCE-OWEN PLAN (456).

Significance
The Contact Group was no more successful in persuading the parties in the Bosnian war to terminate their military actions than the many efforts made by delegations from the United Nations, the Conference for Security and Cooperation in Europe, or the European Union. The NATO members of the Contact Group were inclined to threaten the use of force, and on several occasions NATO aircraft attacked Serbian positions. The most significant attack pressured the Serbs to seek a negotiated settlement. U.S.-Russian differences over the NATO air campaign, however, strained relations within the Contact Group.

Peacemaking: Northern Ireland   453

Seeking a peaceful solution for the problem of Northern Ireland. After decades of conflict, and the sacrifice of several thousand lives, diplomatic efforts by Great Britain and the Republic of Ireland paid off in 1994 with an agreement to discuss avenues for peaceful settlement. The Anglo-Irish Agreement signed at Hillsborough on 15 November 1985 by Prime Minister Margaret Thatcher of Britain and Prime Minister Garrett Fitzgerald of Ireland provided the background for these later developments. In their agreement the two leaders called for a closer working relationship to promote peace and stability in Northern Ireland, reconcile Protestants and Catholics, create a climate of friendship, and cooperate in combating terrorism. They established a joint ministerial conference and a permanent secretariat to monitor political security, as well as the legal question and other issues of concern to the Catholic minority of Northern Ireland. Thus, by 1994 the principals in the struggle—the Irish Republican Army's (IRA) Sinn Fein and the Ulster Defense Force—were prepared to carry the process forward. They called for a cessation of their terrorist assaults while the negotiators searched for a political formula favorable to both sides. The most immediate issue concerned the need to disarm the parties who were most reluctant to yield their weapons. Britain refused to be fazed by this problem, and its willingness to negotiate directly with Sinn Fein while continuing its talks with Dublin departed from standing British policy. As a terrorist organization, Sinn Fein never received London's recognition as a legitimate negotiating partner, especially following the numerous IRA-organized bombing incidents in London. Britain nevertheless put aside that policy and arduously pursued a full-fledged peace conference that could involve all the parties, whether or not they had been sufficiently disarmed.

Significance
The breakthrough in Northern Ireland's long period of civil strife came when Sinn Fein leader Jerry Adams offered to halt IRA actions in Ulster and Britain proper in return for direct talks with British authorities. London agreed to the trade-off in concert with the Irish government, and the cease-fire arranged between the parties provided the first opportunity in a quarter-century for the people of Northern Ireland to experience relative tranquility. The IRA demand that British troops in Northern Ireland not only stand down but withdraw met with positive British reaction, but the implementation of a withdrawal was predicated on the success of the IRA disarmament program. Along with the arsenal of weapons under IRA control, London insisted on the destruction of IRA stores of the plastic explosive Semtex, which had been used against targets in Britain. IRA reluctance to yield such weapons meant British peacemaking operations in Northern Ireland would continue during the period of tedious negotiations. In 1995, in a sharp difference of opinion over IRA disarmament, Ireland's prime minister, John Bruton, openly aligned himself with the IRA, claiming that the IRA-allied Sinn Fein party should be brought into multiparty negotiations even if the IRA refused to dispose of its weapons.

Peacemaking: Peacebuilding ⏐454⏐
The focus on the removal of the structural causes of conflict (social, economic, humanitarian, ethnic, sectarian, and environmental conditions that contribute to the outbreak of violence). Until these conflict elements are satisfactorily addressed, no amount of peacekeeping can have lasting effect. Peacekeeping measures are ephemeral if they cannot provide for a more or less general settlement of a dispute. Peacekeepers may contain the physical violence necessary to provide humanitarian assistance and they may succeed in leading the protagonists to the conference table, but if the underlying problems are not addressed, they will continue to provoke the actions of the more violence-prone members of a troubled society. The threat that hostilities can be reignited at any time taxes the energy and will of the peacekeepers. Therefore, peacekeeping efforts are rewarded only when peacebuilding is successfully pursued. But peacebuilding is far more difficult than peacekeeping. To have a measure of success, peacebuilding must be launched before a peacekeeping mission begins, and must remain in place long after the peacemaking campaign is completed. The long-term commitment to peacebuilding assigns responsibilities to peacekeepers and peacemakers that they are reluctant to assume, given the cost to them in financial and human terms. The United Nations has assumed the role of the major peacekeeper and peacemaker, but it has failed in many of its missions because the more significant role of peacebuilder cannot be shouldered by an international organization dependent on the quixotic support it receives from the world's major powers. Indeed, the expense of UN peacekeeping operations following the Cold War has bankrupted the organization, and the failure of peacebuilding efforts threatens its very foundations. *See also* PEACEKEEPING (443); PEACEKEEPING: UNPROFOR (451); PEACEMAKING: UNOSOM II (455).

Significance
Peacebuilding is a more controversial subject than peacekeeping because it projects long-term involvement in a country's internal affairs. Moreover, it is expensive and does not necessarily enhance the national interest of the states supplying the peacebuilding elements. Critics of peacebuilding ventures argue that the long-term presence of a peacebuilding force, no matter how humanitarian its outlook, will be judged an unwanted force by the indigenous population. What begins as an act of compassion, they assert, will degenerate into ugly confrontations between the still-unreconciled groups within the target society. They cite the failed peacebuilding operation in Somalia that began as an effort to feed a starving population and quickly deteriorated into a factional conflict that consumed the peacekeepers and peacebuilders alike. The UN retreat from Somalia in March 1995 is cited as proof that peacebuilding is not a realistic program for the United Nations. Opposition to peacekeeping, let alone peacebuilding, in the United States reached crescendo force in 1995. U.S. criticism of the United Nations is revealed in the United States' reluctance to meet its financial obligations to the organization. By 1995 the UN debt had risen to more than $4 billion, with the United States and Russia the countries most in arrears. UN peacebuilding efforts seem likely to diminish in the years ahead.

Peacemaking: UNOSOM II $\boxed{455}$
United Nations Operation in Somalia. Originally a peacekeeping force, it later assumed peacemaking responsibilities that were sanctioned by Security Council Resolutions 794 and 814. UNOSOM was comprised of essentially Asian and African contingents following the withdrawal of U.S. forces, which had initiated the Somali intervention. The UN resolutions authorized UN Secretary-General Boutros Boutros-Ghali to assume responsibility from the U.S.-led Unified Task

Force (UNITAF) that invaded Somalia in December 1992. The Americans had been dispatched to Somalia by President George Bush to protect relief workers attempting to feed Somalia's destitute population. Famine relief had been made impossible by roving bands of Somali gunmen in the pay of regional headmen. They had dominated the Somali political scene following the overthrow of the long-term Somali dictator, Siad Barre. UNITAF opened Mogadishu's seaport and airfield for a major relief program, neutralized many of the armed groups, and orchestrated a conference of reconciliation between Somali headmen in March 1993. Given the general success of the initial operation, the UNITAF mission was expanded into a peacemaking operation by the UN secretary-general, who ordered the disarming of the militias of the rival headmen prior to beginning the process of organizing a formal government for Somalia. Under the principle of "assertive multilateralism," the Clinton administration arranged for the commingling of the UNITAF mission with that of UNOSOM II when the latter assumed primary responsibility for the UN operation in Somalia on 4 May 1993. However, Somali factional leaders opposed UNOSOM, and on 5 June 1993, 23 Pakistani members of the UN force were ambushed and killed while attempting to search a weapons depot controlled by the militia of Mohammad Farah Aidid, a leading headman in Mogadishu. The UN Security Council issued still another resolution calling for the apprehension of Aidid, and Resolution 837 increased the number of troops attached to UNOSOM. The Aidid faction's assault on a small contingent of American UNITAF troops caused a number of American deaths. The dead soldiers were dragged through the streets of Mogadishu, and cameras caught the sequence for transmission around the world. Despite a substantial effort, neither U.S. nor UN forces were able to capture Aidid, and growing criticism in the U.S. Congress over the change in the Somali mission forced the Clinton administration to withdraw the UNITAF force. Subject to continuing factional struggles by rival Somali clans, the United Nations approved Resolution 865, establishing March 1995 as the date for terminating the UN peacekeeping operation in Somalia. *See also* PEACEKEEPING: UNPROFOR (451); ASSERTIVE MULTILATERALISM (618).

Significance:
UNOSOM II nurtured a desperate population, but it could not ensure an elected government nor provide for functioning institutions. Most important, it could not reconcile the competing clans. UNOSOM's tasks proved to be a "mission impossible," and with the U.S. departure, the force—lacking in coordination or discipline, limited in expertise, and totally inept at fathoming the character of the Somali tribal order—was an easy target for Somali gunmen. Although the Somali intervention achieved some humanitarian successes, UN peacekeeping and peacemaking suffered grievous setbacks. Moreover, given the demonstrated weakness of the United Nations in Bosnia, the United Nations' role as the primary guarantor of the peace was significantly undermined. UNOSOM II's humiliating retreat from Somalia in March 1995 required the return of an U.S. protective force, giving a negative twist to "assertive multilateralism." It also hinted at the future failure of other UN peacekeeping and peacemaking missions.

Peacemaking: Vance-Owen Plan

$\boxed{456}$

A 1992–1993 UN-sponsored peace plan aimed at stopping the bloodshed in Bosnia (formerly a constituent unit within the Yugoslav Federation). Drawn up by international mediators Cyrus Vance, a former U.S. secretary of state, and Lord David Owen, a British European Community representative, the plan sought to placate all sides in the conflict over the final disposition of Bosnia. In this struggle between Bosnian Serbs, Croats, and Muslims, the Muslims claimed the right to rule over Bosnia-Herzegovina as originally constituted during the late Yugoslav Federation. The Bosnian Serbs rejected this claim and, provided with support from brother Serbs in Serbia, launched attacks on the other ethnic groups with the intention of allowing the battlefield to determine the ultimate status and character of the territory. Insofar as the Serbs were largely successful in their military campaign against both the Croats and the Muslims, the United Nations pressed for a political settlement that more or less reflected the political realities on the ground. Given the failure of the European Union and the Conference on Security and Cooperation in Europe to mediate the conflict, the United Nations advanced the Vance-Owen Plan. The plan called for dividing Bosnia-Herzegovina into ten largely autonomous, ethnic-based provinces with a centralizing government comprising the different ethnicities. However, by the terms of the plan, the Bosnian Serbs would have been required to forgo much of the territory seized during the hostilities, and they rejected it outright. The Bosnian Muslims were no more inclined to accept the plan, which appeared to rule out the creation of an independent Bosnia. In the end, the plan was rejected by all the warring parties, and the conflict raged on pending still another solution. *See also* POPULATION TRANSFER (180).

Significance
The Vance-Owen Plan never had much chance of success considering the established independence of Croatia and Slovenia prior to Bosnia's declaration of independence. More important, Serbia, with Montenegro, was determined to establish Greater Serbia. The earlier and largely successful Serbian campaign against the Croats heralded a significant clash between Serbs and Bosnian Muslims in Bosnia-Herzegovina, where the Serbs had a substantial minority population. The Vance-Owen Plan therefore satisfied none of the belligerents, and the political geography it described was acknowledged to be more of a stimulant to continue the hostilities than a promise of

their termination. Vance retired from the scene after the failure of the plan, and although Owen teamed up with another European, Count von Stoltenberg, to press still another arrangement (the Owen-Stoltenberg Plan), these efforts were no more successful. Owen remained in the middle of the diplomatic effort until June 1995, when he announced his retirement. Former president Jimmy Carter offered his good offices in the fall of 1994; he was able to get little more than a cease-fire that simply allowed all the sides additional time to acquisition new stores of arms. The failure of the Vance-Owen Plan was an early signal that even-handed diplomacy would not succeed in the Bosnian conflict. The Vance-Owen negotiations, however, did have a positive dimension. They prepared the groundwork for subsequent diplomatic efforts, notably the one led by U.S. assistant secretary of state Richard Holbrooke during the summer and fall of 1995. Moreover, the Holbrooke Plan for peace in Bosnia was something of a modified Vance-Owen Plan, but deemed to be more realistic and hence more workable. Although the Holbrooke proposal reduced Bosnian Serb gains, it left them with a sizeable portion of the state. Most important, the territorial divisions called for coherent and contiguous territories that enhanced communication and transportation, promoted unity, and avoided unnecessary fragmentation. The Holbrooke Plan in fact called for a confederation of Bosnia-Herzegovina that included a separate Republika Srpska drawn from 49 percent of the territory. This Serb entity was to be loosely affiliated with the 51 percent of the region that was to be governed from Sarajevo. The Holbrooke Plan supposedly left Bosnia a unified country, but it also acknowledged Bosnian Serb control of almost half the original territory of Bosnia-Herzegovina. Although achieving the necessary support from the parties, the details of the plan waited on a cessation of hostilities and a more concerted effort at bringing peace to the region.

Recognition: Governments | 457 |

An official act, such as an exchange of ambassadors, that acknowledges the existence of a government and indicates readiness to engage in formal relations with it. Recognition of a new state cannot be accomplished without recognizing the government in power. For this reason, confusion often arises concerning recognition of states and recognition of governments. Recognition of a state, once accomplished, continues for the life of the state, even when a particular government of that state is not recognized. After the Russian Revolution of 1917, for instance, the United States continued to recognize the Russian state even though it did not recognize the Soviet government until 1933. Recognition of a government is not perpetual and may be granted or withheld with each change of regime. A break in diplomatic relations, however, is not a withdrawal of recognition.

Significance
International lawyers are divided on whether or not recognition of governments is a matter of legal right and duty. The practice of states, however, indicates that recognition is regarded as essentially a unilateral political decision. Although historically the United States granted recognition to new governments that demonstrated effective control, during President Woodrow Wilson's administration the United States made "constitutionality" or "legitimacy" of a new regime the prerequisite for U.S. recognition. In a statement of doctrine associated with his name, in 1930 Foreign Minister Don Genaro Estrada of Mexico held that the granting or withholding of recognition for political reasons was an improper and insulting intervention in the domestic affairs of another sovereign state because it constituted an external judgment of the legal qualifications of a foreign regime. Opponents of the Estrada Doctrine point out that the purpose of recognition is not the passing of judgment but merely the unavoidable necessity of establishing the essential representative character of a

new regime. In 1932 Secretary of State Henry Stimson stated, in reaction to the Japanese conquest of Manchuria, that the United States would not recognize the validity of political changes brought about in violation of international obligations or treaty rights (Stimson Doctrine). The Cold War encouraged the granting and withholding of recognition as a discretionary political technique governed by decisionmakers' interpretations of the state's national interest, as in the refusal of the United States to recognize the government of the People's Republic of China from 1949 to 1979.

Recognition: States | 458 |

The process by which a political entity becomes an international person in international law and is accepted by existing states as a new member of the community. Once recognition of statehood has occurred, this status continues regardless of internal organization or changes in government so long as the sovereign character of the state continues.

Significance
Recognition is a complex and controversial topic of international law because it permits discretionary application of the principles involved. Failure to recognize either a new state or government tends to isolate it and diminish its prestige by restricting its ability to engage in normal diplomatic and legal relations. One of the moot points of international law is whether recognition is declarative or constitutive. If declarative, the new state or regime has rights and obligations prior to recognition. Recognition would therefore indicate a wish to establish normal diplomatic relations and a desire to establish access to national and international courts where rights and duties in the legal relations of the two parties can be defined and controversies resolved. This view appears to have more authoritative support than the constitutive theory, which holds that, as far as the international community is concerned, recognition creates the state or regime. The latter theory raises

questions, such as the number of recognitions required and whether an unrecognized state or regime is free to violate international law. Under the constitutive theory, for example, by ratifying the Treaty of Versailles in 1919 the signatories were recognizing and thus creating the states of Czechoslovakia and Poland. Each state is free to apply the declarative or constitutive theory, with the decision in fact usually based on political expedience.

Recognition, *De Facto* | 459 |

An indefinite and provisional recognition by the government of one state that a particular regime in fact exercises authoritative control over the territory of a second state.

Significance
De facto recognition is extended pending evidence of the stability of the new regime, or for a practical consideration such as the maintenance of trade. The legality of the assumption of authority by the regime so recognized is immaterial, and such recognition is not necessarily a precondition for the establishment of *de jure* or formal diplomatic relations.

Recognition, *De Jure* | 460 |

Complete, unqualified recognition of one government by another. Once *de jure* recognition has been granted and trouble arises with the government so recognized, its representative character is not denied nor is recognition withdrawn. Instead, diplomatic relations with the offending government are broken.

Significance
De jure recognition always involves the establishment of normal diplomatic relations. Such recognition is termed *express* when it is accomplished by a formal act such as an exchange of notes expressing both desire and readiness to engage in regular diplomatic relations. De jure recognition is termed *tacit* when accomplished by an act that implies intention to recognize, such as a consular convention.

When Israel declared its independence in 1948, the United States recognized it *de facto*, and waited before extending *de jure* recognition. On the other hand, the Soviet Union recognized Israel *de jure* from the outset.

Transparency   461

The necessity for "openness" in diplomatic settlements. The term *transparency* developed in the years leading up to the termination of the Cold War and is much utilized by states engaged in critical matters that affect or influence their national interests. Transparency emphasizes the open character of agreements and the credibility of the states entering into them. It emphasizes the need to place everything, notably military capabilities and maneuvers, in the public view. The purpose is to avoid suspicion between states, on the one side, and to instill confidence between them, on the other. Transparency is considered essential in arrangements between formerly adversarial states, but the term also applies to friendly states in their relations with one another. Thus, for example, the relationship between NATO and the Western European Union (WEU) emphasizes the need for transparency in their operations. *See also* ALLIANCE: EUROCORPS (282); ALLIANCE: WESTERN EUROPEAN UNION (WEU) (291); ARMS CONTROL: VIENNA DOCUMENT, 1992 (382); ARMS CONTROL PRINCIPLE: TRANSPARENCY AND NUCLEAR WEAPONS (384); REGIONAL MILITARY GROUP: WESTERN EUROPEAN UNION (WEU) (559).

Significance
Confidence building between the states is as important in the post–Cold War period as it was during the years of acute global rivalry. Transparency represents a willingness to share experiences, to communicate matters generally believed to be delicate but nonetheless of importance in creating conditions that permit the development of good-faith agreements. Transparency does not prevent states from pursuing national objectives, but it does require states to declare their intentions prior to taking actions that are destined to raise questions about the state's motives. The failure of Russia to adhere to the 1992 Vienna Document on security-building measures when it moved against the breakaway state of Chechnya in December 1994–1995 is an important illustration of the difficulty in sustaining transparency. Whereas the European states and the United States did not fault Russia for seeking to sustain its territorial integrity, under the terms of the Vienna Document, to which it was a signatory, Russia was required to announce its military preparations in advance of the assault on the Chechens, and in so doing the action might have been avoided altogether. More predictable behavior appeared likely with the establishment of the Forum of Consultation, which institutionalized dialogue between Eastern and Western Europe. Projected to meet twice each year at the ambassadorial level, and at the monthly convening of the Counsellors Group, the forum brought together the WEU members with representatives from Bulgaria, the Czech Republic, Estonia, Hungary, Latvia, Lithuania, Poland, Romania, and Slovakia. Meetings of the forum were suspended, however, when these East European states were given associate status with the WEU (Kirchberg Declaration) in May 1994, thus demonstrating the success of a policy of transparency.

International Law

Citizen

A legal status whereby an individual has both the privileges and responsibilities of full membership in the state. The status of citizen can be acquired (1) at birth, by *jus soli*, or citizenship by place of birth; (2) by *jus sanguinis*, or citizenship at birth determined by the allegiance of the parents; (3) by naturalization, the formal transference of allegiance. *See also* CITIZENSHIP: *JUS SANGUINIS* (466); CITIZENSHIP: *JUS SOLI* (467); CITIZENSHIP: NATURALIZATION (469).

Significance
The status of citizen ensures for the individual the protection that his country's laws and power afford. The citizen performs certain duties, such as paying taxes and serving in the armed forces, and enjoys certain privileges, such as voting, and when abroad, calling on the services of his or her country's diplomatic and consular missions. The status of citizen may be lost for reasons that vary among countries. Typical reasons for loss of citizenship include extended residence abroad, serving a foreign state without permission, taking a foreign oath of allegiance, and denaturalization. An individual may have dual citizenship, depending on the laws of the countries involved, or, more seriously, may be stateless and thus unable to claim the protection of any country as a matter of right.

Citizenship: Alien

A person who is not a citizen or national of the state wherein he or she is located. As a general principle of international law, states possess internal sovereignty and are free to admit or exclude aliens as they choose. States extend to aliens most of the same civil, but not political, rights enjoyed by citizens. These usually include the rights of freedom of speech and religious worship, the right to follow certain professions and licensed occupations, and the rights of contract and of holding, inheriting, and transmitting real property. International law recognizes distinctions between resident aliens, who have established a domicile, and transient aliens. Resident aliens may be expected to perform many of the same duties as citizens, such as paying taxes and serving in the armed forces. In the public interest they may be subjected to specific restrictions, such as the obligation to inform the government periodically as to their location and occupation. Aliens may also be expelled, provided the expulsion does not discriminate against the citizens of any particular foreign country.

Significance
International law concerning the rights and duties of aliens and the rights and duties of states is undergoing a process of transition because of increased travel and communication. Sharp controversy revolves around discrimination against citizens of specified countries, usually in the form of exclusive immigration policies. As a result of wars and revolutions, large numbers of citizens have acquired alien status as refugees. Other problems relating to aliens involve stateless persons who can claim the protection of no country, and large ethnic groups who are often treated as cultural aliens in their country of residence. Because of the flood of illegal as well as legally admitted aliens inundating the United States in the 1990s, programs are being developed at state and national levels to stem the tide. All attempts aimed at restricting alien entrance have been controversial. Proposition 187, approved by California voters in 1994, denied the use of public revenue to illegal aliens for medical and educational as well as general welfare purposes. The Clinton administration's decision to deny entrance to those fleeing Castro's Cuba was a sharp departure from long-term U.S. policy to admit such persons. At the heart of the dilemma is the concern that aliens seek entrance to the United States for economic purposes, not because they confront physical or psychological harm in their own countries.

Citizenship: Dual Nationality | 464 |
Citizenships simultaneously held in more than one country. Dual nationality can occur when an individual acquires citizenship in one country through his or her parents (*jus sanguinis*) and citizenship

in a second country in which he or she is born (*jus soli*). Dual citizenship also results where a person is a citizen by birth in one country and by naturalization in another when the country of birth does not recognize the right of the individual to renounce his or her allegiance.

Significance
Dual nationality becomes a problem for a person who moves between two states, each of which claims the individual's allegiance on different grounds. He or she is thus subject to two sets of rights and duties, some of which may conflict. Foreign offices have been plagued by cases involving the individual's duty to perform military service in either or both countries. In the absence of specific agreements on the subject, claims are frequently resolved in favor of the state possessing *de facto* jurisdiction over the individual. A person with dual nationality is well-advised to investigate his or her status thoroughly before moving between different jurisdictions claiming his or her allegiance.

Citizenship: Expatriation | 465 |
The act whereby an individual is released from citizenship by his or her government through some specific action on the individual's part or at his or her own request. Actions that constitute grounds for expatriation in most countries include taking an oath of allegiance to another state, serving in foreign military services without permission, voting in foreign elections, and public renunciation of citizenship. The key to expatriation lies in a voluntary action undertaken by the individual rather than by a government. *See also* CITIZEN (462); CITIZENSHIP: NATIONALITY (468).

Significance
Persons who expatriate themselves are often unaware that they are doing so and may not understand the consequences of their actions. Unless the expatriate is assured of naturalization elsewhere, he or

she may become a stateless person unable to obtain a residence permit, passport, or visas to travel to other countries. In short, the person could claim no protection as a matter of right from any state.

Citizenship: *Jus Sanguinis* | 466 |

The "law of blood," or the rule that at birth a person acquires the citizenship of his parents. *Jus sanguinis* is one of two legal rules that states follow in determining citizenship by birth. The other rule is *jus soli*, or the "law of the soil." *See also* CITIZEN (462); CITIZENSHIP: JUS SOLI (467).

Significance

States that follow the rule of *jus sanguinis* establish nationality through that of the parents rather than through the place of birth. Under this rule, for example, children born to British parents outside the jurisdiction of the United Kingdom are citizens of Great Britain even though the basic rule followed by Great Britain is *jus soli*. Most continental European countries follow the rule of *jus sanguinis*.

Citizenship: *Jus Soli* | 467 |

The "law of the soil," or the rule that a person's citizenship is derived from his place of birth. *Jus soli* is one of two legal rules that states follow in determining citizenship by birth. The other rule is *jus sanguinis*, or the "law of blood." *See also* CITIZEN (462); CITIZENSHIP: JUS SANGUINIS (466).

Significance

Jus soli is the rule of citizenship followed by most English-speaking and Latin American countries. Children born within the jurisdiction of the United States, for example, are U.S. citizens even if their parents are ineligible for citizenship, although the 1995 Congress is considering abandoning that principle. Children born to foreign diplomats serving in countries that follow the rule of *jus soli* are not granted citizenship in those countries.

Citizenship: Nationality | 468 |

The legal relationship between an individual and a state whereby the individual claims protection from the state, and the state in turn requires allegiance and the performance of certain obligations. Nationality is acquired by birth or by naturalization, although the rules covering each method vary from country to country. The principle that an individual can be divested of nationality is commonly accepted in the state system, and diverse methods recognized by states include denationalization, denaturalization, expatriation, and renunciation. *See also* CITIZEN (462).

Significance

Nationality implies membership in a state. Conflicts over the nationality of an individual can arise between a state that follows *jus sanguinis* and another that asserts the rule of *jus soli*. Similarly, conflict can occur when a person born in a state that follows the doctrine of inalienable allegiance becomes the naturalized citizen of another state. Since individuals move between states in large numbers, such conflicts over questions of nationality affect the relations of states and are responsible for protracted efforts at codifying international law on the subject.

Citizenship: Naturalization | 469 |

The legal process whereby an individual changes citizenship from one country to another. Details vary from country to country, but normally include a formal renunciation of allegiance to one sovereign and an oath of allegiance to the new state. *See also* CITIZEN (462).

Significance

Naturalization is the only way in which a person who cannot claim citizenship in a state by right of birth (*jus sanguinis or jus soli*) can acquire citizenship in that state. Immigrants from other countries are naturalized individually. Collective naturalization can occur, however, by a treaty or legislative enactment granting citizenship to the people of a newly acquired territory. In this manner the United States conferred citizenship on the people of Alaska, Florida, Hawaii, Louisiana, and Texas. Whether individual or collective, naturalization cannot be claimed as a matter of right. It is a discretionary prerogative of the granting state, which, in the absence of specific treaty commitments, is free to establish conditions.

Citizenship: Passport $\boxed{470}$

A legal document issued by a state that identifies an individual and attests to his or her nationality. Passports are issued to citizens who wish to travel abroad and entitle the bearer to the protection of his or her country's diplomatic and consular representatives. They are also requests to foreign governments to allow the bearer to travel or sojourn within their jurisdiction and to grant lawful aid and protection. Diplomatic passports, which are issued to emissaries of foreign governments, identify their official status and ensure their receipt of appropriate diplomatic privileges and immunities. *See also* CITIZENSHIP: VISA (472); DIPLOMATIC PERSONNEL: DIPLOMAT (422).

Significance
A passport is essentially a travel and identity document that attests to the bearer's claim to protection by the issuing government and provides prima facie evidence of nationality. Passports are not only essential to legitimate foreign travelers, but are also sought by those who would enter another country fraudulently. Cleverly faked passports can command a high price in black markets in many places around the world. Prior to World War I, passports were not generally required for international travel. In recent years some countries have moved toward discontinuing passport requirements by special agreements, as, for example, among the members of the European Union.

Citizenship: Statelessness $\boxed{471}$

The condition of an individual who is not recognized by any state as one of its nationals. Statelessness may result from dislocations caused by war or revolution, from a conflict of nationality laws, or by some act of denationalization undertaken by a government against some of its citizens. An individual act of expatriation that is not followed by the acquisition of a new allegiance would also result in statelessness. *See also* CITIZEN (462); CITIZENSHIP: NATIONALITY (468); POPULATION EXCHANGE (76); WAR: REFUGEE (313).

Significance
Statelessness means that a person has no legal claim to protection from any country. In the case of political refugees, individuals may have no legal right to be where they are, nor are they likely to be able to secure passports or the necessary visas to go elsewhere. The international and human problems of statelessness and refugees are of particular concern to such international agencies as the UN General Assembly, the Economic and Social Council, the International Law Commission, and the Office of the High Commissioner for Refugees. In 1961 the General Assembly opened for signature a Convention on the Reduction of Statelessness, which establishes circumstances under which a country could be required to grant nationality.

Citizenship: Visa $\boxed{472}$

An endorsement on a passport by an official of the country to be entered, authorizing admission to that state. The visa indicates that the identity and nationality of the individual have been authenticated and reasons for entry approved. *See also* CITIZENSHIP: PASSPORT (470).

Significance
Many governments require foreigners to secure visas before admitting them to the country. In U.S. practice, foreigners wishing to enter the United States must present a valid passport to a U.S. consular officer abroad. The consul exercises final discretionary power in granting nonimmigrant visas to businessmen, tourists, students, and other visitors. Before grant-

ing an immigrant visa to aliens wishing to settle in the United States, the consul must determine that the annual quota for the alien's country has not been filled and that the individual meets other immigration requirements. Although a worldwide trend developed in the 1970s to eliminate visa requirements, they assumed new importance in the 1990s as governments, troubled by the worldwide AIDS epidemic, endeavored to protect their citizens by screening persons seeking to enter their countries.

Contract Debt: Calvo Clause | 473 |

A clause sometimes inserted by Latin American governments in public contracts with aliens. The Calvo Clause requires that, in case of differences arising under the contract, the alien party will rely solely on local remedies and will not appeal to his or her government for diplomatic interposition on his or her behalf. International arbitral tribunals and mixed claims commissions have split in their decisions as to whether, under international law, the inclusion of the clause in such a contract can prevent the foreign government from entering the dispute. The clause is named after Carlos Calvo, the Argentine jurist who wrote extensively on the subject. *See also* CONTRACT DEBT: DRAGO DOCTRINE (474).

Significance

Supporters of the Calvo Clause assert that aliens have no claim to better treatment than that accorded to nationals, and that foreign interference in such matters does violence to the principle of the sovereign equality of states. Opponents hold that although an individual may sign such a contract, the act cannot prevent his or her government from insisting that other governments remain responsible for dealing with him or her according to the standards established by international law.

Contract Debt: Drago Doctrine | 474 |

A position opposing the use of force by states in the recovery of contract debts.

The Drago Doctrine was enunciated in 1902 by the foreign minister of Argentina. The doctrine held that a state's defaulting on its public debt owed to aliens did not give another state the right to intervene forcibly on their behalf to collect that debt, or the right to occupy the territory of the debtor state. *See also* CONTRACT DEBT: CALVO CLAUSE (473); MONROE DOCTRINE (657); WAR MEASURES: INTERVENTION (324).

Significance

The Drago Doctrine was occasioned by the 1902 naval blockade of Venezuela established by Great Britain, Germany, and Italy when Venezuela defaulted on its public debt and other claims held by nationals of those countries. The Drago Doctrine was defended by the United States as supportive of the principle of European nonintervention in the hemisphere proclaimed in the Monroe Doctrine. In 1907 the United States by treaty assumed control of the customs houses of the Dominican Republic to ensure the payment of foreign debts and thus forestall European intervention. Current practice indicates that forcible intervention for such purposes by any state is legally inadmissible. The debtor state may, however, be subject to a charge of denial of justice under the standards of international law if it fails to provide local judicial and administrative remedies to the claimants. In that event, a foreign government could intervene diplomatically on behalf of its citizens.

ICJ: International Court of Justice | 475 |

The principal judicial organ of the United Nations. The International Court of Justice is the successor to the Permanent Court of International Justice (PCIJ), which functioned from 1922 to 1946. All UN members are automatically parties to the Statute of the International Court of Justice, and the General Assembly, on recommendation of the Security Council, establishes conditions under which nonmembers—such as Switzerland—may accede to the statute. The court is competent to hear any case brought to it by parties to a dispute who accept its jurisdiction in a particular case or who have accepted its compulsory jurisdiction under the Optional Clause. The ICJ may also render advisory opinions on legal questions referred to it by states, the principal organs of the United Nations, and most of the specialized agencies. To reach a decision, the court applies (1) treaties, (2) international customs, (3) general principles of law, and (4) judicial decisions. With the consent of the parties, the court may also apply teachings of qualified international jurists. Also with the consent of the parties, the court may render a decision *ex aequo et bono* (based on justice and fairness rather than law). Decisions are arrived at by majority vote and cannot be appealed. The Security Council and the General Assembly, voting separately, elect the 15 judges for nine-year terms. Five judges are elected every three years, and all are eligible for reelection. Article 9 of the Statute of the ICJ provides that the judges should be selected on the basis of their individual qualifications and that they should represent the main forms of civilization and the principal legal systems of the world. *See also* ICJ JURISDICTION, COMPULSORY (479); ICJ JURISDICTION: EX AEQUO ET BONO (477); INTERNATIONAL LAW (480); LEGAL SETTLEMENT: ADJUDICATION (521); LEGAL SETTLEMENT: ADVISORY OPINION (522).

Significance
The International Court of Justice represents the broadest effort to date to substitute the rule of law for the use of force in settling international disputes. The ICJ has heard over 50 contentious cases, rendered final judgments in 22, and issued about 20 advisory opinions. The court has not settled any major international disputes, largely because states appear reluctant to submit their vital interests to the finality of its decisions, and because of disagreement as to the norms to be applied. The judicial independence of the court, although questioned on occasion in the heat of partisan controversy, has never been successfully challenged. Nev-

ertheless, political considerations, such as whether or not a country is represented on other principal organs of the United Nations, have influenced the selection of judges. The principle of equitable geographic distribution has also been applied by the General Assembly and the Security Council, even though this criterion for selection of judges is not prescribed by the statute of the court. Practice also reveals the continuous presence on the court of a national of each of the five permanent members of the Security Council. Regardless of statute criteria for selection of judges, many Afro-Asian states have expressed dissatisfaction with the court on the ground that they are inadequately represented on the bench. The International Court of Justice is nonetheless the high point of efforts by the state system to develop dispute-settlement procedures through international judicial tribunals.

ICJ Jurisdiction: Connally Amendment   476

The reservation attached by the United States to its acceptance in 1946 of compulsory jurisdiction under the Optional Clause of Article 36 of the Statute of the International Court of Justice (ICJ). The Connally Amendment denies the court compulsory jurisdiction in "disputes with regard to matters which are essentially within the domestic jurisdiction of the United States of America as determined by the United States of America." The practical effect of the amendment is to destroy the intended compulsory feature of the court's jurisdiction because the United States is free to determine what is a domestic matter and therefore beyond the purview of the court. *See also* ICJ JURISDICTION, COMPULSORY (479); JURISDICTION (498).

Significance
The role of the International Court of Justice has been substantially reduced by the Connally Amendment's restriction of the jurisdiction of the court in its handling of contentious cases. Many states that have accepted the optional clause followed the

U.S. example by attaching similar reservations. The impact of the Connally Amendment and other reservations is multiplied by their reciprocal application in cases involving other states that have not attached such reservations to their acceptance of the Optional Clause. The result is that in most legal disputes the parties continue to determine whether the court has jurisdiction.

ICJ Jurisdiction: *Ex Aequo et Bono* | 477 |

A basis for a decision by an international court on the grounds of justice and fairness. The *ex aequo et bono* concept, set forth in Article 38 of the Statute of the International Court of Justice (ICJ), can be applied by the court as the basis for arriving at a decision only if the parties so agree. It is a variation from the more usual bases for reaching decisions in the ICJ by applying the rules of positive and customary international law. *See also* ICJ: INTERNATIONAL COURT OF JUSTICE (475).

Significance

A decision *ex aequo et bono* looks beyond specific law for justice and, in this sense, is somewhat analogous to the concept of equity found in Anglo-Saxon jurisprudence. The International Court of Justice has never been called upon to decide a case *ex aequo et bono*. The concept has been used, however, by international arbitral tribunals in resolving such disputes as the Guatemala-Honduras boundary issue in 1933, and in the settlement of the Gran Chaco conflict between Bolivia and Paraguay in 1938.

ICJ Jurisdiction: Optional Clause | 478 |

A method outlined in Article 36 of the Statute of the International Court of Justice (ICJ), by which states may agree in advance to accept the compulsory jurisdiction of the court in certain circumstances. If a state accepts compulsory jurisdiction, it agrees to submit to the court all legal disputes involving questions of treaty interpretation, international law, breaches of international

obligations, and amounts of reparations to be awarded. *See also* ICJ: JURISDICTION, COMPULSORY (479); ICJ JURISDICTION: CONNALLY AMENDMENT (476).

Significance

The purpose of the Optional Clause is to overcome the inability of the court to exercise jurisdiction over sovereign states, which otherwise could refuse to appear in court. More than 50 states have accepted compulsory jurisdiction, either unconditionally or on the condition of reciprocity by other states in similar types of cases. The United States accepted compulsory jurisdiction under the Optional Clause but reserved the right to interpret the application of compulsory jurisdiction (Connally Amendment), which had the effect of rendering its acceptance almost meaningless. The failure of the Optional Clause to achieve a satisfactory system of compulsory jurisdiction indicates that most states are not yet ready to entrust the court with the settlement of disputes over vital issues.

ICJ Jurisdiction, Compulsory | 479 |

The power of an international court to hear and decide certain classes of cases without the necessity of both parties agreeing in advance to accept the jurisdiction of the court in each case. The Statute of the International Court of Justice provides for compulsory jurisdiction in its "Optional Clause" (Article 36), which specifies that "The states parties to the present Statute may at any time declare that they recognize as compulsory *ipso facto* and without special agreement, in relation to any other state accepting the same obligation, the jurisdiction of the Court in all legal disputes concerning (1) the interpretation of a treaty; (2) any question of international law; (3) the existence of any fact which, if established, would constitute a breach of an international obligation; (4) the nature or extent of the reparation to be made for the breach of an international obligation." *See also* ICJ JURISDICTION: CONNALLY AMENDMENT (476); JURISDICTION (498).

Significance
Compulsory jurisdiction depends on prior agreement and is designed to facilitate peaceful international relations by providing for advance acceptance of legal techniques for dispute settlement. The compulsory jurisdiction of the court has been weakened, however, by reservations that states have attached to their acceptance of the "Optional Clause." Nevertheless, compulsory jurisdiction is also provided for in more than 600 international treaties stipulating that issues arising over their interpretation and application shall be decided by the court. No national legal system could function effectively if its courts lacked compulsory jurisdiction, but in the international arena the concept of compulsory settlement of legal disputes before an international court runs head-on into conflict with the doctrine of sovereignty. State officials and scholars continue to advocate voluntary acceptance of compulsory jurisdiction by all nations as the means for resolving this conflict and building a stable world legal order.

International Law 480
The system of rules on the rights and duties of states in their mutual relations. International law is based on the concept of the sovereign equality of states and rests ultimately on agreement among them. The sources of international law include (1) treaties or specific bilateral or multilateral agreements between the states; (2) international custom, as evidenced by practice so long continued as to be considered binding; (3) general principles of law based on such ideas as justice, equity, and morality recognized by civilized nations; and (4) a subsidiary source of law found in judicial decisions and in the teachings of the recognized legal publicists of the various nations. Although international law is applied by international judicial tribunals, it is most frequently interpreted and applied by national courts. Based initially on precedents of earlier eras, international law has developed in the modern state system

since the Peace of Westphalia of 1648. Hugo Grotius, author of the celebrated treatise *De Jure Belli et Pacis* (1625), is often regarded as the father of modern international law.

Significance
International law provides a guide for state action and a technique for peacefully resolving disputes between states by reference to agreed norms of conduct rather than by resort to force. Because the modern state system developed first in Western Europe, international law, which assumes universal applicability, is largely a product of Western culture. Yet the community of states has more than doubled since World War II, with the vast majority of new states located in Asia and Africa—areas that had little or no part in developing existing rules of international law. Consequently, many non-Western states challenge many aspects of the law in its present form. The challenges are based on cultural and ideological differences, nationalistic pride, and antipathy for rules created by former colonial masters. Thus, a major problem in establishing the rule of law among nations is the creation of a new international legal system to which all can agree. Such UN agencies as the Economic and Social Council and the International Law Commission, special committees created by the General Assembly, and various regional organizations are leading the way. The process involves attempts to codify existing law and, through law-making treaties, attempts to create new law according to the needs of a worldwide community of states.

International Law: Conflict of Laws 481
Legal situations in which the laws of more than one country may be applied. Conflict-of-laws situations typically involve such subjects as torts, contracts, inheritance, acquisition and transmittal of property, nationality, domicile, and marriage and divorce. The conflict-of-laws rules of the state determine whether or not, and to what extent, effect will be

given to the acts of another state. The conflict of laws is also known as private international law.

Significance

A major problem of conflict of laws involves the relationship between private international law and public international law. Some states, particularly in Continental Europe, hold conflict-of-laws rules to be a branch of international law and hence binding on all states. The Anglo-American countries treat such rules as a branch of national law. Practice indicates that, in the absence of specific treaties, the Continental view has not been fully accepted by international tribunals. Thus, international law does not generally require one state to give effect to the conflict-of-laws rules of another. Much work is being done, however, to codify rules of private international law and bring about uniformity in national legislation on these rules.

International Law: Customary Law | 482 |

Rules of international conduct based on practices and usages accepted by states to be obligatory. As customary law is applied over the years, its precepts tend to become clarified and its uncertainties reduced. Often, important rules of customary law are transmuted into positive law by their inclusion in treaties. Article 38 of the Statute of the International Court of Justice (ICJ) specifies that "International Custom, as evidence of a general practice accepted as law" is one of the sources of international law to be applied by the court. *See also* INTERNATIONAL LAW: POSITIVISM (485).

Significance

Specific rules of customary law are difficult to ascertain with precision. By its nature, evidence of customary rules must be found in observed practices rather than in specific international enactments and agreements. Evidence of usage believed to be binding as law may be sought in instructions to diplomatic and military officers, in national legislation, and in the opinions of national and international courts. The difficulty of demonstrating the establishment of a new custom in international law, however, has led to increasing use of the law-making treaty. In addition, the emergence of many new states that played no part in the development of customary law has weakened its general applicability.

International Law: Neutrality | 483 |

The legal status wherein a state takes no part in a war and which establishes certain rights and obligations vis-à-vis the belligerents. The rights of a neutral state recognized by belligerents include (1) freedom from territorial violations, (2) acceptance of the fact of the neutral's impartiality, and (3) freedom from interference with its commerce except to the degree sanctioned by international law. Neutral duties include (1) impartiality, (2) refraining from aiding any belligerent, (3) denying to belligerents the use of neutral territory, and (4) permitting belligerents to interfere with commerce to the extent specified by international law. *See also* WAR: CONTRABAND (307).

Significance

The concept of total war has brought into question the use of neutrality as a legal restraint on belligerents. In a total war, any commerce between a third party and a belligerent can be interpreted as aiding the enemy. When such commerce is cut off, the neutral can only acquiesce or enter the war. In cases of aggression, a policy of strict neutrality could be branded as immoral because it makes no distinction between the perpetrator and the victim of aggression. The legitimacy of neutrality is further called into question by the United Nations Charter obligation that all members oppose aggression. Nevertheless, the permanent neutrality of Switzerland is recognized in international law, and Switzerland is not a member of the United Nations. Switzerland's legal neutrality, however, should not be confused with political neutralism, which usually implies nonalignment in conflict or potential conflict. Political neutralism is a political concept, whereas neutrality is a legal principle. The confusion surrounding neutrality is further complicated by the United Nation's role in peacekeeping operations because the world body claims a certain neutrality in interposing itself between warring camps. That neutrality has been seriously questioned in conditions requiring enforcement action in pursuit of humanitarian objectives, as in the situation in Somalia or Bosnia. Calling upon NATO to threaten retaliation against those assaulting UN peacekeepers, or to ensure the security of areas described by the United Nations as "safe havens," seemingly violates the principle of UN neutrality.

International Law: *Pacta Sunt Servanda* | 484 |

The rule of general international law that treaties are binding and should be observed. *Pacta sunt servanda* is the principle that establishes the legal basis whereby treaties constitute binding contracts between signatory states. *See also* DIPLOMATIC TOOL: TREATY (429); INTERNATIONAL LAW: REBUS SIC STANTIBUS (486).

Significance
The rationale of *pacta sunt servanda* is that, in the absence of an international enforcement agency, each member of the international community has the responsibility to keep its agreements. To assume otherwise would be to question the very existence of international law in a community of sovereign states. When a treaty is violated, the offending state usually attempts to justify its act not in terms of the absence of the norm but in terms of extenuating circumstances, which, it asserts, should release it from the operation of the rule (*rebus sic stantibus*). Such attempts at self-justification constitute indirect admission of the existence and validity of *pacta sunt servanda* as a general rule of law.

International Law: Positivism | 485 |

The doctrine that holds that international law consists only of those rules by which states have consented to be bound. Positivism, which emphasizes the concept of state sovereignty, asserts that consent may be granted expressly in the form of a treaty, or by implication through adherence to international customary practices. *See also* DIPLOMATIC TOOL: TREATY (429).

Significance
Positivism is the principal method of international legal reasoning in an age dominated by nationalism, and recognizes the nation-state as the ultimate form of human organization. A weakness of the positivist approach, according to some legal scholars, involves the validity of the concept of implied consent as an explanation for the binding force of international law. The issue concerns the question of whether a sovereign state can be bound except by formal consent. Nevertheless, positivism has contributed to understanding the nature of modern international law by emphasizing state practice rather than a priori reasoning as the source of legal norms.

International Law: *Rebus Sic Stantibus* | 486 |

The international law doctrine that an essential change in the conditions under which a treaty was concluded frees a state from its treaty obligations. *Rebus sic stantibus* is a rationalization for unilateral, unauthorized denunciation of a treaty commitment. The doctrine asserts that every treaty contains an unwritten clause to the effect that substantial changes in the conditions that existed at the time the treaty was signed alter the obligations established by the treaty. *See also* DIPLOMATIC TOOL: TREATY (429); INTERNATIONAL LAW: PACTA SUNT SERVANDA (484).

Significance
Stability in international relations requires that agreements should be observed (*pacta sunt servanda*). *Rebus sic stantibus*, however, might be invoked by a state if its existence was threatened by its performance of a treaty obligation. The assertion of the doctrine is of more questionable validity when a state feels that its

obligations are inconvenient, onerous, incompatible with a change in its status, or damaging to self-esteem. The doctrines of *pacta sunt servanda* and *rebus sic stantibus* are not necessarily incompatible in principle. The sanctity of treaties must be admitted if international relations are to be conducted on the basis of the rule of law, but at the same time treaty obligations must be kept reasonable through periodic renegotiation or adjustment lest the strict application of the law precipitate chaos and conflict.

International Law: Sovereignty

487

The supreme decision-making and decision-enforcing authority possessed by the state and by no other social institution. The doctrine of sovereignty arose in the sixteenth century as a defense of the monarch's right of complete territorial jurisdiction in opposition to the claims of lesser local princes, the papacy, and the Holy Roman Emperor. By the end of the Thirty Years' War (1618–1648), the doctrine had become an accepted political fact, and the modern nation-state became the most important unit of political organization in the world. Sovereignty does not mean that states enjoy absolute freedom of action. State conduct is conditioned by the proscriptions and restraints of international law and by the rules of the various international organizations to which states belong, under the theory that supreme power can be modified by consent. Sovereignty also implies state equality, but only in the sense of equal capacity to acquire rights and to be subjected to obligations. Sovereign states are further limited in their freedom of action by the informal restraints imposed by a state system in which varying capabilities must be harmonized with specific objectives. *See also* DEMOCRATIC PATTERN: SUBSIDIARITY (705); ICJ: INTERNATIONAL COURT OF JUSTICE (475); INTERNATIONAL LAW (480); MAASTRICHT TREATY (432); POWER (26).

Significance
The doctrine of sovereignty implies the decentralization of power in the community of states and legitimates the freedom of the individual state to make independent decisions. It has come under increasing attack by those who point to the unrestrained pursuit of national self-interest as a fundamental cause of war, and who look to a more highly centralized state system as the means for regularizing interstate relations. State sovereignty is incompatible with a centralized state system, just as independent power exercised by a feudal nobility was incompatible with absolute monarchy. Thus, as long as the doctrine of sovereignty prevails, international law will remain a relatively weak, decentralized legal order when compared with the internal legal systems of the individual members of the international community. Theoretically, integration of the world community cannot proceed beyond the confederal stage, typified by the United Nations, because adherence to the doctrine of state sovereignty requires that the ultimate power of decision remain with the individual members of the group. Since the end of World War II, certain aspects of sovereignty have been surrendered on a regional scale with the development of such organizations as the European Union. True political integration in Western Europe was stalled, however, by the continued vitality of sovereignty and nationalism in Great Britain and France, and in Germany following its formal reunification in 1990–1991. Elsewhere, among the older states, nationalism and the conflict over values strengthens dedication to the doctrine of sovereignty. The independence of the newer states of the world is emphasized in the United Nations by their dedication to the concept of sovereign equality. Moreover, the demand for self-determination, i.e., sovereign status, by ethnic and religious groups in contemporary times not only threatens the political status quo, it also promotes the further fragmentation of the state system and encourages the spread and deepening of anarchic conditions. Sovereignty remains the central feature of political community at all levels because, in a given area, there can be only one supreme law-making and law-enforcing authority.

International Law: State   488

A legal concept describing a social group that occupies a defined territory and is organized under common political institutions and an effective government. Some publicists add the qualification that the group must be willing to assume the international legal obligations of statehood. As political abstractions, states do not need to be recognized by other states in order to exist, but for legal purposes they are more generally operational when recognized by other individual members of the international community. *See also* INTERNATIONAL LAW: SOVEREIGNTY (487); RECOGNITION: STATES (458).

Significance

States are the primary units of the international political and legal community. States emerged out of the collapse of the feudal order in Europe, and they stand in a relationship of sovereign equality to one another. As sovereign entities, states have the right to determine their own national objectives and the techniques for their achievement. State freedom of action is conditioned, however, by the formal restraints of international law and international organization, and by the relationship between state power and the informal situational factors that characterize the international environment at any given time.

International Lawmaking: 489
Aggression

An improper intervention or attack by one country against another. Aggression as a legal phenomenon implies that (1) there is a common standard of conduct or a system of norms within which international relationships are to be conducted and (2) action in violation of the standard warrants condemnation and punishment by the community of states. The literature of international law is replete with efforts to define "aggression" and to distinguish between it and legitimate acts of individual or collective self-defense. Ideological cleavages of the Cold War also aggravated the problem of defining "an act of aggression." With no common interna-

tional standard, some countries may laud as justifiable "wars of national liberation" that other countries regard as acts of aggression. A further definitional complication is created by the concept of indirect aggression, which may involve subversion, propaganda, economic penetration, and military aid to insurgents. *See also* INTERNATIONAL LAWMAKING: INTERNATIONAL LAW COMMISSION (ILC) (494); INTERNATIONAL LAWMAKING: WAR CRIMES TRIALS (497).

Significance

The efforts of the state system to develop general agreement on a comprehensive definition of "aggression" that could be applicable to specific actions of states have been unsuccessful but are continuing. One major obstacle is the perception of states; some states would view a violent act against another as an act of aggression, while another group of states would judge the same action a matter of self-defense. For example, Japan faces pressure both at home and abroad to atone for its aggressive actions during World War II, and some Japanese have called the behavior of their country during that period aggressive. Nevertheless, many Japanese engaged in this 1990s debate argue that any admission of guilt by Japan would dishonor their war dead. Thus, in June 1995, the Japanese parliament approved a resolution that called for an apology to Asian nations affected by the war, but it refused to sanction a statement that would label the Japanese the aggressors of World War II in the Pacific. In fact, the parliament argued that Japan, like other nations in the conflict, acted violently for a particular cause, but that it was not the aggressor or the only aggressor in World War II. In practice, therefore, it is international bodies that determine, usually after the fact, that aggression has taken place. The International Military Tribunals at Nuremberg and Tokyo, for example, found some Axis leaders to have been guilty of the crime of waging aggressive war. The Charter of the United Nations calls for the suppression of acts of aggression by members of the international community. The fact of aggression is determined, however, by the votes of a majority of states in the General Assembly or Security Council, as when the latter declared North Korea to be an aggressor in 1950. The International Law Commission (ILC) has tried for a number of years to establish standard categories of aggression leading to a comprehensive definition. Thus far, the ILC has not been able to recommend the draft of a law-making treaty to the General Assembly. Agreement is unlikely so long as a number of states challenge the justice of the international status quo.

International Lawmaking: Codification   490

The systematic organization and statement of the rules of international law. Codification is necessary for the progressive development of international law because of the length of time over which rules of state conduct have been accumulating, the changing circumstances in which the rules are applied, and the differing interests and interpretations of the rules by various states. Codification has been attempted by (1) setting forth the rules actually in force, (2) setting forth the rules as amended to conform to present conditions and standards of justice, and (3) re-creating the entire system in accord with an ideal standard of law. *See also* INTERNATIONAL LAW (480).

Significance
Major efforts at codifying international law have been undertaken at international conferences on a specialized topical basis. Important contributions were made on military and related subjects, for example, by the Hague Conferences of 1899 and 1907, and in the Geneva Convention of 1929, on such topics as occupation of territory and prisoners of war. The League of Nations Codification Conference in 1930 produced wide agreement on the subject of nationality. Other successful efforts included the Geneva Conferences on the Law of the Sea (1958, 1960, and 1982), and the Vienna Conferences on

Diplomatic Privileges and Immunities in 1961 and on Consular Relations in 1963. Article 13 of the Charter of the United Nations charges the General Assembly with promoting the codification of international law, and in 1947 the assembly created the International Law Commission to carry on studies in this field.

International Lawmaking: Genocide   491

The destruction of groups of human beings because of their race, religion, nationality, or ethnic background. World concern over genocide was aroused by the mass murders perpetrated by the Nazis against the Jews and other racial and national groups. In 1948 the UN General Assembly adopted an International Convention on the Prevention and Punishment of the Crime of Genocide, which became effective in 1951 after 20 nations ratified it. Categories of crime recognized in the convention include killing, causing physical or mental harm, inflicting poor conditions of life, enforced birth control, or transferring children from one group to another. Persons committing or inciting acts of genocide are liable to punishment whether they are public officials or private individuals. *See also* INTERNATIONAL LAWMAKING: GENOCIDE (491); INTERNATIONAL LAWMAKING: INTERNATIONAL CRIMINAL COURT PROPOSAL (493); INTERNATIONAL LAWMAKING: WAR CRIMES TRIALS (497).

Significance
Genocide, recognized by the contemporary world as one of the most despicable crimes, requires international action because it may be perpetrated by a government or with its consent. The United States was a leader in drafting the convention, which became effective in 1951, but the Senate refused to ratify it because of public indifference and the belief that some provisions of the convention might contravene federal law and some of the reserved powers of the states. The convention was finally approved by the Senate in 1986. Although the convention establishes virtually unprecedented indi-

vidual responsibility under international law for acts of genocide, no permanent institutions for international enforcement have been established. Acts involving genocide were identified with the war in Bosnia in the 1990s. A war crimes tribunal was established by the United Nations in The Hague, Netherlands, under the leadership of Richard Goldstone, a South African jurist. Its purpose was to identify and try individuals deemed responsible for atrocities committed during the protracted conflict in Bosnia. Some lesser members of the Bosnian Serb army were among the first to be apprehended during the war, and their trials commenced while hostilities continued to ravage the country. Rwanda, the scene of a senseless slaughter of Tutsi by Hutu in 1994, also organized trials following a cessation in the hostilities and the installation of a Tutsi government. These proceedings, however, did not receive the international attention accorded the Bosnian affair because they were carried out by a national government rather than by an international tribunal. Moreover, Rwanda had neither lawyers, judges, nor proper courts to handle the cases, and Hutu were arbitrarily arrested, accused of genocide, and threatened with summary punishment. Such war crime trials might be anticipated following the horror of tribal and ethnic slaughter, but they are less a legal proceeding than a matter of retribution by one group against another. The trials in Ethiopia, following the fall of the Mengistu Haile Merriam regime, or in Cambodia, where more than a million people were said to have been murdered by the Khmer Rouge, can also be placed in the latter category.

International Lawmaking: Hague Peace Conferences (1899 and 1907) | 492 |

The first general international conferences called to codify and develop rules and procedures related to the problems of armaments and war. The Hague Conferences, with 26 states participating in the first and 44 in the second, produced conventions on the pacific settlement of international disputes, rules for the conduct of war and the treatment of prisoners, the rights and duties of neutrals, and rules regulating action to collect international debts. No general agreement was produced in the crucial areas of disarmament, arms limitation, and compulsory arbitration. *See also* ARMS CONTROL: HAGUE PEACE CONFERENCES (1899 AND 1907) (358).

Significance
The most notable contribution of the Hague Conferences to the cause of peace was the creation of the Permanent Court of Arbitration at The Hague. Participating states were encouraged but not bound to submit their disputes to the court rather than resort to war. Although the conferences were concerned with the prevention of war, war was not outlawed, and 12 of the 14 final agreements related only to its regulation. The conferences are of historic importance because participation approached universality for the first time, great and small states participated on the basis of sovereign equality, international peacekeeping machinery was established, and the parliamentary diplomacy that characterized the meetings set a precedent for the League of Nations and United Nations systems.

International Lawmaking: International Criminal Court Proposal | 493 |

Problems encountered in establishing a legal institution to deal with crimes against humanity. An International Criminal Court was envisaged after World War I but never received the required support from the major nation-states. Following World War II, the horrific character of the war, especially the inhumane treatment reserved for millions of defenseless and largely innocent minorities in both Europe and the Far East, demanded action. The defeat of the Axis Powers meant more than victory over aggressive states. World War II was fought for moral objectives, and the end of the war demanded that the moral purpose of the war be represented in legal proceedings. This led to the creation of the Nuremburg and Tokyo tribunals, and the trying of the instigators of the war for crimes against humanity, indeed, as war criminals. A line was drawn between political acts taken in the name of and for the defense of the state, and acts that were clearly personal and had nothing to do with the war effort or the security of the state. The Nuremburg and Tokyo proceedings were ad hoc affairs, however, and although the trials received considerable publicity, they did not result in the establishment of a permanent court. In fact, the nation-states most responsible for the proceedings rejected the recommendation that such a court be established. The humanitarian law that emerged after World War II therefore ranged alongside public international law of long-standing significance, and international law was geared to serve the interests of nation-states, not general humanity. The Geneva Conventions of 1949 attempted to bridge the gap between existing international law and the desire to promote humanitarian law, but not until 6 October 1992, when the United Nations called for the establishment of a war crimes commission to develop "conclusions on the evidence of [international crimes] committed in the territory of the former Yugoslavia," did movement toward the creation of an International Criminal Court gain genuine support from the important nation-states. A unanimous Security Council resolution on 23 February 1993 mandated the establishment of a war crimes tribunal (perhaps the foundation for an international criminal court) to prosecute persons "responsible for serious violations of humanitarian law" in the former Yugoslavia. Distinguished jurists were named to serve on the tribunal, in The Hague. *See also* INTERNATIONAL LAWMAKING: GENOCIDE (491); INTERNATIONAL LAWMAKING: WAR CRIMES TRIALS (497).

Significance

The creation of an International Criminal Court is a matter of considerable contro-versy, despite public statements by governments and world leaders that such a tribunal is necessary in order to counter actions and practices that are, or verge on being described as, crimes against humanity. The work of an International Criminal Court will impact the sovereign states in ways that could diminish their prerogatives. It would place government officials under particular scrutiny, evaluating their motives as well as actions in the performance of their duties. The possibility that the leaders of one state would be singled out while another's behavior is ignored frames the difficulties in operationalizing such a court. States jealously guard their sovereignty, and the actions taken by their leaders, particularly during periods of violent conflict, are generally justifiable in international law. An important attribute of the state is being permitted the right to make war under certain conditions. With this being the prevailing interpretation of international law, even the Nuremberg and Tokyo trials were not without their critics. In addition, judges, prosecutors, and defense attorneys struggled over the question of culpability. Was the action a state action, or one more personal in character and in execution? U.S. secretary of state Lawrence Eagleburger's 1992 public statement accusing Serbia's president Slobodan Milosevic of promoting a policy of "ethnic cleansing" and declaring that he should be tried as a war criminal found an echo in April 1995 when Radovan Karadzic, the leader of the Bosnian Serbs, was cited as a war criminal. The International Criminal Court, however, was not formally established and the ad hoc tribunal lacked the power or real authority to try these Serbian leaders. The United Nations itself lacked the power and the authority, and it lacked the will to invade their domains. The tribunal therefore attempted to satisfy its mandate by trying lower ranking officials or members of the Bosnian Serb army accused of high personal crimes in the Bosnian conflict. The UN-sponsored War Crimes Tribunal in The Hague began serious proceedings against alleged Serbian war criminals in October 1995.

International Lawmaking: International Law Commission (ILC) | 494

An agency created by the UN General Assembly in 1947 to aid it in carrying out its charter responsibility (Article 13) to "initiate studies and make recommendations . . . encouraging the progressive development of international law and its codification." The International Law Commission consists of 21 experts on international law who represent the world's main legal systems and forms of civilization. Chosen on the basis of equitable geographic distribution, the commissioners serve five-year terms in their individual capacities rather than as representatives of governments. The ILC has presented a variety of reports to the UN General Assembly and numerous draft conventions with the recommendations that the assembly convene international conferences to consider the drafts. When this procedure is followed, the conferences adopt law-making treaties that bind the states ratifying them. The ILC has concerned itself with such subjects as recognition, state succession, jurisdictional immunities, the high seas, territorial waters, nationality, statelessness, aliens, asylum, the law of treaties, state responsibility, and arbitral procedure. *See also* INTERNATIONAL LAWMAKING: CODIFICATION (490).

Significance

The International Law Commission has made its chief contributions in the codification of law rather than in the development of a new universal system of norms. Present international law is largely the product of the older states in whose interests it was created, and they are reluctant to see it undergo rapid change. Pointing to the law's Western origin, some of the non-Western states have called for a "modernized" system in keeping with "current political realities." The ILC is unlikely to produce a new universal system until a worldwide political consensus emerges on which it can be based. While the ILC continues to make progress in codifying existing law, new law on a variety of subjects such as road traffic, political rights of women, and freedom of information is also emerging in draft conventions from other agencies, such as the Economic and Social Council and its commissions.

International Lawmaking: International Legislation | 495

Multilateral treaties or conventions designed to codify, modify, and initiate legal rules to be followed by states in their mutual relations. International legislation can be accomplished only by a law-making treaty because states insist, as a function of sovereignty, that they can be bound only by their consent. Law-making treaties can be written by ad hoc conferences, regional institutions, and international organizations such as the specialized agencies and the General Assembly of the United Nations. A procedure followed by the United Nations for the creation of international legislation includes (1) a study by the International Law Commission (ILC), which results in the writing of draft articles of agreement and their submission to the General Assembly; (2) a resolution by the assembly calling an international conference to consider the draft; (3) approval and subsequent ratification by the individual states; and (4) registration of the instrument by the secretary-general of the United Nations. Recent illustrations of international legislation by law-making treaty include the Geneva Conventions on the Territorial Sea and Contiguous Zone (1958) and on Fishing (1958), and the Vienna Conventions on Diplomatic Relations (1961) and Consular Relations (1963).

Significance

International legislation as a concept indicates the intention to create rules for orderly relationships between states. This intent suggests an analogy with national legislation that is helpful in the study of international relations, although the legislative processes in each level are not the same. There is no world legislative body comparable to a national legislature, and in writing the United Nations Charter in 1945, proposals for conferring legislative powers on the General Assembly were overwhelmingly rejected.

International Lawmaking: Law of the Sea | 496 |

International legal rules that pertain to the maritime rights and duties of the states. The law of the sea, which is the oldest branch of international law, has grown out of ancient codes based on customs related to the maritime rights and duties of merchants and ship owners. Precedents include the Rhodian Laws (ninth century), the Tabula Amalfitana (eleventh century), the Laws of Oleron (twelfth century), the Laws of Wisby (thirteenth and fourteenth centuries), and the Consolato del Mare (fourteenth century). Sources of the law of the sea include international custom, national legislation, treaties, and the work of international conferences on the subject. *See also* JURISDICTION: HIGH SEAS (508); JURISDICTION, ADMIRALTY (516).

Significance

The law of the sea is based on two fundamental principles: (1) the freedom of all states to use the high seas without interference and (2) the responsibility of each state to maintain law and order on the sea. Each state exercises jurisdiction over its own ships and within its territorial waters. Vessels in the territorial waters of a foreign state remain under the jurisdiction of the state whose flag they fly unless they threaten the peace and good order of the coastal sovereign. The Geneva Conferences of 1958 (UNCLOS I) and 1960 (UNCLOS II) augmented the law of the sea with conventions on (1) the definition of baselines for measuring territorial seas and contiguous zones, (2) innocent passage, (3) the recovery of food and minerals from the subsoil of the continental shelf and from the seabed, and (4) the conservation of animal and plant sea life. A new series of Law of the Sea Conferences took place from 1973 to 1982 (UNCLOS III). Considerable agreement has evolved concerning (1) national jurisdiction over a 12-mile territorial sea, (2) coastal state rights over a 200-mile exclusive economic zone (EEZ), and (3) transit through, over, and under straits used for international navigation. The major unresolved issues relate to the nature of control over deep-sea resource mining and other forms of exploitation of the wealth of the sea beyond the 200-mile national exclusive economic zones. These issues are tied to the extent of the authority to be granted to a proposed United Nations International Seabed Authority. This authority would govern exploration and exploitation of deep-sea resources if agreement can be reached on such key issues as voting, licensing, and collection of royalties. Dissatisfaction with such provisions led President Ronald Reagan's administration to reject the 1982 United Nations Convention on the Law of the Sea. Although it has not officially sanctioned the treaty, the United States nevertheless observes the vast majority of items detailed in the Law of the Sea Treaty. New issues arose in 1995 that tested a basic feature of the treaty: the extent of sovereign jurisdiction over waters otherwise described as the high seas. Canada attempted to enforce conservation measures by denying further exploitation of its North Atlantic fisheries to European vessels. Spain was especially incensed when Canada seized some of its oceangoing fishing vessels and cut the nets of others. Canada asserted the right to extend its jurisdiction beyond the 200-mile exclusive economic zone in carrying out its conservation program, arguing that not to do so would result in the exhaustion, if not the extinction, of vital fish resources. Although the dispute was not resolved legally, it was momentarily neutralized by a diplomatic understanding developed between Canada and the European Union limiting the catch of specific species of fish.

International Lawmaking: War Crimes Trials | 497 |

Trials of persons from defeated states to determine their individual—as opposed to national—guilt and punishment for criminal acts committed in the course of war or in bringing on war. After World War I, the Treaty of Versailles set a precedent by providing for the trial and punishment of the German emperor and individuals in the armed forces, although the Allies never carried out the trials. After World War II, 22 major German war criminals were tried at Nuremberg by the International Military Tribunal, representing Great Britain, France, the Soviet Union, and the United States. Charged with crimes against peace, war crimes, and crimes against humanity, 12 defendants were sentenced to death, others received jail sentences, and 3 were acquitted. Under the Charter of the International Military Tribunal for the Far East, major Japanese war criminals were tried in Tokyo on similar charges by judges representing the 11 countries at war with Japan. *See also* INTERNATIONAL LAWMAKING: GENOCIDE (491); INTERNATIONAL LAWMAKING: INTERNATIONAL CRIMINAL COURT PROPOSAL (493).

Significance
The Nuremberg and Tokyo war crimes trials opened a new page in the development of the international law of war. Prior to World Wars I and II, customary law provided that, on the termination of war, an amnesty be granted all individual enemies for any wrongful acts connected with their military service. The ferocity of total war and the bitter hatreds engendered by ideological conflict raise the question of whether a general amnesty will ever again be granted. Juristic reaction to the Nuremberg and Tokyo trials has varied. The judgments regarding war crimes and crimes against humanity have brought little criticism because customary law has long recognized the right of the victor to try individual members of enemy armed forces for violations of the international laws of war. The concept of crimes against peace, however, opens new ground. Legal questions relating to that charge include: (1) Can a clear distinction be properly made between aggressive war as a crime in itself and crimes committed during the course of war? (2) Does the Kellogg-Briand Pact, which makes aggressive war illegal, also imply individual criminal responsibility? (3) Is the distinction between aggressive war and defensive war sufficiently clear to assess individual criminal responsibility? (4) Could the Nuremberg court, composed of judges from only four states, be considered an international tribunal representing the world community? The United Nations has sought to legitimate the principle of individual responsibility underlying the war crimes trials by developing a code of international law on crimes against the peace and security of mankind. The General Assembly has charged the International Law Commission (ILC) with preparing a draft code, but the problem of developing a generally acceptable definition of aggression has delayed the process. The convening of a UN war crimes tribunal in 1995 to try individuals accused of war crimes in the war in Bosnia had little chance of success because all sides to the conflict were culpable, even though a majority of the accused were Serbs. Moreover, the Bosnian Serbs, apparent victors in the conflict, had seized approximately half of the state's territory. Bringing leading members of a victorious army before the bar of justice had never been attempted, and it remains to be seen if this proceeding would be the exception to that record. In fact, only a few low-ranking members of the Bosnian Serb army, captured by the Bosnian Muslims and turned over for trial by the UN authorized tribunal, have been found guilty of rape and the killing of innocent citizens in preliminary proceedings. More formal work of the UN War Crimes Tribunal began its work in The Hague in October 1995.

Jurisdiction   498

The right of a state or a court to speak or act with authority. Jurisdiction involves the assertion of control over persons, property, subjects, and situations in a given juridical, political, or geographic area. Under international law, jurisdiction over territory can be acquired by accretion, cession, conquest, discovery, and prescription.

In a world of over 180 independent sovereign states, questions of jurisdiction comprise a major share of the subjects of international conflict, negotiation, and adjudication. Jurisdictional conflicts between states are common in such areas as citizenship, boundaries, airspace, high seas, fishing rights, territorial waters, innocent passage, and outer space.

Jurisdiction: Accretion | 499 |

Acquisition of title to territory created through the slow depositing of materials by rivers and seas, which vests in the mainland or riparian state. The principle of accretion—that natural additions to the original territory come under the same jurisdiction—can be traced back to Roman law through the work of Hugo Grotius. Such additions may occur on riverbanks or ocean shores, or may take the form of islands or deltas.

Significance
The accretion method of territorial acquisition may create serious political and economic questions related to territorial jurisdiction. These may involve islands raised in rivers used as international boundaries, or islands or deltas in the maritime belt, which extend a state's territorial waters farther out into the ocean.

Jurisdiction: Airspace | 500 |

The sovereignty of a state over the airspace above its territory. Jurisdiction over the national airspace was recognized by the Chicago Convention on International Civil Aviation (1944) and is limited only by the bilateral and multilateral treaties to which a state may be a party. The Chicago conference established the International Civil Aviation Organization (ICAO) to implement the principles of the convention and develop rules for international air travel. Freedom of the air as a general principle exists only over the high seas and any other portions of the earth's surface not subject to the control of any state, such as Antarctica. Military and other

state aircraft that are not common carriers always require special authorization before using the airspace of another state. *See also* ARMS CONTROL: OUTER SPACE TREATY (367); UN SPECIALIZED AGENCY: INTERNATIONAL CIVIL AVIATION ORGANIZATION (ICAO) (608).

Significance
Jurisdiction over national airspace has become a subject of increasing concern as technology advances the speed and volume of airborne commerce. Prior to World War I, two theories of airspace jurisdiction were expounded: (1) freedom of the air and (2) national control. Demonstrations of the effectiveness of aerial surveillance and bombardment brought general acceptance of the idea of national jurisdiction. Technological developments since World War II have raised to a practical level the question of how far above its territory a nation's sovereignty extends. The launching and return to earth of rockets, missiles, satellites, and spacecraft are opening new areas of conjecture and negotiation in the international development of airspace law.

Jurisdiction: Annexation | 501 |

Acquisition of legal title to territory by the announcement of the acquiring state that it has extended its sovereignty over and will exercise jurisdiction in the area.

Significance
The extension of sovereignty by annexation may be based on such claims as discovery, occupation, or continuous possession. In 1938 Germany simply announced the annexation of Austria based on an act of the Austrian government converting that country into a state (*Land*) of the German Reich. Annexation may be uncontested by third parties, as in the case of the annexation of Jan Mayen Island by Norway in 1920. The announcement of annexation may also arouse considerable protest and the assertion of counterclaims, as in the case of the legal status of Eastern Greenland in 1933. The rival claims of Denmark and Norway were submitted to the determination of the

Permanent Court of International Justice, which held in favor of Denmark. Israel annexed the strategic Golan Heights from Syria in 1981, proclaiming the territory an integral part of Israel. Diplomatic efforts launched by the United States in 1994 were aimed at restoring the territory to Syrian sovereignty in return for a guarantee of peace and a formal peace treaty between Syria and Israel. In June 1995 Israel's prime minister, Yitzhak Rabin, cited the Golan as Syrian domain and indicated that his government would return the region to Syrian sovereignty under conditions that guaranteed the security of the Jewish state.

Jurisdiction: Avulsion 502

A rule of international law that determines the location of an international boundary between two states separated by a river. When a sudden shift in the location of the main channel occurs, under the avulsion rule the boundary remains in its prior location. *See also* JURISDICTION: THALWEG (515).

Significance

The sudden shift of a main river channel may involve a considerable amount of territory compared to the changes brought about by gradual erosion and accretion. In the absence of such a rule, this could cause serious international problems, such as the Chamizal Tract Dispute between the United States and Mexico. In 1864 the Rio Grande suddenly changed its course and the question of jurisdiction over the territory between the old and the new channels was not finally resolved until 1967.

Jurisdiction: Cession 503

The transfer of sovereignty over territory by agreement between ceding and acquiring states. Cession may involve all or a portion of the territory of the ceding state. In the former instance, the ceding state disappears by absorption into the acquiring state. *See also* PEACEFUL SETTLEMENT: PLEBISCITE (442).

Significance

A treaty of cession legitimates the acquisition of territory by formal transfer of sovereignty, describes the territory in question, and sets forth the conditions of the transfer. The legality of a cession does not necessarily depend on the consent of the people of the ceded territory. The principle of self-determination, however, makes an expression of consent desirable. Cession of territory may be voluntary, as in the Louisiana Purchase, or involuntary, as imposed by the terms of a peace treaty.

Jurisdiction: Condominium 504

A dependent territory governed jointly by two or more sovereigns. In a condominium the legal systems of the states exercising control operate side-by-side, and questions of jurisdiction are governed by an agreement between the sovereigns. Examples of joint control through condominium arrangements include the Sudan (Great Britain and France, 1914) and Canton Island and Enderbury Island (Great Britain and the United States, 1938).

Significance

In a condominium, no external sovereign has exclusive jurisdiction, nor does sovereignty reside in the people of the territory. In international relations and law, the condominium as a form of territorial jurisdiction is a relatively rare phenomenon. The control exercised by Great Britain, France, the Soviet Union, and the United States over Germany after World War II did not constitute a condominium, but rather a form of military occupation.

Jurisdiction: Contiguous Zone 505

An area beyond the territorial waters in which the coastal state remains free to enforce compliance with its laws. The extent of the contiguous zone and the jurisdiction of the coastal state are defined in Article 24 of the Geneva Convention on the Territorial Sea and Contiguous Zone (1958) as follows: "1. In a zone of the high seas contiguous to its territorial sea, the coastal state may exercise the control necessary to: (a) Prevent infringement of its customs, fiscal, immigration, or sanitary regulations within its territory or territorial sea; (b) Punish infringement of the above regulations . . . 2. The contiguous zone may not extend beyond twelve miles from the baseline from which the breadth of the territorial sea is measured." *See also* JURISDICTION: TERRITORIAL WATERS (514).

Significance
The contiguous zone concept implies the existence of a specified area of the high seas wherein the coastal state may not claim sovereignty, but nevertheless may exercise jurisdiction for certain limited purposes such as the enforcement of customs laws. All states recognize that coastal states have jurisdiction over a band of territorial waters at least 3 miles wide. Beyond territorial waters, however, there has been little general agreement on the extension of national jurisdiction, although individual states have asserted various jurisdictional claims. Great Britain and the United States, for example, have traditionally asserted a right to extend limited jurisdiction to a zone extending 12 miles beyond their shores. The concept of the contiguous zone was finally accepted in the discussions of the International Law Commission (ILC) and at the Geneva Conference on the Law of the Sea, and became part of international law in 1964 for those signatories that ratified the Territorial Sea Convention.

Jurisdiction: Extradition $\boxed{506}$

The procedure whereby fugitives from justice found in one state are surrendered to the state where the law violations occurred. Extradition is initiated by a formal request from one state to another and is governed by the specific obligations set forth in extradition treaties between states. *See also* JURISDICTION (498).

Significance
The apprehension by the authorities of one state of a fugitive found within the jurisdiction of another state without the permission of the latter constitutes a grave violation of independence and sovereignty. Mutual interest in the application of justice and the maintenance of law and order, however, has led states to cooperate in surrendering fugitives from justice. Such cooperation is based on carefully drawn agreements that establish conditions and list the specific offenses under which extradition can be demanded. Normally, political crimes are not considered to be extraditable offenses, and states have often been unwilling to surrender their own citizens for trial in another state. Extradition is governed mainly by bilateral treaties, which have produced a tangled web of law that is unlikely to be simplified until states can come to agreement on more uniform rules. In contemporary times, the extradition of terrorists allegedly involved in bombings and other actions has drawn worldwide attention. The 1995 extradition by Pakistan to the United States of a key suspect in the New York World Trade Towers bombing of 1993 contrasts with the reluctance of the Libyan government to yield two individuals believed responsible for the destruction of Pan Am 103 over Lockerbie, Scotland, in 1988.

Jurisdiction: Extraterritoriality $\boxed{507}$

The exercise of jurisdiction by one state within the territory of another. Extraterritoriality is established by a treaty that specifies the persons, the subject matter, and the degree to which local jurisdiction will not be applied to the citizens of the treaty partner. Examples of extraterritoriality antedate the modern state system. "Capitulations" were a form of extraterritoriality, establishing certain privileges for Christians in countries under Muslim rule. The first capitulations were established between the Ottoman Empire and France in 1535. Ostensibly developed to benefit both parties, the capitulations became a major and overwhelming advantage for the grantee when the granting nation became weak. The spread of extraterritorial advantages and privileges, wherein the European imperial states, the United States, and Japan penetrated nations under stress (e.g., China in the nineteenth century), was a manifestation of the age of imperialism. *See also* JURISDICTION (498).

Significance
Extraterritoriality was often imposed by a powerful state on a weaker state during the era of Western imperialism and colonialism. The object of extraterritoriality was to protect the citizens of the dominant state when the cultures and legal systems of the two were markedly different, as between Western countries and those of the Near and Far East. Through the capitulations, however, subjects or citizens of a state who were employed by a foreign company within that state also avoided the enforcement of laws of their own country. Extraterritoriality was also used to gain economic and commercial advantages for the privileged state, and more than likely allowed the intervening company or state to establish military units in the granting country. The United States maintained gunboats on Chinese inland rivers, and when Japan attacked China in the 1930s, a U.S. warship, the *Panay,* was struck and American lives lost. Because extraterritorial privileges or capitulations meant that foreigners accused of crimes were tried under their own law and judges rather than the law of the place, such treaties (normally lacking reciprocity) were bitterly resented as unequal limitations of sovereignty. The Chinese monarchy finally fell in 1911–1912 as a consequence of the increasing resentment by Chinese nationalists and patriots toward a government that was repeatedly pressured to make concessions to foreigners. The United States was the last country to yield its special privileges in China, doing so during World War II. In a special sense, however, extraterritoriality continues to exist in that diplomats are immune from legal process in the host country, and in connection with "status of forces" treaties that accord special rights and duties to the troops of one country stationed within the territory of another.

Jurisdiction: High Seas | 508 |

All of the world's oceans, seas, connecting arms, bays, and gulfs that lie outside the national territorial waters of coastal states. The high seas are open to commerce and navigation by all countries. States may extend jurisdiction to vessels flying their flags on the high seas, but not to the seas themselves. *See also* JURISDICTION, ADMIRALTY (516).

Significance
Under the 1958 Geneva Convention on the High Seas, "no state may validly purport to subject any part of them to its sovereignty." By international law, all states have equal rights to engage in such activities on the high seas as fishing, laying of submarine cables and pipelines, and overflight by aircraft. The exercise of the freedom of the seas by any state is qualified by the general requirement that in the exercise of their freedom to use the high seas, reasonable regard is due the interests of other states.

Jurisdiction: Hot Pursuit | 509 |

The international legal doctrine that permits the apprehension on or over the high seas of vessels or aircraft suspected of having violated national laws within national territorial jurisdiction. Under international law, hot pursuit must be (1) begun within the jurisdiction of the offended state, (2) engaged in only by the public vessels or aircraft of the territorial sovereign, (3) continuous until the pursued vessel is arrested, or (4) broken off when the vessel has passed into the territorial waters of another state. *See also* JURISDICTION: INNOCENT PASSAGE (510); JURISDICTION: TERRITORIAL WATERS (514).

Significance
Hot pursuit means that an offending vessel cannot escape the consequences of its acts merely by moving its location into the high seas, which by law belong to no state. Should suspicions of the arresting

state prove to be unfounded, it may become liable for the payment of compensation. The doctrine is justified in international law as necessary to the efficient exercise of territorial jurisdiction.

Jurisdiction: Innocent Passage | 510 |

The right of foreign vessels to traverse the territorial waters of another state without capricious interference by the coastal sovereign. Innocent passage includes stopping and anchoring, but only when incidental to ordinary navigation or made necessary by *force majeure* (superior force) or distress. *See also* JURISDICTION: TERRITORIAL WATERS (514).

Significance
Passage is innocent provided it does not prejudice the peace, good order, or security of the coastal state. Under international law, vessels in innocent passage are subject to normal rules of transport and navigation and to the laws of the coastal sovereign. In return, the vessels of all states are afforded the advantage of using the most expedient route. Under these same conditions, the 1958 Geneva Convention on the Territorial Sea and the Contiguous Zone recognizes the right of innocent passage for warships.

Jurisdiction: Outer Space | 511 |

International authority over the area beyond the airspace. Although no state exercises jurisdiction over outer space, the subject has become one of increasing international concern since the first Earth satellite was orbited in 1957. In 1959 the United Nations established a permanent Committee on the Peaceful Uses of Outer Space. In 1961 the General Assembly unanimously proclaimed that "International law, including the Charter of the United Nations, applies to outer space and celestial bodies," and that "Outer space and celestial bodies are free for exploration and use by all States in conformity with

international law, and are not subject to national appropriation." In 1963 these principles were augmented by the Declaration of Legal Principles Governing Activities in Outer Space, which provided that (1) space exploration and use are to be for the benefit of all mankind; (2) states conducting such activities bear international responsibility for their acts; (3) all space activity shall be guided by the principles of cooperation and mutual assistance; (4) states launching objects and personnel retain jurisdiction over them in outer space and on their return to Earth wherever they may land; (5) states are liable for any damages on Earth, in the airspace, or in outer space caused by objects they launch into outer space; and (6) astronauts are to be considered envoys of mankind in outer space, and in case of accident, all states are to render them every possible assistance and to return them promptly to the state of registry of their space vehicle. These principles were embodied in the Outer Space Treaty, which was adopted by the General Assembly in 1966 and entered into force for ratifying states in 1967. *See also* ARMS CONTROL: OUTER SPACE TREATY (367); JURISDICTION: AIRSPACE (500).

Significance
Outer space and airspace are recognized in international law as two distinct zones, but the demarcation between them remains unclear. Some authorities define "airspace" as the area of aerodynamic flight. Outer space is therefore beyond national sovereignty, whereas airspace is within the jurisdiction of the subjacent territorial sovereign. The principles enunciated in UN declarations were merely suggestive until the Outer Space Treaty was ratified in 1967.

Jurisdiction: Partition | 512 |

A way of establishing or rearranging territorial jurisdiction by the division of territory between two or more sovereignties. Partition is a device that has often been used to resolve disputes over territorial claims. *See also* DIVIDED STATE (40); PEACEFUL (PACIFIC) SETTLEMENT (438); PEACEFUL SETTLEMENT: PLEBISCITE (442).

Significance
Partition of territory is as old as the history of the nation-state. Historically Russia, Prussia, and Austria had a continuing interest in the partition of Poland to the point that the latter disappeared as a state until resurrected after World War I. Partition may be called for in a peace settlement and may or may not include a plebiscite (vote) of the people involved. In 1947 British India was partitioned into Hindu and Muslim majority regions, thus creating the two sovereign states of India and Pakistan. The creation of these states on the basis of the "two-nation theory," one Hindu and one Muslim, was somewhat questionable, given the 1971–1972 sovereign formation of predominantly Muslim Bangladesh (formerly the province of East Pakistan) by India after its successful war against Pakistan. Growing antagonism among the victorious Allies after World War II led to the partition of Germany into the Federal Republic of Germany (West Germany) and the German Democratic Republic (East Germany). The unification of the two Germanys had to wait for the passing of the Cold War in 1990–1991. Following decades of Japanese occupation, Korea regained its freedom with Japan's defeat in World War II, but was divided by the forces of the Cold War into two sovereign states, the Republic of Korea (South Korea) and the Democratic People's Republic of Korea (North Korea). Some Koreans have endeavored to unify their two countries but, unlike German unification, that goal remains elusive. On the other hand, Vietnam was divided between the Communist north and the non-Communist southern region following World War II. Both the Vietnamese Communists and the French attempted to reunify the country, but even after the Vietnamese Communists defeated the French, they were unable to unify the country because of U.S. intervention. Vietnam remained divided between North and South and yet another war ensued, this time between the North Vietnamese and the Americans, who supported the government in the South. The U.S. withdrawal from the region in 1973 was intended to leave both Vietnams intact, but the North moved south and in 1975 unified the country under its authority.

Jurisdiction: Prescription   513

A method recognized in international law whereby one state, through long and uninterrupted dominion, acquires title to territory previously claimed by another state. The prior sovereign's long-term acquiescence in the exercise of jurisdiction by another state constitutes the grounds for the transference of valid title.

Significance
Prescription can create title for one state only when sovereignty over the territory previously resided in another state; in the absence of a prior sovereign, title would be acquired by discovery. Prescription implies that mere ownership is not enough to maintain title; it must be accompanied by the exercise of effective jurisdiction over the territory. International law does not specify any particular time period following which title passes to the state that has enjoyed uninterrupted use. When claims based on prescription are contested before a court or arbitral tribunal, each case is decided on its merits in line with rules of international law. The Palmas Island Arbitration (1928) between the United States and the Netherlands, for example, recognized the Dutch title on the basis of long, uninterrupted exercise of jurisdiction.

Jurisdiction: Territorial Waters   514

The belt of water immediately adjacent to the coast of a state over which the state exercises sovereignty. Territorial waters 12 miles wide have largely replaced the more historic 3-mile limit as the minimum generally recognized by the states of the world. There is no generally accepted maximum width, although a number of states claim more than 12 miles and, in individual cases, up to 200 miles. The 1982 Law of the Sea Treaty established a 12-mile territorial waters jurisdiction for coastal states, but many states have yet to ratify the treaty. *See also* JURISDICTION: INNOCENT PASSAGE (510).

Significance

The extent of territorial waters has always been a matter of international controversy. The 3-mile minimum limit was accepted in the eighteenth century as the range that could be covered effectively by cannon fire from the shore. Claims to a greater distance were usually of a political or strategic nature, or were based on the location of some resource, such as fisheries or oil, over which the coastal state wished to establish exclusive jurisdiction. Although the Geneva Conferences on the Law of the Sea (1958 and 1960) produced conventions on the high seas, the continental shelf, the conservation of fisheries, and the regime of territorial waters (rules governing their use), they failed to produce the two-thirds vote necessary to establish a uniform limit for territorial waters. The Law of the Sea Treaty of 1982, however, stressed the legality of the 12-mile limit and there appears to be significant consensus that this distance has replaced the 3-mile limit in vogue for approximately two centuries.

Jurisdiction: Thalweg　515

The rule of international law that determines the exact location of the boundary between two states separated by a navigable river. The thalweg, or "down-way," is the middle of the main channel or downstream current. *See also* JURISDICTION: AVULSION (502).

Significance

Rivers may shift their course as a result of natural causes. Unless the boundary can be determined with precision, problems can arise over such matters as customs duties, tolls, jurisdiction over vessels, and fugitives from justice. The thalweg rule can also be applied to estuaries and bays.

Jurisdiction, Admiralty　516

State authority over maritime affairs. Admiralty jurisdiction is a highly technical area of jurisprudence dealt with in states' municipal laws concerned with seaborne commerce and navigation, and their regulation. Admiralty law includes such subjects as jurisdiction over vessels, ports, seamen, and territorial waters; civil and criminal suits; liabilities of vessels and cargoes; passenger carriage; the rights of crew members; and safety regulations.

Significance

The increasing importance of maritime trade and commerce to a growing number of states has produced a vast quantity of national rules and regulations that in turn bring recognition of the need for greater uniformity. Efforts to bring about such uniformity of maritime law by treaty and implementing legislation have met with considerable success in such areas as sanitary regulations, salvage and assistance, collisions, safety at sea, load lines, use of maritime ports, high-seas fisheries, and territorial seas. In the absence of such treaties, admiralty jurisdiction is determined by national laws.

Jurisdiction, Domestic　517

Those spheres of national life that are regulated exclusively by national law and within which the validity of international law is denied. Domestic jurisdiction is thus a concomitant of national sovereignty. Article 2 of the Charter of the United Nations provides that "Nothing contained in the present Charter shall authorize the United Nations to intervene in matters which are essentially within the domestic jurisdiction of any state or shall require the Members to submit such matters to settlement under the present Charter." *See also* ICJ JURISDICTION: CONNALLY AMENDMENT (476); UNITED NATIONS: DOMESTIC JURISDICTION CLAUSE (578).

Significance

The concept of domestic jurisdiction implies that international law is not universal but is limited in its application to those subjects that have been accepted by the sovereign states that comprise the international community. In establishing boundaries between national and international jurisdiction, problems of interpretation inescapably arise. Some of the most difficult to resolve involve questions of human rights and self-determination. In the case of the United States' acceptance of compulsory jurisdiction of the International Court of Justice (ICJ), the practical question of who is to determine what constitutes domestic jurisdiction was resolved by the Connally Amendment in favor of national determination.

Jus Civile   518

The early civil law of the primitive Roman city-state, which applied to citizens only. *Jus civile* may be contrasted with the *jus gentium*, which applied to the diverse peoples of the empire. *See also* JUS GENTIUM (519).

Significance
The *jus civile* became one of the bases for the later development of various systems of national law. Along with the *jus gentium* of the Roman legal system, *jus civile* provided precedents and established principles later used in the development of international law.

Jus Gentium   519

The body of Roman law and equity that applied to all foreigners resident in the empire. The *jus gentium* governed relations between foreigners and between foreigners and citizens, and was based on common ideas of justice found in the laws and customs of the various peoples of the empire. Because it was thought to be simple, reasonable, and adaptable, early jurists regarded the *jus gentium* as universal in its applicability. *See also* JUS CIVILE (518); JUS NATURALE (520).

Significance
The *jus gentium* of Rome can be viewed as a system of private international law that

came to be associated with the *jus naturale* and with the Greek idea of a natural and therefore universal law. Based on these associations, the *jus gentium* has provided modern international law with many useful analogies in such fields as the occupation of territory, property rights, contracts, and treaties.

Jus Naturale   520

A Roman adaptation of the Greek Stoic concept of a set of principles that ought to govern the conduct of all men. The *jus naturale*, or natural law, is founded in the explanation of the nature of man as a rational and social being. This law of reason based on what ought to be, coupled with the universalism of the *jus gentium*, gave Roman law the adaptability and progressiveness that enabled diverse peoples to live together in relative peace despite changing conditions. *See also* JUS GENTIUM (519).

Significance
The concept of *jus naturale*, based on reason and existing above citizens and states, influenced Grotius and other early founders of international law who sought to establish a system of orderly relations between states. Natural-law formulations still evident in international law include such concepts as international morality, equality, justice, and reason. The natural-law school of international law was gradually displaced in the eighteenth and nineteenth centuries by the advocates of legal positivism, who hold that only custom, legislation, and treaties can create rights and duties for sovereign states.

Legal Settlement: Adjudication   521

A legal technique for settling international disputes by submitting them to determination by an established court. These techniques differ in that adjudication involves an institutionalized process carried on by a permanent court, whereas arbitration is an ad hoc procedure. The first international court of general competence was the Permanent Court of International Justice (PCIJ), which functioned as part of the League of Nations system from 1920 until the league's demise in 1946. It was succeeded by the present International Court of Justice (ICJ), one of the principal organs of the United Nations. *See also* ICJ: INTERNATIONAL COURT OF JUSTICE (475).

Significance
Adjudication has been used sparingly to resolve disputes and has been most effective in settling issues of less than vital importance. Advocates of adjudication assert the advantage that there is no international question to which a court could not give a final answer, and hence no international dispute need remain unresolved. States are hesitant to accept adjudication because, in submitting a case to an international court, they must agree in advance to be bound by a decision that might be detrimental to their vital interests. Since the doctrine of sovereignty means that a state cannot be forced into court against its will, defendant states are usually unwilling to submit to adjudication. Adjudication can have the advantage of avoiding the problem of national prestige, however, because a state that abides by an adverse judgment is thereby regarded as supporting the rule of law rather than submitting to the pressure of another state. As a settlement tool, adjudication has been weakened in the contemporary era by revolutionary developments in technology, the East-West conflict, and the emergence of new states and regimes that reject many traditional Western concepts of international law.

Legal Settlement: Advisory Opinion | 522 |
A legal opinion rendered by a court in response to a question submitted by an authorized body. The advisory opinion procedure differs from contentious proceedings in that there are no parties before the court as complainant and defendant. *See also* ICJ: INTERNATIONAL COURT OF JUSTICE (475).

Significance
An advisory opinion informs and clarifies but does not bind the requesting body unless it formally approves the opinion of the court. The United Nations Charter (Article 96) authorizes the General Assembly or the Security Council to request an advisory opinion from the International Court of Justice (ICJ) on any legal question. The General Assembly can also authorize other organs and specialized agencies of the United Nations to request advisory opinions on legal questions arising within the scope of their activities. Under the Headquarters Agreement of 1947, the advisory opinion procedure may also be used in connection with disputes arising between the United States and the United Nations. Although the advisory opinion technique is readily available, it has been used infrequently since 1946.

Legal Settlement: Arbitration | 523 |
An ancient procedure for the peaceful settlement of disputes. Arbitration has several essential features, including (1) a compromise, or agreement by the parties as to the issues to be resolved and the details of the procedure to be followed; (2) judges chosen by the parties; (3) a decision based on respect for international law; and (4) prior agreement that the decision will be binding. *See also* LEGAL SETTLEMENT: ADJUDICATION (521); LEGAL SETTLEMENT: COMPROMISE (525).

Significance
Arbitration, like adjudication, is a legal technique for dispute settlement and is to be distinguished from political methods involving a form of diplomatic negotiation, such as good offices, mediation, inquiry, and conciliation. Arbitration may be arranged ad hoc, or may be compulsory if a treaty to that effect exists between the parties. History records many bilateral arbitration treaties on a variety of subjects. The Hague Conference of 1899 institutionalized the procedure by creating the Permanent Court of Arbitration at

The Hague. Arbitration is also listed as a proper method of settling disputes between countries by the Covenant of the League of Nations (Article 13) and by the Charter of the United Nations (Article 33). In 1970 the United States acceded to the 1959 United Nations Convention on the Recognition and Enforcement of Foreign Arbitral Awards.

Legal Settlement: Award |524|

A judgment in the form of an indemnity or compensation of a monetary nature handed down against a state by an international arbitral tribunal, court, or claims commission. An award can be made in favor of an individual or an individual's government. If the award is made to a government, its distribution becomes a matter of domestic jurisdiction. *See also* LEGAL SETTLEMENT: ARBITRATION (523); LEGAL SETTLEMENT: COMPROMISE (525).

Significance

The granting of an award is an amicable mode of redressing grievances between states that have decided to employ legal techniques for the peaceful settlement of their dispute. The *compromis,* or preliminary arbitral agreement, establishes the general principles and specific rules by which a tribunal is guided in making an award. Under the principle of *res judicata* (the case having been decided), awards are final and binding unless reopened by the consent of the parties in a new agreement, or unless the award is voided by the tribunal's having exceeded its authority as laid down in the compromise.

Legal Settlement: |525|
Compromis

A preliminary agreement by the parties to a dispute that establishes the terms under which the dispute will be arbitrated. The *compromis* specifies the jurisdictional limits of the arbitral tribunal by (1) defining the subject of the dispute, (2) setting forth the principles that are to guide the tribunal, and (3) establishing the rules of procedure to be followed in

deciding the case. Specific questions relating to its jurisdiction are decided by the tribunal under the terms of the *compromis.* An award or decision by the arbitrators may be null and void if the tribunal exceeds its authority as laid down by the parties in the *compromis. See also* LEGAL SETTLEMENT: ARBITRATION (523).

Significance

The decision to arbitrate implies the presence of an international dispute and the necessity of negotiating a *compromis.* By its nature, arbitration cannot take place unless a *compromis* is first established, regardless of whether the arbitration is agreed to ad hoc or whether it is provided for in a prior bilateral or multilateral treaty. With a dispute already in existence and the level of tension rising, the disputants may find it difficult to arrive at the required preliminary agreement. In such a case, arbitration may be facilitated by a preexisting arbitration treaty under which the fundamental procedures detailed in a *compromis* have already been settled.

Legal Settlement: Justiciable |526|
and Nonjusticiable Disputes

A formulation that results from the assertion of the existence of two distinct categories of international disputes: legal and political. Justiciable disputes are those that lend themselves to legal settlement by arbitration or adjudication. Nonjusticiable disputes are those to which techniques of political settlement are applied by bilateral diplomacy, good offices, mediation, inquiry, or conciliation. *See also* PEACEFUL (PACIFIC) SETTLEMENT (438).

Significance

Whether or not a dispute is justiciable depends less on the nature of the dispute than on the importance of the issues to the parties involved and their decision as to which set of settlement norms to apply, if either. The idea of peaceful settlement through arbitration experienced a considerable vogue during the opening decades of the twentieth century, as evidenced by the creation of the Permanent Court of

Arbitration (1899), the Root arbitration treaties (1908), and the Taft-Knox arbitration treaties (1911). Nevertheless, the distinction between legal and political (and therefore justiciable and nonjusticiable) disputes arose because states wished to exempt from the finality of legal settlement those matters touching on national independence and vital interests as interpreted by themselves. That states may not wish to settle disputes by law does not mean that there is no law applicable to the dispute.

Legal Settlement: Permanent Court of Arbitration | 527 |

A panel of internationally recognized jurists who stand ready to serve as arbitrators in any international dispute. The Permanent Court of Arbitration, with headquarters at The Hague, was established by the Convention for the Pacific Settlement of International Disputes as adopted and revised by the Hague Peace Conferences of 1899 and 1907. The panel of available arbitrators includes four jurists of recognized competence appointed by each signatory. Each party to a dispute selects two judges, only one of whom may be a national. These four arbitrators then select a fifth to serve as umpire. Thus, the court is not a standing body but only a panel from which arbitral tribunals can be selected. The parties identify the points at issue, define the authority of the tribunal, and agree that a decision made within these limitations will be accepted as legally binding. *See also* LEGAL SETTLEMENT: ARBITRATION (523).

Significance
The chief value of the Permanent Court of Arbitration lies not in the extent of its jurisdiction but in its existence prior to a dispute and in its readily available machinery. Signatories of the convention are not obligated to use the personnel and procedures of the court. This decision is made in each case by the parties, although their actions may be governed by preexisting arbitration treaties or arbitration clauses found in other treaties. Most arbitration treaties follow the example of the Anglo-French Treaty of 1903, which re-

quired differences of a legal nature and those related to the interpretation of treaties to be referred to the court. In most arbitration treaties, questions involving the vital interests, independence, or honor of the parties and the interests of third parties have usually been exempted. In U.S. practice, the Senate regards each decision to arbitrate under a general treaty as a separate treaty requiring Senate approval. The Hague court represents an early effort at institutionalizing the peaceful settlement of disputes through the rule of law and was the forerunner to the Permanent Court of International Justice (PCIJ) during the League of Nations era and of the International Court of Justice (ICJ) of the United Nations. A successful arbitration under the auspices of the Permanent Court of Arbitration was the Rann of Kutch dispute between India and Pakistan in the 1960s. Although this settlement illustrated a capacity for cooperation between the two countries, the Rann arbitration did nothing to improve the relations between them.

Legal Settlement: Sanctions | 528 |

Penalties meted out as consequences of illegal conduct. In international relations sanctions involve the collective effort of the international community to force a law-breaking state to comply with international law when diplomatic and legal techniques of dispute settlement have failed. Authority to impose sanctions was embodied in the Covenant of the League of Nations and in the Charter of the United Nations. The league suffered a mortal wound when the sanctions it imposed on Italy for its invasion of Ethiopia were secretly violated by the British and French (Hoare-Laval Agreement). *See also* UNITED NATIONS: SANCTIONS (586).

Significance
In the absence of an international executive to enforce the law, the imposition of sanctions depends on the degree of consensus in the international community and on the willingness of each member of the state system to accept responsibility

to uphold the law. To be effective in specific cases, sanctions must create more hardship for the offending state than is created for the states applying the sanctions. The contemporary use of sanctions against South Africa, Libya, Iraq, Haiti, Cuba, etc., have not brought those countries into greater compliance with international rules and principles, but they nevertheless isolated these states from the activities of the larger world. Such isolation could, and in some instances did, have a cumulative effect.

International Organization

Human Rights | 529 |

Protection for individuals from arbitrary interference with or curtailment of life, liberty, and equal protection of the laws by government or private individuals and groups. Domestic guarantees embodied in national constitutions and laws are supplemented by international protection afforded through the actions of international organizations. Many nations also regard the safeguarding of the economic and social rights of individuals—for example, the right to employment, medical protection, and leisure—to be equal in importance to the older concept of political rights. Several regional organizations also provide guarantees for human rights. *See also* HUMAN RIGHTS: EUROPEAN CONVENTION (530); HUMAN RIGHTS, UNIVERSAL DECLARATION (531).

Significance

International activity in the field of protecting human rights has been carried on since 1946 mainly within the UN framework by the General Assembly and the Economic and Social Council and their various committees and commissions. These activities include (1) the enunciation of principles to serve as voluntary norms for member states, as in the Universal Declaration of Human Rights; (2) the adoption of multilateral conventions that constitute enforceable guarantees within states that have ratified them, as in the United Nations covenants outlawing genocide and slavery and protecting the political rights of women; (3) providing information and assistance to national governments, as in the annual Yearbook on Human Rights; and (4) undertaking action against flagrant violators through assembly condemnations and, as in the case of South Africa, the levying of an arms embargo and economic sanctions. Much controversy has arisen in the United Nations between those states that define human rights in traditional, civil, and political terms and those that place primary emphasis on economic and social rights. On the regional level, examples of human rights systems include the European Convention on Human Rights, authored by the Council of Europe and signed in 1950, the 1975 Helsinki Accord developed by the Conference on Security and Cooperation in Europe, and the Inter-American Convention on the Granting of Civil Rights to Women.

Human Rights: European Convention   530

A treaty, in force since 1953, that establishes international machinery for the protection of human rights in controversies arising among signatory states. Developed under the auspices of the Council of Europe, the European Convention has been accepted by 15 states (Austria, Belgium, Cyprus, Denmark, Germany, Great Britain, Greece, Iceland, Ireland, Italy, Luxembourg, the Netherlands, Norway, Sweden, and Turkey). Only three Council of Europe members—France, Malta, and Switzerland—decided not to become parties to the convention. Ten of the ratifying states further agree that appeals on human rights issues by individuals and private groups can be carried beyond their state courts to an international body. Petitions are first reviewed by a Commission on Human Rights composed of 15 members selected from member states. If the complaint is admissible, the commission reports its findings and recommends action to the Committee of Ministers of the Council of Europe. If the Committee of Ministers is unable to work out an amicable settlement, it may decide the case by a two-thirds vote. Finally, a losing party may appeal to the European Court of Human Rights if he or she is a citizen of one of the states that has ratified an optional protocol accepting its jurisdiction. Each of the members of the Council of Europe is represented on the court whether or not it has accepted the protocol. Enforcement of court decisions depends on voluntary compliance by affected states because no sanctions are provided by the convention. *See also* HUMAN RIGHTS (529); REGIONAL POLITICAL GROUP: COUNCIL OF EUROPE (564).

Significance

The European Convention on Human Rights provides the most extensive international machinery for the protection of human rights in the history of the state system. Yet, in practice it has not served as a vigorous defender of individual liberties. Of several thousand complaints brought to the commission, only a few have been found admissible, and the court has considered only a handful of cases. In 1979, in a typical case, the European Court of Human Rights ruled by an 11–9 vote that a British court injunction prohibiting London's *Sunday Times* from publishing an article because it would prejudice a lawsuit against the manufacturer of thalidomide violated the European Convention on Human Rights. The convention's most important impact has been in breaking new ground for international action in a field in which individuals are increasingly demanding more protection than is provided by their own governments. The European system serves as a model for other regional groups and may contribute to the building of a global system under the aegis of the United Nations. The sovereignty of nations, however, militates against outsiders assisting those faced with human rights abuses in their own countries. The end of the Cold War led many to prematurely conclude that regional and international organizations would play a more effective role in protecting the weak and defenseless within given societies. But in the face of hard realities in Rwanda, Kashmir, Haiti, Cambodia, Sri Lanka, and so many other places, it became clear that human rights, even those developed in Europe, were still a long way from being realized.

Human Rights: Universal Declaration   531

A proclamation intended to establish a "common standard of achievement for all peoples and all nations" in the observance of civil, political, economic, social, and cultural rights. Prepared by the Commission on Human Rights and the Economic and Social Council, the Universal Declaration was adopted by the General Assembly on 10 December 1948, since designated Human Rights Day. Since 1954 the General Assembly has been working on two draft covenants—one containing civil and political rights, the other economic, social, and cultural rights—intended to make the rights proclaimed in the Universal Declaration effective by national ratification. In addition, nations that accept the first of these covenants may also ratify an Optional Protocol to the Covenant on Civil and Political Rights by which individuals would be authorized to bring complaints to an international body. *See also* HUMAN RIGHTS (529).

Significance
Although most of the rights set forth in the Universal Declaration have not yet been adopted as international legislation through the treaty ratification process, they are not a dead issue. Many of the new nations have been guided by the document in writing their national constitutions. In all states, the declaration can be used as a yardstick to measure the congruity of national protection of individual rights with this international standard. In several cases, such as Rhodesia and South Africa, the Universal Declaration has served as a basis for condemning national constitutional systems that permit discrimination against racial, religious, social, or political groups. Within the United Nations, the Universal Declaration has established international norms that influence the making of decisions in all principal organs and subsidiary bodies.

League of Nations $\boxed{532}$
A global international organization established by the victors of World War I to preserve peace and security and to promote economic and social cooperation among its members. A covenant consisting of 26 articles included in the Treaty of Versailles served as the constitution for the organization. Although President Woodrow Wilson provided the leadership in developing the league and was chairman of the committee that wrote the covenant, the United States failed to join when the Senate refused to consent to the treaty. Neutral states were invited to be-

come original members, and defeated enemy states were in time permitted to join, resulting in near universality, with the United States the only major holdout. Sixty-three countries ultimately accepted membership, although the maximum number of members at any one time was 58. A council and assembly, resembling the UN Security Council and General Assembly, were the major organs, each requiring unanimity for reaching decisions. Subsidiary bodies aided the two major organs in carrying out their responsibilities in such fields as mandates, disarmament, and economic and social welfare. A Permanent Court of International Justice (PCIJ), forerunner of the present International Court of Justice (ICJ), and the International Labor Organization (ILO) were independent of the league, but coordinated their activities with it. The heart of the league's peacekeeping system called for the members to accept political or legal settlement of their disputes with sanctions to be levied by the league community against any state that went to war in violation of its covenants.

Significance
Unlike the United Nations Charter, which would outlaw war in given situations, the league covenant aimed at making all war illegal. Although the League of Nations' record in resolving many dangerous disputes and situations during the first decade was generally satisfactory, it failed to act decisively when confronted with the challenge of direct aggression by Japan against China in the Manchurian crisis of 1931. In 1935, following an attack by Italy on Ethiopia, for the first and only time the league levied sanctions against an aggressor, but it failed to deter the conquest. The sanctions were undermined from the outset by a secret treaty between Britain and France (Hoare-Laval Treaty) that permitted Italy to purchase oil from their companies and move supplies through the Suez Canal, which was under British control. The Italians were thus allowed to succeed in their imperial venture, and their actions encouraged further aggressions by Nazi Germany,

Japan, and the Soviet Union prior to the outbreak of World War II. Clearly, the League of Nations could not call for collective action when Britain and France were engaged in abetting the Italian operations against Ethiopia. Given the duplicity of its key members, the league failed in its mission to maintain the peace in East Africa, but it nevertheless helped settle many disputes, and it also encouraged technical cooperation among members and worked to improve economic and social conditions in a number of states. The league's utter inability to prevent the outbreak of World War II, however, is often traced to its largely idealistic foundation. In 1946 the league met for a final session in Geneva, voted itself out of existence, and turned over its assets to the United Nations, which was described as a more realistic representation of the world of nation-states. Today, league buildings in Geneva constitute the European headquarters of the United Nations.

League of Nations: Covenant | 533 |

A multilateral treaty (Part I of the Treaty of Versailles) that created the League of Nations. The covenant of the league resembled a national constitution in that it provided for the establishment of major organs and a decision-making system and enunciated principles to guide the actions of its members. *See also* LEAGUE OF NATIONS (532).

Significance
The covenant delineated the procedures whereby the league's twofold objectives of preserving peace and security and promoting international cooperation could be achieved. The brief document of 26 articles and general language provided flexibility for adjusting to changing world conditions. The collapse of the league resulted not from internal constitutional weaknesses but from the failure of key member states to support its principles and the refusal of the United States to join the organization.

League of Nations: Mandates System | 534 |

The arrangement whereby the colonial territories of the defeated Central Powers of World War I (Germany and Turkey) were placed under the guardianship and tutelage of Allied nations. Each Mandatory Power was responsible to the League of Nations in the administration of its mandate. Mandated territories were classified into three groups according to their relative stages of development. Class A mandates (Arab territories formerly under Turkish dominion) were regarded as ready for independence and self-government after a minimal period of tutelage. Class B mandates (German East and West Africa) were given no promises of early independence and were to be governed as colonies with certain fundamental rights guaranteed. Class C mandates (German South-West Africa and Pacific islands) were to be governed as "internal portions of the [Mandatory Power's] territory," with no promise of eventual independence. A Permanent Mandates Commission of ten private experts was established under the covenant to oversee the administration of the mandates and report its findings to the League Council. *See also* UNITED NATIONS: TRUST TERRITORY (588).

Significance
The mandates system, adopted at the Versailles peace conference as an alternative to annexation by the victors, established the precedent that the international community has a responsibility for the well-being of subject peoples. Several mandates—Iraq, Syria, and Lebanon—achieved independence; all other mandates except South-West Africa were placed under the trusteeship system of the United Nations in 1946. South-West Africa's exclusion was a matter of deliberate policy by the government of South Africa, which controlled the mandate. Thus, each of the UN trust territories eventually gained their independence. The only exception was the Trust Territory of the Pacific Islands, which was placed under a special arrangement

known as a "strategic trust," and made the responsibility of the United States. South-West Africa, the one remaining mandate, remained under South African rule long after the demise of the League of Nations, but in 1990 it too achieved independence as Namibia, following a long guerrilla war fought by the South-West African Peoples Organization (SWAPO). In 1966 the UN General Assembly adopted a resolution extending its jurisdiction over South-West Africa (Namibia), but the Republic of South Africa resisted all international efforts pressuring it to accept the will of the people in the territory. The United Nations did not yield to South Africa, and finally, in the 1980s, a settlement was negotiated by the world body. UN peacekeepers were dispatched to the region, and a peaceful transfer of power was accomplished. Namibia became the 160th member of the United Nations in March 1990.

Political Community 535

Any social unit or group holding common values, utilizing mutual institutions for decision making, and complying with decisions made. The level of integration within a political community is determined by the volume of social transactions carried on, the extent to which decision making is centralized, and the degree of nonviolent resolution of conflict among members of the community. A political community may take the form of (1) a regional organization that fosters limited cooperation among members in specific areas, (2) a federal system with the central authority possessing supranational powers, or (3) a unitary community resulting from the merger of previously sovereign entities. *See also* CONSENSUS OF VALUES (106).

Significance
The creation of political communities beyond the level of the national state has become commonplace in the contemporary state system. Functionalism provides the main integrating force for the

new movement; for pragmatic reasons, states have joined in cooperative attacks on common economic, social, and political problems. More than 30 major regional groups have been established since World War II. The Commission of the European Union illustrates supranational organization in that it can make decisions binding on its members. Unitary communities have been created by the merger of two or more state units, as in the case of Tanganyika and Zanzibar (Tanzania).

Political Community: Atlantic Community 536

The concept of a partnership among the states of Western Europe and North America to solve common security, economic, social, and political problems. The Atlantic Community idea, based on a common Western cultural heritage, received added impetus from the threat of aggression by Eastern Europe. Although no regional organization includes all Atlantic Community states, the Organization for Economic Cooperation and Development (OECD) and the Council of Europe have memberships that include most of the 25 states in the region. Other groups that have helped to integrate the policies of the states in the region include the North Atlantic Treaty Organization (NATO), the European Union (EU), and the European Free Trade Association (EFTA). The Atlantic Council of the United States, based in Washington, is the primary spokesman for the Atlantic Community, and especially for NATO. It functions as a high-powered creator and distributor of information on all matters affecting the Atlantic Community, and has among its members many of the leaders in American political, business, and academic life. *See also* POLITICAL COMMUNITY (535).

Significance
The development of the Atlantic Community idea helped to produce a rapprochement between former enemies of World War II and a unity of policy fostered

through joint consultations on major issues. In the 1960s and 1970s, France's withdrawal from NATO, U.S. preoccupation with the Vietnam War, and the reduced threat of aggression from Eastern Europe contributed to a weakening of Atlantic Community ties. Resurgent nationalism slowed progress toward the original goal of an Atlantic union based on a supranational institutional framework for political decision making. The Atlantic Community prevailed over that of the Eastern bloc of Communist states, and since the disappearance of the Soviet Union in 1991, the community has been under pressure to justify its continuation, especially the NATO alliance. The 1994 formation of the Partnership for Peace, which links the former Soviet republics and formerly Communist states of Eastern Europe with NATO and the Atlantic Community, appears to reinforce the argument that NATO remains important. Nevertheless, the extension of the NATO arena advances the notion of an Atlantic Community that stretches all the way to the Pacific Rim and well into the Caucasus and Central Asia.

Political Community: Confederation | 537

An association of states that seeks to achieve national objectives through common political or economic institutions. A confederation differs from a federation in that its members retain full sovereignty, whereas in a federation political authority is constitutionally divided between a central and regional units of government. Global organizations such as the League of Nations and the United Nations and regional organizations such as the North Atlantic Treaty Organization (NATO), the Organization of American States (OAS), and the Organization of African Unity (OAU) embody the confederation principle. Decisions may be made by unanimity, majority voting, or weighted vote, but no state can be forced to accept a majority decision against its will or if it considers the decision a threat to its national interests.

Significance
Confederation is a halfway house between independent state action and the establishment of a federal system. Advocates of world federation regard a global confederation like the United Nations as an evolutionary step toward a higher level of political integration, as occurred in the U.S. experience. Although a confederation lacks the powers to make and enforce laws, its decision-making authority is as extensive as the consensus developed within the association.

Political Community: Functionalism | 538

The theory that postulates the building of a world community slowly and cumulatively through progressively expanding programs of economic and social cooperation rather than by direct political integration. Functionalism is based on the premise that economic and social problems tend to be worldwide in scope; therefore, a coherent attack upon these problems necessitates common action by members of the state system. In addition, habits of cooperation that result from successful progress toward objectives in economic and social fields may then be transferred into political integration.

Significance
Functionalism as a theory of international integration helps to explain the evolution of a consensus among nations, which enables them to move to higher levels of cooperation. The ultimate consequence of the process, functionalists assert, could be a form of world government based on interlocking functional units. But more immediately, the functional approach in international affairs involves the development of coherent regional organizations wherein several or more states agree to pool their efforts and resources, usually in economic and technical matters, to maximize their advantages in the larger world. The Common Market in Western Europe used this strategy to assemble the European Economic Community, ultimately the European Community and

today's European Union. Prior to the development of the Common Market in the 1950s, serious effort went into creating a unified, integrated Western Europe by stressing its security needs. That attempt at forging a larger community did not succeed. The functionalist approach was more successful because it represented a form of "federalism without tears," and in fact proved to be a boon to the European states recovering from the ravages of World War II. Moreover, as the base of economic and social cooperation expanded in Western Europe, a "spinoff" or "spillover" effect occurred that encouraged the building of a more successful supranational political community. Functionalist theory has been used by scholars who seek to understand the larger implications of systems transformation among the world's nation-states.

Political Community: International Organization 　539

A formal arrangement transcending national boundaries that provides for the establishment of institutional machinery to facilitate cooperation among members in security, economic, social, or related fields. Modern international organizations, which began to emerge more than a century ago in the Western state system, have flowered in the twentieth century—the age of international cooperation. Two types of international organizations are active: public arrangements between two or more states, and private associations of individuals or groups known as nongovernmental organizations (NGOs). Public international organizations include global political arrangements (the League of Nations and the United Nations), regional groups (for example, the North Atlantic Treaty Organization [NATO], the Organization of American States [OAS], and the Arab League), and public international unions (the Universal Postal Union and the World Health Organization [WHO]). Examples of private international organizations include Rotary International, the International Confederation of Free Trade Unions, and the International Red Cross.

Significance

International organizations of great variety and institutions of varying degrees of integration exist in the contemporary world. It is difficult to assess the degree to which such institutions contribute to peace, international understanding, and well-being. Critics tend to polarize their views; one group prefers a unilateral approach to security and greater national flexibility in economic and social affairs, and the other views international organization as ineffectual and calls for a stronger union in the form of one or several federal arrangements. Supporters of international organization assert that it offers means by which states can achieve many objectives; in each case, however, the extent of cooperation necessary to produce useful results depends on the degree of common interest among the members.

Political Community: Nongovernmental Organization (NGO) 　540

Private international groups that serve as a mechanism for cooperation among private national groups in international affairs, especially in the economic, social, cultural, humanitarian, and technical fields. Under the United Nations Charter (Article 71), the Economic and Social Council is empowered to make suitable arrangements for consultation with NGOs on matters within their competence. NGOs are also known as transnational associations. *See also:* TRANSNATIONAL PATTERN: CHARACTER OF NONGOVERNMENTAL ORGANIZATIONS (NGOs) (711).

Significance

Nongovernmental organizations have been active in international affairs for many years, some dating back over a century. Thousands of NGOs are active in today's world, and more than 300 have become consultants for the Economic and Social Council (ECOSOC). Examples of NGOs include environmental, consumer and producer associations, religious groups, teacher organizations, professional legal and medical societies, trade unions, and pressure groups concerned with armaments and their distribution.

Political Community: NGO, International Center for Peace Initiatives (ICPI)   541

A nongovernmental organization established in Bombay, India, in 1990 to develop and promote innovative approaches to peace at global, regional, and national levels. The International Center for Peace Initiatives acts as a catalyst in partnership with leading institutions in India and around the world whose concerns are international peace and security. In the global context, the ICPI advocates a cooperative security regime free of nuclear weapons. Regionally, it is engaged in exploring ways and means of conflict resolution with particular reference to South Asia. In recognition of the fact that global demilitarization and regional conflict resolution need to be accompanied by policies of economic growth, the ICPI brokers discussions between Indian business leaders and government officials.

Significance
The International Center for Peace Initiatives points to the need in South Asia as well as globally for clearer expositions on the subject of peace and security. In this regard it has organized a steering committee to guide the process of conflict resolution. ICPI collaborates with relevant institutions in developing research projects, preparing blueprints for political action, and by opening its own diplomatic forum, which engages lay public organizations. The significance of ICPI work cannot be overstated in the climate of confrontation and conflict pitting two nuclear powers—India and Pakistan—in a deadly game of threat and counterthreat. The long unresolved dispute over Kashmir, and the intensification of the conflict in the Himalayan state in 1995, points to the failure of traditional diplomacy and the special role played by nongovernmental organizations like ICPI in

attempting to address the problem in the cold light of rational thought.

Political Community: Regionalism   542

The concept that nations situated in a geographical area or sharing common concerns can cooperate with one another through a limited-membership organization to meet military, political, and functional problems. Regionalism provides a middle-level approach to problem solving, between the extremes of unilateralism and universalism. The UN Charter encourages regionalism as complementary to the world organization's objectives and activities, but provides that all regional actions be consistent with the purposes and principles of the United Nations. Regional organizations include (1) military-alliance systems, such as the North Atlantic Treaty Organization (NATO); (2) economic arrangements, such as the European Union (EU), the European Free Trade Association (EFTA), Benelux, the Latin American Integration Association (LAIA), and the Central American Common Market; and (3) political groupings, such as the Organization of American States (OAS), the Council of Europe, the Arab League, and the Organization of African Unity (OAU). (*For specific regional organizations, see* Index.)

Significance
The prolific growth of limited-member organizations since World War II stems from a new emphasis on regional integration as a means for achieving national interest goals. The role of regional alliances has been the most controversial during this period, superimposing several balance-of-power systems upon the collective-security approach of the United Nations. Observers differ as to whether military groups have added to the threat of war or contributed to the maintenance of peace and security. In pacific settlement cases, jurisdictional controversies have also arisen between those supporting regional handling of the disputes and those seeking to bring them under the aegis of the United Nations.

Jurisdictional disputes arose, for example, between the Organization of American States (OAS) and the United Nations during the Cuban, Dominican, Nicaraguan, El Salvadoran, and Guatemalan crises. Functional organizations have received the most support and have been the least controversial outgrowths of regionalism, although increasing trade discrimination by rival groups could reverse the trend toward freer world trade. Psychologically, individuals are more likely to give their support to limited-member groups than to a distant world organization. Regionalism is sometimes seen as a "gradualist" approach to the building of international communities and political federations beyond the nation-state. Some observers of the international scene are convinced that the nation-state has already given way to the region-state in several parts of the world.

Political Community: Supranationalism | 543 |

Power exercised by international institutions to make majority-vote decisions that are binding upon all member states or their citizens. Supranationalism involves a transfer of decision-making authority in prescribed areas from constituent units to a central body. Members must accept supranational decisions or withdraw from the system. Decisions may be made either by representatives of member governments or by an institution that functions as an integral unit of the international arrangement. Supranationalism in effect establishes a limited federal system with powers divided between the two levels. *See also* POLITICAL COMMUNITY (535).

Significance

Supranationalism is possible when states voluntarily delegate some of their sovereignty to central institutions. Yet supranationalism has received little support in a world composed of independent, sovereign states whose leaders jealously guard against any loss of their decision-making prerogatives. The Commission of the European Union is a rare example of a supranational institution that initiates policies, functions as an executive body, and makes decisions within prescribed areas that are binding upon member states and private groups and individuals. The Security Council, unlike other UN organs, is empowered under the charter to make supranational decisions in peace and security matters that are binding upon the members. The council exercised this power during the Gulf War of 1990–1991 when it authorized action against Iraq in order to restore the sovereign independence of Kuwait, which Iraq had overrun and absorbed. The council also acted as a supranational body when it levied compulsory economic sanctions on Rhodesia in 1966.

Political Community: World Government | 544 |

A concept of a global political entity that strives for peace and security through the establishment of a higher authority over that of the independent states. Most advocates of world government envisage the establishment of a federation having a central authority vested with specifically delegated powers, while the residue of governmental powers would remain with the constituent units or states. A world law directly applicable and enforceable upon individual states would emanate from the central world government. The most active organization promoting the idea of world government in the United States is the World Federalist Association, whose campaign in 1995 was entitled "Campaign for Global Change." The association believes that only an effective world government is capable of providing sufficient law and the necessary power to control the world's destructive forces. Linked to the World Federalist Association was the World Federalist Movement, presided over by actor Peter Ustinov and Yul Anderson, founder of the African American Future Society. Former correspondent and TV anchorman Walter Cronkite was also an active supporter of the idea of world government. *See also* PATTERNS OF POWER: WORLD GOVERNMENT (25).

Significance
Proponents of world government are split between those who believe that the establishment of a world federal system should be given highest priority, and those who regard the evolutionary development of a world community based on common values and objectives as a necessary antecedent to the political structure. The American experience with federalism is often cited by advocates of world government as a precedent that should be emulated on the global level. The practical question of how to obtain a consensus from almost 200 diverse states on the establishment of a "higher authority" that would abolish their sovereignty in the most critical areas has never been satisfactorily answered. Several disarmament proposals advanced by the great powers would, if put into effect, provide for a limited form of world government to ensure that the agreement would be kept through inspection and enforcement by an international agency. In the Third Law of the Sea Treaty (1982), provision was made for the creation of an International Seabed Authority that would exercise supranational powers in regulating the extraction of wealth from the seabed of the world's oceans. Opponents of the world government idea, however, were more prevalent in the 1990s than those supporting it. The antagonists often took extreme positions, the most reactionary being identified with the militia movement in the United States that centered its attack on the United Nations. The militias in the different states all pressed the same argument: The United Nations is intent on destroying the U.S. Constitution, with help and encouragement from U.S. officials and other notables, such as those in the Trilateral Commission, as a first step before invading and physically taking over the country. Up to the 1990s, World Federalists were always viewed as a marginal group of well-meaning, if overly idealistic people. The aggressive verbal assault on the United Nations from American right-wing groups, however, fell heavily on these same people, bringing the issue of world government from somewhere in outer space down to earth.

Regional Economic Group: Amazon Pact $\boxed{545}$

A treaty for the purpose of coordinating the development of the Amazon river basin and protecting the region's environment through rational use of its resources. Parties to the 1978 treaty include Bolivia, Brazil, Colombia, Ecuador, Guyana, Peru, Surinam, and Venezuela. Treaty provisions include (1) careful use of the region's water resources, (2) the right of each to develop its Amazon territory so long as it does not adversely affect other members' territories, (3) free navigation on all rivers in the region, (4) improvement of health and the building of a transportation and communication infrastructure, (5) encouragement of a common research effort, and (6) promotion of tourism. An Amazon Cooperation Council, composed of ministers from each member country, meets annually to carry out the provisions of the treaty and develop policies and programs.

Significance
The Amazon Pact is an excellent example of how independent nations within a geographical region can, despite their different political and social systems, unite to cope with common ecological and developmental problems. Although it is not a powerful and united supranational group, its ability to elicit cooperation demonstrates that certain kinds of problems can be dealt with through interstate cooperation even though no state can be bound against its will. Its main objective—to stop a ruthless, ecologically disastrous plundering of the resources of the Amazon basin—has not been achieved, but progress has been made. Moreover, the potential for war growing out of national competition in opening the vast area to economic exploitation has been reduced. The Amazon Pact has practical and symbolic value, and both tend to contribute to the improvement of relations among the pact's signatories.

Regional Economic Group: Andean Common Market | 546 |

An economic group established in 1969 to improve its members' bargaining power within the larger Latin American Free Trade Association (LAFTA) and foster trade and development. Members of the Andean Group include Bolivia, Colombia, Ecuador, Peru, and Venezuela. Chile was an original member but withdrew in 1976. Concerned with the slow pace of economic integration within LAFTA, these nations reached agreement to establish a common market as a means for reinvigorating LAFTA. Objectives pursued by the Andean Group include (1) eliminating trade barriers among members by establishing a common market, (2) establishing common external tariff rates, (3) encouraging industrialization through specialization by assigning industry rights among members, (4) giving special concessions to the poorer members, and (5) extending control over multinational corporations operating within the common market. The Andean Group set up a Mixed Commission at its headquarters in Lima, Peru, that functions as the Supreme Organ, aided in its decision making by a Council and a Consulting Committee of Experts. A Development Corporation, which helps finance developmental projects, is also part of the institutional structure. *See also* REGIONAL ECONOMIC GROUP: LATIN AMERICAN INTEGRATION ASSOCIATION (LAIA) (553).

Significance
The Andean Common Market was originated largely as a means to overcome the lack of progress within LAFTA. Unlike the other two major economic groups in Latin America—LAFTA and the Central American Common Market—the Andean nations reject free-trade and market economics in favor of "central planning," "directed economies," and "regional cooperation" as the best approaches to achieving modernization. Virtually all tariffs have been eliminated within the common market, and a common external tariff has been constructed. The Andean Group continues to function within

LAFTA despite its conflicts with the larger, more conservative members of that group.

Regional Economic Group: Asian and Pacific Council (ASPAC) | 547 |

A regional organization established in 1966 to encourage economic, social, and cultural cooperation among members. ASPAC's membership includes: Australia, Japan, Malaysia, New Zealand, Philippines, South Korea, Taiwan, and Thailand. The initiative to establish ASPAC originated with South Korea. ASPAC conferences are held annually in major cities of member states. Between general conferences, the ambassadors of member states to Thailand meet monthly in Bangkok as a standing committee under the chairmanship of the Thai foreign minister. Thailand also provides the secretariat for the organization.

Significance
The Asian and Pacific Council professes to be nonmilitary, nonaligned, and nonideological. ASPAC has issued proclamations and declarations on matters of common interest, such as its condemnation of nuclear testing in the Asia-Pacific area. Most programs inaugurated or under consideration by ASPAC, however, relate to joint efforts in solving problems of economic development.

Regional Economic Group: Association of Southeast Asian Nations (ASEAN) | 548 |

A regional organization established in 1967 to accelerate economic growth, social progress, and cultural development in Southeast Asia. The members of the ASEAN group are Indonesia, Malaysia, Philippines, Singapore, Thailand, Brunei, and Vietnam. The Republic of Vietnam was admitted to membership in ASEAN in July 1995, following the country's formal recognition by the United States earlier in the month. The regional organization is an expanded version of the

Association of Southeast Asia (ASA), established in 1961 by Malaysia, Philippines, and Thailand.

Significance

The Association of Southeast Asian Nations represents an effort to develop Asian solutions to Asian problems in a cooperative arrangement, consisting wholly of nations in the region. Mainly concerned with economic and social problems, the preamble to the declaration establishing ASEAN nevertheless affirmed that all foreign bases in the region are "temporary and remain only with the expressed concurrence of countries concerned." Although ASEAN has only partially met its economic and social objectives, it has become the most dynamic political association in the region's history. Singapore is associated with the Pacific Rim group known as the "four tigers" (the others are Taiwan, Hong Kong, and South Korea); Brunei has one of the highest per capita incomes in the world; and Thailand, Malaysia, and Indonesia are moving aggressively forward in their economic and financial development. Only the Philippines lags behind, but it too anticipates an improved standing as a consequence of its membership in ASEAN. The matter of including other countries within the association centered on Vietnam and, to a lesser extent, Cambodia. Vietnam was eager to join the charmed economic circle of nations on the Pacific Rim, and its newly energized market economy has already opened the country to the larger world. Vietnam's inclusion in ASEAN in July 1995 followed American recognition and illustrated the changing character of international relations on the Pacific Rim. Vietnam's orientation away from ideological matters and toward economic development had already brought the commercial world into its everyday life, and its inclusion in ASEAN confirmed that the Southeast Asian country was no longer a perceived military, let alone a Communist, threat to the region.

Regional Economic Group: Benelux | 549 |

A customs union agreement established by Belgium, Luxembourg, and the Netherlands to eliminate trade barriers, establish a single external tariff, and foster economic union among the three. The agreement, signed in London during World War II and entered into effect on 1 January 1948, abolished most internal tariffs and established a common external tariff. A treaty to harmonize the fiscal and monetary policies of the three by establishing an economic union came into force in 1960. Benelux countries have also agreed to negotiate and enter economic and trade treaties and arrangements as a unit, with no separate national treaties to be concluded. Benelux organization includes a Conference of Cabinet Ministers, a Council for Economic Union, an Administrative Council on Customs Duties, an Administrative Council to provide for a common foreign economic policy toward other states, and a secretariat located at Benelux headquarters in Brussels. *See also* ECONOMIC INTEGRATION: CUSTOMS UNION (216).

Significance

The full realization of economic integration objectives has not been achieved by Benelux, but much progress has been made. Benelux has been increasingly overshadowed by the larger framework of the European Union (EU) as the means for securing integration. At the same time, Benelux has proved useful in combining the bargaining power of the three smallest members of the EU against that of the larger members (France, Germany, Great Britain, Italy, and Spain). One of the major difficulties preventing the achievement of full Benelux integration objectives has been that of harmonizing domestic policies between a laissez faire–oriented Belgian economy and the more extensive direction of economic activity by the Dutch government. Nevertheless, Benelux has levied a common system of excise taxes and a uniform tariff on non-EU imports, and has concluded uniform trade and emigration agreements with non-EU countries.

Regional Economic Group: Caribbean Community and Common Market (CARICOM) | 550 |

A regional economic group established by the Treaty of Chaguaramas of 1973, which set up a customs union with free trade among members and a common external tariff and called for the harmonization of the domestic economic policies of its members. CARICOM's basic charter objectives include maximizing the balanced development of members, achieving the highest level of economic integration possible, developing a common bargaining position toward other regional economic groups, and fostering import protection through a Common Protective Policy aimed at encouraging local industry and agriculture. The group emerged as a successor to the Caribbean Free Trade Association (CARIFTA). CARICOM membership has included a number of Caribbean independent states, semi-independent states still "associated" with Great Britain, and several colonies. All remaining nonsovereign entities, however, are moving toward full independence. For decision-making purposes members are divided into two categories: (1) the More Developed Countries (MDCs), which include the independent states of the Bahamas, Barbados, Guyana, Jamaica, and Trinidad and Tobago; and (2) the Less Developed Countries (LDCs), which include Antigua and Barbuda; Belize; Dominica; Grenada; Montserrat; St. Christopher and Nevis; St. Kitts, St. Lucia, and St. Vincent; and the Grenadines. CARICOM functions through a Heads of Government Conference (HGC), its central governing body. It also uses a Common Market Council (CMC) to make recommendations to the HGC, and a Caribbean Community Secretariat serves both CARICOM and CARIFTA. Subsidiary agencies also help the organization make progress, including the Caribbean Development Bank. The Caribbean Basin Initiative (CBI), a Reagan-administration

program, also sought to encourage trade and development through private investment and a liberalized tariff policy.

Significance

The Caribbean Community and Common Market has moved a long way toward realization of its basic charter objectives. It serves as a model for other Third World developing countries searching for a breakthrough approach that will show them the way to modernization. Using the European Union as a model, CARICOM is making slow but steady progress toward economic and political integration. The main barrier to a more rapid transition toward unity is the built-in conflict between the MDCs and the LDCs. As in most such groupings, members with stronger economies tend to push for freer trade, whereas members with weaker economies are reluctant to give up many governmental programs of protection for their industry and agriculture. Other threats to CARICOM's continued growth include conflicts among members over the role of foreign investment and whether free enterprise or socialism should provide the basic guidelines for the future.

Regional Economic Group: Central American Common Market (CACM) | 551 |

A regional organization that endeavors to promote economic development in member states through a customs union and industrial integration scheme. Five Central American states—Costa Rica, El Salvador, Guatemala, Honduras, and Nicaragua—ratified an Economic Integration Treaty of 1960 that, together with several protocols and supplementary agreements, provided for a significant integration of their economies. The assumption underlying the common-market system was that industrialization and specialization would be encouraged by the broader market and free-trade arrangement, so that foreign investment capital in sizable amounts would be attracted to the region. Common Market decisions are made by (1) the Central American

Economic Council, which is composed of members' economic ministers and develops policies concerning the integration of their economies; (2) an Executive Council, which implements decisions made by the Economic Council; and (3) a secretariat, which provides technical and administrative assistance at the Guatemala City headquarters. The Central American Bank for Economic Integration functions within the system by helping to finance the development program. *See also* REGIONAL POLITICAL GROUP: ORGANIZATION OF CENTRAL AMERICAN STATES (OCAS, also known as ODECA) (572).

Significance
The Central American Common Market eliminated virtually all customs duties, and trade increased substantially during the 1960s and 1970s. The common market idea had to overcome much nationalist rivalry dating back more than a century, and the CACM represented the highest level of economic integration yet obtained in Latin America. Although it has not provided an easy shortcut to development, significant progress has occurred and investment capital is being increasingly attracted from the United States.

Regional Economic Group: European Free Trade Association (EFTA) | 552 |

A regional organization established by the Stockholm Convention of 1959 to eliminate tariffs and other trade barriers among members and harmonize internal production-cost factors. In addition to setting up a timetable to eliminate industrial tariffs by 1970, EFTA's original members (Austria, Denmark, Great Britain, Norway, Portugal, Sweden, and Switzerland) agreed to try to reduce trade barriers on agriculture and fish. In 1961 Finland joined EFTA as an associate member through the FINEFTA treaty, which provided for extension of the free-trade area to Finland, a special council to resolve questions relating to Finnish membership, and the continuance of Finland's special trade arrangements with

the Soviet Union. In 1970 Iceland became a full member. Heading EFTA's simple organizational structure is a Council of Ministers, which settles disputes, reviews complaints, makes recommendations to member governments, and serves as the agency for negotiating major decisions. Six standing committees make recommendations to the council on policy questions, a secretariat functions at the Geneva headquarters, and representatives of EFTA countries to the Consultative Assembly of the Council of Europe meet informally at Strasbourg during annual sessions. EFTA's role was greatly weakened but not destroyed by the decision of three members—Great Britain and Denmark in 1973, and Portugal in 1986—to join the rival European Economic Community (EEC). A free-trade area comprising all EEC and EFTA members was established by a customs union agreement in 1977.

Significance
Dubbed from the outset the "Outer Seven," EFTA in the main represented an effort to secure a sound bargaining position with the "Inner Six" of the Common Market in the early 1960s. All tariffs and other barriers to trade in industrial goods among members were abolished, but little progress was made in reducing tariffs on fish and agricultural products. EFTA's future once depended on the success or failure of the larger, more powerful EEC, and on whether EFTA nations could compete effectively with it. Since the further integration of Western European states in the European Union, and especially after the Maastricht Treaty calling for political union among members of the European Community, EFTA members, preferring their independence, find strength in promoting their individual and collective needs unencumbered by supranational demands.

Regional Economic Group: Latin American Integration Association (LAIA) | 553 |

A regional group, established by a treaty signed in Montevideo in 1980, that seeks to increase regional economic development through joint action. The Latin American Integration Association supersedes the Latin American Free Trade Association (LAFTA), which was set up by the 1960 Treaty of Montevideo. LAIA is also known by the Spanish acronym ALADI, for Asociaciõn Latinoamericana de Integraciõn. Unlike LAFTA, it does not plan to eliminate all tariffs among its members by a specified date. Rather, LAIA wants tariff concessions to be granted individually, based on the economy of each member. Under the new arrangement, the richer members are expected to grant more liberal concessions to the poorer ones. To encourage such actions, the treaty creating LAIA divides the 11 signatory states into three groups according to their level of development: (1) less developed (Bolivia, Ecuador, and Paraguay), (2) medium developed (Chile, Colombia, Peru, Uruguay, and Venezuela), and (3) more developed (Argentina, Brazil, and Mexico). *See also* DEVELOPMENT: THIRD WORLD DEBT CRISIS (196).

Significance
The membership of the Latin American Integration Association includes the most important countries of Latin America, with three-fourths of the population south of the U.S. border. The creation of the new organization was a direct result of the failure of LAFTA to reach its goal of a regional free-trade area. The decision to replace LAFTA was made at a final meeting of that organization in 1980. LAFTA's stagnation was the result of such factors as different levels of development among members, demands by powerful groups and industries for continued protection of local products, communication and transport problems in the region, conflicting economic systems, and political and economic changes. The threefold classification system adopted by LAIA is directed at overcoming some of these problems. Whether the new organization can surmount the difficulties that plagued LAFTA for its 20 years of existence remains problematical. Many of LAIA's members are deep in debt to Western public and private financial institutions, adding to their trade and development problems.

Regional Economic Group: Organization for Economic Cooperation and Development (OECD) | 554 |

A regional economic organization established in 1961 to promote economic growth and freer trade and to expand and improve Western aid to the developing countries. OECD's 24 members include 12 from the European Union (Belgium, Denmark, France, Germany, Great Britain, Greece, Ireland, Italy, Luxembourg, the Netherlands, Portugal, and Spain), the members of the European Free Trade Association (EFTA) (Austria, Finland, Iceland, Norway, Sweden, and Switzerland), and Australia, New Zealand, Turkey, Canada, the United States, and Japan. Before its dissolution, Yugoslavia had a special status with OECD. The OECD replaced the Organization for European Economic Cooperation (OEEC), established in 1948 to elicit common action among Marshall Plan–recipient countries to aid their recovery from World War II. Major organs include a Council of Representatives from all member countries, an Executive Committee of ten members elected annually by the council, and a secretariat, headed by a secretary-general, located at its Paris headquarters. Subsidiary bodies include the Development Assistance Committee (coordinates aid programs to developing states), the Economic Policy Committee (recommends policies to encourage economic expansion), and the Trade Committee (strives to resolve trade issues).

Significance
The Organization for Economic Cooperation and Development represents a major effort on the part of the advanced Western nations to harmonize their internal and foreign economic policies. Major subjects of concern for the OECD are consumer demand, output, employment, costs, prices, foreign trade, and the problem of eliciting cooperation

among members to combat inflation and OPEC oil pricing. U.S. objectives sought through the OECD framework have included opening European markets to overcome discrimination fostered by EU and EFTA preferential trading systems, correcting the deficit in the U.S. balance of payments, and equalizing the foreign-aid burden among the industrialized states. The OECD has been most active in trying to harmonize national programs of technical and developmental assistance. It has established general policies and principles to guide member nations and holds an annual review conference in which representatives of member countries defend their programs and policies in open inquiry. Major decisions are typically initiated by the six largest members—Canada, France, Great Britain, Japan, the United States, and Germany—with the United States playing a key role in policy development.

Regional Military Group: Central Treaty Organization (CENTO) | 555 |

A regional alliance established on U.S. initiative in 1955 to provide security in the Middle East against Communist aggression and to foster economic and social cooperation among its members. CENTO was known as the Baghdad Pact until Iraq withdrew in 1959, following the revolutionary overthrow of its pro-Western government. Membership after 1959 included Great Britain, Iran, Pakistan, and Turkey. Although never a formal member, the United States functioned as an associate and concluded bilateral agreements with Iran, Pakistan, and Turkey that committed it to take action to aid the signatories in resisting a Communist attack. A council was set up to function as the supreme organ of the organization, aided by four main committees (military, economic, countersubversion, and liaison), and a secretariat headed by a secretary-general was located at CENTO headquarters in Ankara. Iran abandoned CENTO following the fall of the shah in 1979, and Pakistan followed, sensing it could no longer support membership in

the alliance despite the Soviet invasion of Afghanistan. However, CENTO was shown to be little more than a paper organization, and did not play a role in that conflict. Although CENTO ceased to function in the early 1980s, it lingered on until the end of the Cold War, when it was allowed to fade away. *See also* ALLIANCE: BAGHDAD PACT (279).

Significance
The Central Treaty Organization was supposed to function primarily as a security alliance, only incidentally concerned with economic and social affairs. Its achievement, however, was its work in provoking the development of the 1964 Regional Cooperation for Development (RCD) among Pakistan, Iran, and Turkey, which later became the Economic Cooperation Organization (ECO). These organizations enabled the "northern tier" states to engage in more intimate economic and cultural programs, and sponsored joint communications between them. CENTO organized joint military programs, and its forces carried out naval, ground, and air exercises. Actions also were undertaken under CENTO auspices to control subversion in member countries. A 3,000-mile military telecommunication service linking Ankara to Teheran and Karachi was developed through CENTO, and efforts were made to construct roads and other infrastructure connecting the Muslim nations. Yet, domestic political problems, differences over tactics and strategies, CENTO's failure to attract Arab states to membership and the reluctance of the United States to become a full treaty member weakened the alliance. In 1979 the Iranian Revolution and the fall of the shah ended any chance that CENTO could develop into a purposeful alliance.

Regional Military Group: Inter-American System | 556 |

The oldest regional society of nations in the world, dating back to the First International Conference of American States held in Washington from November 1889 to April 1890. The concept of collective security emerged as a major element in the Inter-American System during the 1930s in response to attempts by the Axis Powers (Germany, Italy, and Japan) to increase their economic and political influence in Latin America. At Inter-American Conferences in Montevideo (1933), Buenos Aires (1936), and Lima (1938), the American states, prompted by Washington and in response to U.S. pledges of nonintervention, agreed that whenever the peace of the hemisphere was threatened, the foreign ministers of the American republics would meet to consult on possible common action. A series of resolutions adopted at the first meetings of foreign ministers (Panama, 1939; Havana, 1940; and Rio de Janeiro, 1942) further developed the inter-American system of collective security as the American states affirmed the principle of hemispheric solidarity against external aggression and established mechanisms to promote defense of the hemisphere. Meeting in Mexico City in March 1945, the American states adopted the Act of Chapultepec, which provided for collective action, including the possibility of the use of armed force, against aggression from either a non-American or hemispheric nation, and pledged the signatories to negotiate a permanent inter-American collective security treaty once World War II ended. The result was the Inter-American Conference for the Maintenance of Continental Peace and Security, convened in Rio de Janeiro in 1947, and the Rio Treaty, which emanated from its deliberations. The Rio Treaty established a permanent inter-American regional security mechanism within the framework of the UN Charter. Signatory states agreed to act collectively in the event of aggression against any one of them, whether it was an armed attack or some other type of threat to territory, sovereignty, or independence. Collective action could be directed against non-American aggressors or any member of the regional community threatening the peace of the area. Decisions on the application of sanctions required a two-thirds majority of a consultative meeting, usually of foreign ministers, and was binding on all members. A member state, however, could not be expected to use armed force without its consent. The Rio Treaty went into effect on 3 December 1948. At the Ninth International Conference of American States, convened in Bogotá in 1948, the American republics took still another major step by approving the Charter of the Organization of American States (OAS). OAS formalized the rights and duties of its members and set forth its guiding principles. The purposes of OAS are: (1) the strengthening of peace and security in the hemisphere and (2) the prevention of disputes among its members, and should disputes arise, assuring that peaceful settlement will be the goal. OAS addressed the matter of collective action against aggressors, and the use of political, juridical, and economic devices in coping with problems within the system. Stressing the rule of law, the conference also approved an American Treaty on Pacific Settlement (Pact of Bogotá), which calls for good offices, mediation, investigation, conciliation, and arbitration. The OAS charter went into force on 13 December 1951. *See also* ALLIANCE: ACT OF CHAPULTEPEC (277); ALLIANCE: RIO TREATY (INTER-AMERICAN TREATY OF RECIPROCAL ASSISTANCE) (288); PATTERNS OF POWER: COLLECTIVE SECURITY (22).

Significance

During the decades of the Cold War, collective-security procedures were applied under both the Rio Treaty and the OAS charter. The majority of cases confronting the Inter-American System involved long-standing regional tensions, rivalries, or territorial disputes, and the collective-security system has been relatively successful in halting hostilities between the disputants. At times the organization has also found answers to the underlying causes of a particular problem. The Permanent Council established by the treaties has been reasonably successful in dealing with these matters, and the foreign ministers have been called on sparingly. Although the Rio Treaty created a political framework for collective security, it did not establish a combined military command (such as NATO) or a military planning agency. Nevertheless, a defense college was created to train military personnel in advanced military science and tactics. But by and large, inter-American peacekeeping forces have been ad hoc and temporary. In 1962, for example, Argentina and the Dominican Republic participated in quarantining Cuba during the Soviet-provoked missile crisis. A majority of American states rejected the organizing of a permanent peace force to serve as the military arm of OAS, and the OAS therefore turned down a U.S. proposal in 1979 to create a combined peace force to restore order in Nicaragua and provide for free elections. The OAS General Assembly also narrowed its area of geographic concern, eliminating Greenland and some high-seas areas. With a majority of OAS states inclined to emphasize the principle of nonintervention and the right of states to choose freely their political, economic, and social organization, the United States insisted on a protocol, including a reservation, that it accepted "no obligation or commitment to negotiate, sign, or ratify a treaty or convention on the subject of collective economic security." The emergence of NAFTA in 1993–1994 initially included only the United States, Mexico, and Canada. Chile has since been added to the Free Trade Area, and other Latin American nations await an invitation of admission. Clearly, in the post–Cold War period, OAS emphasis has been placed more and more on economic cooperation; the fact that the military arm of the Inter-American System has never been developed seems to have little significance. The military intervention in Haiti in 1994, precipitated by the United States with some OAS member state support was transferred in January 1995 to the United Nations, not to an inter-American collective-security system.

Regional Military Group: North Atlantic Treaty Organization (NATO)   557

A regional organization established in 1949 to provide mutual security for its members in the North Atlantic area. NATO served as the means for pursuing the security objectives established by the collective-action provisions of the North Atlantic Treaty. Its 14 active members—Belgium, Canada, Denmark, Germany, Great Britain, Greece, Iceland, Italy, Luxembourg, the Netherlands, Norway, Portugal, Turkey, and the United States—used NATO as a framework for cooperation in military, political, economic, and social matters. France and Spain, also members, remained militarily independent and, although they cooperated with NATO forces, did not participate in NATO exercises, that is, not until 1995 when French aircraft joined their NATO counterparts in striking Bosnian Serb targets. During the Cold War, the alliance blocked the threat of Soviet military aggression in Europe by combined conventional forces and through the protection afforded by the U.S. nuclear deterrent. The complex NATO organizational structure includes (1) the North Atlantic Council, which developed and executed basic alliance policies; (2) a military command structure built around the Supreme Headquarters Allied Powers Europe (SHAPE), the Supreme Allied Commander Europe (SACEUR), the Supreme Allied Commander Atlantic (SACLANT), the Channel Committee, and the Canada-U.S. Regional Planning Group; (3) various production and logistic organizations; (4) major council committees that comprised the main consultative structure within NATO; and (5) the NATO secretariat, which was led by a secretary-general who also functioned as the civilian chairman of the council. *See also* ALLIANCE: NORTH ATLANTIC TREATY ORGANIZATION (NATO)—COLD WAR (284); ALLIANCE: NORTH ATLANTIC TREATY ORGANIZATION (NATO)—POST–COLD WAR (285); ALLIANCE: PARTNERSHIP FOR PEACE (286); ALLIANCE: PARTNERSHIP FOR PEACE SIGNATORIES (287).

Significance
NATO functioned as a cornerstone of the Western system of defense against the threat of Communist aggression in

the North Atlantic area during the years of the Cold War. Its political-military framework served as an instrument for resolving many of the issues that arose within the alliance. The alliance was strained by growing polycentrism, notably in the case of France, which insisted on its own nuclear deterrent (Force de Frappe); U.S. preoccupation with Latin American, Southeast Asian, and Middle Eastern affairs; and controversies over nuclear strategy and policies. In an act of French chauvinism, France withdrew its troop units from the integrated NATO command in the 1960s. In 1966 President Charles de Gaulle demanded the removal of NATO headquarters from France; Brussels, Belgium, became the organization's new home. Although France and Spain continued their commitments under the North Atlantic Treaty for joint action against an aggressor, their actions effectively removed them as members of NATO. Despite these internal cleavages, NATO represented the most formidable counter to perceived Soviet aggression against Western Europe, and indeed, Europe enjoyed more than four decades of peace during the Cold War, something it had not experienced in centuries. Although the NATO mission requires redefinition in the post–Cold War era, its continuation seems assured because individual nations are no longer capable of managing their defenses in isolation. Moreover, the creation of the Partnership for Peace in 1994 moves NATO beyond Western Europe to much of Eurasia.

Regional Military Group: Warsaw Treaty Organization (WTO) | 558 |

A regional military group of Eastern European Communist states, established during the Cold War to implement the Treaty of Friendship, Cooperation, and Mutual Assistance concluded in Warsaw on 15 May 1955. The founder members of the Warsaw Treaty Organization were the then-Communist states of Albania, Bulgaria, Czechoslovakia, the German Democratic Republic, Hungary, Poland, Romania, and the Soviet Union. Albania

ceased attending Warsaw Pact meetings in September 1961, and in September 1968 withdrew its membership. Romania called for the dissolution of all military alliances in 1966 and distanced itself from the Warsaw Pact. Bucharest entered into commercial arrangements with Western nations and received most-favored-nation status from the United States. The WTO carried on in the absence of these members and supplemented a series of bilateral mutual-aid pacts between the Soviet Union and several East European states that had been concluded between 1943 and 1948. Decisions of the organization were made by a Political Consultative Committee, which met sporadically and only when called by the Soviets. Each member nation was represented on the committee by a high government or party delegate. A military Unified Command anticipated by the treaty was never established, however, and the position of commander in chief was filled by Soviet marshals. Subsidiary organs included a secretariat and a permanent subcommittee to coordinate members' foreign policies. Membership in WTO imposed a responsibility to contribute immediate military assistance to a victim of an armed attack and to consult at once on joint measures to meet the aggression. *See also* ALLIANCE: WARSAW PACT (290).

Significance

The Warsaw Treaty Organization represented a Soviet response to the formation of NATO and, more particularly, to the 1954 Paris Accords by which West Germany was accepted as a NATO member. As a military alliance, the WTO helped to restore some semblance of equilibrium to the East-West balance following German rearmament. Yet, growing polycentrism in Eastern Europe during the 1970s and 1980s weakened the WTO by preventing development of its full structure and anticipated role as a unified military group. Dissatisfaction among the members was generally prudent, given Soviet domination of the alliance, but nevertheless sapped its unity. Trade between the East European and West European nations also weakened WTO's role, and when the Berlin Wall was torn apart by East European youths, the WTO could no longer be sustained. Eastern Europe had always been a questionable region in terms of its support of the Soviets. The uprising in East Berlin in 1953, the Hungarian rebellion in 1956, and the Czechoslovakian defiance in 1968 all required the use of Soviet troops to quell the disturbances behind the Iron Curtain, but none of these affairs solidified the alliance, and it remained a questionable fighting force up to its dissolution in 1991.

Regional Military Group: Western European Union (WEU) | 559 |

A regional alliance established in 1955 to defend Western Europe from attack, control German rearmament, and cooperate with NATO in the defense of the Atlantic Community. WEU was an expansion of the Brussels Pact, linking up its original members (Belgium, France, Great Britain, Luxembourg, and the Netherlands) with two former enemy states (Germany and Italy). Greece, Spain, and Portugal joined later. Associate members—Iceland, Norway and Turkey—participate in most WEU activities. Five observer nations that are members of the EU but not parties to the modified Brussels Treaty are Austria, Denmark, Finland, Ireland, and Sweden. More recently WEU has added as associate partners Bulgaria, the Czech Republic, Estonia, Hungary, Latvia, Lithuania, Poland, Romania, and Slovakia. In November 1994 WEU members began the formulation of a common European defense policy that included all 27 members. The structure of the alliance includes a council of foreign ministers, which could be called into session by any member to consult on threats to the security of Western Europe; a headquarters in Brussels; an assembly, which meets in Strasbourg and consists of delegations of WEU nations to the Council of Europe's Consultative Assembly; and a secretariat, which services the two major organs and the special bodies created to achieve alliance goals. *See also* ALLIANCE: EUROCORPS

(282); ALLIANCE: WESTERN EUROPEAN UNION (WEU) (291).

Significance

The continuing development of the Western European Union from the Brussels Treaty Organization of 1955 signifies belief that the organization still has a major role in European security. Given new vitality and purpose by the 1991 Maastricht Treaty, WEU joins with NATO and the Eurpoean Union in reaffirming European unity and transatlantic solidarity, but it also stands to emphasize Europe's desire to sustain its identity and somewhat distance itself from U.S. influence.

Regional Political Group: Antarctic System (ATS) | 560 |

Accommodation and cooperation at the South Pole. The Antarctic Treaty System (ATS) was established in 1961 and reaffirmed in 1991. Emerging from the Antarctic Treaty of 1959, ATS united those countries active in Antarctica in a uniquely successful agreement for the peaceful uses of the continent. ATS provided an example of how nations can successfully work together to preserve a major part of the planet for the benefit of all—as a zone of peace, where the environment is protected, and the advancement of science is preeminent. The strength of the treaty continues to grow as the original membership of 12 swelled to more than 40 in the 1990s, representing more than 70 percent of the world's population. The original members were Argentina, Australia, Chile, France, New Zealand, Norway, the United Kingdom, Belgium, Japan, South Africa, the United States, and the former Soviet Union. Of these, the claimants to territorial control of Antarctica are the first seven. *See also* ARMS CONTROL: ANTARCTIC TREATY OF 1959 (352).

Significance

Who owns Antarctica has been a source of controversy since the first flag was placed on the barren region. The world has long been organized on the basis of territorial nation-states, which means territories have been parceled out among the states and delineated by generally acceptable legal frontiers. Sovereignty (the right to exercise jurisdiction over a territory to the exclusion of other states) has been claimed over virtually every part of the earth's land surface. Moreover, the UN Convention on the Law of the Sea (UNCLOS), signed in 1982, clarifies maritime jurisdiction concerning a state's claim to a 200-mile exclusive economic zone (less the deep seabed, which has been declared the common heritage of mankind). Thus, no matter where a person stands, that individual essentially stands on the domain of a single sovereign state. That is not the case in Antarctica. The Antarctic Security System strives to maintain the frozen continent as a region open to all nations who wish to join in its preservation and scientific discovery. The treaty's Consultative Parties, comprising the claimants and almost 20 other states, are responsible for maintaining the letter of the treaty. Although the 1982 Falkland Islands War between Argentina and Britain highlighted some of the territorial differences in the region, and led some observers to articulate the possibility of an Antarctic dimension to the conflict, the Antarctic Treaty System oversees the continued peaceful uses of the territory by the larger world community. In an age of improved technology, the parties to the treaty cannot ignore the fact that Antarctica is larger than China, India, or the United States and Mexico combined, accounting for 10 percent of the world's land surface and 30 percent of all the land in the Southern Hemisphere. Antarctica may once have been considered as little more than a vast wasteland, but currently it is believed that the continent possesses 45 billion barrels of petroleum and 115 trillion cubic feet of natural gas. There is also some evidence that Antarctica holds many strategic minerals, not the least of which is platinum. These minerals have not yet been found in exploitable and economically viable deposits (in part, because the Protocol on Environmental Protection calls for a permanent ban on mining in the region), but Antarctica already yields a significant

financial return from the exploitation of its marine resources.

Regional Political Group: Arab League | 561 |

An Arab regional group, encouraged by the British following World War II, formed in 1945 to coordinate the members' political activities, safeguard their independence and sovereignty, and promote cooperation in economic, social, and cultural matters. The Arab League's original members are Egypt, Iraq, Jordan, Lebanon, Saudi Arabia, Syria, and Yemen. They were later joined by 15 additional states (Algeria, Bahrain, Djibouti, Kuwait, Libya, Mauritania, Morocco, Oman, Qatar, Somalia, Sudan, Tunisia, the United Arab Emirates, the Yemen People's Democratic Republic, and the Palestine Liberation Organization [PLO]). (The two Yemens were merged in 1990.) The supreme decision organ of the league was the Majlis, or Council, which met twice each year and was composed of a representative from each member. Binding decisions could be made only by unanimous vote, as in a decision to repel aggression, but those reached by a majority "bind only those that accept them." In addition, permanent committees function under council authority to study economic and social matters and to elicit support for joint projects and programs. A secretariat headed by a secretary-general was located at league headquarters in Cairo, but Egypt was suspended from membership in 1979 following its peace treaty with Israel. Egypt was later reinstated, and the headquarters again established in Cairo.

Significance

Although the Arab League did not achieve Arab unity and a common military position, it nevertheless represented an attempt by the Arab states to combine their resources and work toward common goals. The Arab League did not oppose Yasir Arafat's 1993 search for accommodation with Israel, nor did it oppose King Hussein of Jordan for entering into a peace treaty with the Israelis in 1994. The Arab world was chastened by the aggressive war launched by Iraq against Kuwait in 1990–1991, and Iraq's defeat at the hands of a U.S.-led coalition changed the tenor of the debate within the Arab League. The league's present focus is on reconciling its relationship with Israel and, to perhaps an even larger extent, combating terrorist organizations within their midst that claim religious sanction for their violent actions. Egypt and Algeria are the most significantly affected where terrorism is concerned, but none of the Arab states is free from the assault on the established bastions of power.

Regional Political Group: Commonwealth of Nations | 562 |

A voluntary association of independent states that were once parts of the British Empire. Commonwealth members include 45 European, African, Asian, Western Hemispheric, and Oceanic countries. Queen Elizabeth is recognized as "the symbol of the free association of its independent member nations and as such the Head of the Commonwealth." Some members—India, Pakistan, Malaysia, Cyprus, and Ghana, for example—have become republics and no longer accept the British sovereign as their national head of state. The essence of the Commonwealth system is free cooperation engendered through consultations among members. No formal treaty ties or permanent institutions exist, except for a secretariat. For many years, adherence to the Commonwealth was encouraged by trade preferences and sterling bloc membership, capital and technical assistance grants by advanced members to developing states, military aid to those whose security was threatened, and common institutions and language. Consultations are carried on at many levels, with meetings of the Commonwealth prime ministers held whenever necessary. *See also* TRADE POLICY ORGANIZATION: IMPERIAL PREFERENCES (270).

Significance
The Commonwealth is a unique political system in that its members freely cooperate and assist one another without specific agreements or commitments. During World Wars I and II, for example, Com-

monwealth states joined Great Britain in declaring war and volunteered large expeditionary forces to fight the common enemy. States granted independence from the empire may freely opt to join or reject membership, and members are free to leave the Commonwealth at any time. For example, Burma and the Maldive Islands, upon gaining independence, chose not to associate with the Commonwealth. Ireland withdrew in 1939 and South Africa in 1961, but following the dramatic changes in South Africa in 1994 that brought the black majority into power, South Africa reversed its decision. Great Britain's membership in the European Union has somewhat weakened the preferential trade system central to the unity of the organization, and the future viability of the Commonwealth depends on how effectively its members reconcile their economic and political differences so that the association can continue to offer channels for cooperation in solving common problems.

Regional Political Group: Concert of Europe | 563 |

An ad hoc system of consultation among the great powers developed after the Napoleonic wars. The concert met sporadically during the nineteenth century to settle major issues that threatened to disrupt the peace. Its members included Austria, England, France, Prussia, and Russia, later joined by Germany and Italy, and smaller powers when they were directly involved in the matter under discussion. The concert system functioned mainly through international conferences called at the initiative of a great power that believed the peace was threatened. The result was the establishment of great power hegemony that functioned effectively until the unity of the great powers was destroyed by a rigid polarization of its members into two rival alliances: the Triple Entente (France, Great Britain, and Russia) and the Triple Alliance (Germany, Austria-Hungary, and Italy).

Significance
The Concert of Europe system contributed much to the stability of European

politics during the nineteenth century, but the breakdown of great-power unity led directly to World War I. The effectiveness of the system—so long as a common interest in maintaining peace persisted—was recognized by the framers of the League of Nations Covenant and the United Nations Charter. In each global organization, a council dominated by the great powers was assigned special responsibilities for maintaining peace and security. The Security Council continues to function as a forum for great-power negotiation in the Concert of Europe tradition.

Regional Political Group: Council of Europe | 564 |

A regional quasi-parliamentary organization that encourages political, economic, and social cooperation and endeavors to develop a sense of "European" unity among its members. The Council of Europe was established at London in 1949 by Belgium, Denmark, France, Great Britain, Ireland, Italy, Luxembourg, the Netherlands, Norway, and Sweden. Eight additional states—Austria, Cyprus, Germany (Federal Republic), Greece, Iceland, Malta, Switzerland, and Turkey—were subsequently admitted to membership. In structure, the council consists of two chambers: a Consultative Assembly, composed of delegates chosen by their national parliaments but free to speak and vote as individuals, and a Committee of Ministers representing member governments. The Consultative Assembly functions as the deliberative organ of the council, while the Committee of Ministers has sole power to make decisions, with each government having veto power. The council makes recommendations to member governments and approves treaties and agreements that, when ratified by member states, constitute international legislation. Both organs are free to debate any matter except military questions. The Committee of Ministers meets monthly; the Consultative Assembly meets in spring, fall, and winter sessions. A secretariat located at council headquarters in Strasbourg serves both organs. *See also*

HUMAN RIGHTS: EUROPEAN CONVENTION (530).

Significance
At its founding the Council of Europe represented an initial step toward an eventual union of states into a European federation. In its early years the Consultative Assembly drafted a statute for a general European Political Community consisting of a parliament, executive, and court directly responsible to the people of Europe. When the French parliament killed the proposal for a European Defense Community in 1954, however, the Political Community idea was abandoned. About 50 conventions and agreements have been signed by the Committee of Ministers in such fields as university admissions, patents, social security, human rights, extradition, and peaceful settlement of disputes. In 1976, for example, the Council of Europe adopted an agreement that political causes would not provide for leniency in punishing or extraditing terrorists who had committed offenses involving lethal devices. Member governments have ratified many conventions, including the European Convention on Human Rights, which permits individuals to appeal beyond their national courts for a binding decision by an international body.

Regional Political Group: European Community (EC) | 565 |

The common political structure established to make economic decisions for the European Coal and Steel Community (ECSC), the European Economic Community (EEC), and the European Atomic Energy Community (EURATOM). The European Community institutions included the Council of Ministers, the Commission, the European Parliament, and the Court of Justice. The council and the commission constituted a dual executive, with the council directly representing the views of the governments of the members and the commission functioning as a supranational organ. Some decisions were made by the council, some by the commission, and others by the council following proposal by the commission. The commission's main function was to initiate EC policy under guidelines provided by the three basic treaties or by the council. Important decisions were given final approval by the council. Large states (France, Germany, Great Britain, Italy, and Spain) had two members on the commission, whereas the small states (Belgium, Denmark, Greece, Ireland, Luxembourg, the Netherlands, and Portugal) had only one. The council made important decisions by unanimity, but others were made by a qualified majority through a weighted voting system, and by a simple majority. The European Parliament, first created as the Common Assembly for the ECSC in 1952, served as a deliberative body and consultative organ for the EC, and as an overseer of its actions. Although it had no power to make laws or decisions binding upon member states, it served as a source for the initiation of new policies of economic liberalization and political unity. Delegates to the parliament, formerly appointed by national parliaments, were elected after 1979 by direct universal suffrage and were organized and voted on most issues as three transnational political groups—Christian Democrat, Socialist, and Liberal—rather than as national blocs. The Court of Justice, also established in 1952, functioned as the common court to interpret and apply EC treaties and resolve disputes between EC organs and member states or within either group. Its powers to interpret and review more closely resembled those of a national supreme court than those of other international courts. Other institutions that operated within the EC framework included the European Investment Bank (EIB), which encouraged balanced EC development through loans and guarantees, and almost 100 specialized committees. In addition, the EC developed arrangements with outside countries, such as Turkey, and with many African, Caribbean, and Pacific states as a result of the Yaoundé Convention of 1963 and the Lomé Convention of 1975, which established special EEC/Associated States trading arrangements. The Euro-

pean Community became the European Union (EU) after the member states ratified the Maastricht Treaty of 1992, and the institutions of the EC became the institutions of the EU. *See also* ALLIANCE: EURO-CORPS (282); ALLIANCE: WESTERN EUROPEAN UNION (WEU) (291); MAASTRICHT TREATY (432); REGIONAL POLITICAL GROUP: EUROPEAN UNION (EU) (566); SUPRANATIONAL PATTERN: SINGLE EUROPEAN ACT (SEA), 1987 (709).

Significance
The common institutions of the European Community represented the highest level of integration achieved in the contemporary state system. They were both products and participants in an integrative process moving Western Europe toward eventual political and economic union. As "European" institutions, they helped to develop concepts of a European person, European solutions to European problems, and the still distant but evolving idea of a United States of Europe. In a more immediate way, they functioned as effective decision-making bodies in resolving common economic problems in coal and steel production, marketing, general trade and commercial policies, tariff negotiations, and atomic energy development. The EC adopted a generalized system of preferences (GSP) to encourage imports of manufactures from developing countries, provided large amounts of foreign aid through its European Development Fund, and concluded numerous trade and cooperation agreements with nonmembers. In 1986 the 12 member states of the Common Market approved the Single European Act, which stated: "The High Contracting Parties consider that closer cooperation on questions of European security would contribute in an essential way to the development of a European identity in external policy matters." The EC emerged from the 1986 Single European Act, and decisions were made to eliminate all border barriers between the member states and to emphasize their cooperation in economic, financial, cultural, and security matters. The success of the EC forecast the more

significant economic and commercial integration of the member states by 1992. The Maastricht Treaty of December 1991 prompted the Treaty on European Union, also at Maastricht, in February 1992, thus transforming the European Community into the European Union. In the area of security, the Treaty of European Union "resolved to implement a common foreign and security plan, including the eventual framing of a common defense policy, which might in time lead to a common defense, thereby reinforcing European identity and its independence. . . ." Noting their intention to promote peace, security, and progress in the world, the original 12 signatories to the Treaty on European Union formally established the European Union. Stemming from the experience of World War II, the European Community/Union resulted from efforts by European statesmen to create a United States of Europe. The Europeans of the immediate postwar period, confronted with a Cold War and multiple challenges, saw survival and growth only in their capacity to overcome age-old fears and suspicions. Although reluctant to shed their political identities, some European states found it possible to cooperate in economic matters that promised mutual benefits. Functionalism—the capacity to pool resources for common material advantage—became the driving force behind European cooperation and accommodation. The success of the Common Market, and the experience gained from working together in joint ventures, left open the possibility of greater integration in the future. Changes in the Soviet Union in the 1980s and the subsequent fall of the Berlin Wall, the unification of Germany, and the demise of the Soviet Union raised new questions about European unity. Integrationists believed the time was ripe for pressing ahead with political structures of an all-European character. Other Europeans, more nationalistic in their thinking, believed the time called for a loosening of some of the constraints imposed and self-imposed on national behavior. The European Community/Union reflects a compromise between the two camps, asserting the right of individual member states to promote their national interests without prejudicing their common security, both economic and strategic.

Regional Political Group: European Union (EU) $\boxed{566}$

The evolution of European unity and the building of supranational institutions. The European Union, comprising France, Germany, Belgium, Italy, the Netherlands, Luxembourg, the United Kingdom, Ireland, Denmark, Greece, Spain and Portugal, is the successor organization to the Common Market, the European Economic Community (EEC), and the European Community (EC). These different designations represented different time frames, with the European Union following the signing of the Maastricht Treaty of December 1991. The treaty sought to capitalize on the expansion and increasing intimacy of the West European states during the decades of the Cold War. The end of the Cold War and the subsequent demise of the Soviet Union, however, brought into question the genuineness of the European Union. The Maastricht Treaty projected not only more significant economic uniformity in trade and finance, it also called for a form of political integration that would irrevocably alter the sovereign status of the members. From the vantage point of the Cold War, the EU seemed the best assurance for overall European peace and security. In the absence of the Cold War, the individual nations comprising the EU questioned the depth of their commitment to the "political union" envisaged by the Maastricht Treaty. *See also* DEMOCRATIC PATTERN: SUBSIDIARITY (705); MAASTRICHT TREATY (432); REGIONAL POLITICAL GROUP: EUROPEAN COMMUNITY (EC) (565).

Significance

The members of the European Union acknowledge their economic interdependence and the necessity for regional cooperation in matters of trade and finance, but in the aftermath of the Cold

War they are noticeably reluctant to yield national sovereignty to a supranational organization. The member states agree to sustaining common external tariffs, their customs union on industrial goods, and their common agricultural policy. They also continue to pursue objectives that will realize a full economic and monetary union, including a common currency, but they display hesitation in committing themselves to mechanisms that would minimize their more exclusive and particular interests. No less significant than the passing of the Cold War and the collapse of the Soviet Union was the unification of Germany and its increasing importance as an independent actor no longer saddled by the consequences of its defeat in World War II, and more than able to chart an independent course in European and world affairs. Coupled with the United Kingdom's long-time reluctance to commit itself to European integration and France's highly individualized policies, the future of the European Union, i.e., the creation of a United States of Europe, remains distant.

Regional Political Group: Expanding Membership in the Council of Europe | 567 |

Promoting European cooperation and accommodation. The Council of Europe was the first post–World War II European organization uniting like-minded partners on the common ground of respect for the basic values of pluralist democracy: human rights and the rule of law. The Council of Europe was established on 5 May 1949 by ten member states. By 1989, the fortieth anniversary of the organization, it had 23 members, extending over the totality of Western European states. In June 1989 the Parliamentary Assembly of the Council of Europe opened its doors to delegations of Central and Eastern European countries, beginning with Hungary, Poland, Yugoslavia, and the Soviet Union. Invited initially as "special guests," by 1995 nine countries from the former Soviet bloc (Bulgaria, the Czech Republic, Estonia, Hungary, Lithuania, Poland, Romania, Slovakia, and Slovenia) had be-

come full members. In addition, Andorra joined in November 1994, swelling the Council of Europe to 33 full members. Eight other states are slated to become members once procedural details have been completed. They are: Albania, Belarus, Croatia, Latvia, the former Yugoslav republic of Macedonia, Moldova, Russia, and Ukraine. The nine in process, as well as Bosnia-Herzegovina, enjoy special-guest status in the interim and are already signatories to a number of Council of Europe conventions. They also participate as observers in intergovernmental expert committees. To the extent required, council members and guest members cooperate with one another toward the creation of functioning democratic institutions that are judged compatible with European legal standards as well as with human rights. Democratic reform is judged essential for membership in the Council of Europe, and particular emphasis is given to fair and free elections, universal suffrage, freedom of expression, protection of national minorities, and the observance of the principles of international law. All member states must also sign the European Convention on Human Rights and accept the convention's supervisory machinery in its entirety. *See also* HUMAN DIMENSION (125); REGIONAL POLITICAL GROUP: COUNCIL OF EUROPE (564).

Significance

The Parliamentary Assembly of the Council of Europe adopted a recommendation on the enlargement of the Council of Europe in October 1994. Membership was to be determined by the following criteria: (1) Member states must be located wholly or partly in Europe and their cultures closely linked with European culture; (2) while acknowledging that the boundaries of Europe have not been comprehensively defined under international law, the Council of Europe bases its understanding of who is a European on the accepted geographic limits of Europe; (3) all member states presently in the Council of Europe are deemed to be European, that is, Austria, Belgium, Bulgaria, Cyprus, the Czech Republic, Denmark, Estonia, Finland, France, Germany, Greece, Hungary, Iceland, Ireland, Italy, Liechtenstein, Lithuania, Luxembourg, Malta, the Netherlands, Norway, Poland, Portugal, Romania, San Marino, Slovakia, Slovenia, Spain, Sweden, Switzerland, Turkey, and the United Kingdom (Andorra was included a month after the declaration by the parliamentary assembly); (4) states with special-guest status, i.e., Albania, Belarus, Bosnia-Herzegovina, Croatia, Latvia, the former Yugoslav republic of Macedonia, Moldova, Russia, and Ukraine, are also considered European; (5) the possibility that Serbia and Montenegro will also be included pending a satisfactory solution to the war in Bosnia; and (6) membership could extend to Armenia, Azerbaijan, and Georgia.

Regional Political Group: Nordic Council | 568 |

A Scandinavian regional organization composed of elected and appointed delegates who meet as a council to recommend common policies and programs to the governments of the member states. Established in 1952, the membership of the Nordic Council includes Denmark, Finland, Norway, Sweden, and Iceland. Delegates are chosen by their national parliaments (Iceland was accorded 5, the other members 16 each), with major political groups and opinions represented. Each state may also appoint as many governmental representatives as it wishes, but voting power is limited to the elected delegates. Ordinary sessions of the council are held annually, but extraordinary sessions may be convoked by two members or 25 elected delegates. A presidium of elected officers directs deliberations, which are concerned with economic, social, cultural, legal, and transport matters.

Significance

The Nordic Council has served its members as a superparliament for deliberative purposes. One of its original objectives—to establish a Scandinavian common market—was suspended by the

establishment in 1959 of the European Free Trade Association (EFTA), with Denmark, Norway, and Sweden as full members and Finland as an associate. The council has also been instrumental in eliminating the requirement of passports for Scandinavian citizens to travel in member countries, providing for a Scandinavian labor market, and promoting common legislation through recommendations in various fields.

Regional Political Group: North Atlantic Cooperation Council (NACC) | 569 |

The institutional comingling of NATO states with those of Eastern Europe. The North Atlantic Cooperation Council was established by the NATO Heads of State and Government in November 1991 to act as a forum for dialogue and consultation on political and security-related issues. It also aimed at promoting practical cooperation between NATO countries and the countries of Central and Eastern Europe and the former Soviet Union. A less structured version of the later Partnership for Peace, it serves to represent virtually all the nations on the European continent. The NACC has given priority to economic issues, notably identifying solutions to the problem of converting to civilian purposes those industrial installations formerly devoted to military production. The successful conversion of defense programs is central to the economic-reform process taking place in many NACC countries. Benefits from conversion include improvements in living standards and reductions in unemployment, as well as decreases in military expenditures and the freeing of resources for civilian use. See also ALLIANCE: PARTNERSHIP FOR PEACE (PFP) (286); DISARMAMENT PROPOSAL: DEFENSE CONVERSION (391); TRANSPARENCY (461).

Significance

The North Atlantic Cooperation Council (NACC) was created to link with the North Atlantic Council (NAC), representing the NATO countries, and promotes dialogue and cooperation among member states. NACC and NAC represent the commingling of West and East European states in ways that enable the democracies of the West to assist the developing democracies of the East. Confidence-building has developed into active cooperation at political, economic, and social levels and has prompted the opening of borders and the free movement of experts and specialists concerned with stabilizing the peace achieved with the end of the Cold War.

Regional Political Group: Organization of African Unity (OAU) | 570 |

A regional organization established in 1963 to develop unity, end colonialism, foster economic development, and provide security for African states. OAU's membership includes more than 50 nations—every independent African state except South Africa. In addition, liberation movements associated with the OAU at one time included (1) the African National Congress (ANC, South Africa), (2) the Pan African Congress (South Africa), (3) Polisario (Spanish Sahara), and (4) the South-West African Peoples Organization (SWAPO, Namibia). ANC and SWAPO achieved their independence in 1994 and 1990, respectively. OAU consists of an Assembly of Heads of State, which meets annually, and a secretariat located at OAU headquarters in Addis Ababa.

Significance

Although the broad objectives of the Organization of African Unity are commonly accepted by its members, it remains a loose association of sovereign states producing joint pronouncements but little in the way of concerted action. Its pan-African wellsprings have been sapped by internal political rivalries, ideological differences, conflicting ties with major powers, and an overriding concern with the preservation of personal power and state sovereignty. Security provisions in its charter have not been implemented or broadened. OAU has been largely ineffective in coping with large-scale malnutrition and famine resulting from high birthrates and severe droughts in the Sahelian region or elsewhere in Africa. It was totally ineffective in reacting to the plight of hundreds of thousands in the Rwanda and Burundi genocides, or to the earlier atrocities in Uganda and Liberia. It is utterly unable to deal with the harsh realities of dictatorship through much of Africa. Nevertheless, it assisted in creating an African Development Bank, and it is striving to organize a common-market arrangement on the continent. In the United Nations, the OAU functions as an effective caucusing group when issues of common interest come before the General Assembly. In that way, the African bloc has played a major role in the decolonization process, as well as in efforts to create a new international economic order. However, the OAU was hopelessly feeble in combating the ebola virus, a disease that struck Zaire in 1995, and the organization was forced to acknowledge the expertise that could be provided only by non-Africans, especially the Europeans and the Americans.

Regional Political Group: Organization of American States (OAS) | 571 |

A regional organization established by the Ninth International Conference of American States at Bogotá in 1948 to determine political, defense, economic, and social policies for the Inter-American System. Twenty-one American states originally subscribed to the OAS Charter, although the Castro government of Cuba was expelled from the organization in 1962. Current membership includes 31 Caribbean and Central and South American nations and the United States. Organs of the OAS include (1) the General Assembly, which functions as the supreme organ of the OAS, meeting every five years to consider any matter relating to the American states; (2) the Meeting of Consultation of Ministers of Foreign Affairs, which takes up pressing security and related problems when a majority of members call for a meeting; (3) the Council, which serves as the coordinating agency for the OAS and meets at its headquarters in Washington, D.C.; (4) the Pan-American Union, which functions as the secretariat for the OAS, coordinating inter-American social and economic activities and promoting the welfare of members; (5) the Specialized Organizations, which carry on cooperative programs in such fields as health, agriculture, education, and child welfare; and (6) the Specialized Conferences, which are called to encourage joint efforts to solve technical problems. In addition, special agencies, such as the Inter-American Development Bank and the Inter-American Peace Committee, function autonomously in support of general OAS objectives. The main activities carried on by the OAS relate to the peaceful settlement of disputes, common action against aggression, and economic and social collaboration among members. *See also* ALLIANCE: RIO TREATY (INTER-AMERICAN TREATY OF RECIPROCAL ASSISTANCE) (288); ALLIANCE FOR PROGRESS (617).

Significance
From its inception in 1948, the Organization of American States has devoted its main efforts to dealing with the threat of communism in the hemisphere. Serious situations in the region included (1) the rise of power of the Castro government in Cuba, (2) several international crises involving the United States and the Soviet Union, (3) the intervention of an OAS Peace Force in the Dominican Republic in 1965 "to prevent another Cuba," (4) revolutionary guerrilla warfare in several states, (5) U.S. intervention in Nicaragua in an effort to overthrow its Sandinista regime, and (6) U.S. involvement in the civil war in El Salvador. Conflicts of jurisdiction between the United Nations and the OAS over handling Latin American disputes have usually been won by the OAS, with the United Nations' role limited to that of debate. The United States plays a dominant role in the OAS, especially in security matters, because most governments depend on it to provide the resources to meet threats of aggression, and in the field of economic development,

because Latin American development programs depend heavily on U.S. financing. The main challenges facing the OAS after the Cold War, however, are two intertwined needs: strengthening democratic experiments and promoting economic growth. Much of the world debt crisis involves the countries of Latin America, many of which are in default and threatened with economic collapse. The Mexican debt crisis of 1995 required significant input from the United States, the World Bank, and the International Monetary Fund. Fear that spreading and deepening financial distress in Mexico would impact the other states of Latin America forced the United States to take drastic action. Moreover, the economic instability in Mexico triggered the rebellion in the southern state of Chiapas in 1994, and even the passage of the North American Free Trade Association in that year did not ameliorate the situation. Overall, the OAS seems unable to cope with post–Cold War issues. In 1994 it played a nonrole in Haiti, and in fact stood by in 1995 as a UN peacekeeping force assumed responsibility for monitoring the peace in that country.

Regional Political Group: Organization of Central American States (OCAS, also known as ODECA) | 572 |

A regional multipurpose organization that fosters political, economic, and social cooperation among Central American states. Established under the terms of the 1951 Charter of San Salvador, OCAS's members are Costa Rica, El Salvador, Guatemala, Honduras, and Nicaragua; Panama has been invited to join. A new charter was negotiated for OCAS in 1962. OCAS organs include (1) a Conference of the Presidents of the Central American Republics, which functions as the supreme body; (2) a Meeting of Ministers of Foreign Affairs, which convenes every two years and serves as the principal decision-making agency, with unanimity required for all substantive decisions; and (3) the Central American Bureau, headed by a secretary-general and functioning as a general secretariat for

OCAS. Members of OCAS have established the Central American Common Market (CACM) to promote economic integration. *See also* REGIONAL ECONOMIC GROUP: CENTRAL AMERICAN COMMON MARKET (CACM) (551).

Significance
The Organization of Central American States has played a substantial role in fostering the unity of the region. Numerous agencies, including the Central American Bank for Economic Integration (CABEI), the Superior University Council of Central America (CSUCA), and the Permanent Secretariat of the General Treaty on Central American Integration (SIECA), have emerged out of understandings encouraged by OCAS.

United Nations: Admission ⎡573⎤
The process of accepting a state for membership in an international organization. In the United Nations, the admission of new members requires a recommendation by the Security Council, followed by a two-thirds vote in the General Assembly. Because the veto is applicable to membership questions, any permanent member of the council may block an application. The charter specifies that states desiring admission to membership (1) be peaceloving, (2) accept the obligations contained in the charter, and (3) in the judgment of the organization, be able and willing to carry out these obligations. International public unions, such as the specialized agencies of the United Nations, generally require a two-thirds vote of the organization to admit a new member. Regional groups such as the European Union usually require a unanimous vote to admit.

Significance
The admission of new members to an international organization may influence its nature, objectives, and decision-making functions. The sizable influx of new members into the United Nations during the 1960s and 1970s resulted in an expanded role for the General Assembly. Charter amendments also increased membership

in the Security Council and the Economic and Social Council (ECOSOC) to provide wider representation and an increased emphasis on Third World approaches to securing the objectives of economic development, human rights, and disarmament. The disintegration of the Soviet Union and Yugoslavia resulted in numerous new nations, all of whom sought admission to the United Nations; all were admitted by 1992. The goal of universalism (admission of all states to membership), however, has not yet been achieved. Switzerland has chosen to remain outside the United Nations because the obligations of membership would violate its traditional neutrality. Other states, such as Western Samoa, have chosen not to apply for admission for financial reasons.

United Nations: Amendment Process ⎡574⎤
Procedures by which formal changes in the constitutions of international organizations are proposed and ratified. The League of Nations Covenant provided in Article 26 that amendments would take effect when ratified by all council members and by a majority of the assembly, and that any member refusing to accept such amendments would cease to be a member of the league. In article 108 of the United Nations Charter it is specified that amendments to the charter come into force for all members when adopted by a vote of two-thirds of the members of the General Assembly and ratified in accordance with their respective constitutional processes by two-thirds of the members of the United Nations, including all the permanent members of the Security Council (i.e., the United States, Russia, Great Britain, France, and China). The United Nations Charter also provides for "a General Conference of the Members of the United Nations for the purpose of reviewing the present Charter may be held at a date and place fixed by a two-thirds vote of the members of the General Assembly and by a vote of any nine members of the Security Council" (Article 109). Article 109 further states that in order to propose alterations in the charter the rec-

ommendation must be made by a two-thirds vote of the conference and then those amendments must be ratified through national constitutional processes by two-thirds of the UN members, including the five permanent members of the Security Council, before they come into force.

Significance
Although the League of Nations adopted numerous amendments to the covenant, they had little impact on the effectiveness of that organization. In the United Nations, two amendments were ratified in 1965, one enlarging the Security Council from 11 to 15 and changing its voting majority from 7 to 9, the other enlarging the Economic and Social Council from 18 to 27 members. A 1973 amendment enlarged the membership of the Economic and Social Council (ECOSOC) to 54. Like most constitutional systems, that of the United Nations has been altered more extensively by interpretation, custom, and usage than by formal amendments. Because any one of the great powers can block an amendment, extensive use of the process in the future is as unlikely as in the past.

United Nations: Caucusing Group | 575 |

Representatives of member states whose common interests impel them to meet regularly to determine group approaches on substantive and procedural issues arising in the General Assembly. Some of the caucusing groups currently acknowledged in the assembly include the African (50 members), Asian (41), Arab (21), Nordic (5), Western European and "other states" (22), Latin American (33), and the Group of Seventy-Seven (128). A considerable overlap in membership exists. A few states—China, Israel, South Africa, the United States, and Yugoslavia—do not caucus with any group. A caucusing group is distinguished from a voting bloc in that members of the caucasing group are not bound to vote in the assembly according to the caucus decision and therefore exhibit less cohesion. The

Group of Seventy-Seven (G-77) functions as the largest caucusing group in the United Nations and in major international conferences. G-77 initially became active at the first UN Conference on Trade and Development (UNCTAD) in 1964 and has expanded from its original 77 members to a current membership of 128 Third World countries. G-77 includes most of the nations of Asia, Africa, Latin America, the Caribbean, Oceania, and the Middle East. The group takes a common stand against what they regard as neo-colonial policies of the First and Second Worlds, and in favor of development aid, human rights, and the creation of a New International Economic Order (NIEO).

Significance
Caucusing groups developed early as the various regions of the world began to fight for an equitable share of the elective seats in the principal UN organs. The emergence of many new nations and the greatly increased membership in the assembly accelerated the process of caucusing before important votes. The first identifiable group to emerge, the Soviet bloc, was also the one having the highest percentage of solidarity in voting—over 95 percent during the Cold War era. The Group of Seventy-Seven, with members scattered about the globe, have generally recorded the highest rate of solidarity in voting, especially on economic issues. Caucusing groups have helped to change the decision process in the assembly from one involving individual sovereign states voting independently on issues to one resembling a continental parliament with its multiparty system, its fleeting coalitions, and the need for compromise among various power blocs to reach agreement on issues. Caucusing groups meet before important sessions of the General Assembly or other organs to hammer out common positions on issues under consideration.

United Nations: Collective Security | 576 |

A concept that provides for a global security system based on the agreement of all or most states to take common action against any nation that illegally breaks the peace. To be effective, a collective-security system requires agreement to defend the status quo against violent change, a definite assurance from member states that action will be undertaken against law-breaking states, and a willingness of states not directly threatened to participate in sanctions against an aggressor. Theoretically, a collective-security system is based on the assumption that no state will be likely to challenge the power of the world community, but that if aggression occurs, all will honor their commitment to take police action. A collective-security system should not be confused with an alliance or balance-of-power system in which states on either side are kept in check and peace is maintained by the tendency toward a power equilibrium. Nor should collective security be equated with mutual-security systems, which bring adversaries into relationships that insulate them against the other's aggressive posturing and compel them to find common ground on salient issues. Collective-security systems are less pragmatic than these. Only two collective-security systems—the League of Nations and the United Nations—have been attempted in the modern world. In the United Nations, primary responsibility to preserve world peace is assigned to the Security Council, which may call upon all members to levy sanctions under Chapter VII of the charter. Since adoption of the Uniting for Peace Resolution of 1950, the General Assembly may authorize collective action against an aggressor when the Security Council is deadlocked by use of the veto, a power enjoyed only by the five permanent members (China, France, Great Britain, the United States, and Russia). *See also* PATTERNS OF POWER: MUTUAL SECURITY (23); UNITED NATIONS: SANCTIONS (586); UNITED NATIONS: UNITING FOR PEACE RESOLUTION (591); UN PRINCIPAL ORGAN: SECURITY COUNCIL (601).

Significance
Collective security meets its most severe test when confronted by an overt or co-vert aggression committed in violation of community norms. The world's first peacekeeping arrangement, the League of Nations, proved unable to meet the pre–World War II crises created by Japan's attack on China, Italy's invasion of Ethiopia, Germany's occupation of Austria and Czechoslovakia, and the Soviet Union's war against Finland. All of these developments, and the failure of the league to organize collective action, resulted in the collapse of the league's security system. In 1950 the United Nations undertook the world's first collective-security action involving military sanctions when the Security Council called upon members to contribute forces to stem the North Korean invasion of South Korea. That call was made possible by the absence of the Soviet Union from the council when the vote was taken. The return of the Soviet Union to the Security Council, and its use of the veto, however, negated the decision. At this point the Uniting for Peace Resolution was passed and the UN role in the Korean War was assumed by the General Assembly, but no longer in the context of collective security. In 1956 the United Nations was confronted simultaneously with two collective-security cases: (1) military repression of the Hungarian revolution by the Soviet Union and (2) an attack by France, Great Britain, and Israel against Egypt. Although the United Nations did not employ sanctions in either situation, it produced a moral condemnation of the Soviet action and helped to pressure the belligerents in the Middle East to stop fighting. The great-power split in the Security Council remained the principal factor militating against the proper use of the United Nations' peacekeeping powers. But the United Nations' collective-security system was given another chance at the close of the Cold War. Following Iraq's aggression in Kuwait in 1990, the Security Council put past differences behind it, and the result was a collective stand. With China agreeing not to veto the decision to intervene, and with the Soviet Union (otherwise considered a friend of the Iraqi state) supporting the action of the Security Coun-

cil, a major force was assembled in Saudi Arabia under U.S. leadership. The United Nations then moved to force Iraq from the country it claimed as its nineteenth province. The UN collective-security system never performed better than during Operation Desert Shield and Operation Desert Storm in 1990–1991. Moreover, the Soviets publicized their intention to channel future world problems through the United Nations, and the U.S. president, George Bush, spoke of a "new world order" based on close cooperation between the major powers. The passing of the Soviet Union left its successor, the Russian Federation, to assume responsibility on the Security Council. The future of the UN collective-security system now rested on numerous factors that were not apparent during the years of the Cold War. The breakup of the Soviet state gave new vigor to the forces of nationalism, and it was uncertain how the UN collective-security system would function in an age of resurgent nationalism, which not only swept the new Russia but also the other permanent members of the Security Council. In 1995, even the United States seemed less inclined to pursue a program of collective security, if in so doing it minimized exclusive American prerogatives.

United Nations: Dispute Settlement Procedures

577

Techniques and tools available for use by agencies of the United Nations in efforts to achieve a peaceful settlement of an international dispute. The charter (Article 33) provides that the parties to a dispute should "first of all, seek a solution by negotiation, inquiry, mediation, conciliation, arbitration, judicial settlement, resort to regional agencies or arrangements, or other peaceful means." If these traditional pacific settlement approaches fail or are inappropriate, the dispute may be brought before the Security Council or General Assembly by a member state or by a nonmember if it agrees to accept charter obligations relating to dispute settlement. The secretary-general, under the charter (Article 99), may also bring any situation that threatens peace and secu-

rity to the attention of the Security Council. Initial actions by the world organization may take the form of an appeal to refrain from aggravating the situation or, if fighting has broken out, a cease-fire order may be issued. The parties to a dispute are given an opportunity to present their cases before the council or assembly, and such discussions may be useful in discovering common ground for a settlement. "Quiet diplomacy," a blend of public and private negotiations carried on at UN headquarters, has proved useful in breaking deadlocks. When mediation and conciliation techniques applied in New York fail, a commission of inquiry and mediation or a UN representative or mediator may be appointed to go to the scene of the dispute to establish the facts and try for an on-the-spot settlement. If a great-power confrontation threatens to expand the dispute, "preventive diplomacy" in the form of a UN "presence" or police force to fill a power vacuum may be employed. Finally, when it is possible to secure the acceptance of both parties, the legal approaches to settlement—arbitration or adjudication—may be used to settle a dispute. *See also* PEACEFUL (PACIFIC) SETTLEMENT (438).

Significance
The United Nations has applied its pacifying and moderating influences to many disputes and situations over its history. Although its appeals and cease-fire "orders" under pacific settlement procedures are merely recommendations, and disputants cannot be compelled to obey them, many hostilities have been arrested by the timely intervention of the United Nations. U.S.-Soviet confrontations also were avoided by filling power vacuums with a UN "presence," as in Lebanon in 1958 and the Congo in 1960. An intractable territorial dispute over the Himalayan entity of Kashmir brought war to India and Pakistan on the day of their independence. Although the problem defied solution, and continues to plague relations between the two subcontinental neighbors into the 1990s, the United Nations played a substantial role in winning

a cease-fire that terminated their first conflict in 1947–1948. Unfortunately, the United Nations could not avoid the wars between these same parties in 1965 and again in 1971. Another conflict spanning the decades is that involving Israelis and Arabs. The United Nations did not have the leverage to deal effectively with this problem; in fact, one of its mediators, Count Folke Bernadotte, was assassinated while furthering UN peacekeeping responsibilities. Though only minimally productive in this dispute, the UN role nevertheless created the environment within which the two states, with the assistance of third-party states like the United States, were able to move the conflict to the conference table. As a general rule, the most effective techniques employed by the United Nations have been those that encourage the parties to engage in such bilateral negotiations.

United Nations: Domestic Jurisdiction Clause | 578 |

The charter limitation (Article 2) placed upon the competence of the United Nations, providing that "nothing contained in the present Charter shall authorize the United Nations to intervene in matters which are essentially within the domestic jurisdiction of any state." Collective action to maintain international peace and security is specifically excluded from the limiting clause, but beyond this, no definition is provided as to what constitutes an "international" problem (hence a proper subject for UN consideration) and what is strictly a "national" or "domestic" question. *See also* JURISDICTION, DOMESTIC (517).

Significance
The domestic-jurisdiction clause proclaims a political principle more than it provides a legal limitation on UN powers. However, it is one of the most frequently invoked sections of the charter. On controversial matters, members opposing UN action typically open their defense by claiming that consideration of the issue by the world organization is an unwarranted intrusion into their sovereign affairs. In the final analysis, questions of domestic jurisdiction are decided by UN organs through their voting procedures. In considering questions dealing with colonialism (e.g., Namibia) and denial of human rights (e.g., apartheid in South Africa), the General Assembly rejected assertions that these were essentially domestic matters.

United Nations: Dumbarton Oaks Conference | 579 |

Preliminary conversations over the nature and functions of the anticipated United Nations organization. The Dumbarton Oaks Conference met August–October 1944 in Washington, D.C. Delegations from the United States, Great Britain, and the Soviet Union joined in the first and most important phase of the talks, while China participated with Great Britain and the United States in the second phase. Views were exchanged, compromises secured, and a preliminary working draft of proposals for the new world organization was hammered out. *See also* DIPLOMATIC POLICY: YALTA AGREEMENT (423).

Significance
Agreement among the great powers concerning the nature of the contemplated world organization was reached on most issues. Those in which agreement was lacking (e.g., use of the veto power, membership, and dispute settlement procedure) were referred for resolution to higher political levels—the Big Three (Prime Minister Winston Churchill, President Franklin D. Roosevelt, and Premier Josef Stalin)—at the Yalta Conference of 1945. The preliminary draft of the proposals, with some alterations and additions, became the United Nations Charter following the work of the San Francisco Conference, April–June 1945.

United Nations: Egalitarianism, Elitism, Majoritarianism | 580 |

Concepts that relate to the basic nature and decision processes of international organs. The principle of egalitarianism embodies the idea of traditional equality of states under international law; because each possesses supreme power (sovereignty), all are juridically equal. Elitism, on the other hand, recognizes that great-power politics makes some states in fact "more equal" than others. Majoritarianism offers a decision-making system in keeping with the practices of democratic institutions within states.

Significance

All three principles—egalitarianism, elitism, and majoritarianism—find numerous applications within international organizations in the contemporary world. The first, for example, is applied in the General Assembly of the United Nations (as it was in the League of Nations Assembly), with each member represented and having an equal vote. The typical general conference of international public unions, such as those used by most of the specialized agencies, and the basic policy-determining organ in most regional organizations are also based on equality of representation and voting. The elitist principle—based on the historical precedents of the Concert of Europe and the League of Nations Council—finds its most notable application in the permanent membership and veto power exercised by the five permanent powers in the UN Security Council. Elitism is also reflected in systems of weighted voting, such as those found in the World Bank (IBRD) and International Monetary Fund (IMF) (member votes are determined by financial contributions), and in the European Parliament, where seats accorded members range from a maximum for France, Germany, Great Britain, and Italy to a minimum for Luxembourg. Majoritarianism has gained wide acceptance among international institutions in the twentieth century. Every principal organ of the United Nations, for example, may reach decisions by less than a unanimous vote.

United Nations: Expulsion, Suspension, Withdrawal | 581 |

Procedures by which membership or the rights of membership in an international organization are terminated or temporarily suspended. Expulsion and suspension are potential sanctions that can be applied against recalcitrant members of an international organization, and the right of withdrawal confirms the sovereignty of all members. The Covenant of the League of Nations provided that (1) any member could withdraw from the organization after giving two years' notice, on the condition that all its obligations were fulfilled (Article 1); (2) a member that had violated any covenant of the league could be expelled by a unanimous vote of the council (Article 16); and (3) a member that refused to accept an amendment adopted to the covenant would terminate its membership (Article 26). The United Nations Charter provides that (1) the rights and privileges of membership may be suspended by the General Assembly upon Security Council recommendation when preventive or enforcement action has been taken against the member (Article 5), (2) a member that persistently violates charter principles may be expelled by the General Assembly upon Security Council recommendation (Article 6), and (3) any member two or more years in arrears in its financial contributions may be deprived of its vote in the General Assembly. Although the charter does not provide for withdrawal, its framers at San Francisco approved a declaration that admitted the right of withdrawal.

Significance

Three members—Germany, Italy, and Japan—withdrew from the League of Nations after committing aggressions, some of the smaller member states left for financial reasons, and the Soviet Union was expelled for its attack on Finland in 1939. In the United Nations, only one member—Indonesia—withdrew (in 1965; Indonesia returned to active membership a year later). Efforts to invoke Article 19 to deprive financially delinquent members of their votes in the General Assembly in 1964 temporarily immobilized the assembly during its nineteenth session. By the mid-1990s, not one of the three available charter provisions to suspend rights or expel members had been invoked. Membership in the United Nations, more so than in the League of Nations, remains a coveted privilege unlikely to be taken from members or voluntarily relinquished by them.

United Nations: Finance   582

The function of raising operating funds to expend on overhead costs and the broad-gauged programs carried on under the aegis of the United Nations. Almost all regular budget income comes from contributions assessed upon member states according to a formula that takes into account their national incomes, per capita incomes, and foreign-exchange earnings. Each state must pay the major portion of its assessment in dollars, with the balance payable in local currencies. Assessments range from about 25 percent for the largest contributor (the United States) to the established minimum of 0.01 percent, required of nearly one-half of the members. Overall operations of the organization are divided into four budgets: (1) the regular budget (general overhead and administrative operating costs), (2) the specialized agencies (WHO, UNESCO, FAO, IBRD, etc.), (3) special voluntary programs (UN Development Program, refugees, and UNICEF), and (4) peacekeeping operations (e.g., UN Emergency Force [UNEF] and UN Operation in the Congo [ONUC]).

Significance
The United Nations' financial costs have increased more than sevenfold since the organization began its operations in 1946. Controversies among the great powers over programs and policies and the poverty of many members have contributed to a sizable deficit, which precipitated a crisis in the organization in the 1960s and again in the 1980s. One budgetary conflict concerns the question of whether members that oppose specific peacekeeping operations can be held financially accountable to pay their share of the costs. Another aspect that contributes to the ongoing crisis is the refusal of the United States, France, Russia (who assumed the Soviet debt), and many Third World

countries to pay their annual assessments because of financial or political reasons. Some supporters of the organization have proposed that member state assessment be supplemented or replaced by independent sources of income to enable the United Nations to carry out voted programs. Some of the suggested new sources include charges levied by specialized agencies for services performed, tolls on the use of international waterways, issuance of charters for the exploitation of minerals and other resources of the seabeds of international waters and Antarctica, and charges for fishing, whaling, and sealing rights in international waters. However, member states show little interest in developing independent sources of income for the world organization that would weaken their control over its decisions. To cope with its crisis, the General Assembly established an 18-member Group of High Level Intergovernmental Experts to study the financial crisis and recommend administrative and financial remedies. But in the aftermath of the Cold War, UN peacekeeping activities have multiplied astronomically, and nations with the financial means are increasingly reluctant to assume the necessary responsibility.

United Nations: General Debate   583

The procedure that permits the representatives of all members of the United Nations to address the General Assembly during the opening weeks of each annual session. Often top leaders of many countries—presidents, prime ministers, and monarchs—go to New York to present their nations' views on world problems during general debate. General debate usually absorbs several weeks of plenary sessions of the General Assembly each fall.

Significance
General debate offers each member government an opportunity to unburden itself of its views on international questions. Although not really a form of debate (it consists of a series of largely unrelated speeches), it serves the purpose of raising issues, denouncing opponents, and prais-

ing friends. Typically, most speakers inveigh against the arms race, military alliances, great-power interventions, and the actions of dispute rivals or neighboring countries that displease them. Three demands voiced during general debate overshadow all others: more effective peacekeeping, greater help in economic development, and broader acceptance of human rights.

United Nations: Important Question   584

An issue placed before the General Assembly that requires a two-thirds vote to reach a decision. The charter (Article 18) stipulates that important questions include (1) recommendations on peace and security, (2) election of members to the three councils, (3) admission of new members, (4) suspension of rights and privileges and expulsion of members, (5) questions relating to the operation of the trusteeship system, and (6) budgetary questions. Assembly proposals for amendments to the charter (Article 108) also require a two-thirds vote. The determination of additional categories of important questions can be made by a simple majority of members present and voting. *See also* UN PRINCIPAL ORGAN: GENERAL ASSEMBLY (599).

Significance

The important-question rule has become more crucial as the General Assembly expands its membership and influence. The Cold War split, regional hostilities among the new nations, and the growth of caucusing groups made it difficult to secure a two-thirds majority until the Third World caucus known as the Group of Seventy-Seven (G-77) developed a unified approach to economic and social issues beginning in 1964. The extension of the rule to add additional important questions by a simple majority vote is a parliamentary tactic that may be used to defeat a measure that might otherwise be adopted. In 1961, for example, the United States succeeded in raising a majority to support a change in the designation of the issue of Chinese representation from an ordinary majority vote to an important question requiring a two-thirds vote. In 1972 a majority of the General Assembly reversed that decision, resulting in the acceptance of the People's Republic as the legal representative of China and the expulsion of Taiwan (Formosa).

United Nations: International Police Force   585

The anticipated agent for collective-security enforcement action called for in the United Nations Charter plan for preserving world peace and security. Article 43 of the charter provides that member states through prior agreements make armed forces and facilities available to the Security Council at its request. These agreements, the heart of the original peacekeeping plan, failed to materialize when in 1946 the council's Military Staff Committee was unable to secure the agreement of the great powers concerning the size and character of their contributions. However, 14 international police forces have subsequently been established under UN auspices to function in a different capacity—as agents of pacific settlement using diplomatic and military tactics to restore peace in situations of limited war and to fill vacuums that might threaten future peace. *See also* PEACEKEEPING (443); PEACEKEEPING: PEACEKEEPERS (447); PEACEKEEPING: UN OPERATIONS (450); PEACEMAKING: PEACEBUILDING (454); UNITED NATIONS: SANCTIONS (586).

Significance

The failure of the Security Council to conclude agreements with member states means it can only recommend that members undertake collective military action (as it did in the Korean conflict of 1950). Through the Uniting for Peace Resolution of 1950, the General Assembly also acquired the power to authorize members to join in a collective police action when the Security Council was stymied by a veto. The pacific settlement role for a small UN police force functioning as a peace-supervising body was developed in the UN Emergency Force (UNEF), the UN Disengagement Observer Force (UNDOF) for the Middle East, the UN Operation in the Congo (ONUC), the UN Observer Group in India and Pakistan (UN-MOGIP), the UN Interim Force in Lebanon (UNIFIL), and the UN Force in Cyprus (UNFICYP). Such international police forces operated under secretariat direction but remained responsible to their parent body, the Security Council or the General Assembly. Although these police forces were not authorized to engage in "combat activity," they had the right to defend themselves. Through the years of the Cold War, the UN police forces were usually composed of troops from Third World countries, and they were reasonably successful. The multiplication of peacekeeping operations in the 1990s necessitated the augmentation of forces from the Third World with troops from the more developed nations. Britain and France assumed a large role in UNPRO-FOR (UN Protection Force), the UN action in Bosnia. Japan became involved in Cambodia, and the United States assumed a major role in Somalia and Haiti. Despite this introduction of peacemaking forces from the major nations, peacekeeping was not a successful activity. By the mid-1990s, the forced UN retreat from Somalia in 1995 and a questionable role in Bosnia weakened UN peacekeeping even further.

United Nations: Sanctions | 586 |

Diplomatic, economic, or military punitive actions undertaken through a collective-security system against an international lawbreaker. Under the League of Nations, each member state could determine for itself whether it would levy sanctions against a nation found in violation of the covenant of the league. The United Nations' security system provides that when the Security Council determines that a "threat to the peace, breach of the peace, or act of aggression" exists, the Security Council may invoke voluntary or compulsory sanctions against the law-breaking state. The charter specifies that the council, assisted by the Military Staff Committee, may call upon members to undertake actions that may include "demonstra-

tions, blockade, and other operations by air, sea, or land forces." Nonmilitary sanctions may include "complete or partial interruption of economic relations and of rail, sea, air, postal, telegraphic, radio, and other means of communication, and the severance of diplomatic relations." Under the Uniting for Peace Resolution of 1950, the General Assembly may, by two-thirds vote, authorize members to take action against an aggressor if the council is unable to act because of a veto. To facilitate the levying of sanctions, the charter (Article 43) provides that member states should conclude special agreements with the council to make available, when needed, armed forces to maintain peace and security. *See also* UN PRINCIPAL ORGAN: SECURITY COUNCIL (601).

Significance
In 1950 the General Assembly under the Uniting for Peace Resolution recommended that members undertake collective measures against North Korea, but there was far less than total compliance, and although sanctions were long-lasting, they did little to influence positive change. UN troops were used as police forces to help keep peace in the Middle East, Cyprus, and the Congo, but no sanctions were levied against an aggressor. In the first application of compulsory sanctions, in 1966 the Security Council levied an economic embargo on Rhodesia, declaring its internal racial situation a threat to international peace and security. Sanctions were imposed on Iraq following the Gulf War, and against Haiti during the period of military rule in the 1990s, but their effectiveness was as much a problem in the post–Cold War world as it was in the interwar period, when efforts were made to sanction Italy for its invasion of Ethiopia. By the same token, sanctions imposed on Serbia did not prevent the Bosnian Serbs from zealously pressing their aggressive objectives. A significant dilemma in making sanctions an effective tool of the international community is the inability to gain total compliance for the measures. Political and economic, if not ideological and psychological, differ-

ences assure the feebleness of international sanctions.

United Nations: Secretary-General | 587 |

The chief administrative officer of an international secretariat, sometimes called director-general. Following nomination by the Security Council, the secretary-general of the United Nations is chosen by the General Assembly for a five-year term. Responsibilities of a secretary-general include preparing an agenda for major organs, compiling the budget and expending funds, providing initiative in developing new programs, supervising day-to-day operations, serving as a diplomatic go-between among the member delegations, and offering political leadership for the organization. The secretary-general also has authority under the charter to place matters relating to peace and security before the Security Council, and sits in on meetings of the assembly and three councils to offer advice when requested. In over 40 years of UN operations, there have been five secretaries-general: Trygve Lie (Norway), Dag Hammarskjöld (Sweden), U Thant (Burma), Kurt Waldheim (Austria), Javier Pérez de Cuéllar (Peru), and Boutros Boutros-Ghali (Egypt).

Significance
The office of secretary-general has evolved over a century, reaching its highest level of development in the United Nations. The extent of powers exercised depends not only on the nature of the organization and its constitutional framework but on the capabilities of the person holding the office, the conception of the role to be played, and the problems and issues that arise. U Thant and Kurt Waldheim, for example, conceived of the office as primarily concerned with administrative duties, whereas Trygve Lie and Dag Hammarskjöld additionally viewed it as a vehicle for providing executive-type leadership for the United Nations. Generally speaking, all the Cold War secretaries-general supported Western objectives over those of the Soviets, which led to the

Soviet proposal for a troika arrangement involving a presidium of three secretaries-general—one representing their rivals, one following their position, and another in acknowledgment of the nonaligned. That demand got nowhere, and was ultimately buried with the Soviet Union. Boutros-Ghali, the first post–Cold War secretary-general, anticipated a lighter responsibility than his predecessors. He expected to center attention on the developmental needs of the poorer countries. But if that was his intention, and the prevailing wisdom, these hopes were dashed by the horrific events that ushered in the new era of "peace." Indeed, there was no "peace dividend" after the fall of the Soviet Union. Ethnic wars, reinvigorated nationalisms, and cultural conflicts spread over the larger world. Even Europe, which had avoided war during the years of the Cold War, was plunged into savage conflict in the Balkans. Boutros-Ghali's efforts on behalf of international tranquility were not well-received. His critics in the United States, Western and Eastern Europe, Russia, the Middle East, and elsewhere comprised a weighty combination. His tours of troubled areas were often opportunities for personal attacks. Some of his detractors vehemently opposed his efforts at peacemaking, and they strenuously lobbied against him, his actions, and those of the organization he led.

United Nations: Trust Territory | 588 |

A former League of Nations mandate or a non–self-governing territory placed under the United Nations' trusteeship system. All league mandates that had not achieved independence by the end of World War II became trust territories in 1946, with the exception of the South African mandate of South-West Africa. Only one additional territory—Italian Somaliland—was placed under trust as a consequence of World War II. Each trust territory was brought into the arrangement by a special agreement drawn up by the administering state and approved by the General Assembly. Supervision over the administration of trust territories is carried on by the Trusteeship Council, using annual reports, petitions from trust peoples, and visiting missions. *See also* LEAGUE OF NATIONS: MANDATES SYSTEM (534); UNITED NATIONS: TRUST TERRITORY OF THE PACIFIC ISLANDS (589); UN PRINCIPAL ORGAN: TRUSTEESHIP COUNCIL (602).

Significance
By 1982, 10 of the 11 trust territories have been granted independence or united with a neighboring country on the basis of a UN-supervised plebiscite. The remaining territory is the Trust Territory of the Pacific Islands, administered by the United States. The Pacific Islands are a strategic trust territory administered under Security Council supervision. Because these islands, captured from Japan in World War II, were considered crucial to U.S. security, they were placed under council jurisdiction, where the veto applies. In 1989 the General Assembly finally convinced the government of South Africa to transfer control of its league-sanctioned mandate to SWAPO, the South-West African People's Organization. Namibia became an independent state in 1990.

United Nations: Trust Territory of the Pacific Islands | 589 |

A territory in the area called Micronesia that is under U.S. strategic trust administration. The Trust Territory of the Pacific Islands was the only UN trust territory to be placed under strategic trusteeship, with ultimate decisions made by the Security Council, where the veto is applicable. Micronesia was colonized by Germany in the nineteenth century, placed under Japanese League of Nations mandate after World War I, and captured by U.S. troops during World War II at a heavy cost in lives. The territory includes approximately 150,000 inhabitants scattered over 2,141 islands and atolls. After many years of demands for self-government by the people of the trust territory, the United States reached agreement in the 1970s and 1980s with the four political groups in the

territory—the Marshall Islands, Palau, the Northern Mariana Islands, and the Federated States of Micronesia. Three have entered into compacts of "free association," whereby they exercise autonomy in domestic affairs but leave foreign relations and defense matters under U.S. jurisdiction. The fourth—the Northern Mariana Islands—concluded a Commonwealth Covenant that entered into force in 1987. *See also* UN PRINCIPAL ORGAN: TRUSTEESHIP COUNCIL (602).

Significance
Of the 11 territories placed under the UN Trusteeship system in 1946, by 1988 all had achieved independence except the U.S.-administered Trust Territory of the Pacific Islands. The United States has not always acted in the best interests of the inhabitants of the territory. In the 1950s, for example, major nuclear bomb tests in the region produced radioactive clouds that seriously impacted the health of some of the region's inhabitants, and some of the islands are no longer habitable. Later, President John F. Kennedy's investigatory mission to the territory reported that the people were living in worse conditions than those suffered during the Japanese occupation. Although the United States is in the process of terminating its trusteeship, it intends to retain certain military bases and oversee the region's foreign policy.

United Nations: Unanimity | 590 |

The voting procedure in international organs that provides that no state may be bound by a decision without giving its consent. The rule of unanimity has generally involved the *liberum veto* (a single member, by voting against a proposal, can defeat it), although some organizations' constitutions provide that the dissenting state either accept the decision of the majority or quit the organization. The principle of unanimity is a modern adaptation of the traditional rule of international law that a sovereign state can be bound only by those decisions to which it consents.

Significance

In international organs the rule of unanimity has progressively given way to decision making by simple or extraordinary majorities. Vast differences of interests and judgments among diverse states have made the change essential for reaching decisions in contemporary institutions, although on matters of vital interest to states' foreign policies most international organizations retain the liberum veto. In the United Nations, none of the six principal organs provides for decision making by unanimity, although in the Security Council the charter requires the unanimity of the five permanent members on substantive decisions. Therefore, a negative vote by China, France, Great Britain, the Soviet Union, or the United States constitutes a veto that blocks action.

United Nations: Uniting for Peace Resolution | 591 |

An assumption of power by the General Assembly to authorize collective action against an aggressor. The assembly's new function was made possible by its adoption of the Uniting for Peace Resolution of 1950, which gives the assembly a backup role to the Security Council when that organ is unable to act because of a veto. Other provisions of the resolution call for summoning the assembly into "emergency special session" within 24 hours in a peace and security crisis, establishment of a Peace Observation Commission and a Collective Measures Committee to aid the assembly in such situations, and a survey of resources that members could make available when needed. *See also* UN PRINCIPAL ORGAN: GENERAL ASSEMBLY (599).

Significance

The United States provided the initiative leading to the adoption of the Uniting for Peace Resolution in the hope that it would enable the United Nations to play a vital role in meeting future threats of Communist aggression and limited war. Its adoption by the assembly followed several months of Security Council inability to deal with the Korean conflict

because of Soviet blocking tactics. Although the assembly of the 1990s retains the power it assumed by virtue of the resolution to authorize collective action and to meet in emergency special session following a veto in the council, other measures provided by the resolution have fallen into disuse. The Uniting for Peace Resolution has been invoked by the assembly in its consideration of crises such as those in Hungary (1956), the Congo (1960), and the Middle East (1956, 1967, and 1973).

United Nations: Veto | 592 |

A vote that forbids or blocks the making of a decision. Most international institutions operate under the principle of unanimity, which gives each member the authority to veto decisions. In the United Nations, however, the veto power is exercised only by the five permanent members of the Security Council: China, France, Great Britain, the United States, and Russia. On substantive questions, as distinguished from procedural ones on which the veto does not apply, decisions can be made by an affirmative vote of 9 of the council's 15 members so long as no permanent member vetoes it by casting a negative vote. An abstention from voting by a permanent member does not constitute a veto. The charter requires that parties to a dispute must abstain from voting when the council considers pacific settlement procedures. Because charter amendments must be ratified by all permanent members, failure to ratify by any of the five would have the same effect as a veto. *See also* UN PRINCIPAL ORGAN: SECURITY COUNCIL (601).

Significance

The veto power accorded to the five great powers by the framers of the United Nations Charter was regarded by them as central to the world organization's major role. In peace and security matters, they reasoned, great-power unanimity must prevail or the organization could be used by one group against another, resulting in a third world war. The Soviet Union used the veto to defend its minority position, and in the first decades of the Cold War it cast more than 100 vetoes. Although in 1945 the United States supported the inclusion of the veto power in the charter, it did not begin using the veto until it lost its majority position in the world body. By the 1970s the veto was a familiar device in U.S. foreign policy, and by the 1980s the United States was using it more often than the Soviet Union. Vetoes all but disappeared after the demise of the Soviet Union in 1991–1992, but there is no gainsaying its reappearance should the permanent powers develop more significant cleavages in their future dealings with one another. Although there have been numerous proposals to moderate or eliminate the veto in council decision making, in the absence of a different United Nations there seems little likelihood of this materializing.

United Nations Charter | 593 |

A multilateral treaty that serves as the "constitution" for the United Nations organization. The charter was drawn up and signed in San Francisco on 26 June 1945, and was ratified by 51 original members and put into effect on 24 October 1945, since known as United Nations Day. The document consists of a preamble and 111 articles that proclaim the purposes and principles of the organization, provide for the establishment of six major organs, and enumerate the procedures and functions of each. *See also* UNITED NATIONS CONFERENCE ON INTERNATIONAL ORGANIZATION (UNCIO) (595).

Significance
The United Nations Charter represents an effort by the community of nations to establish norms of international conduct to outlaw war, provide for the peaceful settlement of international disputes, regulate armaments, govern trust territories, and encourage cooperation among nations in dealing with economic and social problems. Like the U.S. Constitution, the charter has proved to be a flexible document, subject to many broad interpretations. Without this feature of adaptability, the United Nations would probably have collapsed under the burden of the Cold War.

United Nations Children's Fund (UNICEF) | 594 |

An organization established by the General Assembly in 1946 to provide emergency supplies of food, medicine, and clothing to destitute children in war-ravaged countries. Originally called the UN International Children's Emergency Fund (UNICEF), when the General Assembly gave it permanent status its name was changed by deleting the words "International" and "Emergency"; however, its well-known acronym, UNICEF, was retained. UNICEF has since expanded its operations to include the underdeveloped countries and has increased its activities to include sponsorship of national projects for better education, improved health, and disease control, with matching funds provided by recipient nations. Increasingly it has called upon specialized agencies, such as the World Health Organization (WHO), the UN Economic and Social Council (ECOSOC), and the Food and Agricultural Organization (FAO) for advice and help in carrying out its programs. Financing for its programs has come from member governments, private contributions, UNICEF holiday greeting card programs, and Halloween "trick or treat" collections by children in the United States.

Significance
Millions of children in Europe, Latin America, Africa, and Asia have been helped by the United Nations Children's Fund. The magnitude of the challenge facing UNICEF is underscored by the fact that two-thirds of the world's children are ill-fed and ill-housed, and suffer from lack of medical and sanitation facilities. UNICEF has placed special emphasis on administering mass health campaigns against epidemic and endemic diseases that attack children, providing milk as a dietary staple, caring for refugee children, and overcoming illiteracy among

the young. It has also been assigned a primary role in the United Nations Development Decade programs for encouraging a substantial rate of economic growth in the developing states.

United Nations Conference on International Organization (UNCIO) | 595 |

The major conference in San Francisco (25 April–26 June 1945) that wrote the charter of the United Nations and approved the statute of the International Court of Justice. The 50 participating states, together with Poland, became the 51 original members of the United Nations. The deliberations at San Francisco were based on the proposals formulated by the four sponsoring governments (China, Great Britain, the Soviet Union, and the United States) at the Dumbarton Oaks Conference of 1944. The work of the San Francisco Conference resembled that of a constituent body drafting a constitution. It was carried on in 4 commissions and 12 committees, with final approval recorded at plenary conference sessions. Leadership was provided by the great powers at each stage. The charter became effective on 24 October 1945 (since designated United Nations Day) when it had been ratified by a majority of signers, including the Big Five. Before the meeting of the first General Assembly in January 1946, the charter had been ratified by all 51 original members. *See also* DIPLOMATIC POLICY: YALTA AGREEMENT (423); UNITED NATIONS: DUMBARTON OAKS CONFERENCE (579).

Significance
The San Francisco Conference, which was held prior to the end of World War II, demonstrated that great-power unanimity was not impossible. The major controversies centered on the character and extent of great-power influence on the organization compared with that allocated to the lesser states. But concern that the major powers would refuse to join the world body was sufficient to deter the smaller powers from pressing their argument for an even playing field. Despite their numerical advantage, they acknowl-

edged the role of the more powerful states and hence refrained from exploiting their voting majority. The charter remains the basic constitution for the United Nations, altered formally by only two amendments: The first, adopted in 1965, increased the memberships of the Security Council to 15 and the Economic and Social Council to 36, and another, in 1973, expanded the latter organ to its present size of 54. Like most constitutions, the United Nations Charter has been altered mainly by interpretation and usage, but in the 1990s states like Japan and Germany began to publicize their interest in joining the original permanent powers. Neither Great Britain nor France, each a permanent power, compared favorably with either of these financial giants, and indeed, even India and Brazil projected greater capacity in all categories defining national power. The world of the 1990s was quite different from the one immediately following World War II. The dilemmas confronting the United Nations in the post–Cold War environment were at least in part a consequence of changed global conditions that no longer focused on the competition of two ideologically opposed superpowers. The increasing number of major actors in Europe, Asia, and Latin America demonstrated the need for a United Nations that more accurately represented the world of nations in the twenty-first century. The United Nations Charter is therefore subject to amendment in critical areas, notably in the number of permanent powers sitting on the Security Council. The work of the Security Council, as well as the United Nations' future, could well hinge on the success or failure of this structural and substantive reform.

United Nations Development Program | 596 |

An international effort aimed at raising the living standards of the world's poorest people. The United Nations Development Program was created in 1965 from the merger of the Special Fund and the Expanded Program of Technical Assistance. The purpose was to achieve better coordination and integration of projects within an overall development program for each country. Although the merger resulted in a single administrative structure for coordinating requests for aid, in fact the two components of the program remained identifiable. By 1993 the UNDP budget was $1.5 billion. Among its many responsibilities is the planning for the Development Decades. The Fourth Development Decade covers 1991 to the year 2000, and is assisted by the Group of Seventy-Seven's Coalition of Developing States, the General Assembly of the United Nations, and the UN Economic and Social Council. The strategy adopted by UNDP is: (1) Increase the role of the UN specialized agencies, (2) help developing nations to control inflation and promote savings and foreign investment, (3) modernize economies, (4) generate appropriate assistance form developed countries, and (5) place greater emphasis on the needs of the most depressed and least developed nations. *See also* TRANS-NATIONAL PATTERN: WORLD DEVELOPMENT MOVEMENT (WDM) (714).

Significance
The work of the United Nations Development Program centers on elevating the poorest segments of the world's populations, but its work is hampered by the worldwide arms race, which impacts most negatively on the least developed nations, and hence those with the more significantly impoverished populations. All the industrialized nations in the Northern Hemisphere have spoken loudly about the need to assist the world's poor and how such assistance promotes democratic development, but their economic and peculiar security interests override these public declarations. Roughly a quarter of annual U.S. aid giving, for example, goes to two countries—Israel and Egypt. Thus, the UNDP has shown that poor countries with big arms budgets get twice as much aid per person as those spending less on arms. El Salvador, it is reported, gets 5 times more aid than Bangladesh, even though the latter

has 24 times as many people and is 5 times poorer. If levels of poverty are the prime indicators for aid, Egypt should receive a small portion, but UNDP reports reveal that the European Union boosted its aid to Egypt by 400 percent following the Gulf War of 1991. By contrast, Ethiopia, a far more impoverished country, received considerably less food aid than Egypt, which by all estimates has a relatively well-fed population. In 1995 the UNDP reported that the industrialized states offered aid amounting to $60 billion a year, yet they earn in compensation $125 billion from military expenditures in the developing world. The organization is convinced that its work will be facilitated only when aid is de-linked from trade—notably the arms trade.

United Nations High Commissioner for Refugees (UNHCR) | 597 |

The primary international organization concerned with the welfare of the world's refugee population. The Office of the United Nations High Commissioner for Refugees replaced the World War II International Refugee Organization, and was charged by the international community with providing international protection to, and seeking durable solutions for, the world's refugees, estimated in 1994 to exceed 25 million. Created in 1951 for a limited period to seek solutions to the problems of refugees and displaced persons still living in camps in Austria, Germany, and Italy following World War II, UNHCR's existence has been prolonged in response to the constant and increasing flows of refugees, and the growing complexity of the refugee phenomenon. In 1993 alone, the number of the world's refugees increased at a rate of some 10,000 a day. UNHCR is involved in large-scale repatriation and rehabilitation programs to help refugees return and rebuild their lives and communities from Cambodia to Mozambique, from Bosnia to Somalia. The growing number of refugees, from 1.4 million in 1960 to more than 25 million in 1994, is a dramatic and tragic reflection

of today's world. *See also* UNITED NA-
TIONS RELIEF AND WORKS AGENCY (UNRWA)
(604); WAR: REFUGEE (313).

Significance

Those who believed that the end of the
Cold War and the collapse of the former
Communist regimes would rapidly pave
the way for the resolution of long-standing
conflicts are no longer so hopeful. While
the reduction in East-West tension creates
new opportunities for international cooperation, the proxy wars of the earlier decades remain, but with a life of their own.
Moreover, the proxy-war patrons left behind devastating weapons that were immediately accessed by rival factions in the
warring states. Thus, states continue to
struggle against both internal and external forces; some are given to fragmentation, others either implode or explode.
But whatever the manifestation, the consequence is an increasing flow of refugees.
UNHCR is charged with the responsibility of addressing people at risk in circumstances beyond their control, and
generally not of their doing. In 1993
UNHCR assisted in the repatriation of
360,000 refugees and displaced persons in
Cambodia alone. It is committed to assist
those in need in Bosnia-Herzegovina, the
region of the most serious humanitarian
crisis that Europe has experienced since
World War II. UNPROFOR, the United
Nations Protection Force that was dispatched to Bosnia under Security Council
Resolution 776, constituted a new type of
involvement for UN emergency forces,
given its humanitarian directive. UNHCR
and UNPROFOR are linked one to the
other, together providing 1,000 metric
tons of assistance each day to the beleaguered inhabitants of the former Yugoslavia. UNHCR also answered the call in
1993–1994 when huge tides of refugees
shuttled between Burundi and Rwanda
to avoid the carnage in their respective
countries. The UNHCR role in Somalia,
Kurdistan, and numerous other areas
around the world point up the heightened rather than diminishing importance
of the agency.

UN Principal Organ: Economic and Social Council (ECOSOC)

| 598 |

A major organ of the United Nations,
which functions under the authority of
the General Assembly in planning and
recommending economic and social programs. ECOSOC is composed of 54 members elected by a two-thirds vote in the
General Assembly for three-year terms,
18 elected each year. Although all UN
members are equally eligible for membership, the major powers have consistently been elected. This situation led to
the enlargement of the council by charter
amendment in 1965 from 18 to 27 members, and again by amendment in 1973 to
54, giving the new nations of Asia and
Africa a larger voice. Major functions of
ECOSOC include (1) research and debate
on economic, social, educational, cultural, and related topics; (2) drafting conventions that, if adopted by the General
Assembly and ratified by member states,
become international law and bind states
domestically; and (3) coordinating the activities of the specialized agencies. To aid
it in its operations, the council established
eight functional commissions (Human
Rights, International Commodity Trade,
Narcotic Drugs, Population, Prevention
of Discrimination and Protection of Minorities, Statistical, Status of Women, and
Transport and Communications) and five
regional economic commissions (Africa,
Asia and the Pacific, Europe, Western
Asia, and Latin America). *See also* UN
SPECIALIZED AGENCY (605).

Significance

The Economic and Social Council has
been mainly concerned with two areas
considered to be of primary importance
by a majority of UN members: economic
development and human rights. In the
field of economic development, ECOSOC
has played a major role in building the
United Nations Development Program
with its technical-assistance and special-
fund approaches to spurring modernization in the developing states. In 1966,
ECOSOC was instrumental in securing

the establishment of the Capital Development Fund to help finance industrialization, culminating a decade of efforts by the developing countries for a Special United Nations Fund for Economic Development (SUNFED proposal). ECOSOC's most notable achievements in the human rights field have been the Universal Declaration of Human Rights, adopted by the General Assembly in 1948, and numerous human rights conventions to expand individual freedom.

UN Principal Organ: General Assembly | 599 |

One of the six principal organs of the United Nations, which functions as a general conference of all member states. Each member is accorded ten delegates and one vote, and each is represented equally on the assembly's seven main committees. Assembly jurisdiction extends to any world problem or internal organizational or procedural problem of the United Nations that a majority of its members wish to consider. Decisions are made by a simple majority of members present and voting, except for "important questions" (defined in Article 18 of the charter), which require a two-thirds vote. Although the assembly cannot make binding decisions or law, it can by resolution recommend various kinds of national and international community action. Through the adoption of conventions or treaties, it can play a role in the development of domestic law within states that ratify them. The assembly annually elects a statesman of international reputation as president, and 17 vice-presidents from major geographical areas of the world. A General Committee, composed of the president, vice-presidents, and chairpersons of the seven standing committees, functions as a steering committee in planning the work of each session. Assembly powers include (1) conciliation of international disputes, (2) recommendation of collective measures against an aggressor, (3) adoption of the organization's budget, (4) supervision of other principal organs and subsidiary bodies, (5) election of members of the three councils and the judges of the international court, (6) admission of new members, and (7) proposal of amendments to the United Nations Charter. *See also* UNITED NATIONS: GENERAL DEBATE (583); UNITED NATIONS: IMPORTANT QUESTION (584); UNITED NATIONS: UNITING FOR PEACE RESOLUTION (591).

Significance
During the years of the Cold War, the General Assembly became a central organ of the United Nations system. Although not specifically related to the charter, the use of the veto in the Security Council caused so many deadlocks that, were it not for the assertiveness of the General Assembly (and most notably, its adoption of the Uniting for Peace Resolution of 1950), the organization could not act. The influx of many new members also contributed to the expanding assembly role. Mainly, however, the importance of the General Assembly has been a natural evolution growing out of broad interpretations of its charter powers, its control over the organization's purse strings, its supervisory powers over other organs, and its role as the only principal organ of the United Nations in which all members are represented. Prior to the demise of the Soviet Union in 1991–1992, the General Assembly was involved in many international disputes, helped to restore peace in several areas, adopted countless resolutions and declarations expounding norms for international conduct, helped promote economic development and freer trade, and expanded the concern for human rights. Most of all, it serves as a center for debate where disputants and aggrieved nations are free to air their complaints before a world forum.

UN Principal Organ: Secretariat | 600 |

An international body of officials and civil servants that performs administrative, budgetary, linguistic, secretarial, and housekeeping functions for an international organization. Individuals who comprise a secretariat are recruited from member states, usually according to a formula that combines the concepts of member state representation and personal competence. Although secretariat personnel retain their national citizenship, they are expected to perform their duties in a professional and objective manner that upholds the principles of the organization. All functioning regional organizations and public international unions, such as the Universal Postal Union, use international secretariats, but the most extensive in the number of personnel and variety of operations is that of the United Nations Secretariat. With about 20,000 persons employed at the New York headquarters and in field staffs in numerous countries, the secretariat functions as one of the six principal organs of the United Nations. It is headed by a secretary-general, who is nominated by the Security Council (with the veto power applicable) and appointed by the General Assembly by majority vote. More than a score of under- and deputy secretaries-general aid the secretary-general in the performance of his or her duties.

Significance
Secretariats face complicated challenges in carrying out their role within the structure of international organizations. Personnel standards must be maintained through recruitment based on merit, yet "geographical distribution" must assure each member state adequate representation, especially in the more important offices. Persons with diverse backgrounds, attitudes, ideologies, abilities, and languages must be integrated into a smoothly functioning bureaucracy. Professional dedication that rejects national partisanship must be cultivated so that members can support the goals and operations of the organization with independence, impartiality, and integrity. Controversies over efforts to develop these characteristics in the United Nations secretariat have kept the secretariat embroiled in the internal politics of the member states. Demands for greater representation in the secretariat, stemming from the influx of new nations into the United Nations, on the one hand jeopardize standards of professional competence, while on the other, the secretariat is an excellent training ground for inexperienced administrators from the Third World.

UN Principal Organ: Security Council $\boxed{601}$

One of the six principal organs of the United Nations. The Security Council is assigned primary responsibility by the charter for maintaining peace and security in the world. The council consists of five permanent members (China, France, Great Britain, the Soviet Union, and the United States) and ten (originally six) elective members that serve two-year terms. Half of the elected members are chosen each year by the General Assembly under a "gentlemen's agreement" that allots the ten elective seats to major geographical areas. Five seats are allotted to Asia and Africa, one to Eastern Europe, two to Latin America, and two to "Western European and other states." All decisions require an affirmative vote of nine members, but substantive decisions—unlike procedural ones—may be vetoed by a permanent member casting a negative vote. Nations not represented on the council may be invited to participate in council deliberations if they are parties to a dispute being considered. A council member that is a party to a dispute must abstain from voting when questions concerning peaceful settlement procedures or terms are brought to a vote. Under the charter, the council's peace preservation role provides for the pacific settlement of international disputes (Chapter VI of the charter) or, following the determination that a threat to the peace, breach of the peace, or act of aggression exists, it may call upon members to undertake collective action against the peace violator (Chapter VII). The office of president of the Security Council rotates monthly among the members, and the council is considered to be in permanent session. *See also* UNITED NATIONS: COLLECTIVE SECURITY (576); UNITED NATIONS: SANCTIONS (586).

Significance
The logic of the charter framers' search for peace was embodied in the formula that delegated primary responsibility to the great powers functioning within the framework of the Security Council. So long as unanimity prevailed among them, no power or group of powers could effectively challenge the peace. Each permanent member was accorded a veto power so that the organization could not be used by one group of great powers against another. Yet, the assumption of the framers that in most cases the great powers would have common cause did not prevail. No other organ of the United Nations suffered a greater disparity between theory and practice during the period of Cold War that pitted East against West and, more significantly, the Soviet Union against the United States. Most of the more serious threats to peace after World War II involved great-power rivalry, either direct or indirect. Ideological hostility framed the struggle between the superpowers, and because of their global involvement, the entire world was caught up in the contest. In the United Nations, disputes over the admission of new members, as well as unrelenting rivalry between the Western powers and the Soviet Union, resulted in the casting of several hundred vetoes. The principal antagonists were quick to organize regional security alliances, which although sanctioned by the charter, nevertheless placed military matters outside the ambit of UN operations. Cold War conflicts could not be adequately addressed by the Security Council, causing an expanded role for the General Assembly and the secretariat, which nevertheless remained feeble and dependent in virtually all peace and security matters. Although the council was challenged by conflict, and in some instances (Korea, Cyprus, and the India-Pakistan wars) helped gain some cease-fires, when great-power interests collided, (Vietnam and Afghanistan, for example), the council was usually paralyzed. Moreover, with the addition of numerous Third World states, the great powers had significant difficulty in influencing voting decisions, es-

pecially in the General Assembly. Third World bloc voting gravitated toward the Soviet bloc, or Arab or Islamic blocs, and more and more the Western nations found themselves on the short end of the balloting. Toward the end of the Cold War, the Security Council seemed to regain its lost stature when Mikhail Gorbachev sought to normalize Soviet relations with the United States and funnel more of the world's problems through the United Nations. The Security Council action against Iraq was a case in point. Despite a treaty of friendship and cooperation with Iraq, Moscow condemned Iraq's conquest and annexation of Kuwait. Moscow also agreed to use the United Nations to pressure Iraq to withdraw its forces from Kuwait and permit the restoration of its monarchy. When Iraq refused to yield, the Security Council, with compliance from both the Soviet Union and China, ordered a U.S.-led coalition of military forces to drive the Iraqis out of Kuwait. The Gulf War of 1990–1991 reinvigorated the Security Council—at just the time the Soviet Union was about to self-destruct. After the disappearance of the most formidable of the Communist states, Russia assumed the Soviet role in the Security Council, and was made one of the permanent powers. Although Russia did not demonstrate the capacity of the former USSR, its significant nuclear arsenal and its retention of a huge military establishment sustained it as a great power in post–Cold War power politics. The Security Council's actions since the fall of the Soviet Union point to more cooperation among the permanent powers, but it is too soon to forecast the full implementation of the United Nations Charter. Moreover, there are Security Council changes in the offing, this time involving the expansion of the rank of permanent powers. In the new environment, it is necessary to take cognizance of the rise of Japan, Germany, Brazil, India, and possibly others to permanent-power status. The future of the United Nations rests on the prospective role played by the Security Council, and the latter will not be able to function if its character and operations do not resemble the world of the twenty-first century.

UN Principal Organ: Trusteeship Council $\boxed{602}$

One of the six principal organs of the United Nations, which supervises the administration of trust territories. The council is subordinate to the General Assembly in its supervision of nonstrategic territories and to the Security Council in its supervision of strategic trusts. Membership on the council includes (1) all trust-administering states, (2) nonadministering permanent members of the Security Council, and (3) additional elective members, to strike a balance between trust-administering and nonadministering states. In 1968, at the peak of its activity, the council consisted of four trust-administering states (Australia, the United Kingdom, the United States, and New Zealand), three permanent members of the Security Council (China, France, and the Soviet Union), and one elective member. In 1987 the Trusteeship Council consisted of only five members: the United States, as a trust territory administrator, and China, France, Great Britain, and the Soviet Union as permanent members of the Security Council. China did not participate in the work of the Trusteeship Council until 1989. Russia assumed the role heretofore occupied by the USSR in 1992. The council carries out its responsibilities through studies and debates, makes recommendations to the General Assembly, hears petitions from trust territory representatives, requires annual and special reports, and sends visiting missions to trust territories for on-the-spot supervision. *See also* UNITED NATIONS: TRUST TERRITORY (588).

Significance

The Trusteeship Council has virtually completed its task of supervising the transition of trust territories to independence. Of the territories originally placed under trusteeship only one, Palau, remained under UN Trusteeship Council supervision by the mid-1990s. British Cameroons was divided into an independent Cameroon state and the remaining portion was absorbed by Nigeria in 1961. French Cameroon became independent in 1960. Naura achieved independence in 1968. New Guinea gained its freedom in 1975. Rwanda-Urundi became the independent and separate states of Rwanda and Burundi in 1962. Somaliland became Somalia in 1960. Tanzanyika, originally independent in 1961, became Tanzania when joined with Zanzibar in 1964. British Togoland joined with the Gold Coast to become Ghana in 1957. French Togoland became independent Togo in 1960. Western Samoa assumed independence in 1962, and although the Marshall Islands and Micronesia remain associated with the United States, they became members of the United Nations in 1991. The remaining former trust territory, the Northern Marianas, is now the U.S. Commonwealth: Northern Marianas. Although the United Nations may consider abolishing the Trusteeship Council, a number of member states are pushing for its transformation into the Trusteeship Council for the Environment.

United Nations Regional Commissions $\boxed{603}$

Commissions established by the United Nations Economic and Social Council (ECOSOC) to foster economic cooperation within major geographical areas of the world. Acting under authority of the United Nations Charter (Article 68), in 1947 ECOSOC established an Economic Commission for Europe (ECE) and an Economic Commission for Asia and the Far East (ECAFE), both intended to aid recovery from World War II. In 1948 ECOSOC recognized an additional role for regional commissions in promoting economic development with the establishment of an Economic Commission for Latin America and the Caribbean (ECLAC). In 1958 an Economic Commission for Africa (ECA) was founded to help the nations of that continent improve their economic lot. In 1974 an Economic and Social Commission for Western Asia (ESCWA) was established, and the ECAFE was redesignated the

Economic and Social Commission for Asia and the Pacific (ESCAP). Although membership in each regional commission is open to countries in the region, Israel has been excluded from ESCWA, and South Africa has been rejected from membership in ECA. Other states from outside the regions, but having a definite interest in the areas, are also members or associate members of each of the commissions. Headquarters for the five commissions are in Geneva, Bangkok, Santiago, Addis Ababa, and Beirut. *See also* UN PRINCIPAL ORGAN: ECONOMIC AND SOCIAL COUNCIL (ECOSOC) (598).

Significance
The five regional commissions play a role in conducting research on economic and social problems, making recommendations directly to member governments, and advising ECOSOC and specialized agencies on matters within their respective competencies. None of their activities can be carried out without the approval of the countries concerned. The regional commissions have promoted economic integration as a means of attacking underdevelopment. In Latin America, for example, ECLAC was directly involved in the establishment of the Central American Common Market (CACM) in 1960, the Latin American Free Trade Association (LAFTA) in 1961, and the Latin American Integration Association (LAIA) in 1980.

United Nations Relief and Works Agency (UNRWA) | 604 |

An organization established by the United Nations in 1949 to care for Arab refugees from the Arab-Israeli War of 1948–1949. Still active through the 1990s, UNRWA provides food, shelter, education and vocational training, and health services for the Arab refugees. The major portion of the annual budget is contributed by the United States. The refugees live in "refugee cities" located in Jordan, Syria, and Lebanon. Those in Lebanon were caught up in the Lebanese civil war that raged between 1975 and 1991. In the Gaza Strip, under Palestine Liberation

Organization (PLO) administration since 1994, and in the West Bank territory, since the September 1995 agreement under Israeli and PLO administration. Palestinian refugees received assistance from UNRWA, but these Palestinians lived in different circumstances from those in the Arab states. In the West Bank, Jericho, and the Gaza Strip, nongovernmental organizations linked with various PLO factions or the Hamas organization serviced the needs of the Palestinian population, often developing schools and medical service units to tend to the needs of their brethren. The PLO and Hamas also have drawn their recruits from the camps, and indeed the same has been done in the Arab states where the refugees are resident. *See also* NATIONALIST MOVEMENT: PALESTINE LIBERATION ORGANIZATION (PLO) (70); UNITED NATIONS HIGH COMMISSIONER FOR REFUGEES (UNHCR) (597); WAR: REFUGEE (313).

Significance
Unlike most refugee organizations, the United Nations Relief and Works Agency has been unable to reduce its problem by the usual methods of resettlement, repatriation, and assimilation. The number of refugees has actually increased from the approximately 800,000 who fled Palestine in 1948–1949 to almost 3 million four decades later. The increases are the result of a high birthrate, poor or reluctant reporting on natural deaths, UNRWA care, the refusal of all the Arab states except Jordan to absorb the refugees, and the Arab-Israeli wars of 1967 and 1973, which forced more people to flee their homes. Not all Palestinian Arabs are camp refugees, however, and indeed the Palestinians are among the most highly educated in the Arab world. Jordan conferred citizenship on them, and in other Arab states (e.g., Egypt, Syria, Libya, and Iraq) they have formed part of the general community even if citizenship was not extended. Palestinians in Saudi Arabia and the other oil-rich Gulf states functioned in significant numbers, at relatively good paying jobs, until the 1990–1991 war that was provoked by Iraqi aggression against Ku-

wait. The Palestinians tended to favor the forces of Iraq and were seen as betraying the Saudi and Gulf governments that had cared for them. The expulsion of tens of thousands of Palestinians from those states following the liberation of Kuwait also added to the refugee population. Libya's 1995 expulsion of Palestinians (allegedly due to Yasir Arafat and the PLO seeking reconciliation with Israel) added to the refugee plight and increased the burden on relief agencies. Thus, the original refugee problem has become far more complicated, and it remains a heavy burden for the United Nations. An additional dilemma is that the Palestinians trace their roots to what is now Israel, and they have always anticipated their return. That hope has been nourished and exploited over the years by the Arab states, the PLO, and other Islamic nations and orders. Israel has reacted in a predictable manner, arguing that the Israeli state would cease to exist if those Palestinians wishing to resettle in the country were in fact permitted to do so. The PLO's national covenant, which remained operative in the 1990s, called for the return of the Arab Palestinians to the land that is now Israel. The same PLO covenant denied the right of settler Israelis and their progeny, even if born in Israel, to remain. The 1995 Israel-PLO accord in fact called upon the PLO to renounce these sections of their covenant. But despite PLO-Israeli progress in their negotiations, and the growing possibility that a Palestinian state will be formed from the West Bank and Gaza before the end of the decade, little has occurred that points to a resolution of the camp-refugee problem. UNRWA was established as a temporary act of humanitarianism, but it has long been used as a political football by all the interests in the area. Will the camp refugees be welcome in the Palestinian state? That is a question not yet addressed by the negotiators.

UN Specialized Agency | 605 |

A functional international organization with broad international responsibilities in the economic, social, cultural, educational, health, or related fields. Although the 16 specialized agencies operate outside the general UN framework, each maintains a relationship with the world organization through a special agreement concluded between the agency and the Economic and Social Council. Each agency has its own budget, although the General Assembly may review it and make recommendations. The common organizational structure of the agencies includes (1) a general conference or assembly of all members, which functions as the chief policy-making organ; (2) an executive council or board, which implements policies between sessions of the general conference, performing executive and supervisory functions; and (3) a secretariat headed by a director or secretary-general, which performs administrative chores at the agency's headquarters. The agencies propose legislation for national enactment by members, draft treaties on matters of common concern, and carry on extensive research, publication, and informational work for the benefit of members. The specialized agencies include the Food and Agriculture Organization (FAO), International Maritime Organization (IMO), International Bank for Reconstruction and Development (IBRD), International Civil Aviation Organization (ICAO), International Development Association (IDA), International Finance Corporation (IFC), International Labor Organization (ILO), International Monetary Fund (IMF), International Telecommunications Union (ITU), United Nations Educational, Scientific, and Cultural Organization (UNESCO), Universal Postal Union (UPU), World Health Organization (WHO), World Meteorological Organization (WMO), World Intellectual Property Organization (WIPO), International Fund for Agricultural Development (IFAD), and the United Nations Industrial Development Organization (UNIDO). Most were created during the UN era, although the origins of some go back to the nineteenth century. Three additional agencies that function much like specialized agencies are the International Atomic Energy Agency (IAEA), the General Agreement on Tariffs and Trade

(GATT), and the World Trade Organization (WTO). (*For specific agencies, see* Index.)

Significance

The decentralized pattern of functional operations provided by the charter for the specialized agencies has permitted all to enjoy freedom of action within their fields of operations while accepting coordination and direction from the United Nations proper. In offering technical assistance to developing nations, for example, each contributes help within areas of its special competence and cooperates with other agencies through the United Nations Development Program to avoid duplication and overlap. Their efforts are part of the functional approach to peace, which postulates the building of a stable world order through cooperation in solving common economic and social problems.

UN Specialized Agency: Food and Agriculture Organization (FAO) | 606 |

A specialized agency of the United Nations, originally created in May 1943. In the preamble to FAO's constitution, members agree to work toward "raising levels of nutrition and standards of living, . . . efficiency in the production and distribution of all food, . . . bettering the conditions of rural populations, and thus contributing toward an expanding world economy." These goals are sought through (1) collecting and distributing information; (2) recommending national and international action to improve conservation, production, processing, marketing, and food distribution; and (3) furnishing technical assistance and organizing agricultural missions. FAO headquarters are located in Rome. *See also* GREEN REVOLUTION (169); UN SPECIALIZED AGENCY (605).

Significance

Considerable progress has been made through the FAO's efforts to increase food production, especially in underdeveloped areas. In many cases, however, population growth has reduced these gains or turned them into losses when measured on a per capita basis. Paradoxically, the FAO's success in helping to avert famines and in improving nutrition has added to its long-range problem of feeding an ever-expanding world population. However, the Green Revolution has turned some net food importers into net exporters by the use of more technology, fertilizer, and improved seeds. The 1974 FAO World Food Conference in Rome made recommendations to participating governments and various UN agencies to (1) increase food production and distribution systems, (2) establish a Global Information and Early Warning System to warn of impending famines, and (3) encourage all governments to create large grain reserves as part of a world disaster stockpile.

UN Specialized Agency: International Atomic Energy Agency (IAEA) | 607 |

An agency of the United Nations established in 1957 to foster cooperation among nations in developing atomic energy for peaceful purposes. The IAEA was first proposed by President Dwight D. Eisenhower in his Atoms for Peace proposals before the General Assembly in 1953. Although technically not a specialized agency, the IAEA functions in a manner similar to the 16 specialized agencies. *See also* DISARMAMENT PROPOSAL: ATOMS FOR PEACE PLAN (389).

Significance

The International Atomic Energy Agency, which reports directly to the General Assembly, was created to reduce the threat of war by encouraging cooperation, especially between the atomic powers and the developing states. It seeks to raise living standards in the world by developing cheap power sources and by teaching the new technology to the scientists of the underdeveloped countries. The IAEA has sponsored numerous research projects, made studies concerning health and safety standards, and furnished fissionable materials to countries for research purposes. Special safeguards, including on-site inspections, have been established to prevent the military use of fissionable materials supplied for peaceful purposes. Creators of the agency hoped that its operations would build the foundation for an eventual international system of control and inspection for nuclear weapons. Despite the obstacles, IAEA is chiefly responsible for monitoring Iraqi nuclear programs since the end of the 1990–1991 Gulf War, and North Korea's nuclear activities since the 1994 crisis.

UN Specialized Agency: International Civil Aviation Organization (ICAO) | 608 |

A specialized agency of the United Nations established in 1947 to develop and regulate international air transportation. The ICAO applies the principles and law incorporated in the Convention on International Civil Aviation signed at Chicago in 1944 and in more recent ICAO conventions. An assembly, composed of all members with each having one vote, meets once every three years to decide general policies of the organization. An executive council elected by the assembly for three-year terms meets regularly to adopt navigation standards, arbitrate disputes among members, and provide extensive information on air transport. Subsidiary bodies appointed by the council study all aspects of international air transportation and make reports to the council. Under the Chicago Convention, members have reciprocal privileges to fly across one another's territories without landing and, under varying circumstances, to land and take on passengers and cargo. Most nations are members of ICAO, whose headquarters are in Montreal. *See also* UN SPECIALIZED AGENCY (605).

Significance

The International Civil Aviation Organization has been one of the most active of the specialized agencies as a result of the expansion in world air transportation. Every international flight today depends heavily upon information, standards, facilities, and services around the globe provided through ICAO programs. The ICAO has also been a leading contributor to the United Nations Development Program by providing experts and missions as consultants to developing states and setting up regional training centers to prepare new nations for the air age.

UN Specialized Agency: International Labor Organization (ILO) | 609 |

A specialized agency of the United Nations, originally established in 1919 by the Treaty of Versailles to improve working conditions in member countries. The ILO was independent of the League of Nations, but coordinated its activities with that organization. The ILO functions by offering advice and providing for information exchange, setting standards, and mobilizing world opinion to support higher labor standards. Its main areas of concern are full employment, migration of workers, social security, workers' health, labor standards, and technical assistance for economic development. The ILO organization includes an all-member International Labor Conference and a smaller Governing Body—both based on a tripartite system of national representation by one employer, one worker, and two government delegates—and an unusually active secretariat, known as the Labor Office. The conference meets annually at the ILO's headquarters in Geneva to determine general policies. Between conferences, the Governing Body functions as an executive, supervising the operations of ILO committees and commissions. *See also* UN SPECIALIZED AGENCY (605).

Significance

The International Labor Organization has encouraged progress in labor affairs in most of the more than 100 member countries. International conventions have helped to improve labor standards simultaneously in many states that otherwise might have refused to take unilateral action because it would place them at a competitive disadvantage. Members that persistently disregard ILO labor rules and principles are placed on a special "blacklist" until they improve their standard. ILO has increasingly directed its efforts toward helping developing states improve their labor productivity, working conditions, and the general well-being of workers. ILO experts provide technical assistance to countries in Asia, Africa, and Latin America. The United States withdrew from the ILO in 1977, charging that the organization had been politicized, particularly in its actions toward Israel, but it resumed membership in 1980.

UN Specialized Agency: International Maritime Organization (IMO)   610

A specialized agency of the United Nations (formerly the Inter-Governmental Maritime Consultative Organization [IMCO]) established to further cooperation in matters relating to shipping, safety, and passenger service on the high seas. IMO, originally IMCO, was formed under a 1948 convention that came into force in 1958 after receiving sufficient ratifications. Its structure includes an assembly, which meets every two years, with all members having an equal vote; a council of 16 members, which functions as an executive body; a Maritime Safety Committee; and a secretariat at its London headquarters headed by a secretary-general. Specifically, IMO advises member governments in maritime navigation and safety matters, including the operation of oil tankers and ecological programs. *See also* UN SPECIALIZED AGENCY (605).

Significance
The International Maritime Organization has been active in diverse fields ranging from the prevention of pollution of the sea by oil to encouragement of tourism. It has sought to reduce governmental discrimination against foreign shipping and restrictive business practices carried on by shipping concerns. Numerous conventions have been hammered out by the as-semblies, convoked periodically since 1959.

UN Specialized Agency: International Telecommunication Union (ITU)   611

A specialized agency of the United Nations established to facilitate all types of telecommunications and harmonize the actions of member states in such fields. The ITU was set up in 1932 as a successor to the International Telegraph Union, which had functioned since 1865. Organs of the ITU include a Plenipotentiary Conference, which meets once every five years to decide basic policies; two Administrative Conferences (one for telegraph and telephone, the other for radio and television), which adopt regulations binding on all members; an Administrative Council to implement policies; and a secretariat, headed by a secretary-general located at ITU headquarters in Geneva. By 1987 almost all nations of the world were members or associate members. *See also* UN SPECIALIZED AGENCY (605).

Significance
The cooperation fostered through the International Telecommunication Union makes possible a global communications network that links national and private telephone and telegraph services. World radio transmission would be chaotic without the allocation of frequencies by the ITU, and television channels may have to be similarly allocated on an orderly basis as international telecasting increases. The ITU's role highlights the necessity for functional cooperation in a technologically tight-knit world. Its main programs provide technical assistance for developing countries.

UN Specialized Agency: United Nations Educational, Scientific, and Cultural Organization (UNESCO)   612

A specialized agency of the United Nations that promotes cooperation among members in the fields of education, science, and culture. Through recommendations to member governments and through its own activities, UNESCO has carried on exchange programs, promoted teaching and research, and sought to advance the ideals of equal rights and educational opportunity. UNESCO machinery includes a General Conference, an Executive Board, and a Secretariat, with its headquarters in Paris. *See also* UN SPECIALIZED AGENCY (605).

Significance
UNESCO and its projects have been the most controversial of the 16 UN specialized agencies. Some critics charge that its efforts to promote better international understanding and reduce the forces of nationalism are steps toward world government. Others assail UNESCO on the opposite ground—that it has failed to contribute effectively to the building of a world community and has done little to spread knowledge and understanding of diverse cultures. UNESCO supporters reject both criticisms and reaffirm its basic principle, as stated in the preamble to UNESCO's constitution, that "since wars begin in the minds of men, it is in the minds of men that the defenses of peace must be constructed." Nonetheless, in 1985 the United States withdrew from UNESCO, followed by Great Britain in 1986; both charged poor management, politicization of issues, and pursuit of "statist" policies. The last of these charges related to the effort of the Third World bloc of members to establish a New World Information and Communication Order (NWICO) that would supposedly produce a more favorable press for them in dealing with major global issues.

UN Specialized Agency: Universal Postal Union (UPU) | 613 |

A specialized agency of the United Nations for integrating national postal services. First established as the General Postal Union by the Berne Treaty of 1874, the UPU adopted its present name in 1878 and entered into an arrangement with the United Nations in 1947. The organization of the union consists of a Congress, which meets every five years; an Executive and Liaison Committee, elected by each Congress; a Consultative Committee on Postal Research; and an International Bureau, located at Berne, which functions as a secretariat. The Universal Postal Convention is revised by each Congress; amendment proposals are circulated by the bureau between congresses and, following ratification by a sufficient number of members, must be acceded to by the others as a condition of retaining membership. *See also* UN SPECIALIZED AGENCY (605).

Significance
The Universal Postal Union illustrates the need for international cooperation in technical fields. Before its establishment, a letter with a foreign destination required special handling and the payment of postage to each country through which it passed. Rates varied widely and were often discriminatory. The UPU has overcome these shortcomings by standardizing national procedures, establishing uniform rates, and setting up compensatory accounts to clear balances. The success of the union has encouraged the creation of additional international public unions in other technical fields.

UN Specialized Agency: World Health Organization (WHO) | 614 |

A specialized agency of the United Nations established in 1948 with the basic purpose of "the attainment by all peoples of the highest possible level of health." WHO carries on some of its programs through advisory services, which combat various maladies and aid in the development of national health administrations. Other programs are administered through central WHO facilities and include international health conventions and the publication of health statistics. WHO machinery includes an annual World Health Assembly, an Executive Board, and a Secretariat, which functions under WHO's director-general at the Geneva headquarters. *See also* UN SPECIALIZED AGENCY (605).

Significance
The record of the World Health Organization has been outstanding, particularly in its effort to control endemic and epidemic diseases such as malaria and smallpox, and in its promotion of maternal and child welfare. Malaria-control programs have been carried out in over 20 countries. WHO has assisted a number of countries in developing their health services and expanding the number of trained health and medical technicians. WHO also aids the victims of natural disasters. In recent years, WHO has provided leadership and helped to coordinate research and other programs in the international campaign to cope with AIDS (Acquired Immune Deficiency Syndrome).

UN Specialized Agency: World Meteorological Organization (WMO)   615

A specialized agency of the United Nations established in 1947 to facilitate worldwide cooperation in weather observation and reporting and to encourage research and training in meteorology. The WMO succeeded the 1878 International Meteorological Organization, composed of national directors of weather services. The new organization has states rather than individuals as members, including most states since 1982. The organization of WMO consists of a World Meteorological Congress, which meets every four years with all members represented and each having one vote; an 18-member Executive Committee, which meets annually and functions as an executive body to implement WMO policies; and a secretariat, headed by a secretary-general, which services the Geneva headquarters and functions as an administrative, research, and information center. *See also* UN SPECIALIZED AGENCY (605).

Significance
The role of the World Meteorological Organization has grown in response to the expanding needs for reliable weather data to provide safety and comfort for the millions who use air- and water-transportation facilities. The WMO has supported the development and use of space satellites for increasing reliability in weather prediction. The growing vulnerability of large urban populations to the destructive forces of nature will increase the need for international cooperation in the field of meteorology.

U.S.
Foreign
Policy

Agency for International Development (AID)

616

A semiautonomous agency operating as a component of the International Development Cooperation Agency (IDCA), established in 1979. Created in 1961 by the Act for International Development, AID now reports to the director of IDCA and administers economic and technical foreign assistance, which involves coordinating security support assistance programs and directing the economic aspects of the Food for Peace program. Differences between the secretary of state and the director of IDCA over aid policy are resolved by the president. *See also* DEVELOPMENT STRATEGY: TECHNICAL ASSISTANCE (215); FOOD FOR PEACE PROGRAM (642); FOREIGN AID (643); FOREIGN AID RECIPIENTS (644).

Significance

Since the days of the Marshall Plan, establishing the proper relationship between foreign-aid programs and the Department of State has been a problem. Organization fluctuates between departmental control of economic foreign policy on the one hand and departmental freedom from the overseas operational functions of such policy on the other. In the same vein, the optimum administrative relationship between economic and military assistance programs has been a matter of continual concern. AID's role under the IDCA is a compromise that emphasizes long-range development plans, agency operational responsibility, and the coordination of the various aid projects within individual countries. By creating the IDCA as an independent agency but having its director report to the secretary of state, administrative experts believe they have resolved the problem of where to locate the AID. In its operations, the IDCA and Treasury Department work closely with the United Nations, the Organization of American States (OAS), the World Bank Group (IBRD), the International Monetary Fund (IMF), and the regional development banks in support of modernization goals. By the 1990s, almost 100 countries received some form of bilateral economic aid from the United States, but in 1995 the U.S. Congress seemed less inclined to sustain the aid program, arguing that the country could no longer afford it. Given congressional desire to eliminate entire federal government departments, AID too was identified as an expendable organization. With plans to reorganize the Department of State, it was suggested that future assistance programs, scaled-back and more limited, could be located in and operate from that altered department. AID was earmarked for extinction.

Alliance for Progress   617

A ten-year development program for Latin America suggested by President John F. Kennedy. Established in 1961 at Punta del Este, Uruguay, by all the American republics except Cuba, the Alliance for Progress plan called for a massive effort to meet the region's desperate need for modernization by means of mutual assistance and self-help. The United States anticipated a flow of public and private capital of approximately $20 billion over the life of the program, mainly from private investors in the capital-surplus countries outside the region. Participants in the program recognized, however, that the Latin American countries would ultimately have to provide four times that amount to meet the program's goal. The program called for regional planning by the Inter-American Economic and Social Council and the Inter-American Development Board, economic cooperation and integration, export price stabilization, land and tax reform, industrialization, and improved health care and educational opportunity. *See also* FOREIGN AID (643); REGIONAL POLITICAL GROUP: ORGANIZATION OF AMERICAN STATES (OAS) (571).

Significance

The Alliance for Progress program, launched so dramatically, languished and disappeared following the assassination of President Kennedy in 1963. The alliance's demise may be explained in part by the dimensions of a task that called for a controlled socioeconomic revolution of continental proportions. In the United States, opposition came from opponents of foreign aid, while in Latin America the established order was slow to bring about the reforms required to ensure the demise of the status quo. Meanwhile, the high rate of population growth throughout the area intensified the need for economic, social, and political modernization. The United States continued to provide modest levels of assistance within the general philosophy of the Kennedy-inspired program, but its original conception was eliminated from U.S. foreign policy.

Assertive Multilateralism   618

The U.S. government's belief that actions involving global security must enjoy international cooperation. This term reflects the central core of the Clinton administration's foreign-policy gambits, but it also lay at the heart of the United States' Cold War strategy. The United Nations was established with that purpose in mind, and the Security Council was given primary responsibility for sustaining the peace following World War II. The passing of the Cold War offered the opportunity to utilize assertive multilateralism in a modified form, and the cooperation received from the Soviet Union (prior to its dissolution) and China enabled the United Nations, rather than the United States, to punish Iraq for its aggression against Kuwait in 1990–1991. Given the success of the United Nation's Iraqi venture, the organization assumed a variety of peacekeeping and peacemaking actions in several parts of the world. A high-profile intervention was the UN action in Somalia, which was prompted by President George Bush and began as a humanitarian intervention to feed a starving Somali population, but quickly developed into a broader UN effort to restore political stability in the strife-torn nation. The United Nations managed the humanitarian peacekeeping problem with some success, but its nation-building peacemaking effort was a dismal failure, and the last UN forces were withdrawn from Somalia in the spring of 1995. If experience was not gained from the Somali affair, the Bosnian fiasco brought the

UN peacekeeping/peacemaking operations to a virtual dead end. Frustrated in its attempts to get the opposed parties to agree to a political settlement, impeded in its humanitarian activities, confronted by savage acts of brutality and callousness, and finally, targeted because of its weakness, the United Nations suffered grievous wounds that some observers considered to be life-threatening.

Significance
Assertive multilateralism lost significance in UN circles, but in so doing appeared to take a new direction as France and, to some extent, Great Britain, supported by the Clinton administration, began to explore ways to refashion the concept. The formation of an international emergency-reaction force, outside the NATO scheme, was envisaged as a method in projecting collective resolve. Assertive multilateralism is a useful concept, but it is no substitute for determined national policy. The term is devoid of meaning if the nations involved in a joint endeavor do not share the same resolve, or if they question the leadership of the coalition or lose the desire to advance its vital purposes. In the absence of a direct national interest, the nations involved in the joint exercise may lack the motivation for high commitment. Assertive multilateralism implies a long-term commitment. When the major actor in an action decides it is no longer interested in pressing the matter, even the United Nations is limited in what it can achieve. For example, the failure of the United States to sustain its Somali intervention weakened the character of collaborative endeavor in general and the United Nations in particular. U.S. ambivalence in the Bosnian conflict had similar consequences. Although the concept, and indeed the strategy, has merit, the difficulty of implementing a plan of assertive multilateralism requires overwhelming support in national institutions and among the general publics. In the absence of the Cold War and a formidable enemy, the people of the United States, and their representatives, are less inclined to join in common endeavor with other nations, even the country's closest NATO partners, if that involvement requires placing U.S. soldiers at risk in remote places that seem unconnected to any vital interest of the United States.

Bipartisanship $\boxed{619}$

Interparty unity in dealing with major problems of U.S. foreign policy. Bipartisanship is based on the idea of collaboration between the two major parties in the Congress, and between the president and the leaders of the opposition. The assumption underlying bipartisanship is that, in times of grave national peril, partisan politics should stop at the water's edge so that a united front can be presented to the outside world.

Significance
Bipartisanship was particularly successful during World War II and in the immediate postwar period of intense Cold War rivalry. The U.S. constitutional system, with its separation of powers and its checks and balances, generates conflict between the executive and legislative branches that could paralyze foreign policy making in the absence of bipartisan unity. Ultimately, a democracy must make a choice between party-developed alternative courses of action with a loyal opposition functioning, or a more unified but less democratic consensual approach to dealing with foreign-policy issues. For bipartisanship to be successful, the minority party must feel that it is actually being "consulted" and not merely "informed" about policy decisions. The key bipartisan foreign-policy gambit, organized in the Congress by Republican leader Arthur Vandenberg at the outset of the Cold War, was the congressional consensus achieved in forming the North Atlantic Treaty Organization (NATO). With the Cold War over, however, Congress had difficulty in projecting a bipartisan foreign policy in the mid-1990s, and indeed, for the first time in 40 years the law-making body had come under Republican leadership. With the presidency in the hands of the Democrats, bipartisanship proved

difficulttoachieve.Congressional leadership went one direction, while the president went in another, on issues such as NATO membership for East European states, the restoration of Bertrand Aristide to power in Haiti, the question of shifting the U.S. embassy in Israel to Jerusalem, and what U.S. policy should be toward Bosnia, Cuba, Russia, and North Korea. In fact, there were few if any foreign-policy issues where Democratic and Republican leaders found common ground. For example, while President Clinton was visiting Moscow and Kiev in May 1995, the Senate majority leader, Bob Dole, ignoring the president's delicate mission, dismissed Clinton's discussions, arguing that they failed to satisfy U.S. interests. It was in this political climate that the bipartisanship forged by Arthur Vandenberg after World War II died.

over the internal repercussion of UN actions such as implementing the Universal Declaration of Human Rights. The net effect of the proposed amendment would have been to reverse the historic trend toward strong executive leadership in foreign affairs. The Case Act of 1972 and the War Powers Act of 1973 are two examples of congressional efforts to redress the balance of decision-making power in foreign affairs. The former requires the president to inform the Congress of all executive agreements the president has concluded. The latter is an effort to limit the president's power to use military force. The National Security Revitalization Act, promoted by a Republican-dominant Congress in 1995, also attempts to limit the president's authority in foreign and national security affairs.

Bricker Amendment | 620 |

A proposed amendment to the U.S. Constitution, introduced in Congress by Senator John Bricker of Ohio in 1953 and 1954. The proposed Bricker Amendment was designed to strengthen the role of Congress in treaty making, limit the president's power to conclude executive agreements, and ensure the primacy of the Constitution over the provisions of any treaty. The proposal was killed when it failed by one vote to secure the necessary two-thirds majority in the Senate. *See also* MISSOURI V. HOLLAND (252 U.S. 416: 1920) (656); WAR POWERS ACT OF 1973 (683).

Significance

The Bricker Amendment was one episode in the history of legislative-executive rivalry over control of U.S. foreign relations. Supporters of the amendment were motivated by a fear that the president might do by treaty that which would be unconstitutional by statute, as had occurred in the famous case of *Missouri v. Holland* in 1920. The amendment also reflected dissatisfaction with the wartime executive agreements concluded at Yalta and Potsdam in 1945, and apprehension

Camp David Accords | 621 |

The September 1978 framework for rapprochement between Egypt and Israel. These Middle East neighbors had lived in a state of war with sporadic hostilities since the creation of Israel in 1948. President Jimmy Carter sensed the ripeness of a moment to make a thrust toward peace in the ongoing Arab-Israeli conflict. He saw the surprise visit of President Anwar el-Sadat of Egypt to Jerusalem in November 1977 as an indication that he and Prime Minister Menachem Begin of Israel might be brought together to discuss mutual problems. Playing on the credibility of the United States in both countries, President Carter provided a neutral and sequestered setting, as well as constant pressure for the two sides to arrange for the resolution of differences. The accords led to the formal peace treaty of March 1979 that ended 30 years of war between Israel and Egypt. *See also* DIPLOMACY: MIDDLE EAST (410); DIPLOMACY, SUMMIT (414); PRESIDENT: CHIEF DIPLOMAT (665); PRESIDENT: CHIEF OF FOREIGN POLICY (667).

Significance

The Camp David Accords exemplify the roles of the U.S. chief executive as chief diplomat and chief of foreign policy. As a result of the accords and peace treaty, Israel gained its first formal recognition from an Arab state, along with the establishment of diplomatic relations, and Egypt regained the Sinai and some relief from the economic burden of a protracted state of war. The United States gained a closer relationship with Egypt and the use of Egyptian military installations, which bolstered its military presence in the Middle East. Anwar el-Sadat was assassinated by disgruntled elements within his own army in 1981, but the United States continued to support the Camp David Accords and the 1979 treaty with billions of dollars in aid to each party, and Israel and Egypt became the two largest recipients of U.S. aid in the 1980s and 1990s. The accords set the scene for all the negotiations between Israelis and Arabs thereafter. An attempt by Lebanon to emulate Egypt failed in 1983. In September 1993 the Palestine Liberation Organization (PLO), under the leadership of Yasir Arafat, entered into an agreement to terminate hostilities with Israel in return for the Gaza Strip and the West Bank city of Jericho. Following a September 1995 Washington-signed agreement, Israel prepared to withdraw its forces from the entire West Bank and transfer its administration to Yasir Arafat's PLO. Jordan signed a treaty of peace with Israel in 1994.

Caribbean Basin Initiative (CBI) | 622 |

A U.S. program to develop stable democratic values and free-market economies in the region, announced by President Ronald Reagan at a meeting of the Organization of American States (OAS) in 1982. Congress enacted the duty-free and tax benefits of the CBI in the Caribbean Basin Economic Recovery Act of 1983. The CBI went into effect for 12 years beginning in 1984 and includes 22 countries. The duty-free provisions encourage development through export diversification. Tax-benefit provisions encourage private U.S. foreign investment in the region.

Significance

The CBI program of political stability and economic growth in the area is important to the American people. Fifty percent of all U.S. trade, including most oil imports, passes through the Caribbean shipping lanes. The creation of local jobs is designed to cut down unemployment as high as 40 percent, which has made the region the second largest source of illegal immigration into the United States. The region is also a major U.S. export market, ranking seventh in the world. The $6.3 billion in U.S. exports is larger than the amount imported by the Russian Federation plus Eastern Europe, or all of Africa, or by France or Italy. U.S. balance-of-payments support, development assistance, and commodity assistance have helped, as has energy-cost assistance from Mexico and Venezuela and a Canadian free-trade program for Caribbean Commonwealth countries. Today, the U.S. budget deficit threatens the absolute level of U.S. aid, economic growth in the basin averages 2 percent, and population continues to grow at 2.5 percent per year.

Case Act of 1972 | 623 |

An act requiring the president to submit to the Congress the text of all executive agreements within 60 days, authored by Senator Clifford Case (R-NJ). Should the president decide that public revelation of terms might endanger national security, the law gives the president the right of transmittal under injunction of secrecy. However, the text still must be given to the Senate Foreign Relations Committee and House Foreign Affairs Committee, exclusively. The act was designed to prevent the executive branch from keeping the legislature in the dark regarding foreign commitments through the use of executive agreement rather than the treaty process. *See also* BRICKER AMENDMENT (620); EXECUTIVE AGREEMENT (640); TONKIN GULF RESOLUTION (676).

Significance
The Case Act illustrates the traditional rivalry between the executive and legislative branches built into the national government by the system of separation of powers and the principle of checks and balances. In 1954 the Bricker Amendment failed by one vote to limit the president's treaty-making power. The repeal of the Tonkin Gulf Resolution in 1970 and passage of the Case Act in 1972 and the War Powers Act in 1973 are examples of congressional efforts to brake the expansion of executive power and reassert the congressional role in the area of foreign policy.

Central Intelligence Agency (CIA) 624

The principal federal agency for the accumulation and evaluation of data gathered by all the units of the national intelligence community. Created by the National Security Act of 1947, the CIA is responsible to the National Security Council (NSC) and to the president. Though not a member of the NSC by law, the civilian director of the CIA usually attends NSC meetings by presidential invitation. In addition to serving as the central receiving and interpreting agency, the CIA also gathers intelligence data and carries on covert operations. *See also* FOREIGN-POLICY PROCESS: INTELLIGENCE (17); NATIONAL SECURITY COUNCIL (NSC) (659).

Significance
The Central Intelligence Agency functions as the principal instrument of the U.S. government for conducting clandestine operations in foreign countries. Its operations and evaluations in the intelligence field appear to have an important impact on foreign-policy decisions made at the highest levels. Revelations of the extent of its sub rosa penetrations of other domestic and foreign programs, both public and private, have stirred political controversy over questions of control. A central issue involves the question of the ultimate effectiveness of White House and State Department control over foreign policy if the gatherer of data also plays a substantial role as a diplomatic actor. Congressional debate over the continuing utility of the CIA in the post–Cold War era reached new levels with the disclosure of traitorous activity by one of its long-term agents in 1994, as well as the agency's complicity in the commission of atrocities involving U.S. citizens in Central America. The general perception was that the intelligence agency not only failed to police its own behavior, but had engaged in actions that at best were sloppy and unprofessional. Although Congress decided to sustain the organization, internal reform was deemed essential.

Civilian Control 625

A constitutional principle, based on British traditions, that ultimate control of the military must be vested in civilian leaders to ensure the maintenance of democracy. Civilian control is established by the U.S. Constitution, which makes the civilian president commander in chief and gives Congress the power to raise and maintain the armed services, make military law, and declare war. Statutory amplification of the principle of civilian control has required that the secretary of defense as well as the secretaries of the army, navy, and air force must also be civilians. The Third Amendment to the Constitution buttresses the principle by forbidding the quartering of troops in private homes without consent, and the Second Amendment ensures the right of the people to keep and bear arms.

Significance
The principle of civilian control has taken on added importance for the United States and for the world as a result of the post–World War II arms race. Military leaders, by offering solutions to military problems, are increasingly influential in determining broader questions of foreign policy. In addition, the bewildering sophistication of military technology forces the Congress to turn for advice on military appropriations to the military services for whose control they are responsible. Whereas Communist gov-

ernments have always remained largely in civilian hands, many Third World countries, from Asia to Africa to Latin America, have come under military control, and many of them know little of civilian government. Nigeria in Africa and Pakistan in Asia are two prominent examples.

Congress | 626 |

The national legislature of the United States, composed of the Senate and the House of Representatives. The principle of state equality entitles each of the 50 states to two senators, who serve six-year terms, one-third of them elected every two years. Membership in the House of Representatives is based on population, and all 435 members face the electorate every two years. The foreign-relations role of the Congress comprises (1) its general legislative power in such matters as creating or eliminating agencies and in establishing or changing trade and immigration policy, (2) the executive powers of the Senate in approving treaties and confirming appointments, (3) control over appropriations, and (4) power to conduct investigations, particularly in relation to the functioning of old law and the need for new law. Congress is also related indirectly to foreign affairs through (1) resolutions indicating the "sense of the Congress"; (2) speeches, travels, and other activities of individual members; and (3) political party activity, which can either diminish or increase the distance between the White House and Capitol Hill.

Significance
The main functions of Congress in foreign affairs fall within the broad framework of the separation of powers and the system of checks and balances established by the Founding Fathers. These principles were intended to ensure that action by one branch of government in the legitimate exercise of its powers would face some form of validating activity in another branch before it could become final. For example, though the president is responsible for the conduct of foreign policy, necessary funds must be voted by the Congress, with appropriations bills starting in the House, and the president cannot take final action on treaties or appointments until Senate approval is secured. During the Cold War, Congress served a policy-validating rather than a policy-making function. The post–Cold War Congress determined to share foreign policymaking operations with the president. Nevertheless, the complex nature of foreign affairs and the leadership role of the United States in the world require constant presidential attention, initiative, and flexibility, which Congress as a deliberative body cannot supply.

Congress: Confirmation of Appointments | 627 |

The function of the national legislature to approve or disapprove nominations made by the president to fill vacancies in executive and judicial positions. The power to confirm appointments is delegated to the Senate by Article II, Section 2, of the Constitution of the United States and is accomplished by a simple majority vote. Confirmation applies only to political appointments (positions not filled by Civil Service procedures or some other formal merit system). *See also* PRESIDENT: APPOINTMENT POWER (664).

Significance
Under the U.S. system of checks and balances, the making of appointments is an executive act shared by the Senate. This ensures that the filling of diplomatic and policy-making positions in the Department of State and other executive agencies will be subject to legislative scrutiny. Through informal consultation with key senators, the president usually tries to determine in advance the acceptability of the candidate for the appointment. Nominees for ambassadorial posts and high positions in the Department of State are usually questioned by the Senate Foreign Relations Committee, the body that makes confirmation recommendations to the full Senate. Presidential appointments in the field of foreign affairs are rarely denied by the Senate.

Congress:
Declaration of War | 628 |

A joint resolution adopted by Congress and signed by the president informing the international community that the nation intends to pursue or defend its interests by military action. Technically, the Congress could pass a declaration-of-war resolution against the wishes of the president; in such a case, the president would have the option of the veto. Except for the War of 1812, every declaration of war by the United States has come at presidential request. Termination of a state of war is also accomplished by joint resolution or treaty. Congress has declared war only five times, but the president has committed troops to action on over 150 occasions without a declaration of war, including in Korea, Vietnam, and the Persian Gulf. *See also* PRESIDENT: COMMANDER IN CHIEF (668); WAR MEASURES: DECLARATION OF WAR (322); WAR POWERS ACT OF 1973 (683).

Significance
The declaration of war as a constitutionally discretionary prerogative of Congress may be of little practical importance because war may be forced by the aggressive acts of other states. Moreover, as director of the nation's foreign affairs, the president may present Congress with a situation leaving no real alternative. Within the limits of the War Powers Act of 1973, as commander in chief the president can order the armed forces into combat situations in the absence of a formal declaration of war, as in Korea and Vietnam. Experience in World Wars I and II, however, indicates that the declaration of war is important for another reason. When the country is formally in a state of war, Congress appears more willing to grant and the courts more reluctant to question the validity of the delegation of vast quasi-legislative powers to the president for the duration. Because of the nature of modern war, this means that the president becomes empowered to virtually reorganize the life of the entire nation for the successful prosecution of the war effort so long as the provisions of the Constitution are not overtly and fla-

grantly violated. The declaration of war also has domestic and international legal consequences in that it fixes the date at which rights and liabilities related to the state of war come into force. Some observers believe that in an age when technology makes possible a virtually instantaneous nuclear exchange with mutual assured destruction (MAD), a declaration of war becomes irrelevant. In the matter of limited war, a declaration of war could spread the conflict, defeating the purpose of a limited war.

Congress: House Foreign
Affairs Committee | 629 |

The standing committee of the House of Representatives that has primary responsibility in the field of foreign affairs. The detailed work of the Foreign Affairs Committee is assigned to standing subcommittees whose members develop expertise by their continued involvement with particular geographic and problem areas. The power of the Foreign Affairs Committee derives from the general legislative power of the House in its authority to conduct investigations, and the role of the House in appropriating the funds necessary for all foreign-policy activities. The committee plays an important role in determining the administrative organization, policy orientation, and budget for such bodies as the Agency for International Development (AID), the United States Information Agency (USIA), and the Department of State.

Significance
Once considered a minor committee, the role of the House Foreign Affairs Committee has increased with U.S. involvement in world affairs. The committee keeps abreast of international developments through the participation of its members in study missions abroad, subcommittee hearings, participation in international and domestic conferences, and by committee representation on the U.S. delegation to the UN General Assembly. Although the Senate Committee on Foreign Relations historically has dominated congressional involvement

with foreign policy, the House Foreign Affairs Committee increasingly insists on a substantive role related to the constitutional powers of the House.

Congress: Joint Resolution | 630 |

A legislative act similar to a statute. To become law, a joint resolution, like a bill, must pass in identical form by simple majorities in both houses of Congress and be signed by the president. When this device is used by the Congress to propose amendments to the Constitution, the president's signature is not necessary. Joint resolutions are labeled "HJ Res" and "SJ Res" to distinguish them from bills.

Significance

Joint resolutions are frequently used in foreign-policy matters to declare or terminate a state of war, approve an action by the president, or attempt a foreign-policy initiative. In certain circumstances, a joint resolution by both houses may be substituted for treaty action by the Senate, with the consequent substitution of simple majority votes in both houses for the two-thirds vote required in the Senate. The annexations of Texas and Hawaii were accomplished by this means. The Tonkin Gulf Resolution was passed in 1964 to give the president an almost free hand in Vietnam, but repealed by Congress in 1970 to demonstrate disapproval of the president's conduct of the war. President George Bush did not insist on a joint resolution to support his decision to send U.S. forces to the Persian Gulf area in 1990–1991, but he nevertheless requested a vote of approval from each house. Substantial opposition permitted only slim majorities.

Congress: Legislative Powers | 631 |

The statute-making authority of the national legislature. Article I, Section 1, of the Constitution provides that "All legislative powers herein granted shall be vested in a Congress of the United States, which shall consist of a Senate and House of Representatives." These powers are detailed in Article I, Section 8. Through its legislative power, the Congress establishes the need for, creates, empowers, diminishes, and eliminates the agencies of the executive branch through which the president conducts foreign policy. Thus, until Congress provides the machinery of government and operating funds, in conducting foreign policy the president is restricted to those few powers allotted in the Constitution. *See also* PRESIDENT: CHIEF LEGISLATOR (666).

Significance

The importance of the legislative powers of Congress in the conduct of U.S. foreign policy is derived from the system of separated powers of government that requires the cooperation of at least two branches if the national government is to operate effectively. As a consequence, subjects of international concern yet unknown will come within the purview of the Congress because U.S. foreign policy depends on statutory implementation.

Congress: Power of the Purse | 632 |

The authority of Congress to control government finances in terms of both revenue and expenditures. The power of the purse exercised by Congress includes the "power to lay and collect taxes, duties, imposts, and excises, to pay the debts and provide for the common defense and general welfare of the United States . . ." (Art. I, Sec. 8), and the restriction that "No money shall be drawn from the Treasury but in consequence of appropriations made by law . . ." (Art. I, Sec. 9). Before a new program can enter into force, it must pass through both chambers of Congress twice—first, as a policy matter to authorize the program, and second, to appropriate the necessary funds. Under the first function, bills are considered by the House Foreign Affairs Committee and the Senate Foreign Relations Committee, whereas the second concerns the appropriations committees of the two houses. Once an appropriation has been made, its expenditure by the executive branch is audited by the General Accounting

Office (GAO), which was created by Congress to ensure that such expenditures fall within the limits set by congressional appropriations.

Significance
The historic power of the purse is the principal vehicle by which Congress can exert control over the foreign-policy process. It is virtually impossible for the president to implement foreign policy without the expenditure of funds. The extent to which Congress uses this power to influence foreign policy depends in large measure on the political relationship between the individuals in the White House and the leaders on Capitol Hill. Once the president commits the nation to a course of action, however, the power of the Congress to deny funds is weakened by a fear that the national interest would suffer.

Congress: Senate Foreign Relations Committee   633

A standing committee of the Senate that serves as its principal agent in the field of U.S. foreign policy. The Foreign Relations Committee functions largely through standing subcommittees patterned on and coordinated with the geographic and topical divisions of the Department of State. The committee's authority derives from the Senate's general legislative and investigatory powers, which are similar to those exercised by the House of Representatives. As a result of the system of checks and balances, the Senate has certain powers not given to the House, such as a share in the executive branch's treaty- and appointment-making powers. Article II, Section 2, of the Constitution gives the president power "by and with the advice and consent of the Senate, to make treaties, provided two-thirds of the Senators present concur; and he shall nominate, and, by and with the advice and consent of the Senate, shall appoint ambassadors, and other public ministers and consuls. . . ." The Senate usually accepts the recommendations of its Foreign Relations Committee in these and other foreign-policy matters.

Significance
The role of the Senate Foreign Relations Committee has expanded with U.S. involvement in world affairs. Its close liaison with the State Department in the development of policy was demonstrated in the negotiations of the United Nations Charter and the North Atlantic Treaty. Presidents frequently consult with the committee's chairman, the ranking minority leader, and other influential members. Perhaps the most dramatic illustration of the committee's power to check the executive involved its role in the Senate's rejection of the Treaty of Versailles and the League of Nations following World War I.

Congress: Treaty Power   634

The participation of the Senate in the executive act of treaty making. The president negotiates treaties, but under the constitutional system of checks and balances cannot ratify them until the Senate, by a two-thirds majority of those present and voting, gives its consent. Under its treaty power the Senate may (1) consent to ratification, (2) refuse consent, (3) consent to ratification after specified amendments have been made, or (4) consent to ratification with specific reservations. In no case, however, is the president legally required to ratify following Senate action. Although the Senate Foreign Relations Committee is the principal focus of the treaty power in Congress, other committees in the Senate and the House also become involved, depending on the treaty's subject matter. The House of Representatives has no treaty power per se, but it has assumed an active role through its Appropriations Committee's insistence on a substantive review of treaty provisions before recommending the funds necessary to implement the treaty. *See also* PRESIDENT: TREATY POWER (670).

Significance
The roles played by the Senate and the House in the treaty process indicate that in treaty making the ratification stage is

often as crucial as the original negotiations. The powers constitutionally fixed in the Senate make it possible for a small bloc of senators representing states inhabited by a minority of the population to negate the wishes of the majority. The treaty process in Congress is typically slow and cumbersome, exacting a price in executive time and tempers by duplicate hearings, amendments, and reservations, and the ultimate ability of the Senate to frustrate the executive will. The president will not automatically be checked, but the possibility can never be ignored. Although most treaties submitted by the president to the Senate are duly approved, some have been voted down and others killed through Senate inaction. Important treaties that have failed to secure Senate consent cover such diverse subjects as the League of Nations Covenant (1919), the Charter of the International Trade Organization (1948), and the Genocide Convention (1949–1986).

Containment | 635 |

The United States' basic Cold War foreign policy and its theoretical assumptions, aimed at halting Soviet expansion. The containment theory started with the assumption that Soviet foreign policy was most likely motivated by the imperatives of a dictatorship modified by Communist ideology and Russian historicism. This formulation is associated primarily with George F. Kennan, chief of the Policy Planning Staff of the Department of State in 1947, but also builds upon Nicholas Spykman's reference to the "Rimland" in his 1944 book *The Geography of the Peace*. The containment theory was implemented by a two-phase policy that dates from the Greek-Turkish aid program in 1947. Phase I, enunciated in the Truman Doctrine, called for halting any further geographical advances by the Soviet Union. It involved drawing a geopolitical "shatter zone" from Norway through Central and Southeast Europe and from the Middle East to South and East Asia. With the containment line thus drawn, Phase II

called for building "situations of strength" through countervailing U.S. power along this perimeter, demonstrated by the string of military alliances that began with NATO in April 1949. These "defensive" alliances were constructed to provide the non-Communist nations with sufficient, immediately available and prepositioned military power to counteract actions taken by the Soviet Union to break the ring. The policy was intended to frustrate achievement of Soviet foreign and domestic objectives and thus intensify the internal pressures and dissatisfactions held to be inherent in the dictatorship. Soviet leaders were to be brought to the realization that, while Soviet interests could not be gained by violence, disorder, and subversion, some of them might be achieved by accommodation through peaceful diplomacy. In point of fact, the Soviets did pierce the containment ring by leapfrogging into the Middle East, initially by way of Egypt in 1955, and later succeeded in penetrating the Western Hemisphere by befriending Cuba after Fidel Castro's rise to power in 1959. The Soviets also developed associations with the Vietnamese Communists, enjoyed good relations with India, and supported African regimes in Angola and Mozambique. Containment was less than successful, but it nevertheless provided the Western alliance with its raison d'être, and in the end it contributed to the demise of the Soviet state. *See also* TRUMAN DOCTRINE (678).

Significance
The containment policy implied action based on a well-developed, long-term, realistic theory of foreign policy rather than on a collection of abstract, idealistic principles that had been developed historically as guides to U.S. foreign policy. Containment, as postulated by Kennan, called for cool nerves, a sense of timing, and a delicate touch. The Soviets were not to be backed into a corner where they might feel forced to turn and fight. They were always to be permitted room to maneuver and save face. The ultimate purpose of containment was not war, but

accommodation. Containment produced a military stalemate that was followed by lessening of tension and a measure of accommodation, first through the Soviet-inspired policy of peaceful coexistence, and later by the joint superpower policy of détente. The containment doctrine was extended to include Chinese Communist expansion in Asia, which led to the U.S. involvement in Korea from 1950 and in Indochina from 1964. Although he was the author of the containment policy, Kennan later vehemently criticized the basic philosophy and strategic considerations embodied within the policy that drew the nation into undeclared wars, notably the one in Vietnam. The containment policy was judged a success following the disappearance of the Soviet state in 1991, but it is obvious that it was not completely successful, nor was it alone responsible for ending the Cold War.

Contra Rebels　636

Counterrevolutionary guerrilla forces opposed to the leftist Sandinista government in Nicaragua. The United States had long supported the dictator Anastasio Somoza, who was finally driven from power in 1979. He was replaced by the increasingly Marxist-oriented Sandinista National Liberation Front (FSLN). The rebel Contra coalition, including numbers of former Somoza adherents and military people as well as disillusioned Sandinistas, established bases in neighboring Costa Rica and Honduras from which to seek the military and political overthrow of the Sandinista regime. In the United States, the Reagan administration identified the Sandinistas as a tool of Cuban and Soviet communism. President Reagan similarly identified the government of the tiny Caribbean island of Grenada before removing it by a sea and air invasion in 1983. *See also* AUTHORITARIAN PATTERN: CAUDILLISMO (684); AUTHORITARIAN PATTERN: PERSONALISMO (690).

Significance
U.S. aid to the Contras became a focus for domestic political conflict over admini-

stration policy in Central America. At one extreme, "domino theorists" warned against Communist victories rolling their way up to the Texas border. At the other end of the scale came warnings of "no more Vietnams." The Soviet Union and Cuba supplied support to the Sandinistas, including massive amounts of military equipment. The Contras received millions of dollars in covert U.S. aid through the Central Intelligence Agency (CIA), which also helped with the mining of Nicaraguan harbors. In demanding U.S. support for the Contras, President Reagan referred to them as "freedom fighters." Congress blew hot and cold, sometimes providing overt assistance and sometimes making government aid to the Contras illegal. Scandals involving the propriety and legality of the diversion of profits to the Contras from the secret sale of arms to Iran (known as "Irangate") involved officials of Reagan's National Security Council staff. These revelations brought the appointment of special prosecutors and congressional investigations, who found that members of the National Security Staff had acted unlawfully. Although the Contra rebels never defeated the Sandinista government forces, the Sandinistas agreed to hold open and fair elections, which brought a non-Sandinista faction to power in Nicaragua. The passing of the Cold War reinforced this electoral victory, but it also permitted the formation of a government of national reconciliation when Sandinistas were included in Nicaragua's ruling cabinet. The collapse of the Soviet Union eliminated the military support that had flowed to the Sandinistas, and in recognition of a considerably diminished threat, the United States sought to renew its normal ties with Nicaragua.

Cultural Exchange　637

Programs aimed at fostering understanding and improving relations between the people of the United States and the people of other countries. Although a Division of Cultural Relations was established in the State Department in 1938, the

Fulbright Act of 1946 marks the beginning of an intensified program of cultural relations, largely administered today by the Bureau of Educational and Cultural Affairs. The Fulbright Act permits the use of foreign currencies and credits (obtained from the sale of surplus U.S. property abroad) to finance study by Americans in foreign universities, and helps foreign students attend American universities. In addition to student and professorial exchanges under the Fulbright program, the Smith-Mundt Act of 1948 and later programs have made possible the exchange of scientists, businesspersons, and governmental and professional leaders.

Significance
Since 1946 executive and congressional leaders of both parties have favored the Fulbright and other cultural-exchange programs over other programs to influence foreign attitudes toward the United States. Supporters of cultural exchange recognize students and teachers as important political elites, particularly in the developing countries. They believe that common educational backgrounds can facilitate good future relationships with the United States by establishing wider paths of communication across national cultural lines. Cultural-exchange programs also reflect American faith in the efficacy of individual contacts to promote long-range acceptance of American perceptions of the nature of the international community.

Defense, Department of | 638 |

The executive department responsible for the military security of the United States, created in 1947. The Department of Defense directs, supervises, and coordinates the Army, Navy, and Air Force departments. These military departments, under civilian secretaries, are subordinate to a single civilian secretary, the secretary of defense, who is a member of the president's cabinet. The military chiefs of staff of each service advise their civilian secretaries and, together with the chief of staff to the secretary of de-

fense, comprise the Joint Chiefs of Staff, the highest military advisory body in the nation. The secretary of defense also receives advice from the Armed Forces Policy Council, which consists of the service secretaries, the Joint Chiefs, and the director of Defense Research and Engineering. The secretary of defense and the chairman of the Joint Chiefs of Staff serve as top-level advisers to the president on military and defense policies, and are members of the National Security Council. *See also* JOINT CHIEFS OF STAFF (654); NATIONAL SECURITY COUNCIL (NSC) (659).

Significance
The Department of Defense is responsible for national military policy, civil defense, maintenance and operation of the armed forces, coordination of military programs with other countries, and the maintenance of overseas bases. Research and development of new and improved weapons systems also is a DOD responsibility. With over 1 million civilian employees, the department accounts for almost half of the federal government's civilian personnel and at times more than half of the entire national budget. Because national security is a fundamental goal of foreign policy, it is often difficult to distinguish between foreign and military policy. Although a unified defense establishment was a primary objective in the creation of the Defense Department, interservice rivalries continue, often with congressional encouragement. The Defense Reorganization Act of 1958, for example, enabled each military service to establish individual contact with Congress, permitted no changes to be made regarding the Marine Corps or the National Guard except by congressional consent, and denied the president power to merge the armed services or create a military general staff system. Each branch remains relatively autonomous, stands guard over its traditional role, competes vigorously for its share of the military budget, and seeks control over new weapons systems. Called to reduce its budget after the Cold War, the Defense Department responded by closing down

dozens of bases within the continental United States, over the objections of congressional members in whose districts the bases were located. The department also emphasized the need to modify its ready forces, given a significant reduction in active personnel. A leaner, better trained, more fully equipped, more mobile and integrated service force was forecast for the future, especially as U.S. armed forces were no longer confronted by a major military establishment of the dimensions represented by the erstwhile Soviet Union. But assuming new mission assignments was no simple matter. The U.S. armed forces were unfamiliar with peacekeeping roles, and when President Bush ordered the military to Somalia, ostensibly to provide humanitarian assistance to a starving population torn by factional strife, the mission got bogged down in the internal wars plaguing that East African nation. During one encounter in 1993, a small U.S. unit was overrun by armed Somalis who killed a number of the troops and then mutilated their bodies before rolling TV cameras. That incident convinced Congress that the U.S. military should not be engaged in actions not directly connected with U.S. national interests. The United States removed its forces from Somalia in 1994, and by March 1995 the UN peacekeeping force also withdrew. The Department of Defense agrees with members of Congress that U.S. forces should not be used for UN programs, especially if those forces are not under firm U.S. command. It is with that understanding that the DOD agreed to send a 25,000-man force to assist with a peaceful settlement in Bosnia.

Dollar Diplomacy   639

Active use of the power of a state against other countries to promote the private foreign-investment interests of its citizens. Dollar diplomacy is associated primarily with U.S. foreign policy toward Latin American countries during the administrations of Theodore Roosevelt, William Howard Taft, and Woodrow Wilson. The policy was based on the idea that U.S. investment abroad would benefit the region as well as the investor, and that constructive investment required political stability in an area of chronic instability. The policy called for U.S. military intervention whenever necessary to ensure stability and prevent foreign intervention, particularly in the vicinity of the Panama Canal.

Significance
Dollar diplomacy involved various forms of intervention, including the use of armed force and the establishment of financial protectorates in Cuba, the Dominican Republic, Haiti, and Nicaragua. The policy led to charges of "Yankee imperialism" and economic imperialism, and produced lasting suspicion and ill will toward the "colossus of the north." The animosities thus engendered continue to affect relations between the United States and Latin America despite the Good Neighbor efforts begun in the Hoover administration and pressed forward by all presidents since Franklin Roosevelt. The growing multilateral cooperation efforts evidenced by the Organization of American States (OAS) and the Alliance for Progress have not ended the concern with intervention exhibited by Latin American states in such episodes as the Guatemalan crisis (1954), the Cuban Bay of Pigs invasion attempt (1961), the initial unilateral intervention by the United States in the Dominican crisis (1965), the invasion of Grenada (1983), the violent assault on Panama in 1989, and, to some extent, the Haitian intervention of 1994.

Executive Agreement   640

An international agreement concluded between heads of state. In the United States, executive agreements are not subject to the formal treaty process, which requires Senate consent before ratification by the president. The categories of executive agreements include:

1. Agreements designed to execute the stipulations of a treaty already approved. Hundreds of agreements, for example, were required to carry out

the North Atlantic Treaty, the cornerstone of U.S. policy in Europe in the post–World War II period.

2. Agreements made by the president under a prior grant of authority from Congress. Under the Reciprocal Trade Act of 1934 and the Trade Expansion Act of 1962, the president was delegated the authority to negotiate reciprocal tariff reductions with foreign governments. The Lend-Lease agreements of World War II were also of this type.

3. Agreements made with subsequent congressional approval. In 1940, before U.S. entry into World War II, President Franklin Roosevelt traded Prime Minister Winston Churchill 50 over-age U.S. destroyers for leases on British territories to be used as air base sites in an arc stretching from Newfoundland to South America. Congress could have repudiated the agreement, but gave its tacit approval when it appropriated the funds to construct the bases.

4. Agreements made by the president based solely on the president's power as commander in chief and general authority over the nation's foreign relations. Examples include the Rush-Bagot Agreement of 1817, whereby Great Britain and the United States limited naval forces on the Great Lakes, and the Yalta and Potsdam agreements of 1945 on the conditions for terminating World War II.

The principal legal distinction between treaties and executive agreements is that agreements cannot change existing domestic law but must operate within it. Treaties, on the other hand, are part of the supreme law of the land under Article VI of the Constitution and can supersede earlier statutes or treaties. Although the Constitution does not mention executive agreements, they have been in use since 1792, during the Washington administration, when the first one was concluded on the subject of reciprocal mail delivery. In recent years, the number of executive agreements has far outstripped the number of treaties. However, a treaty or trade statute may require the negotiation of any number of agreements to carry it out, so it is of questionable value to compare the frequency of the two without a subject-matter analysis in each instance. *See also* BRICKER AMENDMENT (620).

Significance
Public criticism of executive agreements is frequently based on the assumption that the executive branch intends to circumvent the Senate's power to check the president in conducting foreign affairs. The charge may or may not be true in the few agreements that can be made without congressional participation. In an international emergency involving national security, publicity might not be in the public interest and could provoke crises. Therefore, agreements made on the sole authority of the president have the advantages of speed and secrecy. The existence of this alternative to the treaty process for reaching international accord may also contribute to Senate acceptance of some treaties. The Case Act of 1972 requires the president to report all agreements to Congress within 60 days.

Executive Office of the President 641

A group of staff agencies directly responsible to the president, created to advise and aid the president in carrying out a wide range of executive duties. Agencies within the Executive Office have varied since its creation by executive order under the Reorganization Act of 1939. The agencies included and the dates of their creation are: White House Office (1939), Office of Management and Budget (OMB) (1921), Office of Policy Development (1970), National Security Council (NSC) (1947), Council of Economic Advisors (CEA) (1946), Office of Science and Technology Policy (1959), Council on Environmental Quality (1969), Office of Administration (1978), and Office of the U.S. Trade Representative (1974).

Significance
The Executive Office, originally established to aid the president in domestic

matters, now reflects the president's equal or greater concern with foreign policy and related matters. Prior to its creation, the president was dependent on the major operating agencies for reports, recommendations, projections, and daily assistance. Today, the Executive Office has institutionalized the presidency. This presidential "team" numbers approximately 2,000 people who aid the president in establishing and implementing broad policies ranging across the spectrum of the executive branch.

Food for Peace Program | 642 |

The disposition of surplus U.S. agricultural products to improve U.S. foreign relations and increase consumption of such commodities abroad. The Food for Peace Program (also called Food for Freedom) was established by Public Law 480 in 1954. *See also* FOREIGN AID (643).

Significance

The Food for Peace Program recognizes that the population explosion makes food supply a matter of increasing importance in international politics. Under the program, agricultural products in excess of usual marketings are sold on credit terms for dollars and to some extent for local currency, which can be used for local purposes to foster U.S. foreign policy. The act also empowers the president to furnish emergency assistance in famine and other extraordinary relief situations.

Foreign Aid | 643 |

Military, economic, and social assistance offered by the United States to foreign countries. The names of the programs and the geographic foci have varied since World War II with the problems involved and the nature of U.S. national interest. From 1948 to 1952, foreign aid was concentrated in massive economic assistance to Western Europe through the Marshall Plan. From 1952 to 1959, the emphasis of foreign aid became predominantly military with the advent of the Korean War and a policy of resisting Soviet and Chi-

nese expansionism. From 1959 until the termination of the Cold War in 1991, the mix of economic and military foreign aid was determined by U.S. national interest and local problems in various regions of the world. In 1993—1995, following the collapse of worldwide communism, and as a result of public and congressional criticism, the emphasis in aid programs shifted from outright grants to long-term, low-interest loans. A greater degree of selectivity has been evident in the awarding of U.S. foreign aid. Generally speaking, the public and its congressional representatives are less inclined to offer foreign aid, especially when national resources are in short supply and, many argue, are more needed at home. The United States is no longer the world's principal aid dispenser. *See also* DEVELOPMENT: THIRD WORLD DEBT CRISIS (196); DEVELOPMENT STRATEGY: FOREIGN AID (210); FOREIGN AID RECIPIENTS (644).

Significance

The vast economic power of the United States is a political fact of international life, and foreign-aid programs, as instruments of U.S. foreign policy, are vehicles for the expression of that power. Foreign aid is used for a number of reasons—some selfish, others humanitarian, some short-sighted and opportunistic, others long-range and visionary. From the start, a core objective of U.S. foreign aid following World War II was to gain time to frustrate the forces leading to violent change, and to establish a world order based on peaceful international processes. After many years of involvement, however, U.S. executive, legislative, and public support for foreign aid has waned. Although the per capita income gap between rich and poor countries has widened since 1949 and was greater in 1995 than at any time since the end of World War II, the portion of the U.S. national budget allocated to foreign aid continues to shrink. Although its population consumes approximately one-quarter of the world's resources, the United States is increasingly more reluctant to engage in programs promoting foreign assistance for the world's most needy nations.

Foreign Aid Recipients |644|

Beneficiaries of U.S. aid and their supporters' lack of support for U.S. policy. U.S. foreign aid has not always produced the desired support from its recipients. Examining UN voting records, it is obvious that nations receiving U.S. assistance do not feel obligated to support the United States in matters coming before the world body. Of the ten largest recipients of U.S. foreign aid in 1995, only Israel voted with the United States almost all the time. The other recipients on this list voted with the United States less than 50 percent of the time. India, the number three recipient, voted against the United States on 84 percent of the votes cast, and Egypt, the second largest recipient, voted against the United States on 65 percent of the questions. The complete list of the top ten recipients is:

Recipient	FY 1995 Aid	UN Votes against U.S. Policies (1994)
1. Israel	$3,003,600,000	5%
2. Egypt	2,121,729,000	65%
3. India	155,479,000	84%
4. Peru	150,516,000	55%
5. Bolivia	134,178,000	56%
6. Bangladesh	112,679,000	64%
7. Ethiopia	92,148,000	61%
8. Haiti	88,813,000	57%
9. South Africa	82,453,000	58%
10. Philippines	74,004,000	61%

Overall, 74 percent of U.S. aid recipients voted against the United States a majority of the time. Russia voted against the United States on only 33 percent of the votes, whereas 95 recipient countries opposed the United States on many more occasions. Indeed, the United States' most consistent supporters, apart from Israel, are found among the former Soviet-bloc countries. *See also* FOREIGN AID (643).

Significance
In an era when U.S. foreign aid is under fire from Congress, the statistical information demonstrating that aid does not necessarily purchase support on world issues makes it all the easier for critics of foreign aid to call for a dramatic scaling back. Efforts by Congress in 1995 to not only eliminate much of the U.S. foreign-aid program but also dissolve the Agency for International Development were reinforced by these data. The U.S. public appeared to support the cutback, if not the outright elimination, of foreign aid, believing it to cost far more than its actual expenditure. Considering that foreign aid, the Department of State, AID, USIA, and associated agencies together drew only 1.3 percent of government revenue in 1995, the foreign-aid component was considerably less than 1 percent and far below U.S. aid-giving practices throughout the years of the Cold War.

Foreign Service |645|

The diplomatic and consular establishment of the United States. Created by the Rogers Act of 1924 and augmented by various foreign-service acts, the career Foreign Service is entered by passing a nationwide competitive examination; advancement is based on a merit system. Personnel are divided into five broad categories: (1) Chief of Mission (CM), either a senior career officer or political appointee who serves as an ambassador or head of a special mission, such as to the United Nations; (2) Foreign Service Officer (FSO), the standard title for the various grades of career diplomatic and consular officers who form the core of the service; (3) Foreign Service Reserve Officer (FSR), a technical expert or specialist, such as a commercial attaché, who may serve for nonconsecutive periods of up to five years at the discretion of the secretary of state; (4) Foreign Service Staff (FSS), which includes diplomatic couriers, executive secretaries, and embassy administrative staff involved in such matters as disbursing, budget, and telecommunications filing; (5) Foreign Service Local Employees (FSL), several thousand noncitizens employed at Foreign Service posts around the world to perform duties ranging from translation to custodial services. See also DIPLOMATIC PERSONNEL: DIPLOMAT (422).

Significance
The U.S. Foreign Service, under the control of the Department of State, is charged with conducting the day-to-day relations between the United States and the other countries of the world. Functions of the Foreign Service include (1) execution of U.S. foreign-policy objectives, (2) protection of U.S. citizens and interests abroad, (3) collection and interpretation of information, (4) negotiation, and (5) staffing delegations to multilateral and regional organizations such as the United Nations and the Organization of American States (OAS).

Foreign Service Examination   646

Written, oral, and physical examinations that constitute the basis for appointment to the career Foreign Service. The Board of Examiners for the Foreign Service determines the nature, scope, and date of the written examination and selects the panels of officers who will conduct the oral examination of those who pass the written test. Physical requirements are similar to those for entering into military service. Upon successful completion of the first three hurdles, passage of the language requirement may be deferred and a provisional appointment to the Foreign Service may be made.

Significance
Appointment to the service by means of a nationwide competitive examination is intended to ensure a high level of preparation and background among applicants. Together with the career concept, the examination is designed to provide the nation with high-quality diplomatic representation in keeping with its status as a great power. Although thousands of capable applicants take the Foreign Service examination each year, only a small, elite group ultimately survives the rigors of the selection process. In the 1980s the Foreign Service entrance examinations were postponed for several years because of complaints registered by female candidates who claimed admissions discrimination on the basis of sex. The women

won their case for affirmative action, and the examination was again offered in the 1990s, this time with a far higher recruitment rate achieved by female applicants.

Foreign Service Institute   647

A division of the Department of State that trains Foreign Service and State Department personnel in the various fields of international relations, administrative operations, management, supervision, and foreign languages.

Significance
The Foreign Service Institute offers Foreign Service officers and other federal personnel thorough indoctrination concerning their overseas responsibilities before they receive foreign assignments. Some observers urge that the institute be expanded into a Foreign Service Academy with a four-year curriculum to train diplomats in the same way that the military services prepare their officers.

Foreign Service Officer (FSO)   648

A U.S. career diplomatic officer. Foreign Service officers usually enter the Foreign Service in Class 6 through competitive examination. Promotion by merit goes through Class 1. Further advancement comes from application and acceptance into the Senior Foreign Service. From this level some are selected to serve as ambassadors and small numbers are promoted to career minister, or receive the highest rank of honor—career ambassador.

Significance
The Foreign Service officer is a skilled professional and the backbone of the Foreign Service. During his or her career, the FSO can expect to serve anywhere in the world. He or she will probably learn two foreign languages, become expert in one geographical area, and perform a range of duties involving political, economic, intelligence, commercial, informational, and consular activities. The personnel of the Foreign Service have been integrated with the diplomatic backup personnel in

the State Department so that each serves in both domestic and foreign posts.

Good Neighbor Policy | 649 |

A U.S. policy toward Latin America intended to overcome the fear and suspicion evidenced by such terms as "Yankee imperialism" and "colossus of the north." In his inaugural address in 1933, President Franklin Roosevelt spoke of the "good neighbor who resolutely respects himself, and because he does so, respects the rights of others." For the first third of the century, U.S. policies characterized by dollar diplomacy, military intervention, unilateralism, and a generally paternalistic attitude engendered much resentment in Latin America. The Good Neighbor Policy was an about-face and embodied the idea that U.S.–Latin American relations should be conducted on the basis of sovereign equality and mutual cooperation.

Significance
Under the Good Neighbor Policy, a nonintervention treaty was signed at Montevideo in 1933. In 1934 the Platt Amendment limiting Cuban sovereignty was abrogated and U.S. troops were withdrawn from Haiti. The good relations that prevailed during World War II resulted in mutual security treaties in 1945 and 1947 and a vast array of cooperative enterprises under the aegis of the Organization of American States (OAS). Nevertheless, the enormous power of the northern partner, its occasional support of unpopular regimes, unilateral acts such as the Bay of Pigs fiasco in 1961, military interventions in the Dominican Republic in 1965 and in Grenada in 1983, the attack on Panama and the seizing of President Manuel Noriega in 1989 all impacted negatively on the United States' neighbors in Latin America.

Implied Power | 650 |

A power possessed by the U.S. government that is inferred from a specific power delegated to it in the Constitution. The power to create an air force may be properly exercised by implication from the power to raise and maintain an army and navy, even though manned flight and intercontinental ballistic missiles did not exist at the time the Constitution was written. The concept was authoritatively set forth by the Supreme Court in *McCulloch v. Maryland* (4 Wheaton 316 [1819]). *See also* CONGRESS: LEGISLATIVE POWERS (631).

Significance
The implied-powers doctrine enables the United States to function effectively in the field of foreign as well as domestic policy without a vast proliferation of amendments to the Constitution. A strong national government would be impossible if its powers were limited exclusively to those enumerated in the Constitution. A loose construction of the Constitution, through the vehicle of the "necessary and proper" clause of Article I, Section 8, enables the national government to adapt itself to contemporary conditions.

Inherent Powers | 651 |

Powers exercised by the U.S. government that are neither enumerated nor implied in the Constitution. Inherent powers are derived from the nature of the United States as a sovereign state and, by definition, the equal of all other such states in the international community. Under this doctrine, the U.S. government can do those things that any national government must do, such as make treaties and acquire territory. *See also* UNITED STATES V. CURTISS-WRIGHT EXPORT CORP., (299 U.S. 304: 1936) (681).

Significance
The inherent-powers doctrine has given the U.S. government, operating under the limitations of a constitutional system, the flexibility to meet the challenges that arise from the interaction of the nation with more than 160 other states. In domestic affairs, the Supreme Court held in *Youngstown Sheet and Tube Co. v. Sawyer* (343 U.S. 579 [1952]) that the powers of the national government must be traced from a specific grant or be reasonably implied from

such a grant. In international affairs, the court has held that the doctrine of the sovereign equality of states provides the necessity and the authority to act even though the Constitution may be silent. Although the national government cannot do anything forbidden by the Constitution, the limits of its inherent powers beyond this point are unspecified.

Interest Group | 652 |

An association of persons who share a particular value orientation and seek government support for the promotion or protection of those values. Interest groups operate through lobbying activities directed toward agencies of government, usually by paid professionals. They also operate by propaganda activities directed toward the general public to build popular support for their particular value or values. The number and diversity of interest groups is astronomical. Some of the most prominent involve the concerns of (1) business, labor, and agriculture; (2) ethnic, national, patriotic, religious, and veterans groups; and (3) consumer and environmental advocates.

Significance
Interest groups, unlike political parties, are not interested in operating the entire government. They are minorities that seek to influence or control policy and those who make and implement policy. Some, like the U.S. Chamber of Commerce, operate continuously. Others, like the National Rifle Association (NRA), become highly active only when a particular value seems threatened. In modern pluralist societies, interest or pressure groups can be viewed as a normal part of the political process.

Isolationism | 653 |

A doctrine that views the national interest of the United States as best served by withdrawing the country from the political entanglements of the international community. Proponents of isolatonism base their arguments on the concept of the geographical, ideological, and cultural separateness of the United States. This attitude was particularly prevalent in the United States in the period between World Wars I and II.

Significance
During the nineteenth and early twentieth centuries, the United States practiced varying degrees of noninvolvement in international politics, but was never actually isolated. The United States has never implemented the principle of noninvolvement in Pacific or Far Eastern affairs to the extent that it did in Europe. The application of the doctrine vis-à-vis Europe helps to explain U.S. efforts at neutrality in the early stages of World Wars I and II. The technological developments of the mid-twentieth century, particularly the splitting of the atom, raise questions about the relevance of the doctrine, but the end of the Cold War and U.S. financial problems, as well as a reluctance to engage in other people's wars—whether ethnic, religious, or subnational—have compelled Americans to rethink their role in the world. Originally inspired to view a "new world order" by President Bush, Americans are no longer enamored of that idea, but as the only remaining major actor in the world (some insist, the only superpower), it is questionable whether the country can return to the interwar years of isolationism. Moreover, the country is intertwined with the other financial and trading nations in a web of interdependencies that appear to rule out a go-it-alone policy. Nevertheless, some American ultranationalists in the post–Cold War period argue that the United States can manage and thrive without the close intimacies of the General Agreement on Tariffs and Trade (GATT) and North American Free Trade Agreement (NAFTA), or other such economic and commercial arrangements.

Joint Chiefs of Staff | 654 |

A top-level military staff agency in the Department of Defense responsible for all matters related to military strategy. The

Joint Chiefs of Staff was created by the National Security Acts of 1947 and 1949 and comprises the chiefs of staff of the army and air force, the chief of Naval Operations, the commandant of the Marine Corps, and the chief of staff to the secretary of defense. A second staff agency, the Armed Forces Policy Council, composed of the civilian and military heads of the Departments of the Army, Navy, and Air Force, advises the secretary of defense on broader policy questions. *See also* DEFENSE, DEPARTMENT OF (638).

Significance
The Joint Chiefs of Staff function as the highest military advisory body available to the president and the secretary of defense. Although intended to present a unified military point of view, the Joint Chiefs also reflect the views of their individual services. Despite the creation of a single Department of Defense, the diversity of advice offered by the Joint Chiefs demonstrates that the integration of the armed services envisioned by the National Security Acts has not been fully accomplished. Consequently, the institution has been criticized because traditional interservice rivalries, budget procedures, and an insistance on a division of labor among the separate services have made it difficult to secure clear strategic guidance.

Marshall Plan | 655 |

A program of massive U.S. assistance to rebuild the European economies ravaged by World War II. Proposed by Secretary of State George C. Marshall in 1947, Congress adopted the plan under the title of the European Recovery Program. Between 1948 and 1952 the United States provided $15 billion in grants and loans to 16 West European countries (17 after West Germany was included). With the encouragement of the United States, the participants formed the Organization for European Economic Cooperation (OEEC) to work cooperatively for economic recovery on a regional rather than strictly national basis. The Soviet Union and the countries of East Europe, though invited, chose not to participate. *See also* FOREIGN AID (643).

Significance
The Marshall Plan provided the catalyst that enabled European experience and enterprise to raise the economies of all the countries involved above prewar levels by 1951. As a result, the Soviet Union was denied the opportunities for exploitation inherent in economic dislocation and in social and political unrest. The cooperative relationships fostered in the OEEC became a precedent for subsequent efforts toward European economic integration, leading to the creation of the European Community, later the European Union, with U.S. encouragement.

Missouri v. Holland (252 U.S. 416: 1920) | 656 |

A leading case in which the U.S. Supreme Court answered affirmatively the question of whether the national government, acting through the treaty power, could establish jurisdiction in areas otherwise reserved to the states. In *Missouri v. Holland,* the Supreme Court upheld the constitutionality of a federal statute implementing a treaty with Great Britain for the regulation and protection of migratory birds flying between Canada and the United States. Previously, in the absence of the treaty, similar legislation had been found by the lower federal courts to be an unconstitutional exercise of national power. *See also* BRICKER AMENDMENT (620); PRESIDENT: TREATY POWER (670).

Significance
The decision in *Missouri v. Holland,* while not destroying the federal principle, enables the national government to accomplish by treaty objectives that which might be unconstitutional in statute form. No treaty has ever been declared unconstitutional. Treaties, however, are part of the supreme law of the land under Article VI of the Constitution, and may be made only on appropriate subjects affecting

international relations. The *Missouri* case gave rise to a fear among opponents of strong national power that the treaty power might be used to subvert the Constitution. This opposition culminated in the unsuccessful effort in the 1950s to secure passage of the Bricker Amendment, which would have seriously weakened the treaty-making powers of the president and Senate. The amendment would have restricted national authority by permitting treaties to become effective only through legislation that would be valid in the absence of the treaty.

Monroe Doctrine | 657 |

A basic principle of U.S. foreign policy, opposing foreign intervention in the Western Hemisphere. The Monroe Doctrine, which began as a unilateral policy statement by President James Monroe in his State of the Union message to Congress in 1823, also stated a reciprocal U.S. intention (since abandoned) to refrain from interfering in the internal affairs of Europe. The statement was occasioned by concern that, with the end of the Napoleonic wars, the Holy Alliance might assist in the reestablishment of the Spanish colonial empire through the subjugation of the newly independent Latin American republics.

Significance

The Monroe Doctrine has provided the basic guidelines of U.S. policy in the Western Hemisphere for over a century and a half. Following the Congress of Vienna of 1815, British sea power established the *Pax Britannica,* which indirectly supported the Monroe Doctrine because of parallel British and U.S. interests in the Western Hemisphere. By the end of the century, U.S. military power was sufficient to back its own doctrine. through interventions, unilateral corollaries, and restatements, it increasingly offended the Latin Americans, but the Monroe Doctrine nevertheless found a place in the Covenant of the League of Nations. Beginning with the Good Neighbor Policy in 1933, however, the doctrine has gone

through a process of multilateralization that has produced political unity in the form of the Organization of American States (OAS) and a common security policy against foreign intervention embodied in the Rio Treaty. Soviet leader Nikita Khrushchev declared the Monroe Doctrine dead following the failure of the U.S.-inspired Bay of Pigs invasion of Cuba in 1961. The Soviets extended their influence into the Western Hemisphere by way of Cuba after that episode, and sought to penetrate both Central and South America at the height of the Cold War. The United States resisted all such efforts, more successfully in South America than in the Caribbean or Central America, but the writ of the Monroe Doctrine was still judged a foundation stone for U.S. foreign policy in the Western Hemisphere. The U.S. intervention in Panama and the arrest, trial, and imprisonment of its head of government, Manuel Noriega, in 1989 dramatized the importance given the Monroe Doctrine almost 200 years after its declaration.

Most-Favored-Nation | 658 |
(MFN) Policy

The importance of most-favored-nation (MFN) policy as a bargaining chip in U.S foreign relations. The most important issue in U.S.-China relations is the linkage of the most-favored-nation policy to matters of human rights. In 1974 the U.S. Congress approved the Jackson-Vanik Amendment, which required annual renewal of most-favored-nation status for any presently or formerly Communist country. The United States denied the Soviets most-favored-nation treatment because the Soviet Union refused to permit the free migration of its citizens to other countries. Most-favored-nation status means that products from one country can be imported into another country at relatively low tariff rates, the same rates set for goods from other countries also receiving most-favored-nation status. The United States extends most-favored-nation status to more than 180 countries, many of them scarcely democratic. Nevertheless, China was singled out in the post–Cold War period in the attachment of human rights issues to those of international trade, and the Jackson-Vanik Amendment is the vehicle for this association. But the more pertinent reason was the 1989 Tienanmen Square massacre perpetrated by Chinese authorities against defenseless members of the Democracy Movement. Congress was appalled by the assault and the resulting carnage, and many congressional leaders called for the termination of most-favored-nation status that China had earlier been granted. The Bush administration could not ignore the passion of the congressional debate, but behind the scenes the administration worked to sustain the prevailing economic arrangements, sensing that more significant matters drew China and the United States into intimate embrace, which had prompted the conferment of most-favored-nation status in the first place. Thus, when faced with an act of Congress granting tens of thousands of Chinese students in the United States extended stays, Bush vetoed the legislation, arguing that it was an unwarranted intrusion into the president's authority in foreign affairs. Bush later issued an order similar to that contained in the congressional bill, but simultaneously dispatched his national security adviser and deputy secretary of state to Beijing to salve Chinese feelings. In May 1990 Bush renewed China's most-favored-nation status. The issue of human rights and trade with China, however, would not die. The Clinton administration was confronted with the same dilemma, and again there was concerted congressional opposition. Like Bush before him, after intense debate Clinton found it necessary to sustain most-favored-nation treatment for China. *See also* TRADE POLICY INSTRUMENT: MOST-FAVORED-NATION CLAUSE (260).

Significance
The mixing of most-favored-nation status with human rights dramatizes the concepts of realism and idealism in U.S. foreign policy. Americans have long demonstrated a penchant for casting foreign policy in moral terms, and the Chi-

nese government's massacre of its own students who were engaged in an openly defiant but nonetheless peaceful demonstration against authority, juxtaposed the original ideal purpose with the real, or pragmatic need for sustaining a working relationship. The United States officially recognized the Beijing government in 1979 knowing full well that it ruled over an authoritarian state and did not respect democratic tradition. Expediency, not morality, governed U.S. decisionmakers from Jimmy Carter to Ronald Reagan to George Bush. All ignored the character of China's repressive political system because (1) it was a major world actor and (2) it had deep differences with the Soviet Union. When China launched its economic reform program in the 1980s and began to test the water in promoting a quasi-market economy, both the Reagan and Bush administrations were keen to herald a new course in Chinese policy. The United States moved with alacrity to normalize relations with its former adversary, and the granting of most-favored-nation status was considered the key element in a new set of intimate relationships. U.S. government officials adopted political realism, ignoring the ongoing ideological and hence emotional debate between competitive systems. The war on Marxism was not forgotten, but in the effort to establish firm and productive relations with Beijing, the issue was certainly muted. Therefore, the Tienanmen Square episode was quickly bypassed, and the prior relationship, with its most-favored-nation gratuity unaffected, was extended. This did not terminate the debate in the United States, but it clearly had less intensity. In 1992 the Clinton administration indicated that it would reverse the Reagan-Bush policy toward China if the latter did not improve its human rights record. But the Chinese government refused to bow to pressure, and another administration has had to acknowledge the need to sustain close ties to Beijing, given more pressing problems in the region (e.g., North Korea's nuclear program). The United States' most-favored-nation policy toward

China did not move that country along a more democratic course, but the policy became the essential component in the relationship between the two countries.

National Security Council (NSC)   659

A staff agency in the Executive Office created by the National Security Act of 1947 to advise the president on the integration of domestic, foreign, and military policies related to national security. The National Security Council's statutory members include the president, the vice president, and the secretaries of state and defense. Also present are the chairman of the Joint Chiefs of Staff and the director of the Central Intelligence Agency (CIA), which operates under the direction of the council. The president invites other officials, such as the director of management and budget or the secretary of the treasury, when he deems their presence to be desirable. The president's national security adviser heads NSC. *See also* CENTRAL INTELLIGENCE AGENCY (CIA) (624); JOINT CHIEFS OF STAFF (654).

Significance
The National Security Council was designed to function as the highest level advisory agency available to the president on national security affairs. However, the president has ultimate constitutional authority in defense matters and decides whether and in what circumstances to use its services. Since its establishment, the degree of reliance on the council has varied with the styles of the presidents. Its intended role was to study major defense-related problems and make recommendations; it was not created to decide strategies, nor to have active responsibility for policy implementation. Some administrations, however, have permitted elements of the council to engage in such activities (e.g., arms to Iran and aid to Nicaraguan Contra rebels). Since the days of Secretary of State Henry Kissinger, presidents have occasionally permitted the influence of their national security advisers on foreign policy to rival or overshadow that of their secretaries of state.

Nicaragua v. the United States   660

An action brought by the Sandinista government of Nicaragua against the United States in the International Court of Justice (ICJ) in 1984. Nicaragua argued that U.S.-assisted mining of Nicaraguan harbors and support for military attacks by Contra rebels against the legitimate and U.S.-recognized government of Nicaragua were violations of international law, and Nicaragua claimed compensation for damages. In anticipation of the suit, the United States denied the jurisdiction of the ICJ in this case. Nicaragua then sought, and over U.S. objection the ICJ granted, a restraining order against aid to the Contras pending hearings on the merits, which took place 12–20 September 1985. The court found against the United States, which in turn ignored the finding. *See also* CONTRA REBELS (636); ICJ: INTERNATIONAL COURT OF JUSTICE (475).

Significance
The ability of the United States to influence world events has weakened in the last quarter of the twentieth century. This change in status has been indicated in a number of foreign-policy moves, mainly during President Ronald Reagan's administration, away from multilateralism in institutions that it had helped to create. These moves demonstrated a return to some form of unilateralism in an age of growing international interdependence. Evidence includes the withdrawal from the International Labor Organization (ILO) and from the United Nations Educational, Scientific, and Cultural Organization (UNESCO), attacks on the roles of the UN secretary-general, the UN General Assembly, and the Security Council, and the denial of the jurisdiction of the ICJ in the Nicaragua case. As a sovereign state, the United States had the legal right to make this determination, though its political wisdom can be challenged. It appears extremely self-serving because the

United States traditionally has stood for the development and use of the rule of law in international dealings. Indeed, it used the ICJ in 1980 when it brought suit against Iran in the diplomatic hostage crisis, and roundly condemned Iran when it denied the jurisdiction of the court.

Peace Corps   661

A program through which U.S. volunteers work in other countries for world peace through development and cultural relations. The Peace Corps was initially created by executive order by President John F. Kennedy in March 1961, and established by statute in September of that year. The act states that the program is designed to aid developing countries upon request "in meeting their needs for trained man power, and to promote a better understanding of the American people . . . and of other peoples on the part of the American people." *See also* CULTURAL EXCHANGE (637); FOREIGN AID (643).

Significance

The Peace Corps represented a new emphasis in the field of foreign assistance by providing human resources to aid nations in their process of modernization. Since its inception, thousands of Americans have served on a voluntary basis, usually for two-year periods, at the grassroots level in over 46 countries. The volunteers receive a period of training in the United States before going abroad to live and work alongside the people they serve. The small salary received indicates that most volunteers are motivated by a desire to help and by a spirit of adventure. Approximately half of the volunteers are teachers and the other half engage in agricultural, health, public works, and community development projects. Although following the Cold War the program is a much smaller version, with a much lower profile than the original, the Peace Corps continues to score high marks from the receiving countries, who find the volunteers helpful additions to their development activities.

Point Four Program   662

A program designed to foster economic development and modernization by making available to the recipient countries U.S. technical knowledge and skills. The Point Four Program resulted from an appeal to Congress to provide foreign technical assistance. The program received its name because it was the fourth major point in President Harry Truman's inaugural address delivered on 20 January 1949. The president advocated the maintenance of peace and freedom by means of "a bold new program for making the benefits of our scientific advances and industrial progress available for the improvement and growth of underdeveloped areas." Implementation was provided in 1950 by the Act for International Development. *See also* FOREIGN AID (643).

Significance

The Point Four Program was popular in the United States for several reasons. There was confidence in the quality of U.S. knowledge and skills, and such a program was comparatively inexpensive ($45 million was appropriated the first year). The economy of the program, however, explains the limited success of Point Four. At the time, there was a failure to realize that there had to be some input of capital to complement the developing country's newly acquired technical competence if the program was to produce the intended results. Point Four was the first of many assistance programs provided by the United States, other advanced countries, and the United Nations to aid developing countries in the process of modernization.

President   663

The central figure in the U.S. system of government. The president is the nation's chief executive, the commander in chief of its armed forces, and represents the nation to the rest of the world. The power of the president in foreign affairs is based on the Constitution, statutes, custom and tradition, judicial interpretations, party leadership, and public support. Each of these sources of power has been developed and applied by the people who have filled the position. The dimensions of the executive office are best understood in terms of the president's roles as chief diplomat, chief of foreign policy, chief legislator, and commander in chief, and in powers of appointment, recognition, and treaty.

Significance
In the field of foreign affairs, the powers arising from the president's combined roles as head of state and head of government, together with the strength of the nation the president leads, make the U.S. chief executive the most powerful in the world. The president serves as the chief architect in developing foreign policy and as the nation's exclusive spokesperson in international relations. Nations and the lives of peoples in many areas of the world are affected by the American people's choice of the person to occupy the White House.

President: Appointment Power | 664 |

Authority to nominate individuals who will serve in government positions. The appointment power (usually an executive function) in the United States is modified by the system of checks and balances. Article II, Section 2, of the Constitution provides that the president "shall nominate, and, by and with the advice and consent of the Senate, shall appoint ambassadors, other public ministers and consuls." The appointment power of the president and the secretary of state has been augmented by statute under the same constitutional clause that states that "the Congress may by law vest the appointment of such inferior officers, as they think proper, in the President alone . . . or in the heads of departments." The president is also empowered to fill vacancies in ambassadorial, ministerial, or consular posts if any occur while the Senate is in recess. If upon the reconven-

ing of the Senate the interim appointment is not confirmed for any reason, the appointee's temporary commission expires at the end of that session. Thus the president's power of appointment is derived directly from the Constitution and augmented by congressional legislation. *See also* CONGRESS: CONFIRMATION OF APPOINTMENTS (627).

Significance
Because the president is ultimately responsible for the conduct of U.S. foreign policy, presidential appointees must be persons who will scrupulously and skillfully implement policies. Consequently, in nominating ambassadors and other diplomats, the president has wide discretion and is rarely checked by the Senate's refusal to confirm the appointment. The president is not required to select high-level diplomatic appointees from among the career Foreign Service officers, and a number of political appointments occur in every administration. The number of career diplomats nominated, however, ranges between 50 and 75 percent. On a more informal basis, the president can also send a personal emissary on a diplomatic mission without the advice or consent of the Senate. The president has power to remove diplomatic officers at any time, because executive and administrative officials serve at the president's pleasure.

President: Chief Diplomat | 665 |

The role of the chief executive as the nation's highest level negotiator with foreign powers. The president as chief diplomat is the official medium through which the government of the United States communicates with foreign countries. The president's powers are derived directly and by implication from Article II of the Constitution. Thus the president can send and receive ambassadors, grant or withhold recognition, sever diplomatic relations, negotiate treaties, and, through the power as commander in chief, focus the military power of the nation in support of U.S. foreign policy. In the formulation and implementation of foreign policy, the president depends most heavily on the secretaries of state and defense and on the executive departments they head. *See also* DIPLOMACY, SUMMIT (414).

Significance
The primacy of the president as chief diplomat has been recognized since the early days of the republic. The Supreme Court, in *United States v. Curtiss-Wright Export Corp.*, held that "the President alone has the power to speak or listen as a representative of the nation." Direct negotiation at the presidential level was carried on by Woodrow Wilson in World War I and by Franklin D. Roosevelt in World War II. In the post–World War II period, summit diplomacy with other heads of government became the most dramatic manifestation of the president's role as chief diplomat, a role enhanced by such developments as the 1963 "hot line" agreement establishing a direct communications link between the White House and the Kremlin. President Richard Nixon's reopening of relations with the People's Republic of China and his discussions with Mao Zedong, Jimmy Carter's Camp David peace talks with Egyptian and Israeli leaders Anwar el-Sadat and Menachem Begin during the 1970s, Ronald Reagan's meetings with Mikhail Gorbachev from 1986 to 1988, and Bill Clinton's sessions with Boris Yeltsin in Washington and Moscow in 1995 further illustrate the presidential diplomatic role.

President: Chief Legislator | 666
A concept that emphasizes the importance of the president's role in the legislative process. The president's legislative powers are based on Article I, Section 7, and Article II, Section 3, of the Constitution, which enable the president to (1) exercise a legislative veto, (2) adjourn the Congress under unusual circumstances, (3) call special sessions of the Congress, and (4) call matters to the attention of the

Congress and recommend legislation in special messages. In an effort to guide national policy, the president also uses equally important but less formal devices. The power and prestige of the office are exerted through the president's position as party leader, the control of patronage, personal persuasiveness, and careful attention to public relations in building public support for the president's leadership. *See also* CONGRESS: LEGISLATIVE POWERS (631).

Significance
The president's role as chief legislator is as vital in foreign affairs as in domestic affairs because foreign policy generally requires legislative support and implementation. Most legislation affecting foreign relations is first drafted in the executive branch and then introduced by legislators friendly to the administration. Whether the item is the annual foreign-aid bill, a request for a new agency like the Peace Corps, or a plan for the reorganization of the armed services, it is generally but not always assured of careful congressional scrutiny when it is known to be an "administration measure" and part of "the president's program."

President: Chief of Foreign Policy | 667
The role of the chief executive as the nation's highest policymaker in the field of foreign affairs. As chief of foreign policy, the president is ultimately responsible for the security and well-being of the nation. Presidential responsibilities derive from the constitutional roles as chief executive officer and commander in chief, which require the president to formulate, develop support for, and carry out foreign policies calculated to maximize the national interests of the United States. The president's leadership function is exercised largely through the secretary of state and Department of State, although foreign-policy leadership can be exercised in a variety of other ways, including the drafting of legislation, messages to Congress, personal diplomacy, public

addresses, press conferences, and press releases. The Monroe Doctrine, for example, was contained in a State of the Union message, and the Point Four Program was first enunciated in President Harry Truman's inaugural address. Public statements by cabinet and other executive officials and by persons known to speak with the authority of the president constitute an informal channel through which the president can reach the peoples and governments of the world. *See also* UNITED STATES V. CURTISS-WRIGHT EXPORT CORP. (299 U.S. 304: 1936) (681).

Significance
The framers of the U.S. system could hardly have anticipated the development of the presidency into a position of individual world leadership. The degree of personal involvement is a matter of individual choice; although the foreign-policy involvement of some presidents has been minimal, others have so directly immersed themselves in foreign-policy matters that they functioned, in effect, as their own secretaries of state. The primacy of the presidential office as the nation's highest official level for developing and implementing foreign policy, however, is grounded in the Constitution and has been clearly set forth by the Supreme Court.

President: Commander in Chief | 668

The role of the chief executive as director of the nation's armed forces. Under Article II, Section 2, of the Constitution the president is designated commander in chief of all U.S. armed forces and of the state militias when they have been called into federal service. *See also* WAR POWERS ACT OF 1973 (683).

Significance
The president as commander in chief exercises the vast war powers affecting the security of the United States and many other nations. Since the president is the nation's highest elected official, the chief executive's legal authority over the military implements the U.S. democratic principle of civilian control. In wartime the president can coordinate and direct military operations and such related activities as arranging an exchange of prisoners and negotiating an armistice. In peacetime the president's disposition of forces and ability to order armed intervention to protect U.S. interests can profoundly affect foreign policy and the state of international relations. The president can commit forces to hostilities commenced by foreign governments, as President Harry Truman did in Korea in 1950. Although the powers granted the commander in chief do not include declaring a state of war, the president can act in ways that leave Congress little alternative, as when President Franklin Roosevelt ordered naval forces to protect convoys of war supplies bound for Great Britain early in World War II before the United States was actually at war with Germany. This freedom of action has been modified to some degree by the War Powers Act of 1973.

President: Recognition | 669

Willingness to establish normal diplomatic relations with another state or government. The president's plenary power of recognition is derived by implication from the power to send and receive ambassadors (Art. II, Sec. 2), and is used at the president's discretion. *See also* RECOGNITION: GOVERNMENTS (457).

Significance
Recognition is a most important step for a great economic and military power such as the United States because it can facilitate or hamper the success of a new state or government in its international relations. It may also promote or impede good relations between the United States and interested parties. U.S. presidents have followed no single line of policy on recognition. At times recognition has been held to be purely a legal act not necessarily implying approval, and at other times it has been considered primarily a political act with the definite implication of ap-

proval. In 1914, during the Mexican Revolution, President Woodrow Wilson's refusal to recognize the Huerta regime because he considered it to be illegitimate led to the collapse of that government. In 1933 President Franklin D. Roosevelt recognized the government of the Soviet Union, which had been in power since 1917. President Harry Truman recognized the state of Israel within hours of its creation in 1948. No president was willing to recognize the government of the People's Republic of China from 1949 to 1979, yet most of the Communist regimes of the states of Eastern Europe were recognized. The president alone has the legal power to grant or withhold recognition, but the effects of the decision are of profound political importance at home and abroad. The president can be expected to weigh legislative, executive, and public opinion against his own concept of the national interest before exercising his exclusive authority.

President: Trebury Power

**President:
Treaty Power** | 670 |

Power of the president as the nation's chief diplomat and chief of foreign policy to direct the negotiating of treaties. The treaty power is set forth in Article II, Section 2, of the Constitution. Under the system of checks and balances, the president can negotiate but cannot ratify a treaty until the Senate has given its consent in the form of a two-thirds vote of approval. Courses of action open to the president in connection with the Senate's role in the treaty process include these possibilities: (1) The president normally will submit the treaty to the Senate and then ratify it after the Senate has consented; (2) if the Senate is hostile, the president may refuse to submit a treaty, and let it die rather than suffer a defeat; (3) under similar conditions, the treaty can be withdrawn from the Senate before a vote has been taken; and (4) if the Senate has approved a treaty with Senate amendments and the president deems renegotiation inappropriate, the president may refuse to ratify. The technical steps in the entire treaty process

are negotiation, signature, ratification, exchange of ratifications, publication, proclamation, and execution. *See also* CONGRESS: TREATY POWER (634).

Significance
The president is properly charged with initiating treaties because of the incomparable resources in the executive branch available to the president, and because it is through the president that foreign governments conduct their relations with the United States. However, Congress, by joint or concurrent resolution, can attempt to induce the president to negotiate a treaty. Since President Woodrow Wilson's experience with the Treaty of Versailles in the Senate, presidents have tried to involve the Senate in the treaty process in the early stages. Certain senators, for example, were appointed to the U.S. delegation to the San Francisco Conference and participated in the negotiation of the United Nations Charter. Key senators, especially members of the Foreign Relations Committee, are likely to be kept informed during the progress of negotiations so that Senate attitudes can be taken into account before submission of the completed document for Senate approval. Depending on the subject matter, the president as chief negotiator also may use the alternative of the executive agreement should the Senate prove intractable.

Pressler Amendment | 671 |

An amendment to a congressional trade act in 1985 requiring the president to certify annually, as a prerequisite to the sale of weapons or a decision to provide assistance, that the country scheduled to receive the arms/aid is not in the process of building or possessing nuclear devices or weapons. Presidents have the authority to waive the restriction, but Congress is generally insistent that the terms of the amendment be complied with.

Significance
The Pressler amendment was designed to pressure Pakistan, the third largest recipient

of U.S. assistance in the 1980s, to relinquish its nuclear weapons program. At the time, Pakistan provided the main channel for the delivery of arms to the Afghan mujahiddin in their struggle with the Soviet Red Army. President Reagan and, later, President Bush ignored the Pressler amendment for the duration of the conflict in Afghanistan, but when the Soviets withdrew their forces in February 1989, President Bush changed direction. Called upon to certify that Pakistan was not building nuclear weapons, Bush said that he could not, and the full force of the Pressler amendment was imposed in October 1990. In 1991 Congress cut off $570 million of assistance and prevented the transfer of fighter aircraft for which Pakistan had already paid. The Clinton administration attempted to get around the Pressler amendment in 1995, following the Pakistani prime minister's visit to the United States, but when he endeavored to release the aircraft, President Clinton found congressional opposition formidable and unyielding.

Reciprocal Trade Agreements Act of 1934 | 672 |

An act that empowered the president on the basis of reciprocity with other countries to raise or lower tariffs up to 50 percent of the existing rates. The Reciprocal Trade Act provided for the most-favored-nation principle, which permitted the best trade concessions negotiated with any participating state to be granted automatically to all states that included the most-favored-nation clause in their trade agreements. Revisions of the act permitted further percentage reductions in the remaining tariff rates, but protectionists secured the inclusion of peril point and escape clause procedures. The peril point is that tariff level at which foreign competition might threaten or injure the domestic producer, in which case the Tariff Commission would so inform the president and Congress. By use of the escape clause procedure, the president could raise the tariff rate to restore protection for the affected industry. *See*

also TRADE POLICY INSTRUMENT: MOST-FAVORED-NATION CLAUSE (260); TRADE POLICY INSTRUMENT: TARIFF (264).

Significance
The Reciprocal Trade Agreements Act was a break in the rampant worldwide economic nationalism of the early days of the Great Depression, and resulted in the negotiation of reciprocal tariff reductions by executive agreements with 43 countries. The act, with its 11 extensions, is sometimes referred to as the Hull Reciprocal Trade Agreements Program after Cordell Hull, secretary of state during the crucial pre–World War II period when international trade policy began to shift toward emphasizing trade expansion. Four additional statutes have guided the U.S. approach to international trade issues and the vicissitudes of the international political economy since World War II. These are (1) the Trade Expansion Act of 1962, (2) the Trade Act of 1974, (3) the Trade Agreements Act of 1979, and (4) the Congress's approval of the General Agreement on Tariffs and Trade (GATT) entered into by the United States in 1994.

Secretary of State | 673 |

Head of the Department of State and chief adviser to the president on foreign policy, for which, however, the president is ultimately and completely responsible. The office of secretary was established in 1789 with the creation of the Department of State. The position is political in nature and is filled by the personal choice of the president. As with any other high-level position, the appointment is subject to senatorial confirmation, but because final responsibility for foreign affairs vests in the president, the Senate is unlikely to refuse confirmation. As a political appointee, the secretary has no fixed term, serving at the pleasure of the president. The importance of the post can be inferred from the fact that the secretary ranks first among cabinet officers and first among the nonelective officials in the line of presidential succession. *See also* STATE, DEPARTMENT OF (674).

Significance
The importance of the office of secretary of state has increased in proportion to U.S. participation in international affairs. Personally and through the department, the secretary seeks to establish specific national interests and to formulate programs calculated to achieve them by suggesting the particular combination of negotiation, propaganda, economic power, and military force to be applied. The degree to which the secretary is free to act as a decisionmaker depends on the relationship between that office and the president. Some presidents, such as Woodrow Wilson and Franklin Roosevelt, have been, in effect, their own secretaries of state. Others, like Dwight Eisenhower and Gerald Ford, have at times permitted their secretaries a virtually free hand in ordering the affairs of the republic among the nations of the world.

State, Department of   674
The primary staff arm of the president in all matters dealing with foreign relations. Since its creation in 1789, and under the direction of the secretary of state, the department (1) advises the president, (2) initiates and implements foreign policy, (3) administers those foreign programs assigned to it by Congress, (4) examines domestic policy in terms of its international impact, (5) provides for coordination among the increasing number of governmental agencies whose activities affect foreign relations, and (6) promotes good relations between the United States and the nations of the world. The pyramidal structure of the department is organized by levels; in descending order these include (1) the Office of the Secretary, which includes the undersecretaries; (2) assistant secretaries in charge of functional bureaus such as Economic Affairs, or of geographic bureaus such as European Affairs; and (3) field missions of various types, mainly diplomatic, staffed largely by Foreign Service officers. Several semiautonomous agencies, such as the Peace Corps and the Agency for International Development (AID), also come under the policy guidance of the department and the International Development Cooperation Agency (IDCA). *See also* SECRETARY OF STATE (673).

Significance
The State Department, as one of the oldest federal agencies, carries on a proud, elite tradition. Because it is mainly concerned with external affairs, a sympathetic reciprocal identification between the department and the U.S. public has been difficult to establish and maintain. "Democratization" in recruitment policies and "professionalization" in the sense of career service have improved this relationship in recent years. The department's freedom of action to develop policy is conditioned by the nature of the U.S. system, in which the president has ultimate responsibility in the field of foreign affairs. Consequently, the role of the department depends in large measure on the relationship between the president and the person the president selects as the secretary of state. The Department of State is the oldest department in the executive branch of the U.S. government, but its longevity does not mean it is free from congressional scrutiny and reorganization. In 1995 the Republican-dominant Congress moved to eliminate several executive departments. High on the list of those to be scrapped were Commerce and Education, while departments like that of State were notified of impending cuts and downsizing. Although the State Department traditionally received the smallest appropriation from the Congress, the long years of the Cold War transferred many of its activities to the Department of Defense, the National Security Council, and the Central Intelligence Agency. National security policy, not foreign policy, dominated U.S. actions in world affairs during that era, and the State Department was little more than an extension of the country's defense needs. It was not surprising, therefore, that while Congress

moved to liquidate whole departments and slash the budgets of others, the Pentagon received immunity from these reductions.

Taiwan Relations Act, 1979 | 675 |

Act ending official U.S. recognition of the Republic of China (ROC) as the only legitimate government of all of China. U.S.–Republic of China (ROC) relations are governed by this act. The withdrawal of official recognition was necessitated by U.S. recognition of the People's Republic of China (PRC). The PRC insisted that it was the only China, and that the price of developing formal relations between itself and the United States was for the United States to sever official relations with the ROC. The United States complied with the Chinese Communist demand, but it nevertheless found a way to sustain "unofficial" political, economic, and even security ties with the ROC. Under the Taiwan Relations Act, the two-way trade between the United States and the ROC continued and even grew, from $9 billion in 1979 to an estimated $44 billion in 1994. The United States also continued to provide Taiwan with defense weapons and state-of-the-art technologies that were needed to keep pace with the ever-changing security needs in the region. Moreover, continued U.S. involvement in Taiwan enabled the country to further develop democratic institutions.

Significance
In September 1994 President Bill Clinton announced several revisions in the U.S.-ROC policy. The president permitted U.S. representatives to hold direct meetings with their counterparts in ROC government offices. Clinton also allowed the ROC government to change the name of Taiwan's representative offices in the United States from Coordination Council for North American Affairs to Taipei Economic and Cultural Representative Office. U.S. officials have since attended conferences in Taipei, and the United States is the ROC's chief sponsor in seeking full admission for Taiwan in the General Agreement on Tariffs and Trade (GATT) and World Trade Organization (WTO), as well as the United Nations. By these actions the United States signaled Communist China that Washington has important relationships with the ROC and it will not be pressured by its relationship with Beijing to ignore a friendly state. In a further gesture of goodwill, the Clinton administration agreed to allow the president of Taiwan to visit the United States in order to deliver a commencement address at Cornell University in 1995. Beijing's reaction was predictably angry and threatening, but the administration seemed prepared to ride out the storm.

Tonkin Gulf Resolution | 676 |

The 1964 joint resolution whereby Congress gave prior approval for the president to take "all necessary measures to repel any armed attacks against the forces of the United States and to prevent further aggression." The resolution was passed after naval forces of North Vietnam reportedly fired on two U.S. destroyers several days earlier in the Gulf of Tonkin, which lies between the North Vietnamese mainland and the large Chinese island of Hainan. Originally, President Lyndon Johnson did not seem to view the resolution as a blank check. He intended limited warfare in the South, coupled with retaliation should the North launch any attacks against U.S. forces. Following his election in 1964, and after this policy failed, however, the president sought to silence his critics. He chose not to seek increased taxes or a declaration of war; the Tonkin Resolution became his vehicle for the escalation of U.S. military effort. Domestic turmoil and opposition escalated to the point that Johnson was constrained to withdraw from the presidential race in 1968. *See also* BRICKER AMENDMENT (620); CASE ACT OF 1972 (623); WAR POWERS ACT OF 1973 (683).

Significance
The vast expansion of the Vietnam War and the resultant clamor of supporters

and opponents resulted in confused demands that the United States simultaneously win and withdraw. This domestic conflict over the interpretation of the national interest was evidenced in strikes, protests, marches, rallies, mob violence, and police brutality, and ultimately symbolized by the killing of four Kent State college students by National Guard troops in 1970. In this context of opposition to an "imperial presidency," the Tonkin Gulf Resolution was repealed in 1970. The history of the resolution symbolizes the traditional ambivalence of Congress toward its own role in foreign policy as it has both supported and attempted to restrain the expansion of presidential power to control foreign affairs.

Trade Agreements Act of 1979   677

An act to carry out the agreements made during the Tokyo Round of multilateral trade negotiations begun in 1973 and concluded in Geneva in 1979. The Trade Agreements Act of 1979 was the fourth in a series of acts governing U.S. international trade posture since the Great Depression. The others are the Reciprocal Trade Agreements Act of 1934, the Trade Expansion Act of 1962, and the Trade Act of 1974. *See also* TRADE POLICY INSTRUMENT: MOST-FAVORED-NATION CLAUSE (260); TRADE POLICY ORGANIZATION: GENERAL AGREEMENT ON TARIFFS AND TRADE (GATT) (269); TRADE POLICY ORGANIZATION: URUGUAY ROUND (274).

Significance
Since World War II, U.S. support for world trade expansion has been implemented through periodic "rounds" of multilateral trade negotiations carried out under the aegis of the General Agreement on Tariffs and Trade (GATT) using the vehicle of the most-favored-nation principle to reduce barriers to trade. However, the United States is no longer the unchallenged giant of international trade. Its position is contested by such phenomena as the economic growth and competitive vigor of the European Union and

Japan and some of their protectionist policies; by economic dislocations caused by the oil crisis; and by inflation, unemployment, and the decline of the dollar. All of these, together with other considerations, combine to raise the level of domestic demands for government protection against "unfair" foreign competition. Such demands coming out of local constituencies are politically difficult for legislators to resist despite executive pressure to hold to the line of liberal trade policy. U.S. interests, particularly in the areas of agriculture and services, were among the topics of the Uruguay Round launched in 1986 and completed in 1994. The revised GATT emerging from the 1994 agreement established a World Trade Organization (WTO) with responsibilities somewhat ill-defined, but nevertheless centered on ensuring the cooperation of GATT members. The problems confronting the WTO were illustrated in the 1995 U.S.-Japanese trade negotiations, which failed to satisfy U.S. demands that the Japanese open their markets to U.S. products. The U.S. appeal to the WTO brought a counterappeal from the Japanese to the same body. Observers concluded that saddling the WTO with so long-term and thorny a problem as U.S.-Japanese trade relations would grievously wound the organization before it had the opportunity to establish its bona fides.

Truman Doctrine   678

The first post–World War II statement of the U.S. policy to aid countries that requested help against Soviet expansion or subversion. The Truman Doctrine began with a dramatic address to a joint session of Congress on 12 March 1947, in which President Harry Truman declared that "it must be the policy of the United States to support free people who are resisting subjection by armed minorities or outside pressures." At the president's request, Congress appropriated $400 million to help Greece resist Communist-led attacks against the government and to bolster

Turkey against Soviet pressure, particularly in the area of the Dardanelles. The United States thereby assumed a commitment in the eastern Mediterranean that the British, for economic reasons, felt compelled to relinquish. *See also* AGENCY FOR INTERNATIONAL DEVELOPMENT (AID) (616); CONTAINMENT (635); FOREIGN AID (643); GEOPOLITICS: RIMLAND THEORY (166).

Significance
As an open commitment of U.S. economic and military power in peacetime, the Truman Doctrine represented a break with U.S. foreign-policy tradition and marked the start of the containment policy. The Truman Doctrine was also the first of the series of economic- and military-aid programs that became a permanent feature of U.S. foreign policy during the years of the Cold War. The enunciation of the Truman Doctrine demonstrated the power of the president to commit the nation to a course of action in foreign policy that Congress was virtually powerless to oppose. The Truman Doctrine was followed by the Eisenhower Doctrine, which extended the arena of U.S. concern to roughly the whole world; the Nixon Doctrine, which sustained U.S. commitments abroad, but nevertheless acknowledged the increasing power of the Soviet Union; the Carter Doctrine, which reaffirmed U.S. concern for the Persian Gulf oil reserves; and the Reagan Doctrine, which combined them all and at the same time called upon the Western world to join the United States in supporting wars of national liberation that were directed against the Soviet Union, e.g., Afghanistan and Angola. Although President Bush was identified with the quest for a "new world order," and President Clinton promoted the Partnership for Peace, the passing of the Cold War has marked a time for moderating presidential doctrines. Furthermore, the president's central role in the making of foreign policy, in the absence of a major primary threat to the United States, has somewhat altered the once dominant role of the American president in international affairs.

United States Information Agency (USIA) | 679 |

The official overseas public-diplomacy organ of the U.S. government formerly known as the International Communications Agency (ICA). Created in 1978 under the Presidential Reorganization Plan, the USIA carries out functions previously performed by the ICA and the State Department's Bureau of Educational and Cultural Affairs. The USIA is closely associated with the State Department, and USIA personnel are attached to overseas diplomatic missions. *See also* IDEOLOGICAL WARFARE (128); PROPAGANDA (137); VOICE OF AMERICA (682).

Significance
The United States Information Agency's activities are aimed at foreign publics and elites to explain and build support for U.S. foreign policy, and to foster an image of U.S. society as being complex, pluralistic, tolerant, and democratic. The message is disseminated through books, periodicals, film, television programs, and exhibits. Perhaps its most widely known activity is the Voice of America (VOA), which broadcasts about 2,000 hours per week in 48 languages. USIA also administers exchange programs involving artists, musicians, dramatists, scholars, educators, students, and athletes. In 1995 there was considerable congressional debate over eliminating USIA altogether, and placing its activities in a modified Department of State.

United States International Trade Commission (ITC) | 680 |

An independent agency created in 1974 to serve as a continuing observer of the foreign-trade position of the United States. The International Trade Commission's main responsibility concerns the impact of imports on U.S. producers. Six commissioners, three from each of the two major political parties, are appointed by the president with the consent of the Senate for six-year terms. *See also* TRADE POLICY INSTRUMENT: ESCAPE CLAUSE (258); TRADE POLICY INSTRUMENT: TARIFF (264).

Significance

The International Trade Commission investigates and reports on matters affecting foreign trade at the request of the president, Congress, the House Committee on Ways and Means, and the Senate Committee on Finance. The ITC replaced the Tariff Commission, which had functioned since 1916. The commission also serves as the agency to provide information to the president that may be used to activate the peril point and escape clause procedures of the Reciprocal Trade Agreements Act of 1934 and subsequent tariff legislation.

United States v. Curtiss-Wright Export Corp. (299 U.S. 304: 1936) | 681 |

A leading constitutional law case that recognized the inherent power of the federal government to control the foreign relations of the nation. The case involved the constitutionality of a broad grant of power by Congress to the president under which the latter embargoed shipment of war supplies to Bolivia and Paraguay in the Gran Chaco War. The Supreme Court recognized the "exclusive power of the President as the sole organ of the Federal Government in the field of international relations." *See also* INHERENT POWERS (651); PRESIDENT: CHIEF OF FOREIGN POLICY (667).

Significance

The *Curtiss-Wright* case established the principle that, whereas the internal powers of the national government are restricted to those delegated by or implied from the Constitution, its external powers are more broadly based. In the field of international relations, the United States as a sovereign state possesses all the powers inherent in its sovereign nature. To hold otherwise, the court noted, would render the United States inferior in comparison to other sovereign states. Justice Sutherland concluded for the court that, even if the Constitution were silent on the subject, such power "would be vested in the national government as a necessary

concomitant of nationality." Hence, in foreign affairs any restrictions on the power of the president to act for the nation must be specified in appropriate provisions of the Constitution. The *Curtiss-Wright* doctrine has greatly facilitated the conduct of U.S. foreign relations under the U.S. constitutional system.

Voice of America (VOA) | 682 |

The broadcasting medium through which the United States Information Agency (USIA) carries out its responsibilities in the area of public diplomacy (propaganda or the selective presentation of data designed to move the object in a direction determined by the user). The VOA broadcasts in approximately 48 languages to give almost global distribution to news programs, music and other cultural programs, and political journalism. Other perhaps less widely known broadcasting efforts include Radio Free Europe, directed toward Eastern Europe; Radio Liberty, aimed at the Soviet Union; and Radio Marti, beamed at Cuba. *See also* PROPAGANDA (137); UNITED STATES INFORMATION AGENCY (USIA) (679).

Significance

Behind the Voice of America and other broadcasting activities lies the assumption that foreign reaction to the United States, its people, and its policies can be positively influenced through the presentation of specially designed communications. From its inception, support for the VOA has been split. Some favor a strong emphasis on selling U.S. foreign policy, while others prefer a broader depiction of life and culture in the United States. Currently, the Voice of America produces and broadcasts radio programs in English and 42 foreign languages for overseas audiences. Programming includes news reports from on-the-scene correspondents, news analyses, feature programs, music, and editorials. Along with the USIA, VOA was judged no longer necessary by Congress, and in 1995 plans were set in motion to eliminate the organization.

War Powers Act of 1973 $\boxed{683}$

An act to limit the war-making power of the president. The president is required to secure congressional authorization for any troop commitment to action within 60 days. An additional 30 days may be approved without a declaration of war if Congress agrees that the safety of the forces involved requires it. After 90 days Congress can, by concurrent resolution, require the withdrawal of U.S. forces. This decision is not subject to presidential veto. *See also* PRESIDENT: COMMANDER IN CHIEF (668).

Significance

The act does not affect the president's power to commit troops to action following a congressional declaration of war. It is designed to curb undeclared wars based solely on the president's authority as chief executive and commander in chief by bringing the Congress back into the decision making on the use of armed force by the United States. The act is a reaction to the growth of presidential power in general and, more specifically, to the heavy and unpopular U.S. involvement in the undeclared wars in Korea and Vietnam. The War Powers Act gives Congress the legal power to participate in decision making in this area, but it will be a political determination as to whether or not Congress will use the power to restrain the president in actions relative to national security.

Patterns
of
Political
Organization

Authoritarian Pattern: Caudillismo | 684 |

The principle of personal or "boss-type" political rule in Latin American politics. The *caudillo* depends on the personal loyalty of his followers. Founded in the feudal systems of Spain and Portugal, *caudillismo* serves as a substitute for formal institutions of government from the local to the national level. *See also* AUTHORITARIAN PATTERN: DICTATORSHIP (686); AUTHORITARIAN PATTERN: PERSONALISMO (690); PEACEKEEPING: UNITED NATIONS MISSION IN HAITI (UNMIH) (449).

Significance
Latin American politics traditionally tend to focus on individual loyalties rather than on issues. Thus, the "boss" can control affairs from a presidential office through direct patronage, as did Juan Perón in Argentina, or through the services of paramilitary and secret police forces, as was the case with Batista in Cuba, Trujillo in the Dominican Republic, or Duvalier in Haiti. *Caudillismo* may cloak itself in the trappings of republicanism, but it more closely resembles absolute monarchy or dictatorship. Building democracy in Haiti in the 1990s meant confronting entrenched *caudillismo*. Paradoxically, it also involved its effective use; Jean-Bertrand Aristide's reinstatement as president of Haiti in 1995 required the use of raw power. Despite Aristide's democratic credentials, Haitian government succeeds or fails on the strength of the leader's *caudillismo*.

Authoritarian Pattern: Constitutional Dictatorship | 685 |

Legal arrangements empowering the executive with the constitutional right to rule by decree, usually for a specified period of time. The scope of the "dictator's power" is generally set forth in the legal instrument that calls upon the executive to act decisively at times of crisis. Constitutional dictatorship usually results from either regional disturbances, e.g., the Indian states placed under "president's rule," or a sustained national crisis, e.g., the transformation of the Turkish nation by Mustafa Kemal Ataturk. Constitutional dictatorship is considered necessary in order to preserve constitutional order and/or protect the state's integrity against both internal forces and external

413

actors. *See also* AUTHORITARIAN PATTERN: DICTATORSHIP (686).

Significance

Constitutional dictatorship is characterized by the delegation of legislative power to the executive, curtailment of economic and political rights, and, at times, by martial rule and the suspension of fundamental rights otherwise guaranteed under the constitution. The temporary suspension of the normal functioning of representative government in democratic countries is triggered by such things as war, rebellion, and economic depression. General Charles de Gaulle, for example, was given temporary authority to rule by decree when the regular French government proved incapable of dealing with the crises brought on by the Algerian war for independence in the late 1950s. Indira Gandhi, although a prime minister, assumed some of the same prerogatives under India's constitution, ruling by decree during the emergency of 1975–1977.

Authoritarian Pattern: Dictatorship | 686 |

Arbitrary rule by an individual or junta not constitutionally responsible to the people or their elected representatives. Changes in government can come about only by death, revolution, coup d'état, war, or voluntary surrender of power. Characteristics of contemporary dictatorships usually include (1) a veneer of democratic jargon and institutions, (2) an ideological rationalization, (3) elimination of active opposition, (4) control of the military, (5) an aggressive foreign policy, (6) a charismatic leader who personifies the state, (7) subordination of the individual to the state, (8) control of the mass media of communication, and (9) a single party, which supports the leader, controls the administration of the state, and transmits government policy to the citizenry. *See also* AUTHORITARIAN PATTERN: CONSTITUTIONAL DICTATORSHIP (685); FASCISM (117); IDEOCRACY (126).

Significance

Dictatorship results from a variety of political, economic, and social factors. These may include frustration with existing institutions, the broad appeal of a sweeping plan to deal with the situation, and the seizure of power by constitutional or extraconstitutional means. Dictatorship can be civilian in nature supported by the armed forces, as in the case of Nazi Germany, or it can be carried on by the military as in pre–World War II Japan or in a number of African states. Totalitarianism, the ultimate degree of dictatorship, implies control over every facet of individual and public life, as in Hitler's Germany. The ultimate problem faced by every dictatorship is that of succession because, by its nature, the system does not provide for predictable and institutional transfer of power.

Authoritarian Pattern: Latifundismo | 687 |

A Latin American pattern of land tenure based on huge landed estates owned by local gentry, absentee landlords, and domestic or foreign corporations. The *latifundia* system, developed by the ancient Romans, was transplanted first to the Iberian Peninsula and thence to the Americas.

Significance

In Latin America, agriculture provides the principal income for two-thirds of the population. Since colonial times, the *latifundia* system has concentrated land ownership in very few hands with large numbers of workers living in conditions resembling peonage. Because agricultural labor is the principal type of employment, political power has been based largely on control of land. Problems of land tenure are closely associated with the slow pace of political, economic, and social modernization in much of Latin America. Mass frustration resulting from the political elite's failure to break up and redistribute the large estates contributes to the threat of revolution throughout the region.

Authoritarian Pattern: Monarchy | 688 |

Hereditary or constitutional rule by a king, emperor, or other royal person.

Significance

Up to the beginning of the twentieth century, monarchy represented the dominant political system in vogue throughout the world. The spread of democracy and republicanism in the nineteenth century, and its expansion after World War I, has all but ended this system of government, largely confining monarchs to ceremonial roles, while others have disappeared altogether. Monarchies of the constitutional variety are found in such democratically oriented systems as those of Great Britain, Norway, Sweden, and Denmark. Some monarchs still represent absolute political power, and are sustained in countries such as Saudi Arabia, Qatar, and Oman. In Southeast Asia, notably Thailand, the monarch plays an ancillary role as a paternal leader and is sometimes called upon to mediate between rival political factions of the mundane variety. Monarchy may not be the political system of choice in the twenty-first century, but popular adoration of personal rulers suggests the institution—indeed, the system—is not yet a matter of history.

Authoritarian Pattern: One-Party System | 689 |

A system of government in which there is only one party, and therefore no political choice. Generally speaking, the less choice offered a people, the greater the degree of control and authoritarianism imposed upon them. Some one-party states justify the absence of choice by citing their perfect credentials, the need to maintain national unity, and the infallibility attributed to those dominating this unidimensional system. *See also* COMMUNIST THEORY: DICTATORSHIP OF THE PROLETARIAT (97); FASCIST THEORY: ELITISM (119).

Significance

One-party systems are repugnant to Western democratic tradition because they violate the requirement of presenting the voter with alternatives. Experience with totalitarian and authoritarian forms like those of Nazi Germany and Fascist Italy prior to and during World War II confirms this sentiment. Yet, a variant of the one-party state developed after World War II with the independence of the former European colonial possessions of Africa, and to some extent of Asia. Asserting that development required discipline and national unity, not the constant bickering of competitive party organizations, many of the emerging states believed themselves justified in their management of one-party, or one-party–dominant, systems. In one-party states like Algeria or Zaire, the consequences meant emboldened dictatorships. In India the Congress party, a representation of one-party dominance, permitted the political opposition to challenge its power, but only in rare circumstances was the monopoly of power enjoyed by the Congress broken.

Authoritarian Pattern: *Personalismo* | 690 |

The Latin American political phenomenon of personalizing political power. Traditionally, many Latin American political parties could be described as bands of loyal followers clustered around, and serving as a vehicle for the expression of, a dominant and colorful personality. *See also* AUTHORITARIAN PATTERN: CAUDILLISMO (684).

Significance

Although *personalismo* is still a force in the political life of Latin America, more programmatic and issue-oriented parties are emerging. The decline of the South American military elite in the 1990s, e.g., Chile and Argentina, points to the possible development of more sophisticated political systems in the region.

Authoritarian Pattern: Soviet Cult of Personality | 691 |

A charge directed by Communist party leaders at individuals who departed from the Marxist-Leninist principle of collective leadership to establish personal rule through self-deification and totalitarian tactics. The concept of the "cult of the individual" or "cult of personality" was used by Nikita Khrushchev in a speech to the Twentieth Party Congress in 1956 to castigate the totalitarian dictatorship and autocratic rule of Josef Stalin, who died in 1953. Khrushchev charged Stalin with ignoring the Politburo and the Central Committee organs of the Communist party, and with arbitrary and despotic rule that produced the "Great Purge" of the 1930s, and thus the deaths of tens of thousands of party members as well as millions of Soviet citizens. *See also* COMMUNIST DOCTRINE: MAOISM (86).

Significance
The downgrading of Stalin by the men who had carried out his orders destroyed the idea of the infallibility of the Soviet Communist party and its leaders. It produced consternation in the USSR and in the once obedient Communist parties in other countries, and precipitated an international crisis. Khrushchev's attack on Stalin caused a weakening of Soviet control over the worldwide Communist movement. Coupled with a growing sense of nationalism within the member states of the Communist bloc, and given the nuclear stalemate between East and West, the monolithic Communist bloc splintered into several groups, one led by the USSR, another by China, and some, such as Yugoslavia, insisting on a national Communist orientation.

Confederal Pattern: Commonwealth of Independent States (CIS) | 692 |
The successor political arrangement to the late union of Soviet Socialist Republics. Formed when the Soviet Union was dissolved in December 1991, the CIS is a pale shadow of the former centralized Bolshevik state. On 8 December 1991, the presidents of Russia, Ukraine, and Belarus, which together represented 73 percent of the former Soviet population and 80 percent of the territory of the once

vaunted superpower, signed an agreement in the Belarus capital of Minsk officially creating a confederation of republics, the CIS. Although Mikhail Gorbachev was technically still the head of the Soviet Union, he was not consulted. The CIS was not very different from the new union that Gorbachev had proposed earlier, because it too called for joint efforts in foreign policy, trade, customs, transportation, communication, currency, emigration, the environment, and combating crime. Because the presidents of the several republics had declared the dissolution of the Soviet Union, Gorbachev denounced the formation of CIS. He called the action illegal and said the USSR could not be dissolved without the formal approval of the USSR Congress of People's Deputies. Gorbachev cited the cataclysmic nature of the decision and predicted that Russia and the other republics would be plunged into a chaos of license and anarchy that inevitably would provoke civil war. The CIS sponsors, however, rejected both Gorbachev's argument and warning. The CIS agreement was quickly ratified by the republic legislatures, and the new commonwealth was officially established on 10 December 1991. By 20 December, five more republics (Kazakhstan, Kyrgyzstan, Tajikistan, Turkmenistan, and Uzbekistan) had joined, and two days later three more (Armenia, Azerbaijan, and Moldova) agreed to accept the new confederation. Georgia and the Baltic states of Latvia, Lithuania, and Estonia opted for total independence and rejected membership in CIS, but later Georgia, under pressure from Russia, reluctantly joined the other 11 republics. *See also* ETHNIC WARS: ABKHAZIA AND GEORGIA (48); ETHNIC WARS: BOSNIA AND CHECHNYA (50).

Significance
The formation of the CIS proved the undoing of the Soviet Union. Russian forces seized the principal assets of the Soviet Union, i.e., the Foreign Ministry, the Supreme Soviet, the KGB, and Gorbachev's private office. Gorbachev found himself the leader of a state that had ceased to

exist, and he resigned as president of the Soviet Union on 26 December 1991. The Supreme Soviet then passed a resolution acknowledging the demise of the Soviet Union. Russia assumed the seat of the USSR in the UN Security Council, and the Soviet Union's embassies abroad removed the Soviet banner and raised the Russian flag in its place. Although the members of CIS declared their intention to establish democratic systems in their respective countries, there was little evidence to show that Western-style democracy could work in the former Soviet republics. Moreover, all the countries of the CIS confronted monumental political, economic, and social problems. All were virtually bankrupt, none were familiar with the workings of the free market, and not one had experience in the building of pluralist democratic institutions. All the states were further burdened by nationality problems that Soviet leadership had capped but not resolved. Each republic was a mosaic of peoples, many of whom now wanted their independence too. Georgia, Tajikistan, and Russia were plunged into veritable civil wars, much as Gorbachev had predicted. Ethnic wars not only threatened the new states and their fragile democratic experiments, they challenged the practicality of the CIS.

Democratic Pattern: Cabinet Government | 693 |

A system based on the British model of a fusion of executive and legislative powers of a cabinet operating under the principle of ultimate parliamentary supremacy. Usually selected from among the leaders of the majority party, the cabinet has collective responsibility for (1) establishing and implementing domestic and foreign policy, (2) coordinating the operations of government agencies, (3) dealing with emergency situations, and (4) maintaining long-range policy objectives. Cabinet-approved measures are introduced and defended in the House of Commons by the appropriate minister. Passage is usually expected because the cabinet leads the party that controls the House. Because any division

within the cabinet is seized upon by the opposition, cabinet unity and collective responsibility for all decisions constitute traditional doctrines of the system, though actual behavior is now more individual. Defeat in Commons on an issue of confidence would require the resignation of the entire cabinet. In this event, the monarch might request the leader of the opposition or another leading statesman to form a new government, or, more likely, the prime minister would ask the monarch to dissolve Parliament. In the latter case, a general election would decide whether the prime minister's party was returned to power or a new political majority appeared. *See also* DEMOCRATIC PATTERN: COALITION GOVERNMENT (694).

Significance
The ultimate power of the House of Commons to bring down the government is to some extent offset by the power of the government to force a dissolution of the Commons. While the threat of a new election exists as a theoretical possibility, a more satisfactory explanation for government dominance of Parliament is party discipline and loyalty. No government in this century has been brought down by defections among its own party members in Commons. The changes that have occurred resulted when the party in power was defeated in a general election. General elections must be held every five years unless called sooner by a prime minister seeking to renew his or her party's mandate to govern. The distinguishing feature of cabinet government in the British parliamentary system is that responsibility for the initiation and administration of policy lies with the prime minister and the cabinet chosen from the Parliament and accountable to it. This system ensures against the kind of deadlock between executive and legislative branches that can occur in the U.S. system when the two branches are controlled by different parties.

Democratic Pattern: Coalition Government | 694 |

A government in which several minority parties form the cabinet when no single party can command a majority. The leader of the strongest party tries to secure agreement from enough smaller parties so that their combined strength will constitute a majority in the legislature. The price of agreement may include promises to pursue, modify, or abandon certain policies and programs, and cabinet or other posts for all parties in the coalition. Coalition government is most likely when a nation lacks broad social consensus, parties have strong ideological orientations, diverse minority groups feel they cannot entrust their interests to major parties beyond their control, and the electoral system is based on a form of proportional representation. See also DEMOCRATIC PATTERN: MULTIPARTY SYSTEM (699); DEMOCRATIC PATTERN: PARLIAMENTARY GOVERNMENT (700).

Significance
Coalition government is inherently more unstable than governments controlled by a single majority party. It requires compromise across lines of party doctrine, and each participant must decide how far compromise can be carried without violating basic party principles. A multiparty government also makes the task of fixing responsibility more difficult for the electorate. In a two-party system, coalitions or governments of national unity may also be formed during a war or other national emergency when partisanship must temporarily be put aside. In coalitions, as in alliances, the least-willing partner controls the level of cooperation. Although it is unusual, a majority party may coalesce with one or several minor parties to strengthen its parliamentary position.

Democratic Pattern: Constituency | 695 |
A voting district or geographical unit represented in a legislature, or the people so represented. The individual voter is called a constituent. Under a single-member district system, a constituency sends one representative to the legislature; under systems of proportional representation, several representatives are elected from each constituency.

Significance
The constituency is the base of representative government. Given the mobility of modern society, one of the continuing problems of democratic representative government is drawing and maintaining constituency or district lines so that each area is roughly equal in population.

Democratic Pattern: Constitution | 696 |
A state's organic or fundamental law, which prescribes the basic organs of government and their operations, the distribution and use of power, and the relationship between the individual and the state. No constitution is completely written or unwritten. In the United States, the written document has been amplified by statute, court interpretation, custom, and usage. Where no specific document exists, as in Great Britain, historic acts of state, basic statutes, judicial interpretation, and custom and convention serve similar functions. In all cases, the function of constitutions is to establish the norms by which the system operates. *See also* DEMOCRACY (108).

Significance
Constitutions may range in complexity and content from the rigid document of the German Weimar Republic to the flexible Constitution of the United States. An extremely rigid, detailed constitution is usually symptomatic of a minimal degree of consensus regarding the ends and means of government. Because of the difficulty encountered in the amending process to keep such constitutions abreast of changing social, economic, and political conditions, they tend to be short-lived. In a consensual society, the constitution can be confined to basic principles and adapted to changing conditions by means of statutory and judicial interpretation

rather than by formal amendment. In Communist or Fascist dictatorial and totalitarian systems, constitutions are used by the regime to provide legitimacy and perpetuate their rule rather than to limit the powers of government.

Democratic Pattern: Federal Government | 697 |

A political system in which power is constitutionally divided between the central government and the nation's constituent subdivisions (provinces, states, regions, etc.). Each of the two sets of governments exercises authority directly on the people; neither owes its powers to a grant of authority from the other, but to a constitution that is superior to both. When a conflict occurs between the national government and a subdivisional government, and each is acting properly within its jurisdictional limits, the case is resolved in favor of the national government as the ultimate focus of sovereignty. To resolve the dispute in favor of the constituent unit would be to convert the system into a confederation of sovereign states. States with federal governments include Australia, Canada, Mexico, Switzerland, the United States, and Germany. *See also* DEMOCRATIC PATTERN: UNITARY GOVERNMENT (706).

Significance
Federal government stands between the concentration of power in a single national government and the diffusion of power in a confederation of sovereign states. Where it has been adopted, it has normally been designed to accommodate a variety of peoples, cultures, languages, and traditions in a single large state. Federalism is one of the most sophisticated systems of government ever devised because of the dual requirement of organizing national unity on common purposes while preserving local diversity in the same society. Success requires that the value consensus holding the federal system together must be stronger than the diversity of local values, which tend to

pull it apart. Yet those who emphasize local values must have confidence, demonstrated in practice, that the central government will respect them. The necessity of balancing unity and diversity makes a federal system difficult to operate effectively, with the result that it has never enjoyed the widespread popularity of unitary government.

Democratic Pattern: List System | 698 |

An electoral system based on proportional representation and used in a number of European countries. Each party presents its list of candidates for the seats to be filled. The party determines the order of names on its list, and seats are filled starting with the top of the list. The voter chooses between lists, and is thus voting for a party rather than an individual. Each party wins the number of seats equated with its fraction of the total popular vote. *See also* DEMOCRATIC PATTERN: MULTIPARTY SYSTEM (699).

Significance
The list system is simple to operate. It adds to the power of party leaders, by restricting the self-expression of individual candidates, and fosters party discipline. It also prevents ticket splitting by the voters, whose freedom of choice is thus restricted, and the process is depersonalized. Variations of the list system allow the voter to establish the rank order of the candidates within a particular list.

Democratic Pattern: Multiparty System | 699 |

A representative democratic system in which more than two parties compete for power. The multiparty system usually requires the formation of a coalition to construct the majority necessary for establishment of a government. It is typical of European parliamentary systems. *See also* DEMOCRATIC PATTERN: LIST SYSTEM (698).

Significance
Proportional representation is usually associated with a multiparty system. The impulse to form minor parties is strong because a minority party can usually count on winning some seats in the legislature even though unable to form or participate in a government. By contrast, the single-member district system of representation, in which the "winner takes all," is more typical of two-party systems. One of the strengths of a multiparty system is that it offers the electorate a wider choice of alternatives. Yet, the price exacted may be one of instability. To form a government in a multiparty system, compromise usually occurs among parties after an election. In a two-party system, compromise takes place within each major party and precedes the election.

Democratic Pattern: Parliamentary Government 700

A system in which legislative and executive powers are fused. Parliamentary government does not require the separate election of the head of government, as in the U.S. system, where powers are separated. The leadership of the majority in the legislature forms the cabinet, which exercises executive power. Leadership of the majority party or parties in the cabinet virtually guarantees the passage of government-sponsored legislation. This form of government operates with either a two-party or a multiparty system, such as those found in Great Britain and in Western Europe. *See also* DEMOCRACY (108); DEMOCRATIC PATTERN: MULTIPARTY SYSTEM (699).

Significance
Parliamentary government in its various forms and adaptations is the most widely used pattern of government in the world. In its classic mold, parliamentary government is based on the ability of the legislature to grant or withhold its confidence in the executive, thus forcing the government to resign or dissolve the legislature. The issue is usually submitted to the people in a national election. The system en-

sures against protracted disagreement between the two branches.

Democratic Pattern: Party Government 701

The decisive role of the majority party in the political decision-making process. In the British system, the party that wins a majority at the polls has the right to form the government. As majority party leaders, the prime minister and the cabinet wield the powers of the Parliament to implement their programs. They can continue so long as the government retains the confidence of Parliament. *See also* DEMOCRATIC PATTERN: CABINET GOVERNMENT (693).

Significance
Party government in Great Britain is based on an essentially two-party system in which the Conservative and Labour parties, by advocating varying public policies, offer the electorate a choice of alternatives. Although Parliament remains legally supreme, its role has been diminished by a dependence on the cabinet as the source for the initiation and determination of policy. Contrasted with the U.S. party system, the British parties are characterized by centralized organization, a degree of ideological unity, and party-whip discipline. Hence, leadership is usually assured of an automatic majority in Parliament on government-sponsored measures. In 1995 the Republican-led U.S. Congress to some extent adopted the British party-government experience. Under the leadership of Newt Gingrich, who assumed the Speaker's role, the Republican majority in the House of Representatives unanimously approved a "Contract with America," a legislative package that ranged over a wide variety of issues.

Democratic Pattern: Proportional Representation (PR) 702

An electoral system in which the seats in a legislative body are distributed to political parties in proportion to the size of each party's popular vote. Forms of proportional representation range from simple to complex, but all are based on voting districts with plural representation. *See also* DEMOCRATIC PATTERN: LIST SYSTEM (698); DEMOCRATIC PATTERN: MULTIPARTY SYSTEM (699).

Significance
Proportional representation affords an opportunity for the direct expression of a wide range of social, economic, religious, ethnic, and political ideas, and is therefore associated with a multiparty rather than a two-party system. Various forms of proportional representation are used in national elections in Europe, and a few U.S. states employ it to fill state and local offices. Proportional representation is an alternative to the "winner takes all" feature of the single-member district system, in which the winning candidate represents all the people in his constituency.

Democratic Pattern: Representative Government | 703 |
A democratic system that enables electors to express their wishes on the formation and implementation of public policy through their chosen representatives. *See also* DEMOCRACY (108); DEMOCRATIC PATTERN: REPUBLIC (704).

Significance
Representative government exists in states that are federal or unitary, parliamentary or presidential, republican or monarchical. The key to representative systems lies in the electorate's delegation of its sovereign authority to periodically chosen and legally responsible officials. Authoritarian regimes often exhibit a façade of representative government by holding elections and seating legislatures, but they are not representative because they are not accountable to the electorate for their actions. The complex nature of modern society has added another dimension to the traditional concept of representation through elections: citizen interests represented through political parties, interest groups, the mass media, technical experts, and lobbyists.

Democratic Pattern: Republic | 704 |
A state in which the government consists of elected representatives. Republicanism may be contrasted with the right of personal rule in a monarchy or oligarchy. The representatives act in the name of and are legally responsible to the electorate. This means that (1) they cannot hold office except by election or through appointment by an elected official, (2) their term in office can be extended only by reelection or reappointment, and (3) they can be required to answer in a court of law for any illegal acts. *See also* DEMOCRATIC PATTERN: REPRESENTATIVE GOVERNMENT (703).

Significance
Although monarchy was once the universal form of government, since the American and French Revolutions most of the states of the world have been organized as republics. The key to republicanism is the legitimating process of elections.

Democratic Pattern: Subsidiarity | 705 |
Seeking the appropriate balance of power between the institutions of supranational community and those of its member states. A traditional federalist concept, subsidiarity on the one side aims to avoid the overcentralization of power, while on the other, it cautions against exaggerated dispersal of governmental power and responsibility. Subsidiarity may have its origin in the Catholic church, a highly centralized institution that nevertheless expressed the need to enhance the role of the localized churches and orders. Adapted to the secular European political experience, subsidiarity is associated with the European Community, where it appeared in the 1975 Tindemans Report on European Union. Subsidiarity was again identified and applied in the 1984 Draft Treaty of the European Parliament, and more specifically in the Single European Act of 1987. Subsidiarity was written into the Maastricht Treaty of 1991 at the insistence of Germany, a leading proponent of federalism in Western

Europe but nevertheless mindful of the need to protect the constitutional position of the German Laender (states). The British, less inclined toward federalism, seized upon the principle of subsidiarity as a means toward accepting the European Union while simultaneously sustaining national interests, policies, and purposes.

Significance
Subsidiarity addresses the need to coalesce, but also the necessity for retaining national political institutions and options. Because it permits the member states within the European Union to avoid total commitment, it elevates the principle of ambiguity to acceptable levels. A common principle of the Maastricht Treaty and the European Union, it has come to mean that decisions will be taken with a view toward the people most affected by them. Therefore, the European Union can take action in areas where it does not have exclusive competence only if the objectives of the proposed action cannot be adequately achieved by the member states. Subsidiarity does not delegate responsibility to the European Union; it only suggests how its competence is to be utilized. Denmark's initial rejection of the Maastricht Treaty demonstrated the determination of the European countries to protect their national institutions and procedures. The question of how to interpret subsidiarity was made the subject of three meetings of the European Council, at Lisbon, Birmingham, and Edinburgh. The proponents of a high degree of subsidiarity lost out to those wishing to defer to subnational dispositions. Thus, while the European Union emphasizes actions that are less than supranational, it nevertheless sets a course for more significant integration in the future. Indeed, through the principle of subsidiarity, the European Court of Justice will enjoy remarkable powers, and through its decisions, prepare the ground for greater interaction by the European Union's political institutions.

Democratic Pattern: Unitary Government | 706 |
A political system in which all power is centralized in the national government. In a unitary system, the subnational units of government are created by the central authority, which grants them whatever powers they exercise. In any modern state, local government is necessary, if only for administrative efficiency, but in the unitary pattern of organization the local units exist legally at the pleasure of the central government. Most of the governments of the world are unitary systems. *See also* DEMOCRATIC PATTERN: FEDERAL GOVERNMENT (697).

Significance
The unitary system of government has the advantage of simplicity when compared to a federal system. Power and responsibility exist in a single straight line between the people and the national government. This creates uniformity in law and administration, and duplication of effort can be avoided. Conversely, unitary government tends to develop large national bureaucracies and reduce local self-reliance by transmitting problems to the national capital for solution.

Government | 707 |
The institutionalized process through which the internal and external aspects of state sovereignty are exercised. Many types of government exist, described by such words as democratic, authoritarian, oligarchic, dictatorial, republican, parliamentary, monarchical, presidential, unitary, and federal. Regardless of type, all governments make and enforce law, provide services for their citizens, and administer justice. The type of government is determined by the way in which legislative, executive, and judicial power is organized and distributed. No matter how it is organized, effective government, or the ability to demonstrate control over the populace, is an essential attribute of statehood under international law. *See also* INTERNATIONAL LAW: STATE (488).

Significance

The government of the nation-state is the most powerful instrument for social control yet devised by man, and takes precedence over other institutions for social control such as family or church. Organized society implies the presence of rules applicable throughout the society, and it is government, exercising the rule-making power and the monopoly of force necessary to ensure ultimate compliance, that prevents anarchy and makes organized social living possible. The extent of control exercised by government is dependent on the relative power of the various groups in the state and the extent of value consensus within the society.

Supranational Pattern: Committee on the Challenges of Modern Society (CCMS) | 708 |

An organization concerned with defense-related environmental issues. The committee brings together West European with Central and East European states to examine and offer solutions for environmental problems that are regional in scope and importance. The CCMS has been placed within the framework of the North Atlantic Cooperation Council (NACC) of the North Atlantic Treaty Organization (NATO), and its activities are organized under the auspices of the annual NACC Work Plan. Following the formation of the Partnership for Peace by NATO heads of state and government in January 1994, NATO's CCMS is further expanding cooperation between NATO and NACC member countries. The annual NACC Work Plan establishes meetings of the CCMS with counterparts from cooperation-partner countries at least once each year. The first CCMS meeting in cooperation session took place in February 1993, with participation from representatives of NATO member states along with those from the Czech Republic, Estonia, Hungary, Latvia, Lithuania, Poland, Russia, Slovakia, and Ukraine. The next meeting took place in January 1994 with NATO members and NACC participants from Belarus, Bulgaria, the Czech Republic, Estonia, Hungary, Latvia, Lithuania, Moldova, Poland, Romania, Russia, and Ukraine. *See also* ARMS CONTROL: CHEMICAL WEAPONS CONVENTION, 1993 (354).

Significance

Although a little-known body outside the working group, the Committee on the Challenges of Modern Society addresses problems of critical interest both regionally and worldwide. A pilot study launched in 1992 on the protection of civil populations from toxic-material spills during movements of military goods examined the potential impact of accidental releases and identified proper emergency procedures to follow regarding all specialized military materials, especially chemical and biological warfare agents. In addition, the committee addressed means of containment, transport of goods, emergency response, and public perception. In 1993 the CCMS examined cross-border environmental problems emanating from defense-related installations and activities. This study focused on radioactive and chemical pollution in the Barents and Kara Seas, the Baltic region, and the Black Sea. In 1994 the CCMS began to investigate environmental aspects of reusing former military lands, with special concern for the conversion of former Soviet bases to civilian use. The contamination of the soil on heretofore military bases and the problems confronted in cleaning the sites have received special attention from NATO members, particularly the United States and Germany.

Supranational Pattern: Single European Act (SEA), 1987 | 709 |

An act that focused European attention on the need to form a genuine single market, free of restrictions on the movement of goods, labor, capital, and services by the end of 1992. The SEA keyed on the 1979 establishment of the European Monetary System, and pressure now centered on the need to go further toward the goal of forming a European Union. With a strong commitment to strengthening the legal framework of the European Community, the SEA demonstrated that national public-finance systems in both federal and unitary states act as interregional "redistributors" insofar as they transfer funds from more developed regions to less developed ones, thereby contributing to what is called "cohesion." The act's success prompted the meeting at Maastricht in 1991, and the formation of the European Union in the following year. *See also* DEMOCRATIC PATTERN: SUBSIDIARITY (705); MAASTRICHT TREATY (432); REGIONAL POLITICAL GROUP: EUROPEAN UNION (EU) (566).

Significance
The Single European Act was yet another building block in the construction of an integrated European community, but in many respects it was the culmination of decades of effort to re-create the European scene. Though focused on economic and financial cooperation, it also sustained previous efforts toward the achievement of political union. Approved during a period of heightened enthusiasm, and elevated in importance by the dramatic changes overtaking the Soviet Union in the mid-1980s, the Single European Act represents Western Europe's intention to erect a more integrated community based upon the principle of Europeanization.

Transnational Anarchic Pattern: Terrorism | 710 |

Transnational activities of state or nonstate actors who use techniques of violence to attain political objectives. Methods used by terrorists include the hijacking of aircraft, the taking of hostages, sabotage, bombing, bank robberies, political abductions, and assassinations. Terrorist organizations typically attempt to gain the attention of the media and the public by their deeds. Most terrorist organizations represent extremist political positions, with leftist groups involved in attempts to touch off a revolution or civil war, and rightist groups seeking to protect the established order. Some terrorists have been described as idealists because

they appear to regard themselves as dedicated patriots or defenders of the people's rights. In the four decades following World War II, many of the national liberation organizations in the existing colonies used terrorist tactics in efforts to advance their independence movements. Many ethnic terrorist groups have also engaged in unconventional as well as orthodox techniques of violence in their efforts to establish a separate state. Some terrorist organizations direct their violence against foreign diplomats, military officials, and corporation executives in the belief that they are fighting to liberate their country from outside domination or neocolonialism. Whatever the form or explanation for terrorism, it is a matter of low-intensity conflict in that it involves warlike actions that can be perpetrated by one person, a small group, or an organized movement. Irrespective of the action, terrorists force established authorities to mobilize significant resources in attempting to prevent or counter their actions. By the same token, whole societies feel less secure when faced with a hidden adversary, rather than an abstract but exposed enemy. *See also* WAR MEASURES: SABOTAGE (328); WAR TYPE: TERRORISM, STATE-SPONSORED (347).

Significance
The terrorists of today often become the patriotic leaders and national heroes of tomorrow. This fact makes it more difficult for national and international communities to combat them. The use of terror tactics by groups to achieve political objectives has many historical precedents, but growing dependence on modern transportation facilities and easy access to weapons and explosive devices have encouraged its use in recent years. Yet, the frequency and magnitude of terrorist activity remains small in contrast to the wide publicity received by the terrorists. When particularly gruesome bombings or murders occur, often two or three terrorist organizations claim credit for the atrocities. Some of the best-known nonstate groups that have employed terrorism include the Palestine Liberation

Organization (PLO) in the Middle East, the Irish Republican Army (IRA) in Ulster, and the right- and left-wing death squads that operated in several Latin American countries, especially Argentina, Chile, Peru, Guatemala, and El Salvador. Many governments also use various forms of terrorism to achieve their political objectives, including air strikes, mass executions, and imprisonment. Efforts have been made by the international community to condemn terrorist activities through the United Nations, but the majority of the world's leaders retains sympathy for guerrilla warfare and terrorism used for pursuit of political objectives with which they agree. For those trying to deal with terrorism, the main problem is whether to adopt a policy of counterviolence against them or undertake political compromises that might placate them.

Transnational Pattern: Character of Nongovernmental Organizations (NGOs)   711

Citizen groups and people's associations covering a whole range of human interests—business, industry, science, the arts, education, culture, religion, sports, social welfare, international relations, and economic and social development. In the mid-1990s, the number of NGOs worldwide was approximately 20,000. NGOs are not subject to specific responsibilities and duties, but they influence the agendas and policy formulation of formal and official organizations, i.e., nation-states, intergovernmental agencies and associations, and international organizations such as the United Nations system with its many organs, associated agencies, programs, and worldwide information systems. NGOs, particularly those possessing considerable financial resources, occupy advantageous political space, making them a force to be reckoned with in more formal decision-making circles.

Significance
The NGOs of the 1990s represent a shift away from the supreme power of the

nation-states to more citizen-based groups that often transcend national circumstances to embrace larger issues. The network relating the NGOs to nation-states and international relations hints at a broader distribution of power and a devolution of responsibility to concerned citizen organizations concentrating on essentially single-issue projects. It is this exclusive concern that permits the NGO to apply intense pressure on national governments and allows it to force its views in international forums. It is important to note that NGOs are generally organized by national sections, and national sections are organized by local branches, so that NGO networks reach directly from individual households to world bodies. No other type of diplomatic activity has this capability. In the United States, for example, almost 6,000 grass-roots peace groups can ultimately influence the highest level of decision making in state, national, and international organizations. Examples of active playgrounds for the work of the NGOs are the Stockholm Conference on the Environment; the Rome World Hunger Conference; the International Women's Decade Conferences in Mexico City, Copenhagen, Nairobi and Beijing; and the World Conference on Poverty in Copenhagen. In the defense and security area, perhaps the most significant NGO is the Global Non-Offensive Defense Network (NOD), which works toward the building of a network of NOD experts and supporters worldwide. NOD participates in world conferences; seeks interviews with relevant decisionmakers, military officials, and academics; publishes a newsletter on NOD and defense conversion; holds seminars and workshops; and generally reaches out to the broader population of world public opinion on matters related to arms control and disarmament.

Transnational Pattern: Proliferation of Nongovernmental Organizations (NGOs)   712

The failure, indifference, or inability of national governments to cope with (let alone satisfy) the demands of different publics, especially in the period after the Cold War. The relationship between subnational, national, and international or supranational systems is observed in the role played by the nongovernmental organizations. Particularly focused on world environmental politics, the NGOs are also major actors in revolutionizing the global economy and in encouraging more significant political and security cooperation between sovereign states. NGOs use their leverage to influence policy in virtually all international organizations, and they are increasingly recognized as legitimate actors in scenarios previously reserved for governmental bodies alone. The importance of NGOs is observed in their proliferation. Compared with international organizations, which increased from less than 40 at the beginning of the twentieth century to more than 300 at its close, NGOs increased from less than 200 to many thousands. In the environmental area alone, the increasing number of NGOs is dramatic. The NGO liaison unit within the United Nations Environment Program includes slightly less than 1,000 organizations, the World Conservation Union has almost 500, and the African NGOs Environment Network represents over 500. Latin America and the Caribbean have more than 6,000 NGOs, most of them formed since the 1970s. The emergence of broad-based international NGO coalitions is also epoch-making. Prominent among these groupings are the Asian NGO Coalition for Agrarian Reform and Rural Development, which joins South and Southeast Asian NGOs, and the International NGO Forum, which brings together Indonesia, Thailand, and Philippines NGOs with those in the Netherlands, Belgium, Germany, and the United States, thus connecting Eurasia with North America. Japanese NGOs formed the Japan Tropical Forest Action Network, which now links counterpart organizations in Asia, North America, Latin America, and Europe. Few matters escape the world of NGOs. Whether it is conservation, human rights, democratic development, economic cooperation, financial exchange, or worldwide security, the NGOs are involved. Moreover, these subnational, sovereignless organizations are directly connected to decision-making processes in international and supranational bodies. NGO input therefore enables lay organizations to compete with intergovernmental organizations and hence to impact the individual nation-states by influencing public policy choice, thereby effecting more significant global cooperation. *See also* DEMOCRATIC PATTERN: SUBSIDIARITY (705); TRANSNATIONALISM (78).

Significance
NGOs are subnational organizations that pressure their respective governments, largely by involving themselves in international and supranational organizations as lobbying and educational agencies. NGOs center their efforts on particular issues, e.g., environmental, women's rights, public health, global security, or economic development. They exploit transnational linkages to publicize and magnify matters that would otherwise be relegated to marginal concern by intergovernmental bodies. The magnitude of NGO intervention into the once exclusive realm of government is witnessed in the proliferation of NGOs. Their increasing popularity in an age of increased communication only hints at the changes in a heretofore state-based international order.

Transnational Pattern: Rapid Reaction Force (RRF) | 713 |

A special transnational military combat unit proposed in June 1995 by Jacques Chirac, the French president, and John Major, the British prime minister. Citing the seizure and humiliation of UN peacekeepers in Bosnia (notably French and British, but others as well) by Bosnian Serbs, the two leaders called for the assembly of a force, essentially free from UN jurisdiction and separate from other established military forces in Europe (NATO, Eurocorps, WEU, etc.). The RRF was conceived as a 10,000-troop quick-response combat unit, heavily equipped and capable of close-support combat operations in difficult terrain. Ostensibly created to identify and contain Bosnian Serb renegade contingents, whom Chirac publicly identified as international terrorists, the RRF was assembled from special units in the French and British army. The Netherlands agreed to join the RRF shortly after its establishment. *See also* DEMOCRATIC PATTERN: SUBSIDIARITY (705); TRANSNATIONALISM (78).

Significance
Both the British and French sought U.S. sanction and cooperation for the RRF. However, because of opposition in the Congress from the Republican majority, led by Senator Bob Dole, the United States refused to provide forces. Although there was initial indication that the United States would offer logistical and other air support, this matter was also delayed. U.S. financial aid was questioned by a skeptical Congress largely opposed to UN peacekeeping operations, and thus little interested in transnational or international activities such as RRF. European leaders questioned whether their Rapid Reaction Force could be operationalized without U.S. involvement. Europe had grown accustomed to U.S. assistance in the security area, and it was now forced to assess its ties and commitment to an Atlantic Community no longer unified. The RRF episode pointed up the different trends: In the United States, nationalism was on the ascendant; in Europe, transnational cooperation, governed by the principle of subsidiarity, was gaining in importance. In spite of these difficulties, on 30 August 1995 the RRF positioned on Mount Igman, a hilltop southwest of Sarajevo, targeted Bosnian Serbs with their artillery in conjunction with NATO air raids around the Bosnian city.

Transnational Pattern: World Development Movement (WDM)

| 714 |

A nongovernmental organization that campaigns for political changes to benefit the world's poor. Founded in 1970, WDM links individuals, local groups, lobby teams, and support staff totaling about 17,000 members, notably from Great Britain. WDM lobbies for cuts in military expenditures and seeks to control arms sales. It also argues for the cancellation of Third World debt, the removal of unfair trade barriers, and aid to the poorest of the world's societies.

Significance
The World Development Movement symbolizes the growth and spreading influence of nongovernmental organizations (NGOs) in arenas previously reserved exclusively for the governments of nation-states. An example of WDM's role was its successful campaign to expose an illegal action by the British government in granting more than $150 million of aid for the Pergau dam project in Malaysia. Evidence amassed by WDM revealed the linkages between aid and arms sales, and exposed the British government's secret arrangement with Malaysia to offer aid in return for a lucrative arms-purchase contract (traced to former prime minister Margaret Thatcher's effort to increase arms sales). The Malaysians drove a hard bargain and forced the British to offer extra trade credits. Malaysia's request for partial payments in commodities like rubber, as well as cash, were embraced by Whitehall. Extra landing rights for Malaysian planes were granted at Heathrow. When Foreign Secretary Douglas Hurd was informed that the Pergau dam was "uneconomic," and that the World Bank and the Malaysian Power Corporation in fact preferred gas-fired power stations, the British government—intent on satisfying its Malaysian arms purchasers—ignored all the negative reports, citing "wider considerations." The British High Court entered the controversy following the pressure exerted by the WDM, and in November 1994 the court found that the government had acted unlawfully and illegally. In the absence of the WDM, the British government's deal would have escaped scrutiny.

Index